2. TIME DIAGRAM

To get an accurate picture of a problem, it is helpful to draw a cash flow or time diagram. This is simply a freehand sketch with a time scale in days, months, or years to fit the problem. The date and size of each transaction are put on the diagram. Analysis of a problem is helped if:

Outflows and dates are put on one side of the time line

Inflows and dates are put on the other side

3. EQUATION OF VALUE

A mathematics of finance problem is solved with an equation of value. This is an equality between outflows and inflows of sums of money *after they have been brought to the same point in time.* When a time diagram has been drawn and a focal date chosen, all flows are brought to the focal date, using appropriate time value formulas. Then the following *equation of value* is set up and solved:

Sum of outflows   Sum of inflows
at the focal date = at the focal date

There are many business and economic applications of the mathematics of finance. The three basic tools are used in analyzing and solving all types of problems.

Mathematics of Finance

Mathematics of Finance

Seventh Edition

Robert Cissell (1913–1973)

Formerly of Xavier University

Helen Cissell

David C. Flaspohler

Xavier University

HOUGHTON MIFFLIN COMPANY   BOSTON

Dallas   Geneva, Illinois   Lawrenceville, New Jersey   Palo Alto

Printed in the U.S.A.

Library of Congress Catalog Card Number: 85-81059

ISBN: 0-395-35645-8

DEFGHIJ-MP-8987

Contents

Preface

The mathematics of finance enables students to identify mathematics with the world they know. Most students will in later life buy a car, home, or other items on time; borrow money; and take out life insurance. Many will seek a second income by putting savings in bonds, stocks, or other investments. A knowledge of the mathematics of finance will enable them to borrow or invest more wisely.

To make this text especially suitable for students of economics, business, and accounting, we have included practical and current material on the mathematics used in modern business transactions. To meet the needs and interests of all students, including those taking liberal arts and general college courses, the book emphasizes financial transactions that are important to individuals and families.

Financial decision making should take into account the time value of money. This is emphasized throughout the book, particularly in the discussion of the important management function of capital budgeting.

Interest, the price paid for credit, plays an important part in the economic progress of nations. Increased governmental emphasis on orderly economic development means new and interesting applications for the mathematics of finance. Material is included on gross national product, the Consumer Price Index, and other economic time series to show how the mathematics of finance is needed for intelligent analysis of the live issues of economics.

A modern treatment of the mathematics of finance should include a discussion of corporate stocks, which are important in both business financing and the financial planning of individuals and families. Because the mathematics required in the chapter on stocks is covered earlier in the book, students should find this material usable even if there is no time for formal coverage in class.

Throughout the book, practical problems illustrate the application of the formulas and tables. Many problems are based on data taken from actual business transactions. "Easy" credit terms may actually conceal a very high rate which can be determined by the methods in this book.

Students find the mathematics of finance more interesting when they know they will benefit financially from what they are learning.

In a mathematics of finance course, most of the problems are word problems. Analyzing word problems and expressing them in equations is invaluable preparation for applying mathematics to real-life problems. Because students have had trouble with word problems in algebra, they expect the mathematics of finance to be difficult. Fortunately, most word problems are not difficult if the student will do two things: make a time diagram and use an equation of value. Both of these are used in the examples throughout the book.

Algebraic derivations are accompanied or illustrated by numerical examples. This is particularly helpful to students who have a limited knowledge of algebra and find it difficult to follow a derivation that is presented only in general terms.

As the use of hand-held electronic calculators has become commonplace, many users of this book prefer to work problems in the *Mathematics of Finance* without reference to tables. We have attempted in this edition to indicate how problems might be solved by using calculators as well as by using tables. We have included a number of problems designed specifically for using a hand-held calculator. These problems have a (c) following the problem number.

The interest rates and dollar amounts used in problems and examples have been made as current as possible to increase the practical value of the book. It is realized, of course, that economic factors can have an enormous impact on rates and prices in very short periods of time. To help this situation somewhat, a table has been included so that the reader will be able to solve practical problems with a wide range of interest rates and terms. We wish to thank Mr. John F. Niehaus, Associate Vice-President for Finance and Computer Services, for the tables which were produced by the Xavier University Computer Center.

So that students can check their progress, answers follow many of the problems. Because the answer to a problem in the mathematics of finance usually does not help determine the method of solution, the answers are given at the end of the problem to save time that would otherwise be spent looking in the back of the book.

Tables are an important part of a mathematics of finance textbook. The tables in this text have been selected carefully and are those used in business firms. Because these tables are well organized and include all necessary functions, they save valuable time that can be used to work more problems. The mathematical tables are also useful for other courses and for solving practical business problems. Because most problems require the use of one or more functions from the tables, they have been placed together at the end of the book and are separated from the text by a colored divider.

We wish to express our appreciation to Dr. Frank C. Genovese, Dean of Graduate Programs, Babson College, who has made many valuable suggestions. The General Editor of earlier editions, Dr. Marshall D. Ketchum, Professor of Finance at the University of Chicago, has helped in many ways to make the book a more useful one for financial analysts. Sincere appreciation is due to Mr. Odin Nielsen of Laventhol Krekstein Horwath and Horwath, CPAs. His detailed analysis has helped make the book more effective for teaching the mathematics of finance in line with business practices.

H. C.
D. F.

Acknowledgments

So that this book will reflect current commercial practices and be of practical value to students, this and previous editions have been checked by authorities in banking, insurance, investments, and other financial fields. Members of the academic community have also checked the text to see that it provides the mathematical preparation students need. We are grateful to the following persons who have helped ensure the inclusion of present commercial practices in a teachable way.

David R. Andrew, Head, Mathematics Department, University of Southwestern Louisiana; Thomas J. Bruggeman, Associate Professor of Mathematics, Xavier University; David W. Cook, FSA, Assistant Actuary, Group Insurance, The Ohio National Life Insurance Company; H. Earl Corkern, Southeastern Louisiana University; Thomas F. Davis, Sam Houston State University; James A. Delaney, Professor of Mathematics, Xavier University; Wayne E. Dydo, Aetna Insurance Company; Rudolph Feige, Lecturer in Mathematics, Xavier University; Dr. Allen O. Felix, Education Director, New York Stock Exchange, Inc.; Robert C. Goggin, FSA, Assistant Actuary, Meidinger and Associates, Inc.; Miles C. Hartley, Chairman, Department of Mathematics, University of Tampa; Victor E. Henningsen, FSA, Senior Vice President, Insurance, The Northwestern Mutual Life Insurance Company; Harry R. Maly, CPA, Associate Professor of Accounting, Xavier University; Martin Markovits, Orange County Community College; Robert Massa, Connecticut Mutual Life Insurance Company; Dr. Z. I. Mosesson, FSA, Assistant Actuary (retired); The Prudential Insurance Company of America; George J. Pawlikowski, Trenton State College; Charles F. Pinzka, Associate Professor of Mathematics, University of Cincinnati; Robert A. Schutzman, CPA, Associate Professor of Accounting, Xavier University; Jacob W. Schweizer, Professor Emeritus of Accounting, Xavier University; William E. Smith, CPA, Associate Professor of Accounting, Xavier University; James B. VanFlandern, Institutional Account Executive and Assistant Vice President, Merrill Lynch, Pierce, Fenner and Smith, Inc.; Edward F. Wilz, CPA, Professor of Accounting,

Xavier University and Vice President of Finance, Blue Cross of Southwest Ohio; Thomas Wood, Xavier University Computer Center; Professor Edward O. Stephany, Chairman of the Department of Mathematics at the State University College at Brockport; and Ann Dinkheller, Instructor in Mathematics, Xavier University.

H. C.
D. F.

narrow money supply = m_1

   a) Currency

   b) demand deposits

   c) traveler's checks

   d) other checkable deposits

broad money supply = m_2

     all the above &

     certain other deposits

Federal Reserve System controls
money supply.

Chapter 1
Simple Interest

1.1 MONEY

"He is (or is not) worth his salt" is an expression that goes back to the time when workers were paid in blocks of salt. Money is anything that is commonly accepted in exchange for goods and services. Wampum, snail shells, beads, slabs of stone, and other objects have served as money. As an economy develops, the money system must be changed to meet new needs. Wampum, which was once used as money by the Indians, will no longer buy food or clothing.

In the United States, money is often defined as the sum of currency (coins and bills) in circulation, demand deposits (checking accounts in commercial banks), travelers' checks, and other checkable deposits. This sum is sometimes called the narrow money supply; it is designated by the symbol M_1. Each of the components of M_1 can be used as a medium of exchange. When certain other deposits are added to the narrow money supply, we get the broad money supply, denoted by M_2.

While there is talk of a moneyless society, facts point the other way. In 1960, currency averaged $160 per person. By 1984 the average was $668. Figure 1-1 shows that the money supply has been increased over the years to meet the needs of a growing economy. The figure also shows that checkbook money, with its safety and convenience, amounts to over three-fourths of the money supply.

The money supply has a marked effect on a country's economic life and the well-being of its people. If there is not enough money, recession occurs, with attendant unemployment and economic hardship for those out of work and their dependents. Too much money means inflation, with runaway prices and economic hardship for those whose incomes do not keep up with prices.

In the United States the primary instrument for controlling the money supply is the Federal Reserve System, which was established by law in 1913. By its control over credit and other means, the Fed provides the country with an elastic money supply – one that should

1

Figure 1-1 Money Supply

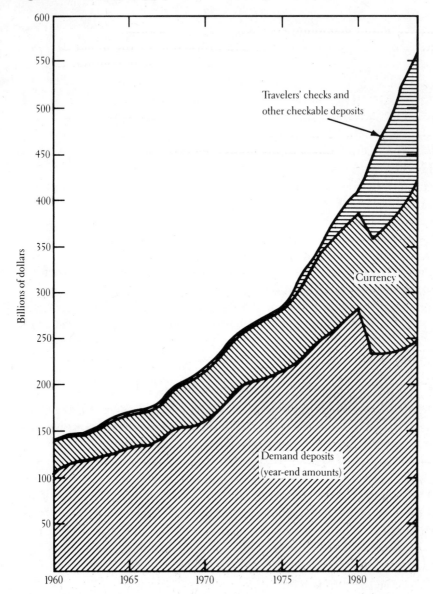

Source: *1985 Economic Report of the President*, Tables B-61, B-62.

expand and contract according to the needs of the people. The Fed attempts to meet the public's changing needs for money in a way that facilitates sound economic growth, a high and growing level of employment, reasonable price stability, and protection of the dollar in international trade and investment. Since these goals may conflict, there is often disagreement over the proper rate and timing of changes in the money supply. Economists argue with one another. The President of the United States and the Chairman of the Federal Reserve Board may disagree on monetary policy. In Chapter 3 the mathematics of finance is used to analyze changes in the money supply.

1.2 PUTTING MONEY TO WORK

Money in your pocket or checking account is always available for making payments, but otherwise it is not doing much for you. With today's high interest rates, surplus cash is an expensive luxury. Smart money managers, those handling individual accounts and those who deal with corporate funds, have a common goal: to put dormant dollars to work. This end can be met by becoming a lender or an owner. Lenders provide funds to be repaid with interest. Owners purchase equities in the hope that the enterprise will be successful and produce profits or capital gains. In each case documents called money market instruments are issued to describe the investment.

Everyone should know how the ownership of money market instruments is transferred. A **bearer** instrument is payable to the holder. It is cashable by anyone who has possession of the paper. Because of increased thefts of bearer instruments, some institutions require evidence of ownership before buying a bearer security. However, even if a thief does have to sell a haul of bearer paper to a "fence" at a large discount, the rightful owner still suffers a total loss. Bearer instruments should be protected as carefully as cash.

Other **negotiable** instruments with the expression "pay to the order of" can have title transferred by endorsement and delivery. Negotiable paper should be safeguarded, for replacement can be costly and time consuming.

There are two markets in which financial instruments are sold. New issues are first sold in the **primary market**. Typically, a new issue is underwritten by an investment banker who purchases the entire issue and forms a syndicate to help sell the issue to new owners.

Outstanding issues are sold by existing holders to other investors in the **secondary, or trading market**. The secondary market consists of organized exchanges located in specific places, such as the New York and American stock exchanges, and the over-the-counter market (OTC). An over-the-counter sale is a transaction not handled on an organized exchange. Over-the-counter sales are often made by dealers who communicate with one another by telephone, by teletype, or electronically.

Financial paper can be negotiable but not **marketable**. To be marketable, a security must be salable on short notice at a reasonable transaction cost in a well-organized secondary market. Marketable instruments may change hands many times after the original sale in the primary market. A negotiable instrument that is nonmarketable is *illiquid.*

1.3 INVESTMENT GOALS

Anyone with idle money can find a place for it to earn money among the many and varied debt and equity instruments in today's money markets. But no one investment will do everything. Money managers study the qualities of different debt and equity instruments so that they can choose the best *mix* of securities to achieve their overall objectives. They consider the strong and weak points of productive assets in terms of the following:

1. Liquidity – ready conversion into money with little or no loss of principal.
2. Safety – protection of principal.
3. Current yield – short-run return from working money.
4. Capital gains – increases in the value of an investment.
5. Marketability – existence of an active secondary market for the asset, which makes for quick sales at reasonable transaction costs.
6. Tax advantages – tax-free current income and favorable rates on capital gains.

1.4 OUR CREDIT-FUELED ECONOMY

Most individuals or families can buy a home only if they have the use of other people's money. Businesses depend on borrowed money for both day-to-day operations and long-term expansion. Government at all levels is a big borrower. The United States, during its two centuries of existence, always has been in debt. The low point was in 1836, when the gross public debt was down to $38,000, less than a cent per person. In 1984 the gross public debt of the federal government was $1.577 trillion, or $6663 per person. No doubt the federal government, along with many states, cities, and corporations, never will be out of debt. But debt is no cause for worry as long as it is within the needs and resources of the borrower. When a person or an institution borrows money, a debt is created. But at the same time, an asset is also created.

Used wisely, credit can help both borrower and lender. A person having money in excess of needs could hide it in a mattress. The money would be available at all times for spending, but it would not grow. If, on the other hand, someone else is allowed to use the money, the lender will have the pleasant experience of watching the money grow. The borrower, although paying for the use of the lender's money, may also gain. The borrower can acquire something needed, such as a home, or can use the money in a business venture that may not only pay the cost of borrowed capital, but also result in a profit for the borrower.

With credit now a way of life and a necessary means for conducting much of the nation's business, it is important that this tool be used wisely. A proper use of credit requires a knowledge of its true price and the ability to determine if a proposed loan is worth the price. Methods developed in this book show how to get the true cost of credit and how to use this cost as a basis for making decisions both in managing personal finances and in operating a business or government agency.

1.5 PRICE OF CREDIT

The price paid for the use of borrowed money is an interest rate. *Time* magazine calls interest rates "the most important regulator of the pace of business and the prosperity of nations."* Basically, interest is a simple idea. Interest is rent paid for the use of money. If the true interest rate is 10% per annum, then the lender receives as interest, or rent, 10 cents for each dollar that the borrower has for a year. Unfortunately, true interest rates are often difficult to determine. Consumers encounter ingenious methods and easy credit claims that conceal high rates. Business executives must solve investment problems that involve many variables and require sophisticated methods to get true rates.

*February 3, 1967, p. 69.

There are great variations in interest rates. In any country at any time, there is a whole spectrum of rates. The lowest rates are paid on almost riskless government securities. The federal government issues four major types of marketable securities: bills, certificates of indebtedness, notes, and bonds. Treasury bills mature in three months to one year, certificates generally mature in one year, notes in one to seven years, and bonds in more than five years. The lowest commercial rate is the prime rate (averaging 12.04% in 1984), which banks charge their largest and most creditworthy business borrowers. The prime rate is a key rate with other bank rates scaled up from it. Changes in the prime rate give a good indication of changes in the cost of money for everyone. Such changes have occurred more frequently in recent years. Borrowers with low and moderate incomes may have to pay from 10 to 42% or more for small loans from legal lenders. Loan sharks illegally charge up to 500% and more for their loans.

During periods of easy money — when money is readily available for borrowing — rates tend to move down together. During times of tight money — when there is less available for borrowing — intererst rates go up. Figures 1-2 and 1-3, from the 1985 *Economic Report of the President*, show recent variations in rates for high-quality or low-risk debt instruments. In general, short-term loans mature in a year or less and long-term obligations in more than a year.

The availability of credit and its price, in the form of interest rates, affects not only individuals and businesses but also the overall well-being of the economy. Rates must be low enough to encourage business to borrow and invest these funds in ways that will result in jobs for a growing labor force. But if low rates cause the demand for goods to outpace the supply, a rapidly rising general price level can mean a lower standard of living for many persons. Monetary authorities seek to avoid both inflation and deflation, and they alter the availability of loan funds and interest rates as part of this endeavor.

An additional complication is a country's international balance of payments, which may cause monetary authorities to attempt to change interest rates. A choice may have to be made between lowering interest rates to spur the domestic economy, and raising them to prevent a serious balance-of-payments deficit. Because of the international mobility of money, interest rates have an important bearing on the flows of funds among nations. If interest rates are high in one nation, capital tends to flow there as investors seek higher returns. This international flow of capital can affect the price structure and economic growth of the countries involved. A healthy development of the world economy requires that all countries take account of the impact of their levels of interest rates on other nations as well as on their own. Usually short-term rates are considered to be more important for balance-of-payment matters and long-term rates for domestic investment decisions.

Whether you will be managing a household budget, a business, or a nation's economy, you will be concerned with the cost of credit. The best way to learn how this cost is determined is to work problems in the mathematics of finance. In this chapter we discuss simple interest, a commonly used method for determining credit cost for loans with maturity of one year or less. Another way to price short-term loans is bank discount, described in Chapter 2.

Figure 1-2 Long-term Interest Rates

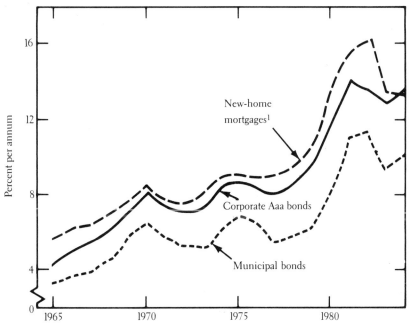

[1] Effective rate on conventional mortgages in the primary market.

Source: *1985 Economic Report of the President*, Table B-66.

1.6 SIMPLE INTEREST

The sum of money borrowed in an interest transaction is called the **principal**. The number of dollars received by the borrower is the **present value** of the loan. In simple interest loans the principal and present value are equal. The **time**, or **term**, of the loan is the period during which the borrower has the use of all or part of the borrowed money. **Simple interest** loans have interest computed entirely on the original principal. **Compound interest**, discussed in Chapter 3, is based on a principal that is increased each time interest is earned.

Principal - sum of money borrowed
present value - # of dollars received

Figure 1-3 Short-term Interest Rates

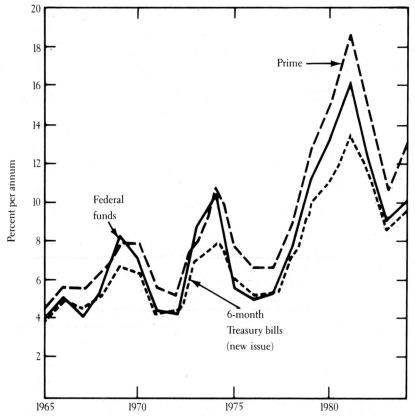

Source: *1985 Economic Report of the President*, Table B-66.

The price of a simple interest loan is expressed as an **interest rate** and is a fixed portion of the principal that is to be paid for its use. Simple interest rates are usually stated as a specified percent per unit of time. One percent means one part in a hundred. If the interest rate is 5 percent (5%) per annum, the interest earned in one year will be $\frac{5}{100}$ = .05 of the principal. An interest rate of $\frac{1}{2}$% per month results in a month's interest of $\frac{5}{1000}$ = .005 of the principal.

Simple interest is defined as the product of principal, rate, and time. This definition leads to the simple interest formula.

$$I = Prt \qquad\qquad (1)*$$

I = simple interest in dollars
P = principal in dollars
r = interest rate or percent of the principal that is to be paid per unit of time
t = time in units that correspond to the rate

Note that r and t must be consistently stated. That is, if the rate is an annual rate, the time must be stated in years; or if the rate is a monthly rate, the time must be stated in months. Before signing a contract, a person should be sure that the time interval associated with an interest rate is stated in writing. In practice, simple interest transactions are often made on a yearly or per annum basis. To avoid repetition in this text, rates are annual rates unless the problem states otherwise.

When an interest rate is stated as a percent, if should be converted to a fraction or decimal in the simple interest formula. If a simple interest rate of 6% is used in formula (1), r would be replaced by $\frac{6}{100}$, or .06. Note that a rate in percent can be changed to a decimal by simply moving the decimal point two places to the left and dropping the percent symbol.

Small differences in interest rates are often expressed in terms of **basis points.** One hundred basis points equal 1 percent. If two securities are quoted at yields of 6.80% and 6.65%, there is a spread of 15 basis points.

basis points

---

*Formulas are numbered consecutively. When used in examples, formulas are identified by number for easy reference in the Index of Formulas in the inside back covers.

[Handwritten note in top margin: 3 types of time deposits:" savings accounts 2) open accounts 3) Certificates of deposit (CD)]

1.7 SIMPLE INTEREST APPLICATIONS

The first experience most people have with simple interest is a **time deposit** in a bank. A time deposit is money held in the bank account of a person or firm for which the bank can require advance notice of withdrawal. There are three types of time deposits: savings accounts, open accounts, and certificates of deposit.

Savings accounts, sometimes called passbook savings accounts, may be subject to prior notice of withdrawal. In practice, however, individuals can usually make withdrawals on request, so these accounts are useful to people who want a return on funds that are still available when needed. Insured savings accounts are a safe place to put money. Although the current return may be modest, savings accounts provide liquidity, safety, and the flexibility of being able to make deposits and withdrawals at any time. Many institutions have savings accounts with the desirable feature of interest from the date of deposit to the date of withdrawal.

Open accounts usually pay somewhat higher rates than savings accounts because of restrictions on deposits and withdrawals. These accounts differ widely in maturity, denomination, and rates of interest. Special passbook accounts may have a minimum initial deposit. Savings certificates have minimum amounts and definite maturity dates. An investor wishing to withdraw funds before the maturity date may be required to present written notice of intent to withdraw. Such notice must be given some fixed time period before the money may be obtained.

An unusual open account is the non-interest-paying Christmas Club. Club members make periodic deposits and have their faithfulness recognized by entries in a special passbook. As the time to make merry draws near, club members get back their deposits without interest. Good money managers save for the holidays in more productive ways. If a Christmas Club appeals to you, look for one that pays interest.

Certificates of deposit (CDs) are money market instruments for fixed sums, time periods, and interest rates. Nonnegotiable, consumer-type certificates that are sold to individual savers are issued in face values of $500, $1000, $2000, and other round amounts. Interest rates are usually higher than the rate being paid on savings accounts. There is some loss in liquidity since the borrowing institution does not have to redeem a CD until maturity. In some cases a certificate may be redeemed earlier, but with loss of interest. Some investors get both liquidity and higher yield by staggering purchases so that at no time is there much of a wait for a CD to mature. Negotiable certificates for large investors are described in Chapter 2.

A **promissory note** is a written promise to pay money. The person who makes the promise and signs the note is called the maker. A promissory note may be made payable to the order of a named person or to "bearer."

The note shown in Figure 1-4 (next page) is typical of various commercial forms in use today. The following expressions are used in notes:

Expression	Example
Face value is the amount of money shown on the note. This amount is usually given in figures and in words.	$600.00
Date is the date the note is made.	June 1, 1978
Term is the time from the date of the note to the maturity or due date.	60 days
Rate is the percent at which interest is to be calculated. (The time period associated with a rate should be stated.)	5% per annum
Payee is the person or firm to whom the note is due.	William Rettig
Maker is the person or firm executing the note, the one who owes the money.	Robert Boster
Maturity date is the date the note is due. This is calculated from the date and term of the note.	July 31, 1978
Maturity value is the face value plus interest, if any. If no interest rate is given in a note, it is non-interest bearing and the maturity value equals the face value. This does not necessarily mean that the original debt did not bear interest. It merely means that the interest, if any, has been added to the principal and the note has been drawn for the maturity of the debt.	$605.00

In addition to interest computations, the simple interest formula has many other applications. Savings and loan associations and credit unions use it to determine dividends on share accounts held by their members. The current yield on common and preferred stocks is obtained by substitution in the simple interest formula.

EXAMPLE 1 A bank pays 8% per annum on savings accounts. Interest is credited quarterly on March 31, June 30, September 30, and December 31. Money deposited by the 10th of the month earns interest for the entire month. A person opens an account with a deposit of $300 on January 8. How much interest will the person receive on March 31?

SOLUTION Since the rate is an annual rate, the time must be expressed in years. Substituting $P = 300$, $r = .08$, and $t = \frac{3}{12}$, or $\frac{1}{4}$, year in formula (1), we find that

$$I = 300 \times .08 \times \tfrac{1}{4} = \$6.00$$

EXAMPLE 2 A couple buys a home and gets a loan for $50,000. The annual interest rate is 12%. The term of the loan is 30 years, and the monthly payment is $514.31. At the end of the month, one spouse says, "Dear, I am going down to make the first payment on our new home." Find the interest for the first month and the amount of house purchased with the first payment.

SOLUTION Substituting $P = 50,000$, $r = .12$, and $t = \frac{1}{12}$ in formula (1), we have

$$I = 50,000 \times .12 \times \tfrac{1}{12} = \$500.00$$

Figure 1-4 A Promissory Note

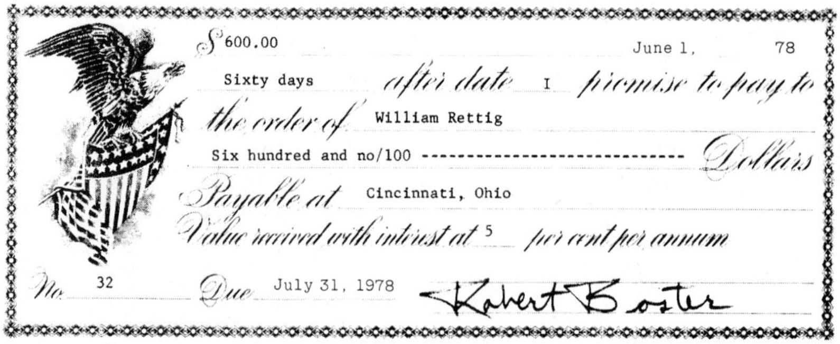

Although homeowning eliminates rent on property, the rent on borrowed money can be substantial. In this case the $514.31 payment buys only 514.31 – 500.00 = $14.31 worth of house.

Of course, you can use algebraic methods to determine the principal, rate, or time if the amount of interest is known. Given any three of the variables, you can solve the equation for the fourth.

EXAMPLE 3   The interest paid on a loan of $500 for 2 months was $12.50. What was the interest rate?

SOLUTION   When a rate is required, ordinarily we get it correct to the nearest hundredth of 1%. We substitute $I = 12.50$, $P = 500$, and $t = \frac{2}{12}$, or $\frac{1}{6}$, in formula (1). It makes no difference which member of an equation is to the left of the equal sign. Many people find it easier to solve equations when the unknown is on the left, as we now show.

$$500 \times r \times \tfrac{1}{6} = 12.50$$

$$r = \frac{6 \times 12.50}{500} = .15 = 15\%$$

EXAMPLE 4   A person gets $63.75 every 6 months from an investment that pays 6% interest. How much money is invested?

SOLUTION   Substituting $I = 63.75$, $r = .06$, and $t = \frac{1}{2}$ in formula (1), we obtain

$$P \times .06 \times \tfrac{1}{2} = 63.75$$

$$P = \frac{63.75 \times 2}{.06} = \$2125.00$$

EXAMPLE 5   How long will it take $5000 to earn $50 interest at 6%?

SOLUTION   Substituting $I = 50$, $P = 5000$, and $r = .06$ in formula (1), we have

$$5000 \times .06 \times t = 50$$

$$t = \frac{50}{5000 \times .06} = \frac{1}{6} \text{ year, or 2 months}$$

EXAMPLE 6 General Motors $100 par value 3.75% preferred stock was quoted at 52. The quote "at 52" means the stock is sold for $52 per share. At this price, what yield will a buyer receive on an investment?

SOLUTION In this problem, two rates are involved. The return in dollars is the stated rate times the par value of .0375 $\times$ 100 = $3.75. This amount will be paid to the owner regardless of what price was paid for the stock. To find the yield rate received by a buyer who paid $52, substitute in formula (1) and obtain

$$52 \times r \times 1 = 3.75$$

$$r = \frac{3.75}{52} = .072 = 7.2\%$$

Although this investment is safe, the market price of $52 is lower than the par value of $100 because interest rates are now much higher than when the stock was issued. Fixed return investments are quite sensitive to interest rates.

EXAMPLE 7 A woman borrows $2000 from a credit union. Each month she is to pay $100 on the principal. She also pays interest at the rate of 1% a month on the unpaid balance at the beginning of the month. Find the total interest.

SOLUTION Note that the rate is a monthly rate. The first month's interest is

$$I = 2000 \times .01 \times 1 = \$20.00$$

The total payment for the first month is $120, and the new unpaid balance is $1900. For the second month the interest is

$$I = 1900 \times .01 \times 1 = \$19.00$$

Since the unpaid balance decreases $100 a month, the interest decreases $1.00 each month. After 19 payments the debt is down to $100, and the last interest payment is

$$I = 100 \times .01 \times 1 = \$1.00$$

The interest payments form an arithmetic progression that can be summed using the formula

$$\text{Sum} = \frac{n}{2} (t_1 + t_n)$$

where n is the number of terms and t_1 and t_n are the first and last terms. In this problem they stand for the first and last interest payments. Substituting, we have

$$\text{Total interest} = \frac{20}{2} (20.00 + 1.00) = \$210.00$$

1.8 AMOUNT

The sum of the principal and the interest is called the **amount**, designated by the symbol S. This definition leads to the formula

$$S = P + I$$
$$= P + Prt$$

Factoring, we have

$$S = P(1 + rt) \qquad (2)$$

EXAMPLE A man borrows $350 for 6 months at 15%. What amount must he repay?

SOLUTION Substituting $P = 350$, $r = .15$, and $t = \frac{1}{2}$ in formula (2), we find that

$$S = 350(1 + .15 \times \tfrac{1}{2}) = 350(1.075) = \$376.25$$

This problem could have been worked by getting the simple interest and adding it to the principal.

$$I = Prt = 350 \times .15 \times \tfrac{1}{2} = \$26.25$$
$$S = P + I = \$350.00 + 26.25 = \$376.25$$

You can solve many problems in the mathematics of finance by more than one method. Look for the easiest way, thereby reducing both labor and the risk of numerical errors. Working a problem more than one way is often desirable as a check.

As the last example shows, the dollar value of a past or future sum of money will vary in accordance with the time and rate. Students who are accustomed to thinking of money only in terms of so much cash should now get into the habit of taking into account these other variables. A debt of $1000 due in 1 year with interest at 6% may be considered as an obligation of $1060 due in 1 year. If a time is not stated, we assume that the designated sum is the present or cash value. Thus if a problem states that the price of a car is $2000, we are referring to the cash price. If a sum is due in the future without interest or if a rate is not stated, we assume that the given value is the maturity value of the obligation. Thus "$3000 due in 6 months" means that 6 months hence the debtor must pay $3000. In the business world, this obligation would be worth less than $3000 before the end of 6 months.

Different amounts of money may be *equivalent in value.* At 5% interest, $100 now is equivalent in value to $105 in a year. What this means in practice is that a borrower is willing to repay $105 in 1 year if the use of $100 can be obtained immediately. The lender is willing to lose the use of $100 for a year if $5 interest is received. The equivalent values of different sums provide the basis for the useful equations of value used throughout the mathematics of finance.

Another way of expressing an interest rate is to say that "money is worth so much." This expression is often used in problems to specify the rate that the parties to a transaction have agreed to use in arriving at a settlement. In practical business usage this rate is usually the current rate for that type of transaction in the particular locality.

1.9 ROUNDING

Money answers in the mathematics of finance are rounded off to values that can be paid in standard coinage. Unless stated otherwise, answers in this book are rounded to the nearest cent. Calculated values ending in half a cent or more are rounded up.

See the table at the top of the next page. Note that in the last case .6749 is rounded down to .67. Since we are rounding to the nearest cent, it would be wrong to make the 4 a 5 in one step and then round to 45.68 in a second step.

Calculated Value	Rounded Value
$45.789	$45.79
45.443	45.44
45.375	45.38
45.4650	45.47
45.6749	45.67

While exceptions to our rule of rounding off are noted as we come to them, we mention a couple now to illustrate how commercial practices affect rounding. Mortgage and other installment lenders customarily round up any fraction of a cent. Thus a monthly payment of $85.142 would be rounded up to $85.15. If the fraction of a cent is dropped, the deficiency that accumulates over a long series of payments will be made up in the concluding payment, making this payment larger than the others. By rounding up, the reverse is true, and the concluding payment will be somewhat smaller. This situation probably makes for happier customers. Some lenders even round up to the nearest dime. A monthly payment of $112.125 would be rounded up to $112.20. Again, no injustice is done, since the overpayment of a few cents each month is offset by the smaller concluding payment.

When data are approximate, rounding should not imply a degree of accuracy that is not possible with the data. Suppose that the market value of a stock has been increasing at about 10% a year. With so many uncertainties involved in the stock market, to predict the price a year from now to the nearest cent would be foolish. A reasonable procedure would be to round off the answer to the nearest dollar and then qualify this value as only a prediction.

Another practical question is how many decimal places to retain when a factor involves an unending decimal. If we want the amount of $4800 at 4% for 1 month, we can substitute in formula (2) to obtain

$$S = 4800(1 + .04 \times \tfrac{1}{12}) = 4800(1.003333\ldots)$$

The second factor must be terminated somewhere. If you have a calculator, a good practice is to carry eight or more decimal places and then round the answer. This practice does not appeal to students who do not have access to a calculator. Yet a thorough understanding of the mathematics of finance requires carrying many problems to the final dollars-and-cents answer. Only in this way can you learn to solve practical problems, including the important decision problems that involve a choice among two or more alternatives. When calculations must be made by pencil-and-paper methods, a good working rule is to round factors to the same number of decimal places as there are digits in the sum of money, including the cents. The required arithmetic can then be done by conventional multiplication. The figure $4800.00 has six digits, so we have

$$S = 4800.00(1.003333) = 4815.9984 = \$4816.00$$

A student using a calculator to do this problem would let the calculator do the work to the limits of its capability. In this problem, the first step is to divide .04 by 12, allowing the calculator to carry its full complement of decimal places. Then add 1 to the result and multiply that answer by 4800 and round off. Following this procedure will yield the most accurate answer possible on that calculator. *When using a calculator, you need not round off at intermediate steps.*

You should look for the easiest way to do problems. This approach conserves time and reduces the risk of errors. In calculating the amount at simple interest, it is often easier to get the interest using formula (1) and then add principal and interest to obtain the amount.

$$I = 4800 \times .04 \times \tfrac{1}{12} = \$16.00$$
$$S = 4800.00 + 16.00 = \$4816.00$$

1.10 TIME DIAGRAMS

All financial decision making must take into account the basic idea that money has time value. A hundred dollars today is worth more than a hundred dollars in a year, because a hundred dollars today can be invested to give a hundred dollars plus interest in a year.

An easy and accurate way to keep track of the varying dollar values of sums of money is to use a time diagram that shows the sums and the points in time at which they have particular dollar values. Students find diagrams to be of great help in the analysis and solution of problems. The simple time diagram in Figure 1-5 shows how the different dollar values of an obligation are placed at the corresponding points in time.

EXAMPLE 1 The current annual dividend rate of a savings and loan association is $5\frac{1}{2}\%$. Dividends are credited to a person's account on June 30 and December 31. Money put in by the 10th of the month earns dividends for the entire month. If money is put in after the 10th, it starts earning dividends the following month. A person opens an account on January 7 with $400. On February 25, $300 is added, and on June 10, $240 is placed in the association. What is the amount in the account on June 30?

SOLUTION In the problem, as in all practical problems, the solution must be based on the rules governing the transaction. Although savings and loan associations pay dividends rather than interest, calculations are made using the simple interest formula. We allow 6 months dividends on the initial $400, although the actual time is a few days less. The $300 gets 4 months dividends although it is in the association a few days longer. Locating the deposits on a time diagram (Figure 1-6) helps us find the length of time each deposit earns dividends.

Figure 1-5

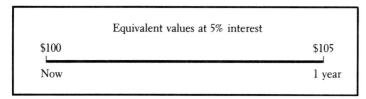

Figure 1-6

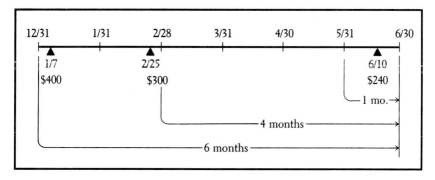

Using formula (1), we compute the dividend on each sum.

$$400 \times .055 \times \tfrac{1}{2} = \$11.00$$
$$300 \times .055 \times \tfrac{1}{3} = 5.50$$
$$240 \times .055 \times \tfrac{1}{12} = \underline{1.10}$$
$$\text{Total dividends} \quad \$17.60$$

Summing all the deposits and dividends, we find that the June balance is $957.60

EXAMPLE 2 The normal fee for travelers' checks is $1 per $100. A seller of travelers' checks advertised an unusual offer during May only — "…just in time for summer vacations you can save as much as $48 [see the following chart] because of this remarkable offer":

Amount of Travelers' Checks	Usual Fee	May Fee	You Save
$ 300	$ 3.00	$2.00	$ 1.00
500	5.00	2.00	3.00
1000	10.00	2.00	8.00
2500	25.00	2.00	23.00
5000	50.00	2.00	48.00

The ad continued, "Many smart people take advantage of our Unusual Offer and buy…Travelers' Checks during May…then keep them on hand throughout the year either for their vacation or against the time they may need cash for an emergency. Why not follow this smart lead?" While this is a smart lead for a person who is leaving soon, it is not so smart for the person whose vacation is several months away.

Instead of buying $1000 worth of travelers' checks on May 1 for an October trip, a person put $1002 in a savings and loan association paying 5% converted quarterly on March 31, June 30, September 30, and December 31. On October 1 the money was withdrawn and used toward the purchase of $1000 worth of travelers' checks. How much did this smart person gain?

SOLUTION The dividend for May and June equals

$$1002 \times .05 \times \tfrac{2}{12} = \$8.35$$

There is now a balance in the account of $1010.35, which gets dividends on September 30 of

$1010.35 \times .05 \times \tfrac{3}{12} = \$12.63$
Balance on October 1 = 1010.35 + 12.63 = $1022.98
Cost of travelers' checks = 1000 + 10.00 = $\underline{1010.00}$
Savings $ 12.98

The advertised plan is a smart one for the issuer of travelers' checks, who has interest-free money as long as the checks are outstanding.

EXAMPLE 3   A national magazine is sponsoring a contest in which the first prize is $100 a month for life. Every month the magazine will deposit $100 in a local bank chosen by the winner. To make the contest more appealing, the magazine mails out sample deposit books that show how the account grows if the bank pays 5% per annum with interest credited on March 31, June 30, September 30, and December 31. This policy means that interest is accumulated and added to the balance every 3 months. The first three entries in the promotional bank book are shown in the following chart. Compute the interest and balance on 12/31/86 using the 5% rate.

Date	Deposit	Interest	Balance
10/1/86	$100.00		$100.00
11/1/86	100.00		200.00
12/1/86	100.00		300.00

SOLUTION   The first payment earns interest for 3 months, the second for 2 months, and the third for 1 month. Substituting in formula (1), we have

$100.00 \times .05 \times \tfrac{3}{12} = \$1.25$
$100.00 \times .05 \times \tfrac{2}{12} = .83$
$100.00 \times .05 \times \tfrac{1}{12} = \underline{.42}$
Total interest $2.50

The balance on 12/31/86 is $302.50. When the payments are equal in size, an equivalent way to get simple interest is to assume that one deposit of $100.00 has earned a total of 6 months interest:

$$100.00 \times .05 \times \tfrac{6}{12} = \$2.50$$

Exercise 1a

1. Find the simple interest on $750 for 2 months at 7% and the amount.
   ($8.75, $758.75)
2. Find the simple interest on $1225 for 3 months at 8% and the amount.
3. The contest passbook in Example 3 shows the following entries for the first 6 months. Compute the interest and balance on 3/31/87.

Date	Deposit	Interest	Balance
10/1/86	$100.00		$100.00
11/1/86	100.00		200.00
12/1/86	100.00		300.00
12/31/86		$2.50	302.50
1/1/87	100.00		402.50
2/1/87	100.00		502.50
3/1/87	100.00		602.50
3/31/87			

($6.28; $608.78)
4. Find the balance on June 30, 1987, for the account in the preceding problem.
5. A woman borrows $30,000 to buy a home. The interest rate is 12% and the monthly payment is $308.59. How much of the first payment goes to interest and how much to principal?
   (interest $300.00; principal $8.59)
6. A $40,000 home loan is to be repaid with monthly payments of $505.78. If the interest rate is 15%, how much of the first payment goes to interest and how much to principal?
7. A savings and loan association advertises a rate of $7\tfrac{1}{2}$%. Deposits made by the 10th of a month earn dividends from the 1st of that month. Deposits made after the 10th earn dividends from the first

of the following month. Dividends are credited on June 30 and December 31. A depositor had $2045 in an account on June 30, 1987, and deposited $1120 on September 7, 1987. How much will be in the account on December 31, 1987?
($3269.69)

8. A man has an account in the savings and loan association described in problem 7. His account had a balance of $1600 on December 31, 1986. He deposited $400 on February 8, 1987, and $600 on April 25, 1987. Find the final entry in his passbook after interest is credited on June 30, 1987.

9. A worker borrowed $150 for 2 months and paid $9.00 interest. What was the annual rate?
(36%)

10. A mechanic borrowed $125 from a licensed loan company and at the end of 1 month paid off the loan with $128.75. What annual rate of interest was paid?

11. If a person invests $3000 at 10%, how long will it take him to get $75.00 interest?
(3 months)

12. How long will it take $8400 to earn $24.50 interest at $7\frac{1}{2}\%$

13. How long a time will be required for $625 to earn $25 interest at 9.6%?
(5 months)

14. How long will it take $9600 to earn $864.00 interest at 8%?

15. What is the amount if $3.6 million is borrowed for 1 month at $9\frac{3}{4}\%$?
($3,629,250)

16. What is the amount if $14.4 million is borrowed for 2 months at $8\frac{3}{4}\%$?

17. A man borrows $95. Six months later he repays the loan, principal and interest, with a payment of $100. What interest rate did he pay?
(10.53%)

18. A loan shark made a loan of $50 to be repaid with $55 at the end of 1 month. What was the annual interest rate?

19. A waitress who was temporarily pressed for funds pawned her watch and diamond ring for $55.00. At the end of 1 month she redeemed them by paying $59.40. What was the annual rate of interest?
(96%)

20. A man had a gambling debt of $150. He repaid it in 1 month with interest of $15. Find the rate.

21. A teacher borrowed $200 from the credit union to which she belonged. Every month for 8 months she paid $25 on the principal plus interest at the rate of 1% a month on the unpaid balance at the beginning of the month. The first interest payment would be 1% of $200, the second interest payment would be 1% of $175, and so on until the loan was repaid. What was the total interest paid on this loan?
   ($9.00)

22. A person borrowed $800 from a credit union that charges 1% per month on the outstanding balance of a loan. Every month for 8 months the person paid $100 on the principal plus interest on the balance at the beginning of the month. Find the total interest.

23. The value of fixed income investments is very sensitive to changes in interest rates. In 1963, when money was relatively easy or cheap, Cincinnati Gas and Electric $100 par value, 4% preferred stock was quoted at 94. Early in 1972, when interest rates were higher, the stock could be purchased for $61. What rates of return or yield rates were received at these prices?
   (4.26% at $94; 6.56% at $61)

24. Philadelphia Electric $100 par value, 3.8% preferred stock was quoted at 41 in the September 30, 1976, issue of the *Wall Street Journal.* What was the yield rate? Find the current yield on this stock. (See Chapter 11 for information on how to read stock tables.)

1.11 EXACT AND ORDINARY INTEREST

When the time is in days and the rate is an annual rate, it is necessary to convert the days to a fractional part of a year when substituting in the simple interest formulas. Interest computed using a divisor of 360 is called **ordinary interest**. When the divisor is 365 or 366, the result is known as **exact interest**.

For a given rate of interest, a denominator of 360 results in a borrower paying more interest in dollars than would be the case if 365 or 366 were used. On individual loans the difference may not be large. When many borrowers each pay a little more, however, the total difference is a substantial sum. This increased revenue makes the 360-day year popular with lenders.

EXAMPLE Figure the ordinary and exact interest on a 60-day loan of $300 if the rate is 15%.

SOLUTION Substituting $P = 300$ and $r = .15$ in formula (1), we have

$$\text{Ordinary interest} = 300 \times .15 \times \tfrac{60}{360} = \$7.50$$
$$\text{Exact interest} = 300 \times .15 \times \tfrac{60}{365} = \$7.40$$

Note that ordinary interest is greater than exact interest and is easier to compute when the work must be done without a calculator.

1.12 EXACT AND APPROXIMATE TIME

There are two ways to compute the number of days between calendar dates. The more common method is the **exact** method, which includes all days except the first. A simple way to determine the exact number of days is to use Table 1 in the back of this book, which gives the serial numbers of the days in the year. Another method is to add the number of days in each month during the term of the loan, not counting the first day but counting the last one. The **approximate** method is based on the assumption that all the full months contain 30 days. To this number is added the exact number of days that remain in the term of the loan.

EXAMPLE Find the exact and approximate time between March 5 and September 28.

SOLUTION From Table 1 we find that September 28 is the 271st day in the year and March 5 is the 64th day. Therefore the exact time is $271 - 64 = 207$ days. If a table of calendar days is not available, we can set up a table as follows:

March	26 (31 − 5)
April	30
May	31
June	30
July	31
August	31
Sept.	28
Total	207 days

To get the approximate time, we count the number of months from March 5 to September 5. Then we can figure that $6 \times 30 = 180$ days.

To this result we add the 23 days from September 5 to September 28, for a total of 203 days.

1.13 COMMERCIAL PRACTICE

Since we have exact and ordinary interest and exact and approximate time, there are four ways to compute simple interest:

1. Ordinary interest and exact time (Bankers' Rule)
2. Exact interest and exact time
3. Ordinary interest and approximate time
4. Exact interest and approximate time

Hence in computing simple interest, as in all problems in the mathematics of finance, both parties to the transaction should understand what method is to be used. In this book, when the time is in days, we use ordinary interest and exact time unless another method is specified. This method is known as **Bankers' Rule** and is the common commercial practice.

When an obligation has a stated time to run, it is necessary to determine the due date. If the time is stated in days, the due date is the exact number of days after the loan begins. If the time is stated in months, the due date is the same as the date on which the term of the loan begins unless the date of the loan is larger than the last date of the month in which the loan matures. When this happens, we take the last date of the month as the maturity date. For example:

Date of Loan	Term of Loan	Maturity Date
June 15, 1988	60 days	August 14, 1988
June 15, 1988	2 months	August 15, 1988
Dec. 10, 1988	4 months	April 10, 1989
Dec. 10, 1988	120 days	April 9, 1989
Dec. 10, 1987	120 days	April 8, 1988 (1988 is a leap year)
December 28, 29, 30, or 31, 1988	2 months	February 28, 1989
December 29, 30, or 31, 1987	2 months	February 29, 1988

EXAMPLE 1 On November 15, 1985, a woman borrowed $500 at 15%. The debt is repaid on February 20, 1986. Find the simple interest using the four methods.

SOLUTION: First we get the exact and approximate time.

Exact time
From Table 1:
November 15 is the 319th day
February 20 is the 51st day
In 1982 there are 365 − 319 = 46 days
In 1983 there are   51 days
                    Total time   97 days

Approximate Time
November 15 to February 15 is three months
Three months X 30 days = 90 days
February 15 to 20   =   5 days
                    Total time   95 days

Ordinary interest and exact time
  (Bankers' Rule) $I = 500 \times .15 \times \frac{97}{360} = \$20.21$

Exact interest and exact time $I = 500 \times .15 \times \frac{97}{365} = \$19.93$

Ordinary interest and approximate time $I = 500 \times .15 \times \frac{95}{360} = \$19.79$

Exact interest and approximate time $I = 500 \times .15 \times \frac{95}{365} = \$19.52$

To encourage prompt payment of bills, many merchants allow discounts for payments in advance of the final due date. Terms of 2/10, n/30 mean that if payment is made within 10 days from the date of the invoice, 2% of the amount of the invoice can be deducted. If the bill is paid after 10 days but on or before the 30th day, the net amount of the invoice must be paid. A buyer who takes advantage of cash discounts in effect lends money to the seller and receives as interest the cash discount. Interest rates earned in this way usually are so high that it is good business practice to take advantage of savings through cash discounts.

EXAMPLE 2 A merchant receives an invoice for $2000 with terms 2/10, n/30. If the merchant pays on the 10th day, what rate of interest is earned?

SOLUTION The cash discount is $40 (2% of $2000), making the principal $1960. Substituting in formula (1), we have

$$1960 \times r \times \frac{20}{360} = 40$$

$$r = \frac{40 \times 360}{1960 \times 20} = .367 = 36.7\%$$

Banks sometimes require business borrowers to keep a **compensating balance** on deposit with the bank as one of the conditions for getting a loan. A borrower who obtains a $1000 loan with a 20% compensating balance will be required to maintain $200 (20% of $1000) in the demand account. If the borrower normally maintains less than $200, part of the loan proceeds must be used to meet the compensating balance requirement. While paying interest at 13% on the full $1000, the borrower will have the use of less than $1000. The effective rate of interest will be greater than the stated 13%. The difference will depend on the size of the compensating balance and the balance the borrower would ordinarily keep anyway.

EXAMPLE 3 A borrower gets a $100,000 loan at 13% at a bank that requires the lender to keep a compensating balance of 20%. If all of this balance is a net increase in the demand account balance that the borrower would normally maintain, what is the equivalent rate paid by the borrower?

SOLUTION The fact that a compensating balance of 20% is required means that the borrower has the use of only $80,000 (20% less than $100,000). The interest on an annual basis figured on the $100,000 base is

$$I = Prt = 100,000 \times .13 \times 1 = \$13,000$$

However, the equivalent is

$$r = \frac{13,000}{80,000} = .1625 = 16.25\%$$

EXAMPLE 4 If the borrower in Example 3 normally keeps a demand deposit balance of $5000, the required balance would result in what equivalent rate?

SOLUTION The borrower is still paying $13,000 interest on an annual basis, and takes $15,000 out of the loan to get the required $20,000 compensating balance. In effect the borrower is paying $13,000 for the use of $85,000. On an annual basis the rate is 13,000/85,000 = .1529 = 15.29%.

EXAMPLE 5   Builders of homes, apartment houses, and commercial buildings often get construction loans. Construction loan funds are not supplied at one time, but rather are advanced gradually as construction progresses. The loan may be repaid in a lump sum shortly after completion of the project.

The builder of an apartment building obtained an $800,000 construction loan at an annual rate of 15%. The money was advanced as follows:

March 1, 1984	$300,000
June 1, 1984	200,000
October 1, 1984	200,000
December 1, 1984	100,000

The building was completed in February of 1985 and the loan repaid on March 1, 1985. Find the amount using ordinary interest and approximate time.

SOLUTION   Interest on each part of the loan is

$$300,000 \times .15 \times 1 \ = \$45,000$$
$$200,000 \times .15 \times \tfrac{9}{12} = \ 22,500$$
$$200,000 \times .15 \times \tfrac{5}{12} = \ 12,500$$
$$100,000 \times .15 \times \tfrac{3}{12} = \ \underline{3,750}$$
$$\text{Total interest} \quad \$83,750$$

Amount of loan = 800,000 + 83,750 = $883,750

Exercise 1b

1. Find the ordinary and exact interest on $750 for 100 days at 6%. ($12.50; $12.33)
2. Find the ordinary and exact interest on $6080.50 for 60 days at $12\tfrac{1}{2}\%$.
3. Find the ordinary and exact interest on $1200 for 45 days at 16%. ($24.00/$23.67)

4. If P = $9800 and r = 15%, find the ordinary and exact interest for a 120-day loan.

5. Use exact time and find the ordinary and exact interest on $300 at 18% from May 5 to September 12 of the same year.
   ($19.50/$19.23)

6. Use exact time and find the ordinary and exact interest on $500 from November 30, 1980, to March 15, 1981, using a rate of $7\frac{1}{2}$%.

7. Do problem 5 using approximate time.
   ($19.05/$18.79)

8. Do problem 6 using approximate time.

Use Bankers' Rule in Problems 9–14.

9. What amount must be repaid on November 21, 1986, if $7000 is borrowed at 16% on November 1, 1986?
   ($7062.22)

10. A person borrows $7760 on December 15, 1986, and repays the debt on March 3, 1987, with interest at 15%. Find the amount repaid.

11. A debt of $500 is due on June 15, 1988. After that date the borrower is required to pay 14% interest. If the debt is settled on January 10, 1989 what must be repaid?
    ($540.64)

12. On May 4, 1987, a person borrows $1850 and promises to repay the debt in 120 days with interest at 12%. If the loan is not paid on time the contract requires the borrower to pay 10% on the unpaid amount for the time after the due date. Determine how much this person must pay to settle the debt on December 15, 1987.

13. A person borrows $3050 on December 15, 1987, at 13%. What amount must be repaid on April 8, 1988? Note that for leap years, the number of the day after February 28 is one more than the number in Table 1.
    ($3176.66)

14. A borrower of $5000 on November 11, 1987, at 11% must repay what amount on March 10, 1988?

15. On December 31 a person has $3000 in an account in a savings and loan association. The money will earn dividends at $5\frac{1}{2}$% if it is left on deposit until the next interest date, which is June 30. Money withdrawn before June 30 does not get any interest. On May 1 the borrower needs $1000. Instead of drawing money out of the account, the borrower makes a passbook loan using the passbook as security. This loan will be repaid from the borrower's account

on June 30 when the interest is received. If the savings and loan association charges 6% for a passbook loan, this plan will save how much money as of June 30? The savings and loan association uses Bankers' Rule to calculate interest on passbook loans.

($17.50)

16. Find the answer to problem 15 if the loan is for $1500 and is made on March 31.

17. A merchant receives an invoice for $2000 with terms 2/10, n/60. If payment is made on the 10th, what rate of interest will be earned?

(14.7%)

18. An invoice for $5000 has terms 3/10, n/45. What rate of interest is earned if payment is made on the 10th?

1.14 PRESENT VALUE AT SIMPLE INTEREST

To find the amount of a principal invested at simple interest, we use the formula $S = P(1 + rt)$. If we know the amount and want to obtain the principal, we solve the formula for P.

$$P = \frac{S}{1 + rt} \tag{3}$$

EXAMPLE If money is worth 5%, what is the present value of $105 due in 1 year?

SOLUTION Substituting $S = 105$, $r = .05$, and $t = 1$ in formula (3), we find that

$$P = \frac{105}{1 + .05 \times 1} = \$100.00$$

Hence $100 invested now at 5% should amount to $105 in a year. Substituting in the amount formula verifies this.

$$S = 100(1 + .05 \times 1) = \$105.00$$

Calculating the present value of a sum due in the future is called **discounting**. When the simple interest formula is used to find the present value, the difference between the amount and the present value is called **simple discount**. Note that the simple discount on the future amount is the same as the simple interest on the principal or present value.

1.15 USE YOUR HEAD

All answers should be subjected to a common-sense check. Many mistakes are whoppers, resuling from such common slips as misplaced decimal points or inverted fractions. There is no disgrace in making such mistakes. Not catching them is another matter. The student who is looking for the present value at 4% of $5000 due in 2 months and writes down $49,668.87 should not expect credit for getting everything right except the decimal point. Common sense should tell the student to expect an answer less than $5000.

1.16 WHAT IS IT WORTH NOW?

The mathematics of finance can be used to find the best answer to many practical business problems. Typical of the many important questions that we consider in this and later chapters are: Should we pay cash or use credit? Is it better to buy or lease? Will a new machine pay for itself?

A good way to compare different plans is to get all of them on a present-value basis. Just as we can compare two items when we know their cash prices, so are we helped to choose between more complicated alternatives when we know what each is worth *now*.

EXAMPLE A person can buy a piece of property for $5000 cash or $5400 in a year. The prospective buyer has the cash and can invest it at 7%. Which method of payment is better and by how much now?

SOLUTION The propositions as they stand cannot be compared because they are at different points in time. By using formula (3), we are able to find that at 7% the $5400 due in a year has a present value of

$$P = \frac{5400}{1.07} = \$5046.73$$

This means that the buyer would have to invest $5046.73 now at 7% to have $5400 in a year. (Check: 5046.73 × 1.07 = $5400.00.) By paying cash, the buyer saves $46.73 now.

If another rate of return on the money was available, the decision might be different. For example:

Rate of Return	Present Value of $5400 Due in 1 Year	Better Plan
7%	$5046.73	Save $46.73 now by paying cash
8%	5000.00	Plans are equivalent
9%	4954.13	Save $45.87 now by paying $5400 in one year

Exercise 1c

1. What is the present value of $1500 due in 9 months if money is worth 8%?
   ($1415.09)
2. At an interest rate of 12%, what is the present value of $4300 due in 3 months?
3. At 6% interest, what is the present value of $600 due in 6 months?
   ($582.52)
4. What is the present value of $600 due in 6 months at: (a) 10% (b) 12%? (c) 14%?
5. What is the present value of $100 due in 1 year at: (a) 8%? (b) 10%? (c) 12%?
   [(a) $92.59; (b) $90.91; (c) $89.29]
6. At 12% find the present value of $2000 due in: (a) 3 months; (b) 6 months; (c) 9 months.
7. A woman can buy a grandfather clock for $3000 cash or $3100 in 1 year. She has the cash but can invest it at 6%. Which is more advantageous to her and by how much now?
   (By paying $3100 in a year, she saves $75.47 now.)
8. If you can earn $7\frac{1}{2}\%$ on money, is it better to pay $1990 cash for an item or to pay $2090 in a year? Give the cash equivalent of the savings resulting from adopting the better plan.

9. A woman can discharge an obligation by paying either $200 now or $208 in 6 months. If money is worth $5\frac{1}{2}\%$ to her, what is the cash equivalent of choosing the better plan?

   (By paying $200 cash, she saves $2.43 now.)

10. A man can settle a debt by paying either $1475 now or $1500 in 2 months. If he can earn 9% on his money, which plan is more advantageous and by how much now?

1.17 PRESENT VALUE OF INTEREST-BEARING DEBT

If we want to find the current value of an interest-bearing debt due in the future, we must first find the maturity value of the debt, using the stated interest rate for the term of the loan. Then we compute the present value of this maturity value for the time between the day it is discounted and the due date, using the rate specified for discounting. Since two rates and two times may be involved, a time diagram may help prevent errors.

EXAMPLE A debtor signs a note for $2000 due in 6 months with interest at 9%. One month after the debt is contracted, the holder of the note sells it to a third party, who determines the present value at 12%. How much is received for the note?

SOLUTION A time diagram is made (Figure 1-7). The maturity value is obtained, and then discounted for the 5 months between the discount date and the due date.

A common error in problems of this type is to use the time between the original loan and the discount date for finding the present value. That would be 1 month in this example. The person who buys the note is not interested in how long it has run, but in how long it still has to run. In this example the buyer of the note is loaning $1990.48 to the holder of the note. The $2090 received 5 months later is a return of the principal with interest at 12%.

1.18 EQUATIONS OF VALUE

Sometimes it is desirable to replace one or more obligations with one or more payments at different times that will be equivalent in value to the original obligations. For example, suppose you owe the same creditor $200 due now and $106 due in a year. You have the cash available to settle all the obligations. However, it would be foolish to make a cash payment of $306 because part of the debt is not due now. You will want the creditor to make some allowance for the early payment of the $106 due in a year. If you are using simple interest to reach a settlement, you and your creditor must agree on a rate. Suppose you decide to use 6%. Then we simply figure the present value at 6% of $106 due in a year.

$$P = \frac{106}{1 + .06 \times 1} = \$100$$

We can add this to the $200 due now to get a total cash settlement of $300. *Note that two sums of money cannot be added until they have been brought to the same point in time.*

In the previous example, suppose that you did not have the cash and asked the creditor to allow you to settle all the debts in a year. You must expect to pay interest on the $200 due now. If the agreed rate is 6%, the $200 would amount to $212 in a year. Because this sum is at the same point in time as the $106, the two can be added, making the total debt $318 *at that time.* The three alternatives we have discussed can be summarized as follows:

Figure 1-7

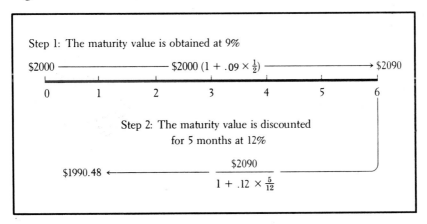

$$\left.\begin{array}{l}\text{\$200 now and \$106 in a year}\\ \text{\$300 now}\\ \text{\$318 in a year}\end{array}\right\} \begin{array}{l}\text{are equivalent in}\\ \text{value if money is}\\ \text{worth 6\%}\end{array}$$

We have gone into this point in detail because of its fundamental importance in the mathematics of finance and the difficulty it causes students. *Always* bring obligations to the same point using the specified rate before combining them. This common point is called a **focal date**, or **comparison date**. When everything has been brought to a focal date, an **equation of value** can be set up and unknown quantities determined. If any obligations are interest bearing, maturity values must be determined before the obligations are moved to the focal date.

A very effective way to solve many problems in the mathematics of finance is to make a time diagram, select a focal date, and then use an equation of value in which the original obligations are set equal to the payments after *both* have been brought to the focal date using the specified interest rate. If obligations are put on one side of the time line and payments on the other side, it is easy to tell them apart when setting up the equation of value.

If you draw a good time diagram, the equation of value will practically write itself.

In simple interest problems the answer will vary slightly depending on the location of the focal date. In compound interest problems the location of the focal date does not affect the answer. You should recognize that the focal date is simply an arbitrary point in time that enables all obligations and payments to be brought to the same time and an equation of value to be obtained.

There are only two ways to move money — backward and forward. Look at any time diagram. If a sum is to be moved forward, use an amount formula; if backward, use a present value formula.

EXAMPLE 1 A person owes $200 due in 6 months and $300 due in 1 year. The creditor will accept a cash settlement of both debts using a simple interest rate of 18% and putting the focal date now. Determine the size of the cash settlement.

SOLUTION A time diagram with the original debts on one side of the line and the new obligations on the other side will make it easy to obtain the correct equation (see Figure 1-8).

To get the $200 to the focal date, we discount it for 6 months. The $300 must be discounted for 1 year. Since the unknown payment is at the focal date, it equals simply x. Now that everything is at the same point in time, we set up the equation of value:

$$x = \frac{200}{1 + .18 \times \frac{1}{2}} + \frac{300}{1 + .18 \times 1} = 183.49 + 254.24 = \$437.73$$

ALTERNATE SOLUTION We could also do this problem by bringing the values to the focal date separately and then combining them.

$$\text{Value now of \$200 in 6 months} = \frac{200}{1 + .18 \times \frac{1}{2}} = \frac{200}{1.09} = \$183.49$$

$$\text{Value now of \$300 in 1 year} = \frac{300}{1 + .18 \times 1} = \frac{300}{1.18} = 254.24$$

$$\text{Value now for both debts} = \$437.73$$

EXAMPLE 2 Solve the preceding problem using 12 months hence as the focal date.

SOLUTION The $200 must be accumulated for 6 months, the $300 is at the focal date, and the unknown payment must be accumulated for 1 year. Then we have the equation of value:

$$x(1 + .18 \times 1) = 200(1 + .18 \times \tfrac{1}{2}) + 300$$

$$1.18x = 218 + 300 = 518$$

$$x = \frac{518}{1.18} = \$438.98$$

This example shows that in simple interest problems the answer varies slightly with the location of the focal date. Thus both parties should agree on *both* the rate and the focal date.

EXAMPLE 3 A person owes $1000 due in 1 year with interest at 14%. Two equal payments in 3 and 9 months, respectively, will be

Figure 1-8

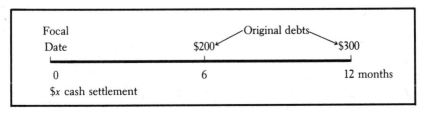

used to discharge this obligation. What will be the size of these payments if the person and the creditor agree to use an interest rate of 14% and a focal date 1 year hence?

SOLUTION   First, find the maturity value of the $1000 debt.

$$S = 1000(1 + .14 \times 1) = \$1140$$

No further use will be made of the original debt of $1000. Now make a time diagram (Figure 1-9), move everything to the focal date, and set up the equation of value.

$$x(1 + .14 \times \tfrac{3}{4}) + x(1 + .14 \times \tfrac{1}{4}) = 1140$$
$$1.105x + 1.035x = 1140$$
$$2.14x = 1140$$

$$x = \frac{1140}{2.14} = \$532.71$$

EXAMPLE 4   A person borrows $2000 at 15% interest on June 1, 1986. The debt will be repaid with two equal payments, one on December 1, 1986, and the other on June 1, 1987. Put the focal date on June 1, 1986, and find the size of the payments. Use approximate time and ordinary interest.

SOLUTION   A time diagram (Figure 1-10) shows in what direction and how far each sum is to be moved.

The $2000 is already at the focal date. The unknown payments are brought back using formula (3). Setting up an equation of value and using reciprocals to simplify computations, we have

Figure 1-9

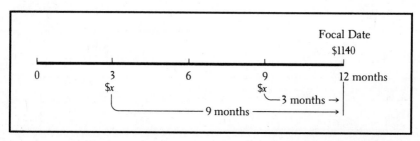

$$\frac{x}{1 + .15 \times \frac{1}{2}} + \frac{x}{1 + .15 \times 1} = 2000$$

$$\frac{x}{1.075} + \frac{x}{1.15} = 2000$$

$$.930233x + .869565x = 2000$$
$$1.799798x = 2000$$
$$x = \$1111.24$$

EXAMPLE 5 Work Example 4 with the focal date on June 1, 1987.

SOLUTION The equation of value is

$$x(1 + .15 \times \tfrac{1}{2}) + x = 2000(1 + .15 \times 1)$$
$$1.075x + x = 2300$$
$$2.075x = 2300$$

$$x = \frac{2300}{2.075} = \$1108.43$$

Note that a different focal date resulted in simpler computations and a slightly different answer.

EXAMPLE 6 A person borrowed $6000 on September 15, 1988, agreeing to pay $2000 on January 15, 1989, and $2000 on May 15, 1989. If the interest rate was 18%, how much was paid on September 15, 1989, to settle the debt? Use approximate time and ordinary

Figure 1-10

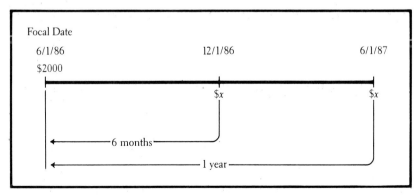

interest. In this problem the logical place for the focal date is September 15, 1989, the final settlement date.

SOLUTION   We put all transactions on a time diagram (Figure 1-11). Using formula (2), we carry forward the debt and two payments to the focal date. Then we write the equation of value.

$$x = 6000(1 + .18 \times 1) - 2000(1 + .18 \times \tfrac{2}{3}) - 2000(1 + .18 \times \tfrac{1}{3})$$
$$= 7080 - 2240 - 2120$$
$$= \$2720.00$$

1.19   INVESTMENT ANALYSIS

Equations of value are often used in the valuation of assets. Acquiring an asset usually means making an immediate outlay for the acquisition cost of the investment, followed by a stream of earnings and costs over time. The immediate outlay and subsequent earnings and costs are called cash inflows and outflows. These flows sometimes occur almost continuously rather than at stated time intervals. A store, for example, has money coming in every day that the store is open. However, it is simpler and usually more satisfactory in making practical decisions to assume that the flows during a time period are concentrated at the end of the period. Some analysts put outflows at the beginning of the period and inflows at the end of the period.

Before an investment decision is made, it is important to try to predict whether or not the investment will be profitable. Cash flow

Figure 1-11

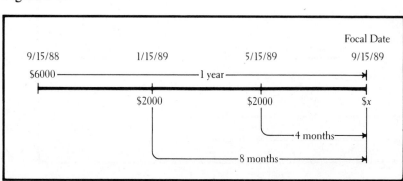

analysis is a general and powerful technique for analyzing investment problems. Both the timing and the size of the cash flows must be taken into account when making investment decisions.

There are two ways to use cash flows to analyze investments. One is to discount all cash flows at a given rate. The algebraic sum of the discounted cash flows is called the **net present value** or simply the **present value** of the investment. If the present value is positive at an acceptable yield rate, the investment is attractive. What constitutes an acceptable rate depends on the cost of capital. This subject is discussed under Capital Budgeting in Chapter 8. The other method is to find the rate that makes the inflows and outflows equal as of a certain point in time. This rate is called the **profit rate**, the **marginal efficiency of investment**, or the **internal rate of return**. This rate must usually be found by trial and error.

In this chapter cash flow analysis is applied to problems involving a limited number of flows and simple interest. When there is a stream of many costs and earnings, it is necessary to use compound interest methods described in later chapters. Regardless of whether there are a few or many flows, a good method of solution is to:

1. Get the inflows and outflows at their proper points in time. If there are more than a couple of flows, draw a time diagram.
2. Select a focal or comparison date.
3. Write an equation of value.

EXAMPLE 1 A project that requires an investment of $1900 is expected to result in a return of $2000 in 6 months. What would be the net present value of this investment based on an interest rate of: (a) 10%? (b) 12%?

SOLUTION We must compare an outflow of $1900 now with an inflow of $2000 in 6 months. Note that outflows are negative. Putting the focal date now and using formula (3) to discount the $2000, we have

$$\text{At } 10\%: \text{ net present value} = -1900 + \frac{2000}{1 + .10 \times \frac{1}{2}}$$

$$= -1900 + 1904.76 = \$4.76$$

$$\text{At } 12\%: \text{ net present value} = -1900 + \frac{2000}{1 + .12 \times \frac{1}{2}}$$

$$= -1900 + 1886.79 = -\$13.21$$

If the investor is satisfied with a 10% return, this investment would be attractive, since it has a positive present value at this rate. The investor who wants 12% would not be satisfied, because the negative net present value indicates that the return is less than 12%.

EXAMPLE 2 Find the rate of return on the project in Example 1.

SOLUTION Since there is only one inflow, this situation can be handled as a problem in simple interest using formula (1).

$$1900 \times r \times \tfrac{1}{2} = 100$$

$$r = \frac{2 \times 100}{1900} = .1053 = 10.53\%$$

CHECK The interest on $1900 at 10.53% = $1900 \times .1053 \times \tfrac{1}{2} =$ $100.04. The 4-cent difference is due to rounding.

EXAMPLE 3 A company can put $3600 in an investment that is expected to result in cash inflows of $1000 in 6 months and $3000 in 1 year. Find the internal rate of return.

SOLUTION A time diagram (Figure 1-12) shows the amount and time of all cash flows.

By trial and error we seek a rate that will make the discounted value of the inflows equal to $3600. Although experience with similar problems is of some help, the first trial rate is largely a guess. At 8%,

Figure 1-12

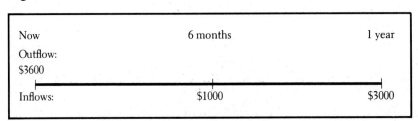

Now	6 months	1 year
Outflow:		
$3600		
Inflows:	$1000	$3000

Present value of inflows $= \dfrac{1000}{1.04} + \dfrac{3000}{1.08} = 961.54 + 2777.78 = \$3739.32$

This result indicates that the rate is much higher than 8%, so we make a bold jump to 16% in the hope that this will bring us below $3600, giving us a bracket on the true rate. At 16%,

Present value of inflows $= \dfrac{1000}{1.08} + \dfrac{3000}{1.16} = 925.93 + 2586.21 = \$3512.14$

Splitting the difference and trying 12%, we have

Present value of inflows $= \dfrac{1000}{1.06} + \dfrac{3000}{1.12} = 943.40 + 2678.57 = \$3621.97$

The rate is now known to be between 12 and 16%. At 14%,

Present value of inflows $= \dfrac{1000}{1.07} + \dfrac{3000}{1.14} = 934.58 + 2631.58 = \$3566.16$

Now we know that the rate is between 12 and 14%. This trial-and-error seeking of the answer, known as **iteration**, can be done rapidly with a computer. In simple problems, however, good judgment in choosing trial rates can quickly take you to a point where you can use interpolation to get an answer that is good enough for making practical decisions.

Interpolation is the way mathematicians read between the lines. Since the mathematics of finance often involves interpolation, it is well to learn a systematic method. Record the closest values on both sides of the unknown and compute differences as shown in the following chart.

Rate		Present value of inflows		
	$\lceil$ 12%	3621.97 $\rceil$		
2%	$d\lceil$ $\lfloor$ _ r	3600.00 $\rfloor$ 21.97	55.81
	$\lfloor$ 14%	3566.16		

Now we have two columns of data. In one column all entries are known; the other contains an unknown value. We assume that r is the same fraction of the distance from 12 to 14% as 3600 is from 3621.97 to 3566.16. We let d represent the unknown increment in the rate and set up a proportion.

$$\frac{d}{2} = \frac{21.97}{55.81}$$

$$d = \frac{2 \times 21.97}{55.81} = .8$$

$$r = 12.0 + .8 = 12.8\%$$

Students often ask if it matters which way they go. The answer is no. All that matters is going the same way in both columns. If we come up from the bottom in this problem, we get

$$\frac{d}{2} = \frac{33.84}{55.81}$$

$$d = \frac{2 \times 33.84}{55.81} = 1.2$$

$$r = 14.0 - 1.2 = 12.8\% \text{ (note subtraction)}$$

An interpolated result is always between the known values. Remembering this fact may catch an arithmetic error or a wrong sign applied to the incremental change.

The method described here is linear interpolation, which assumes a straight-line change between values. Although many mathematics of finance functions are curved, linear interpolation usually leads to results that are accurate enough for practical work. If a very high degree of precision is required, more refined methods of interpolation can be found in books on numerical analysis and in the Compound Interest and Annuity Tables published by the Financial Publishing Company.

Exercise 1d

1. A person owes $200 due in 4 months and $800 due in 8 months. What single payment 6 months hence will discharge these obligations if the settlement is based on an interest rate of 12% and the focal date is 6 months hence?
   ($988.31)

2. A person owes $350 due in 3 months and $525 due in 6 months. If money is worth 16%, what single payment in 6 months will settle both obligations? Put the focal date at 6 months.

3. A person owes $200 due in 6 months and $400 due in 1 year. What cash payment will retire both debts if money is worth 15%? Use now as the focal date.
   ($533.88)

4. Debts of $500 and $1500 are due in 3 and 6 months, respectively. What cash settlement will settle these debts if it is based on an interest rate of 10% and the time of the cash settlement is used for the focal date?

5. A debtor signs a note for $1000 due in 1 year with interest at 12%. Three months after the debt is contracted, the holder of the note sells it to a third party who determines its value at 16% simple interest. How much does the seller of the note receive?
   ($1000.00)

6. A borrower signs a note for $2500 due in 6 months with interest at 15%. Two months after the note is signed, the holder of the note sells it to a buyer who charges 18% simple interest for discounting. How much does the seller receive?

7. A debtor owes $1000 due in 1 year. He agrees to pay $500 in 3 months. If money is worth 13%, what payment must he make 15 months hence to retire the rest of the debt? Put the focal date 15 months hence.
   ($467.50)

8. A woman owes $4000. She and her creditor agree that she can pay $2000 now and the balance in 6 months. Find the payment in 6 months if the settlement is based on an interest rate of 16% and the focal date is 6 months hence.

9. A man incurs a debt for $1500 due in 3 months with interest at 13%. One month later he pays $500 on the debt. What balance will he owe on the original due date if the two parties to the transaction agree to use 13% in arriving at a settlement? Use the due date as the focal date, and approximate time and ordinary interest.
   ($1037.92)

10. A family buys merchandise and agrees to pay $2000 in 2 months. One month later they pay $800 on the debt. What balance will they owe on the due date if the creditor agrees to use 18% in arriving at a settlement? Use the due date as the focal date, and approximate time and ordinary interest.

11. A company has an investment opportunity that would require spending $9200 now. The investment is expected to be worth

$10,000 in 1 year. What is its net present value at: (a) 8%? (b) 10%?

[(a) $59.26; (b) −$109.09]

12. An investment requires a cash outlay of $4200. It is estimated that the investment will return $5000 in 1 year. Find the net present value at: (a) 18%; (b) 20%.

13. Find the internal rate of return for problem 11.

    (8.7%)

14. Find the internal rate of return for problem 12.

15. An investment costs $18,500, and is expected to produce cash inflows of $10,000 in 6 and 12 months. Find the net present value at 10%.

    ($114.72)

16. An investment requires a cash outlay of $2750, and is expected to produce a cash inflow of $1000 in 6 months and $2000 in 12 months. Find the net present value at 8%.

17. Find the internal rate of return for problem 15.

    (10.9%)

18. Find the internal rate of return for problem 16.

1.20   PARTIAL PAYMENTS

When a person borrows money, it is desirable to have an agreement with the creditor under which the interest can be reduced by making partial payments before the due date. There are two common ways to allow interest credit on short-term transactions: **Merchants' Rule** and **United States Rule**. Under Merchants' Rule the entire debt earns interest to the final settlement date. Each partial payment also earns interest from the time it is made to the final settlement date. The balance due on the final date is simply the difference between the amount of the debt and the sum of the amounts of the partial payments. Note that we have what is essentially a focal date problem using the given interest rate and putting the focal date at the final settlement date. Merchants' Rule is used frequently with short-term obligations.

Under United States Rule the interest on the outstanding principal is computed each time a partial payment is made. If the payment is greater than the interest, the difference is used to reduce the principal. If the payment is less than the interest, it is held without interest until another partial payment is made. The two payments are then added. If they exceed the interest at that time, the difference is used to reduce the principal. The final settlement is the last outstanding principal carried to the final settlement date.

In the following examples, solutions are given in tabular form instead of the usual equation of value form. The tabular method of solution may be preferred by some for this type of problem.

EXAMPLE 1 A debt of $1000 is due in 1 year with interest at 15%. The debtor pays $300 in 4 months and $200 in 10 months. Find the balance due in 1 year using Merchants' Rule and United States Rule.

SOLUTION BY MERCHANTS' RULE This method is equivalent to putting a focal date at the time of the final settlement. A diagram (Figure 1-13) helps determine the time each sum is to be moved.

Computations are given in Table 1-1.

SOLUTION BY UNITED STATES RULE Instead of having one point to which all sums are brought, we base the solution on what amounts to a floating focal or comparison date. Each time a payment is made, the preceding balance is brought at interest to this point and a new balance is obtained. In this problem intermediate balances are obtained at 4 and 10 months and a final settlement at 12 months. A diagram (Figure 1-14, page 49) helps to find the time from one payment to the next.

Figure 1-13

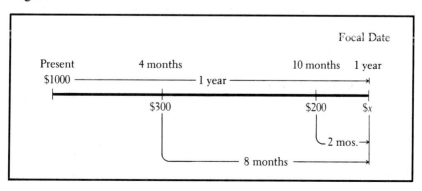

Computations are given in Table 1-2.

Note that the two methods lead to different concluding payments. Again, we see why the two parties to a business transaction must agree on the method of calculating interest.

EXAMPLE 2 On June 15, 1987, a person borrows $5000 at 16%. Payments are made as follows: $2000 on July 10, 1987; $50 on

Table 1-1 Merchants' Rule

Original debt		$1000.00
Interest on $1000 for 1 year		150.00
		$1150.00
First payment	$300.00	
Interest on $300 for 8 months	30.00	
	$330.00	
Second payment	$200.00	
Interest on $200 for 2 months	5.00	
	205.00	
Sum of partial payments accumulated to the final settlement date		535.00
Balance due on final settlement date		$ 615.00

Table 1-2 United States Rule

Original debt	$1000.00
Interest on $1000 for 4 months	50.00
Amount due after 4 months	$1050.00
Deduct first payment	300.00
New balance due	$ 750.00
Interest on $750 for 6 months	56.25
Amount due after 10 months	$ 806.25
Deduct second payment	200.00
New balance due	$ 606.25
Interest on $606.25 for 2 months	15.16
Balance due on final settlement date	$ 621.41

Figure 1-14

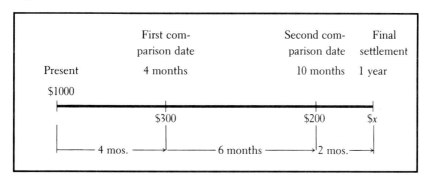

November 20, 1987; $1000 on January 12, 1988. What is the balance due on March 10, 1988, by United States Rule?

SOLUTION This example shows how to handle a payment that is smaller than the outstanding interest. See Table 1-3.

An important application of United States Rule is getting the month-to-month balance on home loans. Home loans usually are repaid with equal monthly payments. The monthly payment depends on the size of the loan, the interest rate, and the number of payments. After the monthly payment is determined using methods given in Chapter 3, simple interest is used to determine how much of each payment goes to interest. The balance of the payment is used to reduce the principal. A long-term loan at a high rate results in very little house being obtained with the early payments.

EXAMPLE 3 A couple gets a $40,000, 30-year, 12% loan. The monthly payment is $411.45. How much of the first two payments goes to interest and how much to principal?

SOLUTION Substituting $P = 40,000$, $r = .12$, and $t = \frac{1}{12}$ in formula (1), we have

$$I = 40,000 \times .12 \times \tfrac{1}{12} = \$400.00$$

Payment to principal = $411.45 - 400.00 = $11.45

The picture now gets brighter. The balance owed on the loan is reduced to $40,000 - 11.45 = $39,988.55.

To find the second month's interest, we return to formula (1) and find that

$$I = 39,988.55 \times .12 \times \tfrac{1}{12} = \$399.89$$

Payment to principal = $411.45 - 399.89 = $11.56

With the second payment the couple gets more house, 11 cents more, as a matter of fact.

The first two payments, totaling $822.90, buy $23.01 worth of house, while the remaining $799.89 is interest. The happy "home-owners" are now renting money instead of an apartment. Near the end of the term of the loan, however, more of the payment goes toward principal.

Table 1-3 United States Rule payment not larger than interest

Debt on June 15, 1987	$5000.00
Interest at 16% from June 15 to July 10	
(25 days)	55.56
Amount due	$5055.56
Payment of $2000 on July 10, 1987	2000.00
	$3055.56
Interest on $3055.56 from July 10 to November 20 (133 days) is $180.62. Since this amount is more than the $50 payment on November 20, this payment is held without interest and no deduction is made.	
Interest on $3055.56 from July 10, 1987 to January 12, 1988 (186 days)	252.59
Amount due	$3308.15
Payments: November 20, 1987 $ 50.00	
January 12, 1988 1000.00	1050.00
Balance as of January 12, 1988	$2258.15
Interest on $2258.15 from January 12, 1988, to March 10, 1988 (58 days). Note the extra day for leap year.	58.21
Balance due on March 10, 1988	$2316.36

Exercise 1e

When calendar dates are given and all payments are made on the same day of the month, base interest computations on approximate time and ordinary interest. For example, take the time between June 1 and September 1 as 3 months or $\frac{1}{4}$ year, and so on. In all other calendar date problems, use Bankers' Rule.

1. A man borrows $5000 at 15%. He pays $2000 in 2 months and $2000 in 4 months. How much would he have to pay in 6 months to cancel the debt by Merchants' Rule? By U.S. Rule?
   ($1225.00; $1233.21)
2. A debt of $7000 is due in 6 months with interest at 14%. Partial payments of $1500 and $2000 are made in 2 and 4 months, respectively. What is the balance due on the final settlement date by Merchants' Rule? By U.S. Rule?
3. The Main Hardware Company was in arrears in its account with the Reliance Supply Corporation to the extent of $1200 on June 1 and was required to pay 15% interest from that date. On July 1 the company paid $400 and on August 1, $300. What was the balance due on September 1 by Merchants' Rule? By U.S. Rule?
   ($531.25; $531.75)
4. An obligation of $650 is due on April 15, after which the borrower must pay interest at 18%. If the borrower pays $200 on June 15 and $100 on August 15, how much will need to be paid on October 15 to discharge the obligation if the final settlement is based on Merchants' Rule? On U.S. Rule?
5. A woman borrows $3000 at 16% on August 15, 1987. She pays $600 on September 15, 1987; $800 on October 15, 1987; $600 on December 15, 1987. If she makes a final settlement on February 15, 1988, how much will she have to pay by Merchants' Rule? By U.S. Rule?
   ($1141.33; $1146.92)
6. A couple purchases a used car on June 1 for $2000 and pays $500 down. They agree to pay interest on the balance at $17\frac{1}{2}$%. If they pay $300 on August 15 and $200 on September 30, how much must they pay on November 1 to own the car by Merchants' Rule? By U.S. Rule?
7. What is the balance due by Merchants' Rule for Example 2?
   ($2302.64)
8. On June 1, 1978, a woman borrowed $1000 at 13% for 1 year. If not paid on the due date, the maturity value of the debt was to bear interest at $16\frac{1}{2}$% from the due date. She paid $300 on July 15,

1979; $15 on November 20, 1979; and $200 on January 10, 1980. What payment was required on April 30, 1980, to settle the debt by Merchants' Rule? By U.S. Rule?

9. A couple buys an $80,000 house and pays $15,000 down. If they get a $65,000, 30-year, $13\frac{1}{2}\%$ loan, the monthly payment will be $744.52. How much of the first two payments will go to interest and how much to principal?

$$\begin{bmatrix} & \text{Payment to} & \\ & \text{Interest} & \text{Principal} \\ \text{First payment} & \$731.25 & \$13.27 \\ \text{Second payment} & 731.10 & 13.42 \end{bmatrix}$$

10. After shopping for credit, the couple in problem 9 finds a lender who will make the loan at 12% with monthly payments of $668.60. Find the payment to interest and principal for the first two payments.

REVIEW EXERCISES FOR CHAPTER 1

1. In July of 1976 a man entered a bank in Cincinnati, Ohio, with $6700 worth of certificates of deposit at 8% taken out in 1919. Suppose that the certificates were purchased on July 1, 1919, and were cashed on July 1, 1976. Assuming the interest was simple, find the interest and the amount.
   ($30,552; $37,252)

2. A company wants to invest $500,000 from July 15, 1986, until September 28, 1986. The company has a choice of four banks in which to invest the money. All four will pay 12% simple interest. Bank A will use ordinary interest and approximate time, bank B will use exact interest and approximate time, bank C will use exact interest and exact time, and bank D will compute using Bankers' Rule. Find the interest each bank will pay on the investment and indicate which bank the company should choose.

3. Suppose that a 1905 nickel increases in value to $2.05 by 1985. Find the rate of increase.
   (50%)

4. Suppose that you borrow $100 at $12\frac{1}{2}\%$ simple interest but the lender refuses to take payment until the time when you must repay $200. How long will it take?

5. The monthly payment on a $40,000, 25-year home loan at $12\frac{1}{2}\%$ is $436.15. Interest is always charged on the outstanding balance. Find the amount of interest paid in the first 3 months.
   ($1249.39)

6. Mrs. U. borrowed $2000 from Ms. S. at 15% to be repaid in 9 months. Three months after the loan, Ms. S. sold the note to Miss A., who wants to get 18% on her money. Find the selling price of the note.

7. A person wants to buy some property. Which selling price is preferable for the buyer and by how much now if money is worth 6%: $1000 now or $1050 in 6 months?

    ($19.42 cheaper to pay $1000 now)

8. The Jones Company owes the Dakota Supply Company $3000 on January 15, 1987, and is required to pay 16% interest from that date. After making payments of $1000 on April 15, 1987, and $1500 on October 15, 1987, what payment on January 15, 1988, will retire the debt using U.S. Rule?

9. Do problem 8 using Merchants' Rule.

    ($800.00)

10. An investment costs $40,000. The return anticipated is $25,000 in 6 months and $20,000 in 1 year. Find the net present value at 10%.

11. A couple wins $10,000 in a lottery and wishes to invest it at 10% simple interest to produce equal amounts of money for each of their two children, now ages 11 and 16, when the children reach age 21. What is the amount each child will get? Put the focal date at 10 years from now.

    ($8000.00)

12. If the terms of a $5000 purchase are 3/30, n/60, how much would the buyer save on the 60th day if money was borrowed from a bank on the 30th day for 30 days at 12% to take advantage of the cash discount?

13. Do problem 11 again using United States Rule. This would be the procedure used in actual practice.

    ($9000.00)

Chapter 2
Bank Discount

2.1 BANK DISCOUNT

The charge for many loans is based on the final amount rather than on the present value. This charge is called **bank discount**, or simply **discount**. The money that the borrower receives is called **bank proceeds**, or just **proceeds**. The rate percentage used in computing the discount is called the **bank discount rate** or **discount rate**.

As an illustration of a bank discount transaction, consider the case of a person who wants to borrow $100 for a year from a lender who uses a discount rate of 6%. The lender will take 6% of $100 from the $100 and give the borrower $94. Thus the computation of bank discount is exactly the same as the computation of simple interest except that it is based on the amount rather than the present value. This realization leads us to the bank discount formula:

$$D = Sdt \qquad (4)$$

D = the bank discount in dollars
S = the amount or maturity value
d = the discount rate per unit of time expressed as a decimal
t = the time in units that correspond to the rate

Since the proceeds or present value of the loan is the difference between the amount and the discount, we can say that

$$P = S - D = S - Sdt$$

Factoring, we have

$$P = S(1 - dt) \qquad (5)$$

Solving this expression for S results in a formula that is useful when a borrower wants a certain amount of cash and the problem is to determine the maturty of the loan to be discounted.

$$S = \frac{P}{1 - dt} \qquad \text{what size loan?} \qquad (6)$$

EXAMPLE 1 A woman borrows $600 for 6 months from a lender who uses a discount rate of 10%. What is the discount and how much money does the borrower get?

SOLUTION Substituting $S = 600$, $d = .10$, and $t = \frac{1}{2}$ in formula (4), we have

$$D = 600 \times .10 \times \tfrac{1}{2} = \$30.00$$

Since the proceeds represent the difference between the maturity value and the discount, the borrower will get $600.00 - 30.00 = \$570.00$.

EXAMPLE 2 A man wants to get $2000 cash with the loan to be repaid in 6 months. If he borrows the money from a bank that charges a 12% discount rate, what size loan should he ask for?

SOLUTION Substituting $P = 2000$, $d = .12$, and $t = \frac{1}{2}$ in formula (6), we obtain

$$S = \frac{2000}{1 - .12 \times \frac{1}{2}} = \frac{2000}{.94} = \$2127.66$$

CHECK $D = 2127.66 \times 0.12 \times \frac{1}{2} = \$127.66$

Proceeds $= 2127.66 - 127.66 = \$2000.00$

Bank discount is sometimes called interest in advance because it is based on the future amount rather than on the present value. Bank discount, requiring only multiplication, is easier to compute than discount at a simple interest rate, which requires division if the amount is known. A given bank discount rate results in a larger money return to the lender than the same simple interest rate. For these reasons, bank discount is commonly used to discount sums of money for periods of time of a year or less.

EXAMPLE 3 Find the present value of $100 due in 1 year: at a simple interest rate of $12\frac{1}{2}\%$; at a bank discount rate of $12\frac{1}{2}\%$.

SOLUTION For a simple interest rate of $12\frac{1}{2}\%$, we substitute $S = 100$, $r = .125$, and $t = 1$ in formula (3):

$$P = \frac{100}{1 + .125 \times 1} = \frac{100}{1.125} = \$88.89$$

For a bank discount rate of $12\frac{1}{2}\%$, we substitute $S = 100$, $d = .125$, and $t = 1$ in formula (4):

$$D = 100 \times .125 \times 1 = \$12.50$$

$$\text{Present value or proceeds} = 100 - 12.50 = \$87.50$$

Note that the present value at $12\frac{1}{2}\%$ bank discount is $1.39 less for the same maturity value than if it were based on a $12\frac{1}{2}\%$ interest rate.

2.2 INTEREST RATE EQUIVALENT TO A BANK DISCOUNT RATE

As the previous example shows, the present value at a given discount rate is less than the present value based on the same interest rate. For comparison purposes, it is desirable to be able to determine the interest rate that is equivalent to a given discount rate. Coupon equivalent is a common expression for the simple interest rate equivalent to a bank discount rate. The reason is that some securities bear coupons that are clipped and cashed to get the periodic interest payments. The dollar value of each coupon is based on simple interest.

A discount rate and an interest rate are equivalent if the two rates result in the same present value for an amount due in the future. To obtain the relationship between r and d, all we have to do is get the present value of an amount S due in the future by formula (3) and set it equal to the present value of the same amount S by formula (5).

$$\frac{S}{1 + rt} = S(1 - dt)$$

Dividing both sides by S, we obtain

$$\frac{1}{1 + rt} = 1 - dt$$

Inverting both sides, we have

$$1 + rt = \frac{1}{1 - dt}$$

Subtracting 1 from both sides and simplifying, we find that

$$rt = \frac{1}{1 - dt} - 1 = \frac{1 - 1 + dt}{1 - dt} = \frac{dt}{1 - dt}$$

Dividing both sides by t yields

$$r = \frac{d}{1 - dt} \qquad\qquad (7)$$

In a similar way we find that the discount rate corresponding to a given interest rate is

$$d = \frac{r}{1 + rt} \qquad\qquad (8)$$

EXAMPLE 1   A bank discounts a $200 note due in a year using a bank discount rate of 12%. What interest rate is the bank getting?

SOLUTION   Substituting $d = .12$ and $t = 1$ in formula (7), we have

$$r = \frac{.12}{1 - .12 \times 1} = \frac{.12}{.88} = .1364 = 13.64\%$$

EXAMPLE 2   A lender charges a discount rate of $13\frac{1}{2}\%$ for discounting a note for $600 due in 2 months. What is the equivalent interest rate?

SOLUTION   Substituting $d = .135$ and $t = \frac{1}{6}$ in formula (7), we find that

$$r = \frac{.135}{1 - .135 \times \frac{1}{6}} = \frac{.135}{.9775} = .1381 = 13.81\%$$

EXAMPLE 3   To earn an interest rate of 11% on a 6 months' loan, a lender should charge what discount rate?

SOLUTION   Substituting $r = .11$ and $t = \frac{1}{2}$ in formula (8), we obtain

$$d = \frac{.11}{1 + .11 \times \frac{1}{2}} = \frac{.11}{1.055} = .1043 = 10.43\%$$

Exercise 2a

1. Determine the bank discount and the proceeds if $1500 is discounted for 3 months at a discount rate of 10%.
   ($37.50; $1462.50)
2. Determine the bank discount and the proceeds if $4400 is discounted at a discount rate of 12% for 2 months.
3. Find the discount on $3200 for 60 days at $13\frac{1}{2}\%$ discount. What are the proceeds?
   ($72.00; $3128.00)
4. Find the discount on $568.30 for 120 days at $10\frac{1}{2}\%$ discount. What are the proceeds?
5. Find the bank discount and the present value of $5000 due in 5 months using a discount rate of 15%.
   ($312.50; $4687.50)
6. An obligation of $6040 is due in 10 months. What is the present value of this obligation at a bank discount rate of 14%?
7. A bank charges 14% for discounting loans. If a man agrees to repay $1200 in 3 months, how much does he receive now?
   ($1158.00)
8. An obligation of $650 is due on August 10. What is its value on April 6 if it is discounted at a discount rate of 12%?
9. Find the bank discount and the proceeds if $450 is discounted for 30 days at $10\frac{1}{2}\%$.
   ($3.94; $446.06)
10. Find the bank discount and the proceeds if $240,000 is discounted for 60 days at 15%.
11. A woman wants $5000 for 3 months. What size loan should she get if her bank charges a discount rate of 16%?
    ($5208.33)
12. A man wants $800 for 6 months. What size loan should he ask for if his bank charges a discount rate of 10%?

13. George Wilson needs $800 on February 10. He plans to repay the money on June 30. What size loan should he request if his bank's discount rate is 11%?
   ($835.75)

14. A borrower needs $4000 on June 1, and expects to repay the loan on July 16. What size loan should the borrower request from a lender whose discount rate is 12%?

15. A bank discounts a sum that is due in 1 year. If the discount rate is 11%, what is the equivalent interest rate?
   (12.36%)

16. If a sum is due in 90 days, what is the interest rate equivalent to a discount rate of 15%?

17. If a sum is due in 6 months, what is the interest rate equivalent to a discount rate of 14%?
   (15.05%)

18. If a sum is due in 1 month, what is the interest rate equivalent to a discount rate of 12%?

19. A lender wants to get a 12% interest rate on a loan being made for 6 months. What discount rate should the lender use?
   (11.32%)

20. To get 15% interest on 120-day loans, what discount rate should be charged?

2.3   PROMISSORY NOTES

Bank discount is used to determine the value of a promissory note at a stated point in time. The proceeds of a note are found as follows:

1. Find the maturity value of the note. This is the face value if it is non-interest-bearing. If the note is interest-bearing, the maturity value is the face value plus interest at the stated rate for the term of the note, the time from the date of the note to the maturity date.
2. Discount the maturity value using the discount rate from the date the note is discounted to the maturity date.
3. Subtract the discount from the maturity value.

EXAMPLE 1 On July 28, 1986, John A. Blalock discounts the note in Figure 2-1 at a bank that charges a discount rate of 12%. Find the proceeds.

SOLUTION Table 1 in the back of the book is helpful in getting the discount period.

Date	Day of year
Maturity date, December 15, 1986	349
Discount date, July 28, 1986	209
Discount period	140 days

Substituting $S = 3000$, $d = .12$, and $t = 140/360$ in formula (4), we have

$$D = 3000 \times .12 \times \tfrac{140}{360} = \$140.00$$

$$\text{Proceeds} = 3000.00 - 140.00 = \$2860.00$$

EXAMPLE 2 On July 28, 1986, John A. Blalock discounts the note in Figure 2-2 at a bank that charges a discount rate of 12%. Find the proceeds.

SOLUTION First, to get the maturity value, we substitute $P = 3000$, $r = .11$, and $t = \tfrac{1}{2}$ in formula (1).

$$I = 3000 \times .11 \times \tfrac{1}{2} = \$165.00$$

$$S = 3000.00 + 165.00 = \$3165.00$$

The elapsed time from July 28 to December 15 is 140 days. Substituting $S = 3165.00$, $d = 0.12$, and $t = 140/360$ in formula (4), we obtain

Figure 2-1 A Non-interest-bearing Note

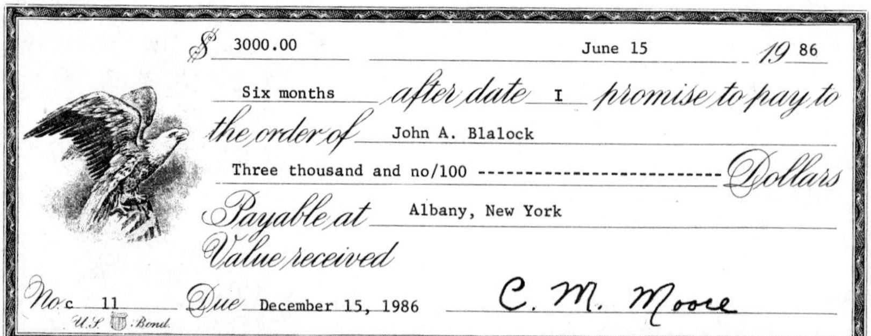

$ 3000.00   June 15   19 86

Six months   after date I promise to pay to
the order of   John A. Blalock

Three thousand and no/100 ------------------------- Dollars

Payable at   Albany, New York
Value received

No. 11   Due December 15, 1986   C. M. Moore
  U.S. Bond.

$$D = 3165.00 \times 0.12 \times \tfrac{140}{360} = \$147.70$$

$$\text{Proceeds} = 3165.00 - 147.70 = \$3017.30$$

A time diagram can be used to illustrate the step-by-step solution of a note problem. Figure 2-3 shows how a time diagram, if drawn approximately to scale, is a help in checking times in a problem.

After working enough note problems to become familiar with the three steps – maturity value, discount, and proceeds – you may prefer to arrange the work in tabular form, as we now show for the previous examples.

Figure 2-2 An Interest-bearing Note

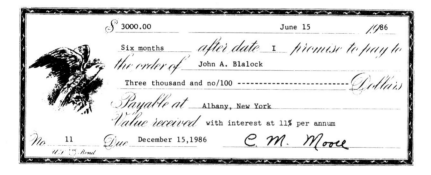

Figure 2-3

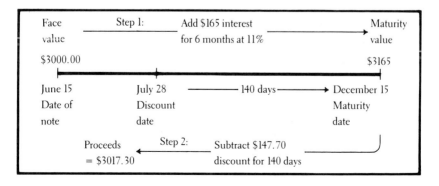

	Non-interest-bearing Note	11% Interest-bearing Note
Face value	$3000.00	$3000.00
Interest for 6 months		165.00
Maturity value	$3000.00	$3165.00
12% discount for 140 days	140.00	147.70
Proceeds	$2860.00	$3017.30

Exercise 2b

If the time in a note is given in months, the due date is the same date of the month as the date of the note. A 3-month note dated March 1 would be due on June 1. If the time is given in days, use exact time when finding the maturing date. When computing the discount, use exact time from the discount date to the due date and a 360-day year.

1. On August 5, 1988, Alice E. Sproul discounts the note in Figure 2-4 at a bank that charges a discount rate of $12\frac{1}{2}\%$. What are the proceeds?
   ($808.92)
2. Find the proceeds if Ms. Sproul discounts the note on July 1, 1988, at a bank charging a discount rate of $12\frac{1}{2}\%$.
3. On February 1, 1987, John P. Foley discounts the note in Figure 2-5 at a bank that charges a discount rate of 10%. How much does

Figure 2-4 Note

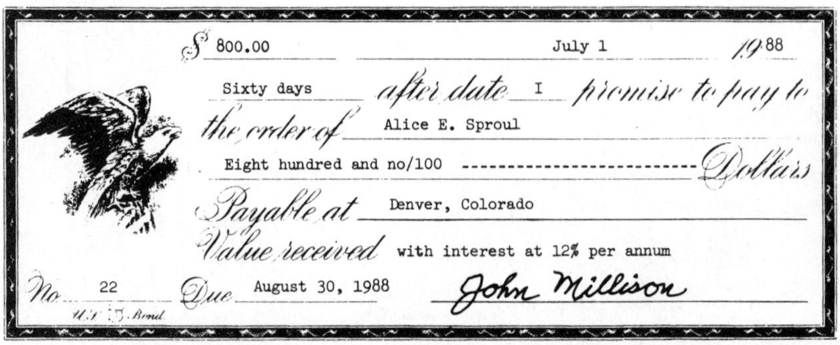
$ 800.00 July 1 1988
Sixty days after date I promise to pay to
the order of Alice E. Sproul
Eight hundred and no/100 ------------------------ Dollars
Payable at Denver, Colorado
Value received with interest at 12% per annum
No. 22 Due August 30, 1988 John Millison

he get?

($7937.78)

4. What are the proceeds if Mr. Foley discounts the note in problem 3 on February 15, 1987, at a bank charging a discount rate of 11%?

5. On December 20, 1986, Francis A. Kuhn discounts the note in Figure 2-6 at a bank that charges a discount rate of 12%. How much does he receive?

($3094.65)

6. What are the proceeds if Mr. Kuhn discounts the note in problem 5 on October 16, 1986, at a bank charging a discount rate of 12%?

Figure 2-5 Note

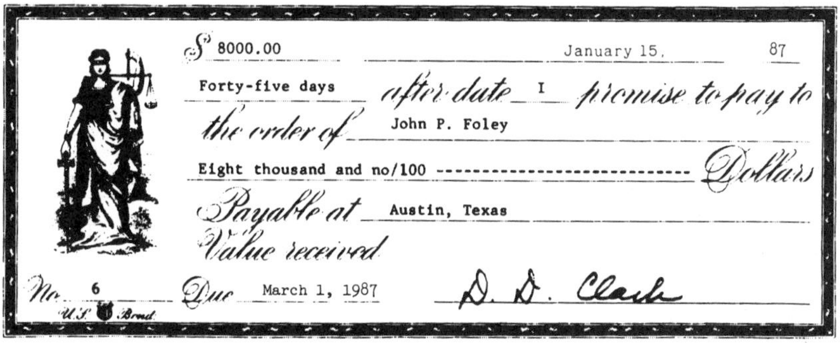

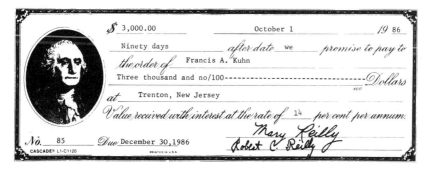

Figure 2-6 Note

7. The Gibson Hardware Company has a note for $1200 dated November 15, 1986. The note is due, in 6 months with interest at 16%. If the Gibson Company discounts the note on January 30, 1987, at a bank charging a discount rate of 15%, what will be the proceeds?
   ($1239.30)

8. A merchant receives a note for $1245.40 that is due in 60 days with interest at 15%. The note is discounted immediately at a bank that charges 16% discount. What are the proceeds?

9. A company holds the following non-interest-bearing notes. The notes are all taken to the bank on August 14, 1989, and the proceeds deposited in the company's account. Find the total proceeds if the discount rate is 12%.

Date of note	Term	Face value
July 15, 1989	90 days	$1000
August 14, 1989	45 days	800
June 25, 1989	60 days	4000
($5754.67)		

10. A company holds the following non-interest-bearing notes. The notes are taken to the bank on November 5, 1986, and the proceeds deposited in the company's account. Get the total proceeds if the discount rate is $12\frac{1}{2}\%$.

Date of note	Term	Face value
September 6, 1986	90 days	$2000
October 16, 1986	60 days	2500
October 12, 1986	30 days	4800

11. A company holds the following interest-bearing notes. The notes are discounted at 10% on June 1, 1988. Find the total proceeds.

Date of note	Term	Face value	Rate
April 2, 1988	90 days	$2000	8%
June 1, 1988	30 days	1000	9%
($3022.10)			

12. A company holds the following interest-bearing notes. They are discounted at 14.2% on July 15, 1986. Find the total proceeds.

Date of note	Term	Face value	Rate
May 16, 1986	120 days	$4200	9%
June 10, 1986	45 days	6000	8%

13. A person buys merchandise costing $340, and wants to give a 30-day non-interest-bearing note that, if the creditor discounts it immediately at $7\frac{1}{2}\%$, will result in proceeds of $340. For what amount should the person make out the note?
($342.14)

14. The owner of a store needs $500 cash for a business transaction and arranges to get the money from a bank that charges a discount rate of 10%. If the note is for 90 days, it should have what face value if the proceeds are to be $500?

15. On April 10 a woman obtains a loan from her bank to be repaid on June 29. If the bank's discount rate is $13\frac{1}{2}\%$, what must be the face value of a non-interest-bearing note that will have proceeds of $485?
($500.00)

16. On July 10 a man needs $2350, which he plans to repay on September 18. He gets a loan from a bank that has a bank discount rate of 14.4%. What will be the face value of the non-interest-bearing note that he signs?

17. On June 1 Fanger and Rampke buy merchandise amounting to $3000. If they pay cash they will get a 2% cash discount. To take advantage of this cash discount, they sign a 60-day non-interest-bearing note at their bank that charges a discount rate of 14%. What should be the face value of this note to give them the exact amount they need to pay cash for the merchandise?
($3010.24)

18. The Economy Appliance store buys merchandise totaling $4560. A 3% discount will be allowed for cash payment. The store manager gets the cash by signing a 30-day non-interest-bearing note at a bank that charges a discount rate of 12%. Find the face value of the note.

2.4 PROMISES AND ORDERS

There are two types of negotiable financial paper – promises to pay and orders to pay.

Time deposits, notes, and certificates of deposit are examples of promises to pay. Drafts and bills of exchange (sometimes called acceptances) are examples of orders to pay.

A **draft** is an order by a first party (drawer) directing a second party (drawee) to make a certain payment to a third party (payee). There are three parties to a draft, but only two persons may be involved. Thus the drawer may make himself or herself the payee.

A common form of draft is the ordinary bank check. When you open a checking account, there is an agreement between you and the bank that the bank will honor your checks (orders for payment) up to the amount you have on deposit. The importance of checks as a means of payment is shown by the fact that a very high percentage of financial transactions by volume are handled by check. Since checks are the first contact most students have with negotiable financial paper, suggestions from the American Bankers' Association on how to write and endorse checks are given in Figure 2-7. Following these suggestions can save you trouble, time, and money.

2.5 MONEY AND CAPITAL MARKETS

Needs of government and business for large sums of money for short periods are met by the **money market**, composed of a group of markets for a wide variety of short-term credit instruments. Maturities may be as long as 1 year, but often they are of 90 days or less and can be arranged for only a few days or even one day.

Capital market instruments, such as bonds and mortgages, have a term to maturity of over a year. When long periods are involved, the market value of a capital market instrument may vary greatly over the life of the instrument due to changes in interest rates and other causes. However, lender and borrower can count on predictable interest income and costs far into the future. We will discuss capital market instruments after we cover compound interest in Chapter 3. A capital market instrument may be considered a money market instrument when it is within a year of its maturity date.

The short terms of money market instruments reduce the risk of loss due to changes in interest rates. There is safety of principal when money market instruments are issued by borrowers in sound financial condition. Money market rates are often below rates on bank loans, so it is advantageous to be able to borrow in the money market. By bringing together lenders with cash surpluses and borrowers with cash deficits, the money market makes possible a more efficient use of

Figure 2-7 Tips on How to Write a Check

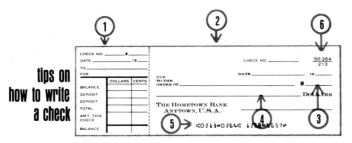

tips on how to write a check

1 Start with the stub.

Fill in check number and amount of check.

Date. Then person to whom the check is written (Payee). The purpose for which the check is written.

Be sure the balance is carried over from the previous stub.

Add latest deposits. Write in amount of this check. Subtract from balance. Carry new balance on to next stub.

2 Fill in the number of the check, the date, and the person to whom the money is to be paid.

3 The Amount of the Check in Numbers: Write it as close to the dollar sign as possible to prevent anyone from adding other numbers.

4 Start at the extreme left — again to prevent any additions. Fill in wavy line after the words, all the way over to "dollars." NOTE: Change is written as a fraction. Write carefully—it's your money you're ordering paid out!

5 These odd-looking numbers are the MICR Numbers (Magnetic Ink Character Recognition). They are the account and bank numbers used for high-speed automatic processing.

6 This number simplifies the process of exchanging out-of-town checks by indicating the proper route and clearing house through which the check should be sent for sorting and exchanging.

Always use ink — no pencil. This is to prevent anyone from altering the check. Never cross out or erase or change a check after it's written.

If an error is made, tear up the check and start another. Mark "void" on the stub.

Commercial Banks offer two kinds of checking accounts: REGULAR and SPECIAL. In addition to personal checks, banks offer CERTIFIED Checks (Payment guaranteed by the Bank) and CASHIER'S or OFFICIAL CHECKS. (Drawn by a bank on itself.)

---

how to endorse a check:

To cash or deposit a check, you must sign your name exactly as it appears on the face of the check. The following are types of endorsements—

Blank: Signature alone. When so endorsed, anyone may be able to cash it. Wait until you reach the bank before signing a blank endorsement.

Restrictive: The signature appears beneath the words "For deposit only."

Transfer to a Second Party (or account): Signature appears beneath "Pay to the order of. . . ."

Misspelling: If your name is misspelled, first sign as it actually appears. Then, sign correctly beneath it.

---

what happens to a check when it's cashed?

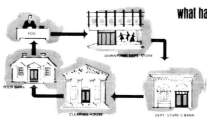

A Example: You send your check to a downtown department store.

B The department store deposits the check in its bank.

C The bank sends your check, along with the others it has received, to a clearing house, where checks are exchanged by banks each day.

D From the clearing house, your check is returned to your bank, which deducts the amount of the check from your account.

E At the end of the month, your bank returns your check to you, along with the other checks you have written and your bank statement.

In the case of an out-of-town transaction, the check travels on a longer journey, with more stops along the way, but the basic process of clearing the check by having the different banks exchange each other's checks is exactly the same.

Source: American Bankers' Association.

money. Lenders temporarily having surplus cash can invest in producing assets until the money is needed for predictable obligations such as tax payments, dividends, and debt repayment. Borrowers who need cash for inventory financing and other short-term requirements can sell money market paper.

While rates on money market instruments tend to fluctuate together, there are times when the return on a particular instrument may get out of line. When alert money managers note abnormal differences between rates, they shift from one instrument to another to improve their position. In time this restores normal rate relations among the various short-term instruments.

A well-managed short-term portfolio may include several types of securities selected for the amount of risk, rate of return, and degree of liquidity consistent with the objectives of the portfolio manager. Many money market instruments are traded on a discount basis. These instruments do not have a stated rate of return. The investor realizes return by appreciation of the instrument to its face value at maturity. Some money market instruments are interest-bearing. These instruments have a maturity value equal to the face value plus interest for the term of the loan. Table 2-1 gives the general characteristics of common money market instruments.

Money market rates vary both over time and among the different instruments. Because of the large sums, a spread of even a few basis points can result in large dollar differences in returns on alternative investments.

2.6   TREASURY BILLS

Treasury bills are the shortest-term security issued by the United States government. Bills are the most liquid of all securities. As Figure 2-8 shows, a bill is a noninterest, bearer instrument. The buyer's return is the difference between the price paid and the face value received from the government when the bill matures. The ownership of vast sums can be transferred with very simple instruments. On the due date, which must be entered on the bill, the bearer of a bill like the one shown would receive $1 million.

The tax anticipation bill is a special form of Treasury bill designed to help the Treasury smooth out its flow of tax receipts while providing companies an attractive investment for funds accumulated for tax payments. Although these bills mature a week after a tax date, they are accepted at par in payment of taxes on the tax date. Like other Treasury bills, tax anticipation bills are sold at a discount in competitive auctions.

Institutions often have idle cash that has been accumulated for payment of obligations of known amounts and due dates, or as a reserve against contingencies. These excess cash reserves can be converted into riskless, earning assets by buying T bills. The highly organized secondary market for bills ensures their easy convertibility into cash should money be needed before bills come to maturity. The short maturities of T bills minimize the risk of price fluctuations resulting from market conditions. T bills form the cornerstone of many short-term portfolios.

Bills are sold at weekly public auctions with competitive bids expressed on the basis of 100 with not more than three decimals. The yield on T bills is reported on a bank discount basis. To obtain the bank discount corresponding to a given bid, we substitute $100 = S$, bid price $= P$, and time in days $= t$ in formula (5) and solve for d.

Table 2-1 Common Money Market Instruments

Money Market Instrument	Basis	Common Denominations	Common Maturities
Treasury bills	Discount	$10,000, $15,000, $100,000, $500,000, $1 million	91, 182, 273, 365 days
Commercial paper	Discount or interest	Multiples of $5000, amounts of $5 million or more	3 to 270 days
Negotiable certificates of deposit	Interest	$100,000, $500,000, $1 million	1 to 4 or more months
Bankers' acceptances	Discount	$25,000 to $1 million	30 to 180 days
Federal funds	Interest	Units of $200,000 and $1 million	1 day
Federal agency issues	Usually interest	Various	Various

$$P = 100\left(1 - \frac{dt}{360}\right)$$

$$\frac{P}{100} = 1 - \frac{dt}{360}$$

$$\frac{dt}{360} = 1 - \frac{P}{100} = \frac{100 - P}{100}$$

$$d = \frac{360}{t}\left(\frac{100 - P}{100}\right)$$

EXAMPLE 1   A bank bids 96.871 for a 91-day, $1 million bill. This means that the bank is willing to pay $968,710 for the bill, which 91 days after its issuance will be worth $1,000,000. If the bid is accepted, what yield will the bank get on a bank discount basis?

SOLUTION

$$d = \frac{360}{91}\left(\frac{100.000 - 96.871}{100}\right) = .12378 = 12.378\%$$

Figure 2-8 Treasury Bill

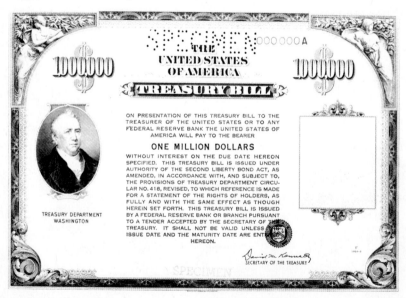

EXAMPLE 2 Find the yield on the bill in Example 1 on a coupon equivalent or simple interest basis.

SOLUTION The discount rate and time are substituted in formula (7).

$$r = \frac{.12378}{1 - .12378 \times (91/360)} = .12778 = 12.778\%$$

The owner of a bill can hold it to maturity and have the Treasury redeem it for face value. If the owner needs cash, the bill can be sold. Yields of outstanding bills normally begin to drop as issues approach maturity. This decrease occurs because there are usually some investors who are willing to accept a lower yield for the privilege of investing in a bill that is close to maturity. A company with several hundred thousand dollars that is not needed for a few days can earn substantial sums by investing in bills. Now the purchase will be made from another owner of bills rather than from the Treasury. Such sales may offer the seller of bills an opportunity to improve the return for the period the bill was held.

EXAMPLE 3 The investor in Example 1 held the bill for 60 days and sold it for $989,750. Find the interest rate earned for the period the bill was held, and the discount and interest rate the buyer will earn.

SOLUTION The cost of the bill was $968,710. The interest earned over the 60 days is 989,750 - 968,710 = $21,040. Substituting in formula (1), we have

$$21,040 = 968,710 \times r \times \frac{60}{360}$$

$$r = \frac{21,040 \times 360}{968,710 \times 60} = .13032 = 13.032\%$$

In effect, the buyer of the bill is bidding 98.975 for a bill that has 31 days to maturity.

$$d = \frac{360}{31} \left(\frac{100.000 - 98.975}{100} \right) = .11903 = 11.903\%$$

$$r = \frac{.11903}{1 - .11903 \times \frac{31}{360}} = .12026 = 12.026\%$$

On this transaction everyone comes out ahead. The buyer of the bill is able to put money to work for 31 days. When the Treasury redeems the bill, the buyer will get $10,250 more than was paid. The seller of the bill has increased the yield rate for the period the bill was held. To improve the yield for the period as a whole, the seller must now reinvest the funds at a suitable rate. If current rates do not favor a sale and new investment, the owner of a bill can simply hold it to maturity.

Firms are finding that holding cash to the minimum needed to meet current obligations increases the productivity of company funds. Use of sophisticated management techniques allows rapid assembly of information on cash positions and better projections of cash inflows and outflows. Some firms are finding portfolio income attractive because it can be obtained at relatively low expense.

2.7 COMMERCIAL PAPER

Negotiable, short-term promissory notes issued by commercial organizations are called commercial paper. This paper is often issued in face amounts of $100,000, $250,000, $500,000, $1,000,000, and combinations thereof. Lenders may also have commercial paper tailored to their specifications. Maturities vary from a few days to 9 months. Commercial paper with a term of 270 days or less is not registered with the Securities and Exchange Commission. There are no interest rate ceilings on commercial paper.

These corporate IOUs enable a corporation temporarily having excess funds to help another company that needs a short-term loan. By issuing commercial paper, a corporate treasurer can bypass banks and escape restrictions on bank credit. The seller (borrower) can get short-term cash at rates lower than would be available with a bank loan. The buyer (lender) gets a higher return than would be received on other short-term money market instruments.

Commercial paper is usually unsecured and may be issued in bearer form. The discount or interest is calculated on the face value of the paper and a 360-day year.

The commercial paper shown in Figure 2-9 is an example of a short-term discount note. This illustration shows how large sums are transferred with very simple instruments.

The purchaser of this note will get $1,000,000 in 90 days. The purchase price will depend on the discount rate. If the discount rate is $8\frac{5}{8}\%$, we get the discount by substituting in formula (4).

$$\text{Discount} = 1{,}000{,}000.00 \times .08625 \times \tfrac{90}{360} = \$21{,}562.50$$

$$\text{Proceeds} = 1{,}000{,}000.00 - 21{,}562.50 = \$978{,}437.50$$

Commercial paper has had a good reputation for safety. However, a cash shortage or other financial problem can be serious when the time comes for a corporation to sell new paper or borrow elsewhere to make payment on the maturity date of an issue of commercial paper. After large operating losses, Penn Central in 1970 was unable to pay off outstanding commercial paper and had to declare bankruptcy. While disasters have been rare, buyers should carefully check the creditworthiness of the issuing corporation. Dealer paper is sold through commercial paper dealers. Directly issued paper is sold directly to investors by the borrowing firm. If a corporation can place its own paper, it may make substantial savings on a large loan.

There is a less active secondary market for commercial paper than for many other money market instruments. For this reason, investors in commercial paper may look for a maturity that coincides with their investment needs. Some dealers and finance companies will repurchase outstanding paper if the buyer requests it. There are large dealers who maintain a market in the paper they underwrite and thereby provide liquidity for investors who need money to meet contingencies.

EXAMPLE 1 A company issued a $5 million piece of commercial paper to mature on June 1, 1978. This paper was purchased by the

Figure 2-9 General Motors Sample Note

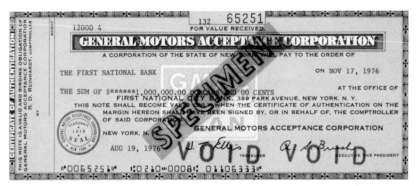

firm of Merrill Lynch, Pierce, Fenner, & Smith on March 3. What was the purchase price if the discount rate was 7%?

SOLUTION We find the time to maturity using Table 1.

Date	Day of the year
June 1	152
March 3	62
	90 days

Substituting in formula (4), we have

$$D = 5,000,000 \times .07 \times \tfrac{90}{360} = \$87,500$$

Purchase price = 5,000,000 − 87,500 = \$4,912,500

EXAMPLE 2 Merrill Lynch sold the paper mentioned in Example 1 in the secondary market to a buyer on April 5. Find the price if based on a discount rate of 6.95%.

SOLUTION We find the time to maturity.

Date	Day of the year
June 1	152
April 5	95
	57 days

Then we can obtain

$$D = 5,000,000 \times .0695 \times \tfrac{57}{360} = \$55,020.83$$

Sale price = 5,000,000.00 − 55,020.83 = \$4,944,979.17

EXAMPLE 3 What interest rate did Merrill Lynch earn while holding the paper?

SOLUTION Interest = 4,944,979.17 − 4,912,500.00 = \$32,479.17. Time from March 3 to April 5 is 33 days. Substituting in formula (1), we have

$$32{,}479.17 = 4{,}912{,}500 \times r \times \tfrac{33}{360}$$

$$r = \frac{360 \times 32{,}479.17}{4{,}912{,}500 \times 33} = .0721 = 7.21\%$$

2.8 CERTIFICATES OF DEPOSIT

A negotiable certificate of deposit is a marketable receipt issued by a bank in exchange for the deposit of money. Certificates may be in registered or bearer form, with the latter more convenient for secondary market trading. The bank agrees to repay the amount deposited plus interest on the maturity date of the certificate. Negotiable CDs are commonly available in amounts of $100,000, $500,000, and $1 million. Certificates are sometimes issued for amounts as low as $25,000 and as high as $10 million or more. Negotiable certificates are issued and traded on a bond yield equivalent or simple interest basis using a 360-day year.

The development of an active secondary market has contributed to the marketability of certificates. In the secondary market, the common trading unit is $1 million. Smaller-denomination CDs issued by smaller banks are less actively traded.

EXAMPLE 1 On March 10, 1977, a bank sold a $1 million CD, which was to bear interest at 6.25% and mature on December 5, 1977. If the buyer held the CD to maturity, what amount was paid by the bank?

SOLUTION We find the time to maturity.

Date	Day of the year
December 5	339
March 10	69
	270 days

Substituting in formula (1), we have

$$I = 1{,}000{,}000 \times .0625 \times \tfrac{270}{360} = \$46{,}875.00$$

$$\text{Amount} = 1{,}000{,}000.00 + 46{,}875.00 = \$1{,}046{,}875.00$$

EXAMPLE 2 On November 5, 1977, the owner of the certificate in Example 1 sold it to a buyer who wanted a return of 6% on a simple interest or bond yield equivalent basis. Find the sale price.

SOLUTION The new buyer collected $1,046,875 when the CD matured in 30 days. To find the purchase price, we substitute in formula (3) to obtain

$$P = \frac{1,046,875}{1 + 0.06 \times \frac{30}{360}} = \frac{1,046,875}{1.005} = \$1,041,666.67$$

2.9 BANKERS' ACCEPTANCES

An **acceptance** is a form of draft or order to pay. An after-date draft is payable a stated time after the date of the draft. An after-sight draft is payable a stated time after the drawee (the person who will make payment) signs the draft and writes the date of acceptance. After-sight and after-date drafts are known as time drafts and may be sold or discounted.

A **trade acceptance** is a draft drawn by the seller of goods on the purchaser and accepted by the purchaser. The buyer of the goods designates the bank at which the acceptance is payable and returns it to the seller, who may hold it or discount (that is, sell) it. An acceptance is two-name paper. It is a primary liability of the purchaser (drawee or acceptor) and a secondary liability of the seller (drawer). The acceptance should be self-liquidating from the sale of the goods.

A **bankers' acceptance** is a time draft drawn by the seller of merchandise on the bank of the buyer and accepted by that bank. Now there is an agreement by a bank to pay a specific bill for a customer when the bill comes due. An acceptance that represents the liability of a well-known bank is a more desirable credit instrument than one drawn on an unknown person or firm. After a draft is accepted by a bank, the payee (the party to whom payment is to be made) may discount it in the money market. Subsequent holders in due course may either hold the acceptance or sell it.

Bankers' acceptances are widely used in international trade. Assume that a retailer in the United States wants to buy clothing from an English firm. The American buyer arranges with a bank to accept the seller's draft with the understanding that the buyer will provide the funds by the due date of the acceptance. The American bank issues a letter of credit in favor of the English exporter. This letter states that the American bank will accept time drafts drawn on the American bank provided that they are drawn in accordance with details of shipment, terms, and amount given in the letter of credit. The obligation for payment is now shifted from the importer to an American bank and the English exporter can be confident that payment will be made. When shipment is made, the English firm prepares a draft on the American bank and discounts this draft at its bank. The draft is sent by the English bank to the American bank. When the time draft drawn by the English firm is marked "accepted" and is signed by an officer of the American bank, it becomes a bankers' acceptance. The draft is now an irrevocable obligation of the American bank. The English bank will probably discount the acceptance with the American bank, which can hold the paper to maturity and collect the face value, or the English bank's United States agent may sell it to a dealer in the acceptance market. Bankers' acceptances have a fine record for safety and are widely traded in secondary markets. Their safety and liquidity make them a useful instrument for investment of short-term funds. Maturities range from 30 to 180 days but are often 90 days.

EXAMPLE 1 A Cleveland importer wants to import a shipment of shoes from an Italian manufacturer. The importer has a bank issue a letter of credit in favor of the Italian firm, giving shipment details including the amount for which the firm may draw a time draft on the bank. When shipment is made, the Italian firm prepares a 90-day draft for $10,000 dated July 10, 1986, drawn on the Cleveland bank. On July 10 the exporter discounts the draft at an Italian bank. Find the proceeds if the bank uses a discount rate of 8%.

SOLUTION Substituting in formula (4), we have

$$D = 10,000 \times .08 \times \tfrac{90}{360} = \$200$$

Proceeds = 10,000.00 − 200.00 = $9800.00

EXAMPLE 2 On July 20 the Italian bank discounts the acceptance of the Cleveland bank. Find the proceeds if the Cleveland bank uses a discount rate of $7\tfrac{7}{8}\%$.

SOLUTION The maturity date of the acceptance, 90 days after July 10, is October 8. We get the time to maturity.

Date	Day of the year
October 8	281
July 20	201
	80 days

Then we find that

$$D = 10{,}000 \times .07875 \times \tfrac{80}{360} = \$175.00$$

$$\text{Proceeds} = 10{,}000.00 - 175.00 = \$9825.00$$

2.10 FEDERAL FUNDS

Banks that are members of the Federal Reserve System are required to keep percentages of their time and demand deposits as reserves. The reserves may be held as nonearning demand deposits with Federal Reserve banks or as vault cash. These deposit balances at Federal Reserve banks are called **federal funds**. Because deposit balances at the Fed do not produce income, banks prefer to keep their reserves near the legally required minimum. One way to do this is to lend excess reserves to borrowing banks, who use the loan proceeds to cover their reserve deficiencies. Both lending and borrowing banks may profit by such loans. The lending bank earns interest, while the borrowing bank has a convenient way to bring its reserves to the required level.

Most federal funds transactions are for 1 day with the cost determined on a simple interest basis using a 365-day year. Among larger banks federal funds are usually traded in units of $1 million. As interest rates have risen, smaller banks have become more concerned about the cost of holding idle funds. As these banks have entered the federal funds market, trading in amounts of $200,000 or less has become more common.

EXAMPLE To correct its reserve position, a bank gets a $5 million loan from another bank that has surplus reserves. Find the cost of the loan if it is for 1 day at 11.68%.

SOLUTION Substituting in formula (1), we have

$$I = 5{,}000{,}000 \times .1168 \times \tfrac{1}{365} = \$1600.00$$

2.11 FEDERAL AGENCY ISSUES

The following federally sponsored credit agencies issue their own securities and borrow directly from the public:

Issuing agency	Types of Securities
Federal National Mortgage Association	Debentures and discount notes
Federal home loan banks	Bonds and discount notes
Federal land banks	Bonds
Federal intermediate credit banks	Debentures
Banks for cooperatives	Debentures

A **debenture** is a debt that is not protected by a lien or mortgage on property.

Money market and capital instruments of federal agencies are issued to finance obligations of the individual agencies. Their financing is carried out separately from the regular debt operations of the federal government. The federal agencies help to channel funds from capital surplus to capital deficit areas in the nation. Agency issues are not part of the public debt, are not a legal obligation of the federal government, and are not guaranteed by the federal government. However, there is probably little difference in risk between federal agency issues and United States Treasury issues. Federal agency issues usually provide a somewhat higher yield than Treasury obligations. The combination of yield, liquidity, and safety make federal agency issues attractive investments. Terms of agency securities range from 30 days to nearly 20 years.

2.12 SUMMARY OF SIMPLE INTEREST AND BANK DISCOUNT FORMULAS

Short-term credit costs can be based either on the present value of a loan (simple interest) or on the maturity value (bank discount). Formulas for the two methods are summarized in Table 2-2.

2.13 TERM STRUCTURE OF INTEREST RATES

The relationship between yield and length of time until a loan becomes due is called the **term structure of interest rates**. A curve that shows yield to maturity as a function of time to maturity is called a **yield curve**. As the price of a fixed income security goes down, the yield goes up. Conversely, a rising price means a decreasing yield. Yield curves should be drawn only for issues of comparable credit quality that differ in time to maturity. Factors that affect the shape of a yield curve include:

1. *Expectations.* What borrowers and lenders think will happen to interest rates in the future has an effect on security prices now.
2. *Liquidity preferences.* Lenders may accept a lower yield on short-term obligations that they can expect to sell with little risk of capital loss.
3. *Transaction costs.* Costs involved in buying and selling securities may affect the length of time an investor prefers to hold securities.
4. *Institutional preferences.* Different types of institutions may have different choices of terms to maturity. A bank, which has large amounts of short-term liabilities in the form of passbook accounts

Table 2-2 Formulas for the Two Methods

Simple Interest	Bank Discount
Cost of credit is based on present value.	Cost of credit is based on maturity value.
(1) $I = Prt$	(4) $D = Sdt$
(2) $S = P(1 + rt)$	(5) $P = S(1 - dt)$
(3) $P = \dfrac{S}{1 + rt}$	(6) $S = \dfrac{P}{1 - dt}$
(7) $r = \dfrac{d}{1 - dt}$	(8) $d = \dfrac{r}{1 + rt}$
I is simple interest.	D is bank discount.
P is present value or principal.	S is maturity value or amount.
r is interest rate.	P is present value or proceeds.
S is amount or maturity value.	d is bank discount rate.
d is bank discount rate.	t is time.
t is time.	r is simple interest rate.

and certificates of deposit, will want short-term earning assets that can be sold readily. An insurance company, which has commitments to pay out funds far into the future, can hedge against changes in interest rates by buying long-term bonds to provide predictable interest income for 20 years or longer.

Curves showing how interest rates vary as a function of term to maturity have a variety of shapes, as shown in Figure 2-10.

Since the term structure of interest rates is affected by anticipated price changes, fluctuations in the level of economic activity, and monetary policy, yield curves should be based on yields as of a certain date. The graphs in Figure 2-11, prepared by the Federal Reserve Bank of Chicago, show that large changes in yield curves can occur over a short period.

2.14 RIDING THE YIELD CURVE

Since marketable securities need not be held to maturity, there are times when a profitable investment strategy is to sell some securities and buy others. Riding the yield curve means buying and selling securities to take advantage of yield differentials on securities of varying maturities. While riding the yield curve is not an exact science, the technique is useful in the hands of an alert portfolio manager. By selling one marketable issue before maturity and buying another, a portfolio manager may be able to improve the overall yield on invested funds.

Suppose that an investor keeps about a million dollars in Treasury bills. The investor buys a 6-month bill that will yield 12% on a discount basis. After holding the bill for 4 months, the investor finds a buyer who is willing to accept a 10% yield on a security that will mature in 2 months. By selling the bill, the investor will increase the return to more than 12% for the 4 months the bill has been held. Before making a sale, the investor should check investment opportunities that are now available. If new Treasury bills are still available at a price that will yield 12% or better, the switch could be a profitable one. Repeated purchases at issuance and sales at lower discount rates before maturity is called *riding the yield curve down.*

Exercise 2c

1. A bank obtained a $1 million, 182-day Treasury bill at a price of 94.200. Find the yield on a bank discount and simple interest

Figure 2-10 Yield Curves

Downward sloping

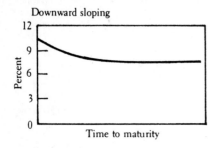

Descending yield curves have been observed during tight money periods when rates are high relative to historical experience. Investors expect rates to go down and the market value of fixed income securities to go up.

Upward sloping

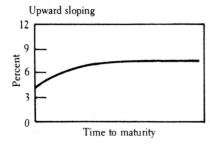

Ascending yield curves have been observed when rates are low. Investors expect rates to go up and the market value of securities to go down. When investors favor short-term issues to minimize capital losses, the pressure on long-term rates results in higher yields for longer maturities.

Relatively flat

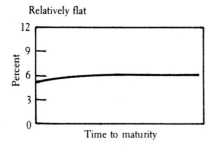

Relatively flat curves occur during periods when little change is expected in future rates. Investors accept slightly lower yields for the more liquid short-term securities.

Humped

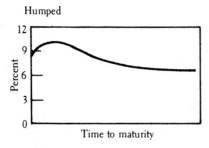

Humped curves have appeared when rates are generally high and credit is tight. When investors expect rates to rise and then fall, a humped curve may result.

Figure 2-11 Examples of Yield Curves

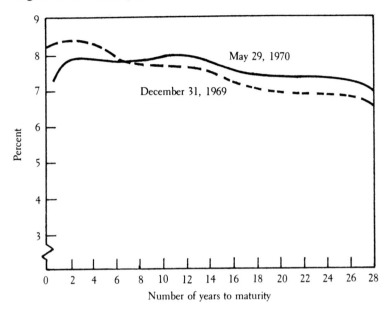

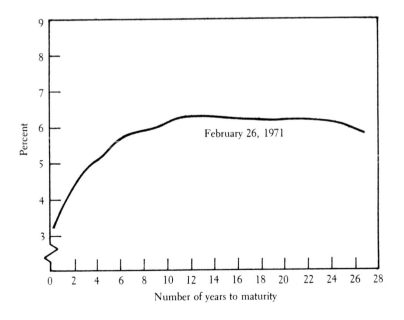

basis.

$(d = 11.47\%; r = 12.18\%)$

2. An investor purchased a $500,000, 91-day Treasury bill at a price of 96.5. Find the yield on a bank discount and simple interest basis.

3. The bank in problem 1 held the bill for 120 days and then sold it in the secondary market for $983,000. Find:
   (a) the interest rate earned by the bank during the period the bill was held.
   (b) the yield the new buyer will get on a discount basis if the bill is held to maturity.
   (c) the yield the new buyer will get on an interest basis if the bill is held to maturity.

   [(a) 13.06%; (b) 9.87%; (c) 10.04%]

4. The investor in problem 2 held the bill for 81 days and then sold it in the secondary market for $498,400. Find:
   (a) the interest rate earned by the investor during the period the bill was held.
   (b) the yield the new buyer will get on a discount basis if the bill is held to maturity.
   (c) the yield the new buyer will get on an interest basis if the bill is held to maturity.

5. A company issued a $2 million piece of commercial paper to mature on August 1, 1984. The paper was purchased by an investor on June 2, 1984. Find the purchase price if based on a discount rate of 12%.

   ($1,960,000)

6. A company issued a $5 million piece of commercial paper on May 31, 1985. The paper is to mature in 45 days. It is purchased on May 31 to yield 11% on a bank discount basis. Find the purchase price.

7. The investor in problem 5 sold the paper on July 12 at a price that gave the new buyer 11.4% on a discount basis. Find the purchase price.

   ($1,987,333.33)

8. On June 30, 1985, the company in problem 6 sold the paper in the secondary market. Find the sale price if based on a discount rate of 9%.

9. On June 5, 1983, a bank sold a $500,000 certificate of deposit that was to mature on August 4, 1983, and bear interest at $13\frac{1}{2}\%$. If the buyer held the CD to maturity, what amount was paid by the bank?
   ($511,250)

10. On December 1, 1983, a bank sold a $100,000 certificate of deposit to mature on March 1, 1984, and bear interest at $11\frac{1}{2}\%$. If the buyer held the certificate to maturity, what amount was paid by the bank?

11. On July 20, 1983, the owner of the certificate in problem 9 sold it in the secondary market to a buyer who wanted a return of 10.8% on a simple interest or bond yield equivalent basis. Find the sale price.
($508,959.68)

12. On February 19, 1984, the owner of the certificate in problem 10 sold it to a buyer who wanted a return of 11% on a simple interest basis. Find the sale price.

13. A Richmond bank arranges to accept drafts from a German exporter. The exporter ships goods to a Richmond firm and prepares a 60-day draft for $30,000 dated May 1 and drawn on the Richmond bank. On May 1 the exporter discounts the draft at a German bank. Find the proceeds if the discount rate is 13%.
($29,350)

14. The bank of a St. Louis retailer agrees to accept drafts from a Scottish exporter. On September 15 the exporter draws a 90-day draft for $25,000 on the St. Louis bank. Find the proceeds if the exporter discounts the draft at a Scottish bank on September 15 and the discount rate is 12.78%.

15. On May 11 the German bank in problem 13 discounts the acceptance at the Richmond bank. Find the proceeds if the discount rate is 13.2%.
($29,450.00)

16. On September 30 the Scottish bank in problem 14 discounts the acceptance at the St. Louis bank. Find the proceeds if the discount rate is 13.05%.

17. A bank gets a 1-day, $10 million federal funds loan at $10\frac{1}{2}\%$. Find the interest.
($2876.71)

18. A bank gets a 1-day, $2 million federal funds loan at $12\frac{3}{4}\%$. Find the interest.

19. If a federal funds loan is made on Friday, the next clearing date is 3 days away and interest is charged for 3 days. A bank borrowed $1 million in federal funds on Friday. If the rate is 11.44%, find the interest due on Monday.
($940.27)

20. A federal funds loan of $5 million was made on Friday. Find the interest for 3 days at $12\frac{1}{4}\%$.

REVIEW EXERCISES FOR CHAPTER 2

1. A 90-day note for $5000 at 15% interest dated June 15 is discounted on July 21 at a bank that charges a discount rate of $13\frac{1}{2}\%$. Find the proceeds.
   ($5082.45)

2. Find the interest rate that the noteholder in problem 1 actually received for the time the note was held.

3. Find the interest rate on a simple interest basis that the bank in problem 1 received on its investment.
   (13.78%)

4. A 6-month note for $2000 at 16% interest was later discounted at a bank charging 12% discount. If the proceeds were $2116.80, how long did the bank that discounted the note have the note?

5. A 60-day note with 15% interest was signed on August 19 and discounted at 14.4% on September 3. The proceeds were $3019.65. Find the face value of the note.
   ($3000.00)

6. A borrower has a choice between an interest rate of 12.25% and a discount rate of 12% for a 4-month loan. Which is preferable for the borrower?

7. A bid of 96.371 is accepted for a 91-day, $1 million Treasury bill. Find the yield on the investment on a bank discount and simple interest basis.
   ($d = 14.36\%; r = 14.90\%$)

8. Suppose that the bill in problem 7 was sold after 60 days for $990,000. Find the interest rate earned by the seller for the period the bill was held and the discount rate and interest rate the buyer will earn.

9. On March 5 an investor buys a 60-day, $50,000 CD with interest at 13.8%. The certificate is sold on March 20 to a buyer who wants a 15% simple interest return on the investment. Find the selling price and the rate of return the original investor actually received on the investment while it was held.
   ($50,208.59; 10.01%)

10. A $10,000, 72-day note was discounted after 12 days at a discount rate of 9%. The proceeds were $10,000. Find the interest rate on the note.

Chapter 3

Compound Interest

3.1 EIGHTH WONDER OF THE WORLD

When Baron Rothschild, one of the world's wealthiest bankers, was asked if he could name the seven wonders of the world, he said: "No, but I can tell you what the Eighth Wonder is. This Eighth Wonder should be utilized by all of us to accomplish what we want. It is **compound interest.**"*

Table 3-1 shows the impressive growth that results when compound interest is applied to a modest starting sum.

Table 3-1 Growth of $100 at Compound Interest

Time in Years	Annual Interest Rate			
	4%	6%	8%	10%
10	$148.02	$179.08	$215.89	$259.37
20	219.11	320.71	466.10	672.75
30	324.34	574.35	1,006.27	1,744.94
40	480.10	1,028.57	2,172.45	4,525.93
50	710.67	1,842.02	4,690.16	11,739.09
60	1,051.96	3,298.77	10,125.71	30,448.16
70	1,557.16	5,907.59	21,860.64	78,974.70
80	2,304.98	10,579.60	47,195.48	204,840.02
90	3,411.93	18,946.45	101,891.51	531,302.26
100	5,050.49	33,930.21	219,976.13	1,378,061.23

*Loraine L. Blaire, *Your Financial Guide for Living* (Englewood Cliffs, N.J.: Prentice-Hall, 1963), p. 62.

Applications of compound interest go far beyond keeping track of bank accounts. Compound interest is used for business and government planning, gauging the health of the economy, making judgments about the growth of the American economy relative to other national economies, estimating future populations, and many other applications. Leonard S. Silk, well-known financial writer, has stated: "Explaining compound interest — for a bank or a nation — is the central problem of economics."*

Figure 3-1 shows the effect of time and rate on the growth of a sum of money at compound interest. With increasing time and higher rates, the curves get progressively steeper. But there are many functions

Figure 3-1 Growth of $100 at Compound Interest, Arithmetic Scale

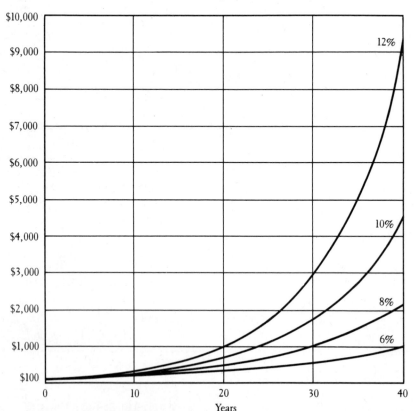

*Leonard S. Silk, *The Research Revolution* (New York: McGraw-Hill, 1960), p. 38.

that have this configuration on an arithmetic graph. On such a graph it is not possible to tell if a time series is growing according to the compound interest law or some other relationship.

There is another method for making such a determination. A special type of graph, called a semilogarithmic or ratio graph, can be used. This graph is based on the principle of logarithms. A description of how it is designed is given in the appendix, page 491. When you plot data that follow the compound interest law on a ratio graph, the result is a straight line. If two time series plot as parallel lines on a ratio graph, their rates of change (interest rates) are the same. If one line is steeper than the other, the steeper one corresponds to a higher interest rate. See Figure 3-2.

Figure 3-2 Growth of $100 at Compound Interest, Ratio Scale

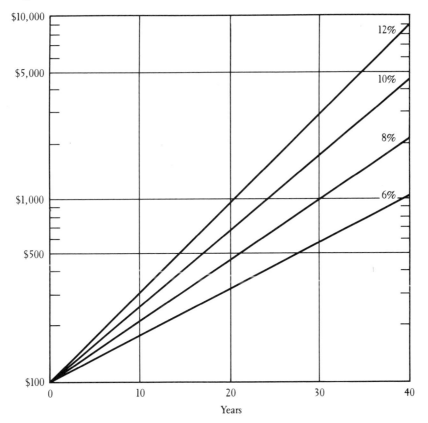

Rates of change are of great importance in economic analysis and forecasting. When a time series plots as approximately a straight line on a ratio graph, the analyst has valuable information. The compound interest law can then be used as a practical tool for making predictions.

3.2 BENJAMIN FRANKLIN'S 1000 POUNDS

An example of the magic of compound interest is a bequest of 1000 pounds that Benjamin Franklin willed to Boston. Dr. Franklin died on April 17, 1790, and what was then the Town of Boston accepted the donation at a town meeting on June 1, 1790. Franklin's will stipulated that the money was to be loaned at interest to young and needy apprentices. The interest was to augment the principal, and at the end of 100 years, part of the fund was to be expended for public works and the balance was to be compounded for a second 100-year period. The administrators of the fund followed Franklin's instructions as closely as possible.

In 1907 the building of the Franklin Institute of Boston was started with $438,742 from the fund. Over 80,000 students have been enrolled in this institute, which opened in 1908. The balance of the fund was left to accumulate and amounted to $3,458,797 in 1980. This money is now being used to make loans at low interest to medical students. All of this from a bequest that was equivalent to about $4570.*

3.3 SIMPLE INTEREST OVER AND OVER

While compound interest is the eighth wonder of the world in terms of results, the concept is basically simple. As the forthcoming example shows, compound interest is simple interest applied over and over to a sum that is increased by the simple interest each time it is earned. This ever-increasing principal explains the snowball effect of compound interest.

An investment of $1000 at 6% simple interest earns $60 per year. In 3 years the simple interest would amount to $180. However, if the interest as it is earned is added to the principal and this new principal

---

*Mr. Michael Mazzola, director of the Franklin Institute, supplied this history of the bequest of Benjamin Franklin. The accomplishments it made possible are impressive evidence of the power of compound interest.

draws interest, the investment increases more rapidly than it would with simple interest. Interest paid on an increasing principal in this way is known as **compound interest**. The following example shows the increase in an investment of $1000 if the interest rate is 6% compounded annually.

Original principal	$1000.00
Interest for first year at 6%	60.00
Principal at the start of the second year	1060.00
Interest for second year at 6%	63.60
Principal at the start of the third year	1123.60
Interest for third year at 6%	67.42
Amount at the end of 3 years	$1191.02

Thus the compound interest earned on the original investment is $191.02 as compared with the $180.00 that would be earned at simple interest in the same length of time. The difference of $11.02 is interest earned on interest. The total, $1191.02, is called the **compound amount**.

Hereafter compound interest is used in all problems in this book except when the time is a single interest period or a part of a period.

Note that compound interest is simply a repeated application of simple interest. If a long time is involved – say, two or three hundred interest payments – the computations using the preceding system would be very laborious. Fortunately, it is easy to develop a formula that gives the final amount without the intermediate computations.

3.4 COMPOUND AMOUNT FORMULA

In the preceding example the interest was computed and added to the principal every year. In many business transactions, the interest is computed annually, semiannually, quarterly, monthly, daily, or at some other time interval. The time between successive interest computations is called the **conversion**, or **interest, period**. This basic unit of time is used in all compound interest problems. The important rate is the **interest rate per conversion period**, which is designated by the symbol i. The symbol for the total number of conversion periods is n.

In most business transactions the practice is to quote an annual interest rate and the frequency of conversion. From this information the rate per period is determined. Thus 6% compounded (or converted) semiannually means that 3% interest will be earned every 6 months. The quoted annual rate is called the **nominal rate** and is indicated by the symbol j. The number of interest conversion periods per year is indicated by the symbol m. The equation relating j, i, and m is $i = j/m$ or $j = im$ ("Jim"). The symbol $j_{(m)}$ means a nominal rate j converted m times a year. When no conversion period is stated in a problem, assume that the interest is compounded annually.

Table 3-2 shows a few examples of quoted or nominal rates and the corresponding conversion periods per year and rate per period.

To eliminate the tedious period-by-period computations used in the example at the beginning of this chapter, we invest P dollars for n periods at a rate of i per period and derive a formula for the final amount. A numerical example is used to illustrate the steps. In this example $P = \$1000$, $i = .04$, and $n = 2$. The principal at the end of the first period will be indicated by P_1; at the end of the second period, by P_2; and so on.

Original principal	P	$\$1000$
Interest	Pi	$1000 \times .04$
P_1	$P + Pi = P(1 + i)$	$1000 + 1000 \times .04 = 1000(1.04)$
Interest	$P(1 + i)i$	$1000(1.04).04$
P_2	$P(1 + i) + P(1 + i)i$	$1000(1.04) + 1000(1.04).04$
	$= P(1 + i)(1 + i)$	$= 1000(1.04)(1.04)$
	$= P(1 + i)^2$	$= 1000(1.04)^2$

Table 3-2 Compound Amount Formula

Quoted or Nominal Rate (j)	Conversion Periods per Year (m)	Rate per Period ($i = j/m$)	
		Percent	Decimal
6% compounded annually	1	6	.06
6% compounded semiannually	2	3	.03
6% compounded quarterly	4	$1\frac{1}{2}$	.015
6% compounded monthly	12	$\frac{1}{2}$	.005
3% compounded quarterly	4	$\frac{3}{4}$	.0075
5% compounded semiannually	2	$2\frac{1}{2}$	.025
5% compounded monthly	12	$\frac{5}{12}$	.004167

If there were more periods, each new principal would be $(1 + i)$ times the preceding value. At the end of n periods the final amount, for which the symbol is S, would equal the original principal times $(1 + i)^n$. This results in the basic formula for compound interest,

$$S = P(1 + i)^n \qquad (9)$$

to find cpd interest

S = the amount at compound interest
P = the principal
i = the rate per conversion period
n = the number of conversion periods

The factor $(1 + i)^n$ is called the **accumulation factor**, or **amount of 1**, and is sometimes designated by the symbol s.

Note that this formula has the same "ingredients" as the formulas for amount with simple interest (2) and amount at bank discount (6) — namely, amount (S), present value (P), rate (i), and time (n). They are applied differently in the different formulas. We can see from Table 3-1 that the amount for 8% is not halfway between the corresponding values at 6% and 10%. With simple interest the value for 8% will be halfway between the 6% and 10% values. The computations in compound interest are somewhat more difficult mathematically, but today we are provided with the machinery to make the computations easy.

The numerical value of $(1 + i)^n$ can be computed by successive multiplication, by logarithms, or by the binomial theorem. In practical business usage the numerical value is usually obtained from previously computed tables, or by using an electronic calculator or a computer. In this book, values of $(1 + i)^n$ for common interest rates will be found in the "Amount of 1" column of Table 2 or Table 3. The columns of data in Table 2 have descriptive headings that tell what the various columns are in a few simple words. At the bottom of each column of data, symbols are given to help you select the correct factor for a problem.

You can easily appreciate the usefulness of Table 2 when you consider how much time it saves. Carrying a sum of money forward by getting the simple interest for each period and adding it to the principal means two arithmetic operations for each period. This calculation involves a lot of work and many chances to make mistakes if many periods are involved. Table 2 makes it possible to carry money forward 20, 30, or more periods just as easily as making one simple interest computation. Figure 3-3 shows how to get the correct factor from Table 2. Table 3 is an extension of Table 2.

Figure 3-3 How to Use the "Amount of 1" Column in Table 2

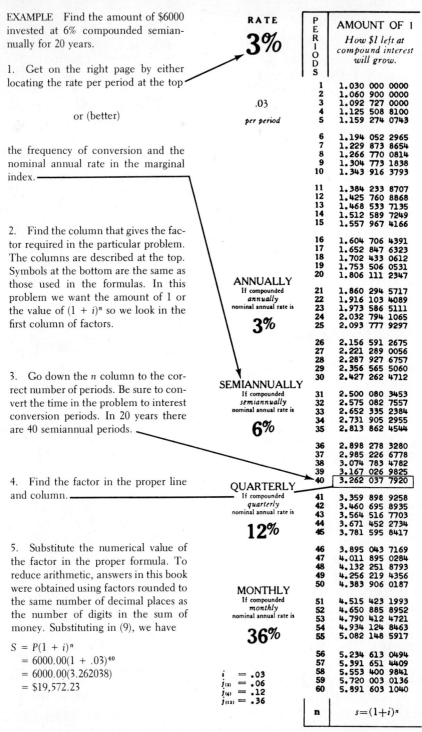

EXAMPLE Find the amount of $6000 invested at 6% compounded semiannually for 20 years.

1. Get on the right page by either locating the rate per period at the top

or (better)

the frequency of conversion and the nominal annual rate in the marginal index.

2. Find the column that gives the factor required in the particular problem. The columns are described at the top. Symbols at the bottom are the same as those used in the formulas. In this problem we want the amount of 1 or the value of $(1 + i)^n$ so we look in the first column of factors.

3. Go down the n column to the correct number of periods. Be sure to convert the time in the problem to interest conversion periods. In 20 years there are 40 semiannual periods.

4. Find the factor in the proper line and column.

5. Substitute the numerical value of the factor in the proper formula. To reduce arithmetic, answers in this book were obtained using factors rounded to the same number of decimal places as the number of digits in the sum of money. Substituting in (9), we have

$S = P(1 + i)^n$
$= 6000.00(1 + .03)^{40}$
$= 6000.00(3.262038)$
$= \$19,572.23$

RATE

3%

.03
per period

ANNUALLY
If compounded annually nominal annual rate is

3%

SEMIANNUALLY
If compounded semiannually nominal annual rate is

6%

QUARTERLY
If compounded quarterly nominal annual rate is

12%

MONTHLY
If compounded monthly nominal annual rate is

36%

$i \ = .03$
$j_{(2)} = .06$
$j_{(4)} = .12$
$j_{(12)} = .36$

P E R I O D S	AMOUNT OF 1 — *How $1 left at compound interest will grow.*
1	1.030 000 0000
2	1.060 900 0000
3	1.092 727 0000
4	1.125 508 8100
5	1.159 274 0743
6	1.194 052 2965
7	1.229 873 8654
8	1.266 770 0814
9	1.304 773 1838
10	1.343 916 3793
11	1.384 233 8707
12	1.425 760 8868
13	1.468 533 7135
14	1.512 589 7249
15	1.557 967 4166
16	1.604 706 4391
17	1.652 847 6323
18	1.702 433 0612
19	1.753 506 0531
20	1.806 111 2347
21	1.860 294 5717
22	1.916 103 4089
23	1.973 586 5111
24	2.032 794 1065
25	2.093 777 9297
26	2.156 591 2675
27	2.221 289 0056
28	2.287 927 6757
29	2.356 565 5060
30	2.427 262 4712
31	2.500 080 3453
32	2.575 082 7557
33	2.652 335 2384
34	2.731 905 2955
35	2.813 862 4544
36	2.898 278 3280
37	2.985 226 6778
38	3.074 783 4782
39	3.167 026 9825
40	3.262 037 7920
41	3.359 898 9258
42	3.460 695 8935
43	3.564 516 7703
44	3.671 452 2734
45	3.781 595 8417
46	3.895 043 7169
47	4.011 895 0284
48	4.132 251 8793
49	4.256 219 4356
50	4.383 906 0187
51	4.515 423 1993
52	4.650 885 8952
53	4.790 412 4721
54	4.934 124 8463
55	5.082 148 5917
56	5.234 613 0494
57	5.391 651 4409
58	5.553 400 9841
59	5.720 003 0136
60	5.891 603 1040
n	$s=(1+i)^n$

Source: Table courtesy of Financial Publishing Company, Boston, Mass.

If you have access to a calculator with exponential capability (a key denoted y^x or x^y), you can perform these computations even more easily. You are not bound by the limitations of any table, but only by the limitations of the calculator. The amount of 1 can be calculated for any rate and any number of periods. The problems throughout this book can be worked using such a calculator. Some examples and exercises are beyond the extent of the tables given in the book; they are indicated by a (C). On such a calculator, it is only necessary to enter the value of $1 + i$ as the base and n as the exponent, and then let the electronics do the work.

3.5   FINDING n

When a sum of money earns interest from one date to another, the elapsed time must be obtained and converted into interest conversion periods or the value of n. One way to get elapsed time is to subtract the earlier calendar date from the later one.

EXAMPLE 1   How many semiannual conversion periods are there from June 1, 1979, to December 1, 1984?

SOLUTION   The dates are put in tabular form to simplify subtraction. After subtracting, we multiply the number of years by the periods per year and divide the number of months by the months in a period. We add these results to get the number of periods.

Year	Month	Day
1984	12	1
-1979	- 6	-1
5 years	6 months	0 days

$$n = (5 \times 2) + 6/6 = 10 + 1 = 11$$

EXAMPLE 2   How many quarterly conversion periods are there from November 15, 1976, to August 15, 1985?

SOLUTION   The dates are set up in the usual way to subtract the earlier date from the later one.

Year	Month	Day
1985	8	15
−1976	−11	−15

Subtracting 11 months from 8 would result in a negative number. To avoid this, we borrow a year and add 12 to the 8 months. It is a good idea to keep a record of what is being done by striking out the numbers that are changed and replacing them with their new values. This procedure is illustrated as follows:

Year	Month	Day
4	20	
198$\not5$	$\not8$	15
−1976	−11	−15
8 years	9 months	0 days

$$n = (8 \times 4) + 9/3 = 32 + 3 = 35$$

3.6 HOW MANY PLACES?

The factors in Table 2 and Table 3 are given to 10 decimal places, making them adequate for handling large sums of money. In the examples worked in the tables published by the Financial Publishing Company, the complete factor is used and the answer is rounded to the cent. If a calculator is available, as it usually is in a business, this method is the sensible one to use in working a problem since it ensures maximum accuracy without any troublesome questions about the number of decimal places to use to get answers correct to the nearest cent.

Since many students have to do calculations manually, we use simple sums in most problems to minimize routine arithmetic. To further conserve your time, we give answers that were obtained by rounding the factors to the same number of decimal places as there are digits in the sum of money given in the problem, *including the cents*. Thus a principal of $25,000 would mean rounding the factor to 7 decimal places, while 4 places would be used for a principal of $25. This practice usually gives an answer that is the same as, or within a penny or two of, what would be obtained using the entire factor.

EXAMPLE 1 Find the compound amounts of $25, $2500, and $2,500,000 invested at 6% converted quarterly for 5 years.

SOLUTION

$$25(1.015)^{20} = 25 \times 1.3469 = \$33.67$$
$$2500(1.015)^{20} = 2500 \times 1.346855 = \$3367.14$$
$$2{,}500{,}000(1.015)^{20} = 2{,}500{,}000 \times 1.346855007 = \$3{,}367{,}137.52$$

EXAMPLE 2 A principal of $1000 is deposited at 6% for 10 years. What will be the compound amount and the compound interest if the interest is compounded annually, semiannually, quarterly, and monthly?

SOLUTION The required factors and final results are summarized in the following chart. As the frequency of conversion is increased, interest is added to principal more often, so the depositor has a larger amount credited.

Frequency of Compounding	Rate per Period (i)	Number of Conversion Periods (n)	Amount of 1 $[(1 + i)^n]$	Compound Amount (S)	Compound Interest $(S - P)$
Annually	.06	10	1.790848	$1790.85	$790.85
Semiannually	.03	20	1.806111	1806.11	806.11
Quarterly	.015	40	1.814018	1814.02	814.02
Monthly	.005	120	1.819397	1819.40	819.40

EXAMPLE 3 Banks and other savings institutions offer certificates of deposit and other savings instruments that permit deferral of interest payment until the deposit matures or is redeemed. This practice makes possible the automatic reinvestment of interest at the rate paid on the original investment. This rate is usually higher than the rate paid by the institution on its passbook accounts.

A person aged 60 put $10,000 in a deferred account paying 8% converted quarterly. The account is to mature in 5 years. Find the amount at that time.

SOLUTION Substituting $P = 10{,}000$, $i = .02$, and $n = 20$ in formula (9), we have

$$S = 10{,}000(1.02)^{20} = 10{,}000 \times 1.4859474 = \$14{,}859.47$$

Tables 2 and 3 list compound interest factors for many rates. The Financial Compound Interest and Annuity Tables published by the Financial Publishing Company give many more. Any set of tables, however, will be able to include only a limited number of values for rates. If you use a calculator with exponential capability, you can work with any rate.

EXAMPLE 4$^{(C)}$ A bank pays 7.8% compounded quarterly on savings accounts. A woman puts $5000 into such an account on July 1, 1985. Find the amount in the account on January 1, 1990.

SOLUTION In this case $i = \frac{.078}{4} = .0195$ and $n = 18$.

$$S = 5000(1.0195)^{18} = \$7078.48$$

EXAMPLE 5 A depositor planned to leave $2000 in a savings and loan association paying 5% compounded semiannually for a period of 5 years. At the end of $2\frac{1}{2}$ years the depositor had to withdraw $1000. What amount will be in the account at the end of the original 5-year period?

SOLUTION First we find the amount in the account at the end of $2\frac{1}{2}$ years.

$$S = 2000(1.025)^5 = 2000 \times 1.131408 = \$2262.82$$

After withdrawal of $1000 the depositor has a balance of $1262.82. During the remainder of the 5 years this amount will grow to

$$S = 1262.82(1.025)^5 = 1262.82 \times 1.131408 = \$1428.76$$

ALTERNATE SOLUTION We could draw a time diagram (Figure 3-4), select a focal date, and solve using an equation of value.

$$\begin{aligned} x &= 2000(1.025)^{10} - 1000(1.025)^5 \\ &= 2000 \times 1.280085 - 1000 \times 1.131408 \\ &= 2560.17 - 1131.41 \\ &= \$1428.76 \end{aligned}$$

In compound interest problems in which transactions occur at interest conversion dates, the answer does not depend on the choice of the focal date. By skillful selection of focal date, you can work problems and check results with a minimum of work.

3.7 LAW OF ORGANIC GROWTH

The compound interest law is often called the *law of organic growth.* This law can be applied to anything that is changing at a constant rate. There are many situations in nature, science, and business where the compound interest law is useful, provided that good judgment is used in applying it. The investigator must be careful about extending past rates into the future. If something has been increasing at approximately a constant rate for several years, that rate can be useful for obtaining predicted values for the next few years. The same rate might lead to absurd long-term predictions. Rates determined under one set of conditions may not apply in another situation. Rats and bugs may increase at certain rates in the laboratory, where they are protected from their natural enemies. But there is no justification for applying these rates to the usual environment with its cats, birds, and other limiting factors.

EXAMPLE 1   During the period 1970–1980, the population of a city increased at a rate of about 3% a year. If the population in 1980 was 300,000, what is the predicted population in 1990?

SOLUTION   Substituting $P = 300{,}000$, $i = .03$, and $n = 10$ in formula (9), we have

$$S = 300{,}000(1.03)^{10} = 300{,}000 \times 1.343916 = 403{,}175$$

Figure 3-4

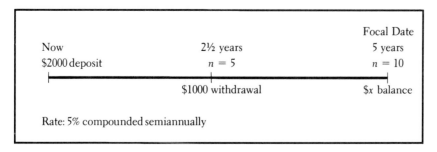

Focal Date

Now   2½ years   5 years

$2000 deposit $n = 5$ $n = 10$

$1000 withdrawal $x balance

Rate: 5% compounded semiannually

In dealing with approximate data, the prediction should usually be rounded off to a reasonable value such as 403,000.

EXAMPLE 2   During the period 1970–1975 the earnings per share of Oklahoma Natural Gas Company common stock increased at about 9% a year compounded. The earnings per share for 1975 was $2.92. Assuming that the same rate of increase continues, predict the earnings per share for 1990.

SOLUTION   Substituting $P = 2.92$, $i = .09$, and $n = 15$ in formula (9), we obtain

$$S = 2.92(1.09)^{15} = 2.92 \times 3.642 = \$10.63$$

EXAMPLE 3   During the period 1970–1980, the population of a city increased 8%. If the population was 500,000 in 1980, what is the estimated population for 2000 assuming that the same rate of growth continues?

SOLUTION   The conversion period is the basic unit of time in compound interest problems. In financial problems this period is usually 1 year or less. In organic problems it may be many years or it may be a few seconds or less. In this problem it is a decade, so for 20 years, $n = 2$. Substituting in formula (9), we have

$$S = 500,000(1.08)^2 = 500,000 \times 1.166400 = 583,200$$

3.8   NONTABULATED RATES

When a problem involves a rate not included in this text or even in the complete tables of the Financial Publishing Company, a calculator can be used to get the amount-of-1 factor. By the law of exponents, $(1 + i)^n \times (1 + i)^m = (1 + i)^{n+m}$, the answer can be obtained quickly. If we need $(1.052)^{15}$, we could multiply the factor by itself to get the square, multiply the 2nd power by itself to get the 4th power, multiply the 4th power by itself to get the 8th power, multiply the 8th power by itself to get the 16th power, and then divide the 16th power by the 1st power to give the 15th power. Sometimes the calculator manufacturer has instruction sheets that show how to reduce time and increase accuracy when making routine calculations. After $(1 + i)^n$ has been obtained, the other compound interest factors can be obtained using the relationships at the bottom of the columns in Table 2.

Exercise 3a

1. A finance company makes consumer loans at a nominal annual rate of 36% compounded monthly. Find j, i, and m.
    ($j = 36\%$, or .36; $i = 3\%$, or .03; $m = 12$)
2. Fill in the conversion periods per year and the rate per period columns in the table below.
3. Find the compound amount and the compound interest if $1000 is invested for 10 years at 7%.
    ($1967.15; $967.15)
4. Find the compound amount and the compound interest if $24,500 is borrowed for 3 years at 9% converted monthly.
5. The day a boy was born, his father invested $200 at 5% compounded semiannually. Find the value of the fund on the boy's 18th birthday.
    ($486.51)
6. On a girl's 8th birthday, her parents place $250 in her name in an investment paying 6% compounded semiannually. How much will she have to her credit on her 21st birthday?

Quoted or Nominal Rate	Conversion Periods per Year (m)	Rate per Period (i) Percent	Decimal
8%			
8% compounded semiannually			
8% compounded monthly			
8% compounded quarterly			
10% compounded monthly			
9% compounded semiannually			
7% compounded semiannually			

7.   A town increased in population at 2% a year from 1970 to 1980. If the population was 18,000 in 1980, what is the estimated population to the nearest hundred for 1990, assuming that the rate of growth remains the same?
      (21,900)

8.   The sales of a business have been increasing at the rate of 3% per year. If the sales in 1981 were $250,000, what are the estimated sales to the nearest thousand dollars for 1986?

9.   Find the amount of $6000 for 8 years at 8% nominal, compounded: (a) annually; (b) semiannually; (c) quarterly; and (d) monthly.
      [(a) $11,105.58; (b) $11,237.89; (c) $11,307.25; (d) $11,354.74]

10.   Find the amount of $10,000 for 10 years at 7% compounded: (a) annually; (b) semiannually; (c) quarterly; and (d) monthly.

11.   What amount of money will be required to repay a loan of $6000 on December 31, 1994, if the loan is made on December 31, 1988, at a rate of 10% compounded semiannually?
      ($10,775.14)

12.   On June 1, 1987, a woman incurs a debt of $3000 that is to be repaid on demand of the lender with interest at 9% converted semiannually. If the lender demands payment on December 1, 1995, how much must the borrower repay?

13.   On June 30, 1985, a man put $15,000 in a deferred savings account paying 8% converted quarterly. Find the amount in the account when it matures on June 30, 1991.
      ($24,126.56)

14.   As part of her retirement program, a woman puts $12,000 in a deferred savings account paying 7% converted quarterly. The investment is made on the day she becomes 57. What will be the maturity value of this account if it matures when she becomes 62?

15.   On June 30, 1986, a man deposits $850 in a building and loan association paying 6% compounded semiannually. How much will he get if he draws out his money on June 30, 1993?
      ($1285.70)

16.   What amount of money will be required to repay a loan of $1835.50 on July 1, 1991, if the loan is made on October 1, 1987, at an interest rate of 12% compounded quarterly?

17.   A woman puts $2500 in a savings and loan association paying 6% converted quarterly. She plans to leave the money there for 6 years and then use it for a trip. At the end of 2 years she has

to withdraw $500. What is the amount left in her account at the end of the original 6-year period?

($2939.26)

18.   What is the answer to problem 17 if the woman withdraws the $500 at the end of 4 years?

19.   On July 1, 1986, a woman puts $5000 in a savings and loan association paying 6% converted semiannually. On January 1, 1988, she withdraws $2500 from her account. What is the balance in the account on January 1, 1991?

($3538.74)

20.   Interest dates for a bank are May 1 and November 1. Interest on savings accounts is 8% converted semiannually. A depositor opens an account on May 1, 1986, with a deposit of $1500. A withdrawal of $500 is made on November 1, 1987, and a deposit of $1000 is made on May 1, 1989. What is the balance in the account on May 1, 1990?

21.   During the period 1970–1975 the annual earnings per share of the U.S. Shoe Corporation increased about 5% per year. If the earnings in 1975 were $1.95 per share, find the predicted per share earnings for 1987 if the same rate continues.

($3.50)

22.   The earnings per share of R. J. Reynolds increased at about 9% annually during the period 1966–1975 to a value of $7.39 in 1975. Assuming that the same rate continues, predict the per share earnings for 1988.

23.$^{(C)}$ Find the amount of an investment of $10,000 for 5 years at $7\frac{3}{4}\%$ compounded semiannually.

($14,625.49)

24.$^{(C)}$ A family has its savings in a building and loan association paying $5\frac{1}{2}\%$ compounded quarterly. Interest is calculated on March 31, June 30, September 30, and December 31 of each year. Suppose that they had $1200 on June 30, 1981. If nothing is deposited or withdrawn, how much will they have on December 31, 1989?

3.9 DAILY COMPOUNDING

The Board of Governors of the Federal Reserve System establishes the maximum nominal rates that member banks may pay on time and savings deposits; the Federal Deposit Insurance Corporation has similar authority with respect to deposits in insured nonmember banks; and the Federal Home Loan Bank Board establishes the maximum rates paid by federally insured savings and loan associations. Since interest rates are the price of credit, this federal freeze on rates is one of our few peacetime examples of price controls. The greatest impact is on small savers. Affluent investors, who have more alternatives for investing money, can find higher rates in other investments.

Since there are no restrictions on the frequency of compounding, banks and savings and loan associations try to attract depositors by increasing the frequency of compounding when the demand for loanable funds is great. With a fixed nominal rate, more frequent compounding results in depositors earning more interest.

For a given nominal rate j the amount-of-1 factor for a 360-day year is computed from the expression $[1 + (j/360)]^t$, where t is the time in days. The amount-of-1 factor for a 365-day year is computed using $[1 + (j/365)]^t$.

EXAMPLE Compute the amount-of-1 factor for 5% converted daily for 1, 2, and 3 days for 360- and 365-day years.

SOLUTION   For a 360-day year, we find that

$$(1 + j/360) = (1 + .05/360) = (1 + .0001388889)$$

We now raise this factor to a power equal to the number of days.

$$(1.0001388889)^1 = 1.0001388889$$
$$(1.0001388889)^2 = 1.0002777971$$
$$(1.0001388889)^3 = 1.0004167245$$

For a 365-day year, $(1 + j/365) = (1 + .05/365) = (1 + .0001369863)$. For 1, 2, and 3 days the amount-of-1 factors are

$$(1.0001369863)^1 = 1.0001369863$$
$$(1.0001369863)^2 = 1.0002739914$$
$$(1.0001369863)^3 = 1.0004110152$$

Some institutions will pay interest based on Bankers' Rule so that at the end of the year $t = \frac{365}{360}$ and the factor is $[1 + (j/360)]^{365}$. This procedure will produce even more interest for the investor. For example, the amount at 8% compounded daily for one year using Bankers' Rule is

$$S = 10,000 [1 + (.08/360)]^{365} = 10,000 \times 1.0844816 = \$10,844.82$$

If the same investment had been made using exact interest and exact time, the value would be

$$S = 10,000 [1 + (.08/365)]^{365} = 10,000 \times 1.0832775 = \$10,832.78$$

Bankers' Rule produces $12.04 in additional interest at the same rate.

3.10 EFFECTIVE INTEREST RATES

To put different rates and frequencies of conversion on a comparable basis, we determine the **effective rate**, r. The effective rate is the rate converted annually that will produce the same amount of interest per year as the nominal rate j converted m times per year.

If the nominal rate is 6% converted annually, the effective rate will also be 6%. But if the nominal rate is 6% converted semiannually, the amount of $1 at the end of one year will be $(1.03)^2 = \$1.0609$. This calculation is simply the accumulation factor for a rate per period of 3% and two periods. The interest on $1 for 1 year is then $1.0609 − 1.0000 = \$.0609$. This result is equivalent to an annual rate of 6.09%. Thus 6.09% converted annually would result in the same amount of interest as 6% converted semiannually. The computations used to get the effective rate of 6.09% in this case can be summarized as follows:

$$1.0609 = (1.03)^2$$
$$r = 1.0609 - 1 = .0609 = 6.09\%$$

To obtain an equation to find the effective rate in general, we assume that the effective rate produces the same amount S from the given principal P in 1 year as the compounded interest. We then have

$$S = P(1 + rt) = P(1 + r)$$

and

$$S = P(1 + i)^m$$

Setting the value of S equal,

$$P(1 + r) = P(1 + i)^m$$

Divide both sides by P:

$$1 + r = (1 + i)^m$$

$$r = (1 + i)^m - 1 \qquad (10)$$

effective rate

As m, the frequency of conversion, is increased, the effective rate corresponding to a given nominal rate gets larger. However, the increase becomes less rapid with large values of m.

To find the effective rate for discrete compounding, we simply look up the amount of 1 corresponding to the nominal rate and the number of conversions in a year and subtract 1 from this factor. For 5% converted monthly, the amount-of-1 factor for 12 periods is 1.051161 and the effective rate is .051161, or approximately 5.12%. Table 3-3 shows the effect of frequency of compounding on the effective rate and the corresponding interest on $10,000 for a year.

While daily and continuous compounding may result in impressive advertisements, these practices do not mean much to the average depositor in terms of income. In a year, $10,000 earns $511.62 at 5% compounded monthly. With daily compounding, the interest is only $1.05 more. When an enterprising ad writer points out that Institution X offers interest compounded continuously for the use of your money, the cost to the borrower is not much more than for daily compounding. What can be of great value to depositors is the policy of some

Table 3-3 Effect of Frequency of Compounding

If the Nominal Rate is 5% Compounded:	The Effective Rate Is:	A Year's Interest on $10,000 Is:	Additional Interest Is:
Annually	5.0000000%	$500.00	—
Semiannually	5.0625000	506.25	$6.25
Quarterly	5.0945337	509.45	3.20
Monthly	5.1161898	511.62	2.17
Weekly	5.1245841	512.46	.84
Daily	5.1267496	512.67	.21
Hourly	5.1270946	512.71	.04
Continuously	5.1271096	512.71	.00

institutions of paying interest on deposits to the date of withdrawal and of using Bankers' Rule.

Because three rates are used in compound interest work, it is a good idea at this point to summarize the meaning of each.

The nominal rate (symbol j) is the quoted or stated rate. When a nominal rate is quoted, the frequency of compounding should be stated. Nominal rates are given in the marginal index of the compound interest tables.

The rate per period (symbol i) equals the nominal rate divided by the number of conversion periods per year (j/m). The rate per period is the value used to compute compound interest factors. This rate is at the top of the page in the compound interest tables.

The effective rate (symbol r) is the rate actually earned in a year. This rate is used to obtain different nominal rates and conversion periods on a common basis for comparison purposes.

EXAMPLE Find the effective rate of interest equivalent to 8% converted semiannually.

SOLUTION The rate per period = 4%, or .04, and m = 2. In getting the effective rate it is usually sufficiently accurate to take the amount-of-1 factor from Table 2 to four decimal places. Substituting in formula (10), we have.

$$r = (1.04)^2 - 1$$
$$= 1.0816 - 1.0000 = .0816 = 8.16\%$$

Thus 8.16% compounded annually will produce the same amount of interest as 8% compounded semiannually.

Exercise 3b

1.   What is the effective rate of interest equivalent to 10% converted: (a) semiannually? (b) quarterly? (c) monthly?
      [(a) 10.25%; (b) 10.38%; (c) 10.47%]
2.   What is the effective rate of interest equivalent to 7% converted: (a) semiannually? (b) quarterly? (c) monthly?
3.   Which gives the better annual return on an investment, $6\frac{1}{8}\%$ converted annually or 6% converted quarterly? Show the figures on which you base your answer.
      (6% converted quarterly)

4.   Which rate of interest gives the better annual yield, 4% compounded quarterly or $4\frac{1}{2}$% compounded semiannually? Show the figures on which you base your answer.

5.   A savings and loan association in California advertises that it is paying 5.25% converted daily. According to the ad, this claim is equivalent to an effective rate of 5.39%. An investor in Ohio has money in an account paying 5% converted quarterly. If the Ohio investor transfers $10,000 to the California association, how much additional interest will be earned in a year? ($30)

6.   A company has $50,000 to invest. What would be the difference in interest at the end of a year between earning 8% converted semiannually and 8% converted quarterly?

7.   Complete the following table showing the effect of frequency of compounding on effective interest rates. Use the 3% values as a check on your work. Answers not available in this text have been obtained from more extensive interest tables.

Nominal Annual Rate	Effective Rate if Compounded:		
	Semiannually	Quarterly	Monthly
3%	3.02%	3.03%	3.04%
6			
9			
12			
15	15.56	15.87	
18			
21	22.10	22.71	
24	25.44		
27	28.82	29.86	
30	32.25	33.55	

8.(C) Find the effective rate of interest equivalent to a rate of $5\frac{1}{2}$% compounded (a) semiannually, (b) quarterly, (c) monthly, (d) daily (based on a 365-day year).

9.(C) Which is preferable to the lender: 6% compounded daily based on a 365-day year or 6.05% compounded quarterly? (6.05% compounded quarterly)

10.$^{(C)}$ Find the effective rate for an investment at 10% compounded daily using Bankers' Rule.

3.11 INTEREST FOR PART OF A PERIOD

When deriving the compound interest formula, we assumed that the time would be an integral number of conversion periods. When there is a part of a period, the usual practice is to allow simple interest for this time on the compound amount at the end of the last whole period.

EXAMPLE At 7% compounded semiannually, $2000 will amount to how much in 3 years and 5 months?

SOLUTION The total time in this case is 6 whole periods and 5 months left over. The compound amount at the end of the 6 whole periods is

$$S = 2000(1.035)^6 = 2000 \times 1.229255 = \$2458.51$$

The simple interest for the remaining 5 months is

$$2458.51 \times \tfrac{5}{12} \times .07 = \$71.71$$

Therefore the amount at the end of 3 years and 5 months is

$$2458.51 + 71.71 = \$2530.22$$

Note that in obtaining the simple interest we use the nominal annual rate and the time in years. A common mistake is to use the rate per period.

The procedure used to get the total amount for a problem involving a part of a period is illustrated in Figure 3-5. The series of dots indicates that part of the time scale has been omitted.

3.12 AMOUNT AT CHANGING RATES

If the interest rate on an investment changes, we can find the final amount by calculating the amount each time there is a change in rate and carrying this value forward at the new rate until there is another change. Consequently, we end up with a series of compound interest problems. The amount at the end of one stage becomes the principal at the beginning of the next stage.

In this text when a problem has two or more stages, we round intermediate answers to the nearest cent. This practice makes the arithmetic as simple as possible. If you have a calculator you might prefer to either carry more places in the intermediate steps or first multiply the factors together.

EXAMPLE A principal of $900 earns 6% converted quarterly for 4 years and then 7% converted semiannually for 2 more years. Find the final amount.

SOLUTION First we find the amount at the end of 4 years (16 periods) using a factor rounded to 5 decimal places.

$$900(1.015)^{16} = 900 \times 1.26899 = \$1142.09$$

Now we go forward 2 more years at 7% converted semiannually. Since there are 6 digits in the new principal, we round the factor to 6 decimal places.

$$1142.09(1.035)^4 = 1142.09 \times 1.147523 = \$1310.57$$

If this problem were worked by first multiplying the complete factors together, we would have

$$900 \times 1.2689855477 \times 1.1475230006 = \$1310.57$$

Figure 3-5

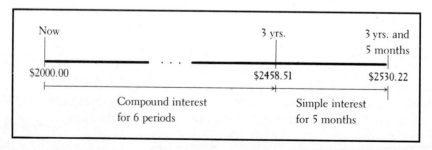

Exercise 3c

1. On June 30, 1977, Charles Moser borrowed $3000 at 8% converted semiannually. How much did he have to repay on September 28, 1984? Use Bankers' Rule for simple interest computation.
   ($5298.93)

2. Find the amount of $750 for $4\frac{1}{2}$ years at 6% effective.

3. If $6000 is borrowed for 5 years and 4 months at 9% converted semiannually, what amount would be required to repay the debt?
   ($9597.34)

4. What is the amount of $40,000 for 6 years and 3 months at 10% converted semiannually?

5. To what sum of money does $2000 accumulate in 3 years and 5 months at 6% compounded semiannually?
   ($2447.80)

6.(C) On June 1, 1983, a debt of $4000 was incurred at the rate of 12% What amount will be required to settle the debt on September 15, 1987? Use Bankers' Rule for simple interest computation.

7. A savings and loan association advertises "instant interest." Funds received by the 10th of the month earn interest from the 1st. Interest is paid at the rate of 8% converted quarterly. Interest dates are March 31, June 30, September 30, and December 31. Interest is paid up to the date funds are withdrawn. A woman deposits $2000 on January 7, 1987. If she closes out her account on January 30, 1989, how much will she get? Allow simple interest for 1 month.
   ($2358.94)

8. Another depositor puts $5000 on April 8, 1987, in the savings and loan in problem 7, and closes out the account on November 30, 1990. What is the balance at that time? Allow simple interest for 2 months.

9. An investment of $4000 is made for 12 years. During the first 5 years the interest rate is 9% converted semiannually. Then the rate drops to 8% converted semiannually for the remainder of the time. What is the final amount?
   ($10,756.96)

10. A principal of $6500 earns 5% effective for 3 years and then 6% compounded semiannually for 4 more years. What is the amount at the end of the 7 years?

11.$^{(C)}$ Dr. and Mrs. William H. Maguire bequeath $400,000 to a university for the construction of a science building. The university receives 12% on this money for 9 years. Then the rate drops to 11%. If the building is constructed 25 years after the gift was received, how much is in the fund at that time?
($5,891,011.30)

12.$^{(C)}$ An investment of $3000 earns $8\frac{1}{2}\%$ for 2 years, then 7.6% compounded semiannually for 4 years, then 9.2% compounded semiannually for 2 years. Find the amount at the end of the 8 years.

3.13   PRESENT VALUE AT COMPOUND INTEREST

In business transactions there are many times when it is necessary to determine the **present value** of a certain sum of money due in the future. The present value is defined as the principal that will amount to the given sum at the specified future date. The difference between the future amount and its present value is the **compound discount.** To find the present value of a future amount, we simply solve the compound interest formula for P:

$$P = \frac{S}{(1 + i)^n}$$

With the aid of a calculator this equation can be used to find P. When the work must be done by hand, it is more convenient to use negative exponents to express the right-hand side. We give the equation in both forms.

$$P = S(1 + i)^{-n} = \frac{S}{(1 + i)^n} \qquad (11)$$

present value at cpd interest

P = the principal or present value
S = the amount due in the future
i = the rate per period
n = the number of periods

The quantity

$$\frac{1}{(1 + i)^n}$$

or $(1 + i)^{-n}$ is called the **discount factor, present worth of 1**, or **present value of 1**. This quantity is also indicated, particularly in insurance problems, by the symbol v^n. Numerical values of the discount factor for common interest rates are given in the "Present worth of 1" column in Table 2. In our examples we follow the common practice of using a negative exponent to indicate that a sum due in the future is to be discounted. If you are using a calculator to solve for the present value, you can divide by the appropriate value in the "Amount of 1" column in Tables 2 and 3. Note that Table 3 has no "Present worth of 1" column. However, the value in the "Present worth of 1" column is always the reciprocal of the corresponding value in the "Amount of 1" column. Using a calculator and Table 3, you can apply formula (11) either by division or by using a reciprocal button $(1/x)$ to calculate $(1 + i)^{-n}$. If your calculator has exponential capability, you can compute $(1 + i)^{-n}$ directly without using the tables.

The "Present worth of 1" column gives the present or current value of a dollar to be paid in the future, taking into account compound interest. For example, at 5% compounded annually, $1 due in 5 years has a present-worth-of-1 factor of .7835261665. In other words, $.78 will grow to $1.00 in 5 years if it earns 5% compounded annually. The present value of any sum due in the future can be obtained by simply multiplying the future amount by the appropriate present-worth-of-1 factor from Table 2.

The concept of present value is one of the most useful and powerful tools in economic analysis. This concept enables the analyst to take sums of money due in the future and determine how much they are worth now.

EXAMPLE 1   Find the present value of $5000 due in 4 years if money is worth 8% compounded semiannually.

SOLUTION   Substituting $S = 5000$, $i = .04$, and $n = 8$ in formula (11) and using the present-worth-of-1 factor from Table 2, we have

$$P = 5000(1.04)^{-8} = 5000 \times .730690 = \$3653.45$$

This statement means that if $3653.45 had been put at interest for 4 years at 8% compounded semiannually, the amount would be $5000. A good exercise for students is to carry money backward and forward in this way to show that the results do check.

EXAMPLE 2   Find the present value of $7500 due in 4 years if money is worth 14% compounded monthly.

SOLUTION   In this case we must use Table 3. We let $S = 7500$, $i = \frac{14}{12}\%$, and $n = 48$.

$$P = 7500 \div \left(1 + \frac{.14}{12}\right)^{48} = \frac{7500}{1.745007} = \$4297.98$$

An alternative method is to compute $(1/1.745006919) = .5730636305$.

$$P = 7500 \times .5730636305 = \$4297.98$$

Using a calculator with exponential capability allows for the use of any interest rate.

EXAMPLE 3$^{(C)}$ How much must be invested in an account paying 8.4% compounded monthly in order to accumulate to $15,000 in 5 years?

SOLUTION   The rate, $i = 8.4\%/12 = .7\%$, is not found in Table 2 or 3. However, using a calculator with $S = 15,000$, $i = .007$ and $n = 60$, we have

$$P = 15,000\,(1.007)^{-60} = \$9870.13$$

When the times involves a part of a conversion period, we bring S back for the minimum number of periods that includes the given time and then compute the simple interest on the principal up to the point at which the present value is wanted.

EXAMPLE 4   A note with a maturity value of $1000 is due in 3 years and 8 months. What is its present value at 6% compounded semi-annually?

SOLUTION   First we bring the $1000 back 4 years or 8 periods, the minimum number of periods that includes 3 years and 8 months.

$$1000(1.03)^{-8} = 1000 \times .789409 = \$789.41$$

Now we take this amount forward 4 months at simple interest.

$$789.41 \times .06 \times \tfrac{1}{3} = \$15.79$$

Adding principal and interest, we get $805.20 as the present value.

On such problems, where it is necessary to move money backward and forward or to keep track of several sums of money, it is good practice to make a time diagram that shows the dollar value of each inflow and outflow of money at the point in time where the flow occurs. Figure 3-6 is a diagram for this problem.

In the preceding examples the maturity value of the obligation was known and it was necessary only to discount this amount. Many times, however, the original debt will be interest-bearing and the maturity value will not be given. Then the *maturity value at the given interest rate must be determined.* Finally, the present value of this maturity value is obtained by discounting at the rate specified for discounting. The two rates may be, and frequently are, different.

EXAMPLE 5 On August 5, 1985, Mr. Kane loaned Ms. Hill $2000 at 12% converted semiannually. Ms. Hill gave Mr. Kane a note promising to repay the loan with accumulated interest in 6 years. On February 5, 1989, Mr. Kane sells the note to a buyer, who charges an interest rate of 16% converted semiannually for discounting. How much does Mr. Kane get?

Figure 3-6

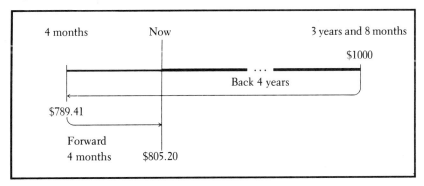

SOLUTION   We must first determine the maturity value of the debt.

$$S = 2000(1.06)^{12} = 2000 \times 2.012196 = \$4024.39$$

Now the original time and the original interest rate have no more bearing on the problem. All that the buyer of the note is interested in is the maturity value, how long the period of time is until collection can be made, and what the note is worth at the specific discount rate.

The note matures on August 5, 1991. From February 5, 1989, to this maturity date is $2\frac{1}{2}$ years, or 5 periods of 6 months each. Therefore the value of the note at 16% compounded semiannually is

$$P = 4024.39(1.08)^{-5} = 4024.39 \times .680583 = \$2738.95$$

Note that the period for discounting is from the time the buyer buys the note to the maturity date. The time at which the original debt was contracted does not enter into this part of the problem except to establish the maturity date. A time diagram (Figure 3-7) will prevent many of the common errors made in dealing with this type of problem.

EXAMPLE 6   A person can buy a piece of property for $4500 cash or for $2000 down and $3000 in 3 years. If the person has money earning 6% converted semiannually, which is the better purchase plan and by how much now?

SOLUTION   We get the present value of $3000 due in 3 years at 6% compounded semiannually.

$$P = 3000(1.03)^{-6} = 3000 \times .837484 = \$2512.45$$

Adding this amount to the $2000 down payment makes the present value of the time payment plan $4512.45. By paying $4500 cash, the buyer saves $12.45 now.

EXAMPLE 7   A piece of property can be purchased for $2850 cash or for $3000 in 12 months. Which is the better plan for the buyer if money is worth 7% compounded quarterly? Find the cash (present value) equivalent of the savings made by adopting the better plan.

SOLUTION We can compare alternative purchase plans by bringing all payments to the same point in time and seeing which plan is better. While the comparison point can be anywhere in time, it is usually best to make the comparison on a present value basis. This method gets all proposals on a "now" basis, the point at which the decision is to be made.

Putting the focal date now and using formula (11) to discount the $3000, we have

$$P = 3000(1.0175)^{-4} = 3000 \times .932959 = \$2798.88$$

The $2850 cash payment is simply $2850 at the focal date. Since the present value of the $3000 due in a year is less than the cash payment, it is better to pay later. The cash equivalent of the savings is

$$2850.00 - 2798.88 = \$51.12$$

Figure 3-7

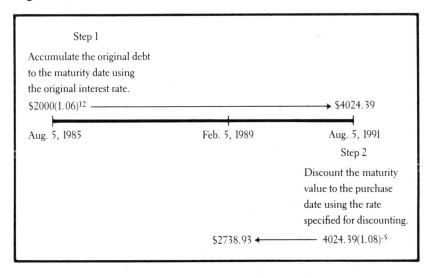

A different rate of interest could lead to a different decision. If the buyer's money was earning only 5% compounded quarterly, the present value of $3000 would be

$$P = 3000(1.0125)^{-4} = 3000 \times .951524 = \$2854.57$$

In this case it is better to pay cash and save 2854.57 − 2850.00 = $4.57 on a cash basis.

Exercise 3d

Use Bankers' Rule for simple interest computations for part of a period when calendar dates are given.

1. What principal is needed to accumulate $3000 in 8 years at 6% converted semiannually?
   ($1869.50)

2. What is the present value at 7% compounded semiannually of $3460 due in 18 months?

3. Find the present value of $5000 due in 5 years if money is worth 8% compounded semiannually.
   ($3377.82)

4. Find the present value of $450.80 due in $2\frac{1}{2}$ years if money is worth 6% compounded semiannually.

5. What is the present value at 9% compounded quarterly of $12,000 due in 18 months?
   ($10,500.29)

6. Find the present value of $3500 due in $4\frac{1}{2}$ years if money is worth 8%.

7. A person owns a note for $2500 due in 5 years. What should a buyer wishing money to earn 14% converted quarterly pay for the note? What is the compound discount?
   ($1256.42, $1243.58)

8. An obligation of $5000 is due on December 1, 1990. What was the value of this obligation on July 16, 1985, at 10% compounded semiannually?

9. On September 3, 1987, Mr. Lovett buys some equipment from the Excello Company. He signs a note promising to pay $3000 with interest at 14% compounded semiannually in 18 months. On December 3, 1987, the Excello Company sells the note to

a finance company that charges an interest rate of 16% converted quarterly for discounting. How much does the Excello Company get for the note?

($3020.69)

10.   A note dated June 1, 1985, calls for the payment of $850 in 6 years. On March 15, 1988, the note is sold at a price that will yield the buyer 9%. How much is paid for the note?

11.   Mr. Durkin gets a note that calls for repayment of $3000 in 5 years together with compound interest at 10% converted quarterly. He sells the note immediately to a buyer who charges an interest rate of 9% converted semiannually for discounting. How much does Mr. Durkin get for the note?

($3165.45)

12.   A note dated September 15, 1987, calls for payment of $400 with annual interest at 9% in 4 years. On December 20, 1989, the note is sold at a price that will yield 8% compounded semiannually. Compute the selling price.

13.   A note of $800 is due in 5 years with interest at 8%. At the end of 3 years the note is discounted at 9%. What are the proceeds at the time of discounting?

($989.36)

14.   A debt of $2500 is due on September 15, 1990. What payment must be made on July 17, 1988, to repay the debt if the borrower is permitted to discount the debt at 12% compounded semiannually?

15.(C)   On August 9, 1987, Miss Lufkin borrows $4000 from Mrs. Feld. She gives Mrs. Feld a note promising to repay the money in 5 years with interest at 11%. On February 9, 1989, Mrs. Feld sells the note to a buyer who charges a rate of 13% compounded semiannually for discount purposes. How much does Mrs. Feld get for the note?

($4337.38)

16.(C)   A note for $2000 dated June 1, 1986, is due in 3 years with compound interest at $13\frac{1}{2}\%$ compounded semiannually. On December 1, 1987, the holder of the note has it discounted by a lender who charges 15% compounded semiannually. What are the proceeds?

17.(C)   Find the present value of $2000 due in 15 months if money is worth 11% converted semiannually.

($1750.07)

18.   A woman can buy a dining room set for $2800 cash or for pay-
       ments of $1500 down and $1500 in 2 years. If she can earn 7%
       on her money, which plan is better?

19.(C) Which would be the better plan for the woman in problem 18
       if she can earn $7\frac{1}{2}\%$ converted annually on her money?
       (She saves $2 now by making two payments.)

3.14 EXTENSION OF THE TABLES

One advantage of using a calculator with exponential capability is that
there is no practical limitation on rates or number of periods. However, for someone using the tables, if the number of periods in the
problem exceeds the number given, the table can be extended using
the law of exponents, $a^m \times a^n = a^{m+n}$. Applying this law in reverse
order to the amount-of-1 factor, we get $(1 + i)^{m+n} = (1 + i)^m \times
(1 + i)^n$. Note that whereas the individual exponents add up to the total
exponent, we obtain the required factor by multiplying the individual
factors.

EXAMPLE 1 It was reported shortly after the United States Bicen-
    tennial celebration in 1976 that the mayor of Piqua, Ohio, was un-
    happy with the amount of money the city was able to afford for its
    festivities. He then contributed $100 to a Mayor's Centennial Fund
    of Piqua to accumulate money for the nation's Tricentennial in
    2076. Find how much his contribution will be worth in 2076 at 5%
    converted annually.

SOLUTION We note that n is 100 and the table goes only to 60.
    However, $(1.05)^{60} \times (1.05)^{40} = (1.05)^{100}$. Using these factors, we
    have

$$S = 100 \times 18.67919 \times 7.03999 = \$13,150.13$$

ALTERNATE SOLUTION When n is easily divisible by table values,
    the work can be simplified by using the same factor more than once.
    In this example $(1.05)^{50} \times (1.05)^{50} = (1.05)^{100}$. Using this fact, we
    obtain

$$S = 100 \times 11.46740 \times 11.46740 = \$13,150.13$$

The required multiplications may be done in any order.

EXAMPLE 2 In his will a college alumnus appointed a trust company to handle his estate. The company was instructed to set aside a sum in a separate account sufficient to pay his alma mater $250,000 at the end of 50 years. What sum should the company deposit in the separate account if it earns 8% converted quarterly?

SOLUTION Substituting $S = 250,000$, $i = .02$, and $n = 200$ in formula (11), we have

$$P = 250,000(1 + 1.02)^{-200}$$

To use Table 2 the present-worth-of-1 factor must be broken down into factors with powers no larger than 60. One solution would be

$$250,000(1.02)^{-60}(1.02)^{-60}(1.02)^{-60}(1.02)^{-20}$$

Since we are dealing with a large sum of money for a long time, complete factors were substituted and calculations made on a calculator.

$$P = 250,000 \times .3047822665 \times .3047822665 \times .3047822665 \times .6729713331 = \$4763.27$$

ALTERNATE SOLUTION Dividing 200 into 4 equal parts, we find that

$$(1.02)^{-200} = [(1.02)^{-50}]^4$$

$$P = 250,000 [(1.02)^{-50}]^4 = 250,000(.3715278821)^4 = \$4763.27$$

EXAMPLE 3 Suppose the interest in Example 2 was compounded monthly. Find the necessary deposit.

SOLUTION

$$P = 250,000(1 + .08/12)^{-600} = 250,000[(1 + .08/12)^{-60}]^{10}$$
$$= 250,000(.6712104444)^{10} = \$4640.10$$

ALTERNATE SOLUTION The solution above would be computationally difficult without a calculator having exponential capability. Table 3 could be used to make the solution easier.

$$P = \frac{250,000}{(1 + .08/12)^{600}} = \frac{250,000}{[(1 + .08/12)^{300}]^2} = \frac{250,000}{(7.3401759637)^2} = \$4640.10$$

With a calculator, these calculations can be done quickly and we have a check on our work even though we are dealing with hundreds of thousands of dollars and hundreds of conversion periods.

Exercise 3e

1. Find the compound amount if $250 is invested at 5% compounded semiannually for 40 years.
   ($1802.39)
2. What is the compound amount of $4500 invested at 8% compounded monthly for 50 years?
3. If $35,000 is invested at 9% compounded semiannually, what will be the amount in 50 years?
   ($2,855,598.13)
4. If $355.60 is invested at 5% compounded quarterly, what will be the amount in 20 years?
5. Find the amount of $4000 invested for 25 years at 6% converted quarterly.
   ($17,728.18)
6. Find the amount of $14,000 invested at 7% compounded quarterly at the end of 22 years and 3 months.
7. How much must be invested today at 6% compounded semi-annually to amount to $10,000 in 50 years?
   ($520.33)
8. How much must be invested today at 6% compounded quarterly to amount to $5000 in 25 years?
9. How much must be deposited now in an investment paying 8% compounded quarterly to amount to $100,000 in 25 years?
   ($13,803.30)
10. How much must be deposited now in an investment paying 10% compounded monthly to amount to $100,000 in 50 years?

3.15 FINDING THE RATE

In the basic formula for compound interest, $S = P(1 + i)^n$, there are four quantities. We have shown how to determine the amount and the present value using Table 2. When the amount, principal, and time are known, the approximate rate can be found by linear interpolation. Since the rate is usually wanted only for information or for purposes of comparison, this method is sufficiently accurate for most practical purposes. If a rate must be determined to several decimal places, refined methods of interpolation will be found in the Compound Interest and Annuity Tables published by the Financial Publishing Company. Logarithmic tables or scientific calculators can also be used following the method given on page 149. If you have access to a calculator that computes arbitrary roots (a button indicated $\sqrt[x]{y}$ or $\sqrt[y]{x}$), you can solve these problems directly.

EXAMPLE If $500 amounts to $700 in 5 years with interest compounded quarterly, what is the rate of interest?

SOLUTION We substitute in formula (9) and get the amount-of-1 factor. Rate problems in this book are based on factors carried to 4 decimal places.

$$500(1 + i)^{20} = 700$$
$$(1 + i)^{20} = \tfrac{700}{500} = 1.4000$$

We must now find the value of i for which $(1 + i)^{20} = 1.4000$. We go along line 20 in Table 2 until we find an amount of 1 of 1.4000 or, as is usually the case, values on each side of the one we are looking for. We put the results in tabular form and let d represent the desired difference.

$$i \text{ in } \% \quad (1 + i)^{20}$$

.250% d 1.750   1.4148 i 1.400   .0531   .0679   1.500   1.3469

$$\frac{d}{.250} = \frac{.0531}{.0679}$$

$$d = .250 \times \tfrac{.0531}{.0679} = .196$$

Therefore the desired rate per period is $1.500 + .196 = 1.696\%$. The nominal rate, compounded quarterly, is $4i$, or $4 \times 1.696 = 6.78\%$.

It is not necessary to write the difference between 1.4148 and 1.3469 as .0679. We can write 679 with the decimal point and zero understood. The number 679 is called the **tabular difference**. Omitting leading zeros is the usual practice and is the one we follow from now on.

If only the nominal rate is required, it is better to use the marginal index and work in terms of nominal rates. This method eliminates multiplying the rate per period by the number of conversions in a year. The symbol $j_{(m)}$ stands for the nominal rate j compounded m times per year. With these simplifications, the problem becomes

$$j_{(4)} \text{ in } \% \quad (1+i)^{20}$$

$$
\begin{array}{ccc}
 & 7 & 1.4148 \\
1 \quad d \quad & j & 1.4000 \quad 531 \quad 679 \\
 & 6 & 1.3469
\end{array}
$$

$$\frac{d}{1} = \frac{531}{679}$$

$$d = .78$$

Therefore the nominal annual rate compounded quarterly is 6 + .78 = 6.78%.

ALTERNATE SOLUTION We can also use a calculator to solve for the rate in this problem. From the above, we have

$$(1+i)^{20} = 1.4000$$

Taking the 20th root of both sides,

$$1 + i = \sqrt[20]{1.4000} = 1.01697$$
$$i = 1.01697 - 1 = .01697$$
$$j = .01697 \times 4 = .0679 = 6.79\%$$

Note that the answers differ slightly. This is not surprising because linear interpolation is an approximation technique and, as a result, will not lead to exactly the correct answer. A good calculator will give somewhat better accuracy. Another advantage of using a calculator is that you are not limited to the rates and number of periods in the tables at hand.

Noting that $\sqrt[n]{x} = x^{1/n}$, a calculator with exponential capability (x^y or y^x) can be used in this problem.

$$1 + i = \sqrt[20]{1.4} = 1.01697$$

The reciprocal function ($1/x$) can be used along with the exponential function to find arbitrary roots.

Another method for solving these problems – logarithms – is given on page 149.

3.16 ECONOMIC ANALYSIS

An important concern of economists is forecasting the future perform-ance of the economy. Business leaders use forecasts to help make investment, production, and marketing decisions that are expected to result in profits for their companies. Based on forecasts, government administrators set policies to promote economic growth, full employ-ment, and stable prices. In the *1967 Economic Report of the President*, the Council of Economic Advisers stated:

> Those concerned with national policies for economic growth have... become aware of the power of compound interest. If the American economy continues to grow at 4 percent a year, output will double in 18 years, triple in 28, quadruple in 35. If that potential is wisely and efficiently shared among competing uses, great advances in the economic well-being of all Americans are assured.*

The American tendency to applaud material growth has resulted in too little attention to the less easily measured quality of life. This tendency may be changing as concern over health care, nutrition, pollution, and other problems indicates a reordering of output prior-ities to emphasize quality as well as quantity. Consideration has been given to the establishment of a Council of Social Advisers to report to the President and the nation about social conditions in the same way that the Council of Economic Advisers reports on economic progress.

Because of the many variables and uncertainties, economic forecasts involve risks that are not present in compound interest problems

*_Economic Report of the President_, January 1967, p. 135.

with definite rates. However, sound forecasting methods reduce risks by making predictions more dependable. Successful forecasting relies on careful and informed analysis of the past. If an economic time series plots as approximately a straight line on a semilogarithmic or ratio graph, the past rate of change was fairly constant. The compound interest law can be used to determine this rate, which can then be used as a help in making forecasts.

Sometimes an economist is interested in monetary changes in the data being studied. Then the economist would work with data expressed in current dollars. At other times the economist might be concerned with changes in real or actual output. This aspect requires data that have been adjusted to eliminate the effect of price changes or changes in the value of money. Data deflated to base year prices or expressed in terms of dollars of constant purchasing power referred to a base year are a measure of volume of output.

An example of the type of time series with which economists are concerned is gross national product. The GNP is the most important key measure of the performance of the economy. It is the total value at current market prices of all final goods and services produced by the nation's economy in a year or at an annual rate. To offset the effect of price changes, deflated GNP figures are also determined. They can be compared to show the year-to-year changes in constant dollars and are a good measure of changes in total physical output.

Figure 3-8 shows how the economy has grown in terms of dollars of constant purchasing power. Although there were periods when there were serious drops in output, it is encouraging to note that during the last 30 years declines have been small in relationship to total output. This trend may provide grounds for confidence in fairly stable growth in the future. Over the years, compounding at seemingly modest rates has resulted in impressive increases in goods and services. Because the GNP in real terms has been increasing faster than population, we have been enjoying a rising standard of living. In 1950 the per capita GNP in 1972 dollars was about $3500. The 1984 value, also in 1972 dollars, was over $6900.

Some economists believe that government fiscal policy – taxing and spending programs – is the important determinant of economic progress. Others think that monetary policy is the dominant influence on the economy. A monetary policy that is suggested by some economists is a steady rate of growth in the quantity of money. Controlling the amount of money is the responsibility of monetary authorities. The money supply must be increased fast enough to be adequate for carrying on the nation's business. But if the money supply is increased too rapidly, there is danger of inflation. An idea of desirable rates of increase can be obtained by studying past trends in relation to other economic variables.

EXAMPLE If the money supply increased from $141.1 billion in 1960 to $170.3 billion in 1966, what was the annual compounded rate of increase?

SOLUTION Substituting in the compound interest formula, we have

$$141.1(1 + i)^6 = 170.3$$

$$(1 + i)^6 = \frac{170.3}{141.1} = 1.207$$

$$i \text{ in } \% \quad (1 + i)^6$$

```
             ┌──── 3.5  1.229 ────┐
        .5 ┌─┤      i  1.207 ──────┤13  │35
           │d └──── 3.0  1.194 ────┘
```

Figure 3-8 How the U.S. Economy Has Grown: Gross National Product, 1972 Prices

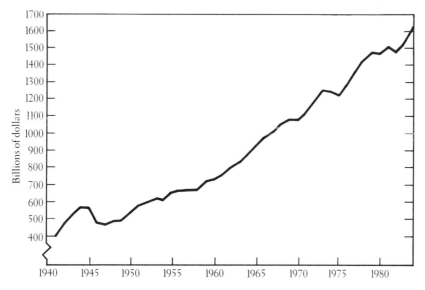

Billions of dollars

1700
1600
1500
1400
1300
1200
1100
1000
900
800
700
600
500
400

1940 1945 1950 1955 1960 1965 1970 1975 1980

Source: *1985 Economic Report of the President*, Table B-2.

$$\frac{d}{.5} = \frac{13}{35}$$

$$d = \frac{.5 \times 13}{35} = .2$$

$$i = 3.0 + .2 = 3.2\%$$

ALTERNATE SOLUTION

$$(1 + i)^6 = 1.207$$
$$1 + i = \sqrt[6]{1.207} = 1.0318$$
$$i = 1.032 - 1 = .032 = 3.2\%$$

Efforts to forecast the future start with a search for regularities in data of the past. When a time series plots as approximately a straight line on semilogarithmic or ratio paper, the period-to-period rate of change has been about the same. Then the compound interest law becomes a promising tool for economic analysis and forecasting.

Because there is always uncertainty as to the extent to which past regularities will hold in the future, economic forecasting and the conduct of economic policy are partly an art. The art is to determine the timing and amount of policy changes needed to keep our large and complicated economy on a course that will result in nearly full employment, relatively stable prices, and growth that includes quality of life as well as quantity of output.

Sometimes a ratio graph of a time series exhibits more than one linear pattern. The Consumer Price Index increased from 147.7 in 1974 to 311.1 in 1984, an annual compounded rate of 7.7%. The individual annual rates were quite different, as one can see from Figure 3-9.

Exercise 3f

In problems 1 to 4, find the answer to two decimal places when expressed as a percent. In problems 5 to 18, find the answer to one decimal place when expressed as a percent.

1.   For a sum of money to double itself in 15 years, what must be the rate of interest converted annually?
      (4.73%)

2. If an investment increases from $5000 to $6500 in 5 years, what is the nominal rate of interest compounded semiannually?

3. If $750 accumulates to $1200 in 6 years, find the nominal rate converted semiannually.

    (7.99%)

4. If an investment increases 50% in 8 years, what is the effective rate of interest?

5. The sales of a business increased from $30.4 million in 1980 to $43.5 million in 1985. What was the annual rate of increase, assuming that it was constant from year to year? (Answer to .1%)

    (7.4%)

Figure 3-9 Consumer Price Index (1967 = 100)

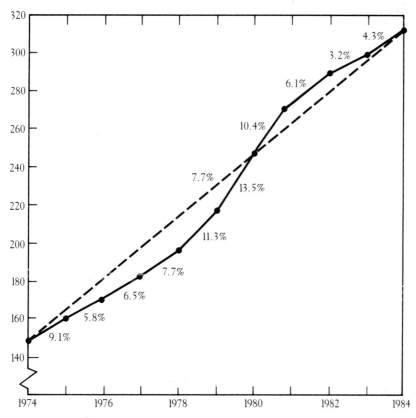

Source: *1985 Economic Report of the President*, Table B-52.

6. If the population of a city increases from 400,000 to 490,000 at approximately a constant rate during a decade, what is the annual rate of increase?

7. A firm organized in 1965 had sales of $30,000 that year. In 1985 the sales were $120,000. What was the annual rate of increase, assuming that it was approximately constant from year to year?

    (7.2%)

8. The sales of a business increased at approximately a constant rate from $5.8 million in 1979 to $7.9 million in 1984. What was the annual rate of increase?

9. A family bought a house for $30,000. In addition to the cost of the house, they paid $300 for legal fees and $100 for a survey. Three years later they sold the house for $40,000, from which the real estate agent deducted a 6% commission. The increased net selling price represents what annual rate of return on the original cost?

    (7.3%)

10.(C) A loan for $10,000 was paid off 15 years later with $40,000. Find the effective rate.

11.(C) A person bought stock in Fly-by-Night Mining Company for $2 per share in 1976. In 1986 the same stock sold for $10. Find the average annual rate of return.

    (17.46%)

12. A person purchased 10 shares of Cincinnati and Suburban Bell Telephone Company stock in 1957 when the price was $77 a share. Commissions and other buying costs totaled $10. The stock was sold in 1963 when the price was $104 a share. Selling costs totaled $12. Find the average annual increase in the net value of the investment.

13. The net income of the General Electric Company increased at approximately a constant rate from $471.8 million in 1971 to $608.1 million in 1974. Find the annual rate.

    (8.8%)

14. Sales of the G. C. Murphy Company increased at an approximately constant rate from $298.54 million in 1965 to $501.32 million in 1974. Find the annual rate.

15. From 1950 to 1965 the gross national product in constant 1958 dollars increased from $355.3 billion to $616.7 billion. Find the annual compounded rate of growth.

    (3.7%)

16.   From 1965 to 1975 GNP in current dollars increased from $688.1 billion to $1449.0 billion. Find the annual compounded rate of growth.

17.(C) Values of disposable personal income for selected years are

Year	Disposable personal income (billions)
1970	695.3
1975	1096.1
1980	1821.8

Find the annual compounded rates of growth for 1970–1975; 1975–1980; 1970–1980;

(9.5%; 10.7%; 10.1%)

18.   The average gross weekly earnings of private nonagricultural workers increased from $53.13 in 1950 to $235.10 in 1980. Find the annual compounded rate of growth.

19.(C) Total mortgage debt on one- to four-family houses increased from $141.9 billion in 1960 to $987.0 billion in 1980. Find the annual compounded rate of growth.

(10.2%)

20.(C) Personal consumption expenses rose from $430.4 billion in 1965 to $1670.1 billion in 1980. Find the annual compounded rate of growth.

21.(C) The mathematics of finance is used in analyzing and comparing rates of change of economic time series. Refer to the latest *Economic Report of the President* and complete the following table to show how annual rates of change in the 1980s compare with those in the 1970s.

Time Series	1970	1980	198–	Annual Compounded Rate of Growth 1970–1980	198–
U.S. population, thousands	204,878	222,807	–	0.8%	–
Gross national product, current dollars, billion	992.7	2,627.4	–	10.2%	–

Time Series	1970	1980	198–	Annual Compounded Rate of Growth 1970–1980	198–
Consumer Price Index (1967 = 100)	116.3	247.0	–	7.8%	–
Corporate after-tax profits, billions	71.4	181.7	–	9.8%	–
Average hourly earnings in manufacturing	3.35	7.27	–	8.1%	–
Employed workers, thousands	78,627	97,270	–	2.2%	–
Public debt, billions	370.1	907.7	–	9.4%	–

3.17 FINDING THE TIME

We now find the time when the principal, amount, and rate are known. To do this, we determine the numerical value of the amount-of-1 factor, $(1 + i)^n$, and then locate this factor, or the values on both sides of it, in Table 2. If no interest is allowed for part of a period, we can take n corresponding to the factor closest to the computed value of $(1 + i)^n$. However, if we want at least a certain amount, we take the n corresponding to the factor larger than the computed value. If simple interest is allowed for part of a period, we can use either the simple interest formula or interpolation to get the exact answer.

EXAMPLE 1 How long will it take $200 to amount to $350 at 7% compounded semiannually?

SOLUTION Substituting in the compound interest formula, we have

$$200(1.035)^n = 350$$
$$(1.035)^n = \frac{350}{200} = 1.75$$

We now look under 3.5% for an accumulation factor of 1.75. As is usually the case, we do not find this exact value. If n is 16, the factor is 1.73399, and if it is 17, the factor is 1.79468. That is, 16 periods or 8 years will produce an amount near to but a little less than $350.

If we let the money accumulate an additional period, the amount will exceed $350. Problems of this type are asked in one of three ways.

1. Find the number of periods that is nearest to the accumulation factor. In this example the solution is 16 periods or 8 years, since 1.73399 is nearer to 1.75 than 1.79468. The amount in this case would be 200 × 1.73399 = $346.80.
2. Find the number of periods required to accumulate at least the amount. In such a case the assumption is made that interest is added only on conversion dates and the investor wants to be sure to accumulate the amount in question. If a problem is stated in this way, the solution is the number of periods corresponding to the first accumulation factor larger than that computed for the problem. If the investor in Example 1 can receive interest only on conversion dates and wants to accumulate at least $350, the answer is 17 periods or $8\frac{1}{2}$ years, because 1.79468 is the first factor that exceeds 1.75. The amount would be 200 × 1.79468 = $358.94.
3. In many cases, interest can be earned for part of a period and the investor can collect at any time. In our example the answer would lie between 8 years and $8\frac{1}{2}$ years. To find the actual amount, we use simple interest for part of a period. After 8 years the amount $S = 200 \times 1.73399 = $346.80. The question is, how long will it take $346.80 to grow to $350 at 7% simple interest?

$$350 = 346.80(1 + .07 \times t)$$

$$1 + .07t = \frac{350}{346.8} = 1.00923$$

$$.07t = 1.00923 - 1 = .00923$$

$$t = \frac{.00923}{.07} = .132 \text{ years, or 48 days based on a 360-day year}$$

Thus we conclude that it would take 8 years and 48 days.

We could also have used interpolation to approximate the solution.

Periods		$(1.035)^n$		
1 period	d	16	1.73399	
or		n	1.75000	1601
180 days		17	1.79468	6069

$$\frac{d}{180} = \frac{1601}{6069}$$

$$d = \frac{1601 \times 180}{6069} = 47$$

Again because interpolation is an approximation technique, the answer may differ slightly from the more exact solution. We could also use trial and error on a calculator to work these problems.

EXAMPLE 2   Draw a graph showing the time required to double your money if interest is compounded annually and no interest is allowed for part of a period.

SOLUTION   The time for any given rate is the smallest value of n that results in an amount-of-1 factor of at least 2. For example, if the rate is 5%, this time occurs at 15 periods. More precisely, at the end of 15 years each dollar will grow to $2.08. (See Figure 3-10.)
   If we use logarithms, we can extend beyond this graph.

Rate	11%	13%	15%	19%	26%	42%
Years	7	6	5	4	3	2

Exercise 3g

1. How long will it take an investment to increase at least 50% in dollar value if the interest rate is 5% converted annually? No interest accrues for part of a period.
   (9 years)
2. Find the time required to triple your money if interest is compounded annually, no interest is allowed for a part of a period, and the rate is: (a) 2%; (b) 3%; (c) 4%; (d) 5%; (e) 6%; (f) 7%; (g) 8%.
3. How long will it take $750 to accumulate to $1000 at 8% converted semiannually? Give the answer to the nearest period.
   (7 periods)
4. How long will it take $4000 to amount to $5000 at 7% converted semiannually? Give the answer to the nearest period.
5. A child 8 years old is left $1600. Under the conditions of the will, the money is to be invested until it amounts to $2500. If the

money is invested at 6%, how old will the child be when the $2500 is received? Give the answer to the nearest birthday.

(16 years old)

6. A man invests $1000 at 6% compounded semiannually on June 1, 1983. No interest is allowed for part of a period. On what date will this account have at least $2000 in it?

7. How long will it take $3000 to amount to $3600 at 6% converted semiannually? Assume that simple interest is allowed for a fraction of a period and give the answer to the nearest day.

(3 years and 30 days)

8. In what time will $200 amount to $250 at 5%? Allow simple interest for a fraction of a period and get the answer to the nearest day.

9. The population of a city has been increasing at the rate of 3% a year. If the population is now 425,000, how long will it take the

Figure 3-10 Double Your Money

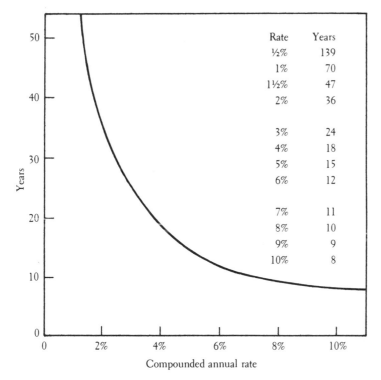

Rate	Years
½%	139
1%	70
1½%	47
2%	36
3%	24
4%	18
5%	15
6%	12
7%	11
8%	10
9%	9
10%	8

Compounded annual rate

city to grow to a population of 500,000, assuming that the annual rate of increase remains at 3%?

(5+ years)

10. The sales of a business have been increasing at approximately 7% a year. If the sales in 1985 were $14.2 million, when will sales reach $21 million, assuming that the rate of increase remains at 7%? Give the answer to the nearest year.

11. A loan company charges 36% a year compounded monthly on small loans. How long will it take to triple money at this rate? Give the answer to the nearest month.

(37 months)

12. An alumnus leaves $75,000 to a university with the provision that it is to be invested until it amounts to $100,000. From then on the interest is to be used each year for scholarships. If the school gets 9% compounded annually, how many years after receipt of the gift will the fund first amount to at least $100,000?

13. How long will it take an investment to increase 33% if it draws interest at 6% compounded quarterly? Answer to the nearest period.

(19 periods)

14. On June 1, 1985, $500 was put in a savings deposit. Interest is allowed at 6% compounded quarterly, but no interest is paid for part of a period. What is the date on which this account will have at least $750 in it? What will be the amount at that time?

15. A person invested $2000 at 7% compounded semiannually on September 1, 1985. No interest is allowed for part of a period. On what date will this investment first amount to at least $3000 and what will be the amount at that time?

(September 1, 1991; $3022.14)

3.18 EQUATIONS OF VALUE

In business transactions it is often necessary to exchange one set of obligations for another set of different amounts due at different times. To do this, it is necessary to bring all the obligations to a common date called a **focal date**. Then we set up an **equation of value** in which all the original obligations at the focal date equal all the new obligations at the focal date. This procedure is based on the fact that we can find the value of any sum of money at any time by accumulating it at compound interest if we take it into the future, or discounting it if we bring it back in time. The equation of value should be thoroughly understood because it is the most effective way to solve many investment problems, particularly the more complicated ones.

EXAMPLE 1   A person owes $200 due in 1 year and $300 due in 2 years. The lender agrees to the settlement of both obligations with a cash payment. Before the problem can be worked, the two parties must agree on an interest rate or value of money to be used in setting up the equation of value. In this case we assume that the lender specifies that 10% compounded semiannually will be used. If this is as much as or more than the borrower can get elsewhere, then the wise decision is to use the cash to cancel the debts. Assume that the borrower is satisfied with this rate of interest, and determine the size of the cash payment.

SOLUTION   The first thing to decide is the location of the focal date. In compound interest problems the answer will be the same regardless of the location of the focal date. Therefore the only consideration is reducing our work to a minimum. If there is only one unknown payment, putting the focal date at the time that payment is made will eliminate division to obtain the solution.

   Most students find a sketch similar to Figure 3-11 helpful in getting times correct in focal date problems. If the original obligations are put on one side of the time scale and the payments on the other side, the equation of value can be quickly and correctly determined from the sketch.

   Figure 3-11 shows that the $200 must be discounted for 2 periods and the $300 for 4 periods to transfer them to the focal date. Be-

Figure 3-11

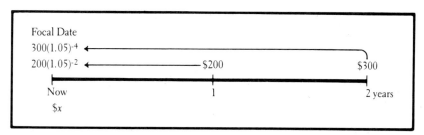

cause the focal date is at the point at which the unknown payment is made, we can set up the equation of value:

$$x = 200(1.05)^{-2} + 300(1.05)^{-4}$$
$$= 200 \times .90703 + 300 \times .82270$$
$$= 181.41 + 246.81$$
$$= \$428.22$$

Thus a cash payment of $428.22 will equitably settle debts of $200 and $300 due in 1 and 2 years if money is worth 10% compounded semiannually.

Because the focal date method of solving problems is so useful in the mathematics of finance, you should both understand and have confidence in this method. To show that this is a fair and correct answer to this problem, let us consider it in another way. Suppose that the borrower had invested $428.22 at 10% compounded semiannually, the rate the borrower and the lender agreed on. At the end of 1 year this would amount to $428.22(1.05)^2$, or $472.11. If the borrower deducts the $200 now owed, a balance of $272.11 remains. Carrying this amount forward for another year results in an amount of $272.11(1.05)^2$, or $300.00. You should check several problems in this way until you are convinced of the utility and the accuracy of the focal date and the equation of value.

EXAMPLE 2   A person owes $500 due now. The lender agrees to settle this obligation with 2 equal payments in 1 and 2 years, respectively. Find the size of the payments if the settlement is based on 9%.

SOLUTION   Since there are 2 unknown payments, it will not be possible to avoid division in the final step. If the focal date is put at 2 years, the coefficient will be as simple as possible and the work will be less than if the focal date were put anywhere else. A sketch (Figure 3-12) shows what factors are needed to get everything to the focal date.

Since the two payments are equal, we designate each of them by x. The value of the first one *at the focal date* is $x(1.09)$. Since the second one is already at the focal date, its value at that point is x.

We now set up an equation of value in which the payments carried to the focal date equal the original obligation at the focal date.

$$x(1.09) + x = 500(1.09)^2$$
$$2.09x = 500 \times 1.18810 = 594.05$$
$$x = \frac{594.05}{2.09} = \$284.23$$

Thus payments of $284.23 in 1 and 2 years will equitably settle a debt of $500 due now if money is worth 9%. Sometimes students think that this answer should be accumulated or discounted from the focal date to the time the payment is made. This assumption is incorrect. The equation of value gives the size of the payment at the time the payment is made.

EXAMPLE 3 A piece of property is sold for $5000. The buyer pays $2000 cash, and signs a non-interest-bearing note for $1000 due in 1 year and a second non-interest-bearing note for $1000 due in 2 years. If the seller charges 8% compounded annually, what non-interest-bearing note due in 3 years will pay off the debt?

SOLUTION A time diagram of the debt and the payments (Figure 3-13) shows that 3 years is a good location for the focal date.
Carrying the $3000 balance and the payments to the focal date, we get the equation of value,

Figure 3-12

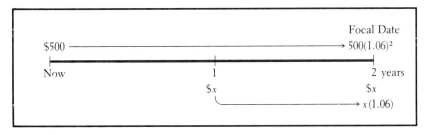

$$x = 3000(1.08)^3 - 1000(1.08)^2 - 1000(1.08)$$
$$= (3000 \times 1.259712) - (1000 \times 1.166400) - (1000 \times 1.08)$$
$$= 3779.14 - 1166.40 - 1080.00$$
$$= \$1532.74$$

This problem can also be worked or checked using United States Rule.

Original debt	$3000.00
Interest for 1 year	240.00
Amount due in 1 year	3240.00
Deduct first payment	1000.00
New balance	2240.00
Interest for 1 year	179.20
Amount due in 2 years	2419.20
Deduct second payment	1000.00
New balance	1419.20
Interest for 1 year	113.54
Amount due in 3 years	$1532.74

EXAMPLE 4 If any obligations bear interest, we must first compute the maturity values. A person owes $1000 due in 3 years with interest at 10% compounded quarterly, and $500 due in 5 years with interest at 8%. If money is worth 9%, what single payment 6 years hence will be equivalent to the original obligations?

SOLUTION First we obtain the maturity values of the debts:

Figure 3-13

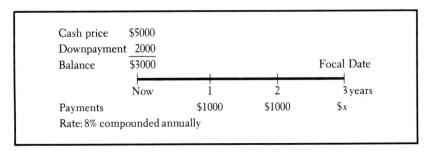

$$1000(1.025)^{12} = 1000 \times 1.344889 = \$1344.89$$
$$500(1.08)^5 = 500 \times 1.46933 = \$734.67$$

Now we sketch the problem (Figure 3-14) and set up the equation of value.

$$x = 1344.89(1.09)^3 + 734.67(1.09)$$
$$= (1344.89 \times 1.295029) + (734.67 \times 1.09)$$
$$= 1741.67 + 800.79$$
$$= \$2542.46$$

EXAMPLE 5 On June 1, 1986, a person obtained a $5000 loan for which payment of $1000 on the principal plus 6% interest on the unpaid balance will be made every 6 months. The repayment schedule for this loan is given in the following chart:

Payment Number	Date	Total Payment	Payment on Interest	Payment on Principal	Balance of Loan
					$5000
1	Dec. 1, 1986	$1300	$300	$1000	4000
2	June 1, 1987	1240	240	1000	3000
3	Dec. 1, 1987	1180	180	1000	2000
4	June 1, 1988	1120	120	1000	1000
5	Dec. 1, 1988	1060	60	1000	0

Figure 3-14

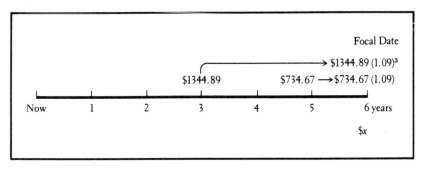

On June 1, 1987, the lender sells this contract to a buyer who wants a yield of 16% converted semiannually. Find the sale price.

SOLUTION   The seller gets the payment due on June 1, 1987. The buyer will get the three remaining payments. A time diagram (Figure 3-15) shows that June 1, 1987, is a good place for the focal date since this is the point in time when the purchase price is to be determined.

Discounting all payments to the focal date, we have

$$x = 1180(1.08)^{-1} + 1120(1.08)^{-2} + 1060(1.08)^{-3}$$
$$= (1180 \times .925926) + (1120 \times .857339) + (1060 \times .793832)$$
$$= 1092.59 + 960.22 + 841.46$$
$$= \$2894.27$$

EXAMPLE 6   A head of a household stipulates in a will that $30,000 from the bequeathed estate is to be placed in a fund from which each of the three children in the family is to receive an equal amount upon reaching age 21. When the head of the household dies, the children are ages 19, 16, and 14. If the fund is invested at 8% converted semiannually, how much does each receive?

SOLUTION   A sketch of the problem (Figure 3-16) helps determine the required times.

Bringing all sums to the focal date at 8% compounded semi-annually,

$$x(1.04)^{-4} + x(1.04)^{-10} + x(1.04)^{-14} = 30,000.00$$
$$.8548042x + .6755642x + .5774751x = 30,000.00$$

Figure 3-15

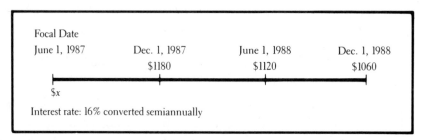

Focal Date			
June 1, 1987	Dec. 1, 1987	June 1, 1988	Dec. 1, 1988
	$1180	$1120	$1060

$x

Interest rate: 16% converted semiannually

$$2.1078435x = 30,000.00$$

$$x = \frac{30,000.00}{2.1078435}$$

$$x = \$14,232.56$$

CHECK The answer should be checked to be certain that everything will come out right, with each child getting the same amount.

Amount in fund at end of 2 years = 30,000.00$(1.04)^4$ = \$35,095.76
Pay oldest child   14,232.56
Balance in fund   \$20,863.20
Amount in fund after 3 more years = 20,863.20$(1.04)^6$ = 26,398.60
Pay second child   14,232.56
Balance in fund   \$12,166.04
Amount in fund after 2 more years = 12,166.04$(1.04)^4$ = \$14,232.55

The 1-cent difference is due to rounding. This problem shows the power of an equation of value that leads directly to the solution. The problem also shows why a lawyer may need an accountant or mathematical economist to help set up a problem like this so that it can be explained to the surrogate court judge.

Figure 3-16

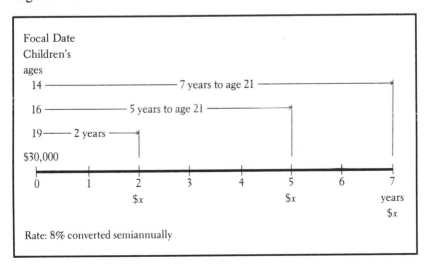

Exercise 3h

1. A person owes $300 due in 2 years and $500 due in 4 years. If money is worth 7% converted semiannually, what single payment 3 years hence will settle the obligations?
    ($788.13)

2. On June 1, 1987, a woman owes $4000, which she is unable to repay. Her creditor charges her 12% converted semiannually from that date. If the debtor pays $2000 on June 1, 1988, how much would she have to pay on June 1, 1989, to discharge the rest of her obligation?

3. Hull owes Graves $300 due at the end of 2 years and $300 due at the end of 3 years. He wishes to replace these two obligations with a single payment due at the end of $2\frac{1}{2}$ years. If the two parties agree that money is worth 14% converted semiannually, what will be the size of the payment?
    ($601.37)

4. Wilson owes Smith $500 due at the end of 2 years and $1000 due at the end of 4 years. Both men agree that Wilson may settle his obligations with a single payment at the end of 3 years using an interest rate of 9%. Solve this problem for the single payment, putting the focal date at 3 years. Solve a second time using 4 years for the focal date.

5. A mother leaves $10,000 to her two children with the provision that they are to get equal amounts when they reach age 21. If the children are 12 and 17 when the woman dies, how much will each receive? The money is invested at 8% compounded quarterly.
    ($8205.67)

6. A man leaves an estate of $30,000 that is invested at 7% compounded semiannually. At the time of his death, he has three children, aged 13, 15, and 19. Each child is to receive an equal amount from the estate upon reaching age 21. How much does each get?

7. Suppose that the woman in problem 5 had left each child $5000 with the provision that the money be invested at 8% compounded quarterly and the amount be given to each child upon reaching 21. How much would each get?
    (12-year-old child, $10,199.44; 17-year-old child, $6863.93)

8.   Suppose that each of the three children in problem 6 received $10,000 upon the father's death with the provision that the money be invested at 7% compounded semiannually until each child reaches age 21. How much would each receive?

9.   A piece of property is sold for $10,000. The buyer pays $2000 cash and signs a non-interest-bearing note for $4000 due in 1 year. If the seller charges 10% converted quarterly for credit, what non-interest-bearing note due in 2 years will pay off the debt?

($5331.97)

10.   Assume that the buyer in problem 9 signs a non-interest-bearing note for $4000 due in 2 years. The remainder of the debt is to be met with a non-interest-bearing note due in 1 year. For how much should this note be drawn if the seller charges 10% converted quarterly?

11.   Instead of taking $3000 cash, the beneficiary of an estate takes 2 equal payments due in 1 and 2 years, respectively. If the investment pays interest at 7% converted quarterly, what will be the size of each payment?

($1663.55)

12.   A mother invests $2000 at 6% compounded semiannually on her son's 12th birthday. If the money is to be paid to the son in 4 equal annual payments starting on his 18th birthday, what will be the size of each payment?

13.(C)   A building is sold for $35,000. The buyer pays $8000 cash and signs a note with maturity value $10,000 due in 1 year and another with maturity value $10,000 due in 2 years. If the seller charges interest on the debt at 10%, what should be the maturity value of a third note due in 3 years that will pay off the remainder of the debt?

($12,837.00)

14.   A woman borrows $5000 on March 1, 1986, agreeing to pay 12% compounded semiannually. She pays $2000 on September 1, 1987. How much will she have to pay to settle the debt on October 16, 1988?

15.   On August 1, 1986, a man bought $300 worth of merchandise and signed a note promising to pay the $300 without interest in 6 months. On November 1, 1986, he bought $500 worth of merchandise and signed a note promising to pay $500 without

interest in 6 months. On December 1, 1986, the holder of the notes sold them to a finance company that charged 18% converted monthly. How much does the finance company pay for the notes?

($755.33)

16. On June 1, 1985, a woman bought $400 worth of goods and gave a note for $400 to be paid in 6 months without interest. On August 1, 1985, she bought $400 worth of goods and signed another 6-month, non-interest-bearing note for this amount. On November 1, 1985, the company that holds the notes had them discounted by a finance company that charges 21% converted monthly. How much was received for the notes?

17. A woman owes $500 due now and $1000 due in 15 months. Her creditor will allow her to pay both debts in 18 months provided that the settlement is based on 16% converted quarterly. What payment in 18 months will settle both obligations?

($1672.66)

18. A man buys machinery worth $6000. He pays $2000 down and agrees to pay the balance in 2 equal payments in 3 and 6 months, respectively. If interest is charged at 16% converted monthly, what will be the size of each payment?

19. A piece of property can be purchased for $28,500 cash or for $10,000 down and 2 equal payments of $10,000 at the end of 1 and 2 years, respectively. To pay cash, the buyer would have to withdraw the money from an investment that is paying 5% converted semiannually. How much will the buyer save now by choosing the better method of payment?

(By paying cash, the buyer saves $77.65 now.)

20. If the buyer in problem 19 has money in stocks that are currently yielding 6% on their market value, would you recommend that the buyer sell the stocks and pay cash? Explain your answer in terms of probable savings by adopting your recommendations.

3.19 NEGATIVE RATES

The compound interest law also applies to quantities that are decreasing at a constant rate. A negative rate is sometimes called a **decay coefficient**. An example from the natural realm is the decay of radioactive substances. The book value of an asset, depreciated according to the double declining balance method (section 8.7), follows the compound interest law with a negative rate. The sales of a nonadvertised product may decline at approximately a constant rate. When only a small number of periods are involved, calculations are easy to handle on a calculator.

EXAMPLE 1 A new car cost $6000 and depreciates 25% a year. Find the book value at the end of each year for 5 years and the annual depreciation in dollars.

SOLUTION Substituting $P = 6000$ and $i = -.25$ in formula (9), we find that

$$S = 6000(1.00 - .25)^n = 6000(.75)^n$$

where n is the number of years. Since values are wanted for each year from 1 to 5, we simply multiply successively by .75 as shown in the following chart.

Year	Book Value	Depreciation Allowance
0	$6000.00	
1	6000.00 X .75 = 4500.00	$1500.00
2	4500.00 X .75 = 3375.00	1125.00
3	3375.00 X .75 = 2531.25	843.75
4	2531.25 X .75 = 1898.44	632.81
5	1898.44 X .75 = 1423.83	474.61

If you want only the book value after 5 years and have a calculator with exponential capability, the solution is straightforward:

$$6000(.75)^5 = \$1423.83$$

With negative rates, the annual depreciation allowance is large at first and then becomes progressively smaller. This tendency corresponds to practical experience with many assets.

Negative rate problems can be solved using logarithms as shown in the appendix and in the example on page 156.

With discrete compounding, going forward at a negative rate is not the same as coming back with a positive rate having the same numerical value. For example, if a $1000 asset is decreasing 8% a year, its book value at the end of 1 year would be $1000(1.00 - .08) = \$920.00$. The present-worth-of-1 factor applied to a future amount of 1000 results in a present worth of $1000 \times .925926 = \$925.93$.

It is possible to use the compound interest table to handle negative rates if Table 2 has a rate with present-worth-of-1 factors equal to the depreciation factors for the negative rate. If the rate of decrease is r, we look for a rate i in Table 2 such that $(1 - r) = (1 + i)^{-1}$.

EXAMPLE 2 An asset with an initial value of $1000 is decreasing in value 7.4% a year. Use Table 2 to find its value at the end of 5 years.

SOLUTION $(1 - r) = (1 - .074) = .926$

Looking in row 1 of the "Present worth of 1" column, we find .925925 for a rate of 8% per year. We can now use the present-worth-of-1 factors for 8% to get the depreciated value of an asset that is decreasing 7.4% a year. At the end of the 5 years the asset will be worth approximately

$$1000(1.08)^{-5} = 1000 \times .680583 = \$681$$

This method should be used with the complete Compound Interest Tables of the Financial Publishing Company to get the closest approximation to the required value.

ALTERNATE SOLUTION Using a calculator directly, the solution is

$$1000(1 - .074)^5 = 1000(.926)^5 = \$680.86$$

3.20 USE OF LOGARITHMS

Logarithms can be used to solve problems when compound interest tables are not available or when the time or rate is not in the table. An explanation of logarithms will be found in the appendix.

When the total time is obtained using logarithms, the assumption is that compound interest is earned for the fraction of a period as well as for the number of whole periods. Hence results will be slightly different from those obtained using the factors from Table 2 and linear interpolation. If time is determined by logarithms and simple interest is to be used for the remaining fraction of a period, the amount should be determined for the integral number of periods. Then the simple interest formula can be used to find the additional time needed for this sum to equal the final amount.

When logarithms are used to get the rate, the result is theoretically correct and not an approximation, as was the case using factors from Table 2 and linear interpolation. Under ordinary business conditions when the rate is needed only for comparison purposes, Table 2 leads to sufficiently accurate results.

The following examples show how logs can be used to solve the four types of compound interest problems. Six-place tables have been used for these problems. Although the method remains the same, more extensive tables are needed to get accurate results with large sums of money.

EXAMPLE 1   Counterfeit notes seized by the Secret Service increased from $9.0 million in 1966 to $15.1 million in 1969. This annual compounded rate of increase is 19%. What would have been the value in 1975 at the same rate of increase?

SOLUTION   Substituting $P = 15.1$, $i = .19$, and $n = 6$ in formula (9), we have

$$S = 15.1(1.19)^6$$

Since 19% is not in Table 2, we take the logarithm of both sides.

$$\log S = \log 15.1 + 6 \log 1.19$$

$$\log 15.1 = 1.178977$$
$$6 \log 1.19 = 6 \times .075547 = \underline{.453282}$$
$$\log S \text{ (adding)} = 1.632259$$

Looking up the antilog of 1.632259, we find that $S = \$42.9$ million. The answer is rounded, since this forecast is based on approximate data. However, the result is accurate enough to indicate that counterfeiting is an increasing threat to the integrity of the dollar.

EXAMPLE 2 Find the present value of $600 due in 8 years if money is worth 5.2% compounded semiannually.

SOLUTION Substituting $S = 600$, $i = .026$, and $n = 16$ in formula (11), we have

$$P = 600(1.026)^{-16}$$

Taking the logarithm of both sides, we obtain

$$\log P = \log 600 - 16 \log (1.026)$$

$$
\begin{aligned}
\log 600 &= 2.778151 \\
16 \log (1.026) = 16 \times .011147 &= \underline{.178352} \\
\log P \text{ (subtracting)} &= 2.599799
\end{aligned}
$$

Looking up the antilog of 2.599799, we have $P = \$397.92$.

EXAMPLE 3 How many years will it take $175 to amount to $230 at 4.4%?

SOLUTION Substituting $S = 230$, $P = 175$, and $i = .044$ in formula (9), we have

$$230 = 175(1.044)^n$$

from which

$$(1.044)^n = \tfrac{230}{175}$$

Taking the logarithm of both sides, we have

$$n \log (1.044) = \log 230 - \log 175$$

$$n = \frac{\log 230 - \log 175}{\log 1.044} = \frac{2.361728 - 2.243038}{.018700} = 6.347 \text{ years}$$

This result means that if compound interest is paid for a part of a period, the time would be 6.347 years. Since this practice is not common, the time would usually be used in one of the following ways. If the interest is paid only on conversion dates, we would say that the closest time is 6 years, which would result in an amount somewhat less than $230. Thus if we want at least $230, the money would have to be left on deposit for 7 years. If simple interest is paid for part of a period, we would take the amount at the end of 6 years and use the simple interest formula to get the additional time necessary for this amount to accumulate to $230.

EXAMPLE 4 If a speculative investment increased in value from $30,000 to $80,000 in 5 years, what was the annual compounded rate of growth?

SOLUTION   Substituting $S = 80,000$, $P = 30,000$, and $n = 5$ in formula (9), we have

$$80,000 = 30,000(1 + i)^5$$

$$(1 + i)^5 = \frac{80,000}{30,000}$$

Taking logarithms of both sides, we obtain

$$5 \log (1 + i) = \log 80,000 - \log 30,000$$

$$\log (1 + i) = \frac{\log 80,000 - \log 30,000}{5}$$

$$= \frac{4.903090 - 4.477121}{5} = \frac{.425969}{5} = .085194$$

Looking up the antilog of .085194, we find that

$$1 + i = 1.2167$$

from which we get

$$i = .2167 = 21.67\%$$

Exercise 3i

1. A company bought a piece of equipment for $10,000. The item depreciates at 20% a year. Find the book value at the end of each year for 5 years and the annual depreciation in dollars.
   (After 5 years the book value is $3276.80.)

2. A crane costs $20,000 and depreciates at 10% a year. Find the book value and annual depreciation for the first 4 years.

3. Do problem 1 if the cost was $15,000.
   ($4915.20 in 5 years)

4. Do problem 2 assuming that the rate is 15%.

5. If an investment pays $9\frac{1}{2}\%$ return, what will be the amount of $100 in 5 years?
   ($157.42)

6. What will be the amount of $234.50 in 8 years at 7.2% compounded semiannually?

7. If an investment pays 10%, how much must be invested today to amount to $250 in 10 years?
   ($96.39)

8. How much must be invested at 7.6% converted quarterly to amount to $500 in 4 years?

9. How long does it take $350 to amount to $500 at 5.75% converted annually? Give the answer to the nearest year.
   (6 years)

10. How many years will it take $45,000 to amount to $72,000 at 3.8% converted annually?

11. How long does it take an investment to at least triple itself at 9.5% compounded annually?
    (13 years)

12. How long will it take a principal of $42,000 to amount to $60,000 at 7.25% converted quarterly? Give the answer to the nearest period.

13. What is the annual rate of interest if an investment of $3500 amounts to $45,000 in 40 years?
    (6.6%)

14. An investment of $6700 amounted to $32,000 in 14 years. What was the annual rate of return correct to .1%?

15. A piece of property was purchased in 1972 for $32,000. In 1987 it was sold for $255,000. What annual rate of return was received on this investment?
    (14.8%)

16. What is the nominal rate of return converted semiannually if $6780 amounts to $18,550 in $8\frac{1}{2}$ years?

17. Over the past several years a business has been increasing at an approximately constant rate of 10% a year. If the business had sales of $2.5 million in 1977, what are the estimated sales for 1987, assuming that the business continues to increase at about the same rate?

    ($6.5 million)

18. The net income of a business has been increasing at about 12% a year. If the net income in 1988 was $23.6 million, what is the estimated net income for 1992?

19. A person estimates that a piece of property will be worth $185,000 in 6 years. If a return of $8\frac{1}{2}\%$ on the investment is expected, what is the property worth today to the nearest thousand dollars?

    ($113,000)

20. The estimated value of a piece of property in 5 years is $75,000. What would it be worth today to a speculator who expects a rate of 10% on the money invested?

21. An investor who bought 100 shares of International Business Machines Corporation common stock for $2750 in 1914 would have had 74,150 shares in 1976 worth approximately $20 million. Find the compounded annual rate of increase in the value of this investment to the nearest percent.

    (15%)

3.21 INFLATION

A common problem of people everywhere is too much month left over at the end of their money. Rapid rises in prices cause hardships for those on fixed money incomes. To help cope with rising prices, workers demand wage increases to compensate for both past and future losses of purchasing power. Increased costs of labor, material, and other inputs cause manufacturers to raise prices on final products.

Price changes are reported in terms of official cost-of-living or price indexes. The agency responsible for determining a price index must determine the types and quantities of goods on which the index will be based. The dollar values of the items in the index are determined for a base year or period. In subsequent years the total cost of the items on which the index is based is determined. This value is then expressed as a percentage of the total cost in the base period.

The domestic purchasing power of a nation's currency is computed from the reciprocal of the price index. When prices are increasing, as is the case now in most nations, the depreciation of money is measured by the rate of decline in the purchasing power of currency.

In the United States, among the most important statistics published by the federal government are the Consumer Price Indexes (CPIs). They measure average changes in prices of goods and services. Since 1978 the Bureau of Labor Statistics has published two CPIs, one for Urban Wage Earners & Clerical Workers (CPI-W) and a new one for all Urban Consumers (CPI-U). The CPI-U reflects the buying habits of about 80% of the noninstitutional, civilian population of the United States. The CPI-W is based on the buying habits of about one-half of the population covered by the CPI for all Urban Consumers. As this is written, both CPIs have a reference base of 1967 = 100. Prices are collected from 85 urban areas for about 265 classes of items selected to represent the movement of prices of goods and services purchased by both groups. The importance or weight of each category differs between the two indexes because buying habits of the two groups are different. Prices are collected from a variety of retail stores and service establishments, such as food stores, barber shops, doctor's offices, and department stores.

To get the value of the dollar from the CPI, we substitute in the expression

$$\text{Value of the dollar} = \frac{1}{\text{CPI}} \times 100 = \frac{100}{\text{CPI}}$$

When the CPI is 125, the value of the dollar is 100/125 = \$.80, or 80 cents.

Movements of the price index and the value of the dollar are usually expressed as percentage changes rather than changes in index points because point changes are affected by the level of the index relative to its base period, whereas percentage changes are not. To get the percentage change from one period to another, use the formula:

Percentage change =
$$\frac{\text{Value for later period} - \text{Value for previous period}}{\text{Value for previous period}} \times 100$$

When the CPI changes from 100 to 125, there is a 25 index point difference. There is also a 25% change, as we now show:

$$\text{Percentage change} = \frac{125 - 100}{100} \times 100 = 25\%$$

When the CPI changes from 125 to 150, there is a 25 index point change. However, the percentage change is

$$\frac{150 - 125}{125} \times 100 = 20\%$$

The CPI change from 125 to 150 means a drop in the value of the dollar from $.80 to $.67 and a percentage change of

$$\frac{.67 - .80}{.80} \times 100 = -16.2\%$$

Note that the percentage change in the value of the dollar is not equal to the corresponding percentage change in the price index. This point is frequently misunderstood and can be clarified by a simple example. If the CPI changes from 100 to 200, there is a 100% increase in prices. However, the corresponding drop in the value of the dollar is 50%.

For countries in all stages of development, reasonable price stability is important for economic progress. Some countries have been more or less successful in slowing inflation with official stabilization policies — higher interest rates, increased taxes, and reduced public spending. The problem is to find policies that curb price increases without resulting in unacceptable levels of unemployment. As ways are sought to achieve relatively stable prices and nearly full employment, compound interest methods will be used to evaluate past results and predict future trends.

To analyze long-range trends in prices, values of the price index are substituted in the compound interest formula. When this formula is solved for the rate, we have the annual compounded rate of change in prices. The result is sometimes called the rate of inflation, particularly by the party not in office. When we substitute the value of money in the compound interest formula, we get the compounded rate of change in the purchasing power of money.

EXAMPLE In 1966 the CPI was 97.2, and in 1975 it was 161.2. Both values are relative to 1967 = 100. Find the annual compounded rate of change of the CPI and of the value of the dollar.

SOLUTION   Substituting the CPI values in formula (9), we have

$$97.2(1 + i)^9 = 161.2$$

$$(1 + i)^9 = \frac{161.2}{97.2}$$

Taking logarithms of both sides, we obtain

$$9 \log(1 + i) = \log 161.2 - \log 97.2$$

$$\log(1 + i) = \frac{2.207365 - 1.987666}{9} = .024411$$

$$1 + i = \text{antilog of } .024411 = 1.058$$
$$i = 1.058 - 1 = .058 = 5.8\%$$

To determine the annual percentage change in the value of the dollar, we first obtain the value of the dollar as explained on page 154.

Year	Consumer Price Index	Value of the Dollar
1966	97.2	$1.03
1975	161.2	.62

Substituting in formula (9), we have

$$1.03 (1 + i)^9 = .62$$
$$9 \log (1 + i) = \log .62 - \log 1.03$$

$$\log (1 + i) = \frac{(.792392 - 1) - .012837}{9}$$

When working with logarithms, we must end with a positive mantissa and an integral characteristic. To achieve this, we can change the form of the logarithm provided that we do not change its numerical value. If we add 8 to the first term in the first logarithm and subtract 8 from the second term in the same logarithm, we can complete the problem. (The value 8 was chosen to be added and subtracted so that the characteristic when divided by 9 would yield an integer value.)

$$\log(1 + i) = \frac{(8.792392 - 9) - (.012837)}{9}$$

$$= \frac{8.779555 - 9}{9}$$

$$= .975506 - 1$$
$$1 + i = \text{antilog}(.975506 - 1) = .945$$
$$i = .945 - 1 = -.055 = -5.5\%$$

Note that the rate of change in the value of the dollar is not numerically equal to the percentage change in the CPI. Here the difference is not large, but it can be large, as it was in the example on page 155.

3.22 CONTINUOUS COMPOUNDING

You may have noticed that if the nominal rate of interest is unchanged but compounding takes place more frequently, the effective rate will get larger. It can be proved that this is always the case. This fact leads us to question what happens when interest is compounded very frequently – daily, hourly, or even every minute or every second. Since the effective rate must be increasing with the frequency of compounding, only two things could occur: either the effective rate becomes infinitely large or it gets nearer and nearer to some value.

In Table 3-4 we see the effective rate for a nominal rate of 10% and various compounding frequencies. We can see that when the number of times the interest is compounded gets very large, the effective rate doesn't change very much. It can be shown, using the tools of mathematical analysis, that there is a point beyond which the effective rate will not go, no matter how often the interest is compounded. If we could determine how to calculate the smallest such quantity, it would represent the largest effective rate possible for the given nominal rate. We would then call that value the effective rate when interest is compounded continuously. This would be very useful for financial institutions that want to pay their investors the largest amount of interest possible but are constrained by law to keep their nominal rate at a particular value. This section will describe how to compute interest when it is compounded continuously.

The limit that occurs in continuous compounding involves a special number called e. An important constant in mathematics, e is a real number whose decimal representation never terminates. A good approximation for our purposes is $e \approx 2.718281828459045$. It can be defined to be the limit of $(1 + 1/m)^m$ as m approaches infinity. That is, this quantity gets nearer and nearer to e as m gets larger and larger. Figure 3-17 shows this fact. We write

$$\lim_{m \to \infty} \left(1 + \frac{1}{m}\right)^m = e$$

It then follows that

$$\lim_{m \to \infty} \left(1 + \frac{j}{m}\right)^m = \lim_{m \to \infty} \left(1 + \frac{j}{m}\right)^{(m/j)j}$$

$$= \lim_{m \to \infty} \left[\left(1 + \frac{1}{m'}\right)^{m'}\right]^j$$

$$= e^j$$

Therefore the effective rate for nominal rate j compounded continuously will be given by $e^j - 1$.

To compute the factor for an amount of money at rate j compounded continuously for time t (measured in years), e is also used. In that case, we have

Table 3-4 Effective Rates for 10%

When Compounded	Periods per Year	Rate per Period	Amount of 1 in 1 Year	Effective Rate
Annually	1	.10	1.10	10.0000%
Semiannually	2	.05	1.1025	10.2500%
Quarterly	4	.025	1.103812891	10.3813%
Monthly	12	.0083333	1.104713067	10.4713%
Weekly	52	.0019231	1.105064793	10.5065%
Daily	365	.0002740	1.105155781	10.5156%
Hourly	8,760	.0000114	1.105170290	10.5170%
Every minute	525,600	.00000019	1.105170481	10.5170%
Continuously	—	—	1.105170918	10.5171%

$$\lim_{m \to \infty} \left(1 + \frac{j}{m}\right)^{mt} = \lim_{m \to \infty} \left[\left(1 + \frac{j}{m}\right)^{m}\right]^{t} = e^{jt}$$

Therefore, if $P is invested at nominal rate j compounded continuously for t years, the amount is given by

$$S = Pe^{jt} \tag{12}$$

We can compute the amount of an investment in the case of continuous compounding if we can determine e^{jt} for the appropriate values of j and t. This may be done using Table 6 or with a calculator having a button marked e^x or e^y. If you have such a calculator, you can obtain e^{jt} by multiplying j times t and then pushing the e^x button.

Some calculators evaluate e^x by using the natural logarithm. The exponential function, e^x, is the inverse of the natural logarithm, $\ln x$. You can compute e^x by taking a combination of the inverse function (INV) and the natural logarithm ($\ln x$). Check the owner's manual to determine how to get e^x on your calculator.

To use Table 6, you can apply the law of exponents, $e^a \times e^b = e^{a+b}$.

EXAMPLE 1 Find $e^{.125}$.

Figure 3-17 Graph of $\left(1 + \dfrac{1}{m}\right)^m$

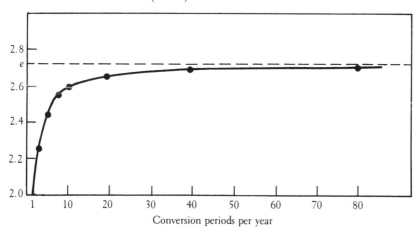

Conversion periods per year

SOLUTION   The exponent is rewritten as the sum of entries found in Table 6.

$$e^{.125} = e^{.12 + .005} = e^{.12} \times e^{.005} = 1.127\ 496\ 8516 \times 1.005\ 012\ 5209$$
$$= 1.133\ 148\ 4531$$

EXAMPLE 2   Find the amount of $10,000 invested for 3 months at 12% compounded continuously.

SOLUTION

$$S = 10,000e^{.12 \times 1/4}$$
$$= 10,000e^{.03}$$
$$= 10,000 \times 1.030\ 454\ 5340$$
$$= \$10,304.55$$

EXAMPLE 3   Find the amount of $1000 at $5\frac{1}{2}\%$ compounded continuously for 5 years.

SOLUTION

$$S = 1000e^{.055 \times 5}$$
$$= 1000e^{.275}$$
$$= 1000e^{.27}\ e^{.005}$$
$$= 1000 \times 1.309\ 964\ 4507 \times 1.005\ 012\ 5209$$
$$= \$1316.53$$

The maximum nominal rate that savings institutions and banks may pay on savings accounts is often limited by law. These institutions must encourage people to use such accounts if they are to have capital to invest or lend. In order to attract customers, many now pay the maximum nominal rate compounded continuously because potential savers are usually aware that the maximum effective rate occurs in that case. The use of continuous compounding by such institutions has increased rapidly in recent years.

To find the present value of an amount when interest is compounded continuously, we need only solve the amount formula for P. Using negative exponents, we have

$$P = Se^{-jt} \qquad\qquad (13)$$

Table 6 gives e to both positive and negative powers.

EXAMPLE 4 How much must be invested now at 8% compounded continuously to amount to $5000 in $2\frac{1}{2}$ years?

SOLUTION

$$P = 5000e^{-.08 \times 2.5}$$
$$= 5000e^{-.20}$$
$$= 5000 \times .818\ 730\ 7531$$
$$= \$4093.65$$

EXAMPLE 5 Find the present value of $25,000 in 3 years at $12\frac{1}{2}\%$ compounded continuously.

SOLUTION

$$P = 25,000e^{-.125 \times 3}$$
$$= 25,000e^{-.375}$$
$$= 25,000e^{-.37}\ e^{-.005}$$
$$= \$17,182.23$$

The amount formula can also be solved for rate and time using logarithms. We will not discuss those techniques at this time.

Exercise 3j

1. One thousand dollars is invested for $2\frac{1}{2}$ years at a nominal annual rate of 6%. Find the amount if interest is compounded: (a) quarterly; (b) monthly; (c) continuously.
   [(a) $1160.54; (b) $1161.40; (c) $1161.83]
2. Solve problem 1 using a nominal annual rate of 9%.
3. Five thousand dollars is invested for 18 months at a nominal annual rate of 8%. Find the amount if interest is compounded: (a) semi-annually; (b) quarterly; (c) continuously.
   [(a) $5624.32; (b) $5630.81; (c) $5637.48]
4. Solve problem 3 using a nominal rate of 6%.
5. An obligation of $10,000 is due in 3 years. Find the present value using a nominal rate of 7% compounded: (a) annually; (b) semi-annually; (c) continuously.
   [(a) $8162.98; (b) $8135.01; (c) $8105.84]
6. Solve problem 5 using a nominal rate of 8%.

7. An obligation of $5000 is due in 5 years. Find the present value using a nominal rate of 10% if interest is compounded: (a) semi-annually; (b) quarterly; (c) continuously.
   [(a) $3069.57; (b) $3051.36; (c) $3032.66]
8. Solve problem 7 using a nominal rate of 7%.

As indicated earlier, financial institutions frequently compound interest continuously in order to maximize the effective rate. Some are using another method to increase the amount a little more. They use Bankers' Rule (ordinary interest and exact time) to compute t. If interest is allowed to accumulate for 90 days, the value for t is $\frac{90}{360}$. However, if the interest accumulates for 1 year, the factor for t is $\frac{365}{360}$, producing a somewhat larger amount of interest for the investor.

EXAMPLE 6 Ten thousand dollars is invested on April 1 at 15% compounded continuously using the method described above. Find the amount and the interest on December 1 of the same year.

SOLUTION Using Table 1, the time from April 1 to December 1 is 335 − 91 = 244 days.

$$S = 10,000e^{.15 \times 244/360} = \$11,070.14$$

$$I = S - P = \$1,070.14$$

EXAMPLE 7(C) Find the effective rate of 10% compounded continuously, using the method described above for computing time.

SOLUTION

$$r = e^{jt} - 1 = e^{.10 \times 365/360} = .1067 = 10.67\%$$

REVIEW EXERCISES FOR CHAPTER 3

1. In July of 1976 a man entered a bank in Cincinnati, Ohio, with $6700 worth of certificates of deposit at 8% taken out in 1919. Suppose that the certificates were purchased on July 1, 1919, and cashed on July 1, 1976. Find the value of the certificates if interest is compounded annually, and compare this with the answer to problem 1 in the Review Exercises for Chapter 1.
   ($538,553.52)

2. Do problem 1 assuming that the interest is compounded semi-annually.

3. When Secretary of State William Seward purchased Alaska for less than 2 cents an acre in 1867, some dubbed it "Seward's Icebox," others "Seward's Folly." Since that time Alaska has yielded nearly 100 times its price in gold alone. If the $7.2 million that the United States paid Russia for Alaska in 1867 had been invested at 4% compounded annually, how much would the investment have been worth in 1967 (to the nearest million)?
   ($364 million)

4. In 1626 Peter Minuit bought Manhattan Island from the Indians for trinkets valued at 60 guilders, or $24. Had this money been put into a savings account paying 3% converted annually, how much would be in the account now? Answer to the nearest $10,000.

5. A note is redeemable in 10 years for $100,000. How much should be paid for the note by a buyer who wants to earn 14% converted quarterly?
   ($25,257.25)

6. How long will it take an investment of $1000 to be worth at least $3000 at 9% converted: (a) annually? (b) semiannually? (c) quarterly? (d) monthly?

7. An investment of $5000 is made at 6% compounded semiannually. How long will it take until the investment is worth $7000?
   ($5\frac{1}{2}$ years plus 68 days)

8. The population of a country increases from 130 million to 148 million in 10 years. Find the annual compounded rate of increase.

9. An illegal money lender makes a loan of $100. Six months later the victimized borrower repays $133.10. On a converted monthly basis, find the rate.
   (59%)

10. A loan of $3000 is partially repaid with payments of $1000 after 6 months and $1500 after 1 year. If the rate is 12% converted semiannually, find the payment in 2 years that will discharge the debt.

11. A person holds a 1-year note that can be cashed at any time for its face value of $5000 or held to maturity to earn interest at 6%. Six months prior to the maturity date, the holder needs $5000. Would it be better for the holder to cash the note or to borrow the money for 6 months at 10% converted monthly?
    (Loan is better by $44.73 in 6 months.)

12. Find the value on July 20 of a note for $2500 to be paid on December 5 of the same year if money is worth 9% converted monthly.

13. The parents of four children, a 13-year-old, a 12-year-old, and 10-year-old twins, die suddenly. Their wills call for a trust fund of $200,000 to be held, with equal amounts of the money to be given to each of the children at age 18. If the fund earns 10% converted quarterly, find the amount each child will get.
    ($96,586.28)

14. Find the amount each child in problem 13 would get if the wills called for a trust fund of $50,000 to be set up for each.

15. Look up the current value of the Consumer Price Index relative to 1967 = 100. Use this value to get the annual compounded rate of change of the CPI and the value of the dollar since 1967.

16. Find the effective rate corresponding to 12% compounded continuously, using both $t = 1$ and Bankers' Rule.

17. Five thousand dollars is invested at 6% for 15 years. Find the amount if the interest is compounded: (a) annually; (b) quarterly; (c) monthly; (d) continuously; (e) continuously using Bankers' Rule.
    [(a) $11,982.79; (b) $12,216.10; (c) $12,270.47; (d) $12,298.02; (e) $12,452.71]

18. An obligation of $10,000 is due in 5 years. Find the present value of this money at 7% compounded: (a) annually; (b) semiannually; (c) monthly; (d) continuously.

Chapter 4
Ordinary Annuities

4.1 TYPES OF ANNUITIES

When most people buy a home, they borrow money and agree to repay it in monthly payments over a period that may range from 10 to 30 years. To compute the interest or discount on 120 to 360 payments one by one would be very laborious. Formulas and tables have been developed that make the solution of a problem involving many payments as easy as the handling of a single sum was in Chapter 3.

The series of equal monthly payments that a person makes in buying a home is called an **annuity**. Interest payments on bonds, premiums on insurance, and payments on installment purchases are also familiar examples of annuities. In general, any set of equal payments made at equal intervals of time form an annuity.

Annuities are divided into annuities certain and contingent annuities. An **annuity certain** is one for which the payments begin and end at fixed times. In most cases the payments on a home form an annuity certain because the payments start on a fixed date and continue until the required number has been made. Even if the buyer of the home dies, any outstanding debt on the home must be paid.

A **contingent annuity** is one for which the date of the first or last payment, or both, depends on some event. Pensions, social security, and many life insurance policies are examples of contingent annuities.

The **payment interval, or rent period**, is the length of time between successive payments. Payments may be made annually, semiannually, monthly, weekly, or at any fixed interval. The **term** of an annuity is the time between the start of the first rent period and the end of the last rent period. The **periodic rent** is the size of each payment in dollars and cents.

In this chapter we work with the **ordinary annuity**, for which the periodic payments are made at the *end* of each period. In the next chapter we discuss the **annuity due**, which has the payments made at the *beginning* of each period.

4.2 AMOUNT OF AN ORDINARY ANNUITY

The final value, or **amount**, of an annuity is the sum of all the periodic payments and the compound interest on them accumulated to the end of the term. In the case of an ordinary annuity, this amount will be the value of the annuity on the date of the last payment.

EXAMPLE Starting 1 year from now, a person deposits $500 a year in an account paying 6% compounded annually. What amount has accumulated just after the 4th deposit is made?

SOLUTION A sketch is often helpful in visualizing annuity problems (see Figure 4-1). In this case we put the focal date at 4 years because we want the amount of all the payments at that time. Starting with the last payment and accumulating all of them to the focal date, we have

4th payment	$ 500.00
3rd payment 500(1.06)	530.00
2nd payment 500(1.06)^2	561.80
1st payment 500(1.06)^3	595.51
Amount of the annuity	$2187.31

4.3 AMOUNT FORMULA

If there are many payments, the preceding method for obtaining the amount would require too much work. Now we derive a general form-

Figure 4-1

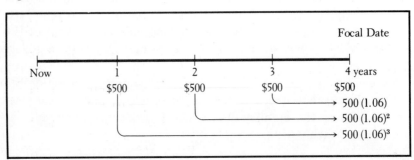

ula for the amount of an annuity of n payments of $1 each and a rate of i per period. As in the preceding example, we accumulate each payment to the end of the term. At this point the last payment will be $1, since it has had no time to earn interest. The next-to-the-last payment will be $1(1 + i)$ or simply $(1 + i)$, because it has earned interest for 1 period. The payment before this will amount to $(1 + i)^2$, and so on. The first payment will amount to $(1 + i)^{n-1}$, because it has earned interest for 1 period less than the number of payments.

We can show the diagram for this ordinary annuity of $1 per period (Figure 4-2). The dots indicate that some of the payments do not appear on the sketch. The symbol $s_{\overline{n}|}$ (read "s sub n" or "s angle n") is used to represent the amount of n payments of $1 each when the interest rate per period is i. Students sometimes prefer to write this as $s_{\overline{n}|i}$ and put in the rate per period as they set up a problem. This method helps them remember what rate to use when they get the numerical value of the factor from Table 2. We follow this practice in some of the examples in this book.

Starting with the last payment and writing the sum of all the payments accumulated to the end of the annuity, we have

$$s_{\overline{n}|} = 1 + (1 + i) + (1 + i)^2 + \cdots + (1 + i)^{n-2} + (1 + i)^{n-1}$$

Figure 4-2

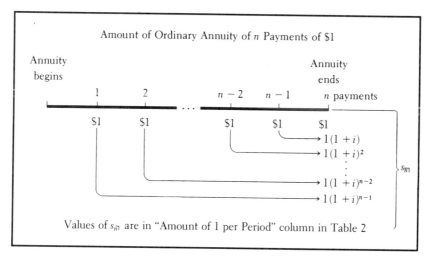

Amount of Ordinary Annuity of n Payments of $1

Values of $s_{\overline{n}|}$ are in "Amount of 1 per Period" column in Table 2

The expression on the right is a geometric progression in which the first term is 1, the common ratio is $(1 + i)$, and the number of terms is n. In algebra it is shown that the sum of the terms in a geometric progression is

$$s = a + ar + ar^2 + \cdots + ar^{n-1} = \frac{a(r^n - 1)}{r - 1}$$

Substituting values $a = 1$ and $r = (1 + i)$ from the annuity problem into this general formula, we get

$$s_{\overline{n}|} = \frac{1[(1 + i)^n - 1]}{(1 + i) - 1} = \frac{(1 + i)^n - 1}{i}$$

Values of $s_{\overline{n}|}$ for common interest rates are given in the "Amount of 1 per period" column of Table 2. This factor is also called the amount of an annuity of 1 per period. If the periodic rent is $\$R$ per period instead of $\$1$, we indicate the total amount of the payments by the symbol S_n. All we have to do to obtain the amount of an annuity of $\$R$ per period is to multiply R by $s_{\overline{n}|}$. Thus the basic formula for the amount of an ordinary annuity is

$$S_n = Rs_{\overline{n}|} = R\,\frac{(1 + i)^n - 1}{i} \tag{14}$$

S_n = amount of an ordinary annuity of n payments
R = periodic payment or rent
$s_{\overline{n}|}$ = amount of 1 per period for n periods at the rate i per period

Students who use the tables or a calculator with preprogrammed financial functions will find the first form of the equation, $S_n = Rs_{\overline{n}|}$, to be more useful. Those who use one of the more common calculators with exponential capability will prefer the second form.

Students using a calculator to compute the factor will need to work out the quantity $[(1 + i)^n - 1]/i$. Again, the advantage is that they will not be limited by any set of tables. If the tables are to be used, many people prefer to work with $j_{(m)}$, the nominal annual rate converted m times a year. They use the marginal index to get on the right page of the compound interest and annuity tables. Numerical values of $s_{\overline{n}|}$ are in the second column of factors in Table 2. Figure 4-3 shows how to find the amount of an annuity.

EXAMPLE 2 Starting 1 year from now, a person deposits $500 a year in an account paying 6% interest compounded annually. What amount is in the account just after the 4th deposit is made?

SOLUTION Substituting $R = 500$, $n = 4$, and $i = 6\%$ in formula (14, we have

$$S_4 = 500s_{\overline{4}|6\%} = 500 \times 4.37462 = \$2187.31$$

This problem is the same as the one on page 166 that took several multiplications and an addition when each deposit was handled separately.

EXAMPLE 3 A woman deposits $200 at the end of each 3 months in a bank that pays 5% converted quarterly. How much will she have to her credit at the end of 10 years?

SOLUTION Substituting $R = 200$, $n = 40$, and $i = 1\frac{1}{4}\%$ in formula (14), we have

$$S_{40} = 200s_{\overline{40}|1\frac{1}{4}\%} = 200 \times 51.48956 = \$10{,}297.91$$

The deposits total $200 \times 40 = \$8000$. Thus the total compound interest is $2297.91.

Exercise 4a

1. Find the amount of an annuity of $5000 per year for 10 years at: (a) 6%; (b) 7%. Interest is compounded annually.
   [(a) $65,903.98; (b) $69,082.24]
2. Find the amount of an annuity of $1200 at the end of each 6 months for 5 years if money is worth: (a) 5%; (b) 6%. All rates are converted semiannually.
3. Every 3 months a person puts $100 in a savings account that pays 5% compounded quarterly. If the first deposit was made

Figure 4-3 How to Use the "Amount of 1 per Period" Column in Table 2

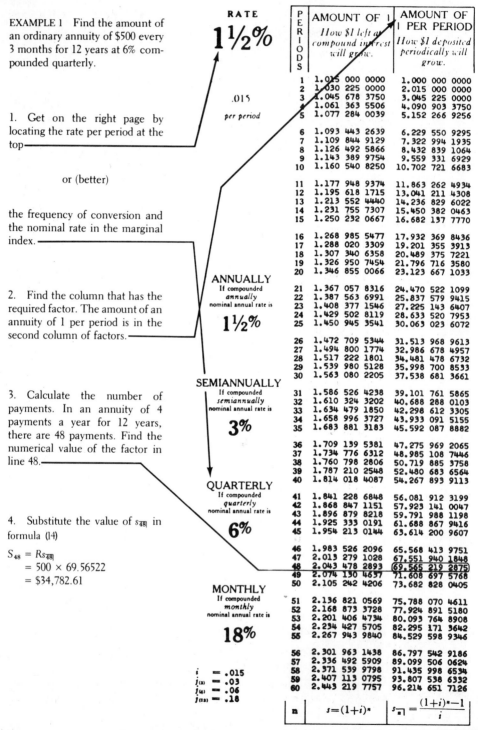

EXAMPLE 1 Find the amount of an ordinary annuity of $500 every 3 months for 12 years at 6% compounded quarterly.

1. Get on the right page by locating the rate per period at the top——

or (better)

the frequency of conversion and the nominal rate in the marginal index. ——

2. Find the column that has the required factor. The amount of an annuity of 1 per period is in the second column of factors. ——

3. Calculate the number of payments. In an annuity of 4 payments a year for 12 years, there are 48 payments. Find the numerical value of the factor in line 48.——

4. Substitute the value of $s_{\overline{48}|}$ in formula (14)

$S_{48} = Rs_{\overline{48}|}$
$\quad = 500 \times 69.56522$
$\quad = \$34,782.61$

RATE

$1\tfrac{1}{2}\%$

.015

per period

P E R I O D S	AMOUNT OF 1 How $1 left at compound interest will grow.	AMOUNT OF 1 PER PERIOD How $1 deposited periodically will grow.
1	1.015 000 0000	1.000 000 0000
2	1.030 225 0000	2.015 000 0000
3	1.045 678 3750	3.045 225 0000
4	1.061 363 5506	4.090 903 3750
5	1.077 284 0039	5.152 266 9256
6	1.093 443 2639	6.229 550 9295
7	1.109 844 9129	7.322 994 1935
8	1.126 492 5866	8.432 839 1064
9	1.143 389 9754	9.559 331 6929
10	1.160 540 8250	10.702 721 6683
11	1.177 948 9374	11.863 262 4934
12	1.195 618 1715	13.041 211 4308
13	1.213 552 4440	14.236 829 6022
14	1.231 755 7307	15.450 382 0463
15	1.250 232 0667	16.682 137 7770
16	1.268 985 5477	17.932 369 8436
17	1.288 020 3309	19.201 355 3913
18	1.307 340 6358	20.489 375 7221
19	1.326 950 7454	21.796 716 3580
20	1.346 855 0066	23.123 667 1033
21	1.367 057 8316	24.470 522 1099
22	1.387 563 6991	25.837 579 9415
23	1.408 377 1546	27.225 143 6407
24	1.429 502 8119	28.633 520 7953
25	1.450 945 3541	30.063 023 6072
26	1.472 709 5344	31.513 968 9613
27	1.494 800 1774	32.986 678 4957
28	1.517 222 1801	34.481 478 6732
29	1.539 980 5128	35.998 700 8533
30	1.563 080 2205	37.538 681 3661
31	1.586 526 4238	39.101 761 5865
32	1.610 324 3202	40.688 288 0103
33	1.634 479 1850	42.298 612 3305
34	1.658 996 3727	43.933 091 5155
35	1.683 881 3183	45.592 087 8882
36	1.709 139 5381	47.275 969 2065
37	1.734 776 6312	48.985 108 7446
38	1.760 798 2806	50.719 885 3758
39	1.787 210 2548	52.480 683 6564
40	1.814 018 4087	54.267 893 9113
41	1.841 228 6848	56.081 912 3199
42	1.868 847 1151	57.923 141 0047
43	1.896 879 8218	59.791 988 1198
44	1.925 333 0191	61.688 867 9416
45	1.954 213 0144	63.614 200 9607
46	1.983 526 2096	65.568 413 9751
47	2.013 279 1028	67.551 940 1848
48	2.043 478 2893	69.565 219 2875
49	2.074 130 4637	71.608 697 5768
50	2.105 242 4206	73.682 828 0405
51	2.136 821 0569	75.788 070 4611
52	2.168 873 3728	77.924 891 5180
53	2.201 406 4734	80.093 764 8908
54	2.234 427 5705	82.295 171 3642
55	2.267 943 9840	84.529 598 9346
56	2.301 963 1438	86.797 542 9186
57	2.336 492 5909	89.099 506 0624
58	2.371 539 9798	91.435 998 6534
59	2.407 113 0795	93.807 538 6332
60	2.443 219 7757	96.214 651 7126

ANNUALLY
If compounded *annually* nominal annual rate is
$1\tfrac{1}{2}\%$

SEMIANNUALLY
If compounded *semiannually* nominal annual rate is
3%

QUARTERLY
If compounded *quarterly* nominal annual rate is
6%

MONTHLY
If compounded *monthly* nominal annual rate is
18%

$i \quad = .015$
$j_{(2)} = .03$
$j_{(4)} = .06$
$j_{(12)} = .18$

n	$s = (1+i)^n$	$s_{\overline{n}|} = \dfrac{(1+i)^n - 1}{i}$

Source: Table courtesy of Financial Publishing Company, Boston, Mass.

on June 1, 1979, how much will be in the account just after the deposit made on December 1, 1988?

($4986.62)

4. Every 3 months a family puts $50 in a savings account that pays 6% converted quarterly. If they make the first deposit on August 1, 1979, how much will be in their account just after they make their deposit on February 1, 1989?

5. What is the amount of an annuity of $100 at the end of each month for 6 years if money is worth 6% compounded monthly?

($8640.89)

6. Find the amount of an annuity of $35 at the end of each month for 12 years if money is worth 7% converted monthly.

7. To provide for his son's education, a man deposits $750 at the end of each year for 18 years. If the money draws 8% interest, how much does the fund contain just after the eighteenth deposit is made? If no more deposits are made but the amount in the fund is allowed to accumulate at the same interest rate, how much will the fund contain in 3 more years?

($28,087.68; $35,382.39)

8. Two hundred dollars at the end of each year for 6 years is equivalent to what single payment at the end of 6 years if the interest rate is 6% effective?

9. A child 12 years old received an inheritance of $400 a year. The money was to be invested and allowed to accumulate until the child reached the age of 21. If the money was invested at 7% effective and if the first payment was made on the child's 12th birthday and the last payment on the child's 21st birthday, what amount will the child receive on reaching age 21?

($5526.58)

10. A man deposits $125 at the end of each 3 months for 5 years in a fund that pays 7% converted quarterly. How much will he have to his credit just after the last deposit is made?

11. A family has been paying $480 a month on their home. The interest rate on the mortgage is 12% compounded monthly. Because of sickness they miss the payments due on May 1, June 1, July 1, and August 1. On September 1 they want to make a single payment that will reduce their debt to what it would have been had they made all their payments on time. What single payment on this date will be equivalent to the 5 payments from May to September inclusive?

($2448.48)

12.   A dealer purchased merchandise and agreed to pay $200 on August 1, September 1, October 1, November 1, and December 1. There was to be a charge of 18% converted monthly on any payments not made on time. The dealer made the August payment but deferred the rest until December. At that time what payment was necessary to settle all the obligations?

13.   A person has an income of $250 every 3 months from preferred stock. This income is deposited in a savings and loan association paying 6% converted quarterly with interest dates on March 31, June 30, September 30, and December 31. If the first deposit is made on June 30, 1986, and the last is made on December 31, 1990, how much will be in the account just after the last deposit?

   ($5449.18)

14.   In 1974 a woman put $500 in common stocks. She continues to make the same deposit every year. If the stocks increase in market value at about 4% a year, what will be the value of the woman's portfolio just after she makes her purchase in 1991?

15.(C) Solve problem 13 if the rate is 9.2%.

   ($5874.05)

16.(C) A person puts $2000 each year for 10 years into an account paying an effective rate of $7\frac{1}{2}\%$. Find the amount at the time of the last payment.

4.4   PRESENT VALUE OF AN ORDINARY ANNUITY

The **present value** of an annuity is the sum of the present values of all the payments of the annuity. To get the present value, we assume an annuity of n payments of $1 each and a rate of i per period. Then we discount each payment to the beginning of the annuity. The sum of these discounted values is designated by the symbol $a_{\overline{n}|}$. See Figure 4-4.

   Writing the sum of all the payments discounted to the beginning of the annuity, we have

$$a_{\overline{n}|} = (1 + i)^{-1} + (1 + i)^{-2} + \cdots + (1 + i)^{-(n - 1)} + (1 + i)^{-n}$$

   The expression on the right is a geometric progression in which the first term is $(1 + i)^{-1}$, the common ratio is $(1 + i)^{-1}$, and the number of terms is n. Substituting these values in the formula for the sum of a geometric progression (page 168), we have

$$a_{\overline{n}|} = \frac{(1+i)^{-1}\{[(1+i)^{-1}]^n - 1\}}{(1+i)^{-1} - 1}$$

Multiplying numerator and denominator by $(1 + i)$ gives

$$a_{\overline{n}|} = \frac{(1+i)^{-n} - 1}{1 - (1+i)} = \frac{(1+i)^{-n} - 1}{1 - 1 - i} = \frac{(1+i)^{-n} - 1}{-i}$$

$$= \frac{1 - (1+i)^{-n}}{i} = \frac{1 - v^n}{i}$$

Values of $a_{\overline{n}|}$ are given in the "Present worth of 1 per period" column of Table 2. If the periodic rent is R per period instead of $1, we indicate the present value of the annuity by the symbol A_n. To get the value of A_n in dollars, all we need to do is to multiply R by $a_{\overline{n}|}$. Thus the basic formula for the present value of an ordinary annuity is

$$A_n = Ra_{\overline{n}|} = R\,\frac{1 - (1+i)^{-n}}{i} = R\,\frac{1 - v^n}{i} \tag{15}$$

A_n = present value of an ordinary annuity of n payments
R = periodic payment or rent
$a_{\overline{n}|}$ = present worth of 1 per period for n periods at the rate i per period
v^n = present worth of 1 [another symbol for $(1 + i)^{-n}$]

Figure 4-4

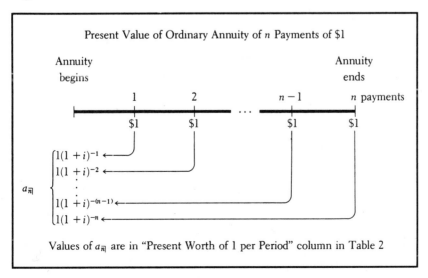

Present Value of Ordinary Annuity of n Payments of $1

Annuity begins

Annuity ends

1   2 $n-1$ n payments

$1 $1 $1 $1

$1(1 + i)^{-1}$
$1(1 + i)^{-2}$
$\vdots$
$1(1 + i)^{-(n-1)}$
$1(1 + i)^{-n}$

$a_{\overline{n}|}$

Values of $a_{\overline{n}|}$ are in "Present Worth of 1 per Period" column in Table 2

Note that we have given the formulas for the amount and present value of an annuity in two forms — one using the factors $s_{\overline{n}|}$ and $a_{\overline{n}|}$, the other using the exponential form as obtained in the original derivation. The form using $s_{\overline{n}|}$ or $a_{\overline{n}|}$ is preferable for the person using the tables or a financial calculator. The exponential form can be used with the more common scientific calculator. Students who wish to use the exponential form should also become familiar with the tables because some types of problems to be encountered later are more easily solved using the tables.

EXAMPLE 1 A donor wants to provide a $3000 scholarship every year for 4 years with the first to be awarded 1 year from now. If the school can get 9% return on its investment, how much money should the donor give now?

SOLUTION Substituting in the present value formula,

$$A_4 = 3000a_{\overline{4}|} = 3000 \times 3.239720 = \$9719.16$$

Note that $12,000 will actually be paid from this gift. The following table shows what will happen to the investment:

Original investment	$ 9,719.16
Interest at 9% for 1 year	874.72
Amount after 1 year	$10,593.88
First scholarship	3,000.00
Investment at beginning of second year	$ 7,593.88
Interest at 9% for 1 year	683.45
Amount after second year	$ 8,277.33
Second scholarship	3,000.00
Investment at beginning of third year	$ 5,277.33
Interest at 9% for 1 year	474.96
Amount after third year	$ 5,752.29
Third scholarship	3,000.00
Investment at beginning of fourth year	$ 2,752.29
Interest at 9% for 1 year	247.71
Amount after fourth year	$ 3,000.00
Fourth scholarship	3,000.00
	0.00

From the annuity problems worked thus far, you should recognize that the annuity formulas, like the compound interest formulas, make it possible to shift financial obligations from one point in time to another point. For further emphasis we restate in summary form the basic principles underlying the mathematics of finance:

1. *Except in cash transactions, the date on which a given sum of money has a certain dollar value must be specified.*
2. *Once the dollar value on a certain date has been specified, the dollar value on any other date can be determined by using the stated interest rate and the appropriate formula.*
3. *Two or more items* must not be *equated unless they have been brought to the same point in time.*

EXAMPLE 2 Wilson agrees to pay Smith $1000 at the end of each year for 5 years. If money is worth 7%, what is the cash equivalent of this debt? If Wilson does not make any payments until the end of 5 years, how much should be paid at that time if this single payment is to be equivalent to the original payments using an interest rate of 7%?

SOLUTION The original debt is $1000 at the end of each year. Thus as each payment is made, it has a dollar value of $1000. If a payment is made before it is due, its dollar value will be less than $1000. If the entire debt is settled immediately, Smith will have use of the money from 1 to 5 years sooner than would otherwise have been the case. Therefore Smith will be willing to write off the entire debt if the present value of the payments is received. This situation is expressed by formula (15):

$$A_5 = 1000a_{\overline{5}|7\%} = 1000 \times 4.100197 = \$4100.20$$

If payment is made after its due date, the dollar value will be increased by the interest. If all of the debt is settled at the end of 5 years, Smith will expect the amount of the payments at that time. This set of events is given by formula (14):

$$S_5 = 1000s_{\overline{5}|7\%} = 1000 \times 5.750739 = \$5750.74$$

Thus $4100.20 now is equivalent in value to the five $1000 payments at the end of each year if money is worth 7%. Likewise, $5750.74 in 5 years is equivalent to the original obligations. As a check on our work, let us see if $4100.20 now is equivalent to $5750.74 in 5 years at 7%. Substituting in formula (9), we have

$$4100.20(1.07)^5 = 4100.20 \times 1.402552 = \$5750.74$$

4.5   FINDING n

In an annuity problem, n is the number of payments. When a problem is stated in terms of calendar dates, students often find that getting n is the most difficult step in solving the problem. The safest approach is to make a time diagram and a careful analysis of each problem.

In determining the value of n, it is important to remember that n is the number of periods from the *beginning of the first period* to the *end of the last period*. You must be careful to distinguish between the date of the first payment and the date of the beginning of the first period of the annuity. In an ordinary annuity the payments are made at the end of each period. The first payment does not occur at the beginning of the first period but at the end. Therefore, it is necessary to read each problem very carefully in order to understand whether the date given is that of the first payment or of the beginning of the annuity. The number of periods from the start of an ordinary annuity until the last payment is equal to n. However, the number of periods from the date of the first payment to the date of the last payment is 1 less than n, so to compute n in this case you must find only the number of periods from the first payment to the last payment and then add 1.

EXAMPLE 1   An ordinary annuity starts on June 1, 1988, and ends on December 1, 1993. Payments are made every 6 months. Find n.

SOLUTION   By the definition of an ordinary annuity, a payment is made at the end of each period (Figure 4-5).

The elapsed time is found from the starting and terminal dates.

Year	Month	Day
1993	12	1
−1988	− 6	−1
5 years	6 months	0 days

Number of time periods = $(5 \times 2) + 6/6 = 10 + 1 = 11$

Since there is a payment at the end of each period, $n = 11$.

EXAMPLE 2 An annuity has payments made every 3 months with the first payment on November 15, 1986, and the last payment on August 15, 1994. Find the number of payments.

SOLUTION When the dates of the first and last payments are given, special care must be used in getting n. We start with a time diagram (Figure 4-6).

Subtracting the starting date from the terminal date gives the elapsed time.

Year	Month	Day
3	20	
199̸4̸	8̸	15
−1986	−11	−15
7 years	9 months	0 days

Number of time periods $= (7 \times 4) + 9/3 = 28 + 3 = 31$

Figure 4-5

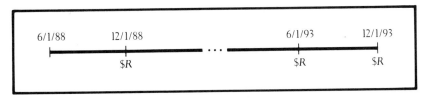

Figure 4-6

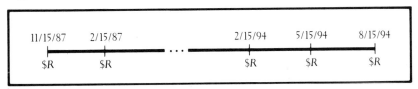

Since the problem gives the dates of the first and last payments, $n = 32$, 1 greater than the number of periods from first to last payment.

The following true story illustrates another way to tackle time problems. At a meeting of a group of scientists, the question came up of how long it would be until the next convention of a professional association. A renowned mathematician held up his hand, carefully ticked off the months on his fingers, and announced the right answer. When a similar problem is first given to a college class, it seems so simple that many students attempt it in their heads. Almost immediately the room is full of instant wrong answers.

Getting n can be so difficult that some students find a combination of time diagram and finger counting the most dependable method. Their solution to the preceding example would be

Payments in 1986 (from the diagram)   1
From 1987 to 1993 inclusive there are 7 years
   (count them) $7 \times 4 = 28$
Payments in 1994 (from the diagram) $\underline{\quad 3}$
                                                    $n = 32$

When this method is used, placing all of the payments in the first and last years on the diagram is desirable.

4.6   AMOUNT OR PRESENT VALUE?

Occasionally a student has difficulty in determining whether the single sum equivalent to a series of payments is an amount or a present value. When in doubt, draw a time diagram. If the payments follow the single sum, it is a present value. If the payments precede the single sum, it is an amount. The diagrams in Figure 4-7 show how the payments of an ordinary annuity are related to the equivalent single sums.

EXAMPLE   A person is paying $200 a month on a debt with the payments due the first of each month. The borrower was unable to make the payments due on April 1 and May 1. Windfall income in May provides enough cash to make all payments that are owed as well as to prepay the payments that will come due during the current year. If the borrower and the lender agree to make a settlement on the basis of 6% compounded monthly, how much should the borrower pay on June 1?

SOLUTION   A time diagram is drawn (Figure 4-8) and the focal date located on June 1, the time of the unknown payment.

The April and May payments precede the single sum that will replace them on the focal date. These payments plus the June payment due on the focal date form an ordinary annuity of 3 payments for which we need the amount. The July-to-December payments follow the focal date, so these 6 payments form an ordinary annuity for which we need

Figure 4-7

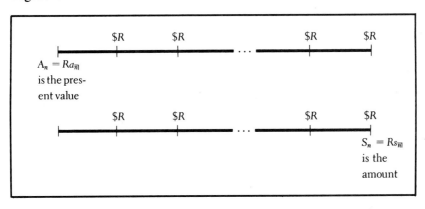

Figure 4-8

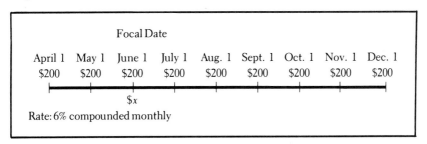

the present value. Combining these results in an equation of value, we have

$$x = 200s_{\overline{3}|} + 200a_{\overline{6}|}$$
$$= 200 \times 3.01503 + 200 \times 5.89638$$
$$= 603.01 + 1179.28$$
$$= \$1782.29$$

Exercise 4b

1. Find n for each of the annuities described as follows:

Date of first payment	Date of last payment	Frequency of payments
(a) April 1, 1982	April 1, 1990	Annual
(b) June 15, 1980	December 15, 1987	Quarterly
(c) June 15, 1980	December 15, 1989	Semiannual
(d) March 1, 1981	July 1, 1987	Monthly
(e) October 1, 1983	September 1, 1993	Monthly

[(a) 9; (b) 31; (c) 20; (d) 77; (e) 120]

2. Find the present value of an ordinary annuity of $5000 per year for 10 years at: (a) 6%; (b) 7%. All rates are converted annually. Carry the present value for the 6% rate forward 10 years. How does the accumulated amount compare with the amount of an annuity of $5000 a year as determined in problem 1(a) of Exercise 4a?

3. Find the present value of an ordinary annuity of $750 a year for 8 years at: (a) 6%; (b) 8%.

[(a) $4657.34; (b) $4309.98]

4. Find the present value of an ordinary annuity of $1200 at the end of each 6 months for 5 years if money is worth: (a) 5%, (b) 6%, and (c) 7%, all compounded semiannually.

5. If money is worth 9% converted semiannually, what is the present value of $145.50 due at the end of each 6 months for 2 years?

($521.99)

6. A television set is bought for $50 cash and $18 a month for 12 months. What is the equivalent cash price if the interest rate is 24% converted monthly?

7. A refrigerator can be purchased for $57.47 down and $20 a month for 24 months. What is the equivalent cash price if the rate is 30% converted monthly?

($415.17)

8. Find the cash value of a used car that can be bought for $400 down and $80 a month for 24 months if money is worth 18% converted monthly.

9. A person receives an inheritance of $500 every half year for 20 years, the first payment to be made in 6 months. If money is worth 6% converted semiannually, what is the cash value of the inheritance?

($11,557.39)

10. A contract for the purchase of a home calls for the payment of $385 a month for 20 years. At the beginning of the 6th year (just after the 60th payment is made), the contract is sold to a buyer at a price that will yield 12% converted monthly. What does the buyer pay?

11.(C) A woman wants to provide a school with a $3000 research fellowship at the end of each year for the next 4 years. If the school can invest money at 10%, how much should the woman give now to set up a fund for the 4 fellowships?

($9509.60)

12. A home was purchased for $6000 down and $200 a month for 20 years. If the monthly payments are based on 12% converted monthly, what was the cash price of the house?

13. A mobile home was purchased for $6000 down and $1000 at the end of each 6 months for 8 years. If the payments are based on 14% converted semiannually, what was the cash price of the mobile home?

($15,446.65)

14. If a person can get 6% converted semiannually on invested money, is it better to pay $11,500 cash or $3000 down and $1000 every 6 months for 5 years?

15. Answer problem 14 if the buyer can get 7% converted semi-annually on the investments.

(By paying on time, the buyer saves $183.39 now.)

16. A man was paying off a car with monthly payments of $150 for 3 years. He made all the payments in the first 2 years; however, shortly after making the 24th payment, he was involved in an accident and was unable to make the next 4 payments. With the insurance settlement he wanted to pay off the entire debt

at the time of the 5th payment in the last year. What single payment will settle the obligation if the interest rate is 12% converted monthly?

4.7 EXTENSION OF TABLES

In some problems the number of payments is greater than can be found directly in the tables. You can solve such problems by dividing the annuity into parts and then accumulating or discounting the amount or present value of each part of the annuity to the desired point in time.

EXAMPLE 1 Find the amount of an annuity of $100 at the end of each month for 30 years at 6% converted monthly.

SOLUTION There are 360 payments, so we divide the annuity into 2 annuities of 180 payments each. The last 180 payments form an ordinary annuity that has an amount of

$$S_{180} = 100 s_{\overline{180}|\frac{1}{2}\%} = 100 \times 290.81871 = \$29,081.87$$

The amount of the first 180 payments just after the 180th payment is also $29,081.87. At the time of the 180th payment, this single sum is equivalent in value to the 180 payments. From here on, all 180 payments can be moved at one time simply by moving this single sum. To find the value of the first 180 payments at the end of the term, we take this equivalent single sum forward at compound interest.

$$S = 29,081.87 \times (1.005)^{180}$$
$$= 29,081.87 \times 2.4540936 = \$71,369.63$$

Adding the 2 amounts gives a total amount of $100,451.50.

A time diagram (Figure 4-9) helps in analyzing and setting up problems of this type. Had there been more than 360 payments, we would have separated the annuity into 3 or more annuities.

EXAMPLE 2 Find the present value of an annuity of $100 at the end of each month for 30 years at 6% converted monthly.

SOLUTION We divide the annuity into 2 annuities of 180 payments each. The first 180 payments form an ordinary annuity that has a present value of

$$A_{180} = 100a_{\overline{180}|\frac{1}{2}\%} = 100 \times 118.50351 = \$11,850.35$$

At a point in time 1 period before the 181st payment, the value of the last 180 payments is also $11,850.35. Now we replace payments 181 to 360 with this single sum. To get the value of the last 180 payments at the beginning of the term, we discount this equivalent single sum.

$$P = 11,850.35(1.005)^{-180}$$
$$= 11,850.35 \times .4074824 = \$4828.81$$

Adding the two results gives a total present value of $16,679.16.

A time diagram (Figure 4-10) helps in finding a systematic solution of the problem.

Whenever possible, the simplest solution is to divide the annuity into equal parts as was done in these examples. If we had 325 payments, we

Figure 4-9

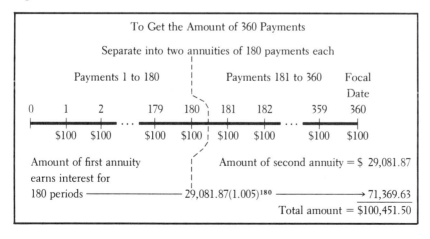

To Get the Amount of 360 Payments

Separate into two annuities of 180 payments each

| Payments 1 to 180 | Payments 181 to 360 | Focal Date |

0   1   2   179   180 ⟍ 181   182   359   360

$100 $100 $100 $100 ┆ $100 $100 $100 $100

Amount of first annuity earns interest for
180 periods ——————————— 29,081.87(1.005)¹⁸⁰ ———————→ 71,369.63

Amount of second annuity = $ 29,081.87

Total amount = $100,451.50

could separate them into annuities of 180 and 145 payments or any other combination that would total 325 with each part 180 or less.

EXAMPLE 3   Check the answers to Examples 1 and 2.

SOLUTION   Since both examples involve the same annuity, we check by taking the present value from Example 2 forward 30 years at 6% converted monthly.

$$S = 16{,}679.16(1.005)^{360} = 16{,}679.16(1.005)^{180}(1.005)^{180}$$
$$= 16{,}679.16(2.4540936)^2 = \$100{,}451.50$$

This result is the same as the amount derived in Example 1.

Of course, there is no need to use this method if Table 3 can be applied or if you are using a calculator with exponential capability. For Example 1:

$$S_{360} = 100\,\frac{(1.005)^{360} - 1}{.005} = \$100{,}451.50$$

For Example 2:

$$A_{360} = 100\,\frac{1 - (1.005)^{-360}}{.005} = \$16{,}679.16$$

Figure 4-10

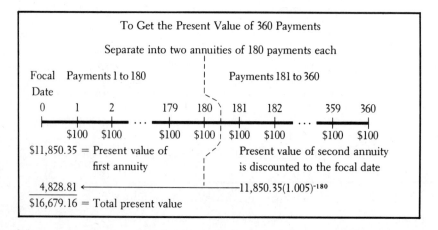

To Get the Present Value of 360 Payments

Separate into two annuities of 180 payments each

For Example 3:

$$S = 16,679.16(1.005)^{360} = \$100,451.50$$

Exercise 4c

1. Find the amount of an annuity of $40 at the end of each year for 80 years if money is worth 6%.
   ($69,864.01)
2. What is the amount of an annuity of $60 at the end of each month for 30 years at 7% converted monthly?
3. Find the present value of the annuity in problem 1.
   ($660.36)
4. Find the present value of the annuity in problem 2.
5. A home can be purchased for $5000 down and $400 a month for 50 years. If the monthly payments are based on 12% converted monthly, find the total cash price of the house.
   ($44,897.85)
6. A condominium can be purchased for $10,000 down and $1000 every 3 months for 18 years. If the payments are based on 9% converted quarterly, find the total cash price.
7.(C) Solve problem 1 if the rate is $7\frac{1}{2}\%$.
   ($173,117.10)
8.(C) Find the present value of the annuity in problem 7.

4.8 PERIODIC PAYMENT OF AN ANNUITY

In practical business problems the amount or present value of an annuity is frequently known and the periodic payment is to be determined. This determination can be made by solving the amount and present value formulas for R.

Solving formula (14), $S_n = Rs_{\overline{n}|}$, for R, we have

$$R = \frac{S_n}{s_{\overline{n}|}} = S_n \times \frac{1}{s_{\overline{n}|}} = S_n \frac{i}{(1+i)^n - 1} \tag{16}$$

R = periodic payment or rent
S_n = amount of annuity of n payments
$\dfrac{1}{s_{\overline{n}|}}$ = periodic deposit that will grow to $1 in n payments

Use formula (16) when the future amount is known. Solving formula (15), $A_n = Ra_{\overline{n}|}$, for R, we have the following formula:

$$R = \frac{A_n}{a_{\overline{n}|}} = A_n \times \frac{1}{a_{\overline{n}|}} = A_n \frac{i}{1 - (1 + i)^{-n}} \qquad (17)$$

R = periodic payment or rent

A_n = present value of annuity of n payments

$\dfrac{1}{a_{\overline{n}|}}$ = periodic payment necessary to pay off a loan of $1 in n payments

Use formula (17) when the present value is known.

While R could be found by dividing S_n or A_n by the correct factor, problems of this type occur so frequently in practice that the reciprocals of these factors have been determined. The numerical values of $1/s_{\overline{n}|}$ are given in the "Sinking fund" column (third column of factors) of Table 2 and $1/a_{\overline{n}|}$ in the "Partial payment" column (sixth column of factors). This availability of values means that the periodic rent can be determined by multiplying as indicated in the final form of formulas (16) and (17). When setting up problems, the rate per period is often included as a subscript. If in doubt about which formula to use, draw a time diagram. If the payments precede the single sum, it is an amount; use formula (16) and the "Sinking fund" column. If the payments follow the single sum, it is a present value; use formula (17) and the "Partial payment" column.

Again we have equations in more than one form. The first is a division form and will be used with Table 3 and a simple calculator. Because these problems occur frequently and division is more difficult to perform by hand than multiplication, Table 2 provides the numerical values of $1/s_{\overline{n}|}$ (Sinking fund) and $1/a_{\overline{n}|}$ (Partial payment). In problems in which Table 2 is used, the second form is used in calculating the periodic payments. Finally, if you are using a scientific calculator, you can apply the last form for any rate and number of periods.

EXAMPLE 1 If money is worth 5% compounded semiannually, how much must a person save every 6 months to accumulate $3000 in 4 years?

SOLUTION A time diagram (Figure 4-11) shows that the $3000 is an amount in the future. Substituting $S_8 = 3000$, $n = 8$, and $i = 2\frac{1}{2}\%$ in formula (16), we have

Form 1: $R = \dfrac{S_n}{s_{\overline{n}|}} = \dfrac{3000}{s_{\overline{8}|2.5\%}} = \dfrac{3000}{8.7361159004} = \$343.40$

Form 2: $R = S_n \times \dfrac{1}{s_{\overline{n}|}} = 3000 \times \dfrac{1}{s_{\overline{8}|2.5\%}} = 3000 \times .114467 = \$343.40$

Form 3: $R = S_n \dfrac{i}{(1+i)^n - 1} = 3000 \dfrac{.025}{(1.025)^8 - 1} = \$343.40$

Note that 8 payments of \$343.40 total \$2747.20. The balance needed to produce an amount of \$3000 comes from the accumulated interest on each payment from the time it is made to the end of the 4 years.

EXAMPLE 2 A couple wants to buy a new automobile costing \$9000. Their down payment, including trade-in, is \$1500. The remainder is to be paid in monthly installments over 4 years at 12% converted monthly. Find the size of the monthly payment.

SOLUTION A time diagram (Figure 4-12) shows that \$7500 is the present value. Substituting $A_{48} = 7500$, $n = 48$, and $i = .01$ in formula (17), we use all three forms:

Form 1: $R = \dfrac{7500}{a_{\overline{48}|1\%}} = \dfrac{7500}{37.9739595} = \$197.50$

Form 2: $R = 7500 \times \dfrac{1}{a_{\overline{48}|1\%}} = 7500 \times .0263338354 = \$197.50$

Form 3: $R = 7500 \times \dfrac{.01}{1 - (1.01)^{-48}} = \$197.50$

Figure 4-11

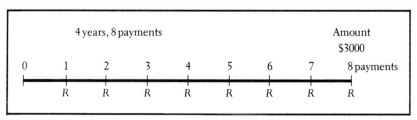

| 4 years, 8 payments | | | | | | | Amount $3000 |

$$
\begin{array}{cccccccc}
0 & 1 & 2 & 3 & 4 & 5 & 6 & 7 & 8\,\text{payments} \\
& R & R & R & R & R & R & R & R
\end{array}
$$

EXAMPLE 3   A family wants to buy a home costing $60,000. If they put $10,000 down and get a 30-year mortgage at 13% with monthly payments, how much will they be required to pay monthly?

SOLUTION   There are 360 payments, so we cannot use Table 2. Applying Table 3 and Form 1 with $n = 360$, $A_{360} = 50,000$, and $i = \frac{13}{12}\%$, we get

$$R = \frac{50,000}{a_{\overline{360}|}} = \frac{50,000}{90.3996054} = \$553.10$$

Note that 360 payments of $553.10 amount to $199,116, making the total interest $149,116.

It is interesting to see that if the family could borrow the $50,000 at 12% compounded monthly, the payment would be

$$R = \frac{50,000}{97.2183311} = \$514.31$$

Hence a reduction of 1 percentage point in the rate results in a savings of $38.79 every month. All of this difference is interest. Over 30 years the savings amounts to $360 \times 38.79 = \$13,964.40$. This sum is not, of course, equivalent to a total cash savings of that amount since the savings are spread over 360 months at the rate of $38.79 per month. The equivalent cash savings will depend on the value of money to the family. For example, at 6% converted monthly, the equivalent cash savings would be

$$38.79 a_{\overline{360}|} = 38.79 \times 166.7916144 = \$6469.85$$

Whether we make the comparison on the basis of the total savings in interest or on the equivalent cash value of the savings, there is no

Figure 4-12

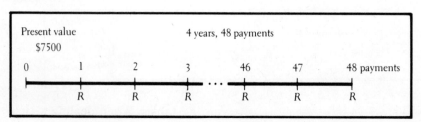

Present value
$7500

4 years, 48 payments

0   1   2   3   46   47   48 payments

R   R   R   R   R   R

doubt that a person should shop around to find the most reasonable rate before borrowing money. An apparently small difference in the rate may translate into the savings of hundreds of dollars.

Another thing to note in the previous example is that with a 12% rate, the interest totaled over $135,000. Interest costs on a home loan can be reduced by making a larger down payment. Savings on interest provide an incentive for people to save money.

EXAMPLE 4   A savings and loan association pays 5% converted quarterly. A savings officer at the association suggests to a couple that they set up a systematic plan for providing a retirement annuity of their own to supplement social security. The husband is now 50 years old. The couple decides to deposit $200 at the end of each 3 months until the husband is 65. Three months after their last deposit they plan to start drawing on the account with equal withdrawals every 3 months over 15 years. Find the size of the withdrawals and the total interest.

SOLUTION   The amount that the couple will accumulate is obtained using formula (14).

$$S_{60} = 200s_{\overline{60}|1.25\%} = 200 \times 88.57451 = \$17,714.90$$

This amount becomes the present value of an ordinary annuity. The couple will now receive 60 quarterly payments with the size determined using formula (17).

$$R = 17,714.90 \times \frac{1}{a_{\overline{60}|1.25\%}}$$

$$= 17,714.90 \times .0237900 = \$421.44$$

Total retirement income = 60 $\times$ 421.44 = $25,286.40
Total deposits = 60 $\times$ 200.00 = 12,000.00
Total interest = $13,286.40

4.9   EXTENSION OF TABLES

In using either of the first two forms of formulas (16) and (17), you are limited to the rates and terms given in the tables. When dealing with a number of periods not included in the tables, use the methods described in Section 4.7 and divide.

To reduce arithmetic, examples and exercises involving extension of tables use factors rounded to the same number of decimal places as there are digits in the sum of money. When a calculator is available, it is good practice to use complete factors and round the final answer as suggested in Section 3.6, page 96.

EXAMPLE 1 How much must be deposited each quarter in an account paying 6% converted quarterly to accumulate $10,000 in 20 years?

SOLUTION $S = 10,000$, $i = 1\frac{1}{2}\%$, and $n = 80$.

$$R = \frac{10,000}{s_{\overline{80}|1\frac{1}{2}\%}}$$

We get $s_{\overline{80}|}$ by using two annuities of 40 payments each.

Amount of last 40 payments $= s_{\overline{40}|}$ $\qquad = 54.2678939$
Amount of first 40 payments $= s_{\overline{40}|}(1.015)^{40}$
$\qquad\qquad = 54.2678939 \times 1.8140184 = \underline{98.4429581}$
$\qquad\qquad\qquad\qquad\qquad\qquad s_{\overline{80}|} = 152.7108520$

If only one problem is to be solved, we can obtain R by dividing 10,000 by $s_{\overline{80}|}$.

$$R = \frac{10,000}{152.7108520} = \$65.48$$

EXAMPLE 2 To help finance the purchase of a home, a couple borrows $30,000. The loan is to be repaid in quarterly payments over 25 years. If the rate is 10% converted quarterly, find the size of the quarterly payment.

SOLUTION Substituting $A_n = 30,000$, $n = 100$, and $i = 2\frac{1}{2}\%$ in formula (17), we have

$$R = \frac{30,000}{a_{\overline{100}|2\frac{1}{2}\%}}$$

We get $a_{\overline{100}|}$ using two annuities of 50 payments each. All payments are discounted to the present.

Present value of first 50 payments $= a_{\overline{50}|}$ $= 28.3623117$
Present value of last 50 payments $= a_{\overline{50}|}(1.025)^{-50}$
$$= 28.3623117 \times .2909422 = \underline{8.2517934}$$
$$a_{\overline{100}|} = 36.6141051$$

$$R = \frac{30,000}{36.6141051} = \$819.36$$

Exercise 4d

1. A person wants to accumulate $3000 in 6 years. Equal deposits are made at the end of each 6 months in a savings account paying 6% converted semiannually. What is the size of each deposit?
    ($211.39)

2. Find the annual payment of an ordinary annuity if the amount is $5000, payments are made for 10 years, and the interest rate is 5%.

3. A family buys a washer that sells for $350 cash. They pay $50 down and the balance in 24 equal monthly payments. If the seller charges 18% converted monthly for time payments, what is the size of the monthly payment?
    ($14.98)

4. A loan company charges 36% converted monthly for small loans. What would be the monthly payment if a loan of $150 is to be repaid in 12 payments?

5. A woman buys a car that lists at $7500. She pays $2000 down and the balance in 36 monthly payments. If the interest rate is 12% converted monthly, what are her monthly payments?
    ($182.68)

6. What would be the monthly payment in problem 5 if the rate was 24% converted monthly?

7. You are the accountant for a male client who is selling a piece of property for $80,000. He is to get $30,000 down at the date of sale. The remainder is to be paid with 12 non-interest-bearing notes of equal face value. The notes are due serially, 1 each 6 months from date of sale. If the settlement is based on 8%

compounded semiannually, each note should be drawn for what amount?
($5327.61)

8. What would be the size of each note in problem 7 if the rate is 9% compounded semiannually?

9. On June 1, 1986, a widow takes the $10,000 benefits from her husband's insurance policy and invests the money at 6% converted monthly with the understanding that she will receive 120 equal monthly payments. If she is to get her first check on July 1, 1986, what will be the size of each monthly payment?
($111.02)

10. If the widow in problem 9 could invest the money at 7% converted monthly, how much would she get each month?

11. A couple expects to need $3000 in 3 years. They plan to accumulate this amount by making equal payments every 6 months in a savings and loan association that pays 6% converted semiannually. If they make the first deposit on July 1, 1988, and the last deposit on July 1, 1991, what is the size of the semiannual payment? They want to have the $3000 just after the last deposit.
($391.52)

12. Find the quarterly payment necessary for an ordinary annuity to amount to $4500 in 4 years at 6% converted quarterly.

13. On June 1, 1987, $8000 is invested at 6% converted monthly. The investment is to be paid out in 96 equal monthly payments with the first payment on July 1, 1987. What is the size of the monthly payment?
($105.13)

14. If the investment in problem 13 is paid out in 48 equal payments, what would be the size of each payment?

15. A family needs a loan of $50,000 to buy a home. One lender charges 12% converted monthly. A second lender offers 11% converted monthly. If the monthly payments are to run for 20 years, what would be the total savings in interest if the family gets the 11% loan?
($8268.00)

16. A mortgage for $70,000 is to be repaid in monthly payments over a period of 15 years. What would be the total savings in interest if the loan is financed at 12% converted monthly rather than 13%?

17. A family buys a home costing $40,000. They pay $10,000 down and get a 30-year mortgage for the rest at 14% converted

monthly. What is the size of their monthly payments? What is the total interest they will pay on this loan?

($355.46 a month; $97,965.60 interest)

18. A woman gets a loan for $8000 to be repaid in monthly payments over a period of 25 years. If the interest rate is $10\frac{1}{2}\%$ converted monthly, what is the size of the monthly payment and the total interest?

19. A $30,000 life insurance policy matures on April 1, 1989, with the death of the insured. The beneficiary is to receive 192 equal monthly payments with the first payment on May 1, 1989. Find the size of the monthly payment and the date of the concluding payment if interest is earned at 6% converted monthly.

($243.43; April 1, 2005)

20. What would be the size of the monthly payment if the money in problem 19 earned 7% compounded monthly?

21. A man wants to accumulate a $100,000 retirement fund. He plans to make semiannual deposits in a savings and loan association that pays 8% converted semiannually. If his first deposit is made on June 30, 1988, and his plan calls for the last deposit to be made on December 31, 2023, what should be the size of each deposit?

($252.49)

22.(C) Work problem 21 if the man can get $7\frac{1}{2}\%$ converted semiannually.

4.10 FINDING THE TERM OF AN ANNUITY

Some problems specify the amount or present value, the size of the payments, and the rate. The number of payments is what needs to be determined. When an integral number of payments is not exactly equivalent to the original amount or present value, one of the following procedures is used in practice. First, the last regular payment can be increased by a sum that will make the payments equivalent to the amount or present value. The second alternative is that a smaller concluding payment can be made one period after the last full payment. In this book we follow the second procedure unless the problem states that the last full payment is to be increased. Sometimes when a certain amount of money is to be accumulated, a smaller concluding payment will not be required because the interest after the last full payment will equal or exceed the balance needed.

EXAMPLE 1 A woman wants to accumulate $5000 by making payments of $1000 at the end of each year. If she gets 5% on her money, how many regular payments will she make and what will be the size of the last payment?

SOLUTION Using formula (14) for the amount of an annuity, we obtain

$$1000s_{\overline{n}|5\%} = 5000$$
$$s_{\overline{n}|5\%} = \frac{5000}{1000} = 5.0000$$

We look in Table 2 under 5% for the factor 5.0000 in the "Amount of 1 per period" column. We find that the factor is 4.310125 for 4 periods and 5.525631 for 5 periods. Therefore the woman will have to make 4 deposits of $1000 and a fifth smaller deposit to be determined. To find the size of this last deposit, we use an equation of value (see Figure 4-13).

Instead of taking the four $1000 payments separately to the focal date, we get the amount of these four payments at the end of 4 years.

$$S_4 = 1000s_{\overline{4}|5\%} = 1000 \times 4.310125 = \$4310.13$$

Now we can take this amount to the focal date using simple interest in the equation of value:

$$4310.13(1.05) + x = 5000$$
$$x = 5000 - 4525.64$$
$$= \$474.36$$

Thus if the woman deposits $1000 at the end of each year for 4 years and $474.36 at the end of the fifth year, she will have exactly

Figure 4-13

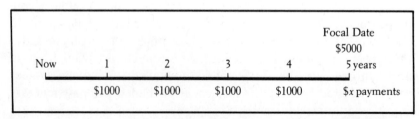

$5000 in her account. In problems like this one, note that the last deposit will never be larger than the others.

ALTERNATE SOLUTION   It is also possible to get the 4 payments to the focal date by looking up $s_{\overline{5}|}$ and subtracting 1 to allow for the fact that no full payment is made at the end. Then the amount becomes

$$1000(5.525631 - 1) = \$4525.63$$

Hence a balance of $474.37 will have to be deposited at the end of the fifth year.

The 1-cent difference in the answers is due to rounding. The second method will be discussed under Annuities Due in the next chapter.

EXAMPLE 2   Do Example 1 again assuming that the woman wants to accumulate $7000.

SOLUTION   Substituting in formula (14), we find that

$$1000s_{\overline{n}|5\%} = 7000$$
$$s_{\overline{n}|5\%} = 7.0000$$

The second column in Table 2 shows that 7.0000 lies between 6 and 7 payments. The amount of 6 full payments is

$$S_6 = 1000 \times 6.801913 = \$6801.91$$

Carrying this amount forward for 1 year at simple interest, we obtain

$$6801.91(1.05) = \$7142.01$$

No smaller concluding payment is required.

EXAMPLE 3   A woman dies and leaves her husband an estate worth $5000. Instead of receiving the full bequest in cash, he is to get monthly payments of $100. How many monthly payments will he receive and what smaller payment 1 month after the last regular payment will settle the estate if interest is at 6% compounded monthly?

SOLUTION   Using formula (15) for the present value of an annuity, we have

$$100a_{\overline{n}|\frac{1}{2}\%} = 5000$$

Solving for $a_{\overline{n}|}$, we obtain

$$a_{\overline{n}|\frac{1}{2}\%} = 50$$

Looking in Table 2 under $\frac{1}{2}\%$ for the factor 50, we find that $a_{\overline{57}|} = 49.49031$ and $a_{\overline{58}|} = 50.23911$. Therefore the widower will receive 57 payments of $100 and a 58th payment that is smaller. To find the size of the concluding payment, we set up an equation of value (see Figure 4-14).

First, we find the amount of the 57 regular payments at the end of 57 months.

$$S_{57} = 100s_{\overline{57}|\frac{1}{2}\%} = 100 \times 65.76361 = \$6576.36$$

Now we take this amount and the $5000 to the focal date and set up the equation of value.

$$6576.36(1.005) + x = 5000(1.005)^{58}$$
$$x = 5000 \times 1.335462 - 6576.36(1.005)$$
$$= 6677.31 - 6609.24 = \$68.07$$

ALTERNATE SOLUTION   As pointed out in Example 1, it is also possible to get the 57 payments to the focal date by looking up $s_{\overline{58}|}$ and subtracting 1. The amount of 57 payments at the end of 58 periods then becomes

Figure 4-14

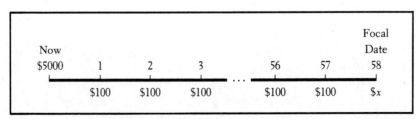

$$100(67.09243 - 1) = \$6609.24$$

For those who have been working with the exponential forms of the annuity formulas, it is possible to solve for n using logarithms.

$$S_n = R \frac{(1 + i)^n - 1}{i}$$

$$\frac{S_n}{R} = \frac{(1 + i)^n - 1}{i}$$

$$\frac{S_n i}{R} = (1 + i)^n - 1$$

$$(1 + i)^n = \frac{S_n i}{R} + 1$$

$$n \log(1 + i) = \log\left(\frac{S_n i}{R} + 1\right)$$

$$n = \frac{\log\left(\frac{S_n i}{R} + 1\right)}{\log(1 + i)}$$

Similarly, using formula (15),

$$n = \frac{-\log\left(1 - \frac{A_n i}{R}\right)}{\log(1 + i)}$$

Of course, n is seldom a whole number when these formulas are used, so that it will be necessary to round the answer and go through procedures similar to those given above in order to find the size of the concluding payment.

EXAMPLE 4(C)   How many quarterly payments of $500 will be necessary to accumulate $5000 if the rate is $5\frac{1}{2}\%$ compounded quarterly?

SOLUTION   Substituting $S_n = 5000$, $R = 500$, and $i = .01375$, we have

$$n = \frac{\log\left(\frac{5000 \times .01375}{500} + 1\right)}{\log(1.01375)} = \frac{\log 1.1375}{\log 1.01375} = 9.43$$

or 9 full payments plus a smaller 10th payment.

EXAMPLE 5^(C)   How many monthly payments of $500 will be necessary to pay off a debt of $50,000 at $10\frac{1}{2}$% compounded monthly?

SOLUTION   Substituting A_n = 50,000, R = 500, and i = .00875, we have

$$n = \frac{-\log\left(1 - \dfrac{50{,}000 \times .00875}{500}\right)}{\log(1.00875)} = 238.69$$

Such a loan requires 238 full payments plus a smaller final payment. To find the size of the debt after the 238th payment,

$$50{,}000(1.00875)^{238} - 500\,\frac{(1.00875)^{238} - 1}{.00875} = \$341.81$$

The final payment will be $341.81 plus interest for one month = 341.80 × 1.00875 = $344.80.

Exercise 4e

1.   Mr. Freeman can afford to set aside $2000 every 6 months from his salary. He plans to buy a resort cottage when he has accumulated $20,000. How long will it take him if he can invest the money at 5% converted semiannually? Give the answer to the nearest payment.
     (9 payments)

2.   How many payments of $150 at the end of every 3 months will be required to accumulate $3000 if interest is earned at 6% converted quarterly? Give the answer to the nearest number of payments.

3.   How many annual payments of $12,000 each and what final smaller payment must be made to accumulate $45,000 if money earns interest at 7%?
     (3 full payments; concluding payment of $3720.68)

4.   A couple deposits $250 at the end of each 6 months in a savings and loan association paying 5% converted semiannually. To accumulate $4500, how many full payments must they make

and what will be the size of the concluding payment if one is needed?

5.(C) A man leaves his wife an estate of $25,000. The money is invested at 7% converted monthly. How many monthly payments of $200 would the widow receive and what would be the size of the concluding payment?

(224 full payments; concluding payment of $116.41)

6.(C) An heiress invests her inheritance of $15,000 at 9% compounded monthly. If she takes the money out in monthly payments of $125, for how many years will she receive payments? Answer to nearest number of years.

7. The present value of an annuity is $7500. Semiannual payments of $500 are made from the $7500, which is invested at 7% compounded semiannually. How many full payments will be made and what will be the size of the concluding payment?

(21 full payments; concluding payment of $321.88)

8. A family has $3000 in a savings and loan association. If they get 6% compounded semiannually, and withdraw $500 at the end of each 6 months, how many withdrawals can they make? What will be the size of the concluding withdrawal if it is made 6 months after the last full withdrawal?

9.(C) Do problem 8 if the rate is $5\frac{1}{2}$% compounded semiannually.

(6 full withdrawals; final withdrawal $325.04)

10.(C) If, in problem 5, the concluding payment was sent with the last regular payment, what total payment would the widow receive at that time?

11.(C) A woman invests $20,000 on June 1, 1987, at 7% converted monthly. She is to receive monthly payments of $250 with the first payment to be made on July 1, 1987. How many full payments will she receive? What will be the date and size of the concluding payment if it is made 1 month after the last $250 payment?

(108 full payments; concluding payment of $18.92 on July 1, 1996)

12. Ten thousand dollars is invested on August 1, 1988, at 6% converted monthly. The investment is to be paid out in monthly payments of $200 with the first payment to be made on September 1, 1988. How many full payments will be made and what will be the size and date of the last payment if it is made 1 month after the last full payment?

13.(C) A house is for sale for $23,500. A couple can pay $8500 down and $150 a month. If they assume a mortgage at 8% converted monthly, how many $150 payments must they make and what will be the size of the concluding payment?

(165 full payments; concluding payment of $51.19)

14.(C) How many full payments must be made and what would be the size of the concluding payment in problem 13 if the rate is 9% converted monthly?

15. A couple can save $150 at the end of each 6 months. How long will it take them to accumulate $3600 if they get 5% converted semiannually on their savings? If they need a partial deposit 6 months after the last $150 deposit, how large should it be?

(19 full deposits; no final deposit)

16. Work problem 15 using a rate of 6% converted semiannually.

17.(C) A piece of property is purchased for $360,000. The buyer pays $60,000 down and agrees to pay $40,000 at the end of each year. If the interest rate is 10%, how many full payments must be made and what will be the size of the concluding payment 1 year after the last full payment?

(14 full payments; concluding payment of $22,275.19)

18. A firm buys a store costing $180,000. The firm pays $30,000 down and $20,000 at the end of each 6 months. If the interest rate is 16%, how many full payments must the firm make and what will be the size of the concluding payment?

4.11 FINDING THE INTEREST RATE

A very practical application of the amount and present value formulas is finding the interest rate. In many business transactions the true interest rate is concealed in one way or another, so it is desirable that the customer be able to determine the rate. In this way one proposition can be compared with another and the least expensive alternative can be selected. The rate can be determined approximately, but with sufficient accuracy for most practical purposes, by linear interpolation using factors from Table 2.

EXAMPLE 1   Find the rate of interest per period and the nominal rate converted quarterly at which payments of $150 every 3 months will amount to $2000 in 3 years.

SOLUTION   Substituting in formula (14) for the amount of an annuity, we have

$$150s_{\overline{12}|} = 2000$$

$$s_{\overline{12}|} = \tfrac{2000}{150} = 13.3333$$

We refer to the "Amount of 1 per period" column in Table 2 and go across the row for $n = 12$ until we find the factor 13.3333 or, as is usually the case, values on each side of this factor. We record these values as follows:

i in %	$s_{\overline{12}|}$

	2.00	13.4121		
.25	i	13.3333		1870
d	1.75	13.2251	1082	

The rate per period in our problem lies between 1.75% and 2%. Using d to indicate the difference between 1.75% and the desired rate, we set up the proportion

$$\frac{d}{.25} = \frac{1082}{1870}$$

$$d = .25 \times \tfrac{1082}{1870} = .144$$

From this result we obtain

$$i = 1.75 + .144 = 1.894\%$$

which is the rate per period. To get the approximate nominal rate converted semiannually, we multiply this value by 4, so that the final answer is

$$4 \times 1.894 = 7.576 = 7.58\%$$

If only the nominal rate is wanted, it is faster and simpler to interpolate between nominal rates as follows:

$j_{(4)}$ in %	$s_{\overline{12}|}$

	8	13.4121		
1	j	13.3333		1870
d	7	13.2251	1082	

$$\frac{d}{1} = \frac{1082}{1870}$$

$$d = \tfrac{1082}{1870} = .58$$

The nominal rate converted semiannually is $7.00 + .58 = 7.58\%$.

EXAMPLE 2   The winner of a lottery can take $1000 cash or $100 a month for 12 months, with the first payment in 1 month. If the monthly payment plan is chosen, what nominal rate of interest will be earned?

SOLUTION   Substituting in formula (15), we have

$$100a_{\overline{n}|} = 1000$$
$$a_{\overline{n}|} = 10.0000$$

We refer to Table 2 and look in row 12 until we find 10.0000 or factors on both sides of it in the column labeled "Present worth of 1 per period." The results are recorded as follows. Note that $a_{\overline{n}|}$ decreases as i increases.

$$j_{(12)} \text{ in } \% \quad a_{\overline{12}|}$$

			$j_{(12)}$ in %	$a_{\overline{12}|}$		
6		d	30	10.2578	2578	3038
			j	10.0000		
			36	9.9540		

$$\frac{d}{6} = \frac{2578}{3038}$$

$$d = 6 \times \tfrac{2578}{3038} = 5.09$$

Then we determine that the nominal rate is $30.0 + 5.1 = 35.1\%$ compounded monthly.

The winner should choose the $100 per month unless an interest rate of 35.1% can be earned on the $1000 prize.

EXAMPLE 3   A used car can be purchased for $500 cash or for $50 down and $35 a month for 18 months. Find the nominal annual rate.

SOLUTION   Subtracting the down payment gives us a present value of $450. Substituting in formula (15) for the present value of an annuity, we have

$$35a_{\overline{18|}} = 450$$
$$a_{\overline{18|}} = \tfrac{450}{35} = 12.8571$$

We refer to Table 2 and look in row 18 until we find either 12.8571 or factors on both sides of this value in the "Present worth of 1 per period" column. The results are recorded as follows. Note that $a_{\overline{n|}}$ decreases as i increases.

$$j_{(12)} \text{ in } \% \quad a_{\overline{18|}}$$

$$\frac{d}{6} = \frac{3326}{5304}$$

$$d = 6 \times \tfrac{3326}{5304} = 3.76$$
$$j = 42.0 + 3.8 = 45.8\% \text{ compounded monthly}$$

Because rates on installment purchases and small loans are often quite high, a buyer should always check the true rate before signing a contract.

EXAMPLE 4 A trombone is priced at $100. The instrument can be purchased for $8 down and $5 a week for 20 weeks. Or it can be obtained for cash at a 10% discount. What nominal interest rate converted weekly is charged the installment buyer?

SOLUTION First, we must get the *true* cash price, which is not $100, but $100 less 10% or $90. Thus the original unpaid balance is $82 ($90 less the $8 down payment). Now we substitute in formula (15) and obtain

$$5a_{\overline{20|}} = 82$$
$$a_{\overline{20|}} = 16.4000$$

From this result we find that

$$i \text{ in } \% \quad a_{\overline{20|}}$$

$$\frac{d}{.25} = \frac{3529}{4015}$$

$$d = .25 \times \tfrac{3529}{4015} = .22$$

$$i = 1.75 + .22 = 1.97\% \text{ per week}$$

Thus the approximate nominal rate is $52 \times 1.97 = 102\%$.

EXAMPLE 5   A dealer extends credit on the basis of 10% add-on. This means that to the unpaid balance is added 10% of the loan for each year that credit is to be extended. Then the total is divided by the number of months to get the monthly payment. If a $2000 loan is repaid over 2 years, what is the nominal interest rate?

SOLUTION

$$\begin{aligned}
\text{Unpaid balance} &= \$2000.00 \\
\text{Add-on} = 2 \times .10 \times 2000 &= \underline{400.00} \\
& \$2400.00
\end{aligned}$$

$$\text{Monthly payment} = \tfrac{2400}{24} = \$100$$

The problem is now an ordinary annuity with a present value of $2000 and a periodic payment of $100. Substituting in formula (15), we have

$$100 a_{\overline{24}|} = 2000.00$$
$$a_{\overline{24}|} = 20$$

Since only the nominal rate is required, we interpolate between the closest nominal rates in Table 2.

$$
\begin{array}{ccll}
 & & j_{(12)} \text{ in } \% & a_{\overline{24}|} \\
3 \left[\; d \left[\rule{0pt}{10pt}\right. \right. & \left. \begin{array}{c} 18 \\ j \\ 21 \end{array} \right. & \begin{array}{l} 20.0304 \\ 20.0000 \\ 19.4607 \end{array} & \left] 304 \; \right] 5697
\end{array}
$$

$$\frac{d}{3} = \frac{304}{5697}$$

$$d = \frac{3 \times 304}{5697} = .160$$

The nominal rate is $18.0 + .16 = 18.16\%$

EXAMPLE 6 A lender makes loans on the basis of 10% discount. For a 1-year loan, 10% of the loan is subtracted. The borrower receives the balance. The monthly payment is obtained by dividing the amount of the loan before the discount by the number of payments. Find the nominal rate paid by a person who borrows $1200 from this lender.

SOLUTION The borrower receives $1200 - 1200 \times .10 = \$1080$. The monthly payment is $1200/12 = \$100$. The problem is now an ordinary annuity with a present value of $1080 and a periodic payment of $100.

$$100a_{\overline{12}|} = 1080$$

$$a_{\overline{12}|} = \frac{1080}{100} = 10.800$$

Using Table 3:

$$j_{(12)} \text{ in } \% \quad a_{\overline{12}|}$$

$$
\begin{array}{c}
.5 \left[\begin{array}{c} d \left[\begin{array}{c} 19.5 \quad 10.8231 \\ j \quad 10.8000 \end{array} \right] 231 \\ 20.0 \quad 10.7951 \end{array} \right] 280
\end{array}
$$

$$\frac{d}{.5} = \frac{231}{280}$$

$$d = \frac{.5 \times 231}{280} = .41$$

The nominal rate is $19.50 + .41 = 19.91\%$.

Monthly installment loans based on add-on or discount result in nominal rates that are about twice the stated value.

4.12 TRUTH IN LENDING ACT

After several years of research and hearings by congressional committees, the Truth in Lending Act became law on July 1, 1969. This law requires that the borrower be told the total finance charge in dollars (except for home loans) and the annual percentage rate. The finance charge includes all costs that must be paid to get credit. There are no distinctions among such items as interest, discount, the time-price differential, and other fees or charges made by the creditor. The annual percentage rate (APR) is based on the actuarial method, which means that a rate is determined that makes the present value of the payments equal to the cash value of the loan. The law also includes the right to rescind certain credit transactions within three business days and the right to sue creditors for not obeying the law.

Since understanding credit costs is important for successful management of personal and family finances, the truth in lending law can be helpful to consumers who are aware of the safeguards it provides. Borrowers can now compare financial terms offered by competing creditors. Since enforcement of the law depends in part on consumer awareness, it is important that consumers learn how the law can help them. As the number of informed borrowers increases, they will exert an influence that will result in a more competitive marketplace for credit that will benefit all borrowers.

A problem that truth in lending does not solve is that of comparing annual percentage rates when the same item is available for different cash prices and time payment plans. The following example shows how this situation can be analyzed using the methods developed in this chapter.

EXAMPLE After a shopping trip a person returns home with the following information for the same item:

Store	Cash price	Down payment	Monthly payment	Number of payments	Cost of credit	Annual rate
A	$110.00	$10.00	$8.75	12	$5.00	9%
B	100.00	10.00	8.25	12	9.00	18%

We want to: (a) check the annual percentage rates claimed by the sellers; (b) determine the total dollar cost for the two stores; and (c) find out what annual percentage rate the time payment plan for store A would represent if based on a cash price of $100.

SOLUTION (a) On the basis of the price of $110, the borrower gets a loan of $100 after the down payment. Substituting in formula (15), we have

$$8.75a_{\overline{12}|} = 100.00$$
$$a_{\overline{12}|} = 11.4286$$

This value is practically the "present worth of 1 per period" factor for a nominal annual rate of 9% compounded monthly.

At the second store the buyer gets a loan of $90 to be repaid in 12 payments of $8.25. Substituting in formula (15), we have

$$8.25a_{\overline{12}|} = 90.00$$
$$a_{\overline{12}|} = 10.9091$$

This is approximately the factor for 18% compounded monthly.

Both merchants are reporting the correct rate for their cash prices.

For part (b) we find that total dollar costs are as follows:

Store A

Down payment	$ 10.00
12 monthly payments of $8.75	105.00
Total	$115.00

Store B

Down payment	$ 10.00
12 monthly payments of $8.25	99.00
Total	$109.00

Store B is the better place to make the purchase because the lower cash price more than offsets the apparently higher credit costs.

Now we consider part (c). If we use a cash price of $100 for store A, the borrower is getting a loan of $90 after the $10 down payment.

Substituting in formula (15), we have

$$8.75a_{\overline{12}|} = 90.00$$
$$a_{\overline{12}|} = 10.2857$$

Interpolating between the closest values in Table 2, we obtain

$j_{(12)}$ in % $a_{\overline{12}|}$

3	d	27 10.4148	1291	1570
		j 10.2857		
		30 10.2578		

$$\frac{d}{3} = \frac{1291}{1570}$$

$$d = \frac{3 \times 1291}{1570} = 2.5$$

The nominal rate is 27.0 + 2.5 = 29.5%

Before buying an item on credit, a person should comparison shop for the total package — merchandise *and* credit. Neither the cash price alone nor the lender's annual percentage rate alone will necessarily indicate which is the best overall proposition. Had merchant A wanted credit terms to sound even better, the "cash" price could have been raised to $115. Now a down payment of $10 and $8.75 a month for 12 months can be advertised as "no charge for credit." The rate is truly zero on the basis of the stated figures.

There is no direct method for solving for *i*. However, you may use a trial-and-error method using various rates on a scientific calculator.

4.13   CHECK THE RATE

Because most students will have to borrow money at least occasionally, it is important to know about the more common sources of credit. In this section we consider consumer loans and installment credit. Large loans for homes and businesses will be discussed in Chapter 6.

The following table gives common rates for various sources of small loans. While this information will be a help in locating the most economical source of credit, the borrower should still check the rate personally, since some lenders vary considerably from the typical values shown.

Source of Credit	Common Rates
Insurance policies	4–12%
Credit unions	9–18%
Commercial banks	6–20%
Automobile finance companies	10–24%
Licensed small loan companies	24–42%
Installment sellers	0–24% and up!
Loan sharks	120–500% and up!

The person who borrows on **life insurance** is in effect getting the use of a personal cash reserve. This practice will be discussed in Chapter 10. Although an insurance policy may be the cheapest source of a small loan, the borrower should remember that the benefits will be reduced by the amount of the loan if the borrower should die.

A **credit union** is really a people's bank. The members of a business, union, church, or other group who have savings put the money on deposit in the credit union and receive interest. Members of the same group who need cash borrow from the credit union. Because operating, investigation, and collection costs are low, a credit union can make small loans at a rate that is usually lower than those charged by commercial sources of credit.

While consumer loan rates charged by **banks** are not high, in terms of modern credit, they are likely to be considerably higher than a good money manager likes to pay.

Automobile finance companies usually charge rates that range from approximately 10 to 24% converted monthly. However, there are a few unethical companies in this field that resort to excessive packing (adding arbitrary amounts to the finance charges), which can make the true interest rate much higher.

Licensed small loan companies charge rates that range from 2 to $3\frac{1}{2}\%$ a *month*. While these rates are high, perhaps unnecessarily so at times, these companies perform a useful service in granting credit to people who could not get a loan from one of the less expensive agencies previously mentioned. Some of these companies advertise how easy it is to get a loan; but borrowers should not forget how hard it is to repay it at the usual rates.

Rates for **installment sales** vary from what is supposed to be zero when there is no charge for credit up to very high rates in other cases. However, if a discount can be obtained for cash, even the "no charge for credit" propositions may actually conceal a high rate of interest based on the *true* cash price.

Loan sharks operate outside the law and will charge whatever they can get away with. Because of their high rates and brutal methods, borrowers should avoid them completely.

We can sum up the wise use of credit by saying that people should pay cash when return on an investment of the same amount would be less than interest on borrowed funds. They should shop for credit if they must borrow, check the true rate of interest, and avoid being swindled by following the rule below:

Read and understand the contract and check financing costs on both a dollar and a percentage basis before signing. Be sure that all blanks are filled in and get a complete copy of the contract.

Exercise 4f

1. The total cost of a used car is $2673.54 cash. The down payment is $873.54. Payments of $70 a month are to be made for 30 months. What is the true annual interest rate converted monthly? Show the answer between the two closest table values.
   $(12–12\frac{1}{2}\%$ converted monthly)

2. A lathe priced at $120 was sold on easy terms for a down payment of $40 and 10 monthly payments of $9. What is the true annual interest rate converted monthly? Show the answer between the two closest table values.

3. If $500 periodic payments per year for 8 years amount to $5000, what is the effective rate of interest?
   (6.28%)

4. Deposits in a building and loan association of $200 at the end of each 6 months for 5 years amounted to $2260. What was the average nominal rate of interest converted semiannually that was earned on this account?

5. A couple saves $200 every 6 months. They made their first deposit in June 1968. If they had $10,000 in their account just after making the deposit in June 1984, what nominal rate of interest converted semiannually did they earn on their savings?
   (4.92%)

6. At the end of each month for 5 years a person put $50 in an investment. If the account then amounted to $4000, what rate of interest converted monthly was earned on the investment?

7. On his 26th birthday Walter Artmeyer put $300 in a savings account. He continues to deposit the same amount every year. If he has $45,000 in his account just after he makes his deposit on his 65th birthday, what average annual rate of return has he earned on his investment?
   (5.86%)

8. A rifle selling for $55 cash can be purchased for $10 down and $10 a month for 5 months. What is the nominal interest rate converted monthly, rounded to the nearest .1%?

9. An electric range lists for $300. Sales tax is 3%. The range may be purchased on time for $25 down and 18 payments of $18.50 a month. What is the nominal interest rate?
(20.8%)

10. A used car is priced at $730. It can be purchased for $64 down and $45 a month for 18 months. What is the nominal rate of interest converted monthly for this time payment plan? Round the answer to the nearest .1%.

11. The cash price of a dishwasher is $360. A buyer can pay $160 down and $12 a month for 24 months. What is the nominal rate converted monthly?
(37.8%)

12. A radio can be purchased for $100 cash. If it is bought on time, the down payment is $10 and the balance is paid in 11 monthly payments of $9 each. Find the nominal interest rate, rounded to .1%.

13. A suite of furniture can be purchased for $431.47 cash, or for $31.47 down and 18 monthly payments of $26 each. What is the nominal rate converted monthly?
(20.5%)

14. A refrigerator lists for $407.47. It can be purchased for $57.47 down and 24 monthly payments of $20 each. What is the nominal rate, rounded to .1%?

15. A gravestone can be purchased for $180 cash, or for $45 down and $7.50 a month for 24 months. What is the nominal rate of interest on the gravestone?
(29.3%)

16. An engagement ring can be purchased for $110. Or it can be obtained with no down payment and monthly payments of $20 at the end of each month for 7 months. Find the nominal rate converted monthly, rounded to .1%.

17. A store advertised a clothes dryer for $300. The ad said that there was no charge for easy terms since the dryer could be purchased for $50 down and $25 a month for 10 months. However, a cash customer could get a 10% discount by asking for it. What nominal rate of interest was actually paid by the installment buyer?
(28.7%)

18. A jewelry store advertised: "No carrying charge for time payments and no down payment." A watch with a price tag of $60 could be

purchased for $5 a month for 12 months. When Muriel Miller asked for a cash discount, she got the watch for $50. Based on the true cash price, what was the nominal interest rate rounded to .1%?

19. A home freezer is listed at $350. If a customer pays $100 down, the balance plus a carrying charge of $20 can be paid in 12 equal monthly payments. If the customer pays cash, a discount of 5% off the list price can be obtained. What is the nominal rate converted monthly if the freezer is bought on time?
(28.6%)

20. A store offers to sell a watch for $60 or for $5 down and $5 a week for 11 weeks. If this same watch can be purchased for $50 cash at another store, what nominal rate of interest is the first store actually charging under their "no carrying charge plan"?

21. A store claims that its credit costs are very low. For example, a $220 washing machine can be bought for $20 down and $17.20 a month for 12 months. Under this plan, the store claims that the buyer is paying only 6% interest. A competitor claims that these carrying charges are low only because the washing machine is over-priced by $15. If this is correct, what nominal interest rate converted monthly is paid by an installment buyer at the first store?
(20.7%)

22. A man borrows $150 from a licensed small loan company and agrees to pay $15.07 a month for 12 months. What is the nominal rate of interest correct to the nearest percent?

23. A woman needs $75 immediately for medical care for one of her children. She gets the money from a small loan company and agrees to pay $9.02 a month for 10 months. What is the nominal rate of interest?
(42%)

24. Shop for some item and obtain the following information:

Item ....
Cash price ....
Tax (if any) ....
Total cost ....
Cash discount (if one is allowed) ....
Down payment ....
Number and size of payments ....
Interest rate as stated by the seller ....

Now compute the nominal rate.

25. You are preparing a report on consumer credit and want to include a table showing true rates corresponding to various stated values. Complete Table 4-1. The given value is from Example 6, page 205.

REVIEW EXERCISES FOR CHAPTER 4

1. A person invests $500 every 3 months in an investment paying 7% converted quarterly. How much will the person have after 10 years?
   ($28,617.07)
2. How much will the person in problem 1 have after 20 years?
3. Suppose that the person in problem 1 pays into the investment for 15 years and then leaves the money to accumulate interest. How much will the investment be worth 5 years after the deposits stop?
   ($74,046.11)
4. A mobile home can be purchased for $1000 down and $200 a month for 3 years. If the interest rate is 12% compounded monthly, find the cash value.
5. A stereo set can be bought for $700 cash or $100 down and $55 a month for a year. If money is worth 8% to the purchaser, which procedure is better and by how much now?
   (Paying cash is better by $32.27 now.)

Table 4-1 True Rates on Loans Repaid in 12 Monthly Payments

If the Charge for Credit per Year Is:	The Quoted Rate Is:	The True Rate per Year Is:	
		For Add-on	For Discount
$4 per $100	4%		
$6 per $100	6%		
$8 per $100	8%		
$10 per $100	10%		19.91%

6. A family wants to save money for a down payment on a summer cottage. If they can invest money at 6% compounded monthly, how much must they invest each month, beginning in one month, to accumulate $10,000 in 5 years?

7. Find the monthly payment on a home loan of $40,000 to be repaid in 20 years if the rate is $12\frac{1}{2}\%$ converted monthly. Also find the total interest paid over the 20 years.
($454.46; $69,070.40)

8. Do problem 7, assuming that the mortgage is to be repaid over 30 years.

9. An automobile is purchased for $4800. The down payment, including the trade-in value of the old car, was worth $1200. The interest is 10% on an add-on basis. The loan is to be repaid in 3 years. Find the nominal interest rate the buyer is paying.
(17.9%)

10. At what interest rate will annual payments of $1000 accumulate to $40,000 in 18 years?

11. How long will it take semiannual investments of $125 to accumulate to at least $2000 at 5% compounded semiannually?
(7 years)

12. To repay a loan of $17,500, a family pays $1000 every 6 months. Find the number of full payments and the size of the concluding payment if the interest rate is 10% converted semiannually.

Chapter 5
Other Annuities Certain

5.1 ANNUITY FUNCTIONS

The amount-of-1-per-period function gives the amount of n periodic deposits of $1 at the time of the last deposit. The symbol for this function is $s_{\overline{n}|}$, and its numerical values are given in the middle column of Table 2 and Table 3. The present-worth-of-1-per-period function gives the present worth of n payments of $1 at a point in time one period before the first payment. The symbol for this function is $a_{\overline{n}|}$, and its numerical values are also given in Table 2 and Table 3.

Ordinary annuities have the payments made at the end of the time periods. The amount of an ordinary annuity is found by simply substituting the value of $s_{\overline{n}|}$ in formula (14), $S_n = Rs_{\overline{n}|}$. The present value of an ordinary annuity is found by substituting the value of $a_{\overline{n}|}$ in formula (15), $A_n = Ra_{\overline{n}|}$.

Now we consider other types of annuities that are evaluated using Table 2. To solve these annuities, we modify or combine the ordinary annuity functions. Since this is a simple matter, publishers of compound interest tables print only numerical values of the ordinary annuity functions.

Before using Table 2 to solve other types of annuities, we should understand exactly what is meant by the tabled values of $s_{\overline{n}|}$ and $a_{\overline{n}|}$. Figure 5-1 shows the points in time at which the ordinary annuity functions give the value of a series of payments.

The value of an annuity may be needed at any point in time from several periods before the first payment to several periods after the last payment. The various possibilities and the corresponding annuity are shown in Figure 5-2.

5.2 ANNUITY DUE

An **annuity due** is one in which the payments are made at the beginning of the payment interval, the first payment being due at once. Insurance premiums and property rentals are examples of annuities due. To find the amount and present value formulas for the annuity due, we modify the formulas already derived for the ordinary annuity so that the ordinary annuity tables can be used with simple modifications.

Figure 5-3 illustrates an annuity due. Note that the diagram starts with a payment and ends one period after the last, or nth, payment.

Figure 5-1

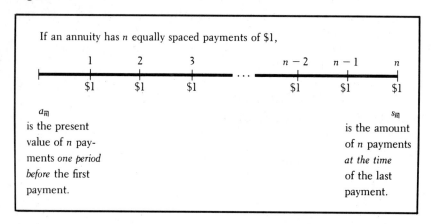

Figure 5-2

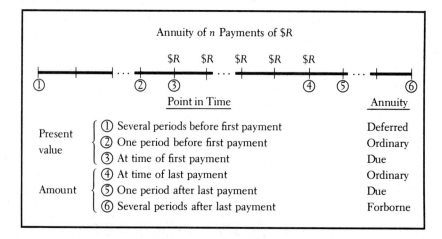

Also included in Figure 5-3 is an illustration of a corresponding ordinary annuity.

Our sketch shows that if we obtain the amount of an ordinary annuity of $n + 1$ payments, we will have the amount of the corresponding annuity due except that we will have included a final payment that is not actually made at the end of the last period of the annuity due. Therefore all we have to do is subtract 1 payment to permit us to use the ordinary annuity tables to get the amount of an annuity due. This procedure leads to the following formula:

$$S_n(\text{due}) = Rs_{\overline{n+1}|} - R$$
$$= R(s_{\overline{n+1}|} - 1)$$
$$= R\left(\frac{(1 + i)^{n+1} - 1}{i} - 1\right)$$
$$= R\,\frac{(1 + i)^{n+1} - (1 + i)}{i}$$
$$= R\,\frac{(1 + i)^n - 1}{i}(1 + i)$$
$$= Rs_{\overline{n}|}(1 + i)$$

$$S_n(\text{due}) = R(s_{\overline{n+1}|} - 1) = Rs_{\overline{n}|}(1 + i) = R\,\frac{(1 + i)^n - 1}{i}(1 + i) \qquad (18)$$

Figure 5-3

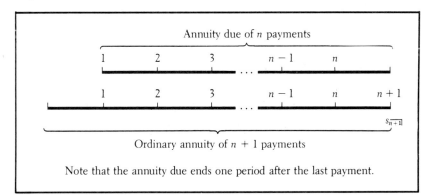

Annuity due of n payments

Ordinary annuity of $n + 1$ payments

Note that the annuity due ends one period after the last payment.

Again we have a factor form of the equation using the factors found in Tables 2 and 3 as well as an exponential form for those using a scientific calculator.

The rather complex appearing quantity that is to be multiplied by R in the first form is quite simple to get. First we add 1 to the number of payments in the annuity due and use the resulting value when we go to the tables. For example, if there are 10 payments, we look up the value for 11 periods. Then we subtract 1 from the factor. For an interest rate of 2% and 11 periods, the factor is 12.1687 (correct to four decimal places). To get the amount of an annuity due of 10 payments, we would use 11.1687 for the factor. All these steps can be done without writing.

To get the present value of an annuity due, we again make a sketch (Figure 5-4) with the corresponding ordinary annuity.

We match the annuity due with an ordinary annuity so that we can get numerical factors from the Compound Interest and Annuity Tables. If we obtain the present value of an ordinary annuity of $n - 1$ payments, we will have the present value of the corresponding annuity due except that we will not have included a payment that is made at the beginning of the term of the annuity due. Therefore all we have to do is add this first payment. This procedure leads to the following formula for the present value of an annuity due:

$$A_n(\text{due}) = Ra_{\overline{n-1}|} + R$$

Figure 5-4

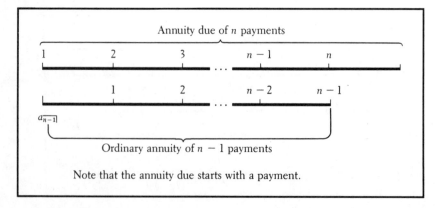

Annuity due of n payments

Ordinary annuity of $n - 1$ payments

Note that the annuity due starts with a payment.

$$= R(a_{n-1|} + 1)$$

$$= R\left(\frac{1 - (1+i)^{-(n-1)}}{i} + 1\right)$$

$$= R\frac{(1+i) - (1+i)^{-(n-1)}}{i}$$

$$= R\frac{1 - (1+i)^{-n}}{i}(1+i)$$

$$= Ra_{\overline{n}|}(1+i)$$

$$A_n \text{(due)} = R(a_{\overline{n-1}|} + 1) = Ra_{\overline{n}|}(1+i) = R\frac{1 - (1+i)^{-n}}{i}(1+i) \quad (19)$$

Again, it is simple to use the ordinary interest tables. First we subtract 1 from the number of payments in the annuity due and use the resulting value when we go to the table. For example, if there are 8 payments in an annuity due, we look up the value for 7. Then we add 1 to the factor. For an interest rate of 6% and 7 periods, the factor is 5.58238. Adding 1 to this factor, we obtain 6.58238 as the present value of an annuity due of 8 payments at a rate of 6%.

EXAMPLE 1 An investment of $200 is made at the beginning of each year for 10 years. If interest is 6% effective, how much will the investment be worth at the end of 10 years?

SOLUTION We use all three forms of formula (18) with $R = 200$, $n = 10$, and $i = 6\%$.

First form: $S_n \text{(due)} = 200(s_{\overline{11}|} - 1) = 200 \times 13.97164 = \$2794.33$

Second form: $S_n \text{(due)} = 200 s_{\overline{10}|}(1.06) = 200 \times 13.18079 \times 1.06$
$= \$2794.33$

Third form: $S_n \text{(due)} = 200\frac{(1.06)^{10} - 1}{.06}(1.06) = \$2794.33$

EXAMPLE 2 A student wants to have $600 for a trip after graduation 4 years from now. How much must she invest at the beginning of each year starting now if she gets 5% compounded annually on her savings?

SOLUTION Substituting in formula (18) and solving for R, we have

$$600 = R(s_{\overline{5}|} - 1) = 4.525631R$$

$$R = \frac{600}{4.525631} = \$132.58$$

ALTERNATE SOLUTION We can check the answer by using an equation of value with the focal date at the time of the last deposit. The 4 payments are brought to the focal date as an ordinary annuity, and the $600 is brought to the focal date by discounting it for 1 period. See Figure 5-5.

$$Rs_{\overline{4}|} = 600(1 + i)^{-1}$$

$$R = 600(1.05)^{-1} \times \frac{1}{s_{\overline{4}|}}$$

$$= 600 \times .952381 \times .232012 = \$132.58$$

This method requires an additional multiplication but no division. We can also work this problem using the second form.

$$600 = Rs_{\overline{4}|}(1.05)$$
$$= R \times 4.310125 \times 1.05$$
$$600 = 4.52563R$$

$$R = \frac{600}{4.52563} = \$132.58$$

EXAMPLE 3 The premium on a life insurance policy is $60 a quarter, payable in advance. Find the cash equivalent of a year's premiums if

Figure 5-5

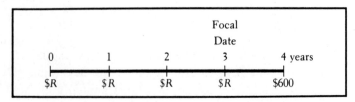

	Focal Date	
0 1 2 3 4 years		
$R $R $R $R $600		

the insurance company charges 6% converted quarterly for the privilege of paying this way instead of all at once for the year.

SOLUTION Substituting $R = 60$, $n = 4$, and $i = 1\frac{1}{2}\%$ into all three forms of formula (19), we have

First form: $A_n(\text{due}) = 60(a_{\overline{3}|} + 1) = 60 \times 3.9122 = \$234.73$

Second form: $A_n(\text{due}) = 60a_{\overline{4}|}(1.015) = 60 \times 3.8544 \times 1.015$
$= \$234.73$

Third form: $A_n(\text{due}) = 60 \dfrac{1 - (1.015)^{-4}}{.015} (1.015) = \$234.73$

Although paying by the quarter is convenient, the savings from paying annually can be substantial.

EXAMPLE 4 The beneficiary of a life insurance policy may take $10,000 cash or 10 equal annual payments, the first to be made immediately. What is the annual payment if money is worth 6%?

SOLUTION Substituting in formula (19) and solving for R, we have

$$10{,}000 = R(a_{\overline{9}|} + 1) = 7.8016923R$$

$$R = \frac{10{,}000}{7.8016923} = \$1281.77$$

ALTERNATE SOLUTION An equation of value with the focal date at the time of the last payment allows us to check our preceding answer. The 10 payments are brought to the focal date as an ordinary annuity, since the focal date is at the time of the last payment. The $10,000 is brought forward 9 (not 10) periods. A time diagram is very helpful in finding the correct values of n in problems like this one. See Figure 5-6.

$$Rs_{\overline{10}|} = 10{,}000 (1.06)^9$$

$$R = 10{,}000 \times (1.06)^9 \times \frac{1}{s_{\overline{10}|}}$$

$$= 10{,}000 \times 1.6894790 \times .0758680 = \$1281.77$$

5.3   OUTSTANDING BALANCE

A common financial problem is determining the outstanding balance on a loan after several payments have been made. The amount of an annuity due provides the easiest way to get the balance one period after a payment.

EXAMPLE 1   A $10,000 loan is to be amortized with payments of $1000 at the end of each year and a final concluding payment. Find the number of full payments and the size of the concluding payment if the rate is 9% converted annually.

SOLUTION   First we substitute in formula (15) for the present value of an ordinary annuity.

$$1000a_{\overline{n}|} = 10,000$$
$$a_{\overline{n}|} = 10$$

When we look for this factor in the "Present worth of 1 per period" column in Table 2, we find that there will be 26 full payments. We draw a time diagram (Figure 5-7) and choose the time of the 27th (and unknown) payment as the focal date.

We get the concluding payment by taking the $10,000 forward as a single sum for 27 years and subtracting the amount of an annuity due of 26 payments.

$$10,000(1.09)^{27} = 10,000 \times 10.2450821 = \$102,450.82$$
$$1000(s_{\overline{26+1}|} - 1) = 1000 \times 101.723134 \quad = \underline{\quad 101,723.13}$$
$$\text{Concluding payment} \quad \$ \qquad 727.69$$

Figure 5-6

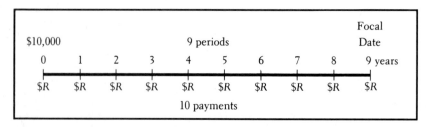

A practice that is sometimes used to take advantage of an unwary borrower is the balloon payment. An item is sold on time for a series of payments that the borrower can meet. At the end there is a much larger payment. If the buyer defaults on the balloon payment, the lender can repossess the merchandise and keep the payments that have been made as well.

EXAMPLE 2 A $2400 used car is sold for $400 down, 17 payments of $100 a month, and an 18th balloon payment. If the interest rate is 24% converted monthly, find the size of the balloon payment.

SOLUTION We draw a time diagram (Figure 5-8), put the focal date at 18 months, and carry everything to the focal date. Since the focal date is one period after the last regular payment, we use formula (18) for the amount of an annuity due.

Figure 5-7

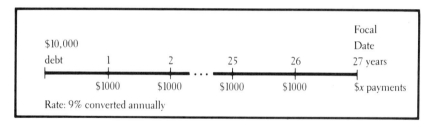

Figure 5-8

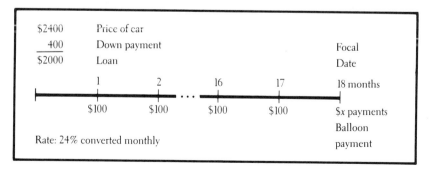

$$2000(1.02)^{18} = 2000 \times 1.428246 = \$2856.49$$
$$100(s_{\overline{17}+\overline{1}|} - 1) = 100 \times 20.41231 = \underline{2041.23}$$
$$\text{Balloon payment} \quad \$815.26$$

Exercise 5a

1. If money is worth 8% converted semiannually, what is the present value of an annuity due of $500 every 6 months for 5 years?
    ($4217.67)

2. At 7% converted monthly, find the present value of an annuity due of $45 every month for 12 years.

3. Find the amount of the annuity in problem 1.
    ($6243.18)

4. Find the amount of the annuity in problem 2.

5. On July 6, 1983, a man deposited $250 in a savings and loan association paying 5% converted semiannually. Interest dates are June 30 and December 31, and deposits made by the 10th of the month can earn interest for the entire month. The man continues to make deposits of $250 every 6 months up to and including January 4, 1989, when he makes his last deposit. How much will be in his account after interest is credited on June 30, 1989?
    ($3535.11)

6. On June 1, 1985, a woman deposited $200 in a savings and loan association that pays 5% converted semiannually. She continues to make $200 deposits every 6 months. If she makes her last deposit on December 1, 1991, how much will be in her account on June 1, 1992? Interest dates are May 31 and November 30. Deposits made by the 10th of any month earn interest for the entire month.

7. A couple expects to need $4000 in June 1989. In June 1985 they made the first of 4 equal annual deposits in an investment paying 6%. What is the size of each deposit needed to accumulate the $4000?
    ($862.61)

8. A debt of $7500 is due in 10 years. The debtor agrees to settle the debt with 10 equal annual payments, the first payment to be made now. Find the size of the payments if money is worth 8%.

9.   The premium on a life insurance policy is $15 a month payable in advance. A policyholder may pay a year's premium in advance. Find the annual premium if it is based on 6% converted monthly.

($175.16)

10.   A life insurance policy has premiums at the beginning of each month of $25. Find the equivalent annual premium at the beginning of each year if it is based on 9% converted monthly.

11.   The annual premium on a life insurance policy is $250 payable in advance. Payments may be made quarterly in advance, in which case the insurance company charges interest at 6% compounded quarterly. Find the size of the quarterly payment.

($63.90)

12.   The annual premium on a life insurance policy is $185 payable in advance. What would be the monthly premium based on 6% converted monthly?

13.   A person has $5000 in a building and loan association that pays 6% compounded semiannually. If $500 is withdrawn at the beginning of each half year, how many withdrawals can be made? What will be the size of the concluding withdrawal?

(Eleven $500 withdrawals and a 12th withdrawal of $325.15)

14.   In problem 13, how many $250 withdrawals could be made and what would be the size of the concluding withdrawal?

15.   Instead of taking $5000 from an inheritance, a person decides to take 60 monthly payments with the first payment to be made immediately. If interest is allowed at 6% converted monthly, what will be the size of each payment?

($96.18)

16.   Instead of taking $20,000 cash from an inheritance, the heir elects to receive quarterly payments for 10 years with the first payment to be made right away. If the money is invested at 7% converted quarterly, what will be the size of each payment?

17.   A man wants to take out enough life insurance to provide 120 monthly payments of at least $150 each to his family. If the first payment is to be made upon proof of the man's death, what size policy should he take out? Round the answer to the next higher $1000. The insurance company pays 6% converted monthly on the money left with them.

($14,000)

18.   A woman is planning an insurance program that will pay 180 payments certain of $200 to her widower. The insurance com-

pany will pay 6% converted monthly on money left with them. If the first payment is to be made on proof of the woman's death, she should take out what size policy? Answer to the next higher $1000.

19.   A store can be rented for $300 a month payable in advance. If the renter pays 3 months in advance, the owner will allow interest at 7% converted monthly. What is the size of the payment at the beginning of each 3 months that is equivalent to $300 at the beginning of each month?
($894.79)

20.   A store can be rented for $350 a month payable in advance. The landlord will accept a single cash payment at the beginning of a year for a year's lease if interest is computed at 6% converted monthly. What would be the cost of a year's lease?

21.   A man knows that if he dies his wife will not get any social security benefits until she reaches age 60. He has several insurance policies. One for $100,000 is to be used to provide monthly income for her between the time he dies and the time she reaches age 60. She is 53 at the time he dies, and she elects to get 84 equal monthly payments from this policy, with the first payment to be made immediately. What will be the size of each payment if 6% converted monthly is paid on the proceeds of the policy?
($1453.59)

22.   The widow in problem 21 decides to wait until age 62 to start receiving social security payments so that they will be larger. She elects to get 108 equal monthly payments from the $100,000 policy, with the first payment to be made immediately. Find the size of the payments.

23.   On June 1, 1985, a couple opened a savings account for their daughter with a deposit of $250 in a bank paying 5% converted semiannually. If they continue to make semiannual deposits of $250 until December 1, 1992, when they plan to make the last deposit, how much will be in the account on June 1, 1993?
($4966.18)

24.(C) A woman invests $300 every year, making her first deposit on August 1, 1985, and her last deposit on August 1, 1995. How much will be in her account on August 1, 1996, if she gets interest at $5\frac{1}{2}$% compounded annually?

25.(C) A man aged 25 is considering two types of life insurance policies. The first is an ordinary life with an annual premium of

$200. The second is a 20-year endowment with an annual premium of $510. He decides to take the ordinary life and to deposit the difference in premiums each year into an investment paying $5\frac{1}{2}\%$ compounded annually. He dies just before making his 17th deposit but after receiving interest for the first 16 deposits. How much was in the account at that time?
($8058.88)

26.   A woman aged 30 is considering two $15,000 insurance policies. The first is an ordinary life with an annual premium of $277. The second is a 20-payment life with an annual premium of $410. She decides to take the ordinary life and put the difference in premiums in an investment paying 5%. How much will her family get from the investment if she dies after interest is earned on the 15th deposit, but before the 16th deposit is made?

27.   A factory owner has fire insurance for which the annual premium is $300 payable in advance. If interest is 6% converted annually, what would be the equivalent single premium that would provide insurance for 5 years?
($1339.53)

28.   A homeowner has been paying insurance at the beginning of each year. The annual premium is $60. At 8% converted annually, what would be the equivalent premium for a 3-year policy?

29.   A $2200 used car is sold for $200 down, 23 payments of $80 a month, and a 24th balloon payment. If the interest rate is 18% converted monthly, what is the size of the balloon payment?
($648.33)

30.   Find the size of the balloon payment in problem 29 if the rate is 21% converted monthly.

5.4   DEFERRED ANNUITY

A **deferred annuity** is one in which the first payment is made not at the beginning or end of the first period, but at some later date. When the first payment is made at the end of 10 periods, the annuity is said to be deferred 9 periods. Similarly, an annuity that is deferred for 12 periods will have the first payment at the end of 13 periods. It is important to understand that *the interval of deferment ends 1 period before the first payment.* In practice attention must be given to this point because in some problems the interval of deferment is given, in others the time of the first payment. When the time of the first payment is given, you must determine the interval of deferment before substituting in the present value formula. For example, if payments are made quarterly and the first payment is made in 4 years, the interval of deferment is 15 periods.

Figure 5-9 shows a deferred annuity of n payments that is deferred for m periods.

To obtain a formula for the present value of a deferred annuity, we begin by assuming that a payment is made at the end of each period during the interval of deferment. If this were the case, we would have an ordinary annuity of $m + n$ payments and the present value would be $Ra_{\overline{m+n}|}$. This value, of course, is too large because it includes the assumed payments during the interval of deferment. These assumed payments also form an ordinary annuity, and their present value is $Ra_{\overline{m}|}$. Therefore, to get the present value of a deferred annuity, all we have to do is subtract the present value of the m assumed payments from the present vaue of the $m + n$ payments.

$$A_n(\text{def}) = Ra_{\overline{m+n}|} - Ra_{\overline{m}|}$$

$$= R(a_{\overline{m+n}|} - a_{\overline{m}|})$$

$$= R\left[\frac{1 - (1+i)^{-(m+n)}}{i} - \frac{1 - (1+i)^{-m}}{i}\right]$$

$$= R\,\frac{(1+i)^{-m} - (1+i)^{-(m+n)}}{i}$$

Figure 5-9

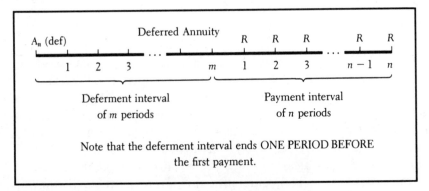

Deferred Annuity

A_n (def)   R R R   R R

1   2   3 m 1   2   3 $n-1$ n

Deferment interval
of m periods

Payment interval
of n periods

Note that the deferment interval ends ONE PERIOD BEFORE
the first payment.

$$= R \frac{1 - (1 + i)^{-n}}{i} (1 + i)^{-m}$$

$$= R a_{\overline{n}|} (1 + i)^{-m}$$

$$A_n(\text{def}) = R(a_{\overline{m+n}|} - a_{\overline{m}|}) = R a_{\overline{n}|} (1 + i)^{-m}$$

$$= R \frac{(1 + i)^{-m} - (1 + i)^{-(m+n)}}{i} \qquad (20)$$

To get the present value of a deferred annuity, from the first form we look up $a_{\overline{m+n}|}$ and $a_{\overline{m}|}$ in the "Present worth of 1 per period" column of Table 2, subtract the smaller value from the larger, and multiply this difference by the periodic payment.

The present value of a deferred annuity can also be obtained by using formula (15) for the present value of an ordinary annuity to get the value of the payments 1 period before the first payment is made. Then this equivalent single sum can be discounted for the m periods in the interval of deferment, and we have

$$A_n(\text{def}) = R a_{\overline{n}|} (1 + i)^{-m}$$

This form of the deferred annuity formula is useful when logarithms are used, and also makes it possible to obtain R without dividing. We can use Table 3 to get the present value of the deferred annuity using the second form and the fact that $(1 + i)^{-m} = 1/(1 + i)^m$. You can use the last form if you have access to a scientific calculator.

EXAMPLE 1 Find the present value of a deferred annuity of $500 a year for 10 years that is deferred 5 years. Money is worth 6%.

SOLUTION We solve using all three forms, substituting $n = 10$, $m = 5$, $R = 500$, and $i = 6\%$.

First form: $A_{10}(\text{def})$ $= 500(a_{\overline{15}|} - a_{\overline{5}|})$
$= 500(9.71225 - 4.21236)$
$= 500 \times 5.49989$
$= \$2749.95$

Second form: $A_{10}(\text{def}) = 500 a_{\overline{10}|}(1.06)^{-5}$
$= 500 \times 7.36009 \times .74726$
$= \$2749.95$

Third form: $A_{10}(\text{def}) = 500 \dfrac{(1.06)^{-5} - (1.06)^{-15}}{.06}$

$$= \$2749.94$$

The 1-cent difference is due to rounding.

EXAMPLE 2 Find the present value of an annuity of \$50 every 3 months for 5 years if the first payment is made in 3 years. Money is worth 5% converted quarterly.

SOLUTION Here $n = 20$ and $i = 1\frac{1}{4}\%$. To find the interval of deferment, we drop back one period from the first payment, so $m = 11$.

$$A_{20}(\text{def}) = 50(a_{\overline{11+20}|} - a_{\overline{11}|})$$
$$= 50(25.5693 - 10.2178) = \$767.58$$

EXAMPLE 3 A woman inherits \$20,000. Instead of taking the cash, she invests the money at 8% converted quarterly with the understanding that she will receive 20 equal quarterly payments with the first payment to be made in 5 years. Find the size of the payments.

SOLUTION The interval of deferment is 19 periods, the present value of the annuity is \$20,000, and i is 2%. Substituting in formula (20), we have

$$20,000 = R(a_{\overline{19+20}|} - a_{\overline{19}|})$$
$$= R(26.9025888 - 15.6784620)$$
$$= 11.2241268R$$
$$R = \dfrac{20,000}{11.2241268}$$
$$= \$1781.88$$

ALTERNATE SOLUTION Using the alternate solution for deferred annuities, we find that

$$20,000 = Ra_{\overline{20}|}(1.02)^{-19}$$
$$R = 20,000 \times 1.4568112 \times .0611567$$
$$= \$1781.88$$

Exercise 5b

1. Find the present value of a deferred annuity of $500 a year for 6 years that is deferred 5 years if money is worth 6%.
    ($1837.26)
2. Find the present value of a deferred annuity of $250 every 6 months for 4 years that is deferred 5 years and 6 months if the rate is 6% converted semiannually.
3. Find the value on September 1, 1988, of a series of $80 monthly payments, the first of which will be made on September 1, 1992, and the last on December 1, 1994, if money is worth 6% compounded monthly.
    ($1649.63)
4. Find the value on June 1, 1988, of a series of payments of $425 every 6 months if the first of these payments is to be made on December 1, 1991, and the last on June 1, 1998. Use an interest rate of 5% compounded semiannually.
5. What sum put aside on a boy's 12th birthday will provide 4 annual payments of $2000 for college expenses if the first payment is to be made on his 18th birthday? The rate is 7% compounded annually.
    ($4830.07)
6. What sum of money should be set aside today to provide an income of $150 a month for a period of 5 years if the first payment is to be made 4 years hence and money is worth 6% compounded monthly?
7. A child aged 12 wins $8000 on a quiz program. This amount is placed in a trust fund earning 8% converted annually. If she takes the money in 4 equal annual payments with the first payment to be made 6 years later, what would be the size of each payment?
    ($3548.97)
8. Under the terms of a will, a child will receive $12,000 on his 18th birthday. He will get $2000 of this amount in cash, and the remainder will be set aside to provide a monthly income from his 21st to his 25th birthday inclusive ($n = 49$). If the money is invested at 7% compounded monthly, what will be the size of the monthly payments?
9.(C) On his wife's 59th birthday, Mr. Jones makes provision for her to receive $1500 a month for 5 years with the first payment to

be made on her 65th birthday. If the investment earns $7\frac{1}{2}\%$ converted monthly, how much money must be set aside?
($48,097.18)

10. On his 57th birthday a man wants to set aside enough money to provide an income of $1000 a month for 10 years with the first payment to be made on his 60th birthday. If he gets 6% compounded monthly on his money, how much will this pension plan cost on his 57th birthday?

11. On June 1, 1985, a woman deposited $3000 in an investment paying 5% compounded annually. On June 1, 1991, she makes the first of 4 equal annual withdrawals from the account. Find the size of the withdrawals if the account is closed with the last of these withdrawals.
($1079.78)

12. If the account in problem 11 had earned 6% interest, what would be the size of the annual withdrawal?

13. A philanthropist gave a college $20,000 on September 1, 1976, with the provision that the money be used to provide annual scholarships of $4000. The first scholarship is to be awarded on the September 1 following the death of the donor. The money is invested at 7%. If the donor dies on June 18, 1991, how many full scholarships can be awarded?
(34)

14.(C) A widower decides to take the $10,000 proceeds from an insurance policy in payments of $200 a month with the first payment to be made in 5 years. How many full payments will he receive if the insurance company allows 6% converted monthly on money left with them?

15. On June 1, 1985, a minor received an inheritance of $6500. This money was placed in a trust fund earning 7% compounded semiannually. On December 1, 1990 the child will reach age 18 and be paid the first of 8 equal semiannual payments from the fund. How much will each payment be?
($1333.86)

16.(C) A school receives $40,000 in 1986 to be used to provide annual scholarships of $7500, with the first to be awarded in 1992. If the money is invested at 10%, how many full scholarships can be awarded? How much will be left in the fund to apply to a partial scholarship 1 year after the last full scholarship is awarded?

5.5 FORBORNE ANNUITY

A **forborne annuity** earns interest for two or more periods after the last payment. Figure 5-10 shows a forborne annuity of n payments followed by p periods during which interest is earned but no payments are made.

To obtain the formula for the amount of a forborne annuity, we begin by assuming a fictitious payment at the end of each period after the last regular payment. Now we have an ordinary annuity of $n + p$ payments and an amount of $Rs_{\overline{n+p}|}$. This result is too large by the amount of the fictitious payments. These assumed payments also form an ordinary annuity, and their amount is $Rs_{\overline{p}|}$. To get the amount of a forborne annuity, we subtract the amount of the p assumed payments from the amount of the $n + p$ payments, which yields

$$
\begin{aligned}
S_n(\text{for}) &= Rs_{\overline{n+p}|} - Rs_{\overline{p}|} \\
&= R(s_{\overline{n+p}|} - s_{\overline{p}|}) \\
&= R\left(\frac{(1+i)^{n+p} - 1}{i} - \frac{(1+i)^p - 1}{i}\right) \\
&= R\,\frac{(1+i)^{n+p} - (1+i)^p}{i} \\
&= R\,\frac{(1+i)^n - 1}{i}(1+i)^p \\
&= Rs_{\overline{n}|}(1+i)^p
\end{aligned}
$$

Figure 5-10

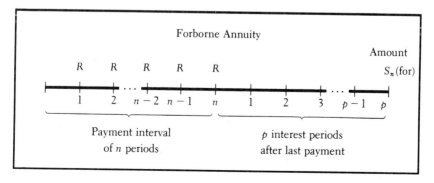

Forborne Annuity

Amount $S_n(\text{for})$

Payment interval of n periods

p interest periods after last payment

$$S_n(\text{for}) = R(s_{\overline{n+p}|} - s_{\overline{p}|}) = Rs_{\overline{n}|}(1+i)^p$$

$$= R\frac{(1+i)^{n+p} - (1+i)^p}{i} \tag{21}$$

As in the earlier cases of annuities, we have three forms of the equation for the amount of a forborne annuity. The most convenient form to use in any one problem depends on the nature of the problem and the tools to be used in its solution.

EXAMPLE 1 Payments of $1000 are made semiannually for 10 years to an account paying 7% compounded semiannually. Find the value of this annuity 5 years after the last payment.

SOLUTION We solve this example with all three forms. Substitute $R = 1000$, $n = 20$, $p = 10$, and $i = 3\frac{1}{2}\%$ into formula (21):

First form: $S_{20}(\text{for}) = 1000(s_{\overline{30}|} - s_{\overline{10}|})$
$= 1000(51.622677 - 11.731393)$
$= 1000 \times 39.891284$
$= \$39{,}891.28$

Second form: $S_{20}(\text{for}) = 1000s_{\overline{20}|}(1.035)^{10}$
$= 1000 \times 28.279682 \times 1.410599$
$= \$39{,}891.29$

Third form: $S_{20}(\text{for}) = 1000\dfrac{(1.035)^{30} - (1.035)^{10}}{.035} = \$39{,}891.28$

The 1-cent difference in answers is due to rounding.

EXAMPLE 2 A savings and loan association pays 6% converted quarterly on passbook accounts. Interest dates are March 31, June 30, September 30, and December 31. On September 30, 1981, a person opened an account with a deposit of $500. Every 3 months $200 was added to the account. The last $200 deposit was made on March 31, 1984. The money was then left to accumulate interest until the account is closed on December 31, 1986. Find the accumulated amount on that date.

SOLUTION A time diagram (Figure 5-11) is drawn to help determine the number of payments and interest periods.

The $500 is carried forward as a single sum from September 1981 to December 1986. The number of periods is found from:

Year	Month
1986	12
1981	9
5	3

$$n = (5 \times 4) + (3/3) = 21$$

The number of $200 payments is the same as the number of periods from September 1981 to March 1984.

Year	Month
3	15
198̸4̸	̸3̸
1981	9
2	6

$$n = (2 \times 4) + (6/3) = 10$$

Now we get the number of periods after the last payment.

Year	Month
1986	12
1984	3
2	9

$$p = (2 \times 4) + (9/3) = 11$$

Figure 5-11

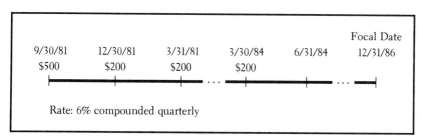

				Focal Date
9/30/81	12/30/81	3/31/81	3/30/84	6/31/84	12/31/86
$500	$200	$200	$200		

Rate: 6% compounded quarterly

We use formula (9) to get the amount of the $500 and formula (21) to get the amount of the forborne annuity.

$$500(1.015)^{21} = 500 \times 1.36706 = \$\ 683.53$$
$$200(s_{\overline{21}|} - s_{\overline{11}|}) = 200(24.47052 - 11.86326) = \underline{\quad 2521.45}$$
$$\text{Total on December 31, 1986}\quad \$3204.98$$

EXAMPLE 3 How much must be invested each year at 8% effective with the first payment in 1981 and the last in 1990 in order to be worth $100,000 in the year 2000?

SOLUTION Substituting in the first form of formula (21) with $n = 10$, $p = 10$, and $i = .08$, we have

$$100,000 = R(s_{\overline{20}|} - s_{\overline{10}|})$$
$$= R(45.76196430 - 14.48656247)$$
$$= 31.27540183R$$

$$R = \frac{100,000}{31.27540183} = \$3197.40$$

ALTERNATE SOLUTION We can also use the second form of formula (21):

$$100,000 = Rs_{\overline{10}|}(1.08)^{10}$$

$$R = \frac{100,000}{(2.15892500 \times 14.48656247)}$$

$$= \$3197.40$$

Exercise 5c

1. A bank pays 6% converted quarterly on passbook accounts. Interest dates are January 31, April 30, July 31, and October 31. Deposits by the first of the month earn interest for the entire month. On May 1, 1986, a man opens an account with a deposit of $100. He continues to make $100 deposits every 3 months until August 1, 1988, when he makes his last deposit. Find the amount in his account on November 1, 1990.
($1223.74)

2.(C)   What would be the amount in problem 1 if the rate is $5\frac{1}{2}\%$ converted quarterly?

3.   A teacher arranges a home loan on which she pays $300 a month during the 9 months, September to May inclusive, when she is paid by her school. The rate on the loan is 10% converted monthly. Because of sickness one year she is unable to make the March, April, and May payments. The lender allows her to defer these payments until September, provided that then she makes a payment that will bring the loan balance up to date if the payments had been made on time. Find the total payment to be made in September, including the September payment.
        ($1238.15)

4.   What would be the amount in problem 3 if the borrower misses only the April and May payments?

5.(C)   A saver wants to have $2000 in an account on December 31, 1990. The plan is to make 4 equal deposits in an account paying $5\frac{1}{2}\%$ converted quarterly with interest payable on March 31, June 30, September 30, and December 31. If the deposits are made on the four interest dates in 1989, what will the size of the deposits be?
        ($463.77)

6.   Find the size of the deposits in problem 5 if the rate is 6% converted quarterly.

7.   A professional athlete wants to provide for her retirement. She deposits $50,000 each year with the first deposit at age 21 and the last at age 35. Find the amount in the account when she reaches age 65 if the interest is 9% effective.
        ($19,477,559.80)

8.(C)   Find the amount in problem 7 if the rate is 10%.

5.6 SUMMARY OF ORDINARY, DUE, AND DEFERRED ANNUITIES

The most effective way for students to solve an annuity problem is to make a sketch, determine at what point in time they want the value of the annuity, and then substitute in the proper formula. This procedure is much better than just reading a problem and then trying to "type" it. Students should recognize that the same series of payments might be treated as one type of annuity at one time and another type at another time. For example, if we want the value of a series of payments one period before the first payment, we would use the present value formula for an ordinary annuity. But if we want the value of the same series of payments one period after the last payment, we would use the amount formula for an annuity due. By comparing your sketches with Figure 5-12, you can eliminate guesswork in solving annuity problems.

The focal date approach is very useful for annuity problems. You should, of course, select a focal date that will minimize computations. Good judgment in choosing a focal date will come from observation and experience. You should also note that even complicated problems can usually be broken down into simple parts. Too often students try to take a word problem of several sentences and immediately set up an equation that will give the final answer. Do one part at a time. Every problem can be broken down into single payments and annuities that can be moved to any point in time. Then you can set up an equation of value.

In this and the preceding chapter we have discussed the common types of annuities certain. All these annuities have one thing in common — a series of equal payments that are equally spaced. The various formulas that were derived were for convenience in calculating the value of the annuity at different times with a minimum of work. Figure 5-12 shows how the formulas we now have enable us to find the value of an annuity at any time.

① To get the value two or more periods before the first payment, use the present value formula for a deferred annuity:

Figure 5-12

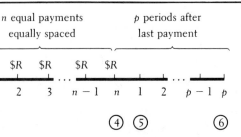

$$A_n(\text{def}) = R(a_{\overline{m+n}|} - a_{\overline{m}|}) = Ra_{\overline{n}|}(1+i)^{-m}$$

$$= R\,\frac{(1+i)^{-m} - (1+i)^{-(m+n)}}{i} \qquad \textbf{(20)}\ \text{page 229}$$

②To get the value one period before the first payment, use the present value formula for an ordinary annuity:

$$A_n = Ra_{\overline{n}|} = R\,\frac{1 - (1+i)^{-n}}{i} = R\,\frac{1 - v^n}{i} \qquad \textbf{(15)}\ \text{page 173}$$

③To get the value at the time the first payment is made, use the present value formula for any annuity due:

$$A_n(\text{due}) = R(a_{\overline{n-1}|} + 1) = Ra_{\overline{n}|}(1+i)$$

$$= R\,\frac{1 - (1+i)^{-n}}{i}\,(1+i) \qquad \textbf{(19)}\ \text{page 219}$$

④To get the value at the time the last payment is made, use the amount formula for an ordinary annuity:

$$S_n = Rs_{\overline{n}|} = R\,\frac{(1+i)^n - 1}{i} \qquad \textbf{(14)}\ \text{page 168}$$

⑤To get the value one period after the last payment, use the amount formula for an annuity due:

$$S_n(\text{due}) = R(s_{\overline{n+1}|} - 1) = Rs_{\overline{n}|}(1+i)$$

$$= R\,\frac{(1+i)^n - 1}{i}\,(1+i) \qquad \textbf{(18)}\ \text{page 218}$$

⑥To get the amount two or more periods after the last payment, use the amount formula for a forborne annuity:

$$S_n(\text{for}) = R(s_{\overline{n+p}|} - s_{\overline{p}|}) = Rs_{\overline{n}|}(1+i)^p$$

$$= R\,\frac{(1+i)^{n+p} - (1+i)^p}{i} \qquad \textbf{(21)}\ \text{page 234}$$

Let us work an example to show how a step-by-step approach using focal dates can solve a problem that at first seems quite difficult.

EXAMPLE A person deposits $2000 today at 6% interest. One year from now the first of 19 annual deposits of $100 each is made in a fund paying 5%. Twenty years from now both of the investments are drawn out, $100 is added to their sum, and an annuity of $200 a month is purchased. The first payment is to be made 1 month after the purchase of the annuity. The purchaser gets 6% converted monthly on the annuity. How many $200 payments are received? What is the size of the concluding payment 1 month after the last full payment?

SOLUTION First we make a sketch of the deposits (Figure 5-13) and find how much the person has when the annuity is purchased 20 years hence.

We put the focal date at 20 years and carry everything to that point. In other words, we allow 6% compound interest on the $2000, get the amount of an annuity due of 19 payments at 5%, and add $100.

$$2000(1.06)^{20} = 2000 \times 3.207135 = \$6414.27$$
$$100(s_{\overline{20}|5\%} - 1) = 100 \times 32.06595 = 3206.60$$
$$\text{Final cash payment} = \underline{100.00}$$
$$\$9720.87$$

This $9720.87 now becomes the present value of an ordinary annuity of $200 per month. Note that the same sum of money may be an amount at one stage of a problem and a present value at another. Using formula (15), the present value formula for an ordinary annuity, we have

$$9720.87 = 200a_{\overline{n}|½\%}$$
$$a_{\overline{n}|½\%} = 48.60435$$

Figure 5-13

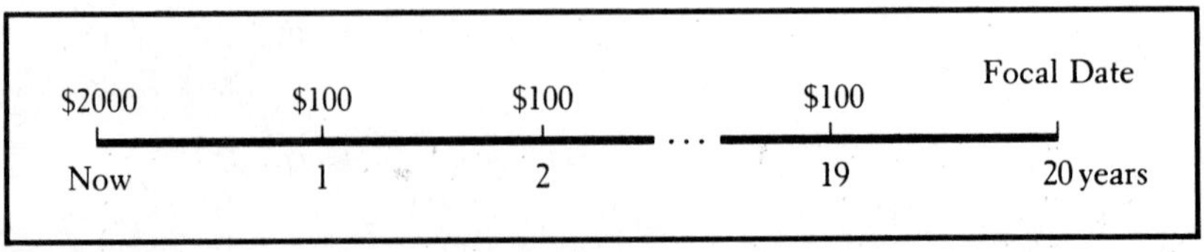

Reference to the "Present worth of 1 per period" column of Table 2 shows that there will be 55 full payments and a smaller 56th payment. To get the size of the concluding payment, we take $9720.87 forward 55 periods and obtain the amount of an annuity of $200 a month for 55 months. Then we allow simple interest on the difference for 1 month.

$$9720.87(1.005)^{55} = 9720.87 \times 1.315629 = \$12,789.06$$
$$200s_{\overline{55}|½\%} = 200 \times 63.12577 = \underline{\;12,625.15}$$
$$163.91$$
$$\text{Interest on } \$163.91 \text{ for 1 month} = \underline{\qquad .82}$$
$$\$\quad 164.73$$

Thus the purchaser will receive 55 payments of $200 and a 56th payment of $164.73.

ALTERNATE SOLUTION   To show how the last part of the problem can be solved in more than one way, we could get the 56th payment by putting a focal date at this point and bringing the 55 payments forward as an annuity due. See Figure 5-14.
Then we would have

$$x = 9720.87(1.005)^{56} - 200(s_{\overline{56}|} - 1)$$
$$= 9720.87(1.322207) - 200(63.44140)$$
$$= 12853.00 - 12688.28$$
$$= \$164.72$$

The 1-cent difference in answers is due to rounding.

Figure 5-14

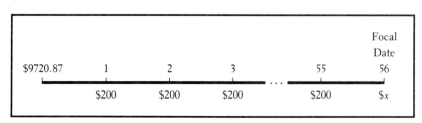

5.7   PERPETUITIES

In some investments only the interest is used and the principal is kept intact. For example, a philanthropist who wants to provide an annual scholarship of $1000 indefinitely must give as an endowment enough money to earn $1000 interest every year. When it is assumed that the regular payments will go on forever, the annuity is called a **perpetuity**. Other examples of perpetuities are dividends on noncallable preferred stock (provided that all dividends are paid), interest on perpetual bonds, and the endowment funds of endowed institutions such as libraries, museums, and so on, that are established with a sum of money that is supposed to maintain them "in perpetuity."

In practice, all perpetuities must end sometime, but the *forever assumption* still underlies the mathematical treatment of perpetuities. Of course, it is impossible to determine the accumulated amount of a perpetuity. Finding the present value is both possible and easy. First we consider the case in which the interest period coincides with the payment period.

To calculate the present value of a perpetual scholarship of $1000 a year, we have to know what rate of interest can be expected on the endowment. Suppose that the school can expect a return of 10%. Then the philanthropist would have to give $10,000 because it takes this amount to earn $1000 interest each year at 10%. As long as only the interest is used and the endowment earns 10%, the $1000 scholarships can be awarded indefinitely. In general terms we can say that

$$A_\infty i = R$$

$$A_\infty = \frac{R}{i} \tag{22}$$

The subscript ∞ is the mathematical symbol of **infinity**. In this case A_∞ denotes the present value of a series of payments that continue indefinitely. The size of each payment is R and the rate per period is i.

Now suppose that instead of using the interest as it is earned, we let it accumulate for more than one period. We use the letter n to indicate the number of conversion periods that elapse before the interest is drawn off, leaving the original principal intact. See Figure 5-15. Letting the present value of this perpetuity accumulate for n periods, we have an amount expressed as

$$A_\infty (1 + i)^n$$

Now we subtract the periodic payment and again have the original present value,

$$A_\infty (1 + i)^n - R = A_\infty$$

To solve the preceding formula for A_∞, we proceed as follows:

$$A_\infty (1 + i)^n - A_\infty = R$$
$$A_\infty [(1 + i)^n - 1] = R$$

$$A_\infty = \frac{R}{(1 + i)^n - 1}$$

Multiplying numerator and denominator by i and rearranging, we have

$$A_\infty = \frac{R}{i} \times \frac{i}{(1 + i)^n - 1}$$

Since

$$\frac{i}{(1 + i)^n - 1} = \frac{1}{s_{\overline{n}|}}$$

this expression can be simplified as follows:

Figure 5-15

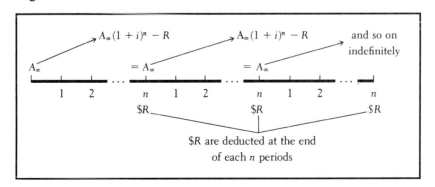

$$A_\infty = \frac{R}{i} \times \frac{1}{s_{\overline{n}|}} = \frac{R}{(1+i)^n - 1} \tag{23}$$

Now we can solve this type of perpetuity with a minimum of work because the factor $1/s_{\overline{n}|}$ can be obtained from the "Sinking fund" column in Table 2.

EXAMPLE 1 An alumnus wants to provide a perpetual yearly scholarship of $1200 with the first scholarship to be given in 1 year. If the money can be invested at 6%, how large must the grant be?

SOLUTION This situation represents the first type of perpetuity. Substituting in formula (22), we have

$$A_\infty = \frac{1200}{.06} = \$20,000$$

EXAMPLE 2 If the money in Example 1 could be invested at 6% converted semiannually, how large a grant would be needed?

SOLUTION Here we must use formula (23), the second perpetuity formula, because interest is converted twice a year although it is used only once a year.

$$A_\infty = \frac{1200}{.03} \times \frac{1}{s_{\overline{2}| 3\%}}$$

$$= \frac{1200}{.03} \times .4926108 = \$19,704.43$$

Just how this initial grant provides the $1200 annual scholarships is interesting to see.

Initial grant	$19,704.43
3% interest for 6 months	591.13
	20,295.56
3% interest for 6 months	608.87
	20,904.43
Scholarship deducted	1,200.00
	$19,704.43

Thus the school can continue to provide $1200 scholarships annually as long as it continues to get 6% converted semiannually on the grant of $19,704.43.

ALTERNATE SOLUTION We can also solve this example using the second form of formula (23):

$$A_\infty = \frac{1200}{(1.03)^2 - 1} = \frac{1200}{.0609} = \$19,704.43$$

Even at today's high interest rates, a very large endowment is needed to earn much of an income on a perpetual basis. Hence an organization such as a private school that does not have enough income from tuition to meet expenses must conduct fund-raising campaigns from time to time to provide funds for operation and expansion.

EXAMPLE 3 Find the nominal rate of return on a 4%, $100 preferred stock with dividends payable quarterly if the stock is selling at $105.

SOLUTION In this problem the stock will pay 1% every 3 months on $100. Thus the person who gets the stock will obtain a perpetuity of $1 every 3 months regardless of what the buyer pays for the stock. However, the rate of return on the investment will depend on the purchase price. The purchase price becomes the present value of the perpetuity and the $1 dividends are the periodic payments. Solving formula (22) for i, we have

$$i = \frac{R}{A_\infty} = \frac{1.00}{105} = .0095 = .95\%$$

The nominal rate is $4 \times .95 = 3.8\%$.

If the stock had been purchased for less than $100, the rate of return would be more than 4%.

EXAMPLE 4 How much must an alumnus give a college to provide an annual scholarship of $500 for an indefinitely long period if the endowment can be invested at 8% and if the first scholarship will be provided: (a) 1 year from now? (b) immediately? (c) 5 years from now?

SOLUTION   (a) If the first scholarship is to be awarded in 1 year, we use formula (22) to get the required grant.

$$A_\infty = \frac{500}{.08} = \$6250$$

(b) If the first scholarship is to be awarded immediately, the grant is the sum of the preceding perpetuity and $500, or $6750.

(c) If the first scholarship is to be awarded in 5 years, the fund will have to contain $6250 in 4 years. At that time it begins to function as a perpetuity and will earn $500 a year interest from then on. The next question we consider is: What sum will amount to $6250 in 4 years at 8%? The answer can be obtained from formula (11).

$$P = 6250(1.08)^{-4} = 6250 \times .735030 = \$4593.94$$

In such problems we advise the use of a time diagram to avoid errors in determining the various times involved. A sketch like Figure 5-16 shows each point in time and the corresponding dollar value of the endowment.

Exercise 5d

1.   Payments of $1000 are made every 6 months, with the first occurring on February 15, 1986, and the last on August 15, 1990. Find the value of this annuity to an account paying 7%

Figure 5-16

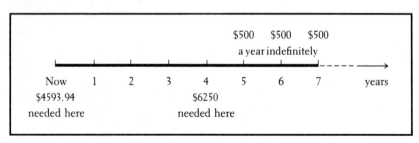

compounded semiannually on: (a) February 15, 1977; (b) August 15, 1985; and (c) February 15, 1986.

[(a) $4634.04; (b) $8316.61; (c) $8607.69]

2. Find the value of the annuity in problem 1 on: (a) August 15, 1990; (b) February 15, 1991; and (c) August 15, 2000.

3. A man wants to provide $1000 every 6 months indefinitely for the support of an orphanage. If the first payment is to be made in 6 months and the fund draws interest at 5% converted semiannually, what size endowment will be needed?

($40,000)

4. What is the present value of a perpetuity of $125 a month if money is worth 6% converted monthly and the first payment is to be made in 1 month?

5. If money is worth 7% converted semiannually, find the present value of an annual $1200 scholarship if the first scholarship is to be awarded in 1 year.

($16,848)

6. What is the present value of a perpetuity of $750 a year if the first payment is to be made in 1 year and the interest rate is 6% converted semiannually?

7. A woman gives a school $15,000 to provide an annual scholarship indefinitely. The first scholarship is to be awarded 1 year after the grant is received. If the fund earns 7% converted semiannually, what will be the size of each scholarship? (When solving practical business problems, always look for the most direct method. Although this is a perpetuity, the perpetuity formulas do not provide the easiest method of solution. Carry the original grant forward for 1 year at compound interest and keep back a sum equal to the original grant. The difference will be accumulated interest, which can be given as a scholarship without touching the original principal.)

($1068.38)

8. If the institution in which the fund in problem 7 is invested starts paying 7% compounded quarterly, what will be the size of the annual scholarship?

9.(C) Ms. Berger wants to provide a research fellowship of $2000 annually. If money can be invested at $7\frac{1}{2}$% compounded semiannually and if the first fellowship is to be awarded in 5 years, how much should Ms. Berger give the school?

($19.498.28)

10.^(C) What sum of money invested at $8\frac{1}{2}\%$ converted semiannually will provide a perpetual income of $3000 at the end of each 2 years?

11. On September 1, 1988, a college receives a grant of $30,000 that was invested at 6%. If annual scholarships are awarded for 20 years from this grant, what is the size of each scholarship if the first one is awarded on: (a) September 1, 1988? (b) September 1, 1998? If the scholarships are to be awarded indefinitely, what will be the size of each if the first is awarded on: (c) September 1, 1988? (d) September 1, 1998?

   [(a) $2467.49; (b) $4418.89; (c) $1698.11; (d) $3041.06]

12. In 1980 an alumnus gave a university $20,000 that was invested at a rate that would provide $2500 scholarships at the end of each year indefinitely. (a) What interest rate was the school earning on the investment at that time? (b) After the scholarship was awarded in 1980, the school had to reinvest the fund at 9%. If the university wants to continue to award scholarships indefinitely, it will have to change the value of each scholarship to what amount? (c) If the university wants to continue to award $2500 scholarships, how many full scholarships will the fund provide at the new rate?

13. What is the value of a perpetuity of $900 at the end of each year if money is worth: (a) 6%? (b) 6% compounded semiannually?

   [(a) $15,000; (b) $14,778.32]

14.^(C) What would be the size of the grants in problem 11 if the college can invest the money at $7\frac{1}{2}\%$?

15. What sum of money invested at 5% converted semiannually will provide $200 at the end of each 2 years indefinitely?

   ($1926.54)

16. How much will it take to provide a hospital with an annual research grant of $5000 indefinitely if the first grant is to be made immediately and if the endowment that is to make the grants possible can be invested at 6%?

17. A school can invest money at 7% converted semiannually. How large a grant would be needed to provide a $1500 research fellowship at the end of each year indefinitely?

   ($21,060.02)

18. What size grant would provide the fellowship in problem 17 if 8% compounded semiannually is earned on the invested funds?

19. A share of preferred stock has a par value of $100 and pays 6% dividends annually. If it is purchased for $94, what yield rate

would the investor get?

(6.38%)

20. If the stock in problem 19 was purchased for $106, what would be the yield rate?

21. To take advantage of the tax benefits of an Individual Retirement Account (IRA), a man decides that he will invest $2000 each year in an IRA paying 8% effective. Suppose that he makes the first payment at age 26 and the last at age 65. (a) How much will be in the account at the time of the last deposit? Withdrawals begin 1 year after the last deposit. (b) How much can the man withdraw annually if there are to be 25 withdrawals? (c) Find the size of the withdrawals if they are to continue indefinitely.

[(a) $518,113.04; (b) $48,536.20; (c) $41,449.04]

22.^(C) Do problem 21 figuring that 10% is earned in the IRA account.

5.8 THE GENERAL CASE

When payments are made more or less frequently than the compounding period, the annuity comes under the **general case**. The first step in solving general annuity problems is to get the payments and the compounding periods to coincide. Then we can complete the problem by using the factors from Table 2 or Table 3, or by using a calculator in the same way that we have been using one to figure simple annuities in which the payments are made at the time interest is earned.

One way to solve general annuities is to convert the given interest rate into an equivalent rate for which the conversion period is the same as the payment period. The second way is to change the original payments to equivalent payments made on the stated interest conversion dates. In this book we follow the latter practice of converting the original payments into equivalent payments that coincide with the compounding periods. This practice results in simpler computations in many cases.

5.9 PAYMENTS LESS FREQUENT
THAN INTEREST

Now we consider problems that have interest compounded more frequently than payments are made. For example, payments may be made annually and interest compounded semiannually; or payments may be made semiannually and interest compounded monthly.

EXAMPLE 1 Find the amount of an ordinary annuity of $500 per year for 10 years if money is worth 8% compounded semiannually.

SOLUTION A good way to analyze a problem of this type is to sketch one payment interval and the corresponding conversion periods. See Figure 5-17. Now we replace the original payments with payments of $R on each interest date. See Figure 5-18. Since the new payments form an ordinary annuity of $R per payment accumulating at 8% converted semiannually, we can set up the following equation of value using formula (16):

$$R = 500 \times \frac{1}{s_{\overline{2}|4\%}} = 500 \times .490196 = \$245.10$$

Figure 5-17

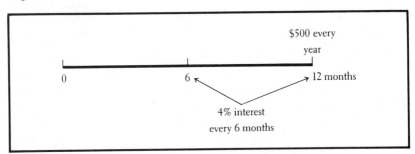

Figure 5-18

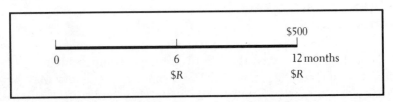

(In the problems and examples in this section, we usually round the equivalent payment to the nearest cent. This practice results in answers that will be the same as those obtained by students who do not have access to calculators and therefore round off intermediate answers to save time. In practical business situations where calculators are available, entire factors can be used throughout the problem without additional labor, and the final answer is then rounded to the nearest cent.)

Now we replace the original payments of $500 every year by payments of $245.10 every 6 months. The problem can then be completed as an ordinary annuity. Note in particular that there are 20 payments in the final annuity because each of the original 10 payments has been replaced by 2 payments. Therefore the final amount using formula (14) is

$$S_{20} = 245.10 s_{\overline{20}|4\%}$$
$$= 245.10 \times 29.77808$$
$$= \$7298.61$$

EXAMPLE 2 Find the present value of an ordinary annuity of 20 semiannual payments of $1000 each if money is worth 6% converted monthly.

SOLUTION A sketch of one payment interval (Figure 5-19) shows that it contains 6 interest conversion periods.

The original payment is to be replaced by 6 equal monthly payments that are equivalent in value to $1000 at the end of 6 months. Substituting in formula (16), we have

$$R = 1000 \times \frac{1}{s_{\overline{6}|\frac{1}{2}\%}} = 1000 \times .164595 = \$164.60$$

Figure 5-19

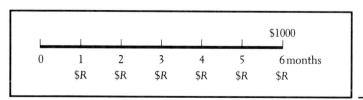

Now we have an annuity of 20 × 6 = 120 payments of $164.60. At 6% converted monthly, the present value of this annuity is

$$A_{120} = 164.60 a_{\overline{120}|\frac{1}{2}\%} = 164.60 \times 90.07345 = \$14,826.09$$

5.10 PAYMENTS MORE FREQUENT THAN INTEREST

We now consider problems in which payments are made more frequently than interest is compounded. For example, payments may be made semiannually and interest compounded annually; or payments may be made monthly and interest compounded semiannually.

The problem is to convert the payments made during an interest conversion period into an equivalent single payment made on an interest conversion date. In making this conversion, as in all problems in the mathematics of finance, we must give close attention to practical conditions pertaining to the problem.

A typical illustration of the practical rules followed by a financial institution can be found in the passbook of a bank. We might find that the bank pays 5% compounded semiannually on May 1 and November 1. Money deposited between these dates earns simple interest until the next conversion date. If money is deposited on the 10th or before, interest is credited from the 1st of that month. If the deposit is after the 10th, interest is credited from the 1st of the following month. Money withdrawn before the semiannual payment date gets no interest for that period. When we work a problem concerning a passbook account at this particular bank, we must follow these rules.

EXAMPLE 1 A man resolves to deposit $120 from his pay at the end of each month in the bank described in the preceding paragraph. If he made his first deposit on May 31, 1980, how much did he have in his account after interest was credited on May 1, 1985?

SOLUTION The first step is to get the semiannual payment that is equivalent to the 6 monthly deposits. A time diagram for the first 6 deposits (Figure 5-20) shows how long each deposit earns simple interest.

Figure 5-20 shows that the last deposit does not earn any simple interest, the 5th deposit earns interest for 1 month, and so on. A chart like the following one will simplify the interest computations.

Deposit	Months Simple Interest Is Earned	Interest	Amount
6th	0	0	$120.00
5th	1	$120 \times .05 \times \frac{1}{12} = .50$	120.50
4th	2	$120 \times .05 \times \frac{2}{12} = 1.00$	121.00
3rd	3	$120 \times .05 \times \frac{3}{12} = 1.50$	121.50
2nd	4	$120 \times .05 \times \frac{4}{12} = 2.00$	122.00
1st	5	$120 \times .05 \times \frac{5}{12} = 2.50$	122.50
	15		$727.50

An equivalent and condensed way to get the simple interest is to assume that 1 deposit of $120 has earned 15 months' worth of interest. (Fifteen is the total number of months that simple interest is earned.)

$$120 \times .05 \times \tfrac{15}{12} = \$7.50$$

Now we replace the 60 monthly deposits of $120 each with 10 semi-annual deposits of $727.50 and work the problem as an ordinary annuity.

$$S_{10} = 727.50 s_{\overline{10}|2.5\%} = 727.50 \times 11.20338$$
$$= \$8150.46$$

In the preceding example simple interest was credited for a part of a period. It is also possible to have compound interest for a part of a period. All that we need to do is to take the basic formula for

Figure 5-20

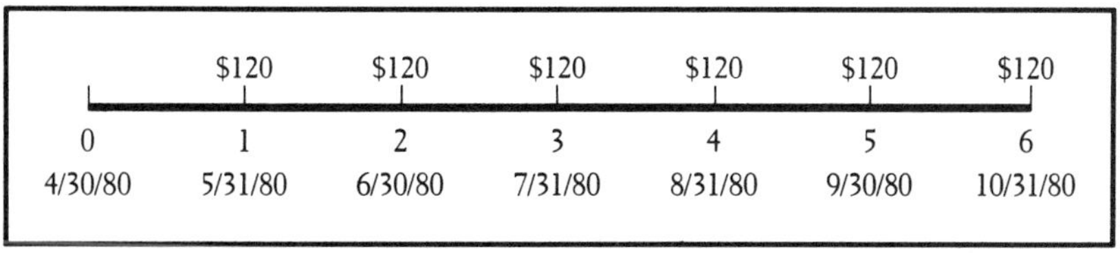

	$120	$120	$120	$120	$120	$120
0	1	2	3	4	5	6
4/30/80	5/31/80	6/30/80	7/31/80	8/31/80	9/30/80	10/31/80

compound interest, $S = P(1 + i)^n$, and substitute the proper value for n.

If $1 is placed at 6% compound interest for 6 months, the amount would be

$$S = 1.00(1.06)^{1/2} = 1.02956$$

Values for $(1 + i)^n$ when n is a fraction can be found using logarithms, a scientific calculator, or the auxiliary tables published by the Financial Publishing Company. In this book, values for compound interest for a part of a period for the more common interest rates are given in Table 4 in the column headed "Amount of 1."

Going back to the previous illustration, suppose that the dollar had been placed at 6% simple interest for 6 months. Then the amount would have been $1.03. This amount is greater than that at 6% compound interest for 6 months. Most people know that money increases more rapidly at compound interest than at the same rate of simple interest if it is left on deposit for more than one interest period. This increase is the result of interest being earned on interest. However, it is not generally known that for less than a conversion period, compound interest results in a smaller amount than simple interest. The difference is not great, but it should be taken into account.

Compound interest for a part of a period is used more frequently in annuity problems than in dealing with single sums. For such problems Table 4, Auxiliary Tables taken from the extensive tables of the Financial Publishing Company, can be used to simplify computations. An example will show how these tables are used.

EXAMPLE 2 What is the amount of $120 at the end of each month for 60 months at 5% converted semiannually if compound interest is paid for part of a period?

SOLUTION The interest conversion period is 6 months and the rate per period is $2\frac{1}{2}\%$. The time interval for payments is 1 month, or $\frac{1}{6}$ of a conversion period. Now we refer to Table 4 under $2\frac{1}{2}\%$ and look opposite 1-6, where we find the factor 6.0621999193 in the column headed "Equivalent per period to a payment of 1." This means that a payment of $6.0621999193 every 6 months is equivalent to a payment of $1 every month if money is worth 5% compounded semiannually. Since our monthly payments are $120, the equivalent semiannual payment is

$$120 \times 6.0621999193 = \$727.46$$

and the amount of 60 deposits is

$$S_{10} = 727.46 s_{\overline{10}|2.5\%} = \$8150.01$$

Note that the answer to this problem is 45 cents smaller than the answer for Example 1. The fact that there is a difference, even though it is not large, shows that you must use the rules that apply to the particular transaction.

EXAMPLE 3 An insurance company pays 8% compounded annually on money left with it. What would be the cost of an annuity of $200 at the end of each month for 10 years?

SOLUTION In Table 4 opposite 1-12 under 8%, we find the factor 12.43389. Therefore the annual payment equivalent to 12 monthly payments is

$$200 \times 12.43389 = \$2486.78.$$

Now we find the present value of an ordinary annuity of $2486.78 per year for 10 years at 8%.

$$A_{10} = 2486.78 a_{\overline{10}|8\%} = 2486.78 \times 6.710081$$
$$= \$16,686.50$$

Exercise 5e

1. Find the present value and amount of an annuity of $400 at the end of every 6 months for 12 years if money is worth 7% converted quarterly.
   ($6402.57; $14,723.34)
2. Find the present value and amount of an annuity of $150 a year for 8 years at 6% converted semiannually.
3. What single payment now at 6% converted monthly is equivalent to payments of $750 at the end of each 6 months for 6 years?
   ($7448.91)
4. Compute the present value of an ordinary annuity of $500 at the end of each quarter for 7 years if money is worth 7% converted monthly.

5. Find the amount of the annuity in problem 3.
   ($10,667.17)
6. Find the amount of the annuity in problem 4.
7. Payments of $200 are made at the end of each month for 5 years in an investment paying 6% converted quarterly. Find the present value and amount of the annuity if: (a) Simple interest is paid for part of a period. (b) Compound interest is paid for part of a period.
   [(a) $10,352.69, $13,943.57; (b) $10,352.52, $13,943.34]
8. Payments of $50 are made at the end of each month for 6 years. The annuity earns 5% compounded semiannually. Find the present value and amount if: (a) Simple interest is paid for part of a period. (b) Compound interest is paid for part of a period.
9. Payments of $500 are made at the end of each 6 months for 10 years in an account paying 5% compounded annually. Find the present value and amount if: (a) Simple interest is paid for part of a period. (b) Compound interest is paid for part of a period.
   [(a) $7818.26, $12,735.12; (b) $7817.10, $12,733.23]
10. An insurance company pays 3% compounded annually on money left with it. What would be the cost of an annuity of $125 at the end of each month for 10 years if compound interest is paid for part of a period?

5.11 FINDING THE PERIODIC PAYMENT

When the amount or present value of a general annuity is known, the **periodic payment** can be found by first getting the equivalent payment per interest conversion period and then converting this amount into payments made according to the particular payment schedule.

EXAMPLE 1   A widow has $10,000 with which she wants to buy an annuity that will provide her a monthly income for 15 years. If she can get 7% converted semiannually on her money, what will be the size of the monthly payments if compound interest is paid for part of a period?

SOLUTION   First we find the equivalent payment at the end of each 6 months.

$$R = 10,000 \times \frac{1}{a_{\overline{30}|3.5\%}} = 10,000 \times .0543713 = \$543.71$$

Now we must convert this semiannual payment to an equivalent monthly payment. Since 6 payments are made during an interest period, we look in Table 4 for $3\frac{1}{2}\%$ and a time interval of 1-6. The factor in the third column is 6.0869147. Since this value is for a payment of 1 per period, our problem becomes

$$R \times 6.0869147 = 543.71$$

$$R = \frac{543.71}{6.0869147} = \$89.32$$

This problem can be solved without division by using the "Payment equivalent to 1 per period" column and multiplying. The payment equivalent to $1 at the end of each 6 months is $.1642868. Therefore the monthly payment that is equivalent to $543.71 every 6 months is

$$R = 543.71 \times .1642868 = \$89.32$$

EXAMPLE 2   A couple would like to accumulate $3000 in 5 years by making deposits at the end of each month in an account paying 5% compounded semiannually. What is the size of each deposit?

SOLUTION   The equivalent semiannual deposit is

$$R = 3000 \times \frac{1}{s_{\overline{10}|2.5\%}} = 3000 \times .089259 = \$267.78$$

Since 6 payments are made during each interest period, we look in Table 4 for $2\frac{1}{2}\%$ opposite 1-6 and find the factor .164957 in the "Payment equivalent to 1 per period" column. Therefore

$$R = 267.78 \times .164957 = \$44.17$$

Exercise 5f

Use compound interest for part of a period.

1. A man leaves his widow a $5000 insurance policy. What monthly income would this policy provide for 8 years if the insurance company pays 6% converted semiannually?
   ($65.53)

2. The present value of an annuity is $12,000. It is to be used to provide a quarterly income for 6 years. What will be the size of the payments if the interest rate is 7% converted annually?

3. What periodic payment at the end of each month for 10 years will be required to accumulate $15,000 if the fund earns interest at 8% compounded quarterly?

   ($82.23)

4. A city wants to accumulate $250,000 in 15 years to redeem an issue of bonds. What payment will be required at the end of each 6 months to accumulate this amount if interest is earned at 6% converted annually?

5.12 OTHER GENERAL ANNUITIES

Other types of general annuities also can be solved by first determining the equivalent payment on interest conversion dates and then solving a simple annuity. As shown in the following examples, time diagrams can be very helpful in the analysis and solution of general annuities.

EXAMPLE 1 Find the present value and the amount of an annuity due of $200 at the beginning of each year for 3 years if money is worth 6% compounded semiannually.

SOLUTION First we make a time diagram of the problem (Figure 5-21).

Figure 5-21

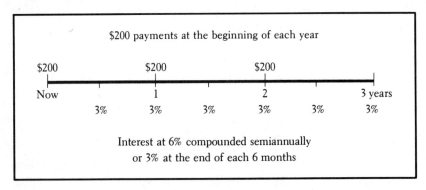

We replace each of the $200 payments with a set of equivalent payments every 6 months. We can make this replacement by letting the $200 be the present value of an ordinary annuity of 2 payments and getting the value of R from formula (17).

$$R = 200 \times \frac{1}{a_{\overline{2}|3\%}} = 200 \times .52261 = \$104.52$$

Now the problem can be illustrated by a diagram (Figure 5-22).

The solution is worked as a simple annuity. From formula (15), we have

$$A_6 = 104.52 \times a_{\overline{6}|3\%} = 104.52 \times 5.41719 = \$566.20$$

From formula (14), we obtain

$$S_6 = 104.52 \times s_{\overline{6}|3\%} = 104.52 \times 6.46841 = \$676.08$$

CHECK $566.20(1.03)^6 = 566.20 \times 1.19405 = \$676.07$

EXAMPLE 2 Find the present value of an annuity of $250 at the beginning of each month for 10 years if money is worth 7% converted semiannually.

SOLUTION The six $250 payments must be replaced with an equivalent payment made on an interest conversion date. A time diagram of the first 6 payments (Figure 5-23) is a help in making this substitution.

Again, we emphasize that in a problem like this the practical conditions that pertain to the problem must be taken into account. There are two possibilities:

Figure 5-22

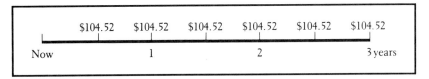

| | $104.52 | $104.52 | $104.52 | $104.52 | $104.52 | $104.52 |
| Now | | 1 | | 2 | | 3 years |

(a) Simple interest is allowed for part of a period. The first payment earns interest for 6 months. Each payment earns interest for 1 month less until we get to the 6th payment, which earns interest for 1 month. Adding the months from 1 to 6, we get a total of 21 months. Using the method described on page 253, we get simple interest on all payments with a single calculation:

$$I = 250 \times .07 \times \tfrac{21}{12} = \$30.63$$

Now we have an equivalent semiannual payment of $1530.63, which has a present value of

$$A_{20} = 1530.63 a_{\overline{20}|3.5\%} = 1530.63 \times 14.212403 = \$21,753.93$$

(b) Compound interest is allowed for a part of a period. To find the equivalent payment, we go to Table 4 for $3\tfrac{1}{2}\%$ and look opposite 1–6 because the payment interval is $\tfrac{1}{6}$ of a conversion period. Multiplying the factor in the "Equivalent per period to a payment of 1" column by the size of our payment, we have

$$250 \times 6.08691 = \$1521.73$$

Since Table 4 gives us the equivalent payment at the time the last payment is made, we must allow interest on this value for $\tfrac{1}{6}$ of a period to get it to coincide with an interest conversion period. Using the "Amount of 1" factor from Table 4 for 1–6 period, we have

$$1521.73 \times 1.005750 = \$1530.48$$

Note that this result is a few cents smaller than the value for simple interest. We now use formula (15) to get the present value:

Figure 5-23

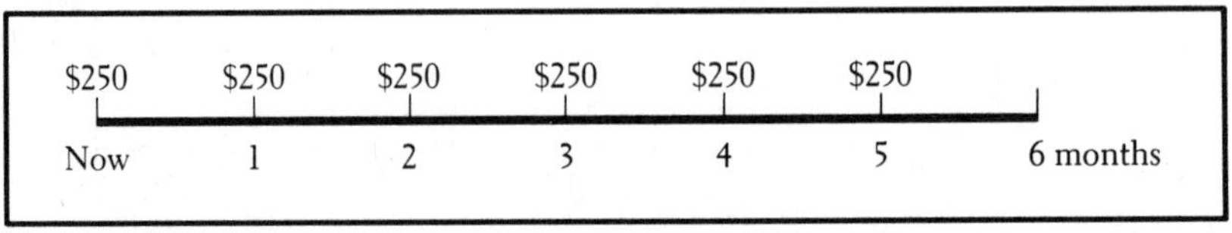

$250	$250	$250	$250	$250	$250	
Now	1	2	3	4	5	6 months

$$A_{20} = 1530.48a_{\overline{20}|3.5\%} = 1530.48 \times 14.212403 = \$21,751.80$$

Of course, you can use a scientific calculator instead of Table 4 for all the general case problems.

Exercise 5g

Allow compound interest for a part of a period.

1. Find the present value and amount of an annuity due of $600 at the beginning of each year for 12 years if money is worth 7% converted semiannually.
   ($5071.88; $11,580.76)
2. Find the present value and amount of payments of $500 at the beginning of each 6 months for 5 years if money is worth 6% converted monthly.
3. Four hundred dollars is invested at the beginning of each 3 months at 6% compounded annually. What is the amount at the end of 5 years?
   ($9355.09)
4. Two hundred dollars is invested at the beginning of each month at 5% compounded quarterly. What is the amount at the end of 3 years?
5. Find the present value of an annuity of $60 at the beginning of each month for 8 years if money is worth 8% compounded annually.
   ($4314.63)
6. What is the present value of an annuity of $100 at the beginning of each month for 5 years if money is worth 5% converted quarterly?

5.13 ANNUITIES AND CONTINUOUS COMPOUNDING

Deposits of $100 each are made four times a year at equal intervals into an ordinary annuity paying 8% compounded continuously. What is the amount at the end of 18 months? With an ordinary annuity the deposits are made at the end of the payment intervals. A time diagram (Figure 5-24) shows that the last payment does not earn interest, the next to the last payment earns interest for $\frac{1}{4}$ year, the payment before that earns interest for $\frac{2}{4}$ year, and so on down to the first payment, which earns interest for $\frac{5}{4}$ years. Since the problem is given in months whereas the rate is a nominal annual rate, we must convert times from months to years, as shown in Figure 5-24.

Individual payments are taken to a focal date at 18 months using $S = Pe^{jt}$. See Table 5-1.

To get a general formula for the amount of an annuity with continuous compounding, we assume that p payments of $1 each are made per year at equal intervals for t years. The total number of payments is $n = pt$. The last payment does not earn interest. Since there are p

Figure 5-24

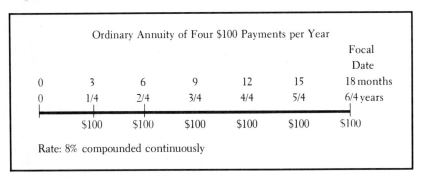

Table 5-1

Payment Number	Years to Focal Date	Amount at Focal Date $100e^{.08t}$	
6	0	$100e^0$ =	100.00
5	$\frac{1}{4}$	$100e^{.02}$ =	102.02
4	$\frac{2}{4}$	$100e^{.04}$ =	104.08
3	$\frac{3}{4}$	$100e^{.06}$ =	106.18
2	1	$100e^{.08}$ =	108.33
1	$\frac{5}{4}$	$100e^{.10}$ =	110.52
			$631.13

payments per year, the next-to-the-last payment earns interest for $1/p$ year. Substituting in $S = Pe^{jt}$, we find that the amount earned by this payment is $e^{j/p}$. The next payment earns interest for $2/p$ year and has an amount equal to $e^{2j/p}$. At the other end of the annuity, the first payment earns interest for $(n - 1)/p$ years. Its amount is $e^{j[(n-1)/p]}$. A time diagram of this annuity is shown in Figure 5-25.

Adding the amounts of the individual payments, we have

$$s_{\overline{n}|} = 1 + e^{j/p} + e^{2j/p} + \cdots + e^{j[(n-2)/p]} + e^{j[(n-1)/p]}$$

This expression is a geometric progression with first term 1, common ratio of $e^{j/p}$, and n terms. Substituting in the formula for the sum of a geometric progression, we obtain

$$S_{\overline{n}|} = \frac{1[1 - (e^{j/p})^n]}{1 - e^{j/p}} = \frac{1 - e^{jn/p}}{1 - e^{j/p}} = \frac{e^{jn/p} - 1}{e^{j/p} - 1}$$

Figure 5-25

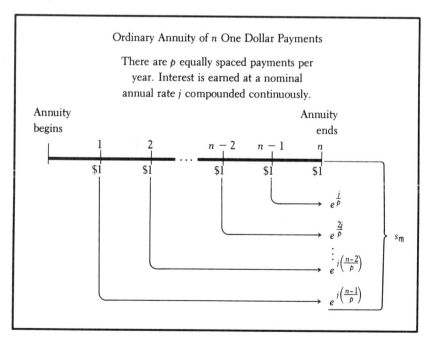

Ordinary Annuity of n One Dollar Payments

There are p equally spaced payments per year. Interest is earned at a nominal annual rate j compounded continuously.

If the periodic payment is R, we multiply by R to get the amount of n payments earning a rate j compounded continuously.

$$S_n = R \, \frac{e^{jn/p} - 1}{e^{j/p} - 1}$$

We now use $P = Se^{-jt}$ to discount this equivalent single sum to get the present value of the annuity. Multiplying by $e^{-jn/p}$,

$$A_n = R \, \frac{1 - e^{-jn/p}}{e^{j/p} - 1}$$

EXAMPLE 1 Payments of \$100 are made at the end of each 6 months into a fund paying 8% compounded continuously. Find the amount at the end of 4 years.

SOLUTION Substituting $R = 100$, $j = .08$, $n = 8$, and $p = 2$ in the above equation for S_n, we have

$$S = 100 \, \frac{e^{.32} - 1}{e^{.04} - 1} = 100 \, \frac{1.37713 - 1}{1.04081 - 1} = \$924.11$$

EXAMPLE 2 Payments of \$500 are to be made at the end of each quarter for 4 years. Find the present value of these payments at 8% compounded continuously.

SOLUTION Substituting $R = 500$, $j = .08$, $n = 16$, and $p = 4$ in the above equation for A_n, we have

$$A_n = 500 \, \frac{1 - e^{-.32}}{e^{.02} - 1} = 500 \, \frac{1 - .72615}{1.02020 - 1} = \$6778.47$$

Exercise 5h

1.   Find the amount at the time of the last payment of \$100 deposits at the end of each 3 months for 5 years if money is worth 8% compounded: (a) quarterly; (b) continuously.
      [(a) \$2429.74; (b) \$2434.75]

2.   Answer problem 1 for a nominal rate of 6%.
3.   Find the amount of an annuity of $1000 every 6 months for 3 years if the rate is 6% compounded: (a) semiannually; (b) continuously.
      [(a) $6468.41; (b) $6475.69]
4.   Answer problem 3 if the nominal rate is 8%.
5.   A contract calls for payments of $200 at the end of each 6 months for 4 years. Find the present value at 8% compounded: (a) semiannually; (b) continuously.
      [(a) $1346.55; (b) $1342.07]
6.   Answer problem 5 if the nominal rate is 10%.
7.   Find the present value of payments of $1000 at the end of each year for 8 years if the rate is 7% compounded: (a) annually; (b) continuously.
      [(a) $5971.30; (b) $5913.71]
8.   Answer problem 7 if the nominal rate is 8%.

REVIEW EXERCISES FOR CHAPTER 5

1.   Deposits of $600 are made every 3 months into an account paying 6% compounded quarterly with conversion dates of January 1, April 1, July 1, and October 1. The first deposit is made on April 1, 1986, and the last is made on October 1, 1995. Find the value of these payments on: (a) July 1, 1982; (b) April 1, 1986; (c) January 1, 1996; (d) July 1, 1999.
      [(a) $14,303.77; (b) $17,883.03; (c) $31,960.73; (d) $39,367.82]
2.   Find the value of the annuity in problem 1 on: (a) January 1, 1986; and (b) October 1, 1995.
3.$^{(C)}$ Do problem 2 assuming that the interest is compounded monthly.
      [(a) $17,595.73; (b) $31,538.17]
4.   Suppose that deposits of $200 are made monthly, beginning February 1, 1986, and ending October 1, 1995, into the account described in problem 1. Using compound interest for part of a period, find the value of these payments on: (a) January 1, 1986; and (b) October 1, 1995.
5.   Do problem 4 using simple interest for part of a period.
      [(a) $17,706.84; (b) $31,645.85]
6.$^{(C)}$ A woman who won $200,000 after taxes in a state lottery placed her winnings in an investment paying 9% compounded

7.   monthly. How many payments of $2000 monthly beginning immediately will she get, and what will be the size of a concluding smaller payment?

7.   How much could the winner in problem 6 get from her investment each month if the payments begin immediately and continue indefinitely?
      ($1488.83)

8.   How much must a person invest to produce $5000 each year indefinitely if the first payment is made: (a) immediately? (b) in 1 year? (c) in 8 years? Assume that the money can be invested at 7% compounded annually.

9.   Do problem 8 assuming that the money is invested at 7% compounded quarterly.
      [(a) $74,580.57; (b) $69,580.57; (c) $42,807.94]

10.   To pay off a debt of $8000, a person begins quarterly payments immediately. Find the size of the 40 equal payments if the interest rate is 8% compounded quarterly.

11.   What would be the size of 120 monthly payments to eliminate the debt in problem 10? The first payment is to be made in 1 month and compound interest is to be used for part of a period.
      ($96.84)

12.   A worker begins to set up a fund to provide a retirement income. On her 45th birthday she deposits $5000 in the fund. She begins making monthly deposits of $100 1 month later, with the last deposit on her 60th birthday. The fund earns 7% converted monthly. The pension is to begin on the worker's 65th birthday with the first of 180 equal monthly payments. Find the size of these payments.

13.   An annuity of $1000 a year for 10 years is to begin with the first payment in 1 year. Find the present value of this annuity at 8% compounded: (a) annually; (b) continuously.
      [(a) $6710.08; (b) $6611.73]

14.   Find the amount of the annuity in both parts of problem 13.

Chapter 6
Amortization and Sinking Funds

6.1 AMORTIZATION OF A DEBT

One of the most important applications of annuities in business transactions is the repayment of interest-bearing debts. First, we consider
the **amortization** method. When a debt is repaid by this method, a
series of periodic payments, usually equal in amount, pay the interest
outstanding at the time the payments are made and also repay a part
of the principal. As the principal is gradually reduced in this way, the
interest on the unpaid balance decreases. In other words, as time goes
on, an increasing portion of the periodic payments is available to
reduce the debt. Sooner or later most of the students who study this
material will purchase a car, home, or other item on time and will
amortize the debt. Developing an understanding of how debts are
amortized and the ability to determine the costs involved can save a
person many dollars by making possible the wise selection of a lender
and of a repayment plan.

The importance of amortization for the well-being of the economy
is indicated by this comment by economist Sumner H. Slichter:

> By far the most important improvement in financial instruments
> during recent years has been the development of the long-term amor-
> tizable mortgage. This instrument has done much to encourage the
> flow of funds into housing. The development of the long-term
> amortizable mortgage was largely the result of the assumption of new
> functions by the federal government. In order to stimulate residential
> building during the depression, the federal government, through the
> Federal Housing Administration, undertook to insure long-term
> amortizable loans secured by residential properties. Later there was
> added the guarantee of similar mortgages by the Veterans Admin-
> istration in connection with housing purchased by veterans.*

*Sumner H. Slichter, *Economic Growth in the United States* (New York: The Free
Press, 1966), p. 154.

6.2   FINDING THE PAYMENT

When a debt is amortized by equal payments at equal intervals, the debt becomes the present value of an annuity. We determine the size of the payment by the methods used to get the periodic rent in the annuity problems in the preceding chapters.

EXAMPLE 1   A family buys a $60,000 home and pays $10,000 down. They get a 25-year mortgage for the balance. If the lender charges 12% converted monthly, what is the size of the monthly payment?

SOLUTION   Here we have an ordinary annuity with A_n = $50,000, $n = 300$, and $i = 1\%$. From formula (17) we find

$$R = \frac{50,000}{a_{\overline{300}|1\%}}$$

$$= \frac{50,000}{94.9465513}$$

$$= \$526.612$$

When a debt is amortized, the common practice is to round up any fraction of a cent. Thus the payment in Example 1 would be rounded to $526.62 if the rounding were to the next highest cent. This ensures complete amortization in the time specified. If each payment were low by a fraction of a cent, there would be a small outstanding debt after the specified number of payments had been made. Instead of rounding up to the cent, a lender may round up to the dime, the dollar, or any other unit of money. This practice does not injure the borrower because the higher periodic payment will be offset by a smaller concluding payment.

EXAMPLE 2   A debt of $10,000 bearing interest at 12% compounded semiannually is to be amortized in 20 semiannual payments. Find the concluding payment if the semiannual payment is rounded up to the: (a) cent; (b) dime; (c) dollar.

SOLUTION   Substituting A_{20} = 10,000, $i = 6\%$, and $n = 20$ in formula (17), we have

$$R = 10,000 \times \frac{1}{a_{\overline{20}|6\%}}$$

$$= 10,000 \times .0871846 = \$871.846$$

Making a time diagram (Figure 6-1), we can see that the simplest method of solution is to set up an equation of value with the focal date at the 20th payment. Then the concluding payment is simply the difference between the $10,000 carried to the focal date and the amount of an annuity *due* of 19 regular payments. Formula (9) takes the $10,000 to the focal date and formula (18) brings forward the 19 payments.

(a) If the payment is rounded up to the cent, $R = \$871.85$.

$$x = 10,000(1.06)^{20} - 871.85(s_{\overline{20}|} - 1)$$
$$= 10,000 \times 3.20713547 - 871.85 \times 35.78559$$
$$= 32,071.35 - 31,199.67$$
$$= \$871.68$$

(b) If the payment is rounded up to the dime, $R = \$871.90$.

$$x = 32,071.35 - 871.90 \times 35.78559$$
$$= \$869.89$$

(c) If we round up to the dollar, $R = \$872.00$.

$$x = 32,071.35 - 872 \times 35.78559$$
$$= \$866.32$$

Figure 6-1

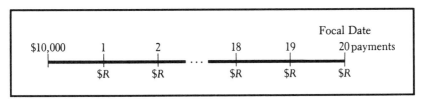

6.3 OUTSTANDING PRINCIPAL

Knowing the principal outstanding at a certain time is often important. The borrower may want to pay off the rest of the debt in a lump sum, or the lender may want to sell the debt that is still owed. To calculate the principal outstanding at any time, we can find the value of the remaining payments at that time.

EXAMPLE 1 To pay off an $8000 debt, a man got a 10-year loan at 12% converted monthly. How much does he still owe after he has paid on it for 5 years?

SOLUTION The monthly payment is $114.78. To find the outstanding principal, we use an equation of value and compare the original debt with the payments that have been made. We put the focal date at the 60th payment and bring everything to this point. See Figure 6-2.

$$x = 8000(1.01)^{60} - 114.78 s_{\overline{60}|}$$
$$= 8000 \times 1.8166967 - 114.78 \times 81.6696699$$
$$= 14,533.57 - 9,374.04$$
$$= \$5159.53$$

Thus far the principal has been reduced by only 8000.00 − 5159.53 = $2840.47, although the man has paid $6886.80 (60 payments × $114.78). During the early years of a long-term amortization program, a large part of the money paid goes for interest. Recognition of this fact leads to a practical point: the buyer of a home should try to borrow from a lender who offers the lowest rate

Figure 6-2

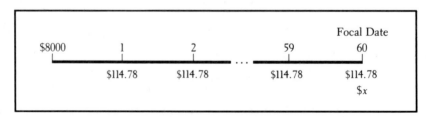

of interest and who will permit the borrower to pay off the mortgage more quickly than the contract requires without charging a fee. Frequently, a borrower will find that an increase in income or an inheritance will allow the payment of more per month on the mortgage than the original terms specified. Since the borrower probably cannot invest this money at as high a rate as that being paid on the mortgage, it is to the borrower's advantage to use it to reduce the debt. It is disconcerting to discover that a small-print provision, which the borrower had not read, in the contract imposes a penalty for this advance payment.

ALTERNATE SOLUTION In this problem we can get a good check on our answer by finding the present value of the remaining 60 payments, which form an ordinary annuity.

$$A_{60} = 114.78a_{\overline{60}|1\%}$$
$$= 114.78 \times 44.95504$$
$$= \$5159.94$$

This result differs by 41 cents from the preceding result because the monthly payment was rounded up to the nearest cent. Carrying the monthly payment to several decimal places would make the two results closer, but there is no reason to go to this trouble, since the payment must be rounded in practical problems.

We could not use this method of checking if the payment had been rounded up to the dime or to the dollar because then the concluding payment would have differed greatly from the other payments.

EXAMPLE 2 On May 15, 1982, a woman borrowed $25,000 at 15% converted monthly. She planned to repay the debt in equal monthly payments over 15 years with the first payment on June 15, 1982. The 12 payments during 1984 reduced the principal by how much? What was the total interest paid in 1984?

SOLUTION We use formula (17) to find the monthly payment.

$$R = 25,000 \times \frac{.0125}{1 - (1.0125)^{-180}} = \$349.90$$

The total reduction in principal in 1984 will be the difference between the outstanding principal in December 1983 and December 1984. A time diagram (Figure 6-3) shows that the outstanding principal must be determined after the 19th and the 31st payments. This determination requires two equations of value using these points as focal dates.

Outstanding on 12/15/83:

$$25{,}000(1.0125)^{19} - 349.90 s_{\overline{19}|} = \$24{,}203.50$$

Outstanding on 12/15/84:

$$25{,}000(1.0125)^{31} - 349.90 s_{\overline{31}|} = \underline{\quad 23{,}594.48\quad}$$
$$\$ \quad 609.02$$

To find the total interest paid in 1984, we subtract the amount applied to principal from the total payments, which equal 12 × 349.90 = \$4198.80. Then we find that the total interest paid is 4198.80 − 609.02 = \$3589.78.

6.4   OWNER'S EQUITY

The owner's equity starts with the down payment and is gradually increased by that part of each monthly payment over and above the interest. On a long-term loan, equity in a home is built up slowly at first because of interest charges. The amount of the owner's equity can be found at any time by subtracting the outstanding principal from the original loan and adding the down payment to this difference.

Figure 6-3

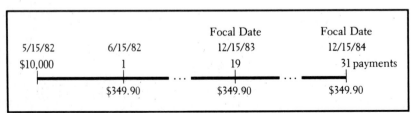

We should recognize that owner's equity calculated in this way makes no allowance for increases or decreases in the value of the property. If a neighborhood or a piece of property deteriorates, an owner may not recover the investment when the real estate is sold. On the other hand, if the property increases in value, the calculated equity is less than the true value of the owner's investment. A long period of rising prices and favorable taxation of capital gains have resulted in attractive financial returns on many pieces of real estate.

EXAMPLE A person buys a $62,500 home and pays $12,500 down. The homeowner gets a 25-year, 12% loan for the balance. Monthly payments are $526.62. What is the owner's equity after 10 years?

SOLUTION The outstanding principal after the 120th payment is found by putting a focal date at that time and taking the original debt and the payments to that point.

$$\text{Outstanding principal} = 50,000(1.01)^{120} - 526.62s_{\overline{120}|}$$
$$= 165,019.34 - 121,142.97 = \$43.876.37$$
$$\text{Addition to owner's equity} = 50,000 - 43,876.37 = \$6123.63$$

At the end of 10 years the homeowner has paid a total of 120 × 526.62 = $63,194.40 to get $6123.63 worth of house. After 10 years the owner's equity is 12,500.00 + 6123.63 = $18,623.63.

Table 6-1 shows how equity is built up in a number of loans of $10,000. The same pattern will occur for a loan of any size. The graphs in Figure 6-4 show how cumulative total payments are distributed between interest and principal over the life of a long-term loan. Early payments go largely for interest. As the debt is reduced, the principal is repaid at an increasing rate. To reduce interest charges, it is often good money management to apply excess funds to outstanding debts. In some cases, however, the tax deduction on interest together with the return on an investment can make it more advantageous to invest extra funds elsewhere.

6.5 AMORTIZATION SCHEDULE

When debts are repaid using the amortization method, it is important to know what portion of each payment goes for interest and how much

Table 6-1 Principal Repayments

After Paying This Many Years	This Much Has Been Repaid on a:				
	10-Year Loan	15-Year Loan	20-Year Loan	25-Year Loan	30-Year Loan
$10,000 Loan at 8%					
5	$ 4,016	$ 2,124	$ 1,248	$ 773	$ 493
10	10,000	5,288	3,107	1,925	1,228
15		10,000	5,877	3,642	2,323
20			10,000	6,199	3,954
25				10,000	6,384
30					10,000
$10,000 Loan at 10%					
5	$ 3,781	$ 1,869	$ 1,020	$ 583	$ 343
10	10,000	4,942	2,699	1,544	906
15		10,000	5,461	3,124	1,834
20			10,000	5,723	3,359
25				10,000	5,870
30					10,000
$10,000 Loan at 12%					
5	$ 3,550	$ 1,635	$ 826	$ 435	$ 234
10	10,000	4,605	2,325	1,224	658
15		10,000	5,050	2,659	1,429
20			10,000	5,265	2,831
25				10,000	5,376
30					10,000
$10,000 Loan at 14%					
5	$ 3,327	$ 1,423	$ 662	$ 319	$ 157
10	10,000	4,277	1,991	961	471
15		10,000	4,656	2,247	1,103
20			10,000	4,826	2,369
25				10,000	4,908
30					10,000

Figure 6-4 The High Cost of Long-term Debt

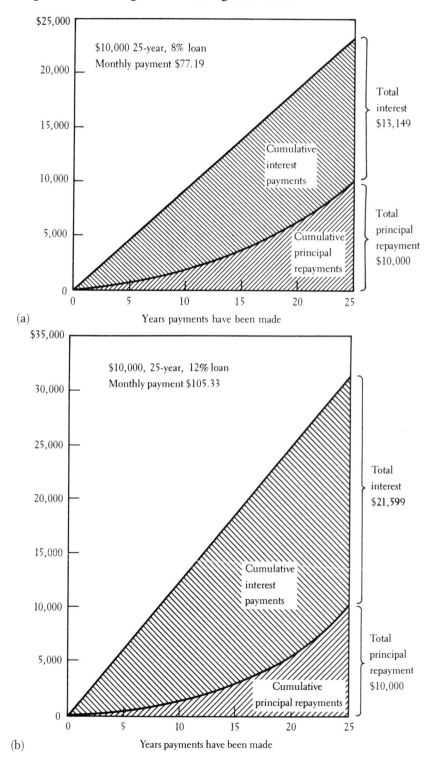

(a)

(b)

is applied to reducing the principal. In the following example we see that interest can be a substantial part of the periodic payment.

EXAMPLE 1   A person buys a home and gets a 25-year, 12% mortgage for $50,000. The monthly payments are $526.62. The buyer entering the lending institution to make the first monthly payment probably thinks that a house is being bought with it. How much house is being purchased with the payment?

SOLUTION   The interest rate is 1% a month. The interest for the first month will be $500. Deducting this amount from the monthly payment means that the homeowner gets only $26.62 worth of house with the payment of $526.62. Of course, things get brighter immediately. After the first payment the unpaid balance drops to 50,000 − 26.62 = $49,973.38. The second month's interest is figured on this principal and amounts to $499.73. With the second payment the buyer gets more house, 27 cents more as a matter of fact. As the payments are continued, more and more of each payment will be applied to the debt. When the debt gets down to approximately $20,000 (this reduction will take about 21 years), the interest will be only about $200 and most of the payment will go for house.

A person who buys a home on an amortization plan should get a periodic statement from the lender showing how much interest has been paid and the amount of reduction of the mortgage. The buyer could also obtain an amortization schedule that shows the exact financial breakdown at any time. The interest column will show the buyer how much interest can be deducted in a calendar year when computing income tax. The same column will show the lender how much must be reported as income. Since there is not space here to show an amortization schedule for 300 periods, we use a shorter problem. The schedule for this problem will include all the steps necessary to construct any amortization schedule.

EXAMPLE 2   A debt of $5000 is to be amortized by 5 quarterly payments made at the end of each 3 months. If interest is charged at the rate of 12% convertible quarterly, find the periodic payment and construct an amortization schedule. Round the payment up to the cent.

SOLUTION   Substituting in formula (17), we have

$$R = 5000 \times \frac{1}{a_{\overline{5}|3\%}} = \$1091.775 = \$1091.78$$

The final payment equals the preceding loan balance plus interest on this balance for the last period. When determining the periodic payment, lenders customarily round up. This ensures that the final payment will be equal to or less than the others. In this example, the last payment is 3 cents smaller than the previous four payments.

Amortization Schedule

(1) Payment Number	(2) Total Payment	(3) Payment on Interest .03 × (5)	(4) Payment on Principal (2) – (3)	(5) Balance of Loan (5) – (4)
				$5000.00
1	$1091.78	$150.00	$ 941.78	4058.22
2	1091.78	121.75	970.03	3088.19
3	1091.78	92.65	999.13	2089.06
4	1091.78	62.67	1029.11	1059.95
5	1091.75	31.80	1059.95	—
	$5458.87	$458.87	$5000.00	

Exercise 6a

Unless stated otherwise, periodic payments are to be obtained by rounding up to the cent.

1. A $6000 loan is to be amortized with 6 equal semiannual payments. If the interest rate is 14%, find the semiannual payment and construct an amortization schedule.
   ($R = \$1258.78$)
2. A loan of $1200 is to be amortized with 12 equal monthly payments. Find the monthly payment and construct a schedule if the rate is 12% converted monthly.
3. A debt of $30,000 with interest at 9% is to be amortized with 4 equal annual payments. Find the size of the payment and construct an amortization schedule.
   ($R = \$9260.07$)

4. Construct an amortization schedule for a debt of $30,000 to be repaid with equal payments at the end of each 6 months over a 5-year period. The rate is 12% converted semiannually.

5. A debt of $8000 with interest at 18% converted quarterly is being amortized with 10 equal quarterly payments. Find the size of the periodic payment and the outstanding principal just after the 5th payment.
($1011.04; $4438.35)

6. A debt of $8500 with interest at 13% converted monthly is being amortized with monthly payments over a period of 15 years. Find the size of the payment and the outstanding principal just after the 90th payment.

7. A couple buys a $40,000 home, pays $8000 down, and gets a 12%, 20-year mortgage for the rest.
   (a) Determine the monthly payment rounded up to the dime assuming that the interest is converted monthly.
   (b) How much of the first payment goes to interest and how much toward reducing the principal?
   (c) How much does the couple owe just after making the 72nd payment?
   (d) How much of the 103rd payment goes for interest and how much for principal?
   [(a) $352.40; (b) $320.00 interest, $32.40 principal; (c) $28,607.40; (d) $263 interest, $89.40 principal]

8. A house worth $75,000 is purchased with a down payment of $15,000 and monthly payments for 30 years. If the interest rate is $12\frac{1}{2}$% compounded monthly, find the size of the monthly payment rounded up to the dime. Complete the first three lines of the amortization schedule. How much is still owed on the house just before making the 90th payment?

9. A $2400 used car is purchased with a down payment of $800 and equal monthly payments for 24 months. If the interest rate is 12% compounded monthly, find the size of the monthly payment and complete the first three lines of the amortization schedule. How much is still owed on the car just before making the 12th payment?
(R = $75.32; $923.00 still owed)

10. Work problem 9 with a rate of 24% converted monthly.

11. A family purchases a home costing $65,000 and makes a down payment of $9000. They get a mortgage for the balance at $13\frac{1}{2}$% converted monthly to be repaid over a 25-year period. If they got the loan in September 1979, and made the first monthly payment

one month later, how much interest could they deduct when preparing their income tax statement of 1979? By how much was the principal reduced in 1979? Base your answers on an amortization schedule.

(Tax deduction, $1889.22; principal reduced by $69.09)

12. A family buys a home for $110,000. They make a 20% down payment and get a 30-year, $12\frac{1}{2}$% loan for the balance that is to be paid off in equal monthly installments. If they make their first payment in November 1987, how much interest can they deduct when they prepare their income tax return for 1987?

13. A debt of $20,000 bearing interest at 16% converted quarterly is to be amortized with payments every 3 months for 10 years. Find the concluding payment if the quarterly payment is rounded up to the: (a) cent; (b) dime; (c) dollar.

[(a) $1010.45; (b) $1007.63; (c) $960.61]

14. Work problem 13 with a rate of 18% converted quarterly.

15. A mobile home is a complete dwelling unit built on a chassis and capable of being towed by a truck. The increased size of mobile homes and the amenities they include have resulted in their becoming widely accepted for family living. Their lower cost makes homeownership available to more people, so that mobile homes now account for the majority of homes sold for under $15,000. Mobile home loans are often made as installment loans, at higher interest rates and on shorter terms than conventional mortgage loans.

A couple buys a $12,000 mobile home and pays $4000 down. The balance is financed at 12% converted monthly over 5 years. Find the monthly payment and the balance due after the 30th payment.

($177.96; $4592.47)

16. Find the answers to problem 15 if the couple gets the loan at 15% converted monthly.

6.6 REFINANCING

After a loan has been partially paid off, sometimes the balance due can be refinanced at a lower rate, which will result in a considerable reduction in the total interest charges. The present value of these interest savings should be balanced against any costs involved in refinancing to see if the change would be a profitable one.

EXAMPLE A family purchased a home and signed a mortgage for $75,000, which required repayment in equal monthly payments over 30 years at 13% converted monthly. Just after making the 60th payment, they have the loan refinanced at 12% converted monthly. If the number of payments remains unchanged, what will the family's new monthly payment be?

SOLUTION   To get the original monthly payment, use formula (17).

$$R = 75,000 \times \frac{i}{1 - (1 + i)^{-360}} = \$829.65$$

Now we get the outstanding balance after 60 payments.

$$75,000(1 + i)^{60} - 829.65\,\frac{(1 + i)^{60} - 1}{i} = 143,164.24 - 69,603.03$$

$$= \$73,561.21$$

The balance becomes the present value of an ordinary annuity of 300 payments. The new payment is obtained using formula (17):

$$R = 73,561.21\,\frac{.01}{1 - (1.01)^{-300}} = \$774.77$$

The difference per month is \$54.88, making the total savings in interest \$16,464. If money is worth 6% converted monthly to the family, the present value of these savings is

$$54.88 \times a_{\overline{300}|\frac{1}{2}\%} = \$8517.75$$

If the cost of refinancing (including any penalty for early payment of the original loan) is less than \$8517.75, the family would be wise to refinance.

6.7 VARIABLE RATE LOANS

With the rapid increase in interest rates in the late 1970s, many lending institutions found themselves in a difficult financial position because they had outstanding loans at lower rates while they were forced to pay high rates to their investors. At the same time they could not invest their money at the available high yields. As a measure to prevent this situation from occurring again, the practice of issuing loans with variable interest rates has become more prevalent. Institutions will usually offer a variable rate loan at a more attractive initial rate than one with a fixed rate. There are several forms of variable rate agreements. One common method is to use a standard benchmark to determine the loan rate. For example, the individual loan rate could be driven by the appropriate Federal Reserve discount rate, the rate quoted for certain U.S. Treasury securities, some measure of the prime rate, or another well-defined measure of yields. A significant change in the benchmark figure would cause a similar change in the loan's interest rate. The borrower and the lender agree that the benchmark will be observed at some regular time interval, such as each month, quarter, or year. If, at that time, the benchmark has changed (either up or down) by some predetermined amount, the loan rate will be changed by a similar quantity. The loan is then, in effect, renegotiated: either the periodic payment or the term is modified in accordance with the new rate.

The frequency and the amount of the possible change in rate are negotiated as part of the original loan agreement. In some cases the two parties agree that the change will not exceed some fixed amount at any one time or that the rate will never go higher or lower than some predetermined values. Borrowers should be aware of the terms of their variable rate agreement. It is possible that the variable rate clause could cause the payment to exceed their ability to pay.

EXAMPLE 1   A variable rate loan for $90,000 is to be repaid with monthly payments over 30 years. The original rate is $12\frac{1}{2}\%$, but the rate is increased to 13% after 5 years. If the payment is modified to maintain the original term, find the change in the payment.

SOLUTION   The loan begins with A_n = $90,000, n = 360, and i = $1\frac{1}{24}\%$.

$$R = \frac{90,000}{a_{\overline{360|}}} = \frac{90,000}{93.6980770}$$

$$= \$960.54$$

In 5 years, 60 payments of $960.54 are made. We must find the outstanding principal after the 60th payment:

$$x = 90,000\left(1 + \frac{.125}{12}\right)^{60} - 960.54 s_{\overline{60}|}$$

$= 90,000 \times 1.8622160851 - 960.54 \times 82.7727442$
$= 167,599.45 - 79,506.53$
$= \$88,092.92$

With the change in rate, there is a new loan for this outstanding balance at 13% for the remaining 25 years. We now can compute the new payment.

$$R = \frac{88,092.92}{a_{\overline{300}|}} = \frac{88,092.92}{88.6654281}$$

$$= \$993.55$$

The payment has been increased by \$33.01, an increase of 3.4%.

EXAMPLE 2[(C)]   Suppose the payment remains constant after the rate change in Example 1, but that the payments are to continue until the loan is repaid. How will this affect the term of the loan?

SOLUTION   We use the logarithmic equation described in section 4.10. The present value is \$88,092.92 and the payment is \$960.54 with $i = 1\frac{1}{12}\%$.

$$n = \frac{-\log\left(1 - \frac{A_{n|}i}{R}\right)}{\log(1 + i)} = 468.02$$

The new rate would require 468 full payments plus a much smaller final payment. The borrower would be required to make 169 more payments than was originally anticipated (approximately 14 more years).

Variable rate loans are often cheaper at the outset, but they can become much more costly later. On the other hand, the borrower may actually save money if the interest rate declines.

EXAMPLE 3   Suppose the rate of the original loan in Example 1 declined to 12% after the first 5 years. Find the new payment if the term is to be unchanged.

SOLUTION The outstanding balance is $88,092.92. We must find the monthly payment for a 25-year loan at 1% per month.

$$R = \frac{88,092.92}{a_{\overline{300}|}} = \frac{88,092.92}{94.946\ 5513}$$

$$= \$927.82$$

This represents a decrease of $32.72 in the monthly payment.

6.8 AMORTIZATION WITH SPECIFIED PAYMENTS

In some transactions the size of the payment is specified, often at some rounded value such as $50, $1000, and so on. Then the number of payments must be determined.

EXAMPLE 1 A debt of $6000 is to be amortized with payments of $1000 at the end of each 6 months. Find the number of payments if the interest rate is 12%.

SOLUTION Substituting in formula (15), we have

$$6000 = 1000a_{\overline{n}|}$$
$$a_{\overline{n}|} = \tfrac{6000}{1000} = 6.00$$

Reference to Table 2 shows that the factor 6.00 lies between 7 and 8 periods. Thus 7 full payments plus a partial payment will be required to amortize the debt.

The concluding irregular payment may be added to the last regular payment, or it may be made one interval after the last full payment. If the concluding payment is small, some lenders prefer to add it to the last full payment. In this book, unless the problem specifies otherwise, follow the common practice of making this payment one period after the last full payment, regardless of its size. On these terms simple interest must be computed on the unpaid balance after the last full payment.

EXAMPLE 2 Find the size of the concluding payment in Example 1 if the last full payment is to be increased by the amount of the outstanding debt.

SOLUTION A time diagram (Figure 6-5) shows that the time of the last full payment is a good place to put the focal date.

The equation of value is

$$x = 6000(1.06)^7 - 1000s_{\overline{7}|}$$
$$= 9021.78 - 8393.84$$
$$= \$627.94$$

The debt would be liquidated with a 7th payment of $1627.94.

EXAMPLE 3 Find the size of the concluding payment in Example 1 if it is made 1 period after the last full payment.

SOLUTION The focal date is put at the time of the 8th payment and the 7 full payments are brought forward as an annuity due. See Figure 6-6.

Figure 6-5

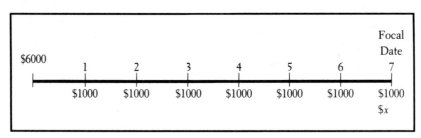

Figure 6-6

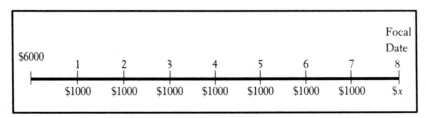

The equation of value is

$$x = 6000(1.06)^8 - 1000(s_{\overline{8}|} - 1) = 9563.09 - 8897.47$$
$$= \$665.62$$

This problem could also be worked by carrying forward the $627.94 balance after the 7th payment in Example 2 at simple interest.

$$x = 627.94(1.06)$$
$$= \$665.62$$

EXAMPLE 4 Construct an amortization schedule for Example 3.

SOLUTION

Amortization Schedule
($6000, 12% Loan with Semiannual Payments of $1000)

Payment Number	Total Payment	Payment on Interest	Payment on Principal	Balance of Loan
				$6000.00
1	$1000.00	$ 360.00	$ 640.00	5360.00
2	1000.00	321.60	678.40	4681.60
3	1000.00	280.90	719.10	3962.50
4	1000.00	237.75	762.25	3200.25
5	1000.00	192.02	807.98	2392.27
6	1000.00	143.54	856.46	1535.81
7	1000.00	92.15	907.85	627.96
8	665.64	37.68	627.96	0.00
	$7665.64	$1665.64	$6000.00	

The 2-cent difference in the final payment in the two examples is due to different frequencies of rounding.

6.9 VARIABLE PAYMENT LOANS

In many consumer loans, the borrower has difficulty making the payments during the early years of the loan but is able to afford the periodic payment much more easily as time goes on. To deal with this situation, some loans are negotiated with variable payments, the size of the payment to increase one or more times during the term of the loan. Usually the lower early payment would at least cover the interest but would decrease the principal much more slowly. Later payments will be higher than those in a standard loan.

EXAMPLE   A home buyer is unable to afford the monthly payment of $1101.09 on a 12%, 20-year loan for $100,000 but agrees to pay $1025 each month for the first 5 years and then bear the monthly cost necessary to repay the full loan in the remaining 15 years. Find the increased payment for the last 15 years.

SOLUTION   Find the outstanding balance after 5 years.

$$x = 100,000(1.01)^{60} - 1025s_{\overline{60}|}$$
$$= \$97,958.26$$

We find the new payment by using formula (17).

$$R = \frac{97,958.26}{a_{\overline{180}|}}$$
$$= \$1175.67$$

ALTERNATE SOLUTION   The loan is repaid with an ordinary annuity of 60 payments of $1025 plus a deferred annuity (deferred 60 months) of 180 unknown payments. We set up an equation of value:

$$100,000 = 1025a_{\overline{60}|} + Ra_{\overline{180}|}(1.01)^{-60}$$
$$100,000 = 46,078.91 + Ra_{\overline{180}|}(1.01)^{-60}$$

$$R = \frac{53,921.09(1.01)^{60}}{a_{\overline{180}|}}$$
$$= \$1175.67$$

This arrangement has the advantage of making the cost more affordable early in the loan's term at the expense of a major increase during the later period. The total cost in interest will be higher. On the other hand, it may make it possible to repay the loan in a shorter time period, thus saving interest costs. The buyer in the example would have been able to afford the monthly payment in a standard 30-year mortgage, but the total interest cost would have been much higher than in the variable payment loan.

6.10   THE POINT SYSTEM

Federal Housing Administration (FHA) and Veterans' Administration (VA) loans have ceilings on interest rates. On conventional mortgages (those not guaranteed or insured by governmental agencies) some states specify a rate ceiling under anti-usury laws. These cases sometimes employ an interesting system called *charging points* to get additional revenue.

A point is a 1% discount from the face value of a loan. Five points means that the lender will advance only 95% of the loan's face value. However, the borrower will be required to repay the loan based on the full face value. For example, if a person needs to borrow $50,000 to purchase a home and is required to pay five points, it will be necessary to take out and repay a loan of $52,631.58. This value is determined by dividing $50,000 by .95. Note that 5% of $52,631.58 is $2631.58. If this amount is deducted from the loan's face value, the needed $50,000 will remain. The borrower gets $50,000 but is required to repay a loan based on the $52,631.58 face value. Therefore the effective rate of the loan is higher than the stated rate.

In some cases the law forbids borrowers to pay points. In those situations the seller assumes the cost of the points. A seller who anticipates the need to pay points will set the price of the property higher to allow for the cost. Sometimes the buyer and the seller split the cost of the points, each paying a part of the discount. In this book we treat all problems as if the buyer (borrower) were paying the points. This approach will give the true interest rate received by the lender.

EXAMPLE 1   A borrower gets a $75,000, 25-year, 13% loan from a lender who charges 4 points. If the borrower pays the points, what is the true interest rate?

SOLUTION   The borrower must get a $78,125 loan in order to receive $75,000. (75,000 ÷ .96 = 78,125.) The monthly payment is based on $78,125. From formula (17) we obtain

$$R = \frac{78,125}{a_{\overline{300}|}} = \$881.13$$

The buyer receives only $75,000, so we have an ordinary annuity with a present value of $75,000 and 300 payments of $881.13. Substituting in formula (15), we have

$$881.13a_{\overline{300}|} = 75,000$$
$$a_{\overline{300}|} = 85.118$$

Reference to the "Present worth of 1 per period" column in Table 3 shows that the nominal rate is between $13\frac{1}{2}\%$ and 14%.

$$
\begin{array}{cccc}
 & j_{(12)} & a_{\overline{300}|} & \\
 & 13.5 & 85.789 & \\
.5 \quad d & j & 85.118 \; \Big] 671 & 2716 \\
 & 14 & 83.073 & \\
\end{array}
$$

$$d = \frac{671}{2716} \times .5 = .12$$

$$j = 13.50 + .12 = 13.62\%$$

Because many students will be confronted with the point problem in their shopping for a home loan, true interest rates corresponding to typical loans and point charges are given in Table 6-2.

These data show the importance of getting the true rate when shopping for credit. Suppose that one lender offers to make a 20-year loan at 12%, but charges the borrower 5 points. A second lender will make the loan at $12\frac{3}{4}\%$, but does not charge any points. The table shows that the $12\frac{3}{4}\%$ loan is the better deal for the borrower.

Because points are charged at the beginning of the loan, none of this charge is recovered if the loan is prepaid. The result is that borrowers who pay off a loan ahead of time pay even higher rates than those shown in the table.

EXAMPLE 2 A person gets a $65,000, 12% loan to be repaid over 30 years. The monthly payment is $668.60. The lender charges 6 points. At the end of 10 years the borrower sells the house and pays off the mortgage. What true rate did the borrower pay?

Table 6-2 True Interest Rates on Discounted Loans

Stated Rate	Points Charged	15-Year Loan	20-Year Loan	25-Year Loan	30-Year Loan
8%	1	8.17%	8.14%	8.12%	8.11%
	2	8.34	8.27	8.24	8.21
	3	8.51	8.41	8.36	8.32
	4	8.68	8.56	8.48	8.44
	5	8.86	8.70	8.61	8.55
	6	9.04	8.85	8.74	8.67
	7	9.22	9.00	8.87	8.78
	8	9.41	9.15	9.00	8.90
	9	9.60	9.30	9.13	9.02
	10	9.79	9.46	9.27	9.15
10%	1	10.18	10.15	10.14	10.13
	2	10.37	10.31	10.27	10.25
	3	10.55	10.46	10.41	10.38
	4	10.73	10.61	10.55	10.51
	5	10.92	10.77	10.69	10.64
	6	11.11	10.92	10.82	10.76
	7	11.31	11.08	10.96	10.89
	8	11.51	11.26	11.11	11.02
	9	11.71	11.43	11.27	11.17
	10	11.91	11.60	11.42	11.31
12%	1	12.19	12.17	12.15	12.14
	2	12.39	12.33	12.30	12.29
	3	12.58	12.50	12.45	12.43
	4	12.78	12.66	12.60	12.57
	5	12.97	12.83	12.76	12.71
	6	13.18	13.00	12.91	12.86
	7	13.39	13.18	13.07	13.00
	8	13.60	13.36	13.23	13.16
	9	13.81	13.55	13.40	13.32
	10	14.03	13.73	13.57	13.48
14%	1	14.20	14.17	14.16	14.15
	2	14.40	14.35	14.32	14.31
	3	14.61	14.53	14.48	14.46
	4	14.82	14.71	14.65	14.62
	5	15.03	14.89	14.82	14.78
	6	15.25	15.08	15.00	14.95
	7	15.47	15.27	15.17	15.12
	8	15.70	15.47	15.36	15.29
	9	15.92	15.67	15.54	15.47
	10	16.16	15.87	15.73	15.65

SOLUTION   After paying the 6 points, the borrower actually received $61,100. The table shows that if the loan was repaid over 30 years, the true rate would be 12.86%. To find the true rate for prepaying the loan, first we get the unpaid balance. A focal date is put at 10 years, and the $65,000 and the 119 payments are brought to this point at the stated rate of 12% converted monthly using the indicated formulas.

$$65,000(1.01)^{120} = \$214,525.15 \qquad (9)$$
$$668.60(s_{\overline{120}|} - 1) = \underline{\ 153,135.27\ } \qquad (18)$$
$$\$\ 61,389.88$$

Now it is necessary to analyze the problem on a cash flow basis. At the beginning of the loan the borrower had an inflow of $61,100. There have been 119 monthly outflows of $668.60 each and a single outflow of $61,389.88 at the end of 10 years. A time diagram (Figure 6-7) helps us to get an overall view of the problem.

The focal date is put at time zero, and the trial-and-error approach is used to find a rate that makes the discounted value of the outflows equal to the $61,100 inflow. We use formula (15) to find the present value of the periodic payments and formula (11) to discount the single sum. At 12% converted monthly the discounted values are

$$668.60a_{\overline{119}|} + 61,389.88(1.01)^{-120} = 46,399.19 + 18,600.81$$
$$= \$65,000$$

Figure 6-7

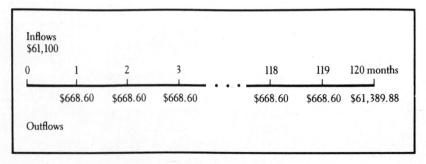

This calculation is really a check on our work. The payments and the balance were computed on the basis of a present value of $65,000 and a 12% rate, so the sum of their discounted values should be $65,000.

To get a present value less than $61,100, we must use a higher rate. At 13% converted monthly, the present value of the outflows is

$$668.60a_{\overline{119}|} + 61,389.88\left(1 + \frac{.13}{12}\right)^{-120} = 44,595.60 + 16,848.07$$
$$= \$61,443.67$$

At $13\frac{1}{2}\%$,

$$668.60a_{\overline{119}|} + 61,389.88(1.01125)^{-120} = 43,732.97 + 16,035.14$$
$$= \$59,786.11$$

We can now use linear interpolation to get an approximation of the true rate.

	Nominal rate	Present value of outflows		
.5	13%	61,444	344	1658
	j 61,100			
	13.5%	59,786		

$$d = \frac{344}{1658} \times .5 = .10$$

True rate = 13.00 + .10 = 13.10%

Exercise 6b

Round all payments up to the cent unless stated otherwise.

1. A 30-year mortgage for $45,000 is being amortized with monthly payments at 14% converted monthly. Just after making the 60th payment, the borrower has the balance refinanced at 12% converted monthly with the term of the loan to remain the same. What will be the total savings in interest?
    ($20,007)

2.   A man gets a $60,000 mortgage on a new home to be repaid in 360 monthly payments at 13% converted monthly. Instead of making the regular 96th payment, he applies $5000 from an inheritance toward the mortgage. At the same time he gets the balance of the debt refinanced at 11% converted monthly with the first payment under the new plan to be made in 1 month. If the duration of the loan remains the same, what is the size of the new monthly payment? If the size of the payments remains the same, how many full payments must he make to pay off the balance?

3.(C)   On September 15, 1984, a couple bought a home. Their loan is to be repaid in 300 payments of $400 each with the first payment on October 15, 1984. If the rate was $12\frac{1}{2}\%$ converted monthly, how much would it cost to pay off the debt on July 15, 1989? Include the payment made on that date.
($35,672.41)

4.(C)   A family buys a $75,000 home with a $15,000 down payment. The remainder is financed with a 30-year variable rate loan having an initial rate of 12.6%. After the 48th payment is made, the lender increases the rate to 12.9%. If the duration of the loan is to remain the same, find the difference in payment at the new rate.

5.(C)   Find the number of payments necessary to repay the loan in Problem 4 if the payment is unchanged.
(389 full payments plus an additional smaller payment)

6.   A loan is to be repaid with $1000 payments every 3 months for 3 years, followed by $2000 quarterly payments for the next 7 years. Find the amount borrowed if the rate is 14% compounded quarterly.

7.   A debt of $8000 is to be amortized with semiannual payments of $1000. How many full payments will be required and what will be the size of the concluding payment 6 months after the last full payment if the rate is: (a) 12%? (b) 14%?
[(a) 11 full payments, concluding payment of $227.63; (b) 12 full payments, concluding payment of $138.12]

8.   A debt of $6500 is to be amortized with semiannual payments of $500. How many full payments will be required and what will be the size of the concluding payment 6 months after the last full payment if the rate is: (a) 10% compounded semiannually? (b) 12% compounded semiannually?

9.(C)   A widow inherits an estate of $12,000 on March 1, 1986. Instead of taking the cash, she invests the money immediately at

6% converted monthly with the understanding that she will be paid $125 each month with the first payment to be made on April 1, 1986. How many $125 payments will she receive? Find the date and size of the concluding payment.

(131 full payments; $14.03 on March 1, 1997)

10.(C)   Work problem 7 if the widow could get 7% converted monthly.

11.   A borrower gets a 5-year, $10,000, 10% loan to be repaid in equal monthly payments. If the lender charges 3 points, what is the true nominal interest rate?

(11.33%)

12.   A person gets a 5-year, $5000, 12% loan to be repaid in equal monthly payments. If the lender charges 4 points, what is the true nominal rate?

6.11   SINKING FUNDS

When a sum of money will be needed at some future date, a good practice is to accumulate systematically a fund that will equal the sum desired at the time it is needed. Money accumulated in this way is called a **sinking fund**. Sinking funds are used to redeem bond issues, pay off other debts, replace worn-out equipment, or provide money for the purchase of new equipment.

Sinking funds are used to retire some loans because the borrower is not allowed to make payments on the principal until the entire debt is due. The creditor may want it this way to avoid the problem of reinvesting a part of the capital every few months. Aside from the extra bother, there is also the possibility that the creditor may have to make the new loan at a lower rate.

Although unequal deposits may be made into a sinking fund at unequal intervals of time, this method is not usually employed because then the problem must be worked sum by sum using the focal date procedure in Chapter 3. A much more common and systematic procedure is to accumulate the fund by equal deposits made at equal intervals. Each periodic deposit is invested on the specified date and allowed to accumulate until the final maturity value is needed. We use this method.

Since the amount needed in the sinking fund, the time it is needed, and the interest rate that the fund will earn are known, a sinking fund becomes simply an ordinary annuity in which the size of the payment is to be determined. When a sinking fund is used to retire a debt, the borrower continues to owe the entire principal on which interest is paid as it falls due to the creditor. The sinking fund is an entirely separate account, and the interest rate it earns will probably be different from the rate paid on the debt.

EXAMPLE A person wants to have $7500 to purchase a new car in 3 years. How much must be deposited every 6 months in an account paying 6% converted semiannually?

SOLUTION Substituting in formula (16), we have

$$R = S_n \times \frac{1}{s_{\overline{n}|}} = 7500 \times \frac{1}{s_{\overline{6}|3\%}}$$

$$= \$1159.49$$

Sinking Fund Schedule

Period	Amount in Fund at Start of Period	Interest Earned on Sinking Fund During Period	Deposit at End of Period	Amount in Fund at End of Period
1	—	—	$1159.49	$1159.49
2	$1159.49	$ 34.78	1159.49	2353.76
3	2353.76	70.61	1159.49	3583.86
4	3583.86	107.52	1159.49	4850.87
5	4850.87	145.53	1159.49	6155.89
6	6155.89	184.68	1159.43[a]	7500.00
		$543.12	$6956.88	

[a] Note that the final payment is somewhat smaller.

Having a schedule that shows how much is in the sinking fund at any time is sometimes desirable. The schedule for the preceding example is shown above.

The advantages of this systematic way of providing for some future purchase are considerable. First of all, the buyer avoids the very high interest rates commonly charged on installment loans. Second, the buyer gets interest on the savings. Third, there is a good chance that the buyer will be able to get a discount when cash is available to pay for the desired item.

6.12 TOTAL PERIODIC CHARGE

In the preceding example we assumed a case in which a person was simply saving money for a future purchase. The most common use of sinking funds is to make provision for retiring a debt. In such cases the borrower must meet two charges — the interest when it is due and the periodic deposits to the sinking fund. Note that there is no relationship between the interest on the debt and the interest earned on the sinking fund. The interest on the debt is not paid from the sinking fund. The two forms of interest are entirely separate. However, for accounting purposes we can add the two to get the total periodic charge, as we show in the following example.

EXAMPLE A person borrows $2000 for 3 years at 10% interest payable semiannually. Periodic deposits are made into a sinking fund earning 5% converted semiannually. Find the total periodic payment and construct a schedule.

Sinking Fund and Interest Schedule

Period	Amount in Fund at Start of Period	Interest Earned on Sinking Fund During Period	Deposit at End of Period	Amount in Fund at End of Period	Interest on Debt	Total Periodic Payment
1	—	—	$ 313.10	$ 313.10	$100.00	$413.10
2	$ 313.10	$ 7.83	313.10	634.03	100.00	413.10
3	634.03	15.85	313.10	962.98	100.00	413.10
4	962.98	24.07	313.10	1300.15	100.00	413.10
5	1300.15	32.50	313.10	1645.75	100.00	413.10
6	1645.75	41.14	313.11[a]	2000.00	100.00	413.11
		$121.39	$1878.61			

[a] The additional penny is needed here because of round-off errors.

SOLUTION The interest every 6 months will be 5% of $2000, or $100. From formula (16), we find the deposit every 6 months to the sinking fund is

$$R = 2000 \times \frac{1}{s_{\overline{6}|\,2\frac{1}{2}\%}} = \$313.10$$

Thus the total cost to the borrower every 6 months will be the sum of these two amounts, or $413.10. Note that the $100 and the $313.10 may be paid to different persons or institutions. However, when the amount in the sinking fund reaches $2000, it will be drawn out and paid to the lender, probably with the last interest payment. The schedule for this example is shown on page 295.

Exercise 6c

Round periodic deposits up to the cent.

1. A firm expects to need $50,000 on May 1, 1994, to replace some machine tools. To provide this amount, the firm makes equal annual deposits into a fund that is invested at 7%. If the first deposit is made on May 1, 1989, and the last deposit is made on May 1, 1994, what will be the size of each deposit? Prepare a schedule for this problem.
    $(R = \$6989.79)$

2. A sinking fund is to accumulate $6000 with 5 equal annual deposits at the end of each year. If interest is earned at 9%, determine the size of the deposits and prepare a schedule.

3. A couple would like to accumulate $40,000 for a down payment on a home by August 1, 1994. They make semiannual deposits in a building and loan association with the first deposit on August 1, 1988, and the last on February 1, 1994. If the building and loan association pays 9% compounded semiannually on February 1 and August 1, how much should the couple deposit every 6 months?
    ($2475.27)

4.(C) What would be the semiannual deposit in problem 3 if the rate is 11% compounded semiannually?

5. A company borrows $80,000 at 12% for 12 years. If a sinking fund is set up at 9% to repay the debt, what is the total annual cost of this obligation?
    ($13,572.06)

6. A woman borrows $5500 for 6 years at 10%. To be sure that she will be able to repay the debt, she makes equal deposits at the

end of each year in an investment paying 6% compounded annually. What is the total annual cost of this loan?

6.13 SINKING FUND WITH SPECIFIED DEPOSIT

In some transactions the size of the payment to the sinking fund is specified, and the problem is to determine the number of payments. Usually in such cases an integral number of payments will not give the exact result desired. This means that an irregular deposit must be made either at the time of the last regular deposit or one period later. In this book we assume the latter procedure unless the problem specifies otherwise.

EXAMPLE A person wants to accumulate $10,000 to start a business. If $750 can be saved every 6 months, how long will it take to accumulate $10,000? The savings at the end of each 6 months are placed in an investment paying 5% compounded semiannually.

SOLUTION Substituting in formula (14), we have

$$10,000 = 750 s_{\overline{n}|\, 2\frac{1}{2}\%}$$

$$s_{\overline{n}|} = \frac{10,000}{750} = 13.33$$

From Table 2 we find that the entrepreneur will have to make 11 deposits of $750 plus a smaller 12th deposit. To get the size of the concluding deposit, the most direct procedure is to get the amount of an annuity due of 11 deposits and subtract this from the $10,000.

$$S_n = R(s_{\overline{n+1}|} - 1)$$
$$= 750(s_{\overline{11+1}|} - 1) = 750(13.79555 - 1)$$
$$= 750 \times 12.79555 = \$9,596.66$$
$$\text{12th payment} = 10,000 - 9,596.66 = \$403.34$$

Note that this or any similar problem can be worked by setting up a focal date and an equation of value. See Figure 6-8.

6.14 COMPARISON OF AMORTIZATION
AND SINKING FUNDS

When a debt is amortized, each payment pays the outstanding interest at that time and the balance is used to reduce the principal. When a sinking fund is used, the entire principal remains unpaid until the due date of the debt. Each interest period, the debtor pays only the interest to the lender. Then a separate deposit is made into a sinking fund that will accumulate to an amount that will retire all or a portion of the debt.

The amortization method has the advantage of being more convenient, since it requires only a single payment each period. The method that will prove to be cheaper depends on the rates of interest. If the rate received on the sinking fund is the same as that charged on the debt, the total periodic cost of the two methods will be the same. If the sinking fund earns a lower rate of interest than is charged on the debt, the periodic cost for the sinking fund method will be greater than that for the amortization method. The reason is that the buyer will be paying one rate of interest on the debt while receiving a lower rate on savings. Conversely, if the borrower can get more interest on the sinking fund than is being paid on the debt, the sinking fund would be preferable. Since such a situation would be very unusual for most borrowers, a person is usually better off amortizing a debt. The effect of different interest rates on the total periodic cost can be shown by an example.

Figure 6-8

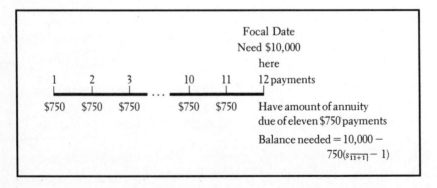

EXAMPLE 1   A person borrows $1000 to be repaid in equal annual installments at the end of each year for 3 years. Find the total annual cost under the following conditions:
(a) The debt is amortized at 8%.
(b) Interest at 8% is paid on the debt and a sinking fund is set up at 7%.
(c) Interest at 8% is paid on the debt and a sinking fund is set up at 8%.
(d) Interest at 8% is paid on the debt and a sinking fund is set up at 9%.

SOLUTION

(a)	(b)
$R = 1000 \dfrac{1}{a_{\overline{3}\,8\%}} = \$388.04$	Interest $= .08 \times 1000 = \$\;\;80.00$
This is the total annual cost since it includes both interest and principal	$R = 1000 \times \dfrac{1}{s_{\overline{3}\,7\%}} = \underline{\;\;311.06}$ Total $\$391.06$

(c)	(d)
Interest $= \$\;\;80.00$	Interest $= \$\;\;80.00$
$R = 1000 \times \dfrac{1}{s_{\overline{3}\,8\%}} = \;\;308.04$ $\overline{\qquad\qquad}$ $\$388.04$	$R = 1000 \times \dfrac{1}{s_{\overline{3}\,9\%}} = \;\;305.06$ $\overline{\qquad\qquad}$ $\$385.06$

Note that this is the same as the amortization plan.

Note that all of the preceding plans allow the entire debt, principal and interest, to be paid in 3 years. Besides simplifying the transaction and usually having a lower periodic cost, the amortization plan has another practical advantage for most borrowers. It literally forces the borrower to reduce the principal along the way. If most people tried to pay future debts by setting up sinking funds, they would probably spend some of the periodic deposits instead of saving them. The result would be that when the debt came due they would not have enough in the sinking fund to pay it. That is why most home mortgages today are paid off with amortization or direct reduction loans.

EXAMPLE 2 A company wants to borrow $1,000,000. One possibility is to borrow the money at 11% converted semiannually and set up a sinking fund at 9% converted semiannually to retire the debt in 10 years. At what rate, converted semiannually, would it be less expensive to amortize the debt?

SOLUTION Find the total periodic payment.

$$\text{Interest}\quad 1,000,000 \times .055 = \$55,000.00$$

$$\text{Payment to sinking fund}\quad 1,000,000 \times \frac{1}{s_{\overline{20}|4\frac{1}{2}\%}} = \underline{31,876.15}$$

$$\text{Total payment every 6 months} = \$86,876.15$$

The total periodic payment becomes the rent of an ordinary annuity with a present value of $1,000,000. Substituting in formula (15), we have

$$86,876.15a_{\overline{20}|} = 1,000,000$$

$$a_{\overline{20}|} = \frac{1,000,000}{86,876.15} = 11.5106$$

Interpolating between the closest nominal rates in Table 2, we obtain

$$
\begin{array}{cccc}
 & j_{(2)} & a_{\overline{20}|} & \\
2\left[d\left[\begin{array}{cc} 10 & 12.4622 \\ j & 11.5106 \\ 12 & 11.4699 \end{array} \right]9516 \right] & & & 9923
\end{array}
$$

$$\frac{d}{2} = \frac{9516}{9923} = .959$$

$$d = 1.92$$

The nominal rate is 10.00 + 1.92 = 11.92% compounded semiannually. If the company can borrow money at less than 11.92% compounded semiannually, it will be less expensive than a straight loan at 11% and a sinking fund of 9%.

Because of the importance of a thorough understanding of the amortization and sinking fund methods, the two are sketched in Figure 6-9 for a debt of $1000 to be repaid with 3 annual payments.

Exercise 6d

Round periodic payments up to the cent.

1. A debt of $50,000 is due at the end of 5 years. To be certain to have this amount when it is due, the borrower decides to set up a sinking fund by making deposits at the end of each year into an account paying 7%. Construct a schedule showing how this fund accumulates.
   (R = $8694.54)

2. A sinking fund is set up to accumulate $85,000 in 6 years. If the fund earns 9% converted annually, what is the size of the deposit at the end of each year? Construct a schedule.

3. A woman wants to accumulate $8000 to start a business. If she can save $800 every 6 months and can invest these savings at 7% compounded semiannually, how long will the accumulation of the necessary capital take her? What is the size of the con-

Figure 6-9 Amortization of a Debt and Sinking Fund

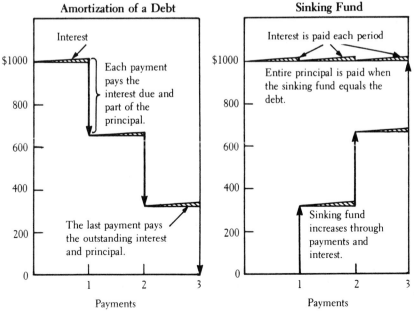

cluding deposit?

(8 full deposits; 9th deposit of $505.20)

4.   A couple wants to accumulate $15,000 for a down payment on a home. If they can deposit $900 at the end of each 6 months in a savings and loan association paying 6% converted semi-annually, how many full deposits must they make and what will be the size of the concluding deposit?

5.   The management of a factory wants to set up a sinking fund to provide $40,000 for the replacement of a machine at the end of 6 years. If equal deposits are made at the end of each 6 months in a fund earning 9% converted semiannually, find the size of each deposit. If the machine has to be replaced at the end of 4 years, how much will be in the fund at that time?

($2586.65; $24,262.81)

6.   Work problem 5 with a rate of 7% converted semiannually.

7.   A man borrows $5000 to be repaid in equal annual installments at the end of each year for 6 years. Find the total annual cost under the following conditions:

(a) The debt is amortized at 8%.

(b) Interest is paid on the debt at 8% and a sinking fund is set up at 6%.

(c) Interest is paid on the debt at 8% and a sinking fund is set up at 8%.

(d) Interest is paid on the debt at 8% and a sinking fund is set up at 9%.

[(a) $1081.58; (b) $1116.82; (c) $1081.58; (d) $1064.60]

8.$^{(C)}$ Find the total annual cost for a loan of $12,000 repaid in 4 equal annual payments under the following conditions:

(a) The debt is amortized at 12%.

(b) Interest is paid on the debt at 12% and a sinking fund is set up at 10%.

(c) Interest is paid on the debt at 12% and a sinking fund is set up at 12%.

(d) Interest is paid on the debt at 12% and a sinking fund is set up at 14%.

9.$^{(C)}$ A firm can borrow $10,000 at $13\frac{1}{2}$% per annum for 5 years. A sinking fund could be set up at 8% converted annually to repay the debt. At what rate would an amortization plan have the same annual cost?

(16.0%)

10.(C)   A company can borrow $100,000 at 12% for 10 years. To repay the debt at the end of 10 years, a sinking fund would be set up at 8% converted annually. Another lender will provide the money at 15% and permit the loan to be amortized with 10 annual payments. Which plan would you choose for the company? Provide the data on which you base your answer.

6.15 AIDS TO COMPUTATION

In most businesses a calculator is available for doing the arithmetic in mathematics of finance problems. The manufacturer's representative should be asked to provide instruction sheets pertaining to the types of problems encountered in the business. These instruction sheets describe the most efficient way to solve problems with the particular make of machine. In some cases, a valuable built-in check is included as a part of the suggested procedure. If you use a calculator to prepare a short amortization schedule using equal payments, you can check the work by noting whether the last payment is within a few cents of the other payments. If you are preparing a long schedule by line-by-line simple interest computations, an error early in the work will be serious if it is not discovered quickly. By using the method described in section 6.3, you can compute the outstanding principal for certain lines (such as every 12th line) before doing the detailed computations. Then you will discover an error as soon as the simple interest computations do not agree with the previously computed principal for that line. Differences of a few cents due to rounding entries to the penny may occur, in which case the value to retain is the one resulting from the line-by-line computations.

Because of the labor required to prepare long amortization schedules, the work is often done by specialists in the field, such as the Financial Publishing Company. The schedules can be prepared quickly and at reasonable cost with modern electronic computing equipment. A computer program for producing amortization schedules is included in the Appendix. A few lines from a long schedule are shown in Table 6-3. The final entry in each line is the outstanding balance after the payment has been made. The schedule shows exactly how much of each payment goes to principal and how much to interest. The schedule given is for a $10,000 loan at 12% converted monthly to be repaid in 30 years with payments of $102.87 a month. You will note that the last payment is somewhat lower.

6.16 SOME PRACTICAL POINTS

Most students will borrow thousands of dollars to buy a home some day. Here are a few rules that can save hundreds of dollars.

1. *Look for a low rate.* Throughout this text many problems have been worked using different rates to show that a small difference in the rate may mean hundreds of dollars difference in interest. For example, on a $10,000 loan at 13% to be repaid monthly over 25

Table 6-3 Schedule of Direct Reduction Loan

Rate: 12%	Payment: $102.87	Loan: $10,000	Term: 30 years
Payment Number	Payment on Interest	Principal	Balance of Loan
1	$100.00	$ 2.87	$9997.13
2	99.97	2.90	9994.23
3	99.94	2.93	9991.30
4	99.91	2.96	9988.34
⋮	⋮	⋮	⋮
119	93.58	9.29	9349.07
120	93.49	9.38	9339.69
121	93.40	9.47	9330.22
⋮	⋮	⋮	⋮
179	86.00	16.87	8583.06
180	85.83	17.04	8566.02
181	85.66	17.21	8548.81
⋮	⋮	⋮	⋮
290	51.96	50.91	5145.01
291	51.45	51.42	5093.59
292	50.94	51.93	5041.66
293	50.42	52.45	4989.21
⋮	⋮	⋮	⋮
358	2.72	100.15	171.53
359	1.72	101.15	70.38
360	.70	70.38	.00

years, the total interest is $23,837. On the same loan at $12\frac{1}{2}\%$, the total interest is $32,712. When a difference of only $\frac{1}{2}\%$ can save $8875 on a relatively small loan, it is easy to see why a little time should be spent looking for the best available rate. If it is necessary to make a loan at a relatively high rate, do not overlook the possibility of having it refinanced later at a lower rate.

2. *Pay off quickly.* As long as you owe thousands of dollars, you will be paying a lot of interest every year even though you have a relatively low rate. The sooner a loan is paid off, the less interest will be charged. A $10,000 loan paid off in 20 years at 12% will cost $16,426 in interest. If the same loan is paid off in 10 years, the interest will drop to $7218, a difference of $9208. Interest charges for common rates and payment periods are shown in Table 6-4.

3. *Keep payments within your means.* The preceding paragraph pointed out the savings that result from paying a loan off quickly. But be careful not to commit yourself to payments that are beyond your means. Table 6-5 shows how the monthly payment varies with the rate and payment period.

4. *Avoid penalty clauses.* Fortunately, there is a way to keep the monthly payments within your means and yet be able to pay the loan off quickly if your income increases or you receive a sum of money from an inheritance or other source. Get a loan that has a monthly payment you can afford but one that can be paid off more rapidly *without a penalty* if you are able at any time to make larger payments. The borrower who has prepaid part of a loan may be helped later if sickness or temporary loss of income prevents the making of some of the regular monthly payments.

5. *Be careful of variable rates.* Variable rate mortgages can begin with a rate that is lower than that for a fixed rate mortgage, but the rate could increase significantly during the term of the loan. You should be confident that an increase in rate will not cause the payment to exceed an affordable amount. Nevertheless, be aware of the frequency of change and the maximum change at any time.

6. *Watch out for points.* If you are thinking of borrowing from a lender who charges points, be sure to compare the true rate of interest on the loan with other sources of credit. It may be that a "12%" loan with points is more expensive than a true 13% from another lender.

7. *Make a large down payment.* The larger the down payment, the less you will have to borrow and the less you will pay in interest. However, don't make the mistake of putting all of your cash into

Table 6-4 Total Interest on a $10,000 Amortization Loan

Payment Period		Nominal Annual Rate			
Years	Months	6%	7%	8%	9%
10	120	$ 3,324	$ 3,933	$ 4,560	$ 5,202
15	180	5,190	6,180	7,203	8,257
20	240	7,196	8,607	10,076	11,595
25	300	9,332	11,204	13,157	15,176
30	360	11,586	13,954	16,417	18,969
40	480	16,414	19,832	23,379	27,027
		10%	11%	12%	13%
10	120	$ 5,859	$ 6,531	$ 7,218	$ 7,918
15	180	9,345	10,459	11,604	12,775
20	240	13,162	14,773	16,426	18,118
25	300	17,264	19,406	21,599	23,837
30	360	21,594	24,286	27,033	29,823
40	480	30,762	34,558	38,408	42,301
		14%	15%	16%	17%
10	120	$ 8,632	$ 9,361	$10,102	$10,856
15	180	13,972	15,193	16,438	17,704
20	240	19,846	21,603	23,391	25,206
25	300	26,114	28,427	30,767	33,134
30	360	32,656	35,522	38,413	41,325
40	480	46,218	50,158	54,114	58,083
		18%	19%	20%	21%
10	120	$11,623	$12,402	$13,191	$13,993
15	180	18,989	20,292	21,613	22,953
20	240	27,042	28,897	30,774	32,665
25	300	35,525	37,931	40,355	42,791
30	360	44,256	47,200	50,160	53,126
40	480	62,058	66,042	70,030	74,024
		22%	23%	24%	25%
10	120	$14,804	$15,626	$16,459	$17,300
15	180	24,304	25,671	27,049	28,441
20	240	34,570	36,490	38,420	40,359
25	300	45,239	47,696	50,159	52,631
30	360	56,096	59,077	62,061	65,046
40	480	78,018	82,011	86,010	90,008

Table 6-5 Monthly Payment on a $10,000 Amortization Loan
(Payment is Rounded up to the Cent)

Payment Period		Nominal Annual Rate			
Years	Months	6%	7%	8%	9%
10	120	$111.03	$116.11	$121.33	$126.68
15	180	84.39	89.89	95.57	101.43
20	240	71.65	77.53	83.65	89.98
25	300	64.44	70.68	77.19	83.92
30	360	59.96	66.54	73.38	80.47
40	480	55.03	62.15	69.54	77.14
		10%	11%	12%	13%
10	120	$132.16	$137.76	$143.48	$149.32
15	180	107.47	113.66	120.02	126.53
20	240	96.51	103.22	110.11	117.16
25	300	90.88	98.02	105.33	112.79
30	360	87.76	95.24	102.87	110.62
40	480	84.92	92.83	100.85	108.96
		14%	15%	16%	17%
10	120	$155.27	$161.34	$167.52	$173.80
15	180	133.18	139.96	146.88	153.91
20	240	124.36	131.68	139.13	146.69
25	300	120.38	128.09	135.89	143.78
30	360	118.49	126.45	134.48	142.57
40	480	117.12	125.33	133.57	141.84
		18%	19%	20%	21%
10	120	$180.19	$186.68	$193.26	$199.94
15	180	161.05	168.29	175.63	183.07
20	240	154.34	162.07	169.89	177.77
25	300	151.75	159.77	167.85	175.97
30	360	150.71	158.89	167.11	175.35
40	480	150.12	158.42	166.73	175.05
		22%	23%	24%	25%
10	120	$206.70	$213.55	$220.49	$227.50
15	180	190.58	198.17	205.83	213.56
20	240	185.71	193.71	201.75	209.83
25	300	184.13	192.32	200.53	208.77
30	360	183.60	191.88	200.17	208.46
40	480	183.37	191.69	200.02	208.35

308 MATHEMATICS OF FINANCE

the down payment. Moving expenses, needed equipment for a new home, and other expenses involved in getting settled may amount to a considerable sum. If you have to get a small loan from a bank or loan company or buy on the installment plan, you may have to pay 15% or more interest a year, as was pointed out in Chapter 4. Too many people try to buy a home with a minimum down payment. It is far better to save money and make a large down payment. The rate of interest charged on a home mortgage is sometimes related to the percentage the down payment bears to the cost of the house. A larger down payment may reduce the rate on the unpaid balance.

8. *Contact several lenders.* Mortgage loans are made by many types of lenders – commercial and savings banks, savings and loan associations (sometimes called building and loan associations), insurance companies, private individuals, and others. Their lending practices, rates, appraisals, closing costs, and down payment requirements vary, so it will pay you to talk with several lenders when you are in the market for a loan. Before you apply for a loan, as in all installment buying, read the application carefully. You may be required to pay a fee even if you decide to get the loan elsewhere. If you are interested in an FHA or VA loan, remember that the money is still supplied by a private lender. No matter where you get a loan, be sure that the principal is reduced as payments are made.

9. *Know what you owe.* Always know how much you still owe and the allocation of your payments to principal and to interest. Home buyers should be sure to claim any tax advantages to which they are entitled. One way to determine how much interest has been paid is to get periodic statements from the lender. Another way is to get an amortization schedule. A portion of a schedule is presented in Table 6-6 to show how much valuable information is contained in a schedule of this type.

This schedule is for a conventional mortgage loan of $10,000 to be repaid over 30 years. The rate is 12% converted monthly. The monthly payment rounded up to the cent is $102.87. Borrowers who get a Federal Housing Administration insured mortgage pay, in addition to the interest, a mortgage insurance premium of $\frac{1}{2}\%$ a year on the average scheduled balance of loan principal outstanding during the year. FHA insurance protects the lender against loss on the loan. It does not protect the borrower against loss; but because of the insurance, lenders are able and willing to make loans on terms that bring homeownership within the reach of many families who otherwise could not afford it. Table 6-6 shows that during the first year $1198.02 goes to interest, leaving only $36.42 to reduce the debt.

   Table 6-7 shows the schedule for the 15th year. After the 180th payment, the halfway point in the term of the mortgage, the borrower still owes over 85% of the principal. The 180 payments, which total $18,516.60, have reduced the mortgage by only $1433.98. Payments to interest are still much greater than the amount going to principal.

   The schedule for the last year is shown in Table 6-8. The principal is being reduced much more rapidly now. Note that the last payment is somewhat lower than the others. This is a result of rounding up when determining the payment. The last line in the table gives the 30-year totals.

10. *Allow for closing costs.* Attorney fees, title insurance, property survey, recording fees, lender's service charges, and other items may require last-minute cash outlays when a house is purchased. Closing costs may run from nothing to several hundred dollars. Get an estimate from the lender and add the money required for closing to your other cash needs.

Table 6-6 Amortization Schedule — The First Year

Loan: $10,000	Term 30 Years	Rate: 12%		Payment: $102.87
Payment Number	Total Payment	Payment to Interest	Principal	Balance of Loan
				$10,000.00
1	$ 102.87	$ 100.00	$ 2.87	9,997.13
2	102.87	99.97	2.90	9,994.23
3	102.87	99.94	2.93	9.991.30
4	102.87	99.91	2.96	9,988.34
5	102.87	99.88	2.99	9,985.35
6	102.87	99.85	3.02	9,982.33
7	102.87	99.82	3.05	9,979.28
8	102.87	99.79	3.08	9,976.20
9	102.87	99.76	3.11	9,973.09
10	102.87	99.73	3.14	9,969.95
11	102.87	99.70	3.17	9,966.78
12	102.87	99.67	3.20	9,963.58
	$1234.44	$1198.02	$36.42	

Table 6-7 The 15th Year

| Payment Number | Total Payment | Payment to | | Balance of Loan |
		Interest	Principal	
169	$ 102.87	$ 87.60	$ 15.27	$8744.44
170	102.87	87.44	15.43	8729.01
171	102.87	87.29	15.58	8713.43
172	102.87	87.13	15.74	8697.69
173	102.87	86.98	15.89	8681.80
174	102.87	86.82	16.05	8665.75
175	102.87	86.66	16.21	8649.54
176	102.87	86.50	16.37	8633.17
177	102.87	86.33	16.54	8616.63
178	102.87	86.17	16.70	8599.93
179	102.87	86.00	16.87	8583.06
180	102.87	85.83	17.04	8566.02
	$1234.44	$1040.75	$193.69	

Table 6-8 The 30th Year

| Payment Number | Total Payment | Payment to | | Balance of Loan |
		Interest	Principal	
349	$ 102.87	$ 11.30	$ 91.57	$1038.02
350	102.87	10.38	92.49	945.53
351	102.87	9.46	93.41	852.12
352	102.87	8.52	94.35	757.77
353	102.87	7.58	95.29	662.48
354	102.87	6.62	96.25	566.23
355	102.87	5.66	97.21	469.02
356	102.87	4.69	98.18	370.84
357	102.87	3.71	99.16	271.68
358	102.87	2.72	100.15	171.53
359	102.87	1.72	101.15	70.38
360	71.08	.70	70.38	0.00
	$ 1202.65	$ 73.06	$ 1129.59	
	$37,001.41	$27,001.41	$10,000.00	

REVIEW EXERCISES FOR CHAPTER 6

Round all payments up to the cent unless otherwise indicated.

1. A family bought a house for $50,000. They paid $10,000 down and got a 30-year mortgage at 9% with monthly payments of $321.85. After making the 144th payment they sell the house. How much of the loan have they paid off?
   ($5631.00)

2. Find the monthly payment on a $35,000, 25-year loan at 13% converted monthly if the payment is rounded up to the: (a) cent; (b) dime; (c) dollar.

3. Find the concluding payment in each part of problem 2.
   [(a) $377.57; (b) $265.27; (c) 299th payment of $213.02]

4. A couple got a 25-year, 12% home loan for $50,000. The first monthly payment of $526.62 was made on June 1, 1980. Just after making the payment on May 1, 1991, the couple re-finances the balance at 11% converted monthly. Find the new payment and the total savings in interest if the duration of the loan remains the same.

5. If money is worth 6% converted monthly to the couple in problem 4, would the refinancing be worthwhile for them if the cost of refinancing is $2500?
   (Worth $529.84 now to refinance)

6.$^{(C)}$ Determine the number of payments if the couple in problem 4 decides when refinancing to continue to pay $526.62 monthly.

7. Find the true nominal interest rate for a $20,000, 12-year loan at 14% converted monthly with 5 points.
   (15.19%)

8. Give the amortization schedule for a $10,000 loan at 10% to be repaid in 5 semiannual payments.

9. A company has a debt of $15,000 to be repaid in 5 years. If all rates are compounded semiannually, find the semiannual cost under the following conditions:
   (a) The debt is amortized at 9%.
   (b) Interest is paid at 9% on the debt and a sinking fund is set up at 8%.
   (c) Interest is paid on the debt at 9% and a sinking fund is set up at 9%.
   (d) Interest is paid on the debt at 9% and a sinking fund is set up at 10%.
   [(a) $1895.69; (b) $1924.37; (c) $1895.69; (d) $1867.57]

10. Set up the sinking fund schedule to accumulate $10,000 in 4 years at 6% converted annually.

Chapter 7

Bonds

7.1 BONDS AND STOCKS

When a corporation or government needs money for an extended period of time, the amount required may be too large to obtain from a single bank or other lender. This situation can be met by issuing **bonds** that are purchased by individuals, insurance companies, and other investors. Thus the buyer of a bond lends money to the organization that issued the bond. A stockholder, on the other hand, is a part owner of the corporation. Interest must be paid on bonds before dividends are declared on stocks. The *face value* or *par value* of a bond, the *interest rate*, and the *term* or *maturity* are quoted in the bond itself. Therefore we are able to use the compound interest and annuity formulas and tables to get either the price to yield a desired return or the return corresponding to a quoted price.

7.2 KINDS OF BONDS

Bonds may be classified in several ways. A bond may be **registered** or **unregistered**. Registered bonds have the name of the owner on them and are valueless to anyone except the person whose name is registered with the issuing company or government. Unregistered, or bearer, bonds do not have the owner's name printed on them. Bearer bonds and bonds registered only as to principal are printed with attached coupons, which are dated serially with the dates on which interest is due. To obtain the interest, the holder of a coupon bond clips each coupon and presents it to a bank or broker for collection.

A coupon bond consists of two parts:

1. The bond itself, which is redeemable on the stated date (see Figure 7-1).
2. Coupons, which can be cashed periodically (see Figure 7-2).

Figure 7-1 City of Warren, Ohio, Bond

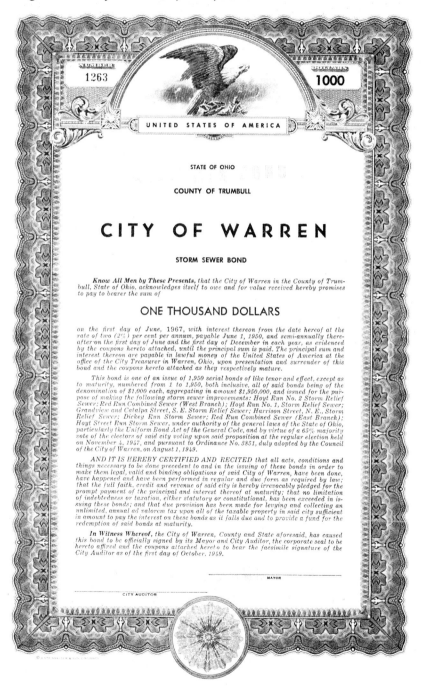

NUMBER
1263

DOLLARS
1000

UNITED STATES OF AMERICA

STATE OF OHIO

COUNTY OF TRUMBULL

CITY OF WARREN

STORM SEWER BOND

Know All Men by These Presents, that the City of Warren in the County of Trumbull, State of Ohio, acknowledges itself to owe and for value received hereby promises to pay to bearer the sum of

ONE THOUSAND DOLLARS

on the first day of June, 1967, with interest thereon from the date hereof at the rate of two (2%) per cent per annum, payable June 1, 1950, and semi-annually thereafter on the first day of June and the first day of December in each year, as evidenced by the coupons hereto attached, until the principal sum is paid. The principal sum and interest thereon are payable in lawful money of the United States of America at the office of the City Treasurer in Warren, Ohio, upon presentation and surrender of this bond and the coupons hereto attached as they respectively mature.

This bond is one of an issue of 1,950 serial bonds of like tenor and effect, except as to maturity, numbered from 1 to 1,950, both inclusive, all of said bonds being of the denomination of $1,000 each, aggregating in amount $1,950,000, and issued for the purpose of making the following storm sewer improvements: Hoyt Run No. 2 Storm Relief Sewer; Red Run Combined Sewer (West Branch); Hoyt Run No. 1, Storm Relief Sewer; Grandview and Catalpa Street, S. E. Storm Relief Sewer; Harrison Street, N. E., Storm Relief Sewer; Dickey Run Storm Sewer; Red Run Combined Sewer (East Branch); Hoyt Street Run Storm Sewer, under authority of the general laws of the State of Ohio, particularly the Uniform Bond Act of the General Code, and by virtue of a 65% majority vote of the electors of said city voting upon said proposition at the regular election held on November 4, 1947, and pursuant to Ordinance No. 3851, duly adopted by the Council of the City of Warren, on August 1, 1949.

AND IT IS HEREBY CERTIFIED AND RECITED that all acts, conditions and things necessary to be done precedent to and in the issuing of these bonds in order to make them legal, valid and binding obligations of said City of Warren, have been done, have happened and have been performed in regular and due form as required by law; that the full faith, credit and revenue of said city is hereby irrevocably pledged for the prompt payment of the principal and interest thereof at maturity; that no limitation of indebtedness or taxation, either statutory or constitutional, has been exceeded in issuing these bonds; and that due provision has been made for levying and collecting an unlimited, annual ad valorem tax upon all of the taxable property in said city sufficient in amount to pay the interest on these bonds as it falls due and to provide a fund for the redemption of said bonds at maturity.

In Witness Whereof, the City of Warren, County and State aforesaid, has caused this bond to be officially signed by its Mayor and City Auditor, the corporate seal to be hereto affixed and the coupons attached hereto to bear the facsimile signature of the City Auditor as of the first day of October, 1949.

MAYOR

CITY AUDITOR

Bonds may also be subdivided according to the security backing them. A **mortgage bond** is secured by a mortgage issued against property of the corporation. A **debenture bond** is secured only by the general credit of the corporation, that is, the reputation of the firm for meeting its obligations. Other types exist, but we do not go into them here because the computations involved in calculating the value of a bond are not affected by the security behind it.

Interest on a bond may accumulate and be paid in one lump sum when the bond matures. Government savings bonds are the most common example of this type of bond. Since the value of government savings bonds at any time after issue is fixed and is printed on the bond, we do not discuss them further. Our discussion is limited to those bonds that have interest payments made periodically, usually semi-annually.

Interest earned on corporation bonds and on bonds issued by the federal government is subject to federal income taxes. State and local government bonds, which are known as **municipal bonds**, are exempt from federal income taxes. Municipals are issued not only by states, towns, and cities, but also by housing authorities, port authorities, and other local government agencies responsible for providing and maintaining community facilities. Most states give preferential tax treatment to their own municipal bonds. However, interest on bonds issued by

Figure 7-2 Coupons for Warren Bond

other states may be subject to tax. Municipals are a favored investment of people in the higher tax brackets. A person in the 50% tax bracket would get the same net return from a municipal paying 6% as from a stock that pays a dividend equal to 12% of the purchase price, and probably with less risk.

The **face value**, or **denomination**, of a bond is usually some simple figure such as $100, $500, or $1000. Most bonds are redeemed at **face value**, or **par**, at maturity.

7.3 CALL PROVISION

The issuer of a bond may have the option of calling the bond before maturity. This **call provision** gives the issuer of the bond the advantage of being able to time repayments to suit financial needs and objectives as they develop. If interest rates decline, a call provision enables a company to call in old bonds and replace them with bonds paying a lower rate. The redemption price of a bond called before maturity is a previously specified percentage of the par value. A $1000 bond redeemable at 102 during a certain year would have a redemption price of $1020 during that year. From the bond owner's standpoint, a call provision has the disadvantage that the call premium may not be enough to provide compensation for having to reinvest funds at a lower rate of interest. To protect buyers of new bonds from early call, most bonds have a stated number of years, typically 5 or 10, of protection against early redemption of the bond. The prospectus that describes a bond issue lists the dates when the bond may be called and the corresponding redemption prices.

7.4 BOND TRANSACTIONS

Bonds are traded on the New York Stock Exchange, the American Stock Exchange, and other exchanges throughout the country. Many large blocks of bonds are traded in the over-the-counter market. This market is not a place but a method of doing business by private negotiation among dealers who use the telephone to buy and sell securities.

Many newspapers publish tables of bond information. Bonds are listed alphabetically by type: corporation, foreign, municipal, and government. Symbols and abbreviations, which vary with different papers, are explained in footnotes. Figure 7-3, from the Otober 22, 1976, issue of the *Wall Street Journal*, is a good illustration of information given in bond tables.

7.5 VALUATION OF A BOND

A fundamental bond problem is the determination of the price an investor can pay for a bond to return the desired yield on the purchase price. This problem involves two rates of interest. One is the rate that the issuing organization pays on the face value of the bond. The other is the yield to maturity that the purchaser gets on the investment. For example, several years ago, when interest rates were lower than they are today, a corporation issued a $1000, 5% bond with semiannual interest payments. The owner of this bond will get $25 every 6 months regardless of what was paid for the bond. If an investor expects more than 5% on money invested in bonds, this 5% bond must be purchased for less than $1000. We must determine what the price would be to produce a specific yield to maturity — such as 8%.

Over the years a special terminology has grown up in connection with the buying and selling of bonds. Since bond valuation is based on formulas already obtained for single sums and annuities, the main problem for students is to gain an understanding of bond terminology, including the symbols we define as follows:

F = the face or par value of the bond.
C = the redemption price of the bond. This price will be the same as the par value of the bond unless stated otherwise.
r = interest rate paid on the bond per period.
Fr = amount of each coupon or interest payment. From now on we use the word *coupon* for any periodic interest payment. Computations are the same whether the bondholder clips a coupon or the company mails a check for the interest.
n = number of interest conversion periods from the given date to the redemption date or the maturity date of the bond.
i = yield or investor's rate per period. This rate of interest is what is actually earned by the investor on the investment.
V = value of the bond.
P = premium.
D = discount.

Figure 7-3 How to Read a Bond Table

Sales for the day on a par value basis.

Bond quotations are on a basis of 100. Most corporation bonds have a face value of $1000. For a $1000 bond a quotation of 107½ means $1075.

"cv" means the bond is convertible into the company's common stock. Details of the conversion can be obtained from a broker.

Annual interest rate and year bond matures. This $1000 bond pays $48 a year interest and matures in 1987.

Abbreviated name of the company. In this case, American Airlines.

Yield rate to the buyer at current price.

Number of bonds sold this day, in 100s. Here, 1300.

For this bond the high for the day was 104¾, low was 104⅝, and the closing price was 104¾. The bond closed ⅝ points or $.625 above the previous closing price.

CORPORATION BONDS

Volume, $18,980,000

Bonds	Cur Yld	Vol	High	Low	Close	Net Chg
ARA 4⅝s96	cv	5	69⅛	69⅛	69⅛	− ⅞
ATO 4⅜s87	cv	1	63⅜	63⅜	63⅜	− ⅛
AddM 9⅜95	9.8	1	95¾	95¾	95¾	+ ¾
AetnCr 9¾86	9.3	1	104⅜	104⅜	104⅜	....
AirRe 3⅞87	cv	27	93	93	93	+2
AlaBnc 8s99	7.9	7	101½	101⅛	101⅛	− ¼
AlaP 8½s01	9.0	9	94	94	94	+ ¾
AlaP 8¼s03	9.0	8	91¾	91¾	91¾	....
AlaP 9¾s04	9.4	5	103¾	103¾	103¾	+ ¾
Ala 8⅞06	..	5	99¼	99¼	99¼	+ ⅛
Alexn 5½96	cv	4	57½	57	57½	− ½
AllgWt 4s98	10.	6	40	39	39	−3¾
AldCh 5.2s91	6.4	13	80⅞	80⅞	80⅞	....
AlldCh 7⅞96	8.0	5	98⅜	98⅜	98⅜	+1¼
AlldPd 7s84	8.8	5	79½	79½	79½	....
AlldSt 4½81	cv	1	149	149	149	+7
AldSu 5¾87	cv	34	49	48	48	− ½
Alcoa 4¼s82	4.9	10	87¼	87¼	87¼	+ ¾
Alcoa 5¼s91	cv	64	107	106½	106½	− ¼
Alcoa 6s92	7.1	40	85⅜	85	85	− ¼
Alcoa 9s95	8.5	2	105¾	105¾	105¾	+1¾
Alco 7.45s96	8.0	25	93⅛	93	93	+1
AluCa 9½95	9.2	5	103½	103½	103½	−1½
AMAX 8s86	8.1	1	99¼	99¼	99¼	....
AMAX 8½96	8.5	5	100⅛	100	100	− ⅛
Amerce 5s92	cv	4	71	71	71	+1
AHes 6¾96	8.4	5	80⅝	80⅝	80⅝	−1⅞
AFoP 4.8s87	6.7	5	71⅝	71⅝	71⅝	....
AForP 5s30	8.3	55	60	59⅝	60	+ ¾
AFor 5s30r	..	5	59¼	59¼	59¼	+ ¼
AAirl 4¼s92	cv	33	55	54¾	54¾	....
AAirln 11s88	10.	5	106⅜	106⅜	106⅜	....
AAirl 10⅞88	10.	5	106	106	106	− ¼
ABrnd 4⅝90	6.4	35	72	72	72	+1
ABrnd 9⅝79	9.0	15	107	107	107	+ ⅜
ABrnd 8⅛85	7.9	5	103⅛	103⅛	103⅛	+ ⅛
ACeM 6¾91	cv	39	55	53	55	+2⅞
AFlet 6¾s78	6.9	4	98	98	98	....
AHoist 5½93	cv	9	82¼	81¾	81¾	− ¼
AHosp 5¾99	cv	11	123½	123½	123½	−1
AInvt 8¾s89	9.6	10	91	91	91	+ ⅞
AMF 4¼s81	cv	1	86	86	86	....
AmMot 6s88	cv	16	62⅞	62⅝	62⅝	− ¼
ASmel 4⅝88	6.7	1	68¾	68¾	68¾	−1¼
ASug 5.3s93	7.4	25	71½	71½	71½	+ ⅞
ASu 5.3s93r	..	2	71	71	71	+1¼
ATT 2¾s80	3.1	13	88¾	88	88¾	+ ½
ATT 3¼s84	4.3	5	75⅞	75⅞	75⅞	+ ⅛
ATT 4⅜s85	5.4	129	80¾	80⅝	80⅝	− ⅛
ATT 4⅜s85r		30	80⅝	80⅝	80⅝	+1⅞
ATT 2⅝s86	3.9	30	68	67½	¾⅞½	+ ¼
ATT 2⅞s87	4.2	1	67¾	67¾	67¾	+1¼
ATT 3⅞s90	5.7	9	68	68	68	....
ATT 8¾2000	8.3	57	105⅞	105¾	105¾	− ⅛
ATT 7.75s77	7.7	37	100½	100⅛	100⅛	− ¼
ATT 8.7s02	8.3	28	105	105	105	....
ATT 7s01	7.8	47	89¾	89¼	89¼	− ⅝
ATT 6½s79	6.5	10	100	100	100	....
ATT 7⅛s03	7.9	53	90⅝	90½	90⅝	+ ⅛
ATT 8.80s05	8.3	33	106	106	106	+ ¼
ATT 7¾s82	7.5	44	103⅜	103	103⅜	+ ¼
ATT 8⅝s07	8.2	26	104¾	104⅝	104¾	+ ⅝
Amfac 5¼94	cv	14	63½	63¼	63½	+ ¼

Source: Reprinted with permission of *The Wall Street Journal*, © Dow Jones and Company, Inc., 1976. All rights reserved.

Now we get the value of a bond on a coupon date, the day on which the organization that issued the bond pays interest. The seller will keep the coupon that is due on that date. The buyer pays for the present value of the redemption price of the bond and the present value of all future interest payments. These present values are to be *computed at the yield rate* because this is the return the investor wants on the investment. The bond rate is used only to calculate the periodic interest payment or coupon.

Adding the present value of the redemption price of the bond and the present value of the annuity formed by the coupons gives us the basic formula for the value of a bond. See Figure 7-4.

$$V = C(1 + i)^{-n} + Fra_{\overline{n}|i} \qquad (24)$$

EXAMPLE 1 Find the value of a $1000 bond with interest at 4% payable semiannually if the bond is bought 3 years before maturity to yield 7% on the investment. This rate is sometimes referred to as a 7% basis.

SOLUTION The semiannual interest payments are 2% of $1000, or $20. The buyer of this bond gets the present value at 7% of $1000 due in 3 years, and the present value at 7% of the 6 interest payments of $20 each. (See Figure 7-5.) We assume that the yield or

Figure 7-4

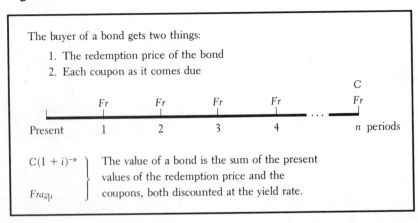

The buyer of a bond gets two things:

    1. The redemption price of the bond

    2. Each coupon as it comes due

	Fr	Fr	Fr	Fr		C, Fr
Present	1	2	3	4	...	n periods

$C(1 + i)^{-n}$ ⎫
⎬ The value of a bond is the sum of the present values of the redemption price and the
$Fra_{\overline{n}|i}$ ⎭ coupons, both discounted at the yield rate.

investment rate is compounded at the same time as the interest is paid on the bond. Thus the yield rate per period is $3\frac{1}{2}\%$, and the problem looks like this:

$$V = (1000 \times .813501) + (20 \times 5.3286)$$
$$= 813.50 + 106.57 = \$920.07$$

A buyer paying \$920.07 for this bond is getting it at a *discount* (or less than the par value) because a yield rate that is higher than the interest rate on the face of the bond (the *coupon rate*) is desired. The buyer will get 7% converted semiannually on the investment of \$920.07. The company that issued the bond will continue to pay 2% every 6 months on the \$1000 face value of the bond regardless of who owns the bond and what was paid for it.

In the case of callable bonds, there is an element of doubt in determining the value because there is no way to know in advance if and when the bond will be called. An investor who wants a certain yield can get the value of the bond assuming both redemption on the earliest call date and redemption at maturity. The lower of these values would be a safe price to ensure the desired yield.

EXAMPLE 2   An Atlantic Richfield Company \$1000, $8\frac{5}{8}\%$ debenture is due on April 1, 2015. Interest is payable on April 1 and October 1. Find the value of the bond on October 1, 1989, to a buyer who wants a return on the investment of 8% converted semiannually, assuming that: (a) the bond is called at 105.05 on April 1, 1995; (b) the bond is redeemed at par on April 1, 2015.

Figure 7-5

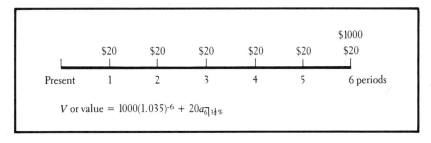

SOLUTION (a) There are 11 periods from the purchase date to the call date. The semiannual interest payments are $43.12 and the call price is $1050.50. We can diagram the dated money flows (Figure 7-6). Substituting in formula (24), we have

$$V = 1050.50(1.04)^{-11} + 43.12a_{\overline{11}|4\%}$$
$$= (1050.50 \times .649581) + (43.12 \times 8.7605)$$
$$= 682.38 + 377.75 = \$1060.13$$

(b) There are 51 periods from purchase to maturity. The time diagram now goes to the due date of the bond (Figure 7-7). Substituting in formula (24), we have

$$V = 1000.00(1.04)^{-51} + 43.12a_{\overline{51}|4\%}$$
$$= (1000.00 \times .135301) + (43.12 \times 21.6175)$$
$$= 135.30 + 932.15 = \$1067.45$$

If the purchaser of this bond can get it for $1060, the yield will be 8% if the bond is called and slightly more if the bond is not redeemed until the due date.

In this example the bond is priced at a *premium* (at more than the par value) because the yield rate is lower than the coupon rate. In the investment market the price of a bond depends on the interest rate of the bond, the yield rate acceptable to investors, the time to maturity, and the degree of safety associated with the particular bond.

Figure 7-6

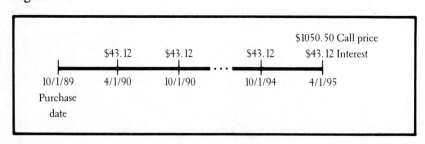

Exercise 7a

Compute the value of the following bonds:

No.	Face Value	Redemption Conditions	Annual Bond Rate Interest Paid Semiannually	Yield Rate Compounded Semiannually	Answer
1.	$1000	8 years at par	4%	10%	$674.87
2.	$1000	6 years at par	5%	8%	
3.	$ 500	10 years at 102	7.5%	12%	$374.08
4.	$5000	5 years at 101	7.2%	14%	

5. A Bethlehem Steel Corporation $1000, 9% debenture is due on May 15, 2014. Interest is payable on May 15 and November 15. The bond may be called at 104 on May 15, 1994. Find the value of this bond on May 15, 1988, if the yield rate is to be 12% converted semiannually, assuming:
   (a) The bond is called at 104 on May 15, 1994.
   (b) The bond is redeemed at par on May 15, 2014.
   [(a) $894.12, (b) $762.08]

6. A Kroger Company $1000, 9% debenture is due on May 1, 2008, with interest payable on May 1 and November 1. The bond may be called at 104 on May 1, 1993. Find the value of this bond on

Figure 7-7

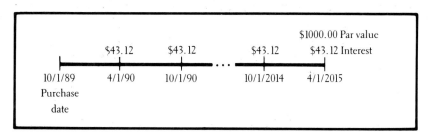

May 1, 1991, if the yield rate is to be 8%, assuming:

(a) The bond is called at 104 on May 1, 1993.

(b) The bond is redeemed at par on May 1, 2008.

7. A Dana Corporation $1000, 6% debenture is due on December 1, 2006. Interest is payable on June 1 and December 1. The bond may be called at 103 on December 1, 1991. Find the value of this bond on June 1, 1988, if the yield is to be 8% converted semiannually, assuming that:

(a) The bond is redeemed at 103 on December 1, 1991.

(b) The bond is redeemed at par on December 1, 2006.

[(a) $962.78; (b) $808.58]

8. A Pacific South West Airlines $1000, 6% debenture is due on October 1, 1999. Interest is payable on April 1 and October 1. The bond may be called at 102 on October 1, 1989. Find the value of this bond on April 1, 1986, if the yield is to be 8% converted semiannually, assuming that:

(a) The bond is called at 102 on October 1, 1989.

(b) The bond is redeemed at par on October 1, 1999.

9. A National Steel Corporation $1000, 8% bond is due on December 1, 2006. Interest is payable on June 1 and December 1. The bond may be called at 104 on December 1, 1991. Find the value of this bond on June 1, 1989, if the yield is to be 9% converted semiannually, assuming that:

(a) The bond is called at 104 on December 1, 1991.

(b) The bond is redeemed at par on December 1, 2006.

[(a) $1010.15; (b) $912.69]

10. A Standard Oil Company of Indiana 6% debenture is due on January 15, 2013. Interest is payable on January 15 and July 15. The bond may be called at 103 on January 15, 1998. Find the value of this bond on January 15, 1995, if the yield is to be 10% converted semiannually, assuming that:

(a) The bond is called at 103 on January 15, 1998.

(b) The bond is redeemed at par on January 15, 2013.

7.6 PREMIUM AND DISCOUNT

Now we develop simplified formulas that can be used for bond valuation when it is assumed that the bond will be paid at par at maturity.

If the interest rate on the bond is greater than the yield rate on the purchase price, the buyer will pay more than the par value of the bond. This difference is called the **premium** and can be obtained as follows:

Since the value at maturity equals the par value, we can substitute F for C in formula (24).

$$V = F(1 + i)^{-n} + Fra_{\overline{n}|i}$$

Because the premium is the difference between the value at the yield rate and the face value, we can say that

$$P = V - F$$

Substituting the value for V that we just obtained, we have

$$
\begin{aligned}
P &= F(1 + i)^{-n} + Fra_{\overline{n}|i} - F \\
&= Fra_{\overline{n}|i} - F + F(1 + i)^{-n} \\
&= Fra_{\overline{n}|i} - F[1(1 + i)^{-n}]
\end{aligned}
$$

Multiplying the last term by i/i will not change the value of the fraction and will enable us to replace $[1 - (1 + i)^{-n}]/i$ with $a_{\overline{n}|i}$.

$$
\begin{aligned}
P &= Fra_{\overline{n}|i} - Fi\frac{[1 - (1 + i)^{-n}]}{i} \\
&= Fra_{\overline{n}|i} - Fia_{\overline{n}|i}
\end{aligned}
$$

$$P = (Fr - Fi)a_{\overline{n}|i} \tag{25}$$

Now we have to look up only one factor to get the value of a bond. Also, as the examples will show, the computations will be simplified. Note that in formula (25), Fr is the coupon and Fi is the face value of the bond times the *yield* rate.

EXAMPLE 1 Find the value on August 1, 1988, of a $1000, $9\frac{1}{2}\%$ bond maturing at par on February 1, 2003, if it is to yield 8% compounded semiannually.

SOLUTION In this problem $Fr = 1000 \times .0475 = 47.50$, $Fi = 1000 \times .04 = 40$, and $n = 29$. Substituting in formula (25), we have

$$P = (47.50 - 40.00)a_{\overline{29}|4\%} = 7.50 \times 16.984 = \$127.38$$

Then the purchase price is $1127.38.

When the buyer of a bond wants a higher rate of return on an investment than the interest rate of the bond, the bond must be purchased at less than the par value, or at a **discount**. This discount equals the par value minus the value at the yield rate.

$$D = F - V$$

To get an equation for the discount, we substitute the value of V from formula (24) and proceed as we did in getting the formula for the premium.

$$D = F - F(1 + i)^{-n} - Fra_{\overline{n}|i}$$
$$= F[1 - (1 + i)^{-n}] - Fra_{\overline{n}|i}$$

$$= Fi \frac{[1 - (1 + i)^{-n}]}{i} - Fra_{\overline{n}|i}$$

$$= Fia_{\overline{n}|i} - Fra_{\overline{n}|i}$$

$$D = (Fi - Fr)a_{\overline{n}|i} \tag{26}$$

EXAMPLE 2 Find the value on May 1, 1989, of a $1000, 6% bond maturing at par on May 1, 1999, if it is to yield 8% compounded semiannually.

SOLUTION In this case $Fi = 1000 \times .04 = 40$, $Fr = 1000 \times .03 = 30$, and $n = 20$. Substituting in formula (26), we have

$$D = (40 - 30)a_{\overline{20}|4\%} = 10(13.5903) = \$135.90$$

Then we can figure the purchase price as $864.10.

Exercise 7b

1. A $1000, $5\frac{3}{4}$% Citicorp bond is due on March 1, 2000. Interest is payable on March 1 and September 1. Find the value on September 1, 1987, to yield 10% converted semiannually. ($700.50)

2. A $1000, 9% Columbia Gas System bond is due October 1, 1999. Interest is payable on April 1 and October 1. Find the value on April 1, 1990, to yield 10% converted semiannually.

3. A Dana Corporation $1000, 5.9% debenture is due February 1, 2006. Interest is payable on February 1 and August 1. Find the value on February 1, 1990, to yield 12% converted semiannually. ($570.44)

4.[C] A $1000, 8% General Motors Acceptance debenture is due on September 1, 2007. Interest is payable on March 1 and September 1. Find the value on September 1, 1987, to yield 11% compounded semiannually.

5. A $1000, 12.05% Gulf Oil bond is due on March 1, 2009. Interest is payable on March 1 and September 1. Find the value on March 1, 1987, to yield 10% converted semiannually. ($1181.04)

6. An American Telephone and Telegraph $1000, 8.7% debenture is due on December 1, 2016. Interest is payable on June 1 and December 1. Find the value on December 1, 1987, to yield 8% converted semiannually.

7.[C] A Jersey Central Power and Light $1000, $7\frac{1}{4}$% bond is due on October 1, 2004. Interest is payable on April 1 and October 1. Find the value on April 1, 1989, to yield $9\frac{1}{2}$% converted semiannually. ($819.35)

8.[C] A Pacific Gas & Electric $1000, $12\frac{3}{4}$% debenture is due on January 1, 2013. Interest is payable on January 1 and July 1. Find the value on July 1, 1987, to yield 11% converted semiannually.

7.7 AMORTIZATION OF THE PREMIUM

When the purchase price of a bond is higher than the maturity value, the buyer can keep the capital intact by setting aside enough from the interest payments to equal the premium when the bond is redeemed. A systematic way to do this involves three steps: Compute the interest at the yield rate on the *book value* of the bond (the value at which the bond is carried on the books of the owner); subtract this result from the bond interest; and apply this difference to periodic reduction of the book value. Under this plan the bond will have a gradually decreasing book value that will equal the face value of the bond when it matures. This method ensures that the investment always earns its yield rate, and what remains from the bond coupon is used to amortize the premium. An example will show how this is done.

EXAMPLE   A $1000, 9.2% bond maturing at par in 2 years was purchased on June 1, 1985, to yield 8%. The interest is paid on June 1 and December 1. Construct a schedule for amortization of the premium.

SOLUTION   Substituting $Fr = 46$, $Fi = 40$, and $n = 4$ in formula (25), we have

$$P = (46 - 40)a_{\overline{4}|4\%} = 6 \times 3.630 = \$21.78$$

Thus the purchase price of the bond is $1021.78. This amount is the initial investment on which the buyer wants to realize 8%. At the end of 6 months, a coupon worth $46 is cashed. However, the interest on the purchase price at the yield rate of 8% for the 6 months is only $40.87. Thus, in effect, the buyer has received $40.87 in interest from the coupon, and the difference between this interest amount and the $46 can be looked on as a partial return of the premium. The $5.13 difference represents capital for reinvestment and is no longer considered part of the investment in the bond. These partial returns of the capital will equal the total premium when the bond matures so that the buyer's capital remains intact. Each period then shows a decreased investment in the bond and an increased part of the bond interest applied to the amortization of the premium. The money invested at any time in the bond is the book value of the bond. The following schedule shows how the book value finally equals the face value of the bond. Long schedules of this type are often prepared on electronic computers.

Amortization of the Premium

Date	Interest on Book Value at Yield Rate	Interest on Bond	Amount for Amortization of Premium	Book Value
June 1, 1985				$1021.78
December 1, 1985	$40.87	$46.00	$ 5.13	1016.65
June 1, 1986	40.67	46.00	5.33	1011.32
December 1, 1986	40.45	46.00	5.55	1005.77
June 1, 1987	40.23	46.00	5.77	1000.00
			$21.78	

7.8 ACCUMULATION OF THE DISCOUNT

If a bond is bought below par, the bond interest will not equal the desired return on the investment. In other words, a portion of the desired interest will not be received with the bond payments but will be obtained when the bond matures at more than the purchase price. Rather than picking up the increase in the value of the bond all at once, the deficit between the desired interest and the bond interest can be applied each period to raise the book value from the purchase price to the maturity value.

EXAMPLE   A $1000, 5% bond maturing in 2 years was bought on May 1, 1986, to yield 10%. The interest is paid on May 1 and November 1. Construct a schedule for accumulation of the discount.

SOLUTION   Substituting $Fi = 50$, $Fr = 25$, and $n = 4$ in formula (26), we have

$$D = (50 - 25)a_{\overline{4}|5\%} = 25 \times 3.5460 = \$88.65$$

Thus the purchase price of the bond is $911.35, and this is the investment on which the buyer wishes to realize 10%. At the end of 6 months, the owner cashes a coupon worth $25. However, 5% of $911.35 is $45.57. The $20.57 in excess of the bond interest must come from the increase in the book value of the bond. The following schedule shows how the periodic differences result in the book value of the bond finally equaling the maturity value.

The 1-cent difference is due to rounding.

Accumulation of the Discount

Date	Interest on Book Value at Yield Rate	Interest on Bond	Amount for Accumulation of Discount	Book Value
May 1, 1986				$ 911.35
November 1, 1986	$45.57	$25.00	$20.57	931.92
May 1, 1987	46.60	25.00	21.60	953.52
November 1, 1987	47.68	25.00	22.68	976.20
May 1, 1988	48.81	25.00	23.81	1000.01
			$88.66	

Exercise 7c

1. A $5000 bond with interest at 10%, payable January 1 and July 1, is to mature at par on July 1, 1989. Construct a schedule showing the amortization of the premium if the bond is bought on July 1, 1986, to yield 8% converted semiannually.
    (Purchase price $5262.11)

2. A $500, 12% bond with coupons payable on March 1 and September 1 is to mature at par on March 1, 1989. Construct a schedule showing the amortization of the premium if the bond was purchased on September 1, 1986, to yield 10% compounded semiannually.

3. A $1000, 5% bond with semiannual coupons on April 1 and October 1 will mature on October 1, 1991. Construct a schedule showing the accumulation of the discount if the bond is purchased on April 1, 1989, to yield 8%.
    (Purchase price $933.22)

4. A $10,000 bond with interest at $5\frac{1}{2}$% is to mature at par on June 1, 1994. The interest is payable annually on June 1. It is purchased on June 1, 1987, to yield 9%. Construct a schedule to show the accumulation of discount.

5.$^{(C)}$ A \$1000, $10\frac{1}{2}\%$ bond with coupons payable on June 15 and December 15 is to mature at par on December 15, 1992. It is purchased on June 15, 1990, to yield 9.8%. Construct a schedule to show the amortization of the premium.

(Purchase price \$1015.20)

6.$^{(C)}$ Construct a schedule to show the accumulation of the discount if the bond in problem 5 is purchased on June 15, 1990, to yield $12\frac{1}{2}\%$.

7.9 BONDS PURCHASED BETWEEN COUPON DATES

In all of the problems worked so far to calculate the purchase price of a bond, the bond was purchased at the coupon date. The seller kept the coupon that was due on that date, and the buyer had to hold the bond for a full period before cashing the first coupon. In practice, of course, bonds are usually purchased between coupon dates. In this circumstance the purchaser will get the full value of the next coupon even though the purchaser has not had money invested for the entire interest period. On the other hand, the seller has had money tied up for part of a coupon period, but will not collect any interest from the institution that issued the bond. The logical solution to this problem, and the one commonly followed in practice, is for the buyer to pay the seller for the accrued portion of the current coupon.

When the buyer pays the interest that has accrued since the last interest payment date, the purchase price includes both the quoted or listed price of the bond and the accrued interest. Thus bonds are sold at a quoted price "and interest." The price that is quoted on the bond market, sometimes called the **market** or **and interest** price, is the price of the bond itself to yield a certain return. The total cost of a bond includes: the *and interest* price; the accrued interest; and, if the bond is traded in the secondary market, the broker's commission.

EXAMPLE A \$5000, 6% bond with interest payable on June 1 and December 1 matures on June 1, 1990. The bond was purchased on October 1, 1988, to yield 8% converted semiannually. Find the purchase price.

SOLUTION To get the *quoted* or *and interest* price, we first determine the value of the bond on the coupon dates immediately preceding and following the purchase date. Then we interpolate to get the *and interest* price on the purchase date. See Figure 7-8.

For June, 1988, we have

$$\text{Discount} = (200 - 150)a_{\overline{4}|4\%} = \$181.49$$

For December 1, 1988, we have

$$\text{Discount} = (200 - 150)a_{\overline{3}|4\%} = \$138.75$$

So the price increases from \$4818.51 on June 1, 1988, to \$4861.25 on December 1, 1988, representing an increase of \$42.74. Now we interpolate to find what part of the increase has occurred by October 1. Since October 1 is $\frac{2}{3}$ of the way from June 1 to December 1, we simply multiply \$42.74 by $\frac{2}{3}$, getting \$28.49.

Thus the quoted price on October 1 is

$$4818.51 + 28.49 = \$4847.00$$

But on October 1, $\frac{2}{3}$ of a coupon has also accrued. This ratio applied to the total interest payment of \$150 equals \$100. Hence the actual selling price on October 1, 1988, would be

$$4847.00 + 100.00 = \$4947.00$$

Figure 7-8

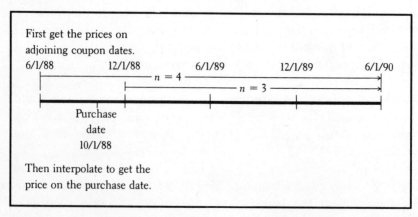

Note that the buyer on this date has 2 months to wait before getting a full coupon of $150. At that time the buyer will be reimbursed for the extra $100 paid to the seller.

Figure 7-9 uses the data from the preceding example to show the relationship between the various prices in bond problems. Note that the *quoted* or *and interest* price approaches the par value of the bond and finally equals it on the maturity date. The actual price equals the *and interest* price only on interest dates.

Figure 7-9 shows why the quoted price of a bond does not include the accrued interest. If the actual purchase price were quoted, there would be a big change in the price before and after an interest date caused by the paying of the bond interest, not by any change in the value of the bond itself.

Sometimes bonds are traded **flat**, or without interest. The market price is the full price paid by the purchaser. A bond may be traded flat when it is in default on interest payments or when there is doubt about the ability of the borrower to meet future interest payments. **Income bonds**, which pay interest only when earned, are also traded flat.

Exercise 7d

1. A Florida Power Corporation $1000, 5% bond is due on June 1, 1994. Interest is payable on June 1 and December 1. Find the *and interest* price and the price including accrued interest if the bond was sold on August 1, 1984, to yield 12% converted semi-annually.
    ($602.19; $610.52)
2. A General Motors Acceptance $1000, 5% debenture is due on March 15, 1993. Interest is payable on March 15 and September 15. Get the *and interest* price and the price including accrued interest if the bond is sold on July 15, 1990, to yield 10% converted semiannually.
3. A Lucky Stores $1000, $8\frac{1}{2}$% debenture is due on April 15, 2009. Interest is payable on April 15 and October 15. Find the *and interest* price and the price including accrued interest on September 15, 1986, to yield 8% converted semiannually.
    ($1051.87; $1087.29)
4. An American Metal Climax $1000, $8\frac{1}{2}$% debenture is due on March 1, 2011. Interest is payable on March 1 and September 1.

Figure 7-9 Bond Purchase Price

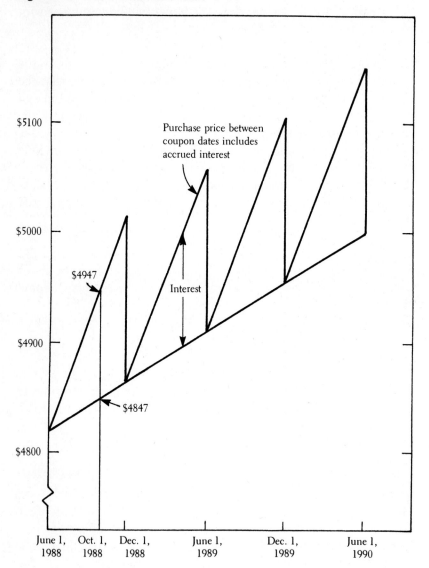

Compute the *and interest* price and the price including accrued interest on July 1, 1988, to yield 8% converted semiannually.

5. An American Telephone and Telegraph $1000, 6% debenture is due on August 1, 2011. Interest is payable on February 1 and August 1. Get the *and interest* price and the price including accrued interest if the bond is sold on September 1, 1984, to yield 12% converted semiannually.
    ($521.72; $526.72)

6. A Boeing Company $1000, 5% debenture is due on August 1, 1996. Interest is payable on February 1 and August 1. Find the *and interest* price and the price including accrued interest if the bond is sold on April 1, 1992, to yield 10% converted semiannually.

7.^(C) A Gulf Oil Corporation $1000, $8\frac{1}{2}$% debenture is due on November 15, 2000. Interest is payable on May 15 and November 15. Find the *and interest* price and the price including accrued interest if the bond is sold on September 15, 1987, to yield 11% converted semiannually.
    ($828.24; $856.57)

8.^(C) A Shell Oil Company $1000, $8\frac{1}{2}$% debenture is due on September 1, 2015. Interest is payable on March 1 and September 1. Get the *and interest* price and the price including accrued interest if the bond is sold on December 1, 1988, to yield 10.5% converted semiannually.

7.10 FINDING THE YIELD RATE

Up to now we have been determining the value of a bond to yield a certain rate of return on the investment. In practice, the quoted or *and interest* price is often given without stating the yield rate. Since the purchaser is interested in the return on the investment, it is necessary to determine the yield rate. The yield that we use is known as *yield to maturity* by investment dealers. It is the true overall rate of return that an investor receives on the invested capital. Another yield that is sometimes used is the *current yield*, obtained by dividing the annual return in dollars by the current price. This yield is very simple to compute, but it is not a true measure of return on invested capital. For this reason, whenever yield rate is used in this text, it means yield to maturity. We get the yield rate in two ways. The first is the Bond Salesman's Method, which is simple and usually leads to fairly accurate results.

EXAMPLE 1 A $1000, 8% bond that matures in 10 years has interest payable semiannually. The quoted price is $1050. What is the yield rate?

SOLUTION Here we have a bond that has a book value of $1050 now and $1000 in 10 years or 20 periods. See Figure 7-10.

We add these two values and divide by 2 to get an *average* investment or book value.

$$\frac{1050 + 1000}{2} = \$1025$$

The periodic interest on this bond is $40, but the bond has been purchased at a premium of $50 that must be amortized over the 20 periods. The average amortization per period is 50/20 = $2.50. This amount is deducted from the interest payments, so that our return per period is $37.50 on an average investment of $1025. Thus the approximate yield rate is 37.50/1025 = 3.66% per period or 7.32% nominal.

If a more accurate value for the yield rate is desired, we use trial and error until we find two adjacent yield rates that bracket the given price. Then we find the yield rate by interpolation. The Bond Salesman's Method showed that the yield rate is close to 3.66% per period. We try the closest table value to this and compute the purchase price.

With our table the closest value is 7% a year or $3\frac{1}{2}$% a period. Using formula (25) for bond premium, we get

Figure 7-10

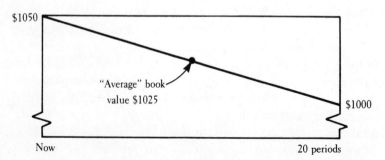

$$P = (40.00 - 35.00)a_{\overline{20}|3\frac{1}{2}\%} = 5.00(14.212) = \$71.06$$

At this rate the purchase price would be $1071.06. Since the actual purchase price was $1050, the yield rate must be higher than $3\frac{1}{2}\%$. The next highest table value is 4%, so we compute the purchase price at that rate.

$$P = (40 - 40)a_{\overline{20}|4\%} = 0$$

and $V = \$1000$.

Now we have one purchase price below the quoted price and another one above. Since our tables do not permit a closer approximation, we interpolate.

<pre>
              i in %   Quoted price

           ┌─── 3.50 $1071.06 ┐
     .50 ┌ d ┌   1050.00 ─┘ 21.06 │ 71.06
        └   └ i   │
           └─── 4.00   1000.00 ─────────┘
</pre>

$$\frac{d}{.50} = \frac{21.06}{71.06}$$

$$d = .148$$
$$i = 3.50 + .148 = 3.648, \text{ or } 3.65\%$$

Then the nominal annual yield is $2i = 7.30\%$.

What this method of determining the yield rate comes down to is finding two adjacent rates in the table such that the quoted price of the bond lies between the prices determined using the two tabular rates. In practical investment work it is usually possible to simplify computations by using bond tables, a calculator, or a computer. We shall work one more example to show how the yield rate is determined if the bond is bought at a discount or between interest dates.

EXAMPLE 2 A $1000, 10% bond with coupons payable semiannually on April 1 and October 1 matures on April 1, 1993. On June 1, 1985, this bond was quoted at 94. What was the yield rate?

SOLUTION First, we use the approximate method to get an estimate of the yield rate assuming that the bond was quoted on the nearest interest date, in this case April 1, 1985. Averaging the quoted price and the redemption price gives

$$\frac{940 + 1000}{2} = \$970$$

The semiannual coupon is \$50. In addition to the interest there will be an increase of \$60 in the value of the bond. Averaged over 30 periods, this increase amounts to \$2 per period. Therefore we have an average return of \$52 on an average investment of \$970, and the approximate yield rate is

$$\frac{52}{970} = .054 = 5.4\% \text{ per period or } 10.8\% \text{ nominal}$$

If we want a more accurate answer, we need to make trial computations using assumed yield rates. We use the value previously obtained as a guide in selecting trial rates.

First, we try 6% (12% nominal).

Date			Quoted price		
April 1, 1985	$(60.00 - 50.00)a_{\overline{30}|} = \$137.65$		$\$862.35$	$\Big]d$	
June 1, 1985			$?$		1.74
October 1, 1985	$(60.00 - 50.00)a_{\overline{29}|} = \$135.91$		864.09		

Since June 1 is $\frac{2}{6}$ of the way from April 1 to October 1, the interpolation to get the June 1 price is

$$\frac{d}{1.74} = \frac{2}{6}$$

$$d = .58$$

The June 1 price for a yield rate of 6% per period is

$$862.35 + .58 = \$862.93$$

This result shows that the true yield rate must be less than 6%. If we use the next table value, 5%, we get

$$P = (50 - 50)a_{\overline{n}|} = 0$$

and $V = 1000$ for each date.
Now we can summarize the results as follows:

Yield rate   **Quoted price on**
per period   **June 1, 1985**

$$
1 \quad
\begin{array}{ccl}
d\; \boxed{} & 5.00 & \$1000.00 \\
 \underline{\qquad} & i & 940.00 \\
& 6.00 & 862.93
\end{array}
\;
\Big\}\,60.00
\;\Big]\,137.07
$$

$$d = \frac{60.00}{137.07} = .44$$

$i = 5.00 + .44 = 5.44\%$ per period, or 10.88% converted semiannually

Exercise 7e

Use Bond Salesman's Method for problems 1 through 4. Interpolate between closest table values for problems 5 through 10.

1. A $1000, 10% bond with semiannual coupons matures at par in 10 years. If this bond is bought for $920, what is the nominal yield rate converted semiannually?
   (11.25%)
2. A $500, 9% bond with semiannual coupons matures at par in 5 years. If this bond is purchased for $480, what is the nominal yield rate converted semiannually?
3. A $1000, 12% bond with semiannual coupons matures at par in 10 years. If this bond is purchased for $1080, what is the nominal yield rate converted semiannually?
   (10.8%)
4. A $1000, 11% bond with semiannual coupons matures at par in 10 years. If this bond is purchased for $1080, what is the nominal yield rate compounded semiannually?
5. Get the nominal yield rate for a $1000, 8% bond quoted at 96 on June 1, 1984, if the bond is to mature at par on December 1, 1991. Coupons are payable on June 1 and December 1.
   (8.74%)
6. A $1000, 8% bond with coupons payable semiannually on March 1 and September 1 was issued on March 1, 1977, to mature in 20 years. On September 1, 1985, this bond was quoted at 102. If

purchased at this price, what would be the nominal yield rate converted semiannually?

7. A $1000, 10% bond issued on August 1, 1981, is to mature at par on August 1, 1991. Coupons are payable semiannually on February 1 and August 1. If this bond is quoted at 95 on February 1, 1989, what is the nominal yield rate converted semiannually? (12.40%)

8. A $1000, 4% Baltimore and Ohio Railroad bond matures on September 1, 1991. Coupon dates are March 1 and September 1. If this bond was quoted at 70 on September 1, 1984, what was the nominal yield rate converted semiannually?

9. A $500, 8% bond with coupons payable January 1 and July 1 matures at par on July 1, 1991. It is purchased on February 1, 1987, for $520 plus the accrued interest. What is the yield rate? (6.93%)

10. A $1000, $9\frac{1}{2}$% bond with coupons payable March 1 and September 1 matures at par on March 1, 2000. It is purchased on May 1, 1995, for $960 plus accrued interest. What is the yield rate?

7.11 BOND TABLES

Companies that buy and sell bonds reduce the computations required to get the price of a bond or the yield rate by using bond tables that cover most of the cases that arise in practice. Bond tables are available in large volumes with answers to four or six decimal places and in pocket-size books with values to two decimal places. The tables give the *and interest* prices of bonds for a wide range of yield and coupon rates and lengths of time until the maturity date of the bond. A sample page from the six-place tables of the Financial Publishing Company is shown in Figure 7-11, and a sample page from the pocket-size book is shown in Figure 7-12. The following examples are based on Figure 7-11, which is for a $100, $2\frac{3}{4}$% bond with interest paid semiannually. The yield rate in the left column is the nominal annual rate converted semiannually.

EXAMPLE 1 A $1000, $2\frac{3}{4}$% bond with interest payable semiannually matures in 23 years. What is the purchase price for a yield rate of 1.5% converted semiannually?

Figure 7-11 Portion of a Page of Bond Tables

2¾% COUPON				23 YEARS	
Yield	Even	1 Month	2 Months	3 Months	4 Months	5 Months
.00	163.250000	163.479167	163.708333	163.937500	164.166667	164.395833
.05	161.736617	161.958989	162.181360	162.403732	162.626104	162.848477
.10	160.239532	160.455235	160.670938	160.886643	161.102349	161.318057
.15	158.758557	158.967716	159.176877	159.386041	159.595207	159.804376
.20	157.293510	157.496247	157.698989	157.901735	158.104486	158.307241
.25	155.844208	156.040644	156.237088	156.433538	156.629995	156.826459
.30	154.410472	154.600726	154.790990	154.981264	155.171547	155.361840
.35	152.992124	153.176312	153.360514	153.544729	153.728958	153.913199
.40	151.588989	151.767227	151.945482	152.123754	152.302043	152.480349
.45	150.200894	150.373294	150.545715	150.718158	150.890622	151.063107
.50	148.827667	148.994340	149.161039	149.327765	149.494516	149.661293
.55	147.469139	147.630195	147.791282	147.952400	148.113549	148.274729
.60	146.125144	146.280689	146.436271	146.591890	146.747546	146.903238
.65	144.795515	144.945656	145.095840	145.246066	145.396335	145.546646
.70	143.480091	143.624931	143.769820	143.914758	144.059745	144.204781
.75	142.178708	142.318349	142.458046	142.597799	142.737608	142.877472
.80	140.891208	141.025751	141.160357	141.295026	141.429758	141.564553
.85	139.617433	139.746977	139.876591	140.006276	140.136031	140.265856
.90	138.357228	138.481870	138.606590	138.731386	138.856264	138.981218
.95	137.110438	137.230273	137.350195	137.470202	137.590296	137.710476
1.00	135.876912	135.992035	136.107252	136.222564	136.337970	136.453472
1.05	134.656500	134.767002	134.877608	134.988317	135.099129	135.210045
1.10	133.449052	133.555024	133.661110	133.767308	133.873618	133.980041
1.15	132.254422	132.355954	132.457609	132.559386	132.661284	132.763304
1.20	131.072465	131.169645	131.266958	131.364401	131.461976	131.559682
1.25	129.903037	129.995952	130.089009	130.182206	130.275545	130.369025
1.30	128.745998	128.834732	128.923618	129.012655	129.101844	129.191183
1.35	127.601207	127.685844	127.770643	127.855603	127.940726	128.026010
1.40	126.468525	126.549147	126.629942	126.710908	126.792048	126.873359
1.45	125.347817	125.424504	125.501375	125.578429	125.655667	125.733087
1.50	124.238946	124.311779	124.384806	124.458027	124.531443	124.605052
1.55	123.141780	123.210836	123.280097	123.349564	123.419237	123.489114
1.60	122.056186	122.121542	122.187115	122.252904	122.318911	122.385134
1.65	120.982035	121.043765	121.105725	121.167914	121.230331	121.292976
1.70	119.919196	119.977376	120.035797	120.094459	120.153361	120.212504

5.00	69.451559	69.389843	69.329321	69.269989	69.211842	69.154874
5.05	68.918721	68.856348	68.795184	68.735224	68.676462	68.618895
5.10	68.391188	68.328179	68.266394	68.205828	68.146474	68.088329
5.15	67.868901	67.805279	67.742894	67.681742	67.621818	67.563116
5.20	67.351804	67.287588	67.224625	67.162909	67.102434	67.043196
5.25	66.839840	66.775052	66.711530	66.649270	66.588265	66.528511
5.30	66.332953	66.267612	66.203553	66.140768	66.079254	66.019004
5.35	65.831089	65.765215	65.700637	65.637348	65.575343	65.514617
5.40	65.334192	65.267805	65.202727	65.138953	65.076477	65.015293
5.45	64.842209	64.775327	64.709769	64.645529	64.582601	64.520978
5.50	64.355086	64.287729	64.221709	64.157021	64.093658	64.031616
5.55	63.872771	63.804956	63.738493	63.673375	63.609597	63.547152
5.60	63.395213	63.326957	63.260068	63.194538	63.130362	63.067532
5.65	62.922358	62.853680	62.786383	62.720458	62.655901	62.592704
5.70	62.454157	62.385074	62.317385	62.251083	62.186161	62.122614

Accrued Interest on $100	5 Months 1.145833	4 Months .916667	3 Months .687500	2 Months .458333	1 Month .229167

Source: Courtesy of Financial Publishing Company, Boston, Mass.

SOLUTION We simply go down the yield rate column to 1.50 and read the purchase price of $124.239 for a $100 bond. A $1000 bond will cost $1242.39.

EXAMPLE 2 A $1000, $2\frac{3}{4}$% bond with interest payable semiannually matures in 23 years and 3 months. What is the purchase price for a yield rate of 5% converted semiannually?

Figure 7-12 Pocket-size Bond Table

2¾%   YEARS AND MONTHS

Mat. Yield	14-1	14-2	14-3	14-4	14-5	14-6	14-7	14-8
.60	130.56	130.73	130.91	131.08	131.26	131.43	131.61	131.78
.65	128.99	129.16	129.32	129.49	129.65	129.81	129.98	130.14
.70	127.45	127.60	127.76	127.91	128.06	128.22	128.37	128.53
.75	126.68	126.83	126.98	127.13	127.28	127.43	127.58	127.73
.80	125.92	126.07	126.21	126.36	126.50	126.65	126.79	126.93
.85	125.17	125.31	125.45	125.59	125.73	125.87	126.01	126.15
.90	124.42	124.55	124.69	124.82	124.96	125.10	125.23	125.36
.95	123.67	123.81	123.94	124.07	124.20	124.33	124.46	124.59
1.00	122.94	123.06	123.19	123.31	123.44	123.57	123.69	123.82
1.05	122.20	122.32	122.44	122.57	122.69	122.81	122.93	123.05
1.10	121.47	121.59	121.71	121.82	121.94	122.06	122.17	122.29
1.15	120.75	120.86	120.97	121.09	121.20	121.31	121.42	121.54
1.20	120.03	120.14	120.25	120.35	120.46	120.57	120.68	120.79
1.25	119.31	119.42	119.52	119.63	119.73	119.84	119.94	120.04
1.30	118.60	118.70	118.80	118.91	119.01	119.11	119.21	119.30
1.35	117.90	118.00	118.09	118.19	118.28	118.38	118.48	118.57
1.40	117.20	117.29	117.38	117.48	117.57	117.66	117.75	117.84
1.45	116.51	116.59	116.68	116.77	116.86	116.95	117.03	117.12
1.50	115.82	115.90	115.98	116.07	116.15	116.23	116.32	116.40
1.55	115.13	115.21	115.29	115.37	115.45	115.53	115.61	115.69
1.60	114.45	114.52	114.60	114.68	114.75	114.83	114.90	114.98
1.65	113.77	113.84	113.92	113.99	114.06	114.13	114.21	114.28
1.70	113.10	113.17	113.24	113.31	113.37	113.44	113.51	113.58
1.75	112.43	112.50	112.56	112.63	112.69	112.76	112.82	112.88
1.80	111.77	111.83	111.89	111.95	112.01	112.06	112.14	112.20
1.85	111.11	111.17	111.23	111.28	111.34	111.40	111.46	111.51
1.90	110.46	110.51	110.57	110.62	110.67	110.73	110.78	110.83
1.95	109.81	109.86	109.91	109.96	110.01	110.06	110.11	110.16
2.00	109.16	109.21	109.26	109.30	109.35	109.40	109.45	109.49
2.05	108.52	108.57	108.61	108.65	108.70	108.74	108.78	108.83
2.10	107.89	107.93	107.97	108.01	108.05	108.09	108.13	108.17
2.15	107.26	107.29	107.33	107.37	107.40	107.44	107.48	107.51
2.20	106.63	106.66	106.69	106.73	106.76	106.80	106.83	106.86
2.25	106.01	106.03	106.06	106.10	106.13	106.16	106.19	106.21
2.30	105.39	105.41	105.44	105.47	105.45	105.52	105.55	105.57
2.35	104.77	104.79	104.82	104.84	104.87	104.89	104.91	104.94
2.40	104.16	104.18	104.20	104.22	104.24	104.26	104.28	104.30
2.45	103.55	103.57	103.59	103.61	103.62	103.64	103.66	103.68
2.50	102.95	102.97	102.98	102.99	103.01	103.03	103.04	103.05
2.55	102.35	102.36	102.37	102.39	102.40	102.41	102.42	102.43
2.60	101.76	101.77	101.77	101.78	101.79	101.80	101.81	101.82
2.65	101.17	101.17	101.18	101.18	101.19	101.20	101.20	101.21
2.70	100.58	100.58	100.59	100.59	100.59	100.60	100.60	100.60
2.75	100.00	100.00	100.00	100.00	100.00	100.00	100.00	100.00
2.80	99.42	99.42	99.41	99.41	99.41	99.41	99.40	99.40
2.85	98.85	98.84	98.83	98.83	98.82	98.82	98.81	98.81
2.90	98.27	98.27	98.26	98.25	98.24	98.23	98.23	98.22
2.95	97.71	97.70	97.68	97.67	97.66	97.65	97.64	97.63
3.00	97.14	97.13	97.12	97.10	97.09	97.08	97.06	97.05
3.05	96.58	96.57	96.55	96.54	96.52	96.51	96.49	96.47
3.10	96.03	96.01	95.99	95.97	95.95	95.94	95.92	95.90

472

Source: Courtesy of Financial Publishing Company, Boston, Mass.

SOLUTION   Since the bond is not being purchased on a coupon date, we must first obtain the *and interest* price and then add the accrued interest. We can obtain both values directly from the table. The *and interest* price is $692.70. From the bottom of the table we get $.6875 for the accrued interest for 3 months on $100. On $1000 it will be $6.88. Adding the two amounts gives a purchase price of $699.58.

EXAMPLE 3   A $1000, $2\frac{3}{4}$% bond that matures in 23 years is quoted at $1250. What is the nominal yield rate?

SOLUTION   The equivalent price for a $100 bond is $125. From the table we see that the yield rate is between 1.45 and 1.50%. If a more accurate answer is needed, we interpolate

Yield rate in %   Quoted price

$$\frac{d}{.05} = \frac{.35}{1.11}$$

$$d = .016$$

The yield rate is $1.45 + .016 = 1.466\%$ converted semiannually.

The following examples are based on the pocket-size tables.

EXAMPLE 4   A $100, $2\frac{3}{4}$% bond matues in 14 years and 6 months. Find the *and interest* price to yield 3% converted semiannually.

SOLUTION   Opposite 3% under 14-6, we find the answer to be $97.08.

EXAMPLE 5   A $2\frac{3}{4}$% bond that matures in 14 years and 3 months is quoted at 105. What is the yield rate?

SOLUTION   The table shows that the rate is between 2.30 and 2.35%. This narrow range is a satisfactory answer for many purposes. Interpolation could be used to get a closer approximation to the true yield rate.

EXAMPLE 6   A $1000, $2\frac{3}{4}$% bond matures in 14 years and 6 months. What should be the quoted price to yield 2%?

SOLUTION   The table value is 109.40 for a $100 bond. Therefore the value of a $1000 bond would be $1094.00.

Exercise 7f

Use the sample bond table on page 339. All yield rates are converted semiannually.

1. A $1000, $2\frac{3}{4}$% bond with interest payable semiannually matures at par in 23 years. What is the purchase price for a yield rate of 5% converted semiannually?
   ($694.52)
2. Work problem 1 for a yield rate of 1.6% converted semiannually.
3. A $1000, $2\frac{3}{4}$% bond with interest payable semiannually matures at par in 23 years and 5 months. Get the *and interest* and the purchase price for a yield rate of 5% converted semiannually.
   ($691.55; $693.84)
4. A $500, $2\frac{3}{4}$% bond with semiannual coupons matures at par in 23 years and 5 months. Find the *and interest* and the purchase price for a yield rate of 1.5% converted semiannually.
5. A $1000, $2\frac{3}{4}$% bond that matures at par in 23 years is sold for $670. What is the nominal yield rate?
   (5.23%)
6. A $500, $2\frac{3}{4}$% bond matures at par in 23 years. If a buyer pays $630 for this bond, what rate of return will be earned on the money?

7.12 BUYING BONDS

Lenders who say, "Here's my money for 30 years," expect a better return than would be earned on shorter investments of comparable safety. When savings accounts are paying 5%, high-grade bonds may be paying 8% and more. To help you determine when and how bonds can be attractive, we consider now the bond facts that are important to investors.

Classified according to the issuing organization, important types of bonds are:

United States Treasury Bonds

These bonds have behind them no tangible assets to guarantee either the payment of interest or the return of invested capital. Yet millions of investors have put billions into Treasury bonds with complete confidence because they know that behind these bonds lies the integrity of the United States. For many years the maximum rate that Congress permitted on long-term debt was $4\frac{1}{4}\%$. Since this rate has not been competitive for several years, the government has stopped issuing $4\frac{1}{4}\%$ bonds. Outstanding Treasury bonds with $2\frac{1}{2}\%$ to $4\frac{1}{4}\%$ coupons are now traded at deep discounts. Congress later authorized the issue of higher-rate bonds whose prices vary with the economy. Some Treasury bonds are redeemable at par and accrued interest for payment of federal estate taxes if the bonds were owned by the decedent and are part of the estate. A person can now buy these bonds at a discount for a safe income while living and, at death, for a lessening of the tax bite for any heirs. Because of their potential tax benefits, these bonds have lower yields to maturity than comparable issues without the estate-tax advantage.

Bonds of Government Agencies and
Sponsored Corporations

Bonds issued by federal agencies and sponsored corporations are not direct obligations of the Treasury, but in one way or another the bonds involve federal sponsorship or guarantee. They are recognized as investment-quality obligations, and many of them are actively traded in secondary markets, enabling owners to combine a high degree of safety and liquidity. Yields are slightly higher than on Treasury bonds of comparable maturity.

Municipal Bonds

These bonds are issued by state and local governments, housing and port authorities, and local government agencies for roads, schools, water works, public housing, and other community services. Regardless of what local government or authority issues the bonds, they are called municipals. The interest income from municipals is exempt from federal income tax and is often exempt from state and local income taxes in the state where the bonds are issued. Municipals are issued in denomina-tions of $1000 and up, with $5000 being the most common.

The tax-free feature of municipal bonds makes them attractive to people in the higher tax brackets. To find the rate that a person would have to earn on a taxable investment to produce the same dollar return as a municipal, we substitute in the formula

$$\text{Required taxable rate} = \frac{\text{rate on municipal}}{1 - \text{tax rate}}$$

To have an after-tax income equivalent to a 7% return from a municipal bond, a person in the 20% tax bracket would need an invest-ment paying

$$\frac{.07}{1 - .20} = \frac{.07}{.80} = .0875 = 8.75\%$$

Table 7-1 shows the equivalent taxable rate for several tax brackets and tax-free rates.

When a person gets into higher tax brackets, municipal bonds can be very attractive investments.

Industrial and Utility Bonds

These bonds are issued by companies from corporate giants down to small local concerns. The usual denomination is $1000, but *baby bonds*

Table 7-1 Taxable Equivalent Yields

Tax Bracket[a]	Taxable Rate Required to Produce Same After-Tax Income as a Tax-Free Rate of:					
	5%	6%	7%	8%	9%	10%
20%	6.25%	7.50%	8.75%	10.00%	11.25%	12.50%
30	7.15	8.57	10.00	11.43	12.86	14.29
40	8.33	10.00	11.67	13.33	15.00	16.67
50	10.00	12.00	14.00	16.00	18.00	20.00
60	12.50	15.00	17.50	20.00	22.50	25.00
70	16.67	20.00	23.33	26.67	30.00	33.33

[a] Total of federal rate and any state and local income taxes that do not apply to municipal bonds.

of $500 and less are sometimes sold. Some companies also issue convertible bonds that give the owner the privilege of converting the bond into a specified number of shares of common stock of the same corporation. From the company's standpoint, convertibles offer lower-cost financing, since rates on convertibles are less than on other bonds of similar quality. These hybrid securities combine features of a stock and a bond. The buyer can count on interest while having a chance of additional profit if the stock of the issuing company goes up. Some companies have been so successful that their convertible bonds now trade at 200 or higher.

7.13 LONG-TERM INTEREST RATES

Over the years there have been great changes in interest rates on bonds. As Figure 7-13 shows, returns on different types of top-grade securities tend to go up and down together.

A bond is a promise to do two things – make periodic interest payments and redeem the bond at maturity. This promise is only as good as the outfit making it. Bond quality ranges from bonds with the least investment risk to those with the greatest investment risk. Bonds are rated by two investment services, and gradations of investment quality are indicated by rating symbols, each symbol representing a group in which the quality characteristics are broadly the same. Starting with the highest investment quality, the ratings are:

Moody's Investors Service, Inc.	Standard and Poor's Corporation
Aaa	AAA
Aa	AA
A	A
Baa	BBB
Ba	BB
B	B
Caa	CCC–CC
Ca	C
C	DDD–D

In general, the higher the quality, the lower the yield, as indicated by the following examples, averages of bond yields for March 1985:

Moody's Ratings	Corporate Bonds	Municipal Bonds
Aaa	12.56%	9.15%
Aa	12.91	9.55
A	13.36	9.76
Baa	13.69	10.16

Beginners and conservative investors are wise to buy bonds of A and higher ratings. The safety and peace of mind provided by high-grade bonds are likely to be more important than the chance of a higher

Figure 7-13 Long-term Interest Rates, 1955–1984

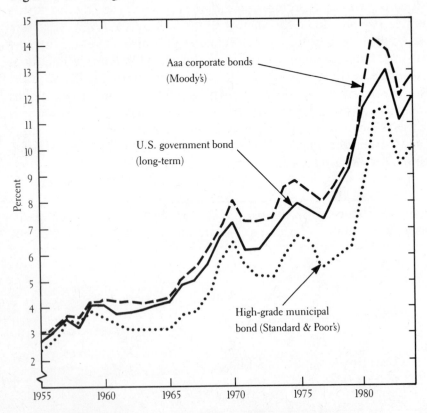

Source: 1985 Economic Report of the President, Table B-66

yield. As a person gains experience and funds, it may be preferable to move down the scale with the hope of increasing the return with speculative buys.

Bonds are usually bought and sold through brokers. The buyer does not pay a commission on bonds of a new issue when the issue is first offered to the public. When an outstanding bond is sold, both buyer and seller pay a commission. The bond buyer should be careful to take the commission into consideration because it can have a substantial effect on the yield.

As interest rates rise, bond prices drop. The reverse is also true up to a point close to the price at which a corporation may call its bonds. If the call price as of a certain date is 106, this becomes in effect a ceiling on the market price of the bond. A bond whose price is being held down because of call provisions is sometimes referred to as a *stymied* bond. Before buying a new issue, it is a good idea to check on the number of years of call protection.

One way to avoid call problems and get desired due dates is to buy seasoned issues, bonds that have been on the market for several years. Since these bonds were issued when rates were lower than they are today, they are now selling at discounts, and so there is little danger of their being called. The yield to maturity on seasoned issues constantly adjusts to the going rate for new issues. At any particular time the yield on older issues may be somewhat lower than the yield on new issues, but that will be offset in part by the lower income taxes on the capital gains between purchase price and redemption price. Yields to maturity can be checked using the methods in section 7.10.

Bond buyers should be aware of the forms of bond ownership. In the case of bonds *registered as to both principal and interest*, the name of the holder appears on the bond and interest checks are mailed by the paying agent to the registered owner. Bonds *registered as to principal only* have the owner's name on the bond. Coupons are attached to the bond, and they are fully negotiable. Both types of registered bonds have the owner's name recorded on the books of the paying agent, and ownership may be transferred only through this agent. Dealers who handle bond sales and purchases usually take care of this transfer in registration. *Bearer bonds* do not carry the owner's name nor is the name recorded on the books of the paying agent. Possession of a bearer bond implies ownership. Replacing a lost or stolen registered bond entails bother and expense, but it can be done. The loss or theft of a bearer bond is a disaster comparable to losing cash.

7.14 YOU NEVER KNOW

Although the interest rate and redemption price of a bond are fixed, the market price is quite sensitive to changes in interest rates and economic trends. Bonds of the highest quality may have wide price movements while retaining their gilt-edged investment status. Bond buyers must be willing to assume a price-level risk that can make life unpleasant if bonds must be sold to get cash. For example, *U.S. News and World Report* in the November 6, 1967, issue had an article entitled "Bargains in Bonds — A Look at Today's Record Yields," which said in part:

> Prices of bonds in the open market, dropping month after month, are now in many cases at the lowest levels ever. For investors, the result is an array of offerings that carry record-high yields.

In large type the article pointed out:

> Many yields are at their highest levels in 46 years. Some are the biggest in nearly a century.

The article included an extensive table of different types of bonds with their yields to maturity. Among the mouth-watering (for 1967) yields were Shell Oil $4\frac{5}{8}$% Triple A bonds of 1986 selling at 84.375 for a yield to maturity of 5.98%. However, interest rates have since set new records, with the inevitable result of lower prices for fixed income securities. In 1971 the Shell bond was down to 76.125. The person who purchased this bond in 1967 and sold it in 1971 would have made about $3\frac{1}{4}$% on the investment.

Although a large drop in the market value of a bond is depressing, the owner of a bond in a sound company knows that the bond will eventually appreciate as it approaches maturity. Even this limited consolation is denied the poor soul who has bonds for which economic or political developments indicate a bleak future. In 1967 Pennsylvania Railroad $4\frac{1}{4}$% bonds were rated Ba and were quoted around 80. In 1971 these bonds had a new rating of Caa and were sold flat at about 17. Other bond holders with little hope are those who bought czarist Russian bonds of 1916, Imperial Chinese Government Hukuang Railways bonds, and other IOUs that have been in default for decades. There is still trading in bonds issued by precommunist governments in countries now behind the Iron Curtain. Some of the price swings have been spectacular. When Lenin annulled foreign loans, czarist bonds dropped to $7.50 for a $1000 bond. Early in World War II the price dropped to $2.50, and then at the time of the Yalta Conference it increased to over $200. Currently, you can get one of these bonds for a few dollars. The speculative interest in old and defaulted bonds is based on the hope that some settlement of ancient debts will be made. Even bonds for which there is no such hope have some trading value as material for papering playrooms.

REVIEW EXERCISES FOR CHAPTER 7

1. A $1000, 8.4% Mobil Oil bond can be called at 104 on October 21, 1999. Coupon dates are April 21 and October 21. Find the value of this bond on April 21, 1989, if the buyer wants to realize 9% compounded semiannually on the investment.
    ($975.66)
2. A $1000 Avco Corporation bond has 11% coupons due on May 1 and November 1. The bond is due on May 1, 2000, but may be called at 102 on November 1, 1992. Find the value on November 1, 1987, to a buyer who wants a yield of 9% compounded semiannually if the bond is: (a) called at 102 on November 1, 1992; (b) redeemed at par on May 1, 2000.
3. An Ozark Airlines $6\frac{3}{4}$%, $1000 bond is due on August 19, 2004. Coupon dates are February 19 and August 19. Find its value on February 19, 1988, to a buyer who wants a yield of 8% converted semiannually.
    ($886.57)
4.(C) A Consolidated Edison 7.9%, $5000 bond is due on December 13, 2007. Coupon dates are June 13 and December 13. Find its value on December 13, 1990, to a buyer who wants to earn 11% converted semiannually.
5. Find the price (including accrued interest) of the bond in problem 3 on April 19, 1989, to a buyer who wants to earn 8% converted semiannually.
    ($901.94)
6.(C) Find the price including accrued interest on September 13, 1993, of the bond in problem 4 to a buyer who wants a yield of 11% converted semiannually.
7. A $1000, 6% bond with semiannual coupons on January 12 and July 12 is due on July 12, 1990. Construct a schedule

showing accumulation of the discount if the bond was purchased on July 12, 1988, to yield 9% converted semiannually.
(Purchase price = $946.19)

8. A $500, 10% bond with annual coupons on July 1 is due on
July 1, 1994. If it is purchased on July 1, 1989, to yield 8%
converted annually, construct a schedule for amortization of
the premium.

9. Use the Bond Salesman's Method to find the yield rate, compounded semiannually, on a $1000, 9.6% bond redeemable at
par on June 1, 1998, that is purchased on June 1, 1988, for
$960. Coupon dates are June 1 and December 1.
(10.2%)

10. Do problem 9 again using the interpolation method.

11. A 7%, $1000 bond is redeemable at par on July 30, 1995.
Coupon dates are January 30 and July 30. If the bond was
quoted at 93 plus accrued interest on December 30, 1988,
use the interpolation method to find the nominal yield rate
converted semiannually.
(8.41%)

Chapter 8

Capital Budgeting and Depreciation

8.1 GROSS NATIONAL PRODUCT

One of the most important measures of the health of the nation's economy is gross national product. GNP is the total value at current prices of all final goods and services produced for sale plus the estimated value of certain imputed outputs. Major components of GNP are shown in Table 8-1.

Table 8-1 Major Components of GNP

	1984		1974	
	Billions of Dollars	Percent of Total	Billions of Dollars	Percent of Total
Personal consumption expenditures	2342.3	64.0	888.1	61.9
Durable goods	318.4	8.7	121.5	8.5
Nondurable goods	858.3	23.4	373.4	26.0
Services	1165.7	31.8	393.2	27.4
Gross private domestic investment	637.3	17.4	228.7	15.9
Net exports of goods and services	−66.3	−1.8	13.4	0.9
Government purchases of goods and services	748.0	20.4	304.1	21.2
Federal	295.5	8.1	111.0	7.7
State and local	452.4	12.4	193.1	13.5
Gross National Product	3661.3		1434.2	

Source: *1985 Economic Report of the President*, Table B-1.

8.2 BUSINESS INVESTMENT

Capital expenditures, money spent by business for structures and the tools of production, amount to about one-tenth of GNP. But this relatively small investment in productive capital plays a particularly important role in determining whether the economy will be in a state of boom or recession. Jobs for a growing labor force, a rising standard of living, stable prices — all depend on maintaining capital formation at a rate that is high enough to meet future needs, yet not so high that inflation results.

Unlike personal consumption expenditures, which are relatively stable through good times and bad, capital expenditures are volatile, with cyclical swings several times as large in percentage terms as the changes in outlays for consumer goods. From 1957 to 1958 business investment dropped 12%. On the other hand, the five-year period from 1959 to 1984 saw nearly a 150% increase in business investment. Figure 8-1 shows the fluctuation in business investments on plant and equip-

Figure 8-1 Annual Business Investment in the United States, 1950–1984 (Nonresidential Net Fixed Investment)

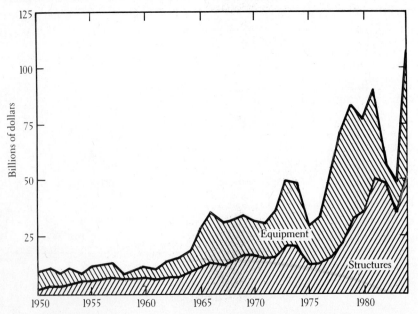

Source: *1985 Economic Report of the President*, Table B-15.

ment in recent years. The instability of investment and the attendant financial fluctuations provide plenty of opportunities either to go broke or to get rich. The mathematics of finance can establish investment planning for individuals, as well as for financial and other organizations, on a sound, rational, and profitable basis.

8.3   WHERE THE MONEY COMES FROM

Investment requires saving, that is, consumption of less than total income. Americans are great savers. Year in and year out individuals and families save an average of 5 to 8 cents out of each dollar of disposable income, the income that is left after taxes. Saving is good for the economy, provided that the savings are borrowed and put to work by others who have reason to spend more than their incomes.

In exceptional years the savings pattern changes. During wartime, when incomes are high and spending opportunities are low, as much as a quarter of each dollar may be saved. In hard times, such as the depression of the 1930s, some people dissave, or spend more than they take in. During these years many families are forced to borrow or use past savings. Figure 8-2 shows both the great fluctuations in abnormal times and the relative stability of the savings rate in normal years, particularly since World War II.

There are frequent changes in the rate of savings. When families become jittery about the economy, they may increase their savings, or in times of high inflation they may lose faith in saving. With disposable income at an annual rate of about $2,500 billion, an increase in the savings rate of even one percentage point means $25 billion less spent on goods and services. As consumer confidence returns, the savings rate drops, and more money is pumped into the spending stream. As this increased spending works its way through the economy, after-tax income is increased. Since consumption expenditures account for over 60% of GNP, consumer behavior is an important determinant of the country's gross national product.

Not all money saved by consumers is used to increase investment. Much of the savings of individuals is used to pay off mortgages and other debts. However, as old debt is extinguished, new debt can be created. Money hoarded at home is not financing a new machine. Money can be transferred from household savings to business investment if it is placed in financial intermediaries such as banks and insurance companies. These efficient financial mechanisms pay interest for the use of the savings of individuals and then make investment loans to businesses in need of funds for the purchase of productive capital. They also help provide liquidity for the whole economy.

Personal savings also become available to finance investment when the savings are used to buy new corporate bonds and stocks. Once bonds and stocks have been issued, they are traded in the various securities markets. This transfer of existing securities does not provide new funds for investment in capital goods. A person buying stock on the stock exchange may say that an investment is being made. This claim may be true in a personal sense, but buying stock is not business investing because the purchase price is transferred to the seller of the stock rather than being used to buy plant or equipment. Although security exchanges do not provide a marketplace for the sale of new

Figure 8-2 Personal Savings as a Percentage of Disposable Personal Income

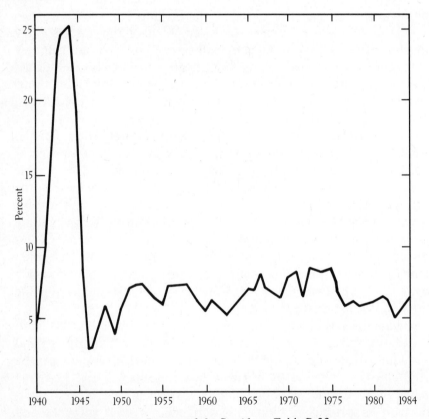

Source: *1985 Economic Report of the President,* Table B-23.

securities, the exchanges do provide a high degree of liquidity for stocks and bonds, thereby making it easier for firms to raise new funds.

Although the savings of individuals are important for investment, they are only a part of the investment funds in a progressive economy. Corporations are important savers, too. They save by not paying out to their stockholders their entire net income. Funds for capital projects are also obtained from depreciation allowances. In 1983, nonfarm, nonfinancial corporations obtained $280.5 billion from internal sources (depreciation allowances and retained earnings) and $155.9 billion from external sources (stocks, bonds, mortgages, and loans).

Regardless of the source of funds — new stock issues, loans, profits, or depreciation — the question to which management seeks an answer is the same: Will a proposed investment show an acceptable profit? Adequate returns are the key requirement for raising the vast sums needed by an advanced technology if it is to become more productive. Individual firms usually have several alternative proposals for the use of limited funds. Present value analysis, using compound interest, can help a decision maker allocate funds in a way that will result in acceptable rates of return on invested capital.

Jobs, as well as profits, depend on investment. Managers of factories and offices tend to employ the number of workers required for efficient operation with the use of equipment on hand. A new job in manufacturing can require an additional investment of $20,000 or more. An adequate level of capital formation is necessary to provide jobs for an increasing labor force.

8.4 WILL IT PAY?

"Will it pay?" is an important and difficult question that the management of a business must face when planning for the future. Finding the right answer is particularly important when management is considering a capital expenditure, that is, a major replacement or addition to plant capacity. Since several years may be required to recover the large initial outlays involved in capital expenditures, errors in capital budgeting can have serious consequences for a company.

As Stewart S. Cort, former president of Bethlehem Steel Corporation, has said: "Of all business activities, capital spending requires the most careful planning. The lives of capital assets are comparatively long and the time lag between the decision to make a particular investment and the beginning of its productive use is usually substantial."*

There may be as much as a decade or more between the time a utility orders a power plant and the time the plant is on line and producing electricity. Because of its size and permanence, a capital spending mistake can affect earnings for a long time. Even after the mistake is written off the books, the memory may linger to prejudice future financing.

Experience and good judgment are essential for making sound capital spending decisions. Although correct compound interest methods cannot take the risks and uncertainties out of capital budgeting, they can help in the analysis and judicious comparison of capital projects.

The combination of the focal date technique developed in earlier chapters with the depreciation methods discussed in this chapter results in useful methods for evaluating proposed capital expenditures. As is the case throughout the mathematics of finance, our analysis is based on the fact that money has a *time value.* A sum of money expected in the future must be discounted if it is to be compared with a cash outlay at another time. Discounting is usually done at a rate that is high enough to include both a reasonable return on the investment and an allowance for risk.

In capital budgeting, the comparison of expenses and income on a present value basis is called *discounted cash flow analysis.* Cash flows include some or all of the following:

Cash Outflows	Cash Inflows
Initial investment	Expected benefits:
Continuing costs	Increased revenues
in future years	Lower costs
	Depreciation allowances
	Salvage value

Since some of the expenses and all of the revenues occur in the future, we discount future cash flows before we compare proposed projects or estimate the rate of return to be expected on an investment.

Wall Street Journal, October 6, 1966, page 16.

Because the future contains many uncertainties, the returns from a proposed investment depend to a considerable extent on forecasting judgment relative to sales, prices, and other variables. Thus in discounted cash flow analysis we are dealing with estimates, not with the mathematical certitude that we had in earlier chapters when considering fixed payment and annuities certain. Predicting cash flows is the most complex and difficult aspect of the capital budgeting process. Once these estimates have been made, it is relatively easy to use mathematics of finance to compare proposed projects and to estimate rates of return.

In predicting the future, two types of risk are involved. One is that the asset may not perform as expected because of early breakdown, high maintenance costs, low productivity, or early obsolescence. The other risk is that future economic conditions and the demand for the product may not develop as expected.

Important in all capital budgeting problems is the recovery of invested capital. Determining the best method of capital recovery requires an understanding of the depreciation methods discussed in the following sections.

8.5 DEPRECIATION IS AN EXPENSE

The cost of a machine, building, or other tangible asset is an expense to be recovered out of revenue during the useful life of the asset. All machinery is headed for the junk heap, and its cost should be recovered before it gets there. As income-producing plants and equipment are used up, depreciation is the allocation of cost that a company writes off against profits.

The earnings of a business are dependent on having adequate capital, materials, and labor. If the costs of assets are not recovered by the end of their useful lives, a company may find itself in serious financial trouble.

One cause of depreciation is wear and tear resulting from use of the asset. Another cause is obsolescence, which means that the asset is out of date because of the development of a better machine, an increase in demand that the present asset cannot meet, or a big decrease in demand for the products that the asset has been producing. A change in the costs of the factors of production may cause obsolescence. For example, increased labor costs may result in the installation of more efficient machinery before the old machinery is worn out.

The importance of allowing for depreciation can be illustrated by a simple example. A person buys a truck for $12,000. Contractors will pay $200 a day for the operator's services and the use of the truck. This $200 must cover maintenance, operating expenses, and wages, as well as earn a reasonable return after taxes on the invested capital. And, if this person hopes to remain in business, the $12,000 should be recovered by the end of the useful life of the truck. Eventually the truck, like any machine, will have to be replaced because it will wear out or become obsolete. Regardless of the reason for replacement, the capital invested in an asset should be recovered from the income of the business. This recovery of invested capital is an expense, and it should be met from current income in the same way that labor, materials, interest, and other costs are recovered from the sale of the goods or services sold by a company

The following terms will be used in depreciation problems:

C = the **original cost** of the asset.
S = the **scrap, salvage**, or **residual value** of the asset at the end of its useful life.
n = the **useful life** of the asset in years.
W = the **wearing value** of the asset. It is the difference between cost and scrap value. $W = C - S$.
R = the **periodic depreciation charge**. This charge is usually annual. It may or may not be equal from year to year depending on the method of depreciation.

Both the estimated life of an asset and its scrap value are estimates made by authorities who are familiar with the particular asset. Since the rate of depreciation is based on judgment of how long an asset will be useful, there may be disagreements as to how much depreciation may be charged against income in any year. In 1962, the Internal Revenue Service published guidelines for depreciation allowances. Industry was classified into about 50 groups, and depreciable lives were assigned to assets in each group. If a company departs substantially from the useful lives established by the guidelines, it may have to show that the claimed depreciation rate is reasonable for the particular business.

Although money recovered through depreciation allowances may be put into securities or other investments to build up a fund that will be used to replace the asset, a much more common practice is to use recovered funds in the operation of the business. In the modern corporation depreciation charges are a major source of funds for capital projects. Used to purchase currently needed assets, the recovered funds usually earn a higher rate of return than could be obtained from income on securities.

The value at which an asset is shown on the accounting records of a company is called **carrying value**, or **book value**. Initially, the book value is the cost of the asset. After the first year the book value equals the amount of capital still invested in the property that must be recovered in the future through depreciation charges and salvage value. As an asset depreciates, it is carried at a decreasing book value. The depreciation allowance each year offsets the decrease in book value. The sum of the depreciation allowances is called the total accumulated depreciation. At all times the book value plus the total accumulated depreciation should equal the cost of the asset.

In general, depreciation charges are on an annual basis. If a company acquires or disposes of property during a year, regular depreciation is allowable for that part of the year the company owns the asset. For example, a company whose accounting year is the calendar year would depreciate an asset purchased on March 1 by an amount equal to the first full year's depreciation times 10/12. To simplify calculations in the examples and exercises in this book, we assume that assets are purchased in time to claim a full year's depreciation for the first year.

Practices differ regarding the handling of scrap values. Some accountants claim that because salvage estimates often require forecasts many years into an uncertain future plus the fact that removal costs may offset recovery income, the best practice is to assume zero scrap value. If this is done and the fully depreciated asset is eventually sold, any receipts from salvage sales would then be reported as income and taxes paid at that time. Others claim that if salvage is likely to be positive, the assumption of zero scrap value is not a sound practice. Since you may encounter either or both practices in later work, we assume in some problems that the company will get something for the asset when they dispose of it, whereas in other cases we depreciate on the assumption of zero scrap value.

There are several ways of allowing for depreciation that meet government regulations. First, we discuss three methods based on time: **straight line**, **declining balance**, and **sum of the years digits**.

8.6 STRAIGHT LINE METHOD

The simplest method of allowing for depreciation is the straight line method. This method spreads depreciation evenly over the useful life of the property. The periodic depreciation charge is obtained by simply dividing the wearing value by the useful life.

$$R = \frac{W}{n} \qquad (27)$$

As an asset is depreciated, the book value at any time equals

Original cost − (periodic charge × number of charges)

EXAMPLE A machine costs $5000 and has an estimated scrap value of $500 at the end of 5 years. Find the annual depreciation charge and the book value at the end of 3 years.

SOLUTION

$$W = C - S = 5000 - 500 = \$4500$$

$$R = \frac{W}{n} = \frac{4500}{5} = \$900$$

Book value at the end of 3 years = 5000 − (3 × 900) = $2300

In many cases the scrap value is assumed to be zero, and a rate is determined from the estimated life of the asset. For an asset with a 5-year life, the rate would be 1/5, or 20%, and the annual depreciation under the straight line method would be 20% of the cost.

8.7 DECLINING BALANCE METHOD

Under this method the depreciation allowance for each year is a constant percentage of the undepreciated or book value of the asset. Since the book value decreases each year, the depreciation charges are largest at first and then become progressively smaller.

New assets having a life of at least three years can be depreciated under this method at twice the straight line rate assuming no salvage value. If it is anticipated that a particular asset will have a significant scrap value, depreciation should stop when cost less this salvage has been recovered, even if this occurs before the end of the useful life. A taxpayer using the 200% or double declining balance method can change to the straight line method at any time. If the asset has no salvage value, a shift will have to be made at some time to the straight line method, since the declining balance method cannot depreciate an asset to zero.

If the declining balance method is applied to used, tangible property acquired after 1953, the rate per year may not exceed 150% of the straight line method, and a change to the straight line method requires the consent of the Internal Revenue Service.

EXAMPLE A new machine costs $5000 and has an estimated scrap value of $500 at the end of 5 years. Find the annual depreciation allowances if the double declining balance method is used for 3 years and the straight line method is used for the last 2 years.

SOLUTION The double declining balance rate is 40%, since it is twice the straight line rate of 20% based on a life of 5 years with no allowance for salvage. Putting the problem in tabular form is a help in making the year-to-year calculations. The last entry in the "Book value" column should equal the scrap value.

Year	Depreciation Charge	Accumulated Depreciation	Book Value
0			$5000
1	$2000[a]	$2000	3000
2	1200[a]	3200	1800
3	720[a]	3920	1080
4	290[b]	4210	790
5	290[b]	4500	500

[a] .40 × book value at end of preceding year.

[b] Straight line charge $= \dfrac{1080 - 500}{2} = 290.$

8.8 SUM OF THE YEARS DIGITS METHOD

This method is a simple one for making the depreciation allowances large during the early years of the useful life of the asset. The depreciation for each year is a fraction of the wearing value. The denominator of the fraction is obtained by numbering the years of useful life and adding.

For example, if the estimated life is 4 years, the denominator = 1 + 2 + 3 + 4 = 10. The numerator for the first year is the estimated useful life. Each year the numerator is reduced by 1.

EXAMPLE 1 A machine costs $5000. It has an estimated scrap value of $500 at the end of 5 years. Find the annual depreciation allowances using the sum of the years digits.

SOLUTION The sum of the digits is 1 + 2 + 3 + 4 + 5 = 15. Depreciation allowances are:

Year	Depreciation Allowance
1	4500 X 5/15 = $1500
2	4500 X 4/15 = 1200
3	4500 X 3/15 = 900
4	4500 X 2/15 = 600
5	4500 X 1/15 = 300
	$4500

Note that most of the cost is recovered early in the life of the asset.

EXAMPLE 2 A store building costs $510,000 and has an estimated life of 50 years. Assume zero salvage value and use the sum of the years digits to get the first 2 years' and the last 2 years' depreciation allowances.

SOLUTION Since the digits from 1 to 50 form an arithmetic progression, we can get their sum quickly and easily by using the formula developed in algebra for the sum of an arithmetic progression.

$$S = \frac{n}{2}(t_1 + t_n)$$

where

S = the sum
n = number of terms
t_1 = the first term
t_n = the last term

Substituting the values in this problem, we have

$$S = \tfrac{50}{2} (1 + 50) = 1275$$

Since the first term in the sum of the years digits is 1 and the last term is n, we can write the sum as

$$S = \frac{n}{2}(1 + n) = n\left(\frac{n + 1}{2}\right) = \frac{n^2 + n}{2}$$

An individual may prefer one form of this formula over the others because it is easier to remember and use. In our problem, we have

$$S = \frac{(50 \times 50) + 50}{2} = \frac{2550}{2} = 1275$$

Year	Depreciation Allowance
1	510,000 X 50/1275 = $20,000
2	510,000 X 49/1275 = 19,600
⋮	
49	510,000 X 2/1275 = 800
50	510,000 X 1/1275 = 400

Since the depreciation allowances form an arithmetic progression with a decrease of $400 each year, a simple way to get each year's depreciation is to subtract $400 from the preceding year's value.

8.9 COMPARISON OF DIFFERENT METHODS

The tables and sketches in Figure 8-3 show how the depreciation is accumulated and the book value reduced under the three methods. All are for an asset costing $5000 with a scrap value of $500 at the end of 5 years.

8.10 DETERMINING THE BEST METHOD

The objective of all depreciation methods is the eventual recovery of the money invested in an asset, but there are differences in the rate of recovery. This consideration is important because the value of a sum of money depends not only on the dollar amount, but also on when it is received. Another consideration is the maximization of a company's net earnings after taxes.

Figure 8-3   Comparison of Depreciation Methods

Straight Line Method

Year	Periodic Depreciation Charge	Total Accumulated Depreciation	Book Value
0			$5000
1	$900	$ 900	4100
2	900	1800	3200
3	900	2700	2300
4	900	3600	1400
5	900	4500	500

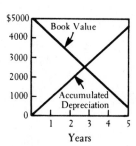

Double Declining Balance
(40% a year for 3 years and then straight line)

Year	Periodic Depreciation Charge	Total Accumulated Depreciation	Book Value
0			$5000
1	$2000	$2000	3000
2	1200	3200	1800
3	720	3920	1080
4	290	4210	790
5	290	4500	500

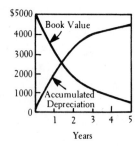

Sum of the Years Digits

Year	Periodic Depreciation Charge	Total Accumulated Depreciation	Book Value
0			$5000
1	$1500	$1500	3500
2	1200	2700	2300
3	900	3600	1400
4	600	4200	800
5	300	4500	500

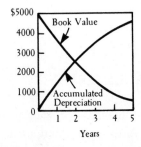

An advantage of the straight line method is its simplicity. There are times when the straight line method offers not only simplicity, but also financial advantages. Individual taxes are dependent on one's tax bracket. In a new business, the owners may be in a low tax bracket while the business is getting established. Large depreciation charges then may be less desirable than later, when the owners expect to be in a higher tax bracket.

The declining balance and the sum of the years digits result in a quick recovery of a large part of the money in an asset. Since depreciation charges reduce the income reported for tax purposes, high depreciation during the early years means savings on income tax during these years. This decrease in tax liability results in more money becoming available sooner for use in the business. A dollar received now is worth more than a dollar to be received in several years because it can be put to use sooner to repay debts, expand the business, or invest at interest.

Accelerated depreciation methods result in large depreciation allowances when the asset is new and repair costs are low and in smaller depreciation allowances later when maintenance costs are higher. The result is a better matching of revenues with expenses throughout the life of the asset.

In times of rising prices with resulting decreases in the purchasing power of the dollar, a rapid write-off may mean that dollars recovered early have more purchasing power than dollars recovered after additional price increases. In many cases, this advantage may be offset at least partially since newer and more expensive machines are also more productive.

Different depreciation methods can be compared on a present value basis by discounting all the depreciation charges. This is shown in Table 8-2 for the $5000 asset discussed in the preceding section. The comparison is based on the assumption that money will earn 8% for the company. The nonuniform payments of the declining balance and sum of the years digits must be discounted one by one using the present-worth-of-1 factor. For comparison purposes, we have also used this factor for the straight line method, although the usual procedure would be to get the total present value with one computation using the present-worth-of-1-per-period factor. Factors that are taken to three decimal places result in answers that are adequate for comparison purposes.

Note that all three methods result in total depreciation charges plus salvage value equal to the cost of the asset. Regardless of the method used, depreciation enables a taxpayer to recover from income the cost of any equipment that is used up in a personal business venture.

Since the timing of depreciation charges depends on the method, there are differences in the total present value of the depreciation charges. Both the double declining balance and the sum of the years digits result in a greater present value than the straight line method.

People who are responsible for preparing income tax reports for a business should understand the various methods of depreciation and be familiar with current tax regulations. Using the most advantageous system of depreciation will result in timing depreciation charges so that they will be of greatest benefit to the business.

If a business grows steadily, accelerated depreciation results in a more or less permanent grant of deferred taxes that may be used for company purposes. This development has contributed to industrial growth in the United States.

Exercise 8a

1. A pick-up truck costs $7000 and has an estimated scrap value of $1000 at the end of 5 years. Prepare depreciation schedules and

Table 8-2 Different Depreciation Methods

		Annual Depreciation Charge			Present Worth of Annual Charge		
Year	Present Worth of 1 at 8%	Straight Line	Double Declining Balance	Sum of Years Digits	Straight Line	Double Declining Balance	Sum of Years Digits
1	.926	$ 900	$2000	$1500	$ 833	$1852	$1389
2	.857	900	1200	1200	771	1028	1028
3	.794	900	720	900	715	572	715
4	.735	900	290	600	662	213	441
5	.681	900	290	300	613	197	204
		500[a]	500[a]	500[a]	340[b]	340[b]	340[b]
		$5000	$5000	$5000	$3934	$4202	$4117

[a] Estimated salvage value.
[b] Present worth of estimated salvage value.

graphs showing the total accumulated depreciation and book value for the straight line method, double declining balance method shifting to straight line method at the end of 3 years, and sum of the years digits method.

2. A machine costs $2500 and has an estimated scrap value of $500 at the end of 3 years. Prepare depreciation schedules and graphs showing the total accumulated depreciation and book value for the straight line, double declining balance shifting to straight line at the end of 1 year, and sum of the years digits methods.

3. An electric generator costs $39,000, has an estimated life of 12 years, and has no scrap value. Compute the first 2 years' depreciation allowances for the straight line, double declining balance, and sum of the years digits methods.

(Straight line: $3250.00, $3250.00; double declining balance: $6500.00, $5416.67; sum of the years digits: $6000.00, $5500.00)

4. A sewing machine costs $400. It has an estimated life of 14 years and a salvage value of $50. Compute the first 2 years' depreciation allowances under straight line, double declining balance, and sum of the years digits methods.

5. An apartment building costs $82,000. Assume a life of 40 years and no scrap value and get the first 2 years' depreciation allowances under straight line, double declining balance, and sum of the years digits methods.

(Straight line: $2050.00, $2050.00; double declining balance; $4100.00, $3895.00; sum of the years digits: $4000.00, $3900.00)

6. A warehouse costs $366,000. It has an estimated life of 60 years and no scrap value. Compute the first 2 years' depreciation under straight line, double declining balance, and sum of the years digits methods.

7. When a $13,000 machine was purchased, the estimated life was 8 years and the estimated salvage value was $1000. However, soon after the machine was put into operation, it became advisable to replace it with a greatly improved model. The replacement was made after the third annual depreciation charge. What was the total accumulated depreciation at this time if depreciation was handled using: (a) straight line? (b) double declining balance? (c) sum of the years digits?

[(a) $4500.00; (b) $7515.63; (c) $7000.00]

8. A machine that cost $7500 has an estimated scrap value of $300 at the end of 12 years. At the end of 5 years, the machine becomes obsolete because of the development of a better machine. What will be the total accumulated depreciation at this time if

the depreciation was handled using: (a) straight line? (b) double declining balance? (c) sum of the years digits?

9. A used truck was purchased for $3000. It has an estimated life of 4 years and a scrap value of $600. Find the first 2 years' depreciation allowances under: (a) straight line; (b) 150% declining balance; (c) sum of the years digits.

   (Straight line: $600.00, $600.00; 150% declining balance: $1125.00, $703.12; sum of the years digits: $960.00, $720.00)

10. A farmer paid $2000 for a used tractor. It has an estimated life of 8 years and a scrap value of $200. Find the first 2 years' depreciation allowances under: (a) straight line; (b) 150% declining balance; (c) sum of the years digits.

8.11 DEPRECIATION BASED ON USE

The depreciation methods discussed so far have been based on the asset having an assumed life in years. Now we consider a method that is based on the hours an asset is used or the number of units it produces. This method allows for more depreciation during a busy period when a factory may be working two or three shifts as compared with one shift during normal times.

EXAMPLE 1 A machine costs $5000 and has an estimated scrap value of $200. Machines of this type have an estimated operating life of 20,000 hours. This machine has been run as follows: first year, 2200 hours; second year, 4000 hours; third year, 1800 hours; fourth year, 3000 hours; fifth year, 4000 hours. Prepare a table showing the depreciation for each year.

SOLUTION The total wearing value is $4800. The depreciation charge for the first year is

$$4800 \times \frac{2200}{20,000} = \$528$$

Continuing this for successive years, we have

Year	Fraction of Useful Life	Periodic Depreciation Charge	Accumulated Depreciation	Book Value
0				$5000
1	2200/20,000	$528	$ 528	4472
2	4000/20,000	960	1488	3512
3	1800/20,000	432	1920	3080
4	3000/20,000	720	2640	2360
5	4000/20,000	960	3600	1400

EXAMPLE 2   A machine costs $5000 and has an estimated scrap value of $200. It is estimated that this machine will produce 50,000 units. The annual production has been: first year, 8000 units; second year, 5000 units third year, 12,000 units; fourth year, 10,000 units; fifth year, 5000 units. Prepare a table showing the depreciation for each year.

SOLUTION   The total wearing value is $4800. The depreciation charge for the first year is

$$4800 \times \frac{8000}{50,000} = \$768$$

Continuing this for successive years, we have

Year	Fraction of Estimated Production	Periodic Depreciation Charge	Accumulated Depreciation	Book Value
0				$5000
1	8,000/50,000	$ 768	$ 768	4232
2	5,000/50,000	480	1248	3752
3	12,000/50,000	1152	2400	2600
4	10,000/50,000	960	3360	1640
5	5,000/50,000	480	3840	1160

Exercise 8b

1. A piece of machinery costs $8000 and has an estimated scrap value of $2000. Machines of this type have an estimated working-hour life of 10,000 hours. This machine is used as follows: first year, 3000 hours; second year, 1200 hours; third year, 1000 hours; fourth year, 2000 hours. Prepare a depreciation schedule for the 4 years this machine has been in use.
2. A machine costs $30,000 and has an estimated scrap value of $4000. It is estimated that this machine will produce 120,000 units during its useful life. The machine produces the following outputs during the first 5 years it is in use: first year, 20,000 units; second year, 15,000 units; third year, 25,000 units; fourth year, 10,000 units; fifth year, 18,000 units. Prepare a depreciation schedule.

8.12   DETERMINING CASH FLOWS

Cash flows, both expenses and revenues, may occur at any time during a time period or more or less continuously during a period. The common practice in capital budgeting is to value all cash flows during a year as if they occur at the end of the year. This practice simplifies computations, is realistic, and is in accord with the practice of making major decisions in business on an annual basis.

Therefore, before starting numerical computations, a good procedure is to combine all cash flows during a year into a single net cash flow for that year. The analyst should take into account expected revenues, expenses, depreciation allowances, taxes, and any other factors that affect the final cash flow for that year.

Depreciation is not only the largest single source of investment funds, it is also the most confusing. The reason is that depreciation is both a noncash expense and a net inflow of cash for the current year. When a company buys a capital asset – a building or a machine – a certain amount of the asset is used up each year, and a cost must be charged for this wear and tear if the company is to keep its capital intact. If no allowance were made for depreciation, a company would be overstating its profits. Depreciation is a legitimate accounting procedure used to arrive at net profits. Inadequate depreciation allowances can contribute to a firm's eventual failure.

However, unlike the costs for labor, materials, and taxes, the company does not send anyone a check or cash to take care of depreciation.

Depreciation costs are handled with entries in the company books showing that the plant or machine is worth so much less than a year ago. This accounting takes care of the noncash expense aspect of depreciation.

For every asset, there was a time in the past when the actual purchase was made. Then as the asset is used up in production, it becomes a legitimate expense that is a part of the total cost of production. Depreciation allowances spread the cost of the asset over its life, and the company must charge enough for its product to cover this cost as well as the costs of labor, material, taxes, and so on. If goods are priced high enough, revenue is derived from sales to cover the cost of depreciation. The depreciation bookkeeping charge against earnings allows the company to reduce current income by writing off assets as they are used up in the business. The depreciation charge before taxes results in the net cash inflow aspect of depreciation.

Note in the examples how net cash inflow from operations is determined. We first get the depreciation, which is deducted as a cost or expense from income. Then taxes are calculated on income less depreciation. Finally the charge for depreciation is added to income after taxes to obtain the net cash inflow from operations.

Sometimes capital budgeting studies are made on the basis of flows before taxes. This approach is reasonable when analyzing government proposals or investment in human capital. However, corporate tax rates are responsible for large cash outflows. For this reason, it is best to use after-tax flows when analyzing private business investment. The examples in this book are based on a tax rate of 48%. This rate may be changed in the future as it has been in the past. Fiscal policy may result in a lower rate when the economy needs such a fiscal stimulus to head off a recession or to initiate a recovery. At other times a higher rate may be desired to slow down an overheated economy that seems headed for inflation. In some cases, it may also be necessary to allow for state taxes. However, the same methods apply regardless of rates. The following example shows how both depreciation and taxes are taken into account in determining the net cash flow for each year.

EXAMPLE 1 A company is considering the purchase of a machine that costs $15,000 and has an estimated salvage value of $3000 at the end of its useful life of 3 years. Annual operating costs are expected to be about $1000 a year. Additional revenue expected from the machine is $7000 a year. Find the net cash flows for this machine assuming a 48% tax rate and: (a) straight line depreciation;

(b) double declining balance for the first year and straight line for the next two years; (c) sum of the years digits.

STRAIGHT LINE

Net income before taxes and depreciation =
additional revenue – additional costs   7000 – 1000 = $6000

Annual depreciation allowance $\dfrac{15,000 - 3000}{3}$ = 4000

Taxable income = net income – depreciation   6000 – 4000 = 2000
Income after taxes = .52 × taxable income*   .52 × 2000 = 1040
Net cash flow = income after taxes + depreciation 1040 + 4000 = 5040

The year-by-year determination of cash flows can be presented quite well in tabular form. The net cash flow for year zero is the cost of the asset and is negative. For subsequent years, the net cash flow is the sum of the depreciation allowance and the income after taxes.

(1)	(2) Net Income before Taxes and	(3)	(4) Taxable Income	(5) Income after Taxes	(6) Net Cash Flow
Year	Depreciation	Depreciation Allowance	(2) – (3)	.52 × (4)	(3) + (5)
0	– $15,000				– $15,000
1	6,000	$ 4,000	$2,000	$1,040	5,040
2	6,000	4,000	2,000	1,040	5,040
3	6,000	4,000	2,000	1,040	8,040[a]
		$12,000	$6,000	$3,120	$ 3,120

[a] Includes $3000 salvage value. The salvage value is added to cash inflow after taxes and depreciation.

DOUBLE DECLINING BALANCE The first year's depreciation is 2/3 of the purchase price, or $10,000. This amount is more than the net income for the year, resulting in a taxable income of – $4000. If the

*Some authors first multiply the taxable income by the tax rate. The tax in dollars is then subtracted from taxable income to get the income after taxes. In capital budgeting problems it is easier and faster to get the after-tax income by multiplying the taxable income by (1 – tax rate). With a tax rate of 48%, the after-tax factor becomes (1.00 – .48) = .52.

company has other income, as will usually be the case, the excess depreciation on this machine can be used to reduce reported earnings by $4000. The result will be a tax shield or tax offset of .48 × 4000 = $1920. Thus the income after taxes from this asset will be – $2080. Since this result is what we get from .52(–4000), we can use the same procedure for getting income after taxes whether the taxable income is plus or minus. If this machine represented all of the company's operations, there could be a carry back or carry forward of the loss.

(1)	(2) Net Income before Taxes and Year Depreciation	(3) Depreciation Allowance	(4) Taxable Income (2) – (3)	(5) Income after Taxes .52 × (4)	(6) Net Cash Flow (3) + (5)
0	– $15,000				– $15,000
1	6,000	$10,000	– $4,000	– $2,080	7,920
2	6,000	1,000	5,000	2,600	3,600
3	6,000	1,000	5,000	2,600	6,600[a]
		$12,000	$6,000	$3,120	$ 3,120

[a] Includes $3000 salvage value. The salvage value is added to cash inflow after taxes and depreciation.

SUM OF THE YEARS DIGITS   The denominator of the annual fraction = 1 + 2 + 3 = 6.

(1)	(2) Net Income before Taxes and Year Depreciation	(3) Depreciation Allowance	(4) Taxable Income (2) – (3)	(5) Income after Taxes .52 × (4)	(6) Net Cash Flow (3) + (5)
0	– $15,000				– $15,000
1	6,000	$ 6,000	$ 0	$ 0	6,000
2	6,000	4,000	2,000	1,040	5,040
3	6,000	2,000	4,000	2,080	7,080[a]
		$12,000	$6,000	$3,120	$ 3,120

[a] Includes $3000 salvage value. The salvage value is added to cash inflow after taxes and depreciation.

Note that the totals are the same for all methods of depreciation, but there are differences in the year-by-year net cash flows.

Time diagrams are quite helpful in presenting net cash flow problems in pictorial form. See Figure 8-4.

Figure 8-5 shows how histograms can be used to give an overall picture of cash flow problems. Sometimes the various inflows and outflows are shaded differently so that a busy reader can see at a glance the different expenses and sources of income.

Figure 8-4

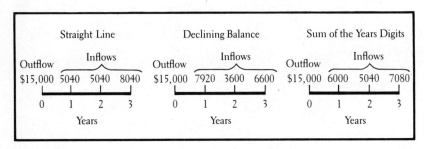

Figure 8-5

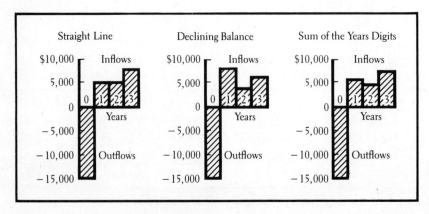

8.13 IMPORTANCE OF TIMING

In the examples in the preceding section, taxable income was $6000 for all methods of depreciation. Regardless of the method of depreciating an asset, total depreciation allowances will be the same. Thus the total income subject to tax will be the same regardless of how an item is depreciated. If tax rates do not change, the government will in the long run collect the same amount of taxes no matter how depreciation is handled. Hence some advocates of fast depreciation have argued that no tax loss will result from accelerated depreciation even if 100% depreciation is allowed the first year. Faster depreciation merely means lower taxes in the early life of an asset and higher taxes in later years.

The total amount written off on any particular asset will be the same regardless of the number of years. However, companies invest every year and the Treasury collects taxes every year. When depreciation is accelerated, the Treasury collects less revenue year by year than it would otherwise get. In 1971 the Asset Depreciation Range System was introduced. This system permits companies to depreciate assets for tax purposes over a period as much as 20% shorter or 20% longer than guideline lives. It was argued that this practice would lead to more investment and modernization of plant and equipment.

The Treasury estimated that the proposed changes would result in a $2.7 billion drop in tax revenue in 1972 and a total drop of $37 billion over a decade. Critics of the change claimed that this lost tax revenue represented additional money for business that might better be used by government to alleviate social problems. Ralph Nader's public interest research group argued that a change like this in tax policy should be made only after adequate public hearings. As informed and concerned citizens gain a better understanding of the time value of money, increased attention will be given to the timing of proposed fiscal policies.

8.14 PRESENT VALUE COMPARISONS

After net cash flows have been determined, compound interest methods can be used in two ways to analyze proposed investments. One way is to use compound discount factors to compute the present value of all flows at a specified rate. The other way is to get the rate that makes the inflows and outflows equal. In either case, the solution is obtained using the focal date approach that is so useful throughout the mathematics of finance. The focal date is usually put at the point at which the major expenditure of funds will be made. If there are relatively small planning expenditures in the years preceding the installation of an asset, these are brought forward at compound interest. Estimated future net cash flows are discounted to the installation date.

The interest rate (often called the discount rate) to be used in getting present values is commonly called the *cost of capital*. This rate is the particular company's best estimate of the return that the firm's creditors and stockholders, its suppliers of long-term capital, expect on their investment.

To help compensate for the uncertainties involved in estimating future cash flows, interest rates in capital budgeting problems are higher than those used in problems where the return is not in doubt. This practice is reasonable, since a firm that could get 8 or 10% on a bond or mortgage will expect a considerably higher return when putting money into a project that involves greater risks. Present investments must be based on forecasts of a future that can be seen only hazily. No one can be sure how business will be in 2 or 3 years, let alone in 5 or 10 years. If there were no premiums for risk taking and no rewards for foresight and good luck, risk capital would not be available for innovation and expansion. When a reasonable allowance for risk taking is added to interest costs, a firm may feel that an after-tax return of 10 or 15% or more on invested capital is required to make a project attractive. The term *invested capital* refers to the money supplied by the owners of the company. In the company balance sheet invested capital is usually called stockholders' equity. Invested capital comes partly from the sale of stock. After a company starts making a profit, a part of earnings probably will be paid out in dividends to the stockholders. The remainder will be retained in the business and recorded as an increase in stockholders' equity. Since profits belong to the owners, retained earnings mean in effect that stockholders are investing more money in the business. If the company continues to prosper, retained earnings will contribute to higher profits and increases in the market value of the stock.

It is interesting to see what some of the top corporations earn as a portion of their total value. The data in Table 8-3, from the annual *Fortune* surveys of American corporations, show after-tax income as a percentage of invested capital.

Some companies had even more impressive profits in 1984. General Dynamics had a 35.9% return on invested capital and Chrysler had 72.0%. A newcomer to the "Fortune 500," Weirton Steel showed 100.0%.

Before accepting a new proposal, the management of a company may insist that the project have an expected rate of return considerably higher than the overall rate for the company. The reason is that the overall rate is calculated after advertising, overhead, and other general expenses are subtracted. A proportionate share of these costs will probably not be allotted in advance to a proposed new project.

When projects are evaluated on a present value basis, the present value of the inflows must be greater than the present value of the outflows for the project to be attractive.

In discounted cash flow analysis, two discount factors are used: present worth of 1, for discounting single sums; and present worth of 1 per period, for discounting a series of equal cash flows equally spaced. These factors are given in Table 5 in the back of the book. Since cash flow analysis is based on estimates, the discount factors are given in Table 5 to three decimal places, sufficient for practical work with uncertain data.

EXAMPLE 1 Determine the net present value of the proposal in section 8.12 using an estimated cost of capital of 8% and the three methods of depreciation.

Table 8-3 Five Largest Industrials

	Net Income as Percent of Equity		
	1984	1979	1975
Exxon	19.2%	19.0%	14.7%
General Motors	18.7	15.1	9.6
Mobil	9.3	19.1	11.8
Ford	29.6	11.2	5.1
Texaco	2.3	16.5	9.6

SOLUTION We discount each net cash flow to the present using the present-worth-of-1 factors. The algebraic sum is the net present value of the project. A tabular arrangement systematizes the work and makes comparisons easy.

Year	Discount Factor at 8%	Straight Line		Double Declining Balance		Sum of Years Digits	
		Net Cash Flow	Present Value	Net Cash Flow	Present Value	Net Cash Flow	Present Value
0	1.000	−$15,000	−$15,000	−$15,000	−$15,000	−$15,000	−$15,000
1	.926	5,040	4,667	7,920	7,334	6,000	5,556
2	.857	5,040	4,319	3,600	3,085	5,040	4,319
3	.794	8,040	6,384	6,600	5,240	7,080	5,622
			$ 370		$ 659		$ 497

The positive net present values show that all of the methods of depreciation would result in the project returning better than 8% provided that the actual net flows are as high as the estimates. The differences in the net present values show the advantages of a rapid write-off.

EXAMPLE 2 Determine the net present values for the preceding example using a cost of capital of 10%.

Year	Discount Factor at 10%	Straight Line		Double Declining Balance		Sum of Years Digits	
		Net Cash Flow	Present Value	Net Cash Flow	Present Value	Net Cash Flow	Present Value
0	1.000	−$15,000	−$15,000	−$15,000	−$15,000	−$15,000	−$15,000
1	.909	5,040	4,581	7,920	7,199	6,000	5,454
2	.826	5,040	4,163	3,600	2,974	5,040	4,163
3	.751	8,040	6,038	6,600	4,957	7,080	5,317
			−$ 218		$ 130		−$ 66

This asset can be expected to produce a 10% return only if the double declining balance method of depreciation is used.

EXAMPLE 3 A company is considering the purchase of a piece of equipment that costs $11,000 and has an estimated scrap value of $1000 at the end of its useful life of 5 years. The equipment is expected to result in operating savings of $5000 a year. Would this investment be attractive to a company that wants a return of 12% a year after taxes? Use straight line depreciation and a tax rate of 48%.

SOLUTION

Annual depreciation allowance = 10,000/5 = $2000
Taxable income = 5000 – 2000   = 3000
Income after taxes = .52 X 3000   = 1560
Net cash inflow = depreciation
   allowance + after-tax income   = 3560

Since the five net cash inflows of $3560 form an ordinary annuity, we get their present value using formula (15) and the present-worth-of-1-per-period factor from Table 5. To this is added the present worth of the scrap value obtained using formula (11) and the present-worth-of-1 factor.

$$\text{Present worth of inflows} = 3560a_{\overline{5}|12\%} + 1000(1.12)^{-5}$$
$$= 3560 \times 3.605 + 1000 \times .567$$
$$= 12,834 + 567 = \$13,401$$

This amount is well above the cost of $11,000. The present value of the asset is 13,401 – 11,000 = $2041. Since the equipment can clearly be expected to return more than 12%, the project is acceptable.

8.15 RATE OF RETURN

The internal rate of return is the rate that will make cash inflows equal to outflows. This rate must be found by trial and error unless the cash flows happen to form an ordinary annuity as in the first example.

EXAMPLE 1 A company is considering the purchase of an asset that costs $6000 and has no scrap value at the end of its useful life of

3 years. Annual net income over operating expenses is expected to be $4200. Find the internal rate of return assuming straight line depreciation and a tax rate of 48%.

SOLUTION

Annual depreciation allowance = 6000/3 = $2000
Taxable income = 4200 – 2000   = 2200
Income after taxes = .52 × 2200   = 1144
Annual net cash inflow = 2000 + 1144   = 3144

Since the net cash inflows in this problem form an ordinary annuity, we find the rate following the method in section 4.11. Substituting in formula (15), we have

$$3144a_{\overline{3}|} = 6000$$

$$a_{\overline{3}|} = \frac{6000}{3144} = 1.908$$

According to the table, the rate is between 25 and 30%. If a more precise answer is required, we interpolate.

$$
\begin{array}{c|cc}
 & i \text{ in } \% & a_{\overline{3}|} \\
\hline
 & 25 & 1.952 \\
5 \quad d \left[\begin{array}{c} \\ i \end{array} \right. & & 1.908 \quad \Big]44 \quad \Big|136 \\
 & 30 & 1.816
\end{array}
$$

$$\frac{d}{5} = \frac{44}{136}$$

$$d = \frac{5 \times 44}{136} = 1.6$$

$$i = 25.0 + 1.6 = 26.6\%$$

Since there are many uncertainties in capital budgeting problems, it is probably well to round this result off to the nearest percentage point. We would simply say that the expected internal rate of return on this project is approximately 27%.

EXAMPLE 2 Work the preceding example using double declining balance for 2 years and straight line for the third year.

SOLUTION The first year's depreciation is 6000 × 2/3 = $4000. Continuing with the solution in tabular form, we have

(1) Year	(2) Net Income before Taxes and Depreciation	(3) Depreciation Allowance	(4) Taxable Income (2) – (3)	(5) Income after Taxes .52 × (4)	(6) Net Cash Flow (3) + (5)
0	– $6000				– $6000
1	4200	$4000	$ 200	$ 104	4104
2	4200	1333	2867	1491	2824
3	4200	667	3533	1837	2504
		$6000	$6600	$3432	$3432

To get the rate of return when the cash inflows are different, we use trial and error until we find a rate that makes the total present value of the inflows equal to the present value of the outflows. By this process we find that the rate is between 25 and 30% because 25% results in a present value greater than $6000 and 30% results in a value less than $6000. The work is summarized as follows:

Year	Cash Inflow	Present Value at 25% Of $1	 Of Cash Inflows	Present Value at 30% Of $1	 Of Cash Inflows
1	$4104	.800	$3283	.769	$3156
2	2824	.640	1807	.592	1672
3	2504	.512	1282	.455	1139
			$6372		$5967

If a more precise answer is required, we interpolate, as shown here:

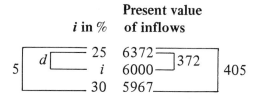

$$
5\begin{bmatrix} d\begin{bmatrix} 25 & 6372 \\ i & 6000 \end{bmatrix}372 \\ 30 & 5967 \end{bmatrix}405
$$

Present value
i in %   of inflows

$$\frac{d}{5} = \frac{372}{405}$$

$$d = \frac{5 \times 372}{405} = 4.6$$

$$i = 25.0 + 4.6 = 29.6\% = \text{approximately } 30\%$$

Going to a more rapid write-off has increased the internal rate of return by three percentage points.

An advantage of the discounted cash flow method is that interest is computed only on the amount of unrecovered capital to date. The rate is not affected by what is done with the recovered capital. Thus we can check a computed rate by finding how long it would take to recover the invested capital if the project were financed at a capital rate equal to the rate of return. If the rate is correct, the period required to recover the investment and the life of the project will be the same.

EXAMPLE 3 A machine that costs $15,925 will produce estimated net cash inflows of $7560 a year for 3 years. Find the rate of return and check.

SOLUTION Since this is an ordinary annuity with a present value of $15,925 and a periodic payment of $7560, we have

$$a_{\overline{3}|} = \frac{15,925}{7560} = 2.106$$

This present-worth-of-1-per-period factor corresponds to a rate of 20%. The following shows that we earn 20% on invested capital and in 3 years recover the investment. The amount of capital recovered equals net cash inflow minus return on unrecovered capital.

Year	Unrecovered Capital at Beginning of the Year	Net Cash Inflow	Return of 20% on Unrecovered Capital	Amount of Capital Recovered
1	$15,925	$7560	$3185	$ 4375
2	11,550	7560	2310	5250
3	6,300	7560	1260	6300
				$15,925

8.16 COMPARISON OF ALTERNATIVES

Discounted cash flow analysis can be used to help managers choose among proposed capital expenditures. One method is to get the rate of return for each proposal. Another method is to rank projects on the basis of net present values. If the proposals differ greatly as to costs and income streams, a method that is preferable to net present value comparisons is the use of a **profitability index**, which is the ratio of the present value of new cash inflows to the present value of outlays. This ratio is also called the **benefit-cost ratio**. Different methods of comparing alternatives do not always lead to the same ranking, as shown in the following example.

EXAMPLE A company is considering two projects that have the following net cash flows after allowing for depreciation, taxes, and other expenses. Find the net present values and profitability indexes using a rate of 16%. Find the internal rates of return for the two proposals.

SOLUTION

Year	Present Worth of 1 at 16%	Proposal A Net Cash Inflow	Proposal A Present Value	Proposal B Net Cash Inflow	Proposal B Present Value
0	1.000	-$30,000	-$30,000	-$30,000	-$30,000
1	.862	0	0	0	0
2	.743	25,000	18,575	0	0
3	.641	25,000	16,025	0	0
4	.552	0	0	34,000	18,768
5	.476	0	0	34,000	16,184
			$ 4,600		$ 4,952
Profitability index			1.15		1.17

The profitability index for proposal A $= \dfrac{18,575 + 16,025}{30,000}$

$$= \frac{34,600}{30,000} = 1.15$$

On the basis of either net present value or profitability index, proposal B would be ranked first.

A trial-and-error determination of the internal rate of return puts proposal A first with a rate of about 23%, as compared with 20% for B. Had the present value comparisons been at a rate close to these true rates of return, A would have also been first on a net present value basis.

Of the methods we have discussed for evaluating alternatives, the net present value and profitability index methods have the advantage of ease of computation as compared with the sometimes tedious calculations required to get the internal rate of return. Another advantage of the present value method is that an allowance for risk can be added to the estimated cost of capital. On the other hand, if the present value analysis is based on an incorrect rate, the ranking of projects may be wrong. When we use the internal rate of return, we can rank proposals in order of yield. Then we can see which ones will probably be most profitable and how far we can go down the list before we reach a point below the cost of capital, where a proposal would be a losing proposition.

It is important to recognize that there is more to decision making than computing a present value or a rate of return for individual proposals. Management is concerned about total return to the firm and takes into account budget constraints. The search is directed toward achieving the best overall combination of capital projects. There is also the problem of reinvesting money. A project that would yield 25% for a year or two might be less attractive than one that would return 20% for five or more years.

There are, of course, situations in which nonmonetary considerations, such as employee morale and community relations, result in adopting proposals that are not financially attractive. In some cases expenditures simply have to be made. Management may have no practical alternative to repairing or replacing a defective roof and installing adequate safety devices.

8.17 HUMAN CAPITAL

Investment in buildings and equipment is not enough to guarantee economic progress. It is also essential to have adequate investment in the health, education, and training of people.

The economic value of a college education is often given in terms of the increased lifetime earnings of college graduates. This gauge is a crude measure that ignores the time value of money. Much of the increased income is far in the future. In the immediate present there is an opportunity cost in the form of forgone earnings that the student could get if he or she were working. There are also immediate cash outlays for school expenses.

However, even when the time value of money is taken into account, money spent on education may be the most profitable investment a person can make. With the increasing demand for skilled and educated workers, expenditures by qualified people on education may be a better form of investment than putting the money into savings accounts, bonds, or stocks. In addition to monetary returns, education has advantages that cannot be expressed as dollars or percentages.

EXAMPLE 1 A student will soon graduate from high school. Upon graduation she can choose between a job paying $7000 more than her current part-time job and going to a four-year college costing $3000 per year in tuition while keeping the part-time job. A high school counselor estimates that the student's lifetime earnings will be about $200,000 more if she chooses college. Estimate the present value of the college education using a rate of 10%.

SOLUTION To simplify the computations, assume that the $200,000 is distributed equally over 40 years, for additional income each year of $5000. Since it is not possible to determine differences in personal tax rates far into the future, comparisons are made on a before-tax basis. No allowance is made for depreciation or scrap value. It is true that some skills become worthless. On the other hand, an employee who continues to learn is one of the few assets that increases in value as years go by. A time diagram (Figure 8-6) helps to visualize the net cash flow.

The outflows (loss of $7000 in earnings plus $3000 cost for each of the first 4 years) form an ordinary annuity with present value $10,000a_{\overline{4}|10\%}$. The inflows are deferred annuity with a present value of $5000(a_{\overline{44}|} - a_{\overline{4}|})$.

$$\text{Present value of the education} = -10,000(3.170) + 5000(9.849 \\ - 3.170)$$
$$= -31,700 + 33,395$$
$$= \$1695$$

EXAMPLE 2 Find the internal rate of return in Example 1.

SOLUTION Since the present value is positive at 10%, the internal rate of return is higher than 10%. Using a rate of 12%, we find that

$$\text{Present value} = -10,000(3.037) + 5000(8.276 - 3.037)$$
$$= -30,370 + 26,195$$
$$= -\$4175$$

Thus the internal rate of return is between 10% and 12%. Interpolating gives a rate of 10.6%.

The best investment opportunity open to many young people is in themselves, provided that they have the foresight and luck to acquire skills for which there will be brisk demand.

8.18 THE PLANNING-PROGRAMMING-BUDGETING SYSTEM

In 1961 the Department of Defense introduced a system called Planning-Programming-Budgeting (PPB). This system is now used as a planning tool in many federal agencies and in some state and local governments. PPB emphasizes the analysis of current outlays within the framework of long-range planning. Goals are identified with care. A search is made for alternative means of reaching goals at the least cost. Performance is measured to ensure an adequate return on expenditures.

An important part of PPB is benefit-cost analysis. Both benefits and costs occur at various points in time, so they are not directly comparable. But if all flows are discounted to the present, we can compute the benefit-cost ratio as follows:

Figure 8-6

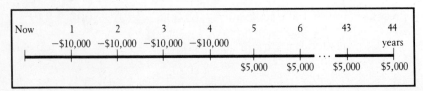

$$\text{Benefit-cost ratio} = \frac{\text{present value of benefits}}{\text{present value of costs}}$$

If this ratio is greater than 1, a proposed project is presumably desirable from an economic standpoint. A ratio less than 1 indicates a loser. Because of its apparent simplicity, the benefit-cost ratio is an appealing device. What could be nicer than to reduce a complicated problem to a single number that signals "go ahead" if it is greater than 1 and warns "do something else" if less than 1? However, before spending millions on the basis of a favorable benefit-cost ratio, we should obtain answers to several questions.

● How good are estimates of benefits and costs? Many proposals, a dam or canal, for example, involve inflows and outflows of money far into the future. Putting a dollar value on them now may be largely guesswork. This limitation does not mean that everything should be held up until the results of a project are practically certain. Life is too unpredictable for that. However, decision makers should be forced to recognize what they do not know and then search for the best available estimates.

● Whose benefits are being measured? There is a difference between whether society as a whole will benefit or whether the returns will go to a small area or to those with special interests.

● Was allowance made for external economies and diseconomies? A project may look good on a benefit-cost basis if only benefits and costs associated directly with the project are included. But if allowance is made for pollution or other external diseconomies, the proposal may be unacceptable. On the other hand, external economies, such as incidental recreation facilities or jobs for ghetto youth, may improve the chances of a proposal that in itself has a marginal benefit-cost ratio.

● What discount rate was used? A particular set of benefits and costs might result in a benefit-cost ratio well above 1 if a discount rate of 4% is used. But a more realistic 6 or 8% might result in the same dollar flows having a benefit-cost ratio less than 1.

We use the same mathematics in benefit-cost analysis that we have used in other discount problems. But the judgment of the person doing the work now can have considerable effect on the data used in the problem and in this way affect the final result. By assuming a long life, limited maintenance, free-spending tourists, and a low discount rate, even pyramid building can be made to look good on a benefit-cost basis!

Although PPB cannot provide final answers to complex political-economic problems, it can help the decision maker by showing where better information is needed, by organizing data, and by logically comparing alternate proposals for achieving government objectives. The development of PPB means that government planners can now use the mathematics of finance to help solve problems that are mathematically similar to those in finance and business.

Exercise 8c

1. A machine costs $20,000. It has an estimated life of 4 years and no scrap value. The machine is expected to increase company revenue by $11,000 a year before maintenance costs, which are estimated at $2000 a year. Assume a tax rate of 48% and find the net present value and profitability index at 16% using: (a) straight line depreciation; (b) double declining balance for 2 years and straight line thereafter; (c) sum of the years digits.

$$\begin{bmatrix} & \text{Net present} & \text{Profitability} \\ & \text{value} & \text{index} \\ \text{(a)} & -\$190 & .99 \\ \text{(b)} & 447 & 1.02 \\ \text{(c)} & 305 & 1.02 \end{bmatrix}$$

2. The management of a company has established an internal rate of return of 14% as the cutoff point for capital projects. In other words, to be acceptable, a proposal must have an expected rate of return of 14% or more after taxes. A department manager recommends installing a machine that costs $12,000 and has an estimated life of 3 years with no scrap value. The manager claims that the machine should reduce labor costs by $8000 a year. Estimated maintenance costs on the machine are $1000 a year. Assume a tax rate of 48% and find the net present value and profitability index using: (a) straight line depreciation; (b) double declining balance for 1 year and then straight line; (c) sum of the years digits.

3. A student will soon get her bachelor's degree. She can start earning $14,000 a year. Or she can go to graduate school and receive an all-expense grant plus $4000 a year. She thinks that she can get her doctor's degree in 3 years. With the higher degree, she believes that she can average about $6000 more a year for 35 years. Is graduate school a profitable investment if the student wants a return of 8% a year before taxes?

(Yes. Present value of forgone income is $25,770; present value of additional income is $55,512. Net present value of additional education is $29,742.)

4. A high school student can get a job at the end of his sophomore year and earn about $5400 a year. Or he can stay in high school and earn about $2250 a year more for 40 years than if he had become a dropout. What is the present value of the 2 additional years of high school at 8% before taxes?

5. A piece of equipment costs $40,000. It has an estimated life of 10 years and a scrap value of $5000. The equipment is expected to increase company revenue $12,500 a year over operating expenses. Assume straight line depreciation and a tax rate of 48% and find the net present value at 14%.
   ($4017)

6. Solve problem 5 using a rate of 16%.

7. A lease on a retail store has 12 more years to run. Fire insurance now costs the store $60,000 a year. If the store installs an automatic sprinkler system at a cost of $180,000, the annual cost for fire insurance will drop to $15,800. Estimated annual maintenance cost of the sprinkler system will be $200. If the system is depreciated to zero on a straight line basis over 12 years and the tax rate is 48%, what after-tax return would be earned on this investment?
   (13%)

8. The lease on a dry cleaning establishment has 10 more years to run. The present cost of fire insurance is $4160 a year. The company can install an automatic sprinkler at a cost of $7600 with estimated annual maintenance costs of $100. The cost of fire insurance will then drop to $900 a year. The sprinkler system can be depreciated to zero over the remaining years of the lease. Assume straight line depreciation and a 48% tax rate and get the internal rate of return.

9. An airport terminal building has an estimated life of 20 years. The annual cost of fire insurance without a sprinkler system would be $2213. With a sprinkler, the cost would drop to $357 a year. Estimated annual maintenance costs are $100. The cost of installing a sprinkler system would be $5120. What would be the approximate rate of return after taxes on this investment if it is depreciated to zero over 20 years on a straight line basis and the tax rate is 48%?
   (20%)

10. What would be the approximate rate of return in problem 9 if the building has an estimated life of 10 years and the sprinkler system is depreciated over 10 years on a straight line basis?

11. A company is considering the purchase of materials handling equipment. The initial cost will be $36,000 and the annual outlay for maintenance, power, and other expenses will be an estimated

$1000. It is expected that the equipment will reduce labor costs by $10,000 a year for 12 years. The estimated life of the asset is 12 years with no salvage value. Assume a tax rate of 48% and straight line depreciation and get the rate of return to the nearest percent.

(13%)

12. A used tractor costs $14,000. It has an estimated life of 6 years and a salvage value of $2000. The annual outlay for maintenance will run about $500. It is expected that this tractor will result in an annual increase in revenue of $5000. Assume a tax rate of 48% and straight line depreciation and find the rate of return to the nearest percent.

13. A company is considering the purchase of an asset that costs $6000 and has no scrap value at the end of its useful life of 4 years. Annual net income over operating expenses, but before taxes and depreciation, is expected to be $3500 a year. The tax rate is 48%. For comparison purposes, find the rate of return to the nearest tenth of one percent assuming: (a) straight line depreciation; (b) double declining balance for 2 years and then straight line; (c) sum of the years digits.

[(a) 25.0%; (b) 27.6%; (c) 26.9%]

14. A company is considering the purchase of a machine that costs $8000 and has an estimated scrap value of 10% of cost at the end of 4 years. It is estimated that this machine will increase the net income before taxes and depreciation by $3000 a year. The tax rate is 48%. For comparison purposes, find the rate of return to the nearest tenth of one percent using: (a) straight line depreciation; (b) double declining balance for 2 years and then straight line; (c) sum of the years digits.

15. A company is considering the purchase of an asset that costs $15,000 and has an estimated scrap value of $3000 at the end of 5 years. It is estimated that this asset will reduce labor costs by $5000 a year. Assume a tax rate of 48% and find the rate of return assuming: (a) straight line depreciation; (b) double declining balance for 3 years and then straight line; (c) sum of the years digits.

[(a) 12.6%; (b) 14.3%; (c) 13.4%]

16. A contractor can purchase a truck for $13,000. Its estimated life is 7 years, and its estimated salvage value is $2000. Maintenance is estimated at $1100 per year. Daily operating expenses are expected to be $200, including the cost of the driver. The contractor can

hire a similar unit and its driver for $250 a day. If the interest rate is taken at 12%, how many days per year must the services of a truck be required to justify the purchase of a truck? Use straight line depreciation. Assume that the daily savings resulting from owning a truck can be lumped together and considered as a single year-end savings. Make no allowance for taxes.

8.19 DEPLETION

Some natural resources, such as mines, oil wells, timber tracts, and sources of natural gas, produce an income for a while and then become used up. This gradual using up of a resource that will not be replaced is called **depletion**. The income from an asset of this type should not only pay a return on the investment, but should also recover the cost of the asset less any resale value it may have when the natural resources are exhausted. Only in this way can the business operate in accordance with the fundamental principle of keeping the invested capital unimpaired.

EXAMPLE 1 A firm buys a mine for $200,000. An annual return of $30,000 over operating costs is expected for the next 15 years. At the end of this time it is estimated that the land can be sold for $10,000. Thus there will be a decrease in the value of the property of $190,000. In this case we assume that the invested capital will be recovered by making periodic deposits to a sinking fund paying 6%. What return is the firm expecting on its investment?

SOLUTION First, we must find the size of the annual deposit to the sinking fund.

$$R = 190,000 \times \frac{1}{s_{\overline{15}|6\%}} = 190,000 \times .04296276 = \$8162.92$$

This amount should be deducted from the $30,000 to replace the invested capital. Thus the net return is

$$30,000.00 - 8162.92 = \$21,837.08$$

The rate of return on the investment then becomes

$$\frac{21,837.08}{200,000.00} = .1092 = 10.9\%$$

If C is the original cost, S the resale value when the natural resource is used up, i the yield rate on the investment, and r the rate earned on the sinking fund, we can write the following general formula:

Annual return = (cost × the yield rate)
+ (annual deposit into sinking fund)

Or using symbols:

$$\text{Annual return} = Ci + (C - S) \cdot \frac{1}{s_{\overline{n}|r}}$$

In this formula we have added the subscript r to the $1/s_{\overline{n}|}$ factor to emphasize that the sinking fund rate is to be used when computing the numerical value of this factor.

In some cases the investor knows what rate of return is desired on the investment, so the problem becomes one of determining a purchase price that will result in the desired yield.

EXAMPLE 2 A mining property is expected to yield an annual return of $40,000 over operating costs for the next 20 years. Then the mine will be exhausted and the property will have a resale value of about $20,000. What could a firm pay for the mine if a return of 10% on the investment is desired and the firm can set up a sinking fund at 7%?

SOLUTION

$$40,000 = C \times .10 + (C - 20,000)\frac{1}{s_{\overline{20}|7\%}}$$

$$= .10C + .02439293C - 487.86$$

$$40,487.86 = .12439293C$$

$$C = \frac{40487.86}{.12439293} = \$325,484$$

Exercise 8d

1.   A sand and gravel company is considering the purchase of a piece of property for $45,000. It is estimated that the property will produce a net annual return over operating costs of $7000 for 10 years, at the end of which time the estimated resale value of the property will be $5000. If the firm can build up a replacement fund for its capital at 5% converted annually, what is the estimated rate of return that can be expected on this investment? Give the answer to the nearest .1%.
(8.5%)

2.   A lumber company leases a tract of timber for 8 years for $60,000. The company expects to get an annual return over operating costs of about $10,000. If a sinking fund at 9% is set up to recover the investment, what return can the company expect on the investment?

3.   A quarry is expected to yield a net income over operating costs of $20,000 a year for 15 years, at which time it will have little or no resale value. If a firm wants a yield of 12% on its investment and can set up a fund at 9% to replace its capital, what could the firm pay for this quarry? Give the answer to the nearest $100.
($129,800)

4.(C)   A company is considering the purchase of some timber land. Company engineers estimate that the land will produce a net return of $30,000 a year over operating costs for 6 years, at which time the land can be sold for about $40,000. How much can the company pay for the land if a return of 10% is desired on the investment and the company can set up a sinking fund at 10% to replace the capital?

5.   A mine is expected to yield an annual return of $40,000 over operating costs for the next 20 years, at which time it will be exhausted and have an estimated resale value of $2000. What could the firm pay for the mine (to the nearest $100) if an annual return of 10% on the investment is sought and the firm can accumulate a sinking fund at 9%?
($334,900)

6.(C)   A gravel pit is expected to produce an average return over operating costs of $7000 a year for 8 years. If the pit will have little or no resale value, what can a firm pay for it if an 8% return on the investment is expected and the firm can accumulate a sinking fund at 11%?

8.20 CAPITALIZED COST

The **capitalized cost** of an asset is the original cost of an item plus the present value of an unlimited number of renewals. First we determine the formulas used for capitalized cost and then discuss their application. The quantities and symbols used in capitalized cost work are

K = the capitalized cost
C = the original cost
S = the scrap or salvage value
W = the wearing value; $W = C - S$
n = useful life in interest conversion periods

To find the present value of the unlimited number of renewals, we use the perpetuity formula (23), substituting $\$W$ for the periodic payment. This is added to the first cost to give us the basic formula for capitalized cost:

$$K = C + \frac{W}{i} \times \frac{1}{s_{\overline{n}|}} \tag{28}$$

In many cases the item has little or no scrap value. In this case the replacement cost equals the first cost and a simpler formula can be derived as follows:

$$K = C + \frac{C}{i} \times \frac{1}{s_{\overline{n}|}}$$

Multiplying C by i/i and factoring C/i, we have

$$K = \frac{C}{i}\left(i + \frac{1}{s_{\overline{n}|}}\right)$$

Replacing $1/s_{\overline{n}|}$ by its exponential form, we obtain

$$K = \frac{C}{i}\left(i + \frac{i}{(1 + i)^n - 1}\right) = \frac{C}{i}\left(\frac{i(1 + i)^n - i + i}{(1 + i)^n - 1}\right)$$

Combining terms and multiplying numerator and denominator by $(1 + i)^{-n}$, we find that

$$K = \frac{C}{i}\left(\frac{i}{1 - (1 + i)^{-n}}\right)$$

Substituting $1/a_{\overline{n}|}$ for the exponential expression, we have

$$K = \frac{C}{i} \times \frac{1}{a_{\overline{n}|}} \tag{29}$$

All of the factors in a capitalized cost problem are estimates: the useful life of the asset, its replacement cost, and the value of money in the future. In spite of these limitations, capitalized cost can be a very useful tool. It can be used to arrive at an estimate of the endowment required for a specific purpose. A more frequent use is to determine which of two or more items would be more economical for a particular job. The capitalized cost formulas enable us to get two assets with different costs and different useful lives on a common basis. The asset with the lower capitalized cost will be the more economical. No actual fund will be set up in cases such as this.

EXAMPLE 1 What is the estimated endowment for the construction of a mess hall at a children's camp if the building costs $20,000 and will need to be replaced about every 25 years at approximately the same cost? By how much will the endowment have to be increased to provide $500 at the end of each year for maintenance? The estimated return on the endowment fund is 8%.

SOLUTION We can use formula (29).

$$K = \frac{20,000}{.08} \times \frac{1}{a_{\overline{25}|8\%}}$$
$$= 250,000 \times .09367878$$
$$= \$23,419.70$$

The annual maintenance costs form a perpetuity. The present value can be found from formula (22).

$$A_\infty = \frac{500}{.08} = \$6250$$

Therefore, to provide for initial construction, replacement every 25 years, and annual maintenance, an endowment of just under $30,000 would be needed.

EXAMPLE 2$^{(C)}$ A machine costs $4500, has an estimated life of 15 years, and has an estimated scrap value of $700. Find the capitalized cost at $9\frac{1}{2}\%$.

SOLUTION Since the rate in this problem is not in the tables, we must use a calculator.

$$K = 4500 + \frac{3800}{(1.095)^{15} - 1}$$

$$= \$5809.75$$

EXAMPLE 3 One grade of floor covering for a store costs $1500 and has an estimated life of 8 years. A better grade has an estimated life of 12 years. If money is worth 6%, the better grade would be worth how much?

SOLUTION To solve this problem, we assume that the two are equally desirable from an economic standpoint if their capitalized costs are equal. In both cases an initial installation and an unlimited number of renewals would be provided for. If C is the unknown cost of the better grade, we can use formula (29) and set the two capitalized costs equal to each other.

$$\frac{C}{.06} \times \frac{1}{a_{\overline{12}|6\%}} = \frac{1500}{.06} \times \frac{1}{a_{\overline{8}|6\%}}$$

$$C = 1500 \times a_{\overline{12}|} \times \frac{1}{a_{\overline{8}|}}$$

$$= 1500 \times 8.383844 \times .161036$$

$$= \$2025.15$$

Therefore if the better grade of floor covering can be installed for less than $2025.15, it will be more economical.

Exercise 8e

1. A memorial library for a town will cost $150,000. The estimated annual maintenance cost is $10,000, and the estimated life is 60 years. If the replacement cost is assumed to be the same as the first cost, what endowment invested at 9% will build, replace, and maintain this library in perpetuity (to the nearest $1000)?
    ($262,000)

2.(C) Work problem 1 if the interest on the endowment is 10%.

3. A philanthropist wants to provide an endowment to construct a community building costing $350,000 and replace it every 50 years. If the estimated return on the endowment is 7%, what size endowment (to the next highest $1000) will be needed?
    ($363,000)

4. The original cost of a shelter house for a park is $12,000. It is estimated that it will have to be replaced every 12 years at the same cost. What donation will be needed to endow this shelter house in perpetuity if the money can be invested at 8%?

5. One type of roof costs $1200 and must be replaced every 8 years. Another type costs $2400 and will last 20 years. If money is worth 8%, which is the more economical?
    (The $1200 roof)

6. A building can be painted for $1200 with a paint that will last 4 years. If a better paint is used, the cost will be $1500 and the job will last 6 years. If money is worth 7%, which paint is more economical?

7.(C) A machine costs $15,000, has an estimated life of 12 years, and has a scrap value of $2000. Find the capitalized cost at $7\frac{1}{2}$%.
    ($24,408.16)

8. A machine costs $7500, has an estimated life of 6 years, and has a scrap value of $1200. What is the capitalized cost at 8%?

9. Timbers used in a certain type of construction work cost $700 and last 12 years. A preservative treatment is expected to increase the life to 18 years. If money is worth 7%, how much can be paid for the preservative treatment?
    ($186.51)

8.21 COMPOSITE LIFE

Usually the assets of a business have probable lives that vary widely. When a plant is to be used as security for a bond issue, it may be necessary to determine the **composite life** of the plant. This is the time necessary for the total annual depreciation charge to equal the total wearing value.

EXAMPLE Find the composite life of the plant described below if depreciation is based on the straight line method.

SOLUTION The following shows how the total annual charge and the total wearing value are obtained.

Item	Life in Years	Cost	Scrap Value	Wearing Value	Annual Charge
Building	60	$120,000	$ 0	$120,000	$2000
Machine tools	15	50,000	5000	45,000	3000
Other machinery	10	30,000	2000	28,000	2800
				$193,000	$7800

Composite life = 193,000 ÷ 7800 = 24.7 years

This example shows that if this plant is to be used as security for a long-term loan or bond issue, the term of the loan should be less than 24 years. To have a reasonable margin of safety, the term should probably be considerably less than the composite life.

Exercise 8f

1. A plant consists of the following: (a) a building worth $70,000 with a life of 50 years and no scrap value; (b) machine tools worth $25,000 with a life of 15 years and a scrap value of $3000; (c) equipment worth $20,000 with a life of 12 years and a scrap value of $1000. Find the composite life if depreciation is based on the straight line method.
   (25– years)
2. If depreciation is based on the straight line method, find the composite life of the plant described as follows:

Item	Life in Years	Cost	Scrap Value
Building	40	$60,000	$ 0
Power plant	15	8,000	500
Machine tools	18	22,000	1000
Dies, jigs, fixtures, etc.	7	6,500	0

REVIEW EXERCISES FOR CHAPTER 8

1. A taxi costs $9000 and has an estimated resale value of $600 at the end of 4 years. Prepare depreciation schedules and graphs showing the total accumulated depreciation and the book value for: (a) straight line; (b) double declining balance shifting to straight line at the end of 2 years; (c) sum of the years digits.
2. Suppose that the taxi in problem 1 can be expected to go 300,000 miles. Prepare a table showing depreciation for each year if it traveled 100,000 miles the first year, 75,000 the second, and 50,000 each the third and fourth years. Here depreciation is to be based on use.
3. Determine the present value of depreciation for each part of problem 1 using an estimated cost of capital of 10%.
   [(a) $7065; (b) $7543; (c) $7382]
4. Suppose that the owner of the taxi in problem 1 estimates that annual operating costs will be $25,000 and that it will produce revenue of $30,000 annually. Find the net cash flow for this taxi assuming a 48% tax rate and using the three methods of depreciation in problem 1.
5. Determine the net present value of the taxi in the previous problems using an estimated cost of capital of 10% and the three methods of depreciation.
   [(a) $2844; (b) $3073; (c) $2995]
6. Find the internal rate of return for each part of problem 5.
7. A student is considering two alternatives after finishing high school. One is to enter a 2-year vocational school where the annual tuition is $2000 and then get a job with a starting salary of around $10,000 a year. The second alternative is 4 years of college at $3000 a year, after which it will be possible to earn about $4000 more annually than in the first alternative. Find the present value

of the 4-year college education using a rate of 12%. Assume 40 years of employment after the 4-year college.

($1755)

8. An oil drilling firm purchased a piece of property for $150,000. It is estimated that the property will produce a net annual return after operating costs of $20,000 a year for 8 years, at the end of which time the resale value of the property will be about $25,000. If the firm can set up a sinking fund at 8% to replace its investment, find the estimated return rate the firm can expect on the investment.

9. What price should the firm in problem 8 pay for the property if they want a return of $7\frac{1}{2}\%$ of their investment (to the nearest $1000)?

($132,000)

10. A swimming facility at a university will cost $250,000 with annual maintenance costs of $5000. If the building can be assumed to last 40 years and can be replaced at approximately the same cost, what endowment at 9% will build, maintain, and replace this facility in perpetuity to the nearest $1000?

11. An automobile costing $6000 can be assumed to last 10 years. A rust-proofing treatment can increase that life to 13 years. If money is worth 6%, how much can be paid for the treatment?

($1216.78)

12. Find the composite life of the plant described as follows if depreciation is based on the straight line method.

Item	Life in Years	Cost	Scrap Value
Building	40	$200,000	$ 0
Machines	10	120,000	10,000
Vehicles	5	40,000	5,000
Tools	12	25,000	1,000

Chapter 9
Life Annuities

9.1 THE MORTALITY TABLE

Up to now we have been dealing with single payments and with annuities that were certain to be paid. Now we will work problems that are contingent on how long a person lives.

Suppose that a group of men who are 18 years old want to set up a fund from which all who are living 20 years from now will receive $1000. How much should each one put into the fund now? To answer this question, we need to be able to predict how many of the original group will be living 20 years from now. While no one can tell who will die during the next 20 years, it is possible to use mortality data to predict approximately *how many* will die during a given period. Before we can work the problem, we must understand the basic tool of the life insurance actuary — the mortality table.

Insurance companies have kept records that show the number of people living and dying at each age of life. These statistics of the march through life are compiled into a table that is called a mortality table.

As life expectancy changes, a mortality table will become obsolete and must be replaced with more recent data. In this book we use the 1958 Commissioners Standard Ordinary (CSO) Mortality Table. This is Table 7 in the back of the book. This table, which is still being used by many insurance companies, became the mandatory nonforfeiture and valuation standard in most states on January 1, 1966. Note that values for females 15 years old and up are the same as the values for males 3 years younger. Values for females age 0 to 14 are given in the complete tables of the Society of Actuaries. In practical applications annuity and insurance contracts may be based on different mortality tables. Since the basic principles involved in life annuity and life insurance problems are the same regardless of the mortality table, all problems in this text are based on the 1958 CSO Table.

The CSO Table starts with 10,000,000 people living at age 0. The l_x column gives the number living at age x. The d_x column gives the number that can be expected to die before reaching age $x + 1$. Thus 70,800 of the 10,000,000 living at age 0 can be expected to die before reaching age 1. The probability of dying within a year for a person age x is indicated by the symbol q_x. This probability is obtained by dividing the number dying at age x by the number living at age x. In symbols, $q_x = d_x/l_x$. An easier figure to work with is the death rate per 1000, which is given in the mortality table under the symbol $1000q_x$.

The Greek letter ω (omega) is the symbol for the terminal age of a mortality table. It is the lowest age at which there are no survivors. For the 1958 CSO Table, $\omega = 100$ for males and 103 for females. Other mortality tables used by insurance companies have different terminal ages, but the formulas derived in this text are applicable regardless of the interest rate or mortality table.

EXAMPLE 1 What is the probability that a 20-year-old man will live to age 50? Of a group of 1000 20-year-old men, what is the predicted number that will live to age 50?

SOLUTION The probability that a 20-year-old man will live to age 50 is simply the number still living at age 50 divided by the number living at age 20.

$$\frac{l_{50}}{l_{20}} = \frac{8762306}{9664994} = .9066$$

Out of 1000 20-year-old men, the predicted number that will live to age 50 is $1000 \times .9066 = 907$.

EXAMPLE 2 What is the probability that a 20-year-old man will die before reaching age 50? Of a group of 1000 20-year-old men, what is the predicted number that will die before reaching age 50?

SOLUTION The probability of a man dying between age 20 and age 50 is the number dying during this period divided by the number living at age 20.

$$\frac{l_{20} - l_{50}}{l_{20}} = \frac{9664994 - 8762306}{9664994} = .0934$$

Note that if we have the probability that a man will live to age 50, we can get the probability that he will die by age 50 by subtracting the probability of living from 1, since he will certainly do one or the other. The probability of dying by age 50 = 1.0000 − .9066 = .0934.

Out of 1000 20-year-old men, the predicted number that will die before reaching age 50 is 1000 × .0934 = 93.

EXAMPLE 3   Find the answers to Examples 1 and 2 for women.

SOLUTION

$$\text{Probability of living} = \frac{l_{50}}{l_{20}} = \frac{8948114}{9713967} = .9212$$

Predicted number living to age 50 = 1000 × .9212 = 921

$$\text{Probability of dying} = \frac{l_{20} - l_{50}}{l_{20}} = \frac{9713967 - 8948114}{9713967} = .0788$$

Predicted number dying before age 50 = 1000 × .0788 = 79

Note the considerably lower mortality predictions for women.

9.2   EXPECTATION OF LIFE

How much longer do you expect to live? Although there is no precise answer for you in particular, you can get an estimate using the expectation of life for persons of your age and sex. The expectation of life is a statistic often used as an index for comparing different mortality tables. The actuarial formula for expectation of life is

$$\mathring{e}_x = .5 + \frac{1}{l_x} \sum_{t=1}^{\omega - x - 1} l_{x+t}$$

where

$\mathring{e}_x$ = expectation of life of a person aged x
l_x = number living at age x
  t = index or variable of summation
ω = terminal age of the mortality table

The symbol Σ is the capital Greek letter sigma. This standard mathematical symbol is used to indicate summation of similar terms.

The index of summation t ranges over the integers 1, 2, 3, ... $\omega -$ $x - 1$. Thus if we want the expectation of life of a person aged x, we start with the number living 1 year later, add the number living 2 years later, and continue in this way to the end of the mortality table. This sum gives the full years of future lifetime for the group of persons age x. When this sum is divided by l_x, the number living at age x, we get the full years of future life for each person *on the average*. This summation makes no allowance for fractional years of life. We assume that complete future lifetimes will exceed by half a year the number of complete years, so we add .5 year to get the complete future lifetime.

To show how this formula is used, we compute the expectation of life for men aged 90 using the 1958 CSO Table. Calculations for younger people are done in exactly the same way but are more tedious because of the larger number of terms in the summation. We substitute 90 for x in the formula and find from Table 7 that $l_{90} = 468,174$. This is the number of men over whom we will average the full years of future lifetime. For $t = 1$, $l_{91} = 361,365$; for $t = 2$, $l_{92} = 272,552$. We continue in this way to the last term in the summation, which is for $t = (100 - 90 - 1) = 9$. For $t = 9$, $l_{99} = 6415$. Arranging the complete problem in tabular form, we have

t	$90 + t$	l_{90+t}
1	91	361,365
2	92	272,552
3	93	200,072
4	94	142,191
5	95	97,165
6	96	63,037
7	97	37,787
8	98	19,331
9	99	6,415
		$1,199,915 = \sum\limits_{t=1}^{9} l_{90+t}$

We substitute in the expectation of life formula the 1,199,915 years of future life that are to be averaged over the 468,174 men living at age 90.

$$\mathring{e}_{90} = .5 + \frac{1199915}{468174} = .5 + 2.56 = 3.06$$

Hence the expectation of life for men aged 90 is 3.06 years based on the 1958 CSO table. Whether a particular person will get more or less than the calculated expectation, only time will tell. Expectation of life for men is given in Table 9-1. To get the expectation of life for women aged 15 and above, look up the value for a man 3 years younger.

Table 9-1 Expectation of Life for Males: 1958 CSO Mortality Table

Age x	$\overset{\circ}{e}_x$	Age x	$\overset{\circ}{e}_x$	Age x	$\overset{\circ}{e}_x$	Age x	$\overset{\circ}{e}_x$
0	68.30	25	45.82	50	23.63	75	7.81
1	67.78	26	44.90	51	22.82	76	7.39
2	66.90	27	43.99	52	22.03	77	6.98
3	66.00	28	43.08	53	21.25	78	6.59
4	65.10	29	42.16	54	20.47	79	6.21
5	64.19	30	41.25	55	19.71	80	5.85
6	63.27	31	40.34	56	18.97	81	5.51
7	62.35	32	39.43	57	18.23	82	5.19
8	61.43	33	38.51	58	17.51	83	4.89
9	60.51	34	37.60	59	16.81	84	4.60
10	59.58	35	36.69	60	16.12	85	4.32
11	58.65	36	35.78	61	15.44	86	4.06
12	57.72	37	34.88	62	14.78	87	3.80
13	56.80	38	33.97	63	14.14	88	3.55
14	55.87	39	33.07	64	13.51	89	3.31
15	54.95	40	32.18	65	12.90	90	3.06
16	54.03	41	31.29	66	12.31	91	2.82
17	53.11	42	30.41	67	11.73	92	2.58
18	52.19	43	29.54	68	11.17	93	2.33
19	51.28	44	28.67	69	10.64	94	2.07
20	50.37	45	27.81	70	10.12	95	1.80
21	49.46	46	26.95	71	9.63	96	1.51
22	48.55	47	26.11	72	9.15	97	1.18
23	47.64	48	25.27	73	8.69	98	.83
24	46.73	49	24.45	74	8.24	99	.50

Reproduced from Society of Actuaries tables with permission of Peter W. Plumley, F. S. A., Executive Director.

For employed persons a statistic analogous to expectation of life is work life expectancy, the average number of remaining years of life in the labor force for persons of a given age and sex. Work life expectancy data are published by the United States Department of Labor. Selected values from the 1960 data are shown in Table 9-2.

Exercise 9a

1. Use the CSO Mortality Table to find the values of: (a) l_{20}; (b) l_{40}; (c) l_{60} for men and for women.
   [Men: (a) 9,664,994; (b) 9,241,359; (c) 7,698,698. Women: (a) 9,713,967; (b) 9,325,594; (c) 8,106,161.]
2. Use the CSO Mortality Table to find the values of: (a) l_{30}; (b) l_{50}; (c) l_{70} for men and for women.
3. Use the CSO Mortality Table to find the values of: (a) d_{20}; (b) d_{40}; (c) d_{60} for men and for women.
   [Men: (a) 17,300; (b) 32,622; (c) 156,592. Women: (a) 15,737; (b) 26,112; (c) 125,970.]
4. Use the CSO Mortality Table to find the values of: (a) d_{30}; (b) d_{50}; (c) d_{70} for men and for women.
5. Find the death rates per 1000 for: (a) 20-year-old; (b) 40-year-old; and (c) 60-year-old men and women.
   [Men: (a) 1.79; (b) 3.53; (c) 20.34. Women: (a) 1.62; (b) 2.80; (c) 15.54.]

Table 9-2 Work Life Expectancy

Age	Work Life Expectancy in Years
20	42.6
25	37.9
30	33.2
35	28.6
40	24.1
45	19.7
50	15.6
55	11.9
60	8.5
65	6.3

6. Find the death rates per 1000 for: (a) 30-year-old; (b) 50-year-old; and (c) 70-year-old men and women.

7. Of a group of 1000 25-year-old men and 1000 25-year-old women, what are the predicted numbers that will die before reaching the age of 45?

   (55 men; 47 women)

8. Of a group of 1000 30-year-old men and 1000 30-year-old women, what are the predicted numbers that will die before reaching the age of 65?

9. A college graduating class has 300 21-year-old men in it. What is the predicted number of living alumni from this group: (a) 25 years; (b) 50 years; and (c) 75 years after graduation?

   [(a) 280; (b) 165; (c) 2]

10. Work problem 9 assuming a group of 300 21-year-old women.

9.3 INTEREST AND LOADING

In determining the premium a policyholder should pay, an insurance company will make allowance for the interest that will be earned on the premiums when they are invested by the company. All computations in this book are based on a rate of $2\frac{1}{2}\%$ compounded annually. The $2\frac{1}{2}\%$ may seem low in the present economy. It should be pointed out that this is not the percentage of return on insurance, but is a figure used by the insurance companies in the determination of premiums.

Actual insurance premiums consist of two parts – the **net premium** and the **loading**. The net premium takes into account mortality and interest on invested premiums. The loading takes care of the insurance company's cost of doing business. Since each company has its own method of allowing for loading, we compute only net premiums. In all cases the present value of the net premiums will equal the present value of all future benefits. Regardless of the type of policy, we derive the formula for net premiums from the basic equation of value:

$$\text{Net premiums discounted to date of issue} = \text{benefits discounted to date of issue}$$

Actuarial symbols used in this book correspond to those used by the Society of Actuaries. Since many of the symbols require multiple subscripts, it is suggested that students use the verbal description of each problem when discussing it. Then you can obtain the right formula by simply referring to the discussion of that type of problem.

Note that the procedures described in this chapter and Chapter 10 will not indicate the cost of annuities or insurance policies because the issuing company's cost of doing business is not included, and also because individual companies could use different sets of tables. They will, however, give an accurate picture of the relative costs for the various types of annuities and policies.

In this book we continue the practice of identifying different annuity and insurance premiums for men and women. Because of sex discrimination suits tried in recent years, not all companies distinguish premiums according to sex. So-called unisex mortality tables are applied in computing net premiums in cases where the sex of the individual is not used. The relative premiums in the various situations will follow the same patterns as those in which sex is used.

9.4 PURE ENDOWMENT

The problem at the beginning of this chapter was what is known as a **pure endowment**, that is, a *single* payment that will go to a person at a certain time *if the person is still living at that time.* To get a formula for a pure endowment, we assume that the size of the payment is 1. Then to solve any problem, all we need to do is multiply by the size of the payment in the particular problem.

If l_x individuals aged x establish a fund to pay \$1 to each member living at age $x + n$, the number of dollars needed in n years will equal the l_{x+n} entry in the mortality table. Since the money is not needed until n years from now, we need to set aside today only the present or discounted value of this amount. If the symbol $_nE_x$ is used to represent each person's contribution to the fund, the total original premiums will equal $l_x \cdot {}_nE_x$, and the problem can be sketched as shown in Figure 9-1.

Discounting the benefits and setting up an equation of value, we have

$$l_x \cdot {}_nE_x = (1 + i)^{-n}l_{x+n}$$

Following actuarial practice, we substitute the letter v for $(1 + i)^{-1}$. Then $v^n = [(1 + i)^{-1}]^n = (1 + i)^{-n}$. Substituting in the preceding formula and solving for $_nE_x$, we have the following expression for the net premium for a \$1 endowment in n years issued to a person aged x years:

$$_nE_x = \frac{v^n l_{x+n}}{l_x}$$

To reduce the numerical work required to solve life annuity and insurance problems, we now introduce the **commutation functions** that are used by life insurance actuaries. These functions simplify formulas and eliminate multiple and tedious computations. They are defined below.

Commutation functions: numerical values are in Table 8

$$D_x = v^x l_x$$
$$N_x = D_x + D_{x+1} + \cdots + D_{\omega-1}$$
$$C_x = v^{x+1} d_x$$
$$M_x = C_x + C_{x+1} + \cdots + C_{\omega-1}$$

Note that all of the commutation functions combine present-worth-of-1 factors and values from the mortality table. Thus a different table of commutation functions is required for each combination of interest rate and mortality table. Commutation functions may involve 100 terms or more. The functions simplify actuarial formulas, and they are indispensable labor savers when calculations are done manually or with calculators.

Figure 9-1

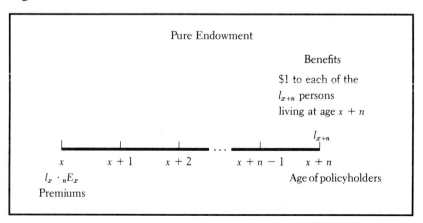

Pure Endowment

Benefits

$1 to each of the l_{x+n} persons living at age $x + n$

l_{x+n}

| x | $x + 1$ | $x + 2$ | $x + n - 1$ | $x + n$ |

$l_x \cdot {}_nE_x$
Premiums

Age of policyholders

The commutation columns in Table 8 were taken from Volume I of the Monetary Tables published by the Society of Actuaries. Examples and answers to problems are based on the complete factors. Because of the numerical work involved if a calculator is not available, some instructors have students substitute complete factors and then permit them to round the values to a specified number of significant figures before completing the problem using logarithms, slide rule, or arithmetic to get the final answer. Answers obtained in this way will usually differ slightly from the more precise answers in the text.

If we multiply the numerator and denominator of the equation for the present value of a pure endowment by v^x, we have

$$_nE_x = \frac{v^{x+n}l_{x+n}}{v^x l_x}$$

Substituting commutation functions, we can write this expression as follows:

$$_nE_x = \frac{D_{x+n}}{D_x} \tag{30}$$

In all formulas in this and the next chapter, x is the age of the person at the time the endowment, annuity, or life insurance is purchased. The meaning of n is defined for each formula. In this formula it means that the person, if still living, will receive the endowment at the end of n years. In some problems we are given the age at which the person is to get the endowment. In such cases, it is not necessary to compute n, since this age equals $x + n$.

EXAMPLE 1 What is the net single premium for an 18-year-old man for a 20-year pure endowment of $1000?

SOLUTION Formula (30) gives the cost of a pure endowment of $1. Therefore we find that a $1000 pure endowment due in 20 years would cost an 18-year-old man

$$1000\frac{D_{38}}{D_{18}} = 1000\frac{3638747.1}{6218174.5} = \$585.18$$

EXAMPLE 2 Solve Example 1 for an 18-year-old woman.

SOLUTION

$$1000\frac{D_{38}}{D_{18}} = 1000\frac{3949851.1}{6727326.8} = \$587.14$$

Note the higher cost to a woman. This is because the woman has a higher expectation of living to the end of the endowment period. Sex discrimination suits have been filed because of the difference in cost. If the premium for an endowment (or annuity) is paid by an employer as part of a retirement plan, female employees receive a lesser dollar return than male employees for the same cost.

EXAMPLE 3 Find the net single premium for an 18-year-old man for a pure endowment of $1000 at age 60.

SOLUTION

$$1000\frac{D_{60}}{D_{18}} = 1000\frac{1749787.7}{6218174.5} = \$281.40$$

This cost is lower than that in Example 1 because the endowment period is much longer. Pure endowments are rarely sold separately. However, they are often a part of life insurance policies. The endowment feature can make such policies quite expensive unless the endowment period is a long one.

Pure endowments illustrate what it means to accumulate a fund with benefit of survivorship. In Example 3, the share of each individual who survives to age 60 is made up in part of the shares forfeited by those who die before reaching 60. Thus each survivor receives more than would be obtained from interest alone. At $2\frac{1}{2}\%$ compounded annually, the $281.40 in Example 3 would amount to $281.40(1.025)^{42} = \$793.83$. With interest and survivorship, those who live to the end of the endowment period get $1000.

Exercise 9b

1. Find the net cost to a 30-year-old man of a pure endowment of $50,000 in: (a) 20 years; (b) 40 years.
   [(a) $28,202.42; (b) $10,983.96]

2. Work problem 1 for a woman.
3. What would be the cost to a 25-year-old man of an endowment of $10,000 when he is 65 years of age?
   ($2644.97)
4. Work problem 3 for a woman.

9.5   WHOLE LIFE ANNUITIES

[handwritten: 1st payment comes one period after the premium is paid". (#31)]

Instead of a single payment, people often prefer to receive benefits from insurance policies and other investments in equal periodic payments. If these payments are to continue as long as the designated person or annuitant lives, the annuity is called a **whole life annuity**. Although the payments can be made at any interval, we shall limit ourselves to the consideration of annual payments. Also, in all of our derivations the size of each payment will be $1. Then to solve any particular problem, all we have to do is multiply the appropriate formula by the size of the payment. As was the case with annuities certain, the first payment can be made one year hence, at once, or several years hence.

We first consider the *ordinary*, or *immediate life*, annuity that provides for annual payments starting in one year, if the annuitant is then living, and continuing throughout the annuitant's lifetime. Our computations will be based on the assumption that l_x persons age x each deposit a_x. Thus the original amount in the fund, $l_x a_x$, plus interest must be adequate to pay each person $1 at the end of each year for life.

One year after the plan is started there will be l_{x+1} persons living, and each of them must be paid out of the fund. Every year from then on, each of the survivors will get $1. This disbursement will continue as long as there are survivors, which is age 99 for men and 102 for women when the CSO Table is used.

Since beginning students find derivations easier to follow when numerical values are used, the formulas in this chapter are derived assuming the CSO Table for males with l_{99} as the last entry in the table. Formulas derived in this way are completely general and are the same as we would get using the expression $l_{\omega-1}$ for the final entry.

To get an equation of value, we discount all future payments to the present date. Thus the present value of the payment to be made in 1 year is $v l_{x+1}$; the present value of the payment to be made in 2 years is $v^2 l_{x+2}$, and so on.

A time diagram of payments and premiums is shown in Figure 9-2. The symbol a_x is used to represent each person's premium.

Bringing everything back to the present and setting up an equation of value, we have

$$l_x a_x = v l_{x+1} + v^2 l_{x+2} + \cdots + v^{98-x} l_{98} + v^{99-x} l_{99}$$

Therefore the cost per person is

$$a_x = \frac{v l_{x+1} + v^2 l_{x+2} + \cdots + v^{98-x} l_{98} + v^{99-x} l_{99}}{l_x}$$

To get the cost of this annuity for a man aged 20, we would have to discount all the annual payments from 21 to 99. To avoid this labor, first we multiply numerator and denominator by v^x.

$$a_x = \frac{v^{x+1} l_{x+1} + v^{x+2} l_{x+2} + \cdots + v^{98} l_{98} + v^{99} l_{99}}{v^x l_x}$$

Then we simplify, using commutation symbols.

$$a_x = \frac{D_{x+1} + D_{x+2} + \cdots + D_{98} + D_{99}}{D_x}$$

Figure 9-2

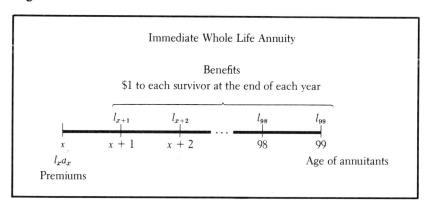

Immediate Whole Life Annuity

Benefits

$1 to each survivor at the end of each year

| | l_{x+1} | l_{x+2} | l_{98} | l_{99} |

x $x+1$ $x+2$ 98   99

$l_x a_x$ Age of annuitants

Premiums

annual pymts as long as person lives [handwritten]

$$a_x = \frac{N_{x+1}}{D_x}$$ (31)

9.6 WHOLE LIFE ANNUITY DUE

1st pymt comes) on the day you pay the premium. (#32) [handwritten]

If the first payment is made at once and payments are made throughout the lifetime of the annuitant, the annuity is called a **whole life annuity due**. The present value of a whole life annuity due of 1 per year is indicated by the symbol $\ddot{a}_x$. Since the only difference between this annuity and the immediate whole life annuity described in the preceding section is the payments made to the l_x individuals at the start, we can say that

$$l_x \ddot{a}_x = l_x + v l_{x+1} + v^2 l_{x+2} + \cdots + v^{98-x} l_{98} + v^{99-x} l_{99}$$

Solving for $\ddot{a}_x$ and multiplying numerator and denominator by v^x,

$$\ddot{a}_x = \frac{v^x l_x + v^{x+1} l_{x+1} + v^{x+2} l_{x+2} + \cdots + v^{98} l_{98} + v^{99} l_{99}}{v^x l_x}$$

$$= \frac{D_x + D_{x+1} + D_{x+2} + \cdots + D_{98} + D_{99}}{D_x}$$

present value of annuity due per yr. [handwritten]

$$\ddot{a}_x = \frac{N_x}{D_x}$$ (32)

Because of its frequent use in annuity work, values of $\ddot{a}_x$ are given in Table 8 along with the commutation columns. By simply subtracting 1 from the values of $\ddot{a}_x$, we can get the present value of an ordinary or immediate whole life annuity of 1 per year. Therefore,

$$\boxed{a_x = \ddot{a}_x - 1}$$

EXAMPLE 1 Find the net single premium for a whole life annuity due of $1000 per year issued to a man who is 50 years old.

SOLUTION Formula (32) gives the net single premium for a whole life annuity due of $1 per year. For annual payments of $1000 the premium is

$$1000 \ddot{a}_{50} = 1000 \times 17.614151 = \$17,614.15$$

EXAMPLE 2 How much would an immediate life annuity of $500 a year cost a man who is 18 years old?

SOLUTION From formula (31) the value of an immediate life annuity of $500 a year is $500a_{18}$. Since the immediate life annuity is the same as the life annuity due except that the first payment is made in 1 year, the value of a_{18} can be obtained by subtracting 1 from $\ddot{a}_{18}$. Therefore the cost is

$$500(\ddot{a}_{18} - 1) = 500(28.963722 - 1.0000) = \$13,981.86$$

EXAMPLE 3 A man dies and leaves his widow a $20,000 insurance policy. If she is 60 years old and elects to receive annual payments for life with the first payment to be made now, what is the size of each payment?

SOLUTION In this problem the present value of the life annuity due is known and the size of the annual payment is to be determined. Letting R represent the size of each payment, we have

$$R\ddot{a}_{60} = 20,000$$

$$R = \frac{20,000}{\ddot{a}_{60}} = \frac{20,000}{14.502179} = \$1379.10$$

EXAMPLE 4 Find the size of the payment in Example 3 if the first payment is to be made in 1 year.

SOLUTION This is an ordinary, or immediate whole life, annuity.

$$Ra_{60} = R(\ddot{a}_{60} - 1) = 20,000$$

$$R = \frac{20,000}{13.502179} = \$1481.24$$

EXAMPLE 5 As compensation for injuries, accident victims sometimes receive cash settlements. Money left after legal and other costs can be used to provide the injured person an income for life. A Chicago construction worker was awarded $696,000 for an injury that resulted in paralysis from the neck down. If the worker, who was 28 years old, put $\frac{2}{3}$ of this money in a whole life annuity due, what would be his annual income?

SOLUTION

$$R\ddot{a}_{28} = 464{,}000$$

$$R = \frac{464{,}000}{\ddot{a}_{28}} = \frac{464{,}000}{26.163201} = \$17{,}735$$

To protect themselves against lawsuits that could result in financial losses, individuals and companies may find it advisable to carry large liability policies.

Exercise 9c

1. Find the net single premium for a life annuity of $10,000 per year for a 30-year-old man if:
   (a) The first payment is to be made now.
   (b) The first payment is to be made in 1 year.
   [(a) $255,189.42; (b) $245,189.42]

2. A man plans to retire at 65. At that time, a life annuity of $10,000 a year would cost how much if:
   (a) The first payment is made at age 65?
   (b) The first payment is made at age 66?

3. A 50-year-old widow wants to use part of her estate to purchase an immediate life annuity of $20,000 a year. Find the net single premium.
   ($358,508.80)

4. A 53-year-old woman wants to buy an annuity that will pay her $10,000 a year for life with the first payment to be made when she is age 54. Find the net single premium.

5. A man will retire at age 65 and start receiving social security benefits of $800 a month. Find the approximate present value of these payments. For this purpose, replace the 12 monthly payments with an approximately equivalent payment of $9600 at the end of each year.
   ($96,354)

6. At age 62, a widow is to receive $750 a month in social security benefits. What is the approximate present value of her benefits?

7. A 20-year-old man takes out a life insurance policy on which the premiums are $100 a year at the beginning of each year for life. Find the net present value of these premiums.
   ($2845.36)

8. A 38-year-old woman takes out a life insurance policy on which the premiums are $250 a year at the beginning of each year for life. Find the net present value of the premiums.

9. A widower who is the beneficiary of a $20,000 insurance policy decides to take an annual income for life. If he is 45 years old, find the size of each payment if the first payment is to be made: (a) now; (b) in 1 year.
   [(a) $1010.97; (b) $1064.79]

10. A 50-year-old man invests $100,000 in a whole life annuity with the first payment to be made in 1 year. What is the size of each payment?

11. In her will, a woman directs that each of her twin children, a boy and a girl, is to receive a life annuity due with a present value of $100,000. At her death, the children are 19 years of age. Find the lifetime annual income of each.
    (Boy, $3482.94; girl $3394.99)

12. A man directs that $\frac{2}{3}$ of his estate is to be used to purchase an ordinary life annuity for his wife and the remaining $\frac{1}{3}$ an ordinary life annuity for his son. The estate amounts to $150,000. When the annuities are purchased, the widow is 62 and the son is 30. Find the annual income of each.

13. On March 5, 1966, a jet plane crashed in Japan, killing all 135 passengers and crew. A series of record-breaking settlements has resulted in millions of dollars being paid to relatives of the victims. A couple who lost two minor children received $541,000. If $\frac{1}{3}$ of this went for legal expenses, the balance would buy an immediate whole life annuity of how much a year for a woman if she purchased the annuity when she was 37 years old?
    ($15,587)

14. The parents of three adult children killed in the accident just described received $172,500. If the mother, at age 57, purchased an immediate whole life annuity with $\frac{2}{3}$ of the money, what would be her annual income?

15. A housewife was blinded by the explosion of a can of drain cleaner. She received $930,000 in damages. If, at age 48, she used $\frac{2}{3}$ of this amount to buy a whole life annuity due, what would be her annual income?
    ($31,340)

16. A pizza baker, skilled at tossing dough high into the air, was injured in an automobile accident. His lawyer claimed that he would no longer be able to throw the dough and please crowds as he had in the past. A jury awarded $335,000 in damages. If the

injured 33-year-old pizza tosser used $200,000 of this amount to buy a whole life annuity due, how much would he receive each year?

9.7 DEFERRED WHOLE LIFE ANNUITY

Another type of annuity is the n-year deferred immediate life annuity. This type is the same as an immediate life annuity with the first n payments omitted. The first payment is made at age $x + n + 1$. The present value of an annuity of 1 per year is denoted by $_{n|}a_x$. The benefits and premiums are shown on the time diagram in Figure 9-3.

Discounting the benefits and setting up the equation of value, we have

$$l_x \cdot _{n|}a_x = v^{n+1}l_{x+n+1} + \cdots + v^{98-x}l_{98} + v^{99-x}l_{99}$$

Solving for the individual premium and multiplying numerator and denominator by v^x, we obtain

$$_{n|}a_x = \frac{v^{x+n+1}l_{x+n+1} + \cdots + v^{98}l_{98} + v^{99}l_{99}}{v^x l_x}$$

Figure 9-3

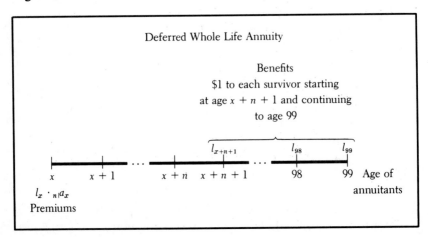

Deferred Whole Life Annuity

$$= \frac{D_{x+n+1} + \cdots + D_{98} + D_{99}}{D_x}$$

$$_{n|}a_x = \frac{N_{x+n+1}}{D_x} \tag{33}$$

In many deferred life annuity problems, we are given the age at which the first payment is to be made. Since this value is equal to $x + n + 1$, we can simply substitute it in the formula and we need not determine n.

EXAMPLE 1 A man 40 years of age wants a life income of $15,000 a year with the first annual payment to be made when he is 65. What is the net cost of this annuity?

SOLUTION Since the first payment is to be made at age 65, $x + n + 1 = 65$. Substituting in formula (33), we have

$$\text{Net cost} = 15,000 \frac{N_{65}}{D_{40}} = 15,000 \frac{15077832.8}{3441765.1} = \$65,712.65$$

EXAMPLE 2 A 15-year-old girl receives an inheritance of $30,000. If she is to get annual payments for life starting on her 21st birthday, what will be the size of each payment?

SOLUTION If R represents the annual payment, we have

$$30,000 = R \frac{N_{21}}{D_{15}}$$

$$R = 30,000 \frac{D_{15}}{N_{21}} = 30,000 \frac{7273432.5}{180101480.3} = \$1211.56$$

All whole life annuity problems can be solved using the following general formula in which R is the periodic payment:

$$\text{Net present value} = R \frac{N_{\text{age at first payment}}}{D_{\text{age when annuity is purchased}}}$$

This verbal form of the whole life annuity formula simplifies solving deferred whole life annuities. When values of $\ddot{a}_x$ are available, as they are in Table 8 in this text, the easiest way to solve immediate whole life annuities and whole life annuities due is to use the $\ddot{a}_x$ function.

EXAMPLE 3 Find the net cost of a $10,000-a-year whole life annuity for a 50-year-old woman if the first payment is to be made when she is: (a) 50; (b) 51; (c) 62.

SOLUTION For parts (a) and (b) we use $\ddot{a}_x$. Part (c) is solved using formula (33) or the general formula given previously.

(a) Net cost = $10,000\ddot{a}_{50} = 10,000 \times 18.925440 = \$189,254.40$

(b) Net cost = $10,000(\ddot{a}_{50} - 1) = 10,000 \times 17.925440 = \$179,254.40$

(c) Net cost = $10,000\dfrac{N_{62}}{D_{50}} = 10,000\dfrac{24883551.1}{2803559.9} = \$88,756.98$

Exercise 9d

1. What is the net cost of a whole life annuity of $5000 a year for a 50-year-old man if the first payment is to be made 15 years hence?
   ($29,572.21)
2. Find the net single premium for an annuity of $10,000 a year issued to a 55-year-old man if the first payment is to be made at the age of 65.
3. Find the answer to problem 1 if the annuitant is a woman.
   ($35,015.96)
4. Find the answer to problem 2 if the annuitant is a woman.
5. A 45-year-old man receives an inheritance of $25,000. He uses this money to buy a whole life annuity, the first payment of which is to be made when he is 60. What will be the size of the annual payment?
   ($3229.85)
6. When his $10,000 endowment policy matures at age 50, a man decides to use this money to buy a life annuity starting at age 65, when his social security payments will begin. What annual payment will be provided by the proceeds of the insurance policy?
7. A woman who is now 51 years old would like to have an annual income of $12,000 starting when she is age 63. What is the net cost of this annuity?
   ($101,800.76)

8. A 58-year-old man wants to use lottery winnings to buy a life annuity that will provide $5000 a year for life to supplement social security, the first payment to be made when he reaches age 65. How much will the annuity cost him now?

9. A woman 50 years old has $15,000 that she wants to invest to produce an income for life beginning at age 60. What annual payment will she receive?
($1461.55)

10. A 42-year-old widower receives $15,000 from an insurance policy. What annual income for life would he get from this policy if the first payment is made: (a) now? (b) in 1 year? (c) when he is age 62?

11. A 44-year-old machinist was also a part-time singer. He was struck by an object protruding from a train and suffered an injury that affected his tenor voice. A jury awarded $150,000 in damages. If the man used $100,000 of this amount to buy a whole life annuity with the first payment to be made when he is 55, what will be the size of the annual payment?
($9304)

12. Find the annual payment in problem 11 if the first payment is to be made when the man is 50.

9.8 TEMPORARY IMMEDIATE LIFE ANNUITY

A temporary life annuity is one that ends after a certain number of years or at the death of the annuitant, whichever occurs first. If the first payment is made one year hence and if the payments are made for n years, we have an *n*-year temporary immediate life annuity. Indicating the present value by $a_{x:\overline{n}|}$ and showing benefits and premiums on a time scale, we have the result shown (Figure 9-4).

Note that this annuity ceases with the final payments to the l_{x+n} individuals living n years after the start of the program. The equation of value becomes

$$l_x \cdot a_{x:\overline{n}|} = vl_{x+1} + v^2 l_{x+2} + \cdots + v^n l_{x+n}$$

Solving for the individual premium, multiplying numerator and denominator by v^x, and substituting commutation symbols, we have

$$a_{x:\overline{n}|} = \frac{D_{x+1} + D_{x+2} + \cdots + D_{x+n}}{D_x}$$

Since

$$N_{x+1} = D_{x+1} + D_{x+2} + \cdots + D_{x+n} + D_{x+n+1} + \cdots + D_{99}$$

and

$$N_{x+n+1} = \qquad\qquad\qquad\qquad D_{x+n+1} + \cdots + D_{99}$$

The numerator can be written as $N_{x+1} - N_{x+n+1}$.

$$a_{x:\overline{n}|} = \frac{N_{x+1} - N_{x+n+1}}{D_x} \tag{34}$$

EXAMPLE   How much would a man aged 18 have to pay for a 5-year temporary life annuity of \$1000 per year if the first payment is to be made when he is 19?

SOLUTION

$$1000a_{18:\overline{5}|} = 1000 \frac{N_{18+1} - N_{18+5+1}}{D_{18}} = 1000 \frac{N_{19} - N_{24}}{D_{18}}$$

Figure 9-4

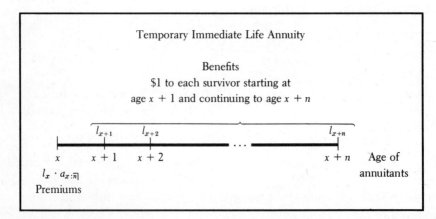

Temporary Immediate Life Annuity

Benefits
\$1 to each survivor starting at
age $x + 1$ and continuing to age $x + n$

l_{x+1} l_{x+2} l_{x+n}

x $x + 1$ $x + 2$ $\cdots$ $x + n$ Age of
annuitants

$l_x \cdot a_{x:\overline{n}|}$
Premiums

$$= 1000 \frac{173883305.8 - 145143761.6}{6218174.5} = \$4621.86$$

9.9   TEMPORARY LIFE ANNUITY DUE

1st pymt made at once

If the first payment is made at once, we have a temporary life annuity due, the present value of which is indicated by $\ddot{a}_{x:\overline{n}|}$. Proceeding in the usual manner, we find that the present value is

$$\ddot{a}_{x:\overline{n}|} = \frac{N_x - N_{x+n}}{D_x} \tag{35}$$

EXAMPLE How much would a 5-year temporary life annuity due of $1000 per year cost a man who is 18 years old?

SOLUTION

$$1000\ddot{a}_{18:\overline{5}|} = 1000 \frac{N_{18} - N_{18+5}}{D_{18}} = 1000 \frac{N_{18} - N_{23}}{D_{18}}$$

$$= 1000 \frac{180101480.3 - 150590927.4}{6218174.5} = \$4745.85$$

9.10   DEFERRED TEMPORARY LIFE ANNUITY

(present value)

A series of annual payments that commences at age $x + n + 1$ and continues for m years if the annuitant survives is called an **n-year deferred m-year temporary immediate annuity**. The symbol for the present value of $1 per year is denoted by $_{n|m}a_x$. Proceeding in the usual manner, we get the following formula for the present value. Note that in this formula, which is given here as it appears in actuarial publications, n stands for the interval of deferment and m is the number of payments.

$$_{n|m}a_x = \frac{N_{x+n+1} - N_{x+n+m+1}}{D_x} \tag{36}$$

EXAMPLE 1 How much would a 5-year temporary life annuity of $1000 a year cost a man aged 18 if he is to receive the first payment when he is 28?

SOLUTION In this problem x, the age of the annuitant, is 18; n, the interval of deferment, is 9; and m, the number of payments, is 5. Substituting in formula (36), we have

$$1000_{9|5}a_{18} = 1000\frac{N_{28} - N_{33}}{D_{18}}$$

$$= 1000\frac{124748159.0 - 102134645.1}{6218174.5} = \$3636.68$$

All temporary life annuity problems can be solved using the following general formula, in which R is the size of the periodic payment:

Net present value =

$$R\frac{N_{\text{age at first payment}} - N_{\text{age at first payment + number of payments}}}{D_{\text{age when annuity is purchased}}}$$

EXAMPLE 2 Find the net cost of a $2000-a-year temporary life annuity for 10 years for a 50-year-old woman if the first payment is to be made when she is: (a) 50; (b) 51; (c) 62.

SOLUTION

(a) Net cost $= 2000\dfrac{N_{50} - N_{60}}{D_{50}}$

$$= 2000\frac{53058604.2 - 28773199.9}{2803559.9} = \$17,324.69$$

(b) Net cost $= 2000\dfrac{N_{51} - N_{61}}{D_{50}}$

$$= 2000\frac{50255044.3 - 26789139.5}{2803559.9} = \$16,740.08$$

(c) Net cost $= 2000\dfrac{N_{62} - N_{72}}{D_{50}}$

$$= 2000\frac{24883551.1 - 10065398.9}{2803559.9} = \$10,570.95$$

EXAMPLE 3 A woman purchased a preparation advertised as a fingernail hardener. Instead of hardening her fingernails, it caused their loss. A jury awarded her $25,000 damages. If the woman was 40 years old and used $15,000 of the settlement to buy a temporary life annuity of 10 annual payments, what would be the size of each payment if the first payment is made when she is: (a) 40? (b) 41? (c) 50 years old?

SOLUTION The present value of the annuity is known and R is to be found. We substitute in the general formula and solve for R.

(a) $15,000 = R \dfrac{N_{40} - N_{50}}{D_{40}}$

$R = 15,000 \dfrac{D_{40}}{N_{40} - N_{50}}$

$= 15,000 \dfrac{3740188.5}{86113147.1 - 53058604.2} = \$1697.28$

(b) $15,000 = R \dfrac{N_{41} - N_{51}}{D_{40}}$

$R = 15,000 \dfrac{D_{40}}{N_{41} - N_{51}}$

$= 15,000 \dfrac{3740188.5}{82372958.6 - 50255044.3} = \$1746.78$

(c) $15,000 = R \dfrac{N_{50} - N_{60}}{D_{40}}$

$R = 15,000 \dfrac{D_{40}}{N_{50} - N_{60}}$

$= 15,000 \dfrac{3740188.5}{53058604.2 - 28773199.9} = \$2310.15$

Exercise 9e

1. Find the net single premium of a temporary immediate life annuity of $1000 per year for 10 years if the annuitant is an 18-year-old man.

   ($8668.66)

2. Find the net single premium of a temporary immediate life annuity of $12,000 a year for 10 years if the annuitant is a 64-year-old man.

3. How much would a 10-year temporary life annuity due of $10,000 a year cost a 31-year-old woman?
   ($88,872.73)

4. Find the net cost of a 15-year temporary life annuity due of $15,000 a year for a 65-year-old woman.

5. At age 58 a woman buys an annuity that will provide her 15 annual payments of $8000. If the first payment is to be made when the woman is age 68, how much will the annuity cost?
   ($48,467.85)

6. How much money must be set aside to provide a 12-year-old boy with $2000 a year for 4 years if he is to receive the first payment when he is 18?

7. Circus elephants doing a dance caused plaster to loosen and fall in the room below. The falling plaster injured a man, who was awarded $18,000 in the United States District Court. If at age 58 he put $10,000 of this settlement in a 5-year temporary life annuity, what would be the size of the annual payment if the first payment is made at age: (a) 58? (b) 59? (c) 65?
   [(a) $2177.67; (b) $2278.44; (c) $3134.82]

8. A boy suffered burns over 40% of his body as a result of a fire started while he was playing with a camera containing an electric flash attachment. A suit on his behalf resulted in a $315,000 settlement. If $200,000 is used to buy a temporary life annuity of 30 annual payments when the boy is 10 years old, what will be the size of each payment if the first payment is made when he is: (a) 10? (b) 11? (c) 21?

9. A 23-year-old woman was awarded $245,000 in a suit against an automobile manufacturer. Her attorney claimed that her permanent injuries were caused by the faulty design of the car. If the woman used $100,000 to buy a temporary life annuity of 40 annual payments, what would be the size of each payment if the first payment is made when she is: (a) 23? (b) 24? (c) 25?
   [(a) $4074.20; (b) $4194.40; (c) $4319.47]

9.11 JOINT LIFE ANNUITIES

All of the annuities in this chapter were based on a single life. Therefore when the annuitant dies, the payments cease. Annuities may also be based on more than one life. For example, a joint life annuity continues in existence as long as all the lives survive, and stops upon the occurrence of the first death. A joint-and-survivor annuity continues as long as any member of the group survives. This type of annuity might be attractive to a retired couple who would want their income to continue as long as both or either of them is living. These other types of annuities are based on the principles given in this chapter. However, the mathematics involved is beyond the range of an elementary text. The various alternatives are mentioned here to acquaint students with the fact that annuities are available to meet those practical situations that involve combinations of two or more lives.

9.12 SUMMARY OF LIFE ANNUITY FORMULAS

The six annuity formulas derived in this chapter can be divided into two general classes:

1. Whole life annuities, which provide equal periodic payments as long as the annuitant lives.
2. Temporary life annuities, in which the payments cease after a specified time or when the annuitant dies, depending on which comes first.

Both of the general classes of annuities are divided into three types, depending on when the first payment is made relative to x, the age of the annuitant at the time the annuity is purchased. Immediate, or ordinary life, annuities have the first payment made at age $x + 1$. Life annuities due have the first payment made at age x. Deferred immediate life annuities have the first payment made at age $x + n + 1$, where n is the interval of deferment.

The formulas in this book are the same as those used by the Society of Actuaries. This usage will acquaint students with actuarial practice. It will also provide a sound foundation for those students who want to continue to more advanced work in insurance.

The annuity formulas are summarized in Tables 9-3 and 9-4 as derived in this chapter and in a second form using verbal subscripts. All formulas are for periodic payments of $1. For other periodic payments simply multiply by the size of the payment.

Table 9-3 Whole Life Annuities

Immediate or ordinary (First payment at age $x + 1$)	$a_x = \dfrac{N_{x+1}}{D_x}$ $(a_x = \ddot{a}_x - 1)$	(31)
Due (First payment at age x)	$\ddot{a}_x = \dfrac{N_x}{D_x}$	(32)
Deferred (First payment at age $x + n + 1$)	$_{n\vert}a_x = \dfrac{N_{x+n+1}}{D_x}$	(33)

All of the whole life annuities can be solved using the following general formula. This is convenient when the time of the first payment is given in terms of the age of the annuitant.

$$\text{Value} = \frac{N_{\text{age at which the first payment is due}}}{D_{\text{age when annuity is purchased}}}$$

Table 9-4 Temporary Life Annuities

Immediate or ordinary
(First payment at age $x + 1$.
  Payments at the end of
  each year for n years.)
	$a_{x:\overline{n}\vert} = \dfrac{N_{x+1} - N_{x+n+1}}{D_x}$	(34)

Due
(First payment at age x.
  Payments at the beginning
  of each year for n years.)
	$\ddot{a}_{x:\overline{n}\vert} = \dfrac{N_x - N_{x+n}}{D_x}$	(35)

Deferred (First payment at age $x + n + 1$. Payments for m years.)	$_{n\vert m}a_x = \dfrac{N_{x+n+1} - N_{x+n+m+1}}{D_x}$	(36)

All of the temporary life annuities can be solved using the following general formula. This is convenient when the time of the first payment is given in terms of the age of the annuitant.

$$\text{Value} = \frac{N_{\text{age at first payment}} - N_{\text{age at first payment + number of payments}}}{D_{\text{age when annuity is purchased}}}$$

REVIEW EXERCISES FOR CHAPTER 9

1. Of a group of 500 18-year-old men, how many can be expected to live to age: (a) 65? (b) 70? (c) 75?
   [(a) 351; (b) 288; (c) 213]
2. Do problem 1 for 500 18-year-old women.
3. Find the net single premium for an 18-year-old woman for a 30-year pure endowment of $25,000.
   ($11,069.40)
4. Do problem 3 for an 18-year-old man.
5. Find the net single premium for a whole life annuity of $10,000 a year for a 50-year-old man if the first payment is to be made: (a) now; (b) in 1 year; (c) at age 60.
   [(a) $176,141.51, (b) $166,141.51; (c) $90,439.81]
6. Do problem 5 for a 50-year-old woman.
7. If the annuitant is a 35-year-old woman, find the net single premium for an annuity of $5000 a year for 10 years beginning: (a) now; (b) in 1 year; (c) in 5 years.
   [(a) $44,370.51; (b) $43,166.40; (c) $38,584.98]
8. Do problem 7 for a 35-year-old man.
9. The beneficiary of a $100,000 life insurance policy wants to use the money to buy an annuity. How much will the beneficiary get annually if the annuity is a whole life annuity with the first payment: (a) immediately? (b) in 1 year? (c) in 20 years? The beneficiary is a 40-year-old woman.
   [(a) $4343.34; (b) $4540.55; (c) $12,998.86]
10. Do problem 9 in the case in which the beneficiary chooses a 20-year annuity.
11. Do problem 9 for a 40-year-old man.
    [(a) 4577.13; (b) $4796.68; (c) $14,927.82]
12. Do problem 10 for a 40-year-old man.
13. A 20-year-old man decides to set up an I.R.A. account. He begins immediately investing $2000 each year into the account, which pays 7% converted annually. He intends to buy a whole life annuity with the first payment at age 65. Upon making the last deposit at age 64, he buys his annuity. Find the annual payment from the annuity.
    ($54,663)
14. How much must a 25-year-old woman invest each year at 8% effective through age 65 inclusive in order to be able to purchase a $20,000 whole life annuity due at the time of the last deposit?

Chapter 10

Life Insurance

10.1 LIFE INSURANCE

Life insurance makes it possible for a head of a household earning a moderate income to provide family income in the event that the wage earner should die. The fundamental principle of the mathematics of life insurance can be illustrated by a simple example.

Suppose that a group of 10,000 18-year-old men in good health want to take out an insurance policy that would pay $1000 to the beneficiary of each of the young men who dies before reaching age 19. If we refer to the CSO Mortality Table, we find that the average death rate for 18-year-old men is 1.69 per 1000. Therefore our group would expect about 17 deaths during the coming year. If each of the 10,000 men pays a premium of $1.70 into a common fund, there would immediately be set up a fund of $17,000 from which the 17 death benefits would be paid.

In practical insurance plans interest is earned on invested funds. An interest rate of $2\frac{1}{2}\%$ will be used in all insurance problems in this book. Gross insurance premiums must be large enough to pay both death benefits and company expenses. We compute only net premiums, making no allowance for loading, for the four most common types of policies: term, straight life, limited payment life, and endowment.

The procedures described in this chapter for determining premiums are used by insurance companies for their own internal accounting purposes. Most companies do not use these methods to set actual premiums. The methods that are used are too technical to be described here. However, the net premium method that we describe will produce premiums reasonably near those that actually will be charged. This method also will point out accurately the relative sizes of premiums charged for the various types of policies.

Before we start computing net premiums, it is interesting to see how the cost of commercial insurance varies with the type of policy. Although there is some variation in cost from one company to another,

Figures 10-1, 10-2, 10-3, and 10-4 are typical of costs from a representative company. The rates are annual rates per $1000 for a man taking out a $10,000 or larger policy. In general, the rates would be somewhat higher for smaller policies. A much larger policy, such as $25,000, would probably have a lower rate. Rates for women may be lower because of their higher life expectancy.

Term insurance has a premium that is based on expected death benefits for a limited period, such as 5 or 10 years. Because mortality rates increase as people get older, the premium for a term policy increases with the age of the insured. Term insurance is quite expensive beyond middle age.

A level premium policy costs more initially than term insurance, but the premium does not increase. During the early years of the policy, this excess premium is set aside as a reserve to help meet increased death benefits later on. The illustrations in this section are for level premium policies issued to a man who is 20 years old.

The most common type of level premium policy is whole life, also known as straight life or ordinary life. The cost of the policy is determined by the age of the insured when the policy is first taken out. The policy can then be carried for the remainder of the person's life at the same premium. (See Figure 10-2.)

Figure 10-1 5-year Renewable Term

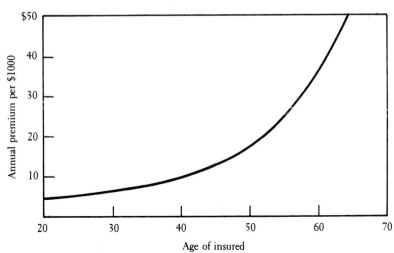

Limited pay life requires payments for a certain number of years, at the end of which time the policy becomes fully paid for the life of the insured. Thus the premiums must be higher than for ordinary or straight life because the reserve must be built up in a shorter time. How much higher will depend on the payment period. (See Figure 10-3.)

Endowment policies provide protection for a stated number of years. At the end of the endowment period, protection ceases and the insured, if still living, receives the face value of the policy. The insurance company must set the premium large enough to take care of the *certainty* that someone, either the beneficiary or the insured, will have to be paid by the end of the endowment period. This reality makes endowment policies very expensive if the endowment period is short. From a representative company a $10,000, 20-year endowment policy would cost a 20-year-old man about $480 a year. Policies with longer endowment periods will have lower premiums. An endowment policy at age 65 for $10,000 would cost a 20-year-old man about $191 from the same company. This policy has an endowment period of 45 years. (See Figure 10-4.)

Figure 10-2 Whole Life

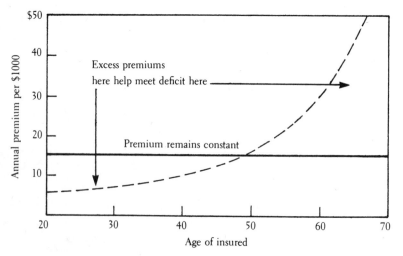

Figure 10-3 20-payment Life

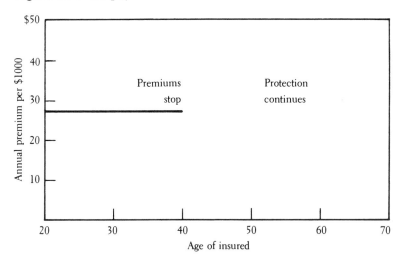

Figure 10-4 20-year Endowment

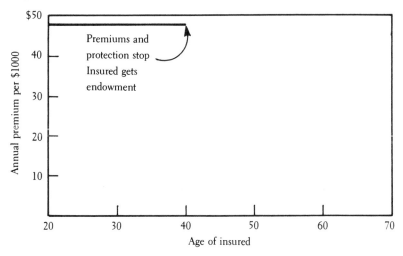

10.2 DETERMINING THE PREMIUM

As an illustration of how net insurance premiums are determined, let us see how we could calculate the premium for an ordinary life policy for an 18-year-old man. We assume that the policy is for $1. Then to get the cost of any policy, all we need to do is multiply our result by the size of the policy. Also we assume that the policy is to be purchased by a net single premium of A.

Referring to the mortality table, we see that there are 9,698,230 men alive at age 18. If each of them took out a $1 whole life policy and paid for it with a single premium, the total premiums plus interest would have to be sufficient to pay the $1 death benefits to the beneficiary of each insured person at the end of the year in which the insured dies. All of the formulas in this book are for payments made at the end of the year in which a person dies. (In practice, insurance companies pay benefits upon proof of death rather than waiting until the end of the year. To take care of this practice, insurance companies make a small adjustment in the net premiums.) Referring to the mortality table, we see that the company would have to pay 16,390 death benefits one year after the policies were issued, 16,846 in two years, and so on to the end of the mortality table. (See Figure 10-5.)

Thus the insurance company will need $16,390 in 1 year, $16,846 in 2 years, $12,916 in 81 years, $6415 in 82 years, and various other amounts in each of the intervening years. The total present value of all these future payments must now be determined by discounting each year's death benefits. Then dividing this total by 9,698,230 will give us the cost per person.

Figure 10-5

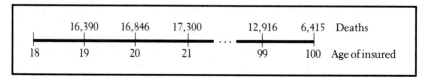

10.3 WHOLE OR STRAIGHT LIFE INSURANCE

To avoid the work involved in discounting many payments, we now derive a formula for getting the premium for a whole, or straight life, policy using the commutation functions. The company issues $1 policies to l_x persons living at age x. At the end of the first year the company will have to pay $\$d_x$ in death benefits. Payments at the end of the second year will be $\$d_{x+1}$, and so on out to $\$d_{99}$. Each of the l_x persons will pay a net single premium, $\$A_x$, for a policy. Thus the number living at age x times the net single premium paid by each must equal the present value of all future death benefits (Figure 10-6). The equation of value is

$$l_x A_x = v d_x + v^2 d_{x+1} + \cdots + v^{99-x} d_{98} + v^{100-x} d_{99}$$

Solving for A_x and multiplying numerator and denominator by v^x, we have

$$A_x = \frac{v^{x+1} d_x + v^{x+2} d_{x+1} + \cdots + v^{99} d_{98} + v^{100} d_{99}}{v^x l_x}$$

Now we can substitute the appropriate commutation functions defined on page 409 and simplify.

Figure 10-6

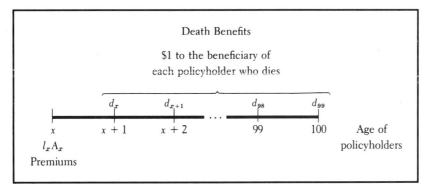

$$A_x = \frac{C_x + C_{x+1} + \cdots + C_{98} + C_{99}}{D_x}$$

$$A_x = \frac{M_x}{D_x} \tag{37}$$

Values of $1000A_x$ are given in Table 8 at the back of the book.

EXAMPLE 1   Find the net single premium for a $10,000 whole life policy for an 18-year-old man.

SOLUTION

$$10,000A_{18} = 10 \times 293.5677 = \$2935.68$$

By paying $2935.68 (plus loading), the man would have a $10,000 policy for the rest of his life.

Because of the larger premium, most young people are not able to buy a whole life policy with a single premium, nor should they. However, a person who has carried insurance for many years may find it advisable to use the cash value of the policy to buy a paid-up policy that will be in effect for life without the payment of additional premiums. At the time a person retires, any children will probably be grown and self-supporting, so less insurance will be needed. At the same time, the person's income may be less. By converting insurance to a paid-up policy, the person can get the necessary protection without having to use money needed to meet other expenses.

EXAMPLE 2   A man retires at age 65. He has been carrying a $20,000 straight life policy that now has a cash value of $11,400. How much paid-up insurance will this buy?

SOLUTION   According to Table 8, we find that

$$1000A_{65} = 730.80721$$

Thus the single premium for a $1 straight life policy is .73080721. Letting y represent the unknown amount of insurance this man can buy with $11,400, we have

$$.73080721y = 11,400$$

$$y = \frac{11,400}{.73080721} = \$15,599.19$$

If this is enough insurance to meet his peresent needs, he would be foolish to continue to pay premiums out of retirement income that is needed for other purposes.

Since the cost of a single premium policy is too large for most people, most insurance payments are made annually or more frequently. Now we determine how to get the annual premium for a straight life policy. The insurance company must take into account the fact that the money received from a policyholder will depend on how long the policyholder lives. Even if a policyholder dies after paying only one annual premium, the beneficiary will get the full value of the policy. The expected death benefits will be the same as in the preceding example. The expected total premium for any year will be the number living at that time multiplied by the net annual premium, which we designate by P_x. The present value of the death benefits must equal the present value of the expected premiums.

Since the premiums are equal and are paid at the beginning of each year, they form a whole life annuity due. The present value of a whole life annuity due of $1 is N_x/D_x [formula (32), page 414]. Therefore the present value of the premiums is $P_x(N_x/D_x)$. This value will equal the present value of the death benefits, which are the same as for a single premium whole life of M_x/D_x [formula 37), page 436]. Setting the present value of the premiums equal to the present value of the death benefits, we have

$$P_x \frac{N_x}{D_x} = \frac{M_x}{D_x}$$

$$P_x = \frac{D_x}{N_x} \cdot \frac{M_x}{D_x}$$

$$P_x = \frac{M_x}{N_x} \tag{38}$$

EXAMPLE 3   Find the net annual premium for a $1000 whole life policy for an 18-year-old man.

SOLUTION

$$1000P_{18} = 1000\frac{M_{18}}{N_{18}} = 1000\,\frac{1825455.4}{180101480.3} = \$10.14$$

Exercise 10a

1. Find the net single premiums for a $1000 whole life policy issued to: (a) a 22-year-old man; (b) a 27-year-old man; (c) a 32-year-old man; and to a woman of the same ages.
   [Man: (a) $318.99; (b) $354.29; (c) $394.03. Woman: (a) $299.72; (b) $332.60; (c) $369.64.]

2. Find the net single premiums for a $1000 whole life policy issued to: (a) a 20-year-old man; (b) a 40-year-old man; (c) a 60-year-old man; and to a woman of the same ages.

3. Find the net single premiums for a straight life policy of $5000 issued to: (a) a 20-year-old man; (b) a 40-year-old man; (c) a 60-year-old man; and to a woman of the same ages.
   [Man: (a) $1530.05; (b) $2335.64; (c) $3393.11. Woman: (a) $1437.62; (b) $2192.23; (c) $3231.44.]

4. Find the net single premiums for a whole life policy of $10,000 issued to: (a) an 18-year-old man; (b) a 28-year-old man; (c) a 38-year-old man; and to a woman of the same ages.

5. Find the net annual premiums for the policies in problem 3.
   [Man: (a) $53.77; (b) $106.91; (c) $257.51. Woman: (a) $49.21; (b) $95.22; (c) $222.82.]

6. Find the net annual premiums for the policies in problem 4.

7. Find the net single premium and the net annual premium for a straight life policy of $25,000 issued to a 25-year-old man and woman.
   (Man: $8491.22; $313.63. Woman: $7974.83; $285.62)

8. Get the net single premium and the net annual premium for a straight life policy of $5000 issued to: (a) a 15-year-old girl; (b) a 27-year-old woman.

9. A father takes out $2000 straight life policies for each of his three boys, who are 9, 11, and 14 years of age. Determine the net annual premium for each policy.
   ($15.65; $16.55; $18.04)

10. Find the annual premiums for the policies in problem 9 if the boys are 19, 21, and 24 years of age.

11. A man who is now 60 years old has a life insurance policy with a cash value of \$7000. He decides to convert this to a paid-up life policy. How much paid-up insurance will he get?
    (\$10,315)
12. A woman who is 50 years old has \$10,000 with which to buy a paid-up policy. How much insurance will she get?

10.4   TERM INSURANCE

Term insurance, as we have seen, has an increasing premium as the insured gets older. Usually the premium is not changed every year, but only every 5, 10, or 20 years. Thus term insurance is usually described as 5-year term, 10-year term, and so on. We now derive a general formula for the net single premium, $A^1_{x:\overline{n}|}$, for a \$1, n-year term policy issued to l_x individuals aged x. The deaths and premiums for the period from age x to age $x + n$ can be sketched as shown in Figure 10-7.

As in the preceding example, we bring everything back to age x and set up an equation of value:

$$l_x A^1_{x:\overline{n}|} = vd_x + v^2 d_{x+1} + \cdots + v^{n-1} d_{x+n-2} + v^n d_{x+n-1}$$

Multiplying through by v^x and substituting commutation functions, we have

Figure 10-7

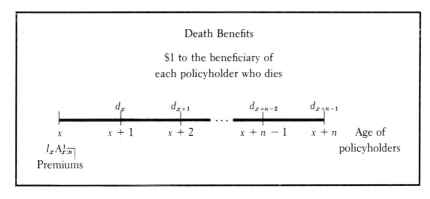

$$A_{x:\overline{n}|}^1 = \frac{C_x + C_{x+1} + \cdots + C_{x+n-2} + C_{x+n-1}}{D_x}$$

Since

$$M_x = C_x + C_{x+1} + \cdots + C_{x+n-1} + C_{x+n} + \cdots + C_{99}$$

and

$$M_{x+n} = \qquad\qquad C_{x+n} + \cdots + C_{99}$$

we can write the numerator as $M_x - M_{x+n}$, so that

$$A_{x:\overline{n}|}^1 = \frac{M_x - M_{x+n}}{D_x} \tag{39}$$

If the policy is paid for with net annual premiums, $P_{x:\overline{n}|}^1$, the premiums form an n-year, temporary life annuity due. The present value of such an annuity of \$1 is $(N_x - N_{x+n})/D_x$ [formula (35), page 423]. Therefore the present value of the premiums is $P_{x:\overline{n}|}^1 \cdot (N_n - N_{x+n})/D_x$. This value will equal the present value of the death benefits, which are the same as for a single premium, n-year term policy, or $(M_x - M_{x+n})/D_x$ [see formula (39)]. Setting the present value of the premiums equal to the present value of the death benefits, we have

$$P_{x:\overline{n}|}^1 \cdot \frac{N_x - N_{x+n}}{D_x} = \frac{M_x - M_{x+n}}{D_x}$$

$$P_{x:\overline{n}|}^1 = \frac{D_x}{N_x - N_{x+n}} \cdot \frac{M_x - M_{x+n}}{D_x}$$

$$P_{x:\overline{n}|}^1 = \frac{M_x - M_{x+n}}{N_x - N_{x+n}} \tag{40}$$

EXAMPLE Find the net single premium and the net annual premium for a 5-year, \$1000 term policy for a man aged 18.

SOLUTION

$$\text{Net single premium} = 1000 A_{18:\overline{5}|}^1 = 1000 \frac{M_{18} - M_{23}}{D_{18}}$$

$$= 1000 \frac{1825455.4 - 1774216.4}{6218174.5} = \$8.24$$

Net annual premium $= 1000P^1_{18:\overline{5}|} = 1000\dfrac{M_{18} - M_{23}}{N_{18} - N_{23}}$

$$= 1000\,\frac{1825455.4 - 1774216.4}{180101480.3 - 150590927.4} = \$1.74$$

Note that when the insured reaches age 23, this policy will have a higher premium.

Exercise 10b

1. Find the net single premium and the net annual premium for a 5-year, $5000 term policy issued to a 30-year-old man and woman.
   (Man: $52.14; $11.00. Woman: $48.16; $10.15.)
2. Find the net single premium and the net annual premium for a 10-year, $5000 term policy issued to a 30-year-old man and woman.
3. Find the net annual premium for a 5-year, $10,000 term policy issued to: (a) a 20-year-old man; (b) a 30-year-old man; (c) a 40-year-old man; (d) a 50-year-old man; (e) a 60-year-old man.
   [(a) $18.09; (b) $21.99; (c) $40.76; (d) $97.31; (e) $236.98]
4. From a representative company get the actual premiums charged for the policies in problem 3 and draw a graph to show the changing annual premium for term insurance. The age of the insured should be plotted on the horizontal axis.
5. Find the net single premiums for the following $10,000 policies issued to a 22-year-old man: (a) 5-year term; (b) 10-year term; (c) 20-year term.
   [(a) $88.35; (b) $172.67; (c) $359.35]
6. Get the net single premiums for the following $20,000 policies issued to a 22-year-old woman: (a) 5-year term; (b) 10-year term; (c) 20-year term.
7. Find the net annual premiums for the policies in problem 5.
   [(a) $18.62; (b) $19.41; (c) $22.90]
8. Determine the net annual premiums for the policies in problem 6.

10.5 LIMITED PAYMENT LIFE INSURANCE

A t-payment life policy is one that provides protection for the lifetime of the insured although premiums are paid for only t years. The present value of the benefits is the same as for an ordinary life policy, M_x/D_x

[formula (37), page 436]. The net single premium for a limited payment life policy is the same as for a straight life policy, since in both cases lifetime protection is provided. The net annual premiums form a t-year temporary life annuity due that has a present value of $(N_x - N_{x+t})/D_x$ for payments of $1 [formula (35), page 423]. If we designate the net annual premium for a t-payment life policy as $_tP_x$, the present value of the premiums will be $_tP_x[(N_x - N_{x+t})/D_x]$. Setting the present value of the premiums equal to the present value of the benefits, we have

$$_tP_x \frac{N_x - N_{x+t}}{D_x} = \frac{M_x}{D_x}$$

$$_tP_x = \frac{D_x}{N_x - N_{x+t}} \cdot \frac{M_x}{D_x}$$

$$_tP_x = \frac{M_x}{N_x - N_{x+t}} \tag{41}$$

Limited payment policies are frequently issued on the basis of being paid up as of a certain age. "Paid up at age 65" means that when the insured reaches age 65, paid-up protection for life that is equal to the face value of the policy is received. The last premium is paid at age 64. A 20-year-old man buying a paid-up-at-age-65 policy makes payments from age 20 to age 64 inclusive, a total of 45 payments. In other words, $x + t$ in formula (41) is 65 or the age at which the policy is paid up. Consequently, it is unnecessary to get t for policies that are paid up as of a certain age. Simply replace $x + t$ with the age at which the policy is paid up.

EXAMPLE 1 Find the net annual premium for a $1000, 20-payment life policy issued to an 18-year-old man.

SOLUTION The net annual premium is

$$1000\,_{20}P_{18} = 1000\,\frac{M_{18}}{N_{18} - N_{18+20}}$$

$$= 1000\,\frac{1825455.4}{180101480.3 - 82372958.6} = \$18.68$$

EXAMPLE 2 Find the net annual premium for a $1000 paid-up-at-age-65 policy issued to an 18-year-old man.

SOLUTION The net annual premium is

$$1000\,\frac{M_{18}}{N_{18} - N_{65}} = 1000\,\frac{1825455.4}{180101480.3 - 15077832.8} = \$11.06$$

Note that this premium is not much higher than the annual premium of \$10.14 for a straight life policy determined in section 10.3.

Exercise 10c

1. Find the net annual premium for a \$5000, 20-payment life policy issued to a 30-year-old man and woman.
   (Man, \$121.15; woman, \$113.27)
2. Find the net annual premium for a \$5000, 30-payment life policy issued to an 18-year-old man and woman.
3. Find the net annual premium for a \$10,000, 20-payment life policy issued to: (a) a 20-year-old man; (b) a 40-year-old man; (c) a 60-year-old man.
   [(a) \$194.85; (b) \$308.36; (c) \$566.59
4. A 35-year-old woman takes out a \$10,000 paid-up-at-age-65 life policy. What is the annual premium?
5. Find the net annual premium for a \$20,000, 30-payment life policy issued to: (a) a 20-year-old man; (b) a 30-year-old man.
   [(a) \$293.67; (b) \$369.86]
6. A 24-year-old woman takes out a \$5000, 20-payment life policy. What is the annual premium?
7. Find the net annual premium for a \$10,000 paid-up-at-age-65 policy issued to a 25-year-old man and woman.
   (Man, \$140.61; woman \$130.67)
8. Find the net annual premium for a \$10,000 paid-up-at-age-65 policy issued to a 35-year-old man and woman.

10.6 ENDOWMENT INSURANCE

An endowment policy provides protection during the term of the policy and a pure endowment equal to the face value of the policy if the insured is still living when the policy matures. Therefore the net single premium for this policy would be the sum of the net single premiums for an n-year term policy and a pure endowment due in n

years. Using the symbol $A_{x:\overline{n}|}$ for the net single premium and combining formulas (39) and (30), we have

$$A_{x:\overline{n}|} = \frac{M_x - M_{x+n}}{D_x} + \frac{D_{x+n}}{D_x}$$

$$A_{x:\overline{n}|} = \frac{M_x - M_{x+n} + D_{x+n}}{D_x} \tag{42}$$

EXAMPLE 1 Find the net single premium for a $1000, 20-year endowment policy issued to a man aged 18.

SOLUTION The net single premium is

$$1000A_{18:\overline{20}|} = 1000\frac{M_{18} - M_{18+20} + D_{18+20}}{D_{18}}$$

$$= 1000\,\frac{1825455.4 - 1629650.6 + 3638747.1}{6218174.5} = \$616.67$$

If an n-year endowment policy is purchased with net annual premiums, the premiums form an n-year temporary life annuity due. Using $P_{x:\overline{n}|}$ to designate the net annual premium and setting the present value of the annual premiums equal to the present value of the benefits, we have

$$P_{x:\overline{n}|}\frac{N_x - N_{x+n}}{D_x} = \frac{M_x - M_{x+n} + D_{x+n}}{D_x}$$

$$P_{x:\overline{n}|} = \frac{D_x}{N_x - N_{x+n}} \cdot \frac{M_x - M_{x+n} + D_{x+n}}{D_x}$$

$$P_{x:\overline{n}|} = \frac{M_x - M_{x+n} + D_{x+n}}{N_x - N_{x+n}} \tag{43}$$

Endowment policies are frequently issued on the basis of the endowment being paid as of a certain age. "Endowment at age 65" means that if the insured lives to age 65, the face amount of the policy will be received. The last premium is paid at age 64. A 20-year-old man buying an endowment at age 65 will make payments from age 20 to 64 inclusive, a total of 45 payments. Then $x + n$ in formula (43) is 65 or the age at which the endowment is paid. In this case it is unnecessary to get n

for endowment policies as of a certain age. Simply replace $x + n$ with the age at which the endowment is paid.

EXAMPLE 2 Find the net annual premium for a $1000, 20-year endowment policy issued to a man aged 18.

SOLUTION

$$1000P_{18:\overline{20}|} = 1000 \frac{M_{18} - M_{18+20} + D_{18+20}}{N_{18} - N_{18+20}}$$

$$= 1000 \frac{1825455.4 - 1629650.6 + 3638747.1}{180101480.3 - 82372958.6} = \$39.24$$

EXAMPLE 3 Find the net annual premium for a $1000 endowment policy at age 65 issued to an 18-year-old man.

SOLUTION Substituting in formula (43), we find that the net annual premium is

$$1000P_{18:\overline{47}|} = 1000 \frac{M_{18} - M_{65} + D_{65}}{N_{18} - N_{65}}$$

$$= 1000 \frac{1825455.4 - 998376.6 + 1366128.5}{180101480.3 - 15077832.8} = \$13.29$$

An interesting type of endowment occurs when a person with a straight life policy outlives the mortality table on which the policy is based. A mortality table has a terminal age ω as a matter of convenience for mathematical analysis. Actuaries know that some people will live beyond age ω. But to simplify computations and formulas, it is necessary to assume a terminal age at which there will be no survivors. Using the CSO Table for males, whole life premiums are based on the assumption that there will be no survivors at age 100. The person who lives to 100 is then statistically dead. The time has come to pay someone. Since the insured is still living, the insured becomes the beneficiary of an endowment equal to the value of the policy.

Exercise 10d

1. Find the net single premium and the net annual premium for a $5000, 20-year endowment policy issued to a 30-year-old man and

to a 30-year-old woman.

(Man: $3099.55; $198.90. Woman: $3092.75; $197.75.)

2. Find the net single premium and the net annual premium for a $25,000, 20-year endowment policy issued to a 28-year-old man and to a 28-year-old woman.

3. Find the net annual premium for a $10,000, 20-year endowment policy issued to: (a) a 20-year-old man; (b) a 40-year-old man; (c) a 60-year-old man.

[(a) $392.84; (b) $416.21; (c) $591.00]

4. Find the net single premium and the net annual premium for a $15,000, 15-year endowment policy issued to a 6-year-old boy.

5. A 25-year-old man and a 25-year-old woman take out a $5000 endowment policy at age 65. Find the net single premium and the net annual premium.

(Man: $2054.25; $85.04. Woman: $2023.01; $82.87.)

6. A 23-year-old woman takes out a $10,000 endowment policy at age 60. Find the net single premium and the net annual premium.

10.7 INSURANCE RESERVES

The net premium for a 1-year term policy is just sufficient to pay the death claims at the end of that year. This premium is sometimes called the natural premium. As people get older (beyond age 10), the probability of death increases and the 1-year term premium becomes greater. As was pointed out in the general description of the various insurance policies, it is possible to avoid this increasing premium by writing level premium policies. These policies have a higher premium than the 1-year term premium for the earlier years of the policy. This excess plus accumulated interest is used to build up a **reserve fund** that will be used to help pay death benefits when the level premium is smaller than the 1-year term premium. In this book we compute **terminal reserves**, which are the reserves at the end of a policy year.

Table 10-1 shows the 1-year term premium for a $1000 policy for a man as his age increases from 20 to 70. Also shown is the level premium for a straight life policy issued to a person at age 20, and the difference in premiums between the 1-year term premium and the level premium.

Figure 10-8 shows how the 1-year term premium and the level premium for straight life compare at different ages.

Table 10-1 Premiums

Age	1-year Term Premium	Level Premium for Straight Life	Excess of Level Premium over 1-year Term
20	$ 1.75	$10.75	$ 9.00
25	1.88		8.87
30	2.08		8.67
35	2.45		8.30
40	3.44		7.31
45	5.22		5.53
50	8.12		2.63
55	12.68		1.93 ⎫
60	19.84		9.09 ⎬ Deficit
65	30.98		20.23 ⎪
70	48.58		37.83 ⎭

Figure 10-8 Net Annual Premium for a $1000 Policy

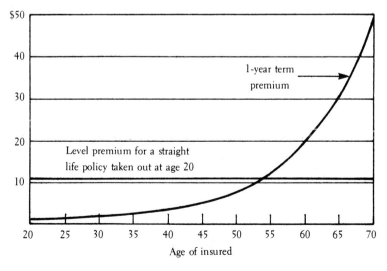

Now we are going to see how the reserve fund is built up when a person takes out a level premium policy. The best way to do this is to work out the financial details when a large group of persons of the same age are insured at the same time. So that the table will be complete and not too long, we work with a $1000, 10-year endowment policy issued to men aged 20. The CSO Table shows that $l_{20} = 9,664,994$. From formula (43) we get an annual premium of $87.98. We now compute the following for the first policy year:

Total premiums $9,664,994 \times 87.98 = \$850,326,172.12$
Fund with interest at $2\frac{1}{2}\%$
    at the end of the year $850,326,172.12(1.025) = \$871,584,326.42$
From the Mortality Table
    $d_{20} = 17,300$. Death
    claims at the end of the
    first year will be $17,300 \times 1000 = \$17,300,000$
Fund at the end of the
    year $871,584,326.42 - 17,300,000.00 = \$854,284,326.42$

The number of survivors at the end of the first year is the same as the number living at the beginning of the second year, or $l_{21} = 9,647,694$. Thus the fund per survivor is

$$\frac{854,284,326.42}{9,647,694} = \$88.55$$

The premiums at the beginning of the second year equal the number of survivors at the end of the first year times the annual premium:

$$9,647,694 \times 87.98 = \$848,804,118.12$$

The fund at the beginning of the second year is the sum of the fund at the end of the first year and the second year's premiums:

$$854,284,326.42 + 848,804,118.12 = \$1,703,088,444.54$$

Values for the full 10 years of the policy are given in Table 10-2. The fund per survivor is given to the nearest cent; other entries are rounded to the dollar.

Table 10-2 Values for 10 Years of Policy

Policy Year	Premiums	Fund at Beginning of Year	Fund with Interest	Death Benefits	Fund at End of Year	Number of Survivors	Fund per Survivor
1	$850,326,172	$ 850,326,172	$ 871,584,326	$17,300,000	$ 854,284,326	9,647,694	$ 88.55
2	848,808,118	1,703,088,445	1,745,665,657	17,655,000	1,728,010,656	9,630,039	179.44
3	847,250,831	2,575,261,487	2,639,643,024	17,912,000	2,621,731,024	9,612,127	272.75
4	845,674,933	3,467,405,958	3,554,091,106	18,167,000	3,535,924,106	9,593,960	368.56
5	844,076,601	4,380,000,707	4,489,500,725	18,324,000	4,471,176,725	9,575,636	466.93
6	842,464,455	5,313,641,180	5,446,482,210	18,481,000	5,428,001,210	9,557,155	567.95
7	840,838,497	6,268,839,707	6,425,560,699	18,732,000	6,406,828,699	9,538,423	671.69
8	839,190,456	7,246,019,155	7,427,169,634	18,981,000	7,408,188,634	9,519,442	778.22
9	837,520,507	8,245,709,141	8,451,851,869	19,324,000	8,432,527,869	9,500,118	887.62
10	835,820,382	9,268,348,251	9,500,056,957	19,760,000	9,480,296,957	9,480,358	1000.00

10.8 THE PROSPECTIVE METHOD

In the preceding section the reserve was determined by accumulating premiums and deducting death benefits. This approach is called the **retrospective method** because it is based on past premiums and past benefits. Formulas can be derived to compute terminal reserves by the retrospective method without constructing a table. Another way to get reserves is to use the **prospective method**, which is based on future benefits and premiums. The two methods give the same numerical result when dealing with net level premium policies. Advanced texts on insurance point out principles that will help the actuary choose the method that will lead to the simpler formula for a particular problem.

The prospective method of computing reserves is based on the general definition of a reserve as the excess of the present value of future benefits over the present value of future premiums. At any time the reserve must be sufficient to make up the difference between the present value of the future benefits and the present value of the premiums. Expressing this as an equation of value, we have

$$\text{Reserve} = \begin{pmatrix} \text{present value of} \\ \text{future benefits} \end{pmatrix} - \begin{pmatrix} \text{present value of} \\ \text{future premiums} \end{pmatrix}$$

EXAMPLE 1 Find the reserve per survivor at the end of the 5th policy year for a $1000, 10-year endowment policy issued to a person who is age 20.

SOLUTION At the end of the 5th policy year, the insured is 25 years old. At that time the value of the future benefits is the net single premium for a 5-year, $1000 endowment policy issued to a person 25 years old. From formula (42) this value is

$$1000 A_{25:\overline{5}|} = 1000 \frac{M_{25} - M_{30} + D_{30}}{D_{25}}$$

$$= 1000 \frac{1754288.5 - 1706575.7 + 4519691.4}{5165008.0} = \$884.30$$

From formula (43) the value for the net annual premium for a 10-year endowment policy for $1000 issued to a person 20 years old is

$$1000P_{20:\overline{10|}} = 1000\frac{M_{20} - M_{30} + D_{30}}{N_{20} - N_{30}}$$

$$= 1000\frac{1804922.4 - 1706575.7 + 4519691.4}{167827046.5 - 115337742.5} = \$87.98$$

Note that the net annual premium is based on the age of the insured when the policy is taken out regardless of the age attained by the time the reserve is to be determined. The five remaining payments of $87.98 form a temporary life annuity due. From formula (35) the present value of this annuity is

$$87.98\ddot{a}_{25:\overline{5|}} = 87.98\frac{N_{25} - N_{30}}{D_{25}}$$

$$= 87.98\frac{139839497.6 - 115337742.5}{5165008.0} = \$417.36$$

Using the symbol V for the terminal reserve, we have

$$V = 884.30 - 417.36 = \$466.94$$

The table for the retrospective method in the preceding section shows a terminal reserve of $466.93 at the end of the 5th policy year for the same policy. The difference is due to rounding values to the penny.

Exercise 10e

1. Complete the first five lines of a reserve fund schedule for a $1000 straight life policy issued to a group of 25-year-old men.
2. Complete the first five lines of a reserve fund schedule for a $1000, 20-payment life policy issued to a group of 25-year-old men.
3. Complete the first five lines of a reserve fund schedule for a $1000, 20-year endowment policy issued to a group of 25-year-old men.
4. Complete the reserve fund schedule for a $1000, 5-year term policy issued to a group of 25-year-old men.
5. Use the prospective method to get the reserve per survivor at the end of the 5th policy year for a $1000, 20-year endowment policy issued to a 30-year-old man.
   ($203.89)

6. Find the reserve for the policy in problem 5 at the end of the 10th policy year.
7. Determine the reserve per survivor at the end of the 10th policy year for a $10,000 straight life policy issued to a 20-year-old man. ($1031.31)
8. Get the reserve for the policy in problem 7 at the end of the 20th policy year.

10.9 BUYING LIFE INSURANCE

Most students in later life will buy life insurance. Since this insurance will mean a considerable expenditure year after year, a person's insurance program should be planned carefully. The experience gained computing net insurance premiums in a course in mathematics of finance is ideal preparation for recognizing the advantages and disadvantages of various commercial policies.

To begin with, you should understand that money can go entirely for protection with term insurance, can go largely for savings with an annuity, or can go for a combination of savings and protection with a level premium policy that builds up a reserve as it goes along. With many types of policies to choose from, it is not surprising that people sometimes take out insurance that does not meet their particular needs. This mistake can be tragic when a family finds that an inadequate and poorly planned insurance program does not begin to provide for its material well-being. The same expenditure on a different type of policy might have met family needs reasonably well. We now consider the four basic types of policies from a practical point of view.

Term insurance provides the most protection for the least cost. It may be the only way for a family of limited means to obtain adequate protection. For other families it can be very handy for special situations, such as additional protection when the children are young or to cover the outstanding debt on a home. The disadvantages of term insurance are the increasing cost as the insured gets older, and the absence of a cash value. If a person gets term insurance with the idea of continuing it or converting it to a level premium plan, the policy should be one that can be renewed to age 60 or older, or converted to another type of policy without a new physical examination. Figure 10-9 shows how the premium charged by a representative company for a term policy varies with the age of the insured. Dollar amounts represent the annual premium per $1000 for a policy of $10,000 or more.

The **ordinary**, or **straight life**, policy has a higher premium than term insurance at first, but the cost will never increase. After the payment of a few premiums, there will be a reserve that can be used to keep the insurance in force if the insured is unable to keep up the premiums. Ordinary or straight life is probably the best all-around protection for most families if they can afford enough protection under this plan.

Limited payment policies, if the payment period is as short as 20 years, require high premiums, so that the average family can carry such insurance only by reducing the amount of protection. Such policies are well suited to people like professional athletes who may have a relatively short period of high earning power and want to pay for their insurance while their income is high.

Endowment policies are expensive because the premium must cover both protection and an endowment. Thus an endowment policy is essentially a term insurance policy plus a pure endowment. Very few people buy pure endowments. Many salespeople do not encourage their clients to buy term insurance. Yet the two placed in one package and sold as an endowment policy become attractive to some people. Short-term endowment policies are primarily savings. If a family wants both

Figure 10-9 Cost of 5-year Level Premium Term Insurance

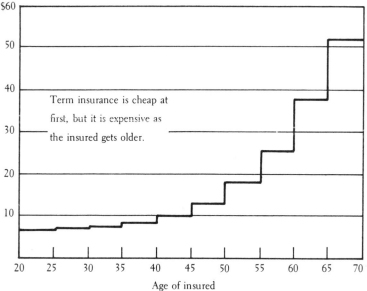

Term insurance is cheap at first, but it is expensive as the insured gets older.

Age of insured

savings and insurance, they should keep most savings separate from insurance so that the family will get both in case of death. In this case the family would carry the less expensive type of insurance and put savings into securities, savings accounts, or real estate.

Besides the basic policies discussed here, there are many combination policies. The buyer of insurance should analyze such policies carefully to see if a combination policy has any advantage over one or more of the four basic types.

10.10 USE OF THE RESERVE

Earlier in this chapter we discussed the reserve that is accumulated as premiums are paid on level premium policies. Many policyholders do not understand the value of this reserve. It can be used in several ways. A holder can surrender the policy and take the cash. Before getting an expensive endowment policy to put a child through college, a couple should consider getting more whole life insurance on the principal breadwinner. Then the family will have more protection while the children are young. When the children reach college age, this whole life policy will have a substantial cash reserve. The reserve can be used if needed, or the policy can be kept in force to provide continued protection. The policy may eventually become a part of the couple's retirement income. If moderate income families understood the great flexibility of the whole life policy, there would be less buying of the more expensive plans with their limited protection.

Instead of taking the cash and dropping the policy, a family may borrow on the cash reserve at a rate that is usually far below the rate for small loans from commercial sources. Generally such loans should be repaid as soon as possible, since the protection is reduced by the amount of the loan. The reserve may also be used as the single premium for a reduced amount of paid-up insurance. Another use of the reserve is to pay for extended term insurance that keeps the entire policy in force for a period dependent on the type of policy and the size of the reserve. If a person stops paying premiums on a level premium policy and does not take the cash, the company may automatically put into effect extended term insurance. Many people do not know this. As a result, there are probably policies thrown away or left lying around in bureau drawers that are worth thousands of dollars, but that will never be collected on because the survivors assume them to be worthless since the insured stopped paying premiums many years before dying.

An insurance agent told us of a widow who received $10,000 from her husband's insurance when she had expected $5000. The man had carried two policies of $5000 in the same company. He paid on one until he died; the other he had dropped years before. When the widow put in her claim, she did not mention the policy that had been dropped, since she assumed that it was worthless. When settling her claim, the insurance company found that death had occurred within the extended term period of the other policy, so the widow collected on both. In most cases there is no way for the insurance company to know that death came during the time of the extended term insurance unless a claim is made.

Insurance companies do what they can to prevent loss of benefits by notifying policyholders that extended term insurance is in effect if a policyholder stops paying premiums. Some companies indicate the exact date on which the coverage expires. The policyholder should file all such papers with the policy. Since papers may be lost or the company may lose contact with a policyholder, a check should be made on any policy that could possibly still be in effect.

The guaranteed values provided by the reserve in a particular policy can be found in the policy. To illustrate the great practical value of insurance reserves, Table 10-3 has been reprinted from the Veterans Administration Bulletin for National Service Life Insurance. These guaranteed values are based on the American Experience Mortality Table with interest at 3%. Thus the values are somewhat different from those that would be obtained using the CSO Table with interest at $2\frac{1}{2}\%$. All values are for a $1000 policy issued to a 25-year-old person. Annual premiums for these policies are

Policy	Annual Premium
Ordinary life	$16.22
20-payment life	25.10
20-year endowment	41.20

Exercise 10f

1. A 28-year-old man can afford to pay approximately $150 a year for life insurance. This amount will cover the net annual premium for what size policy of each of the following types: (a) 5-year term? (b) whole life? (c) paid-up-at-age-65? (d) 20-payment life? (e) 20-

Table 10-3 Guaranteed Values at Age 25 — $1000

Ordinary Life (Participating)

End of Policy Year	Cash Value	Paid-up Insurance	Extension Years	Extension Days	End of Policy Year	Cash Value	Paid-up Insurance	Extension Years	Extension Days
1	$ 8.60	$ 23.78	1	34	13	$134.77	$ 304.26	15	355
2	17.47	47.55	2	87	14	147.39	326.76	16	297
3	26.61	71.28	3	158	15	160.36	349.05	17	190
4	36.04	94.99	4	249	16	173.67	371.09	18	41
5	45.76	118.66	5	354	17	187.34	392.91	18	215
6	55.77	142.24	7	111	18	201.37	414.49	18	352
7	66.09	165.75	8	240	19	215.77	435.81	19	91
8	76.72	189.16	10	6	20	230.50	456.82	19	165
9	87.67	212.47	11	133	25	309.14	556.79	19	197
10	98.94	235.64	12	244	30	394.11	646.17	18	220
11	110.55	258.68	13	325	35	482.33	723.44	17	52
12	122.49	281.56	14	364	40	570.12	788.29	15	145

20-Payment Life (Participating)

1	$ 17.81	$ 49.24	2	110	13	$287.07	$ 648.09	31	51
2	36.24	98.63	4	294	14	314.97	698.27	32	126
3	55.31	148.16	7	193	15	343.86	748.47	33	188
4	75.06	197.84	10	166	16	373.77	798.65	34	263
5	95.49	247.61	13	195	17	404.76	848.91	36	27
6	116.64	297.48	16	241	18	436.85	899.18	37	269
7	138.54	347.45	19	236	19	470.12	949.55	40	40
8	161.21	397.48	22	121	20	504.58	1,000.00	—	—
9	184.66	447.52	24	237	25	555.22	—	—	—
10	208.95	497.64	26	232	30	609.92	—	—	—
11	234.09	547.76	28	124	35	666.72	—	—	—
12	260.12	597.92	29	300	40	723.24	—	—	—

(cont. on next page)

Table 10-3 Guaranteed Values at Age 25 — $1000 (continued)

20-year Endowment (Participating)

End of Policy Year	Cash Value	Paid-up Insurance	Extension Years	Extension Days	Pure Endowment
1	$ 34.45	$ 57.51	4	219	—
2	70.16	114.30	9	345	—
3	107.19	170.35	16	10	—
4	145.58	225.65	16	—	$68.76
5	185.39	280.18	15	—	145.19
6	226.67	333.91	14	—	218.78
7	269.49	386.85	13	—	289.63
8	313.91	438.99	12	—	357.82
9	359.98	490.30	11	—	423.46
10	407.79	540.79	10	—	486.65
11	$ 457.41	$ 590.47	9	—	$547.46
12	508.90	639.28	8	—	605.94
13	562.37	687.28	7	—	662.21
14	617.88	734.43	6	—	716.35
15	675.54	780.75	5	—	768.40
16	735.46	826.23	4	—	818.47
17	797.73	870.88	3	—	866.59
18	862.49	914.73	2	—	912.85
19	929.87	957.77	1	—	957.31
20	1,000.00	1,000.00	—	—	—

Students who are interested in getting more information on life insurance can obtain practical and interesting publications from the Institute of Life Insurance, 277 Park Ave., New York, New York, 10017.

year endowment? Give the answer to the nearest $1000.

[(a) $72,000; (b) $11,000; (c) $10,000; (d) $6000; (e) $4000]

2. Work problem 1 for a 28-year-old woman.

3. Assume that the insured dies while the policies in problem 1 are in force. The benefits are to be paid out in 120 payments certain, with the first payment to be made 1 month after the insured dies. If the company allows 3% converted monthly on the proceeds left with it, what will be the size of the monthly payments for the five policies? The partial payment factor is

$$\frac{1}{a_{\overline{120}|\frac{1}{4}\%}} = .0096560745$$

[(a) $695.24; (b) $106.22; (c) $96.56; (d) $57.94; (e) $38.62]

4. Determine the size of the benefit payments for the policies in problem 2 if the payments are made from the proceeds for 120 months and 3% converted monthly is earned on the balance left with the company. (The partial payment factor is given in problem 3.)

10.11 SUMMARY OF INSURANCE FORMULAS

The formulas used to determine life insurance premiums are summarized in Table 10-4.

REVIEW EXERCISES FOR CHAPTER 10

1. Find the net single premium for a 21-year-old man for a $20,000: (a) whole life; (b) 5-year term; (c) 20-year endowment policy.

[(a) $6248.57; (b) $174.30; (c) $12,342.04]

2. Find the net annual premium for each of the policies in problem 1.

3. Find the net annual premium for the buyer in problem 1 for a: (a) 30-payment life; (b) paid-up-at-65 policy.

[(a) $300.17; (b) $244.41]

4. Do problem 1 for a 21-year-old woman.

5. Find the net annual premium for each of the policies in problem 4.

[(a) $202.71; (b) $34.73; (c) $784.74]

6. Find the net annual premium for the buyer in problem 4 for a $20,000: (a) 30-payment life; (b) paid-up-at-age-65 policy.

Table 10-4 Insurance Premiums (All Formulas Are for a Policy of $1)

Type of Policy	Net Single Premium		Net Annual Premium	
Whole life	$A_x = \dfrac{M_x}{D_x}$	(37)	$P_x = \dfrac{M_x}{N_x}$	(38)
Term policy (for n years)	$A^1_{x:\overline{n}} = \dfrac{M_x - M_{x+n}}{D_x}$	(39)	$P^1_{x:\overline{n}} = \dfrac{M_x - M_{x+n}}{N_x - N_{x+n}}$	(40)
Limited payment life (payments for t years)	(Same as whole life)		$_tP_x = \dfrac{M_x}{N_x - N_{x+t}}$	(41)
Endowment policy (for n years)	$A_{x:\overline{n}} = \dfrac{M_x - M_{x+n} + D_{x+n}}{D_x}$	(42)	$P_{x:\overline{n}} = \dfrac{M_x - M_{x+n} + D_{x+n}}{N_x - N_{x+n}}$	(43)

7. A 30-year-old woman has $500 a year to use for life insurance. This amount will cover the net annual premium for what size policy if the policy is: (a) 10-year term? (b) whole life? (c) paid-up-at-age-65? (d) 30-payment life? (e) 15-year endowment? Answer each to the nearest $1000.

   [(a) $229,000; (b) $37,000; (c) $32,000; (d) $29,000; (e) $9000]

8. A 20-year-old man inherits $5000. He wants to buy as much paid-up life insurance as possible with the money. This amount will cover the net single premium for what size policy if the policy is: (a) 20-year term? (b) whole life? (c) 20-year endowment? Answer to the nearest $1000.

Chapter 11
Stocks

11.1 THE ELEMENT OF UNCERTAINTY

Mathematically, there are no doubts about the results obtained for simple and compound interest problems and annuities certain. The times and amounts of all payments are specified definitely. Although a death or business failure may result in unpredictable changes, no allowance is made for such possibilities when the problem is solved.

In the case of life annuities and life insurance, payments are contingent on a person's age, time of death, and other factors. These uncertain events can be taken into account with a high degree of accuracy *on the average* if the actuary has reliable mortality data on which to base calculations. Although the company cannot make money on every policy, the actuary probably can set premiums that are low enough to be competitive and high enough for the company to make a profit.

Now we consider the application of the mathematics of finance to corporate stocks, even though we can neither make certain calculations for individual problems nor use actuarial data to make predictions that will be true on the average. In spite of the uncertainties, the mathematics of finance can be profitably applied to the buying of stocks.

Most students are interested in stocks, although not always for the right reason. Having heard of someone who made a killing by putting money in a stock that went up like a rocket, they want to know how to do likewise with their first few paychecks. If we knew how, we would be busily doing it.

11.2 KINDS OF STOCKS

In the chapter on bonds, we saw that a person who buys a bond is lending money to a corporation or a government agency and is entitled to interest on the money and the eventual return of the capital. A stockholder is a part owner of the company and must take chances on the fortunes of the company. The stockholder's place is at the end of the line after the government, workers, suppliers, and bondholders. The actual piece of paper that is evidence of ownership of stock in a corporation is called a *stock certificate.* Watermarked paper finely engraved with delicate etching is used to discourage forgery. (See Figure 11-1.)

There are two basic types of stocks: *preferred* and *common.* Preferred stock has a stated return that is given on the stock certificate. Holders of preferred stock receive dividends only if declared by the board of directors. Preferred stock has a claim on earnings before payment may be made on the common stock, and preferred is usually entitled to priority over common stock if the company liquidates. However, owners of preferred rank below bondholders and other creditors. Most preferred is *cumulative*, which means that if any dividends are omitted, they accumulate and must be paid before the common stockholders get anything. Some preferred stock is *convertible*, which means that it may be converted into common. Generally, preferred stock has no voting privileges unless a stated number of dividends have not been declared on the preferred. Preferred stocks are usually redeemable at the company's option at fixed prices. This call feature, of no value to the investor, is important to the corporation because it enables the company to retire stock when the capital market is favorable.

At one time preferred stocks were used extensively by corporations to obtain capital. Today, aside from public utilities, preferred stocks are not often used for new financing. From the investor's standpoint, preferred stocks rank below bonds in safety and below common stocks in opportunities for growth and a share in the increasing profits of a successful corporation.

The venture capital that permits new firms to start and existing ones to expand is often obtained by selling common stock. Common stockholders assume the risks of ownership and, in the event of a failure, may lose all or part of their investment. On the other hand, there is no ceiling on their possible profits. If their firm is successful, they may benefit from both increasing dividends and a rising market price for their stock. As a rule, common stockholders may vote for the directors of a corporation and may suggest changes in corporate policy or practice. Dividends depend primarily on what a company earns in any given year and on anticipated return on reinvested earnings. The board of directors decides what dividends will be paid.

Figure 11-1 Stock Certificate

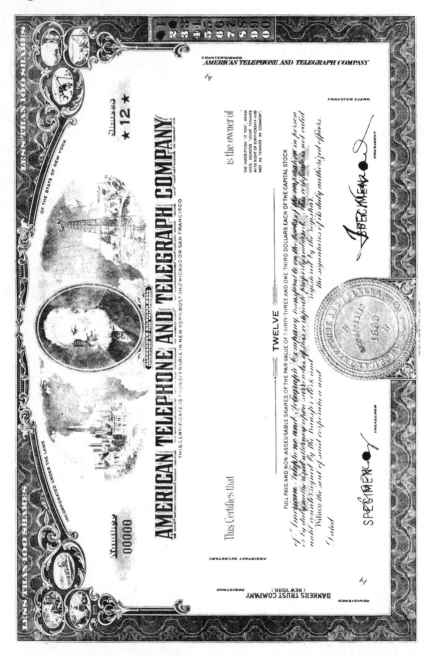

Permission for use granted by American Telephone and Telegraph Company.

In the case of common stock, par value indicates the dollar amount assigned to the share by the company's charter. Par may also be used to compute the dollar amount of the common shares on the balance sheet. Many companies today issue no-par stock. Par value is of little significance in the case of common stock. It has nothing to do with dividends and is no indication of what an investor would receive if the firm were liquidated. The market value of common stock is a matter of supply and demand as buyers and sellers consider earnings, dividends, growth prospects, quality of management, and the general business climate.

There are thousands of different stocks. Many of these are traded on the floor of the New York Stock Exchange, the American Stock Exchange, and various other exchanges throughout the country. Other stocks and bonds, called unlisted securities, are bought and sold in the over-the-counter market. This market is not a place, but a method of doing business by private negotiation among dealers who use the telephone to buy and sell securities.

Many newspapers include tables of stock market information. Stocks are listed alphabetically under column headings that are easy to interpret. Although symbols and abbreviations may vary somewhat with different newspapers, Figure 11-2, illustrating New York Stock Exchange transactions from the October 22, 1976, issue of the *Wall Street Journal*, is a good example of information found in stock tables.

11.3 PRICE TRENDS

Over the long run, the general trend of prices in this country has been upward. The same statement can be made about the trend in common stock prices. Figure 11-3 shows how prices have varied as measured by the Department of Labor's Consumer Price Index (CPI). This index shows the overall variation in the prices of goods and services purchased by middle-income city families. The stock price graph is based on Standard and Poor's Index of 500 Stock Prices. The graphs are plotted on semilog, or ratio, scales on which equal percent changes take the same vertical distance regardless of the magnitude of the variables. The steeper a line on such a graph, the faster the rate of change. This graph shows that from 1929 to 1932 stock prices dropped much more quickly than consumer prices. However, over the long term, particularly from 1942 on, stock prices have, on the average, risen more rapidly than prices of consumer goods. These rising long-term trends have made stock buying attractive for the long pull during the last 30 years. Wise investors recognize that money, like wampum, is only a medium of

Figure 11-2 How to Read a Stock Table

Highest and lowest prices per share during the indicated period.

Abbreviated name of the company. In this case, Acme Cleveland.

"pf" following the name indicates a preferred stock.

Number following name shows indicated annual dividend, in this case \$1.28. This is an estimate based on recent dividends. Letters following the dividend indicate other information which is usually given in footnotes at the end of the table.

The price-earnings ratio of the stock. Described in section 11.7.

Number of round lots traded. On this day there were 86 lots of 100 shares. This number does not include odd lot sales, that is, quantities less than 100 shares for most stocks. When a letter z appears before this number, the number indicates the actual number of shares traded. When the letter x appears, it means ex dividend or without dividend. This is shown on the day the stock goes ex dividend. If a person buys stock when it is selling ex dividend, he will not receive that dividend. It goes to the previous owner.

For this stock, high for the day was $36\frac{1}{2}$, low for the day $35\frac{5}{8}$, and the stock closed at $35\frac{7}{8}$. The closing price was \$.125 less than the closing for the previous day, as indicated by the net change of $-\frac{1}{8}$ point.

–1976– High	Low	Stocks	Div.	P-E Ratio	Sales 100s	High	Low	Close	Net Chg.
		– A–A–A –							
36⅜	32⅜	ACF Ind	1.80	8	13	34⅜	34	34	– ½
4	1⅞	AJ Indust		7	46	3¾	3¾	3¾	......
24⅜	17⅞	AMF Inc	1.24	10	148	19⅜	19⅛	19¼	– ⅛
17⅜	12¾	APLCorp	1	5	15	13¾	13⅝	13¾	– ⅛
60⅝	47¾	ARASv	1.20	13	73	49¾	48¾	49¾	+ ¾
33	12⅝	ASALtd	.80	..	104	15⅞	15⅝	15⅞	+ ⅛
11¾	7¼	ATOInc	.28	5	36	8	7⅞	8	......
55⅛	37¾	AbbtLab	.88	17	144	54	53½	53⅝	......
10¼	8⅛	AcmeClv	.50	13	10	8⅞	8¾	8⅞	+ ⅛
4½	2⅝	AdmDg	.04	5	20	2⅞	2¾	2¾	+ ⅛
12⅜	9⅞	AdmEx	.91e	..	65	11⅞	11⅝	11⅞	+ ⅛
5¾	3⅞	AdmsMillis		6	8	3⅞	3⅞	3⅞	– ⅛
13½	7¾	Addrssg	.10e	12	127	10	9¾	9⅞	......
35⅛	22½	AetnaLf	1.08	11	621	32⅜	31⅜	31½	– ¾
52½	36¼	AetnaLf	pf 2	..	12	49½	48¼	48¼	– ¼
9⅝	4⅜	Aguirre Co		94	26	9⅝	9⅜	9⅜	– ¼
14⅜	9⅝	Ahmans	.22	6	41	13⅞	13⅝	13⅝	– ⅛
6⅞	2½	Aileen Inc		63	27	3¼	3	3⅛	+ ⅛
39¾	32	AirProd	.20	15	283	33⅞	33⅛	33¾	+ ⅝
13⅞	11	AirbnFrt	.50	11	26	12⅛	11¾	11¾	– ⅛
34⅜	17¼	AircoInc	1.15	6	96	29	28½	28½	......
25¾	14⅞	Akzona	1.20	12	2	15⅞	15⅞	15⅞	– ⅛
15⅞	13⅛	AlaGas	1.28	7	21	14⅞	14¼	14¼	– ⅝
112½	104½	AlaPw	pf 11	..	z270	111¾	111½	111½	– ¼
102½	89	AlaP	pf 9.44	..	z100	102	102	102	......
89½	78	AlaP	pf 8.16	..	z10	90	90	90	+ 1
17½	11⅛	AlaskIn	.45e	6	28	15⅞	15	15	– ⅞
21¾	14	AlbanyIn	.72	10	12	17½	17½	17½	+ ⅛
23⅞	17⅞	Albertsn	.72	9	34	19¾	19½	19½	– ¼
30⅝	19⅜	AlcanAlu	.40	79	104	25⅜	25⅛	25⅛	– ⅛
18½	14⅛	AlcoStd	.72	6	97	17½	16⅞	17⅜	+ ½
28	19¾	AlconLb	.28	15	460	19⅝	19⅜	19⅜	– ⅜
9¼	5½	Alexdrs	.36e	5	17	5⅝	5½	5⅝	......
11⅜	7½	AllegCp	.90e	21	11	10	9¾	9¾	– ⅛
43¼	26½	AllgLud	1.80	6	382	34¼	33¾	33¾	– ¼
45½	33¼	AllgLud	pf 3	..	158	40	39½	39½	– ½
21½	16¾	AllgPw	1.60	7	89	20⅛	19¾	20	......
20	9¾	AllenGrp	.60	6	32	13⅛	12⅝	12⅞	– ⅝
44⅞	33½	AlldCh	1.80	8	201	36⅛	35½	35½	– ⅞
13⅝	9⅞	AlldMnt	.64	7	3	11⅜	11⅛	11⅜	+ ⅜
59¼	40¾	AlldStr	1.80	6	86	43¼	42¾	42¾	– ⅛
6	2¼	AlldSupmkt		..	27	2⅞	2¾	2⅞	......
30	11⅞	AllisChal	.60	6	245	25⅞	25¼	25¼	– ½
9¾	6¾	AllrtAut	.60	9	10	8¾	8¾	8¾	– ⅛
11	6½	AlphaP Ind		13	9	10¾	10¾	10¾	+ ⅛
61¼	38½	Alcoa	1.40	26	874	55⅜	53¾	53¾	– 1⅛
41½	30	AmalSug	3a	3	8	34	33½	33½	– ¾
60¼	47	Amax	1.75	13	89	54⅛	53¾	54	– ⅛
146	115	Amax	pf5.25	..	1	130½	130½	130½	– ¾
58¾	52⅞	Amax	pfB 3	..	5	54	53¾	54	......
22¾	11¾	AMBAC	.80	7	31	19¾	19¼	19⅜	+ ⅜
21¾	16¼	Amerce	1.20	7	6	18⅜	18⅜	18⅜	+ ¼
37½	29½	Amrc	pf 2.60		1	[illegible]	34⅝	34⅝	– ⅛
25⅞	16⅝	AHess	.60	7	272	25¾	25¼	25⅜	– ¼
62	45⅞	AHes	pf 3.50	..	38	61½	60¾	61	– ¾
21¼	13¾	AAirFilt	.56	8	31	16⅜	15⅝	15¾	– ½
16⅜	8⅝	Am Airlin		17	441	12¾	12⅜	12½	+ ⅛
10	4⅞	Amcord	.36	7	45	8¾	8½	8⅝	......
15⅜	11¾	AmBaker	1	5	5	13¾	13¾	13¾	+ ⅛
43½	38⅛	ABrnds	2.80	8	334	42⅜	40½	41⅛	– 1¼
26	21	ABrnd	pf1.70	.	5	24⅜	24	24	– ⅜
39⅛	19⅞	AmBdcst	.80	23	292	35¾	34⅞	34⅞	– ⅝
12¼	8¾	AmBldM	.40a	6	10	9	8⅞	8⅞	– ⅛
38½	30⅝	AmCan	2.40	7	94	36½	35⅝	35⅞	– ⅛
23⅛	21	ACan	pf 1.75	..	22	23	22¾	23	+ ¼
3	1⅛	AmCen Mtg		..	15	1⅝	1½	1⅝	+ ⅛
16⅞	12½	AmCredit	.26e	5	65	15⅜	15⅛	15¼	– ⅛
28⅛	23½	ACyan	1.50	9	725	25⅝	25	25	– ½
11	7¾	AmDistill		..	5	8⅝	8½	8½	– ⅛

Source: Reprinted with permission of *The Wall Street Journal.*

exchange. What really counts economically is maintaining the ability to buy goods.   Although there is no certainty that trends in either consumer or stock prices will be the same in the future as in the past, the likelihood of further increases should be taken into account when making investment decisions.

These graphs show why a fixed investment, such as a bond, mortgage, or savings account, has a risk connected with it; the price-level risk is the risk of a loss in purchasing power as a result of price increases. The history of prices in the United States shows that the risk of inflation

Figure 11-3 Consumer and Stock Price Indexes

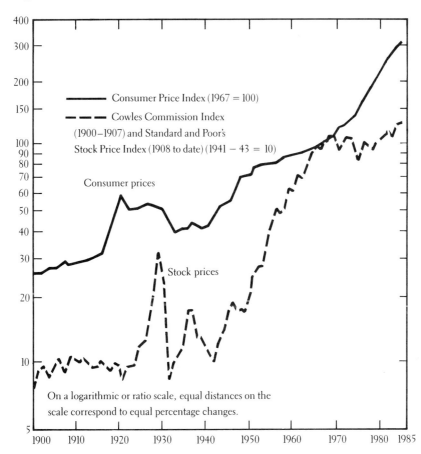

Sources: *Historical Statistics of the United States, Colonial Times to 1970*, Tables E-135, X-495; *1985 Economic Report of the President*, Tables B-52, B-90.

is a real one. There is a good chance that people who loan money will be repaid in dollars of depreciated purchasing power.

Stocks over the years have provided a long-run hedge against inflation. We emphasize the long run because over shorter periods stock prices have not always kept abreast of consumer prices. There have even been years when stock prices went down while the CPI was rising. But in spite of temporary setbacks, investors with diversified portfolios of quality stocks are likely not only to preserve their purchasing power, but also to come out ahead in terms of real income over the years. This eventual gain is what makes stocks attractive to the investor who is interested in the long pull, not a quick profit.

To compare the real value of an investment at one time with its real value at another time, we multiply the number of dollars the investment is worth by the value of the dollar. As explained on page 154, the value of the dollar = 100/CPI. When the CPI = 100 (actually 100%), the value of the dollar is 100/100 = $1.00. If the CPI is 125, the dollar is worth 100/125 = $.80. A CPI of 90 means that the dollar is worth 100/90 = $1.11.

To compare the value of the dollar at one time with its value at another time requires that all values be relative to the same base period. Occasionally the Bureau of Labor Statistics adopts a new base period for the CPI, and past index values are adjusted and spliced to the new series so that a continuous picture of price changes is obtained. Because of their importance for reference purposes and for solving problems in this chapter, the value of the CPI-W and the corresponding value of the dollar are given in Table 11-1. All values are relative to the latest base period, 1967 = 100.

Figure 11-4 shows the long-term trend in the purchasing power of the U.S. dollar. This trend shows the risk in owning fixed-dollar investments. Since 1940 the value of the dollar has increased in only two years, 1949 and 1955. From 1940 to 1952 the value of the dollar dropped from $2.38 to $1.26, an annual compounded rate of depreciation of 5.2%. During the 15 years from 1952 to 1967, the annual rate of depreciation was only 1.4%. During these years many people found themselves better off in terms of real income because their dollar incomes increased at a higher rate than prices of consumer goods. People living on pensions or other fixed incomes were not so fortunate, since even small year-to-year increases in prices can soon mean trouble for those who are barely getting by.

As this text is being written, inflation has again become a serious problem. From 1970 to 1984 the dollar depreciated at an annual compounded rate of 6.8 percent.

Table 11-1 Value of CPI-W and the Dollar*

Year	CPI 1967 = 100	Value of the Dollar	Year	CPI 1967 = 100	Value of the Dollar
1915	30.4	$3.29	1950	72.1	$1.39
1916	32.7	3.06	1951	77.8	1.29
1917	38.4	2.60	1952	79.5	1.26
1918	45.1	2.22	1953	80.1	1.25
1919	51.8	1.93	1954	80.5	1.24
1920	60.0	1.67	1955	80.2	1.25
1921	53.6	1.87	1956	81.4	1.23
1922	50.2	1.99	1957	84.3	1.19
1923	51.1	1.96	1958	86.6	1.15
1924	51.2	1.95	1959	87.3	1.15
1925	52.5	1.90	1960	88.7	1.13
1926	53.0	1.89	1961	89.6	1.12
1927	52.0	1.92	1962	90.6	1.10
1928	51.3	1.95	1963	91.7	1.09
1929	51.3	1.95	1964	92.9	1.08
1930	50.0	2.00	1965	94.5	1.06
1931	45.6	2.19	1966	97.2	1.03
1932	40.9	2.44	1967	100.0	1.00
1933	38.8	2.58	1968	104.2	.96
1934	40.1	2.49	1969	109.8	.91
1935	41.1	2.43	1970	116.3	.86
1936	41.5	2.41	1971	121.3	.82
1937	43.0	2.33	1972	125.3	.80
1938	42.2	2.37	1973	133.1	.75
1939	41.6	2.40	1974	147.7	.68
1940	42.0	2.38	1975	161.2	.62
1941	44.1	2.27	1976	170.5	.59
1942	48.8	2.05	1977	181.5	.55
1943	51.8	1.93	1978	195.4	.51
1944	52.7	1.90	1979	217.4	.46
1945	53.9	1.86	1980	246.8	.41
1946	58.5	1.71	1981	272.4	.36
1947	66.9	1.49	1982	289.1	.35
1948	72.1	1.39	1983	298.4	.34
1949	71.4	1.40	1984	311.1	.32

*The CPI used in this book is the one for Wage Earners & Clerical Workers (CPI-W).

11.4 MEASUREMENT OF GROWTH
AND DECLINE

If a quantity has been changing over the years, we can determine the constant annual rate that would have produced this change. We simply solve for the rate on a compound interest basis using formula (9), $S = P(1 + i)^n$. If time series data plot as approximately a straight line on a semilog or ratio graph, a rate based on past trends may be helpful in making predictions.

EXAMPLE 1   The Standard and Poor's Index of 500 Industrial Stocks was 55.85 in 1960 and 118.78 in 1980. Find the annual compounded rate of growth.

SOLUTION

$$55.85 \, (1 + i)^{20} = 118.78$$

$$(1 + i)^{20} = \frac{118.78}{55.85}$$

$$= 2.1268$$

Figure 11-4 The Shrinking Dollar

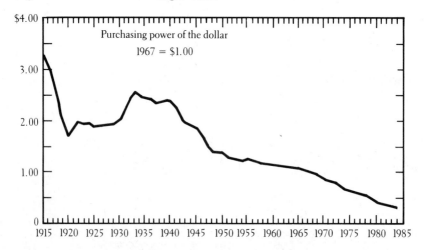

Source: *1985 Economic Report of the President*, Table B-52.

$$i \text{ in } \% \quad (1+i)^{20}$$

$$.5 \left[\begin{array}{c} d \left[\begin{array}{cc} 3.5 & 1.9898 \\ i & 2.1268 \end{array} \right] 1370 \\ 4.0 \quad 2.1911 \end{array} \right] 2013$$

$$\frac{d}{.5} = \frac{1370}{2013}$$

$$d = .34$$
$$i = 3.84\%$$

EXAMPLE 2 The CPI was 94.5 in 1965 and 246.8 in 1980. Compute the annual compounded rate of change.

SOLUTION

$$94.5 \, (1+i)^{15} = 246.8$$

$$(1+i)^{15} = \frac{246.8}{94.5}$$

$$= 2.6116$$

Using a calculator

$$1 + i = (2.6116)^{1/15}$$
$$= 1.06609$$
$$i = .06609 = 6.61\%$$

EXAMPLE 3 In 1965 the value of the dollar was $1.06 and in 1980 it was $.41. Find the annual compounded rate of change.

SOLUTION

$$1.06 \, (1+i)^{15} = .41$$

$$(1+i)^{15} = \frac{.41}{1.06}$$

$$= .38679$$

$$1 + i = (.38679)^{1/15}$$
$$= .93864$$
$$i = -.06136 = -6.14\%$$

Note that the annual percentage drop in the value of the dollar is not numerically equal to the annual percentage rise in the CPI. A larger change makes it easier to see why this is so. When the CPI goes from 100 to 200, there is a 100% rise in prices. There is a corresponding drop in the value of the dollar from $1.00 to $.50, a decrease of 50% — not 100%. The dollar may be shrinking, but it has not disappeared entirely.

11.5 CHANGES IN STOCK VALUES

Some buyers of stocks are interested primarily in receiving a liberal income. Others, who do not need the immediate income, look for stocks that they hope will increase greatly in market value over the years. One way to evaluate past price trends is to get the annual compounded rate of growth by substituting in formula (9) and solving for i.

EXAMPLE 1 On December 31, 1961, Standard Oil of New Jersey common stock was $50\frac{1}{2}$. By December 31, 1980, the company had changed its name to Exxon Corporation and the stock had split 2 for 1 and was at $80\frac{5}{8}$. What was the annual rate of growth in market value of the stock on a compound interest basis?

SOLUTION Substituting in formula (9) and adjusting for the split, we have

$$50.5(1 + i)^{19} = 161.25$$

$$(1 + i)^{19} = \frac{161.25}{50.5} = 3.1931$$

Referring to Table 2, we find that the annual rate is between 6% and 7%. A more precise value is 6.30%.

EXAMPLE 2 On December 31, 1958, Procter and Gamble stock was selling at 57. On December 31, 1980, it was quoted at $68\frac{7}{8}$. There were 2-for-1 splits in 1961 and 1970. What was the annual compounded rate of growth over this period?

SOLUTION   Allowing for splits, we have

$$57(1 + i)^{22} = 275.5$$

$$(1 + i)^{22} = \frac{275.5}{57} = 4.8333$$

Using a calculator,

$$1 + i = \sqrt[22]{4.8333} = 1.0742$$
$$i = .0742 = 7.42\%$$

As long as an investor holds a security, a gain such as this is a paper profit that may be increased or decreased by changes in the market.

Stock prices can go down, in which case the owner of a security has the unpleasant experience of watching an investment depreciate in value.

EXAMPLE 3   An investor bought Chesapeake and Ohio in 1959 at 67. Three years later the price was 52. What was the average annual rate of depreciation in the value of this stock?

SOLUTION

$$67(1 + i)^3 = 52$$

$$\log (1 + i) = \frac{1.716003 - 1.826075}{3}$$

Practical work with logarithms requires that we have positive mantissas and integral characteristics. Therefore we add 30 to the first log in the numerator and offset this addition by subtracting 30.

$$\log (1 + i) = \frac{(31.716003 - 30) - 1.826075}{3} = \frac{29.889928 - 30}{3}$$

$$= 9.963309 - 10$$

Looking up the antilog of 9.963309 − 10, we find that $1 + i = .919$. Therefore

$$i = .919 - 1 = -.081 = -8.1\%$$

On the average, the market value of the stock dropped about 8% a year over the 3-year period. If this downward trend is reversed, the stock may in time recover this loss in market value. Careful investors maintain a cash reserve to avoid being forced to sell at a loss stocks that they would like to hold for anticipated future gains.

ALTERNATE SOLUTION

$$67(1 + i)^3 = 52$$

$$(1 + i)^3 = \frac{52}{67} = .776119$$

$$(1 + i) = \sqrt[3]{.776119} = .91899$$
$$i = -.08101 = -8.10\%$$

EXAMPLE 4 In 1940 a person purchased a savings bond for $75, cashing it in 1950 for $100. Compare the purchasing power of the investment at the two times.

SOLUTION The purchasing power of an investment depends on the number of dollars and the value of the dollar. Putting this investment at the two times on a comparable basis:

Year	Value of the Dollar (1967 = 100)	Value of Investment	
		Current Dollars	Dollars of Constant Purchasing Power
1940	$2.38	$ 75	$178.50
1950	1.39	100	139.00

In spite of accumulated interest, the buying power of this investment dropped about 22% over the period. Rapidly rising prices are particularly hard on people who have their money in fixed-dollar investments.

Exercise 11a

Find annual compounded rates of change to the tenth of one percent.

1. What was the annual compounded percentage change in prices and in the value of the dollar from 1974 to 1984?
   (Prices up 7.7% a year; value of dollar down 7.3% a year.)

2. Compare the annual compounded percentage increase in prices for the period 1915–19 with the period 1941–45. Get the corresponding changes in the value of the dollar.

3. Find the annual compounded rate of change in prices and the value of the dollar from 1930 to 1933.
   (Prices down 8.1% a year; value of dollar up 8.9% a year.)

4. Find the annual compounded rate of change in prices and the value of the dollar from: (a) 1940 to 1950; (b) 1950 to 1960; (c) 1960 to 1970; (d) 1970 to 1980. Compare with the answer in problem 1.

5. From 1954 to 1984, the Standard and Poor's Index of Industrial Stock Prices (1941–43 = 10) went from 29.69 to 160.46. Find the annual compounded rate of increase.
   (5.8%)

6. From 1950 to 1960, the Standard and Poor's Index of Public Utilities Stocks went from 20.59 to 46.86. Find the annual compounded rate of increase.

7. On December 31, 1962, Westinghouse Electric common stock was selling for $32 a share. The stock was split 2 for 1 in 1971. The December 31, 1984, price was $26\frac{1}{8}$. What was the annual compounded rate of growth?
   (2.3%)

8. At the end of 1960, General Motors common was $40\frac{3}{4}$. The closing price in 1984 was $78\frac{3}{8}$. Find the annual compounded rate of increase.

9. Kroger common stock was quoted at $37\frac{7}{8}$ a share on December 31, 1964. On December 30, 1966, the price was $22\frac{1}{8}$. Find the annual compounded rate of change.
   (−23.6%)

10. Alcan Aluminum was 34 in December of 1959. In December of 1966 the price had dropped to 28. Find the annual rate of depreciation over this period.

11. Standard and Poor's Composite Index of Stock Prices dropped from 26.02 in 1929 to 6.93 in 1932. What was the annual compounded rate of change over this period?
    (−35.7%)

12. Standard and Poor's Composite Index of Stock Prices increased from 15.23 in 1949 to 62.38 in 1962. What was the annual compounded rate of increase over this period?

11.6 COMMISSION COSTS

When stocks are purchased and sold, a fee is paid to the brokers who handle the transaction. Such fees are called *commissions.* The commission costs can be an important factor in the cost of the stock and therefore in the ultimate profit (or loss) in the transaction.

Prior to May 1, 1975, minimum commissions were set by the New York Stock Exchange, and these were generally the commissions charged by brokers in stock transactions. Since that time, however, commission charges have been negotiable. This change has had little effect on the small investor, but it has made a large difference for institutions who buy and sell large quantities of stock.

Stocks are traded in round lots and odd lots. For most stocks, a *round lot* is 100 shares, although a few stocks have round lot figures of 50, 25, or even 10 shares. Any number of shares less than a round lot is called an *odd lot.* The broker's fee for handling odd lots may increase the commission cost to the client.

Since brokers' commissions are negotiable, it is not possible to give the exact cost of a purchase here. However, Tables 11-2 and 11-3 give approximations of the commissions that brokers charge for various round and odd lot transactions. The tables can be used to estimate the total cost of a stock transaction and the return that the buyer will get on an investment. Keep in mind that these commissions are only

Table 11-2 Approximate Round Lot Commissions

Shares per Order	Price of Stock									
	$5	$10	$20	$30	$40	$50	$60	$80	$100	$120
100	$ 18.04	$ 27.50	$ 41.80	$ 53.90	$ 63.80	$ 71.50	$ 80.73	$ 80.73	$ 80.73	$ 80.73
200	36.08	55.00	77.00	109.30	131.65	154.01	161.46	161.46	161.46	161.46
300	54.12	73.70	116.75	150.28	183.82	217.35	242.19	242.19	242.19	242.19
400	68.20	90.20	146.56	191.27	235.98	280.69	310.50	322.92	322.92	322.92
500	81.95	106.70	176.36	232.25	288.14	325.40	362.66	403.65	403.65	403.65
600	93.50	139.10	206.17	273.24	325.40	370.12	399.92	459.54	484.38	484.38
700	105.05	157.73	235.98	310.50	362.66	402.41	437.18	506.74	565.11	565.11
800	116.60	176.36	265.79	340.31	394.96	434.70	474.44	553.93	633.42	645.84
900	128.15	194.99	295.60	370.12	422.28	466.99	511.70	601.13	690.55	726.57
1000	139.70	213.62	325.40	399.92	449.60	499.28	548.96	648.32	747.68	807.30
1500	210.52	294.35	424.76	499.28	573.80	648.32	722.84	871.88	1020.92	1169.96
2000	263.30	375.08	499.28	598.64	698.00	797.36	896.72	1095.44	1294.16	1492.88
2500	316.09	437.18	573.80	698.00	822.20	946.40	1070.60	1319.00	1567.40	1815.80

Table 11-3 Approximate Odd Lot Commissions

Shares per Order	Price of Stock									
	$5	$10	$20	$30	$40	$50	$60	$80	$100	$120
5	$ 1.65	$ 3.30	$ 7.04	$ 8.14	$ 9.24	$10.34	$11.44	$13.64	$15.84	$18.04
10	3.30	7.04	9.24	11.44	13.64	15.84	18.04	22.44	25.30	28.16
20	7.04	9.24	13.64	18.04	22.44	25.30	28.16	33.88	39.60	45.32
25	7.59	10.34	15.84	21.34	25.30	28.88	32.45	39.60	46.75	51.70
30	8.14	11.44	18.04	23.87	28.16	32.45	36.74	45.32	51.70	57.64
50	10.34	15.84	25.30	32.45	39.60	46.75	51.70	61.60	71.50	80.73
75	13.09	21.34	32.45	43.18	51.70	59.13	66.55	80.73	80.73	80.73

approximations. The charge on a given transaction may be higher or lower. Remember, too, that a commission will also be charged on the sale of the stock, and this will have an effect on the profit picture.

In the examples and problems that follow, we assume that 100 shares is a round lot and we use the approximate commissions given in the tables.

EXAMPLE 1 If the market price of Sperry Corporation is $50 a share, find the cost of: (a) 10 shares; (b) 100 shares; (c) 1000 shares.

SOLUTION

(a) Sale price = 10 × 50   = $500.00
     Commission   =   15.84
     Total cost $515.84

(b) Sale price = 100 × 50 = $5000.00
     Commission   =   71.50
     Total cost   = $5071.50

(c) Sale price = 1000 × 50 = $50,000.00
     Commission   =   499.28
     Total cost   = $50,499.28

Note that the cost per share is $51.58 for 10 shares, $50.72 for 100, and $50.50 for 1000 shares. The price per share is lower for the buyer who purchases more shares.

EXAMPLE 2 Suppose that Rockwell International is paying an annual dividend of $2.50 and is selling at 60. Find the rate of return to an investor who buys: (a) 50 shares; (b) 100 shares; (c) 1000 shares.

SOLUTION

(a) Sale price = 50 × 60 = $3000.00
     Commission   =   51.70
     Total cost   = $3051.70

At the given dividend rate, the owner will get annual dividends of 50 × 2.50 = $125.00.

$$\text{Rate of return} = \frac{125}{3051.70} = .0410 = 4.10\%$$

(b) Sale price = 100 × 60   = $6000.00
     Commission   =   80.73
     Total cost   = $6080.73
     Total dividend = 100 × 2.50   = $250

$$\text{Rate of return} = \frac{250}{6080.73} = .0411 \quad = 4.11\%$$

(c) Sale price = 1000 × 60   = $60,000.00
     Commission   =   548.96
     Total cost   = $60,548.96
     Total dividend = 1000 × 2.50 = $2500

$$\text{Rate of return} = \frac{2500}{60,548.96} = .0413 = 4.13\%$$

EXAMPLE 3 If Texaco is paying an annual dividend of $2.00 and is selling at 30, find the return to an investor who buys: (a) 20 shares; (b) 200 shares; (c) 2000 shares.

SOLUTION

(a) Sale price = 20 × 30   = $600.00
     Commission   =   18.04
     Total cost   = $618.04
     Total dividend = 2 × 20   = $40

$$\text{Rate of return} = \frac{40}{618.04} = .0647 \quad = 6.47\%$$

(b) Sale price = 200 × 30   = $6000.00
     Commission   =   109.30
     Total cost   = $6109.30
     Total dividend = 200 × 2   = $400

$$\text{Rate of return} = \frac{400}{6109.30} = .0655 \quad = 6.55\%$$

(c) Sale price = 2000 × 30   = $60,000.00
     Commission   =   598.64
     Total cost   = $60,598.64
     Total dividend = 2000 × 2   = $4000

$$\text{Rate of return} = \frac{4000}{60,598.64} = .0660 = 6.60\%$$

Exercise 11b

1. An investor bought Bristol Myers at 80 when the dividend was
   $1.80. Find the cost including commission and the rate of return
   for: (a) 10 shares; (b) 50 shares; (c) 500 shares.
   [(a) $822.44, 2.19%; (b) $4061.60, 2.22%; (c) $40,403.65, 2.23%]
2. An investor bought St. Regis Paper when the price was 50 and the
   dividend was $1.52. Find the cost including commission and the rate
   of return for: (a) 25 shares; (b) 300 shares; (c) 2500 shares.
3. An investor bought General Foods at 30 when the dividend was
   $1.50. Find the cost including commission and the rate of return
   for: (a) 50 shares; (b) 400 shares; (c) 2000 shares.
   [(a) $1532.45, 4.89%; (b) $12,191.27, 4.92%; (c) $60,598.64, 4.95%]
4. An investor bought Ford Motor Company when the price was 50
   and the dividend was $3.20. Find the cost including commission and
   the rate of return for: (a) 5 shares; (b) 50 shares; (c) 500 shares.
5. An investor bought Continental Oil preferred stock with a $2.00
   dividend at 100. Find the cost including commission and the rate of
   return for: (a) 10 shares; (b) 100 shares; (c) 1000 shares.
   [(a) $1025.30, 1.95%; (b) $10,080.73, 1.98%; (c) $100,747.68, 1.99%]
6. General Cinema stock with a dividend of $.68 was purchased at 20.
   Find the cost including commission and the rate of return for:
   (a) 25 shares; (b) 300 shares; (c) 2500 shares.

11.7 HOW MUCH IS A STOCK WORTH?

The price of a stock on a free market, such as the floor of a stock
exchange, is determined by many factors: facts and rumors, hopes and
fears, yields expected by investors, general business conditions, the
outlook for particular industries and companies, and many other things
such as tax changes, presidential heart attacks, and what the dictators
of distant countries are expected to do next. With so many unpredictable variables influencing stock prices, are there any objective mathematical standards by which the value of a stock can be judged? There
are some useful standards of this type that can be used as guidelines in
conjunction with other information in arriving at buy or sell decisions.

For investors who depend on stocks for income, yield rates and
consistent dividends are important considerations. Many stocks have
paid dividends every 3 months for 25 years or more. Some have even
had an uninterrupted flow of dividends for a century or more. Al-

though this does not guarantee anything for the future, a history of payments over a long period including, at times, adverse economic conditions is an indication of underlying strength in a company's operations. Even with such stocks, there is an inherent risk in using past results to predict an uncertain future. Present merits must also be considered in evaluating the outlook for future dividends. Will they be maintained, reduced, or increased?

Although there is no guarantee that dividends and, therefore, yield rates will continue into the future, a careful consideration of past performance may result in conclusions that are at least quite possible. Suppose that a middle-aged couple would like to invest some money now in a security that will pay them a moderate yield at this time with a good prospect of increased dividends in the future. They decide to invest in an electric utility because they think that in most areas the utility will have an increasing business regardless of general business fluctuations. Their broker suggests the following as representative companies that meet their needs:

Company	Closing Price 3/29/85	Indicated Dividend	Indicated Yield
Consolidated Edison	$32\frac{1}{4}$	$2.40	7.4%
Duquesne Light	16	2.06	12.9
Pacific Gas and Electric	$17\frac{5}{8}$	1.72	9.8
Public Service Electric & Gas	$27\frac{3}{8}$	2.72	9.9
Southern Company	20	1.92	9.6

Since commission costs cannot be determined until an order is placed, yield rates in material supplied by brokers are determined by simply dividing the dividend by the price. Actual net yields to the investor, determined as in the preceding section, will be slightly lower than these published figures.

Although a fixed investment, such as a savings and loan account or an industrial bond, might pay a somewhat higher return now, the fact that these companies have a past record of increasing dividends is attractive to this couple because returns a few years from now are of greater importance than present yields. This tabulation is, of course, only a preliminary guide for further and more detailed study of these and other companies, since past dividend trends may not be continued and may even be reversed.

The *price-earnings ratio*, computed by dividing recent market price by latest 12 months per share earnings, can be a useful guide in making investment decisions. On Wall Street there is considerable support for the idea that a historic norm for this ratio is about 15. However, there is no absolute standard for deciding what the price-earnings ratio should be. It varies from company to company, from industry to industry, and as the economic outlook changes. Unusually good or poor 12-month periods should be taken into account in evaluating the significance of the ratio. The price-earnings ratio for a growth company may be high and yet the stock will be quite attractive for certain investment objectives. Thus the price-earnings ratio is a relative matter and is useful only when used for comparison purposes. It is one of the tools that a wise investor uses in conjunction with other information.

For some investors, a liberal income is important. Consider a retired couple who need the income from their investments to meet current living expenses. They will be able to find many stocks that yield 5% or more.

Typical of such stocks are those listed in the following table:

Company	Closing Price 3/29/85	Per Share Earnings	Indicated Dividend	Indicated Yield	P/E Ratio
Exxon	$50\frac{1}{4}$	$6.77	$3.40	6.8%	7.4
General Telephone and Electronics	$40\frac{1}{4}$	5.32	3.08	7.7	7.6
Goodyear	$26\frac{7}{8}$	3.87	1.60	6.0	6.9
Mobil	30	3.11	2.20	7.3	9.6
Tenneco	$42\frac{3}{4}$	4.01	2.92	6.8	10.7

Now we consider an investor who is not dependent on present income from stocks. For this investor, a price-earnings ratio of 15 or more may be acceptable if the stock seems to have the promise of a large growth potential. The following stocks may be of interest to this investor:

Company	Closing Price 3/29/85	Per Share Earnings	Indicated Dividend	Indicated Yield	P/E Ratio
AT&T	$21\frac{5}{8}$	$1.25	$1.20	5.5%	17.3
Clark Equipment	$30\frac{1}{8}$	1.28	1.10	3.7	23.5
Hewlett Packard	34	2.19	.22	0.6	15.5
Wendy's	$17\frac{5}{8}$	.94	.21	1.2	18.8
Weyerhaeuser	$28\frac{1}{4}$	1.52	1.30	4.6	18.6

An idea of whether or not the price-earnings ratio for a growth stock is reasonable might be obtained by using the past growth record of the company to predict the future. Suppose that the earnings of the company are now $10 a share and have been increasing at about 15% a year. If the approximately 15%-a-year increase continues for another 5 years, earnings will be about $20. This picture fit International Business Machines fairly well in the 1970s. It is on prospects such as these that certain growth stocks are actively traded at high P/E ratios.

Exercise 11c

1. An investor is interested in buying stock in a drug company. A broker suggests the following stocks. Determine the yields and price-earnings ratios.

Stock	Closing Price 3/29/85	Per Share Earnings	Indicated Dividend	(Yield)	(P/E)
Bristol Myers	$57\frac{1}{2}$	$3.45	$1.88	(3.3%)	(16.7)
Merck and Co.	$104\frac{7}{8}$	6.71	3.20	(3.1)	(15.6)
Pfizer	$42\frac{7}{8}$	3.08	1.48	(3.5)	(13.9)
Upjohn	$80\frac{1}{2}$	5.67	2.56	(3.2)	(14.2)

2. Compute the yields and price-earnings ratios for the following retailers:

Stock	Closing Price 3/29/85	Per Share Earnings	Indicated Dividend
Federated Department Stores	$55\frac{7}{8}$	$6.77	$2.54
Macy's	$44\frac{3}{4}$	4.19	1.16
J. C. Penney	$47\frac{3}{8}$	5.81	2.36
Sears Roebuck	$34\frac{1}{8}$	4.01	1.76

3. Bring the data and solutions in problem 1 up to date and note any significant changes.
4. Bring the data and solutions in problem 2 up to date and note any significant changes.
5. Compute the yields and price-earnings ratios for the following banks:

Bank	Closing Price 3/29/85	Per Share Earnings	Indicated Dividend	(Yield)	(P/E)
Bankers' Trust	$63\frac{5}{8}$	$9.52	$2.70	(4.2%)	(6.7)
Chase Manhattan	$51\frac{1}{2}$	9.01	3.80	(7.4)	(5.7)
Citicorp	$43\frac{1}{4}$	6.45	2.26	(5.2)	(6.7)
Manufacturer's Hanover	$35\frac{7}{8}$	7.12	3.20	(8.9)	(5.0)

6. Compute the yields and price-earnings ratios for the following oil companies:

Company	Closing Price 3/29/85	Per Share Earnings	Indicated Dividend
Texaco	$36\frac{1}{8}$	$1.03	$3.00
Occidental Petroleum	$29\frac{7}{8}$	3.08	2.50
Phillips	38	5.26	2.40
Shell Oil	$59\frac{5}{8}$	5.73	2.00

7. Bring the data in problem 5 up to date.
8. Bring the data in problem 6 up to date.

11.8 SOUND INVESTMENT PRINCIPLES

A sound investment program may include several types of investments, such as real estate, bonds, and stocks. Real estate is likely to require relatively large sums of money and skilled management. High-quality bonds have the advantage of safety of principal and, at the present time, good rates of return. There are many fine industrial and utility bonds being sold today at prices that will result in a high yield. Some investors put part of their money in bonds for safety of principal and liberal returns. Another part may go into common stocks, some of which are chosen because they pay good dividends and some because of their potential growth.

Although stocks can be an attractive investment, investors should be sure that they can afford them. This means more than just having a few dollars on hand. It costs money to buy stocks, and they can go down as well as up. People should buy stocks only if they feel reasonably sure that they will not be forced to sell at a loss to get cash. They should be able to answer "Yes" to the following questions:

1. Do I have enough to cover living expenses comfortably? For the home buyer this includes a substantial equity in the house.
2. Do I have adequate life insurance to protect my family and an adequate retirement plan?
3. Do I have a cash reserve or savings account for emergencies?

How much for living expenses, how much insurance, and how large a cash reserve depend on the circumstances of the particular individual or family. When you think that you have enough for your particular circumstances, you may reasonably start investing in stocks. Note that an honest appraisal of the situation would result in not buying stocks if there are consumer installment loans. We have seen in earlier chapters that such loans often involve interest charges of 12% or more. Since this is a higher rate than can be expected from most stocks, such debts should be repaid before investing. An investor who is satisfied that stocks are affordable should then decide on personal investment objectives.

Common stocks may offer one or more of the following: probable safety of principal, liberal income, and growth. Some stocks may meet a couple of these objectives to an attractive degree. Thus a high degree of safety and a liberal dividend rate may be found in the same stock. Or a stock with good growth prospects may pay moderate dividends. However, do not expect to find an all-purpose stock that is very safe, pays large dividends, and is sure to go up.

Before buying, get facts. Do not buy on tips or rumors, or on the recommendation of a high-pressure telephone salesperson. Deal with a reputable broker who can suggest industries and particular companies that will meet your investment objectives. Consider the prospects of the various industries. After deciding on an industry that meets your objectives, ask your broker to supply fact sheets on specific companies. Study these and then make your own decision. The more you know about various companies, the better equipped you will be to make a wise choice. Check on a company's profits, the future for its products, its price-earnings ratio, and the quality of its management. In any industry, some companies will be much better than others. Management is the critical factor that makes the difference.

When a person is in a position to afford stock in several companies, there are advantages to diversification. Some industries will move ahead more quickly than others; some may even regress as their products are replaced by new inventions. Diversification protects the investor against the overall loss that would result from having all available money in a failing company. Having stocks in a reasonable number of industries and companies also improves a person's chances of making a profit as a result of one or more of the companies growing at a high rate.

Although diversification reduces risk, some investors prefer not to diversify. They are willing to accept a higher degree of risk in the hope of having a larger-than-average gain. Even a person who diversifies should not own stocks in so many companies that reasonable supervision of each investment is impossible. As one authority has said, "Stocks are perishable." Only by keeping abreast of industry trends and the fortunes of particular companies can a person decide whether to buy more stock in a company, sell what is owned, or simply hold. Also as a person gets older or the family situation changes, investment objectives may change, calling for shifts from one type of security to another.

To keep commissions to a small percentage of the value of stocks, a person can defer the purchase of stocks until at least several hundred dollars are available for investing.

There is no system that will enable a person to consistently buy when the market is low and sell when it is high. A system that some investment counselors recommend is dollar averaging. A person who follows dollar averaging puts a certain number of dollars into the stock of a particular company. At regular intervals, the person again invests about the same amount in this company. When prices are low, this fixed amount buys more shares than when prices are high. Acquiring more shares when prices are low and fewer shares when they are high is the theory behind dollar cost averaging. When stock prices rise, a person's profit will be greater because of the larger number of shares purchased when prices were down. Dollar cost averaging means that a person must have the courage and the cash to keep right on buying in line with a plan to buy fixed-dollar amounts at regular intervals. The success of dollar cost averaging depends on the market value of a buyer's stocks having a generally upward trend in spite of inevitable reverses at times.

We have mentioned the advantages of a person diversifying an investment portfolio by getting stocks in different industries and companies. In this way, poor choices are likely to be offset by stocks that do well. Somewhat the same thing can be accomplished by investing in the shares of investment companies. An *investment company* or *investment trust* is a concern that uses the capital supplied by individuals to buy a diversified group of securities. There are two principal types: closed-end and open-end. The capitalization of *closed-end companies* is fixed. Their shares are bought and sold just like other stocks. Some closed-end companies are listed on stock exchanges.

Open-end investment companies, usually called *mutual funds*, continue to offer new shares of stock for sale. The shares of mutual funds are bought and sold on the basis of their net asset value, which is continually changing because the value of the fund's investments is continually changing. Such funds will redeem outstanding shares at any time at the current asset value per share.

The owner of shares of either a closed-end company or a mutual fund gets diversification and professional management. However, a price is paid for these benefits. The buyer of shares in most mutual funds may be required to pay a load that covers commissions and other costs of distribution. The load may be as much as 8%. This may be more than the commission rates on common stocks and the shares of closed-end companies. Shares of mutual funds can usually be sold without paying another commission, although there may be a small redemption fee.

In all investment companies, both closed-end and open-end, the owner of shares must pay a management fee. This fee varies with the size of the fund, but a typical figure is $\frac{1}{2}$ of 1% of net assets. This may seem small, but note that it is on assets. As a percentage of earnings, it may be as high as 15% or more. Mutual funds are usually sold by salespeople operating on a commission. Any investment should be *bought* only after the investor has made a thorough study and compared different investment possibilities. Only in this way can a person make a selection that is best from the standpoint of personal resources, objectives, and temperament. Mutual funds are available for different types of stocks and industries.

Arranging to purchase stocks for cash is a rather simple procedure. After establishing financial responsibility and opening an account with a broker, orders are placed through the broker. But behind the scenes there is an amazingly complex and efficient system that is described in literature available from the exchanges and brokers. A visit to a broker's office will provide a student or potential investor with an interesting overall picture of the operation of the stock market.

The government, the exchanges, and ethical brokers and investment firms help to protect the stock buyer from gyps and swindles. That gyps and swindles still exist is due in part to unwary and greedy buyers. They let themselves be taken by high-pressure salespeople peddling questionable stocks. By direct mail or long-distance calls, suckers learn that they are the lucky ones for whom some kind dealer has set aside a block of two or three hundred shares of low-priced stock at a special bargain price. Unless the buyer acts within a day or two, it will be too late. The chance of a lifetime to make a killing will be gone for good. What is really meant is that it will be gone for the salesperson, who would make a large commission. "Investigate before you invest" should be the invariable rule of the buyer of stocks. Only in this way will the buyer have a good chance to do well in the interesting and potentially profitable but uncertain stock market.

REVIEW EXERCISES FOR CHAPTER 11

1. Find the most recent value for the CPI and calculate its annual rate of return since: (a) 1950; (b) 1960; (c) 1970; (d) 1980.
2. Do problem 1 for the value of the dollar.

In problems 3 through 10, find recent price, dividend, and earnings figures for the stock, and compute the yield and price-earnings ratios.

3. Coca-Cola
4. Pepsi-Cola

5. IBM
6. Burroughs
7. Exxon
8. Shell Oil
9. General Motors
10. Ford
11. Using the commission tables at the nearest values, find the cost including commission and the rate of return for 100 shares of: (a) Exxon; (b) Shell Oil.
12. Do problem 11 for: (a) General Motors; (b) Ford.

Appendix
Computational Methods

Problems in the mathematics of finance are solved by methods that range from pencil-and-paper computations to programmed solutions on electronic computers.

An efficient way to solve problems requiring only a few computations is to use a calculator. The manual for the particular machine should be consulted for proper operating procedures. Sometimes additional help for common business problems is available in the form of specific instruction sheets with suggested short cuts and checks.

At one time logarithms were used extensively in computational work, but they have been superseded for most routine calculations by calculators and electronic computers. However, logarithms still have some importance in business analysis. They form the basis for semilogarithmic or ratio graphs and in some cases are the only method for solution of a problem.

One of the great recent technological developments is that of the electronic calculator. The electronic calculators now available vary from very simple and inexpensive machines that perform the four arithmetic operations almost instantaneously to very sophisticated machines that might well be called computers. Some of the latter (particularly the scientific and business models, as well as those that can be programmed like a computer) have the capability of calculating table values in the mathematics of finance in seconds. Thus the advanced calculators are reducing the need, in practice, for extensive tables.

A.1 LOGARITHMS

Business problems involving rates of change that would be difficult or impossible to solve with arithmetic can be done with ease using logarithms. Graphs with logarithmic scales are valuable tools for business analysis.

A *logarithm* is an exponent, and computations with logarithms are based on the laws of exponents. The exponential expression $10^2 = 100$ becomes in logarithmic form: $\log_{10} 100 = 2$. This is read "log of 100 to the base 10 equals 2." Although any positive number other than 1 can be used as the base for a system of logarithms, 10 is the best base for computational work and is the one we use. When the base is not indicated, 10 is understood. In all cases, the log of a number will be the power to which 10 must be raised to equal that number. A few numbers with the corresponding exponential expressions and logs are given here:

Number N	N as a Power of 10	Logarithm of N
.01	$\frac{1}{100} = 10^{-2}$	-2
.1	$\frac{1}{10} = 10^{-1}$	-1
1	10^0	0
10	10^1	1
100	10^2	2
1000	10^3	3

The preceding chart shows that the logs of numbers that are integral or 0 powers of 10 can be determined by finding the power to which 10 must be raised to equal the number. The logs of other positive numbers are also powers of 10, but their numerical values must be determined by higher mathematics. Fortunately, their values have been tabulated in tables that can be used by anyone who has a knowledge of elementary algebra.

The previous chart also gives us an idea of the numerical value to expect for the logs of other numbers. Since 2 is between 1 and 10, log 2 must be between log 1 and log 10. Hence log 2 is a decimal between 0 and 1. In a similar way, the logs of numbers like 20 and 200 will lie between integral powers of 10, which is shown at the top of the next page.

Soon we shall show how a log table will give us the numerical value: $\log 2 = .301030$. In exponential form, $2 = 10^{.301030}$. An advantage of logs to the base 10 is that if we know the log of a number such as 2, we can easily get the log of 20, 200, or any other number that consists of 2 multiplied or divided by some power of 10.

N	$\log N$
1	0
2	0 + a decimal between 0 and 1
10	1
20	1 + a decimal
100	2
200	2 + a decimal
1000	3

EXAMPLE   If log 2 = .301030, find log 20 and log 200.

SOLUTION

$$20 = 2 \times 10 = 10^{.301030} \times 10^1 = 10^{1.301030}$$

Since the exponent to the base 10 is the log of the number, then log 20 = 1.301030.

$$200 = 2 \times 100 = 10^{.301030} \times 10^2 = 10^{2.301030}$$

Thus log 200 = 2.301030.

The preceding example emphasized the fact that logs are exponents and follow the laws of exponents. If we keep this in mind, we can omit writing the logs as exponents and simply say

$$\log 20 = \log 2 + \log 10 = .301030 + 1.000000 = 1.301030$$

$$\log 200 = \log 2 + \log 100 = .301030 + 2.000000 = 2.301030$$

In the same way, we can get the log for any other number in which 2 is preceded or followed by zeroes. Thus all we need to get the log of any number is a log table that covers the numbers from 1 to 10, since we can get the log of any number by adding a whole number to the decimal from the table.

Working with logarithms requires the following steps:

1. Finding the *mantissa.*
2. Finding the *characteristic.*
3. Finding the *antilogarithm.*

The whole-number part of a logarithm is the characteristic. The decimal part is the mantissa. For example:

The characteristic depends on the size of the number and is determined by the students, as we will soon describe.

$$\log 20 = 1.301030$$

The mantissa depends on the sequence of significant digits and is obtained from a table.

Getting the Mantissa

A section from Table 9 in the back of the book is shown in Figure A-1. In a log table, decimal points are omitted to save space. The column headed N is for numbers. The digits 100 under N mean 1.00, and so on. To get the mantissa for 1.1, we read down the N column to 110, and read next to it the digits 041393, which have a decimal point understood before the first digit. The first two digits are sometimes omitted.

Figure A-1 How to Use a Log Table

1. Go down the N column to 117
2. Go across the top row to 6
3. Locate the mantissa opposite 117 and under 6

Six-Place Logarithms of Numbers | 100-150

Proportional Parts

N	0	1	2	3	4	5	6	7	8	9	D
100	00 0000	00 0434	00 0868	00 1301	00 1734	00 2166	00 2598	00 3029	00 3461	00 3891	432
101	4321	4751	5181	5609	6038	6466	6894	7321	7748	8174	428
102	8600	9026	9451	9876	01 0300	01 0724	01 1147	01 1570	01 1993	01 2415	424
103	01 2837	01 3259	01 3680	01 4100	4521	4940	5360	5779	6197	6616	420
104	7033	7451	7868	8284	8700	9116	9532	9947	02 0361	02 0775	416
105	02 1189	02 1503	02 2016	02 2428	02 2841	02 3252	02 3664	02 4075	4486	4896	412
106	5306	5715	6125	6533	6942	7350	7757	8164	8571	8978	408
107	9384	9789	03 0195	03 0600	03 1004	03 1408	03 1812	03 2216	03 2619	03 3021	404
108	03 3424	03 3826	4227	4628	5029	5430	5830	6230	6629	7028	400
109	7426	7825	8223	8620	9017	9414	9811	04 0207	04 0602	04 0998	397
110	04 1393	04 1787	04 2182	04 2576	04 2969	04 3362	04 3755	4148	4540	4932	393
111	5323	5714	6105	6495	6885	7275	7664	8053	8442	8830	390
112	9218	9606	9993	05 0380	05 0766	05 1153	05 1538	05 1924	05 2309	05 2694	386
113	05 3078	05 3463	05 3846	4230	4613	4996	5378	5761	6142	6524	383
114	6905	7286	7666	8046	8426	8805	9185	9563	9942	06 0320	379
115	06 0698	06 1075	06 1452	06 1829	06 2206	06 2582	06 2958	06 3333	06 3709	4083	376
116	4458	4832	5206	5580	5953	6326	6699	7071	7443	7815	373
117	8186	8557	8928	9298	9668	07 0038	07 0407	07 0776	07 1145	07 1514	370
118	07 1882	07 2250	07 2617	07 2985	07 3352	3718	4085	4451	4816	5182	366
119	5547	5912	6276	6640	7004	7368	7731	8094	8457	8819	363
120	9182	9543	9904	08 0266	08 0626	08 0987	08 1347	08 1707	08 2067	08 2426	360

n\d	435	430	425	420
1	44	43	43	42
2	87	86	85	84
3	131	129	128	126
4	174	172	170	168
5	218	215	213	210
6	261	258	255	252
7	305	301	298	294
8	348	344	340	336
9	392	387	383	378

n\d	415	410	405	400
1	42	41	41	40
2	83	82	81	80
3	125	123	122	120
4	166	164	162	160
5	208	205	203	200
6	249	246	243	240
7	291	287	284	280
8	332	328	324	320
9	374	369	365	360

n d	395	390	385	380
1	40	39	39	38
2	79	78	77	76
3	119	117	116	114
4	158	156	154	152
5	198	195	193	190
6	237	234	231	228
7	277	273	270	266
8	316	312	308	304
9	356	351	347	342

If only four digits are shown, find the first two digits by looking up the same column until you see a six-digit mantissa.

The numbers across the top of the table permit us to get the mantissas for four-digit numbers. To find the mantissa for 1.176 (or 11.76, 117,600, .001176, or any other number derived from 1176 by multiplying or dividing by a power of 10), we proceed as shown below.

Since 1.176 is between 1 and 10, its log will consist only of the decimal part or mantissa. Therefore log 1.176 = .070407. The mantissas for other numbers with the same sequence of significant digits, such as 11,760,000 and .001176, would also be .070407, but there would be a nonzero characteristic to be determined, as shown below.

Getting the Characteristic

Put your pencil behind the first nonzero digit from the left. Count the number of places to the decimal point. The characteristic is positive if you move to the right. It is negative if you move to the left. Note that this is the system used to find the exponent of 10 when a number is put in scientific notation.

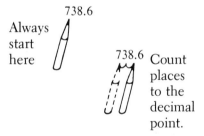

EXAMPLE 1   If the decimal point is behind the first nonzero digit, the characteristic is 0. Any number that is 1 or more but less than 10 will have a characteristic of 0.

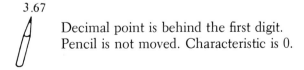

EXAMPLE 2   If the number is 10 or more, the pencil will be moved to the right and the characteristic is positive (+).

738.6

Two places to the right.
Characteristic is 2.

EXAMPLE 3 If no decimal point is shown, it is understood to be behind the last digit.

86,600,000

Seven places to the right.
Characteristic is 7.

EXAMPLE 4 If the number is less than 1, the pencil will be moved to the left and the characteristic is negative (−).

.000426

Four places to the left. Characteristic is −4. Negative characteristics should be written to the right of the mantissa, since the mantissa from the table is positive. The expression may be handled in various ways, depending on the problem. Some of the ways in which log .000426 could be written are

$$\log .000426 = \begin{cases} .629410 - 4 \\ 6.629410 - 10 \\ 56.629410 - 60 \end{cases}$$

Note that in all of these expressions the *net* value of the characteristic is −4.

Finding the Antilogarithm

To find the number corresponding to a logarithm, we go into the body of the table to find the mantissa and then write down the sequence of digits corresponding to this mantissa. To locate the decimal point in the answer, put the pencil behind the first nonzero digit from the left and move it one place to the right for each unit in the characteristic if it is positive, and one place to the left for each unit in the characteristic if it is negative. The final result is the antilogarithm, or antilog.

EXAMPLE 1 If $\log N = 3.170262$, find N.

SOLUTION The sequence of digits corresponding to a mantissa of .170262 is 148. We put the pencil behind the 1 and count three places to the right, making the answer 1480.

EXAMPLE 2 If $\log N = .554731 - 2$ or $8.554731 - 10$, find N.

SOLUTION The sequence of digits corresponding to a mantissa of .554731 is 3587. We put the pencil behind the 3 and count two places to the left, making the answer .03587.

Interpolated Values

To get the mantissa of a number that has more significant figures than the table we are using, we interpolate between the two closest tabular values. *Interpolation* means reading between the lines of a table of data; it is done frequently in the mathematics of finance and other business applications of mathematics.

EXAMPLE 1 Find the log of 2246.3.

SOLUTION We find the mantissas for the numbers immediately preceding and following 22463 and arrange them in tabular form, omitting decimal points:

	Number	Mantissa	
	22470	351603	
10 3	22463	351410 + d d	193
	22460	351410	

Since 22463 is $\frac{3}{10}$ of the way from 22460 to 22470, the mantissa will be $\frac{3}{10}$ of the way from 351410 to 351603. Letting d represent the unknown difference, we set the two ratios equal to each other. This equality of ratios, or proportion, is solved like any fractional equation.

$$\frac{d}{193} = \frac{3}{10}$$

$$d = \frac{3(193)}{10} = .3(193) = 57.9$$

Correct to 2 digits, the result is 58. Therefore the mantissa of 22463 is 351410 + 58 = 351468. Since the characteristic is 3, log 2246.3 = 3.351468.

When using Table 9, numbers with more than 5 significant digits should be rounded to 5 before getting the mantissa.
Interpolation is also used to find antilogs.

EXAMPLE 2   Find N if log N = 8.681650 – 10.

SOLUTION   We record the numbers corresponding to the mantissas on both sides of .681650.

	Number	Mantissa	
	48050	681693	
10 $\quad$ d	48040 + d	681650 $\quad$ 47	90
	48040	681603	

$$\frac{d}{10} = \frac{47}{90}$$

$$d = \frac{10(47)}{90} = 5$$

Correct to 1 digit, the result is 5. The sequence of digits in the answer is 48040 + 5 = 48045. Since the characteristic is – 2, N = .048045.

The preceding examples show in detail the basic method of interpolation that is applicable not only to log tables, but also to compound interest and other tables used in business. Interpolation with logs can be simplified by using two features of the tables in this book. The difference between successive mantissas can be obtained from the D column. The tenths of a difference can be obtained from the Proportional Parts Tables, in which n/d indicates tenths. From Table A-1, we

Table A-1 Six-place Logarithms of Numbers 450–500

N	0	1	2	3	4	5	6	7	8	9	D
450	65 3213	65 3309	65 3405	65 3502	65 3598	65 3695	65 3791	65 3888	65 3984	65 4080	96
451	4177	4273	4369	4465	4562	4658	4754	4850	4946	5042	96
452	5138	5235	5331	5427	5523	5619	5715	5810	5906	6002	96
453	6098	6194	6290	6386	6482	6577	6673	6769	6864	6960	96
454	7056	7152	7247	7343	7438	7534	7629	7725	7820	7916	96
455	8011	8107	8202	8298	8393	8488	8584	8679	8774	8870	95
456	8965	9060	9155	9250	9346	9441	9536	9631	9726	9821	95
457	9916	66 0011	66 0106	66 0201	66 0296	66 0391	66 0486	66 0581	66 0676	66 0771	95
458	66 0865	0960	1055	1150	1245	1339	1434	1529	1623	1718	95
459	1813	1907	2002	2096	2191	2286	2380	2475	2569	2663	95
460	2758	2852	2947	3041	3135	3230	3324	3418	3512	3607	94

Proportional Parts

n/d	97	96
1	9.7	9.6
2	19.4	19.2
3	29.1	28.8
4	38.8	38.4
5	48.5	48.0
6	58.2	57.6
7	67.9	67.2
8	77.6	76.8
9	87.3	86.4

n/d	95	94
1	9.5	9.4
2	19.0	18.8
3	28.5	28.2

see that the difference between mantissas in the 450 row is 96. In the Proportional Parts Tables, we see that $\frac{1}{10}$ of 96 is 9.6, $\frac{7}{10}$ is 67.2, and so on.

EXAMPLE 3   Find the log of 450.68.

SOLUTION   The sequence of digits 45068 lies $\frac{8}{10}$ of the way between the tabular values 45060 and 45070. To get the mantissa for 45068 we:

1. Find the mantissa for 45060.   653791
2. Note that the difference, D, is 96.
3. Find $\frac{8}{10}$ of 96 under the Proportional Parts Table and $\underline{\hspace{0.4cm}77}$
   round off.   653868
4 Add to get the interpolated mantissa.
5. Add the characteristic, obtaining log 450.68 = 2.653868.

EXAMPLE 4   Find the antilog of 1.653440.

SOLUTION   To find an antilog, the steps are:

1. Find the sequence of digits corresponding to 653405, the mantissa immediately smaller than 653440.   45020
2. Subtract to find the difference between mantissas, in this case: 653440 − 653405 = 35.
3. Under the Proportional Parts Table for a D of 96, find the value closest to 35. This value is 38.5, which corresponds to $\frac{4}{10}$ in the n/d column. $\underline{\hspace{0.4cm}4}$
4. Add to get the interpolated sequence of digits.   45024
5. Point off to get: antilog 1.653440 = 45.024.

With these tables and practice, much of the work involved in interpolation can be done mentally.

For the smaller numbers in a log table, the difference between mantissas in a line is not constant, so the D column gives an average value. This value is sufficiently accurate for most practical purposes for the entire line. Also, space does not permit all the Ds to be shown under Proportional Parts. If a particular D such as 412 is not included, a close result can be obtained by interpolating mentally between the values for 410 and 415.

Computations with Logs

Each of the laws of exponents can be applied to problems worked by logarithms. The following types of problems are those met most frequently.

Products and Quotients By the multiplication law for exponents, $a^m \cdot a^n = a^{m+n}$, we are able to multiply numbers by adding their logs, since logs are exponents.

   To save time when working with logs, we set up the problem before going to the tables. This procedure is illustrated in the first example. In subsequent problems in the text, only the final step is shown.

EXAMPLE 1   Evaluate by logs: 386 × 71.92.

Skeleton Solution with Required Logs and Steps Indicated	**Skeleton Solution Filled in with One Reference to Log Tables**
$\log 386 = 2.$	$\log 386 = 2.586587$
$\log 71.92 = 1.\underline{\hspace{2cm}}$	$\log 71.92 = \underline{1.856850}$
Adding, $\log N =$	Adding, $\log N = 4.443437$
	$N = 27{,}761$

   Note that this is not an exact answer because we can interpolate to only one digit beyond the four given in the table. Interpolation can be omitted if the answer is needed to only three or four significant figures.

   By the division law for exponents, $a^m/a^n = a^{m-n}$, we are able to divide numbers by subtracting the log of the denominator from the log of the numerator.

EXAMPLE 2   Evaluate by logs: $\dfrac{79.6}{28.3}$.

SOLUTION

$$\begin{aligned}
\log 79.6 &= 1.900913 \\
\log 28.3 &= \underline{1.451786} \\
\text{Subtracting, } \log N &= .449127 \\
N &= 2.8127
\end{aligned}$$

Since log tables contain only positive mantissas, it is sometimes necessary to change the form of a log, without changing the numerical value, so that negative mantissas will not appear.

EXAMPLE 3   Evaluate by logs: $\dfrac{3.3}{188}$.

SOLUTION   To avoid getting a negative mantissa, we add 10 to the log of 3.3 and then offset this addition by subtracting 10.

$$\begin{aligned}
\log 3.3 &= 10.518514 - 10 \\
\log 188 &= 2.274158 \\
\text{Subtracting, } \log N &= 8.244356 - 10 \\
N &= .017553
\end{aligned}$$

Powers and Roots   By the power of a power law for exponents, $(a^m)^n = a^{mn}$. Using this law, we raise a number to a power by multiplying the log of the number by the power.

EXAMPLE 4   Evaluate $(1.095)^{20}$.

SOLUTION   Since $\log 1.095 = .039414$, this problem can be written $(1.095)^{20} = (10^{.039414})^{20} = 10^{.788280}$. In practice, all we do is multiply the log of the quantity by the exponent, as follows:
Let $N = (1.095)^{20}$. Then

$$\begin{aligned}
\log N &= 20 \log 1.095 = 20(.039414) = .788280 \\
N &= 6.1416
\end{aligned}$$

EXAMPLE 5   Evaluate $\sqrt{18}$ by logs.

SOLUTION

$$\begin{aligned}
N &= \sqrt{18} = 18^{1/2} \\
\log N &= \tfrac{1}{2} \log 18 = \tfrac{1}{2}(1.255273) = .627637 \\
N &= 4.2426
\end{aligned}$$

The characteristic must be a whole number. In raising a number to a fractional power, it may be necessary to change the form of a log to avoid a fractional characteristic. In changing the form of a log we must:

1. Keep the numerical value unchanged.
2. Finish with a positive mantissa.
3. Finish with a characteristic that is a whole number.

EXAMPLE 6 Find $(.882)^{1/4}$

SOLUTION

$$N = (.882)^{1/4}$$
$$\log N = \tfrac{1}{4}(\log .882) = \tfrac{1}{4}(.945469 - 1)$$

To avoid a fractional characteristic, we rewrite this as

$$\tfrac{1}{4}(39.945469 - 40) = 9.986367 - 10$$
$$N = .9691$$

Negative exponents should be handled as follows:

EXAMPLE 7 Evaluate $(1.05)^{-20}$ by logs.

SOLUTION Write $(1.05)^{-20}$ as $1/(1.05)^{20}$.

$$
\begin{array}{rl}
\log 1 = & 10.000000 - 10 \\
20 \log (1.05 = 20(.021189) = & \underline{.423780} \\
\text{Subtracting,} \qquad \log N = & 9.576220 - 10 \\
N = & .37690
\end{array}
$$

Practical problems often require two or more of the basic operations.

EXAMPLE 8 Evaluate $2500(1.085)^{-5}$.

SOLUTION The multiplication and raising to a power can be done in a single series of operations, as follows:

$$
\begin{array}{rl}
\log 2500 = & 3.397940 \\
-5 \log 1.085 = -5(.035430) = & \underline{-.177150} \\
\log N = & 3.220790 \\
N = & 1662.6
\end{array}
$$

Solving for Bases and Exponents

Logarithms can be used to solve compound interest and other types of problems in which a constant rate of change is involved.

EXAMPLE 1   The following equation comes from a compound interest problem. Determine i, which represents the interest rate.

$$625(1 + i)^{10} = 3530$$

SOLUTION   We must first solve for the quantity $(1 + i)$.

Operation	Computations
Divide both sides by 625.	$(1 + i)^{10} = \dfrac{3530}{625}$
Take the logarithm of both sides.	$10 \log (1 + i) = \log 3530 - \log 625$
Look up the required logs and divide both sides by 10.	$\log (1 + i) = \dfrac{3.547775 - 2.795880}{10}$
Do the indicated arithmetic.	$\log (1 + i) = \dfrac{.751895}{10}$ or $.075190$
Look up the antilog of .075190.	$(1 + i) = 1.189$
Isolate i by subtracting 1 from both sides.	$i = 1.189 - 1 = .189$
Convert i to a percent if required.	$i = 18.9\%$

EXAMPLE 2   Over a 6-year period, an investment depreciated in value from $32,000 to $23,500. Determine r, the annual compounded rate of depreciation.

SOLUTION   We substitute in formula (9), replacing i with $-r$.

$$32,000(1 - r)^6 = 23,500$$

As in the preceding example, we first solve for the quantity $(1 - r)$.

Operation	Computations
Divide by 32,000.	$(1 - r)^6 = \dfrac{23,500}{32,000}$
Take the logarithm of both sides.	$6 \log (1 - r) = \log 23,500 - \log 32,000$
Look up the logs and divide both sides by 6.	$\log (1 - r) = \dfrac{4.371068 - 4.505150}{6}$
To avoid getting a negative mantissa in the numerator when we subtract, we add 10 to 4.371068 and subtract 10 from the resulting 14.371068. Thus the form of the first term is changed without changing its value.	$\log (1 - r) = \dfrac{(14.371068 - 10) - 4.505150}{6}$ $= \dfrac{9.865918 - 10}{6}$
To avoid getting a fractional characteristic, we must change the -10 to a number divisible by 6. An easy way to do this is to subtract 50 from the -10, making it -60, and then add 50 to the first part of the log so that its value remains the same.	$\log (1 - r) = \dfrac{59.865918 - 60}{6}$ $= 9.977653 - 10$

Solve for the quantity $(1 - r)$ by finding the antilog of $9.977653 - 10$. Solve for r.

$$(1 - r) = .94985$$

$$r = 1 - .94985 = .05015$$
$$= \text{approximately } 5\%$$

In practice, some of the operations described in detail can be combined, as shown in the following example.

EXAMPLE 3 Solve for r:

$$15,600 (1 - r)^{15} = 1500$$

SOLUTION

$$(1 - r)^{15} = 1500/15,600$$

$$15 \log (1 - r) = \log 1500 - \log 15,600$$

$$\log (1 - r) = \frac{3.176091 - 4.193125}{15}$$

By adding 150 to the first term and then subtracting 150, we can do the subtraction and division with one change in the form of the logs.

$$\log (1 - r) = \frac{(153.176091 - 150) - 4.193125}{15}$$

$$= \frac{148.982966 - 150}{15}$$

$$= 9.932198 - 10$$

Solve for the quantity $(1 - r)$ by finding the antilog of $9.932198 - 10$.

$$1 - r = .8555$$

Solve for r.

$$r = .1445 \text{ or } 14.45\%$$

The following examples show how logarithms can be used to solve for the exponent in rate-of-change problems.

EXAMPLE 4 Solve for n:

$$380(1.07)^n = 1100$$

SOLUTION

Operation	Computations
Divide both sides by 380.	$(1.07)^n = \dfrac{1100}{380}$
Take the logarithm of both sides.	$n \log (1.07) = \log 1100 - \log 380$
Divide both sides by log (1.07).	$n = \dfrac{\log 1100 - \log 380}{\log (1.07)}$
Look up the logs and do the subtraction in the numerator. We now have a problem in division that, like any such problem, can be done by arithmetic or by logs. If we use arithmetic, we have:	$n = \dfrac{3.041393 - 2.579784}{.029384}$ $n = \dfrac{.461609}{.029384} = 15.71$
If we use logs, we take the log of both sides of the new equation, getting:	$\log n = \log .461609 - \log .029384$
Arrange the problem for ease of computation and round numbers to five significant figures before getting the logs.	$\log .46161 = 9.664275 - 10$ $\underline{\log .029384 = 8.468111 - 10}$
Subtracting,	$\log n = 1.196164$
Look up the antilog of 1.196164.	$n = 15.71$

In many practical problems the exponent needs to be determined to only three significant figures. The long division can be done rapidly with a slide rule or calculator.

EXAMPLE 5   Find n to three significant figures.

$$6500(1.12)^n = 2000$$

SOLUTION

Operation	Computations
Divide both sides by 6500.	$(1.12)^n = \dfrac{2000}{6500}$
Take the logarithms of both sides and solve for n.	$n = \dfrac{\log 2000 - \log 6500}{\log (1.12)}$
	$= \dfrac{3.301030 - 3.812913}{.049218}$
Use slide rule accuracy.	$n = \dfrac{-.511883}{.049218} = -10.4$

EXAMPLE 6 Solve for n.

$$7380(1 - .25)^n = 1000$$

SOLUTION

Operation	Computations
Rewrite the problem in a form suitable for taking logarithms.	$(.75)^n = \dfrac{1000}{7380}$
Take the logarithms of both sides and solve for n.	$n = \dfrac{\log 1000 - \log 7380}{\log .75}$
	$= \dfrac{3.000000 - 3.868056}{.875061 - 1}$
	$= \dfrac{-.868056}{-.124939}$
	$= 6.95$

Note that in the last three examples n is simply a number, not a logarithm. In other words, we do the indicated arithmetic on the right of the equal sign without having to be concerned about negative decimals and other details of form that are important when we are solving for the logarithm of the unknown.

Problems

Find the logarithm of each number.

1. 8654	(3.937217)
2. .0004057	(6.608205 – 10)
3. 87 million	(7.939519)
4. 400.86	(2.602993)
5. 53,278	(4.726549)
6. .0038765	(7.588440 – 10)

Find the numbers corresponding to the following logarithms.

7. 9.905850 – 10	(.8051)
8. 2.286905	(193.6)
9. 6.700704 – 10	(.0005020)
10. 4.324950	(21,132)
11. 2.407148	(255.36)
12. 9.845700 – 10	(.70097)

Evaluate by logarithms.

13. $1578.2 \times .8675$	(1369.1)
14. $851/47.9$	(17.766)
15. $(3.89)^5$	(890.74)
16. $(.376)^{.25}$	(.78306)
17. $(1.005)^{100}$	(1.6466)
18. $(1.04)^{-10}$	(.67557)

Solve for the unknown.

19. $650(1 + i)^{10} = 2430$	(14.1%)
20. $88.2(1 + i)^3 = 420.6$	(68.32%)
21. $7830.50(1 - r)^5 = 1000$	(33.74%)
22. $15,500(1 - r)^{20} = 2500$	(8.72%)
23. $(26.2)^x = 1650$	(2.2685)
24. $50,000(1.10)^n = 100,000$	(7.2725)
25. $47,255(1.095)^n = 130,000$	(11.151)
26. $5000(1.08)^n = 2100$	(-11.272)

A.2 SEMILOGARITHMIC GRAPHS

The principle behind the semilogarithmic, or ratio, graph involves a simple application of the rules of logarithms. Note that the basic compound interest formula,

$$S = P(1 + i)^n$$

is a special case of the general formula

$$y = ab^x$$

In fact, any situation involving a constant percentage growth or decline (called geometric growth or decline) will involve a formula of this type. Now if we take the logarithm of both sides of the latter formula, we have

$$\log y = \log a + (\log b)x$$

or

$$\log y = A + Bx$$

This is the equation of a straight line in which the variables are x and $\log y$.

Therefore, if the geometric growth or decline equation is appropriate in a problem, we can use a straight line to graph the data if we merely use the logarithm of the y variable rather than y by itself. Also, we can see that the geometric law is being met if the graph is a straight line.

This could be very convenient, because the straight line is the easiest type of geometric figure to graph and to recognize. On the other hand, it appears inconvenient here because it necessitates looking up the logarithm of each y value. To avoid this problem, semilogarithmic graphs were devised.

On a semilogarithmic graph the points on the horizontal, or x, axis are equally spaced, just as on ordinary graph paper. However, the vertical, or y, axis is scaled differently. The intersection of the axes is not 0 but some power of the number 10 (10, 100, 1000, 1, .1, .01). The hash marks on this axis are not equally spaced. They are determined by the logarithms of the values. For example, in Figure A-2 the *y* values begin at 100, the next mark represents 200, and so on until 1000 is reached. After this point the marks are 2000, 3000, ..., until 10,000 is reached, and so on. Setting up the graph paper in this manner enables us to use the actual *y* values and to plot them on this irregularly scaled graph. The scaling has saved us the trouble of looking up all these logarithms. With a little practice, working with semilogarithmic graphs becomes very easy. Any set of data that graphs as a straight line on such a graph must correspond to the geometric laws of growth or decline. This technique makes the determination significantly easier. We have used semilogarithmic graphs frequently in this book. Figure A-2 shows how compound interest tables for various percentages yield straight lines on this type of graph.

Figure A-2 Growth of $100 at Compound Interest, Ratio Scale

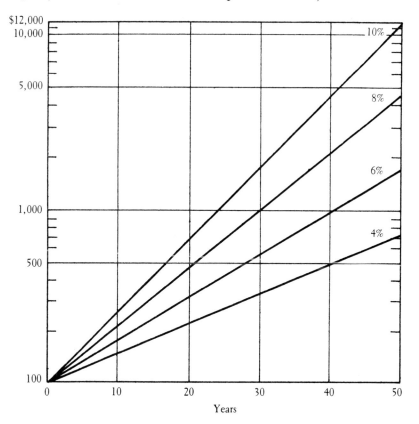

A.3   COMPUTER PROGRAMS

The advantages of electronic computers are great speed and high accuracy. Before a problem can be solved on a computer, skilled specialists must prepare a program or set of instructions for the machine. This program must be absolutely complete and specific, with no omission of details. Only a program that will be used many times will justify the costs involved in developing and checking it.

Computers are particularly helpful in solving problems that require repeated line-by-line computations and problems that must be solved by an iterative or trial-and-error process. Amortization schedules and interest tables for nontabulated rates are examples of the first application. Determining the yield rate on a bond is an example of an application using iteration.

The following pages contain programs prepared by the staff of the Xavier University Computer Center under Mr. John F. Niehaus, Director. The first three programs are written in basic FORTRAN IV with output on the high-speed printer. Students can solve practical problems using these programs or a modification of them to utilize local computer facilities and forms of output.

Program for Amortization Schedule

The first program produces an amortization schedule for two cases. The first uses the balance, rate, payment, and number of conversions per year as input and produces the appropriate schedule. The second uses the balance, rate, number of conversions per year, and duration and produces a schedule. The program adjusts the size of the last payment to exactly amortize the debt.

```
C THIS PROGRAM PRODUCES AN AMORTIZATION SCHEDULE FOR THE FOLLOWING
C TWO CASES***************
C INPUT BALANCE,RATE,PAYMENT,AND NUMBER OF CONVERSIONS PER YEAR
C INPUT BALANCE,RATE,CONVERSIONS PER YEAR, AND DURATION
      DIMENSION ANAME(20)
      DOUBLE PRECISION PMT,PEROD,XINT,BAL ,DUR,RATE,PRIN,ARATE,BRATE
  900 READ (1,1025) ANAME
      WRITE (3,1026) ANAME
C
C  READ BALANCE,RATE,PAYMENT,AND NUMBER OF PERIODS PER YEAR,DURATION OF LOAN
C
   50 READ (1,101) BAL,ARATE,PMT,PEROD,DUR
      NPEROD=PEROD
      LCNT=0.0
      IF(BAL) 999,900,901
C
C  FIND PERIODIC INTEREST RATE
```

```
C
  901 RATE=ARATE/PEROD
      IF(PMT) 500,500,902
C
C  CONVERT DECIMAL RATE TO PERCENTAGE RATE
C
  500 NUMPAY=PEROD*DUR
      PMT=BAL*(RATE/(1.-1./((1.+RATE)**NUMPAY)))
      KPMT=(PMT*100.)+.999999999999
      PMT=KPMT
      PMT=PMT/100.
  902 BRATE = ARATE*100.
C
C  PRINT TITLE INFORMATION
C
      WRITE (3,103) BAL,BRATE,NPEROD
      WRITE (3,107) PMT
      WRITE (3,104)
      WRITE (3,108) BAL
C
C  SET COUNTER FOR PAYMENT NUMBER
C
      N = 0
    2 N = N+1
C
C  COMPUTE INTEREST AS PERIODIC RATE X BALANCE
C
      XINT = RATE*BAL
C
C  ROUND INTEREST TO NEAREST CENT
C
      INT = (XINT + .005)*100.
      XINT = INT
      XINT = XINT/100.
C
C  COMPUTE AMOUNT TO PRINCIPLE
C
      PRIN = PMT-XINT
C
C  CHECK AMOUNT TO PRINCIPLE--IF NEGATIVE OR ZERO, PAYMENT IS TOO SMALL
C
      IF (PRIN) 3,3,4
C
C  INFORM OF TOO SMALL PAYMENT
C
    3 WRITE (3,106)
C
C  READ ANOTHER CASE
C
      GO TO 50
C
C  COMPUTE CURRENT BALANCE AS PREVIOUS BALANCE MINUS AMOUNT TO PRINCIPLE
C
    4 BAL = BAL-PRIN
C
C  CHECK BALANCE--IF NEGATIVE OR ZERO, LAST PAYMENT HAS BEEN REACHED
C
      KBAL=BAL*100.
      IF(KBAL)5,5,6
C
C  OUTPUT PAYMENT NUMBER, AMOUNT OF PAYMENT TO INTEREST, AMOUNT TO PRINCIPLE
C  AND BALANCE DUE
C
    6 WRITE (3,102) N,XINT,PRIN,BAL
      LCNT=LCNT+1
      IF(LCNT-42)2,700,700
  700 WRITE(3,110)
      LCNT=0
C
C  TRANSFER TO COMPUT NEXT PAYMENT
C
      GO TO 2
```

```
C
C   LAST PAYMENT COMPUTATION
C
    5 PRIN = PRIN + BAL
      BAL = 0.00
      WRITE (3,102) N,XINT,PRIN,BAL
      WRITE (3,105)
C
C   TRANSFER TO COMPUTE NEXT SCHEDULE
C
      GO TO 50
  999 CALL EXIT
  110 FORMAT(1H1)
  101 FORMAT(2F20.0, 3F10.0)
  102 FORMAT (1H ,15X,I4,7X,F10.2,5X,F10.2,4X,F10.2)
  103 FORMAT (1H ,29X,21HAMORTIZATION SCHEDULE/1H0,25X,F10.2,17H = AMOUN
     1T OF LOAN ,/1H0,9X,F9.4,35H PERCENT YEARLY INTEREST CONVERTED ,I2,
     216H TIMES EACH YEAR )
  104 FORMAT (1H0,15X,7HPAYMENT,12X,10HPAYMENT TO,14X,7HBALANCE/1H ,15X,
     16HNUMBER,7X,8HINTEREST,6X,9HPRINCIPLE,7X,7HOF LOAN/1H )
  105 FORMAT (1H1)
  106 FORMAT (21H0PAYMENT IS TOO SMALL /1H1)
  107 FORMAT (1H0,25X,F10.2,19H = PERIODIC PAYMENT)
  108 FORMAT (1H ,55X,F10.2)
 1025 FORMAT(20A4)
 1026 FORMAT(1H1/20A4)
      END
```

EXAMPLE

EXAMPLE A debt of $1200 is to be amortized in 12 monthly payments. The interest rate is 12% converted monthly. Prepare an amortization schedule.

SOLUTION

AMORTIZATION SCHEDULE

1200.00 = AMOUNT OF LOAN

12.0000 PERCENT YEARLY INTEREST CONVERTED 12 TIMES EACH YEAR

106.62 = PERIODIC PAYMENT

PAYMENT NUMBER	PAYMENT TO INTEREST	PRINCIPLE	BALANCE OF LOAN
			1200.00
1	12.00	94.62	1105.38
2	11.05	95.57	1009.81
3	10.10	96.52	913.29
4	9.13	97.49	815.80
5	8.16	98.46	717.34
6	7.17	99.45	617.89
7	6.18	100.44	517.45
8	5.17	101.45	416.00
9	4.16	102.46	313.54
10	3.14	103.48	210.06
11	2.10	104.52	105.54
12	1.06	105.54	0.00

Program for Compound Interest Tables

This program will produce a compound interest and annuity table for a range of rates and periods. This program is useful when a rate is not included in available tables. The amount of 1, the amount of 1 per period, and the present worth of 1 per period are given in modified scientific notation due to the range these numbers can span. The number following the D is the power to which 10 is raised. For example, D 02 is equivalent to 10^2. A computer entry of .1862625392D 02 equals 18.62625392 in conventional notation. As input, this program uses a starting rate, an ending rate, a rate increment, a starting period, an ending period, and a period increment.

```
C THIS PROGRAM WILL COMPUTE COMPOUND INTEREST AND ANNUITY TABLES
C
C FOR A RANGE OF RATES AND A RANGE OF PERIODS
C
      DIMENSION NYEAR(49),ANAME(20)
      DOUBLE PRECISION ANS(49,6),RTHIGH,RTSTRT,RTSTOP,A,ANMULT,RTINK,B
  100 READ (1,1025) ANAME
      WRITE (3,1026) ANAME
C
C INPUT STARTING RATE, ENDING RATE, RATE INCREMENT, STARTING PERIOD
C
C ENDING PERIOS, AND PERIOD INCREMENT
C
    2 READ (1,1000) RTSTRT, RTSTOP, RTINK, NSTRT, NSTOP, NINK
      IF(RTSTRT)999,999,600
  600 IF(RTINK)601,601,602
  601 RTINK=1.
  602 IF(NINK)603,603,3
  603 NINK=1
    3 A=NSTOP-NSTRT+NINK
      B=NINK*48
      NUMPGE=(A/B)+.999999999999
      RTHIGH=RTSTRT-RTINK
      M=48
    5 RTHIGH=RTHIGH+RTINK
      ANMULT=(1.+RTHIGH)**NINK
      DO 8 J=1, NUMPGE
      DO 4 I=1, M
      NYEAR(I)=0
      DO 4 K=1, 6
    4 ANS(1, K)=0.
      IF(NSTRT) 27, 27, 28
   27 ANS(1, 1)=1.
      GO TO 29
   28 ANS(1, 1)=(1.+RTHIGH)**((48*(J-1)*NINK)+NSTRT)
   29 ANS(1, 2)=(ANS(1, 1)-1.)/RTHIGH
      IF(ANS(1, 2)) 32, 32, 31
   32 ANS(1, 3)=99.9999999999
      GO TO 33
   31 ANS(1, 3)=1./ANS(1, 2)
   33 ANS(1, 4)=1./ANS(1, 1)
      ANS(1, 5)=(1.-ANS(1, 4))/RTHIGH
      IF(ANS(1, 5)) 35, 35, 34
   35 ANS(1, 6)=99.9999999999
      GO TO 36
   34 ANS(1, 6)=1./ANS(1, 5)
   36 DO 11 M=1, 48
      NYEAR(M)=(NSTRT-NINK)+(48*NINK*(J-1))+(M*NINK)
      IF(NSTOP-NYEAR(M)-NINK+1) 12, 12, 11
```

```
  11 CONTINUE
     M=48
  12 DO 13 N=2, M
     ANS(N, 1)=ANS(N-1, 1)*ANMULT
     ANS(N, 2)=(ANS(N, 1)-1.)/RTHIGH
     ANS(N, 3)=1./ANS(N, 2)
     ANS(N, 4)=1./ANS(N, 1)
     ANS(N, 5)=(1.-ANS(N, 4))/RTHIGH
  13 ANS(N, 6)=1./ANS(N, 5)
     WRITE (3,1001) RTHIGH
     WRITE (3,1007)
     DO 20 L=1, M
  20 WRITE (3,1002) NYEAR(L), (ANS(L, KK), KK=1, 6)
     WRITE (3,1003)
   8 CONTINUE
     IF(RTSTOP-RTHIGH-RTINK+.000000000001) 2, 2, 5
1000 FORMAT(2F20.0,F10.0,3I10)
1001 FORMAT(43X36HCOMPOUND INTEREST AND ANNUITY TABLES/4X2HI=, F15.10/4
    1X115H----------------------------------------------------------------
    2----------------------------------------------------/4X8HIPERIOD
    3I, 5X11HAMOUNT OF 1,4X1HI, 6X9HAMOUNT OF, 5X50HI  SINKING FUND I P
    4RESENT WORTH I  PRESENT WORTH I,4X7HPARTIAL, 4X1HI)
1002 FORMAT(4X1HI, I5, 2H I, 2(E19.10, 2H I), 2(F14.10, 2H I), E15.10,
    12H I, F14.10, 2H I)
1003 FORMAT(4X115H----------------------------------------------------------------
    1----------------------------------------------------/1H1
    2)
1007 FORMAT(4X1HI,6X1HI,20X1HI,4X12H1 PER PERIOD,4X1HI,15X1HI,6X4HOF 1,
    115X18HIOF 1 PER PERIOD I,4X7HPAYMENT, 4X1HI/4X115H----------------
    2----------------------------------------------------------------
    3-------------------------------)
1026 FORMAT(1H1,20A4)
1025 FORMAT(20A4)
 999 CALL EXIT
     END
```

EXAMPLE Produce a compound interest and annuity table for .6875%.

SOLUTION

COMPOUND INTEREST TABLE FOR .6875% FOR TWENTY PERIODS

COMPOUND INTEREST AND ANNUITY TABLES

I= 0.0068750000

IPERIOD	AMOUNT OF 1	AMOUNT OF 1 PER PERIOD	SINKING FUND	PRESENT WORTH OF 1	PRESENT WORTH OF 1 PER PERIOD	PARTIAL PAYMENT
1	0.1006875000E+01	0.1000000000E+01	1.0000000000	0.9931719429	1.9931719429E+00	1.0068750000
2	0.1013797266E+01	0.2006875000E+01	0.4982871380	0.9863905081	1.1979562451E+01	0.5051621380
3	0.1020767122E+01	0.3020672266E+01	0.3310521341	0.9796553774	1.2959217828E+01	0.3379271341
4	0.1027784896E+01	0.4041439387E+01	0.2474365948	0.9729662346	1.3932184063E+01	0.2543115948
5	0.1034850917E+01	0.5069224283E+01	0.1972688412	0.9663227656	1.4898506829E+01	0.2041438412
6	0.1041965517E+01	0.6104075200E+01	0.1638249804	0.9597246585	1.5858231487E+01	0.1706999804
7	0.1049129030E+01	0.7146040717E+01	0.1399376297	0.9531716038	1.6811403091E+01	0.1468126297
8	0.1056341792E+01	0.8195169747E+01	0.1220230979	0.9466632936	1.7758066384E+01	0.1288980979
9	0.1063604142E+01	0.9251511539E+01	0.1080904451	0.9401994226	1.8698265807E+01	0.1149654451
10	0.1070916420E+01	0.1031511568E+02	0.0969451076	0.9337796872	1.9632045494E+01	0.1038201076
11	0.1078278971E+01	0.1138603210E+02	0.0878269085	0.9274037862	1.1055944928E+02	0.0947019085
12	0.1085692139E+01	0.1246431107E+02	0.0802290631	0.9210714202	1.1480520700E+02	0.0871040631
13	0.1093156272E+01	0.1355000321E+02	0.0738007205	0.9147822919	1.1239530299E+02	0.0806757205
14	0.1100671721E+01	0.1464315948E+02	0.0682912729	0.9085361062	1.1330383910E+02	0.0751662729
15	0.1108238840E+01	0.1574383120E+02	0.0635169411	0.9023325698	1.1420617167E+02	0.0703919411
16	0.1115857982E+01	0.1685207004E+02	0.0593398910	0.8961713915	1.1510234306E+02	0.0662148910
17	0.1123529505E+01	0.1796792803E+02	0.0556547198	0.8900522820	1.1599239534E+02	0.0625297198
18	0.1131253771E+01	0.1909145753E+02	0.0523794476	0.8839749542	1.1687637030E+02	0.0592544476
19	0.1139031140E+01	0.2022271130E+02	0.0494493535	0.8779391227	1.1775430942E+02	0.0563243535
20	0.1146861979E+01	0.2136174244E+02	0.0468126607	0.8719445043	1.1862625392E+02	0.0536876607

Rate of Return on a Bond

This program uses an iterative scheme to compute the periodic rate of return on a bond given the present value (sale price), the number of coupons, the iterative tolerance, the flows, and the times at which the flows occur. This program assumes that the redemption price of the bond is included with the last coupon. The program can also be used to compute the periodic rate of return on a set of inflows and/or outflows at irregular intervals.

```
C PROGRAM TO CALCULATE INTERNAL RATE OF RETURN
      DIMENSION A(30),V(30),ANAME(20)
    1 READ (1,1000) ANAME
      WRITE (3,1001) ANAME
    2 RATE=1.1
C
C READ NUMBER OF FLOWS, PRESENT VALUE, ITERATION TOLERANCE
C
      READ (1,1002) NUMFLO, PV, TOL
      IF(NUMFLO)999,1,3
    3 IF(NUMFLO-30)5,5,4
    4 WRITE(3,1003)
      GO TO 999
C
C READ PERIOD AND ASSOCIATED FLOW
C
    5 READ (1,1004) (V(I),A(I),I=1,NUMFLO)
      IF(TOL)19,19,20
   19 TOL=.001
   20 TOL=TOL/2.
    6 CNPV=0.
      DO 7 N=1,NUMFLO
    7 CNPV=CNPV+A(N)*RATE**(-V(N))
      IF(ABS(PV-CNPV)-.1E-30)9,30,30
   30 IF(CNPV-PV)10,9,8
    8 ARATE=(2.*(RATE-1.))+1.
      IF(ABS(RATE-ARATE)-TOL)17,17,11
   11 RATE=ARATE
      GO TO 6
   10 ARATE=((RATE-1.)/2.)+1.
   16 ANINT=ABS(RATE-ARATE)
      IF(ANINT-TOL)17,17,12
   12 RATE=ARATE
      CNPV=0.
      DO 13 N=1,NUMFLO
   13 CNPV=CNPV+A(N)*RATE**(-V(N))
      IF(ABS(PV-CNPV)-.1E-30)9,31,31
   31 IF(CNPV-PV)15,9,14
   14 ARATE=RATE+(ANINT/2.)
      GO TO 16
   15 ARATE=RATE-(ANINT/2.)
      GO TO 16
   17 RATE=ARATE
      CNPV=0.
      DO 18 N=1,NUMFLO
   18 CNPV=CNPV+A(N)*RATE**(-V(N))
    9 TOL=2.*TOL
      RATE=RATE-1.
      WRITE (3,1005) PV,TOL,(V(N),A(N),N=1,NUMFLO)
      WRITE (3,1006) RATE,RATE,CNPV
      GO TO 2
  999 CALL EXIT
 1000 FORMAT(20A4)
 1001 FORMAT(1H1,20A4)
```

```
1002 FORMAT(I2,2F14.2)
1003 FORMAT(29H1MAXIMUM NUMBER OF FLOWS= 30.)
1004 FORMAT(6F12.0)
1005 FORMAT(1H0,26X14HPRESENT VALUE=,     F14.2/1H0,28X10HTOLERANCE=,F14
    1.8/1H0,31X16HPERIOD      FLOW/(32XF4.0,F14.2))
1006 FORMAT(1H0,24X25HRATE OF RETURN PER PERIOD,
    9                          F14.8/1H0,5X40HCALCULATED NET PRESENT
    1 VALUE, USING R OF,F14.8,2H =,F14.2/1H1)
    END
```

EXAMPLE A $1000, 4% bond with semiannual coupons is sold for $980 on June 1, 1973. The bond matures on December 1, 1980. Find the periodic yield rate.

SOLUTION

```
              PRESENT VALUE=          980.00

                 TOLERANCE=      0.00001000

                 PERIOD        FLOW
                    1.          20.00
                    2.          20.00
                    3.          20.00
                    4.          20.00
                    5.          20.00
                    6.          20.00
                    7.          20.00
                    8.          20.00
                    9.          20.00
                   10.          20.00
                   11.          20.00
                   12.          20.00
                   13.          20.00
                   14.          20.00
                   15.        1020.00

          RATE OF RETURN PER PERIOD     0.02157354

 CALCULATED NET PRESENT VALUE, USING R OF     0.02157354 =        980.02
```

Amortization Program in Basic Language

To show the use of another computer language, the amortization program given earlier in this section has been rewritten in BASIC-PLUS. This program was designed for a PDP-11 system and may require some modification for other systems. At the end of the program is the output for the same example given with the FORTRAN program.

```
10 REM THIS PROGRAM PRODUCES AN AMORTIZATION SCHEDULE FOR THE FOLLOWING
20 REM TWO CASES ******************************
30 REM INPUT BALANCE, RATE, PAYMENT, AND NUMBER OF CONVERSIONS PER YEAR
40 REM INPUT BALANCE,RATE,CONVERSIONS PER YEAR, AND DURATION
50 PRINT
60 REM
```

```
70 REM   INPUT BALANCE, RATE, PAYMENT, AND NUMBER OF PERIODS, DURATION OF LOAN
80 REM
90 READ B,R1,P,P1,D
100 LET N = INT (P1)
110 LET L = Ø
120 IF B<Ø THEN 9999
140 REM
150 REM   FIND THE PERIODIC INTEREST RATE
160 REM
170 LET R=R1/P1
180 IF P> Ø THEN 270
190 REM
200 REM   CONVERT DECIMAL RATE TO PERCENTAGE RATE
210 REM
220 LET N1=P1*D
230 LET P=B*(R/(1-1/((1+R)**N1)))
240 LET P=(INT((P*100)+.999999999999))/100
270 LET B1=R1*100
280 REM
290 REM PRINT TITLE INFORMATION
300 REM
310 PRINT TAB(29);"AMORTIZATION SCHEDULE"
320 PRINT
325 LET M$=SPACE$(23)+'#,###,###.## = AMOUNT OF LOAN'
330 PRINT USING M$,B
340 PRINT
345 LET M$='####.#### PERCENT YEARLY INTEREST CONVERTED ## TIMES EACH YEAR'
347 LET M$=SPACE$(9)+M$
350 PRINT USING M$,B1,N
360 PRINT
365 LET M$=SPACE$(23)+'#,###,###.## = PERIODIC PAYMENT'
370 PRINT USING M$,P
380 PRINT
390 PRINT TAB (15);"PAYMENT";TAB(34);"PAYMENT TO";TAB(58);"BALANCE"
400 PRINT TAB(15);"NUMBER";TAB(28);"INTEREST";TAB(42);"PRINCIPLE";
405 PRINT TAB(53);"OF LOAN"
410 PRINT
420 LET M$=SPACE$(53)+"#,###,###.##"
430 PRINT USING M$,B
440 REM
450 REM SET COUNTER FOR PAYMENT NUMBER
460 REM
470 LET N1=Ø
480 LET N1=N1+1
490 REM
500 REM   COMPUTE INTEREST AS PERIODIC RATE X BALANCE
510 REM
520 LET X=R*B
530 REM
540 REM   ROUND INTEREST TO NEAREST CENT
550 REM
560 LET X=(INT((X+.005)*100))/100
570 REM
580 REM   COMPUTE AMOUNT TO PRINCIPLE
590 REM
600 LET P2=P-X
610 REM
620 REM   CHECK AMOUNT TO PRINCIPLE - IF NEGATIVE OR ZERO, PAYMENT TOO SMALL
630 REM
640 IF P2>Ø THEN 750
650 REM
660 REM   INFORM OF TOO SMALL PAYMENT
670 REM
680 PRINT 'PAYMENT IS TOO SMALL'
690 REM
700 REM   GO READ ANOTHER CASE
710 REM
720 GOTO 90
730 REM
740 REM   COMPUTE CURRENT BALANCE = PREVIOUS BALANCE - PRINCIPLE
750 REM
760 LET B=B-P2
770 REM
780 REM   CHECK BALANCE - IF NEGATIVE OR ZERO, LAST PAYMENT HAS BEEN REACHED
790 REM
800 LET K=INT(B*100)
810 IF K<=Ø THEN 1040
820 REM
```

```
830 REM  OUTPUT PAYMENT NUMBER, AMOUNT OF PAYMENT TO INTEREST,
840 REM  AMOUNT TO PRINCIPLE, AND AMOUNT DUE
850 REM
860 LET M$=SPACE$(15)+"####     #,###,###.##   #,###,###.##  #,###,###.##"
870 PRINT USING M$,N1,X,P2,B
880 REM
890 REM  TRANSFER TO COMPUTE NEXT PAYMENT
900 REM
1000 GO TO 480
1010 REM
1020 REM  LAST PAYMENT COMPUTATION
1030 REM
1040 LET P2=P2+B
1050 LET B=0
1060 PRINT USING M$,N1,X,P2,B
1070 PRINT
1080 PRINT
1090 PRINT
1100 REM
1110 REM  TRANSFER TO COMPUTE NEXT SCHEDULE
1120 REM
1130 GO TO 90
7970 REM
7980 REM  ENTER DATA STARTING AT LINE 8000
7990 REM
8000 DATA 1200,.12,0,12,1
9985 REM
9990 REM  DUMMY DATA TO END PROGRAM
9992 REM
9995 DATA -1,0,0,0,0
9999 END
```

AMORTIZATION SCHEDULE

1,200.00 = AMOUNT OF LOAN

12.0000 PERCENT YEARLY INTEREST CONVERTED 12 TIMES EACH YEAR

106.62 = PERIODIC PAYMENT

PAYMENT NUMBER	PAYMENT TO INTEREST	PRINCIPLE	BALANCE OF LOAN
			1,200.00
1	12.00	94.62	1,105.38
2	11.05	95.57	1,009.81
3	10.10	96.52	913.29
4	9.13	97.49	315.80
5	8.16	98.46	717.34
6	7.17	99.45	617.89
7	6.18	100.44	517.45
8	5.17	101.45	416.00
9	4.16	102.46	313.54
10	3.14	103.48	210.06
11	2.10	104.52	105.54
12	1.06	105.54	0.00

Ready

Index

Mathematical Tables

Index of Tables

TABLE 1 THE NUMBER OF EACH DAY OF THE YEAR

For leap years the number of the day after February 28 is one greater than that given in the table.

DAY OF MONTH	Jan.	Feb.	Mar.	April	May	June	July	Aug.	Sept.	Oct.	Nov.	Dec.	DAY OF MONTH
1	1	32	60	91	121	152	182	213	244	274	305	335	1
2	2	33	61	92	122	153	183	214	245	275	306	336	2
3	3	34	62	93	123	154	184	215	246	276	307	337	3
4	4	35	63	94	124	155	185	216	247	277	308	338	4
5	5	36	64	95	125	156	186	217	248	278	309	339	5
6	6	37	65	96	126	157	187	218	249	279	310	340	6
7	7	38	66	97	127	158	188	219	250	280	311	341	7
8	8	39	67	98	128	159	189	220	251	281	312	342	8
9	9	40	68	99	129	160	190	221	252	282	313	343	9
10	10	41	69	100	130	161	191	222	253	283	314	344	10
11	11	42	70	101	131	162	192	223	254	284	315	345	11
12	12	43	71	102	132	163	193	224	255	285	316	346	12
13	13	44	72	103	133	164	194	225	256	286	317	347	13
14	14	45	73	104	134	165	195	226	257	287	318	348	14
15	15	46	74	105	135	166	196	227	258	288	319	349	15
16	16	47	75	106	136	167	197	228	259	289	320	350	16
17	17	48	76	107	137	168	198	229	260	290	321	351	17
18	18	49	77	108	138	169	199	230	261	291	322	352	18
19	19	50	78	109	139	170	200	231	262	292	323	353	19
20	20	51	79	110	140	171	201	232	263	293	324	354	20
21	21	52	80	111	141	172	202	233	264	294	325	355	21
22	22	53	81	112	142	173	203	234	265	295	326	356	22
23	23	54	82	113	143	174	204	235	266	296	327	357	23
24	24	55	83	114	144	175	205	236	267	297	328	358	24
25	25	56	84	115	145	176	206	237	268	298	329	359	25
26	26	57	85	116	146	177	207	238	269	299	330	360	26
27	27	58	86	117	147	178	208	239	270	300	331	361	27
28	28	59	87	118	148	179	209	240	271	301	332	362	28
29	29		88	119	149	180	210	241	272	302	333	363	29
30	30		89	120	150	181	211	242	273	303	334	364	30
31	31		90		151		212	243		304		365	31

TABLE 2 COMPOUND INTEREST AND ANNUITY TABLES

A Word about the Marginal Index

Down the side margin of each page runs an index designed to save much of the adjustment of rates that makes the ordinary table so confusing to the novice. It will help you.

All figures in the tables are calculated at some *rate per period.* This period may be anything from a day to five years or more, depending on how often the interest is calculated. However, you usually have the *annual* rate quoted and that is what you can look up in the marginal index. Suppose that a bank pays 2% per annum compounded *semi-annually* (that is, adds interest each half year). Use the marginal index in the part where "SEMIANNUALLY" appears in capital letters, and find "2%" in that part. You have the table you want. Actually you realize that 2% per annum compounded semiannually means 1% per period where each period is a half year — but you do not need to make this adjustment in advance, simply use the index.

Caution: The number of periods in the table is not necessarily the number of years. It is the number of whatever unit you are using. When you use the "SEMIANNUALLY" index, it is the number of half-years. If you use the "MONTHLY" index, it is the number of months.

The marginal index is there to help you. Use it.

What the Tables Are in a Few Simple Words

1. *Amount of 1.* If you put a dollar in the bank and leave it there, it grows. This table (left-hand column on left-hand page) shows to what sum it does grow. If the rate is 2% to be figured each year, then at the end of 1 year you have $1.02 in the bank. The second year this amount grows to 1.02 × 1.02, or 1.0404. The third year this 1.0404 becomes 1.0404 × 1.02 or 1.061208. Observe that each result at the 2% rate can be obtained by multiplying the preceding result by 1.02, which is the ratio of increase at 2%. The table at any interest rate can be constructed by successive multiplication by its ratio of increase. There is nothing complicated in that concept.
2. *Amount of 1 per period.* If you do not just put a dollar in the bank and leave it there, but at periodic intervals you go back and deposit

another dollar each time, this table (middle column on left-hand page) shows what happens and how your money grows. Note that this table assumes that the deposit is made at the *end* of each period. The figure for one period is 1, meaning that $1 has just been deposited at the end of the period and has not had a chance to grow. At the end of the second period, this first dollar has grown (at 2%) to $1.02 and the second $1 has just been deposited, so the table shows $2.02.

Observe that this is just like the table for compound amount (left-hand column) in that the deposit of $1 is the basic event, and each $1 deposited starts to grow as shown in that table; but here we have a whole series of $1 deposits all growing at the same time, and each deposit successively has been in the bank for one more period than the next deposit, right down to the latest deposit. Therefore this table consists merely of adding all the items in the first table (left-hand column) down to the point desired. That feature of payment at the *end* of the period must be watched because it throws us out by one period. If you want to check the entry for five periods, you could add up the first four entries in the left-hand column and then add 1 for the final deposit that has just been made. You end up with the tabulated result.

This explanation is only here to show you that this table is just the combined total of a lot of $1 deposits, each growing for a different length of time in the manner shown in the left-hand column. Perhaps this concept is a little complicated, but there certainly is no dark mystery involved.

3. *Sinking fund.* This table (right-hand column on left-hand page) shows how much money you must deposit each period in order to have $1 when you need it in the future. Each result is obtained merely by dividing 1 by the entry in the middle column beside it. For if $1 per period will grow to $25, then how much will be needed to grow to $1? Obviously, $1 divided by $25, or 4¢. You will not find any such simple unit figures in the tables but the reasoning is the same. It is entirely a matter of simple proportion. To put it concisely, each entry in this table is the *reciprocal* of the corresponding entry in the column to its left.

4. *Present worth of 1.* If you want to have $1 in the bank at some time in the future, this table (left-hand column of right-hand page) shows you how much you must deposit today. Obviously, since the table for "Amount of 1" shows how money grows when left in the bank, this table is directly related to it. In other words, if $1 left in

the bank will grow to $5, how much money will be needed to grow to $1? Obviously one-fifth of $1, or 20¢. Again, you will not find such simple figures in even units in the table, but it is just a matter of simple proportion. To put it concisely, each entry in this table is the *reciprocal* of the corresponding entry in the table for the amount of 1.

5. *Present worth of 1 per period.* We just saw that the preceding table showed us how much money we must put in the bank today to be able to draw out $1 at some specified date in the future. Now suppose that we want to draw out $1, not on some one single occasion in the future, but $1 for each periodic interval for some length of time into the future. That is what is shown in this table.

Obviously, since we are going to draw $1 at each date, we could use the preceding table for each of them, and add the entries. In fact, that is what the table is. If you will add the first five entries in the "Present worth of 1" table you will get the result shown for 5 periods in the "Present worth of 1 per period" table. To express it concisely, each entry is the cumulative total of the figures in the column to the left of it.

6. *Partial payment table.* The preceding table shows what amount you must have today in order to get periodic payments of $1 in the future; but if you have $1 today, what size periodic payments will it get you in the future? Again, it is a matter of simple proportion. To put it concisely, each entry is the *reciprocal* of the corresponding entry in the column to the left of it. Usually, as the title indicates, this table will be used to show what you will have to pay at each period in the future if you borrow $1 today, but the explanation still stands.

Another basic relationship should be understood. In the "Sinking fund" table we are concerned with the sum that must be set aside to grow to $1; but in this "Partial payment" table we are concerned with paying off a loan of $1, which is the same thing as building up a sinking fund to pay the loan except that it includes the interest on the loan of $1. Therefore if you have the entry in the "Sinking fund" table and add interest (always the *i* at the top of the page), you will get the corresponding entry in the "Partial payment" table.

P E R I O D S	AMOUNT OF 1 *How $1 left at compound interest will grow.*	AMOUNT OF 1 PER PERIOD *How $1 deposited periodically will grow.*	SINKING FUND *Periodic deposit that will grow to $1 at future date.*
1	1.005 000 0000	1.000 000 0000	1.000 000 0000
2	1.010 025 0000	2.005 000 0000	.498 753 1172
3	1.015 075 1250	3.015 025 0000	.331 672 2084
4	1.020 150 5006	4.030 100 1250	.248 132 7930
5	1.025 251 2531	5.050 250 6256	.198 009 9750
6	1.030 377 5094	6.075 501 8788	.164 595 4556
7	1.035 529 3969	7.105 879 3881	;140 728 5355
8	1.040 707 0439	8.141 408 7851	.122 828 8649
9	1.045 910 5791	9.182. 115 8290	.108 907 3606
10	1.051 140 1320	10.228 026 4082	.097 770 5727
11	1.056 395 8327	11.279 166 5402	.088 659 0331
12	1.061 677 8119	12.335 562 3729	.081 066 4297
13	1.066 986 2009	13.397 240 1848	.074 642 2387
14	1.072 321 1319	14.464 226 3857	.069 136 0860
15	1.077 682 7376	15.536 547 5176	.064 364 3640
16	1.083 071 1513	16.614 230 2552	.060 189 3669
17	1.088 486 5070	17.697 301 4065	.056 505 7902
18	1.093 928 9396	18.785 787 9135	.053 231 7305
19	1.099 398 5843	19.879 716 8531	.050 302 5273
20	1.104 895 5772	20.979 115 4373	.047 666 4520
21	1.110 420 0551	22.084 011 0145	.045 281 6293
22	1.115 972 1553	23.194 431 0696	.043 113 7973
23	1.121 552 0161	24.310 403 2250	.041 134 6530
24	1.127 159 7762	25.431 955 2411	.039 320 6103
25	1.132 795 5751	26.559 115 0173	.037 651 8570
26	1.138 459 5530	27.691 910 5924	.036 111 6289
27	1.144 151 8507	28.830 370 1453	.034 685 6456
28	1.149 872 6100	29.974 521 9961	.033 361 6663
29	1.155 621 9730	31.124 394 6060	.032 129 1390
30	1.161 400 0829	32.280 016 5791	.030 978 9184
31	1.167 207 0833	33.441 416 6620	.029 903 0394
32	1.173 043 1187	34.608 623 7453	.028 894 5324
33	1.178 908 3343	35.781 666 8640	.027 947 2727
34	1.184 802 8760	36.960 575 1983	.027 055 8560
35	1.190 726 8904	38.145 378 0743	.026 215 4958
36	1.196 680 5248	39.336 104 9647	.025 421 9375
37	1.202 663 9274	40.532 785 4895	.024 671 3861
38	1.208 677 2471	41.735 449 4170	.023 960 4464
39	1.214 720 6333	42.944 126 6640	.023 286 0714
40	1.220 794 2365	44.158 847 2974	.022 645 5186
41	1.226 898 2077	45.379 641 5338	.022 036 3133
42	1.233 032 6987	46.606 539 7415	.021 456 2163
43	1.239 197 8622	47.839 572 4402	.020 903 1969
44	1.245 393 8515	49.078 770 3024	.020 375 4086
45	1.251 620 8208	50.324 164 1539	.019 871 1696
46	1.257 878 9249	51.575 784 9747	.019 388 9439
47	1.264 168 3195	52.833 663 8996	.018 927 3264
48	1.270 489 1611	54.097 832 2191	.018 485 0290
49	1.276 841 6069	55.368 321 3802	.018 060 8690
50	1.283 225 8149	56.645 162 9871	.017 653 7580
51	1.289 641 9440	57.928 388 8020	.017 262 6931
52	1.296 090 1537	59.218 030 7460	.016 886 7486
53	1.302 570 6045	60.514 120 8997	.016 525 0686
54	1.309 083 4575	61.816 691 5042	.016 176 8606
55	1.315 628 8748	63.125 774 9618	.015 841 3897
56	1.322 207 0192	64.441 403 8366	.015 517 9735
57	1.328 818 0543	65.763 610 8558	.015 205 9777
58	1.335 462 1446	67.092 428 9100	.014 904 8114
59	1.342 139 4553	68.427 891 0546	.014 613 9240
60	1.348 850 1525	69.770 030 5099	.014 332 8015
n	$s=(1+i)^n$	$s_{\overline{n}|}=\dfrac{(1+i)^n-1}{i}$	$\dfrac{1}{s_{\overline{n}|}}=\dfrac{i}{(1+i)^n-1}$

.005

per period

ANNUALLY
If compounded annually nominal annual rate is

½%

SEMIANNUALLY
If compounded semiannually nominal annual rate is

1%

QUARTERLY
If compounded quarterly nominal annual rate is

2%

MONTHLY
If compounded monthly nominal annual rate is

6%

$i = .005$
$j_{(2)} = .01$
$j_{(4)} = .02$
$j_{(12)} = .06$

PRESENT WORTH OF 1 *What $1 due in the future is worth today.*	PRESENT WORTH OF 1 PER PERIOD *What $1 payable periodically is worth today.*	PARTIAL PAYMENT *Annuity worth $1 today.* *Periodic payment necessary to pay off a loan of $1.*	PERIODS	RATE $\frac{1}{2}\%$
.995 024 8756	.995 024 8756	1.005 000 0000	1	
.990 074 5031	1.985 099 3787	.503 753 1172	2	
.985 148 7593	2.970 248 1380	.336 672 2084	3	.005
.980 247 5217	3.950 495 6597	.253 132 7930	4	
.975 370 6684	4.925 866 3281	.203 009 9750	5	*per period*
.970 518 0780	5.896 384 4061	.169 595 4556	6	
.965 689 6298	6.862 074 0359	.145 728 5355	7	
.960 885 2038	7.822 959 2397	.127 828 8649	8	
.956 104 6804	8.779 063 9201	.113 907 3606	9	
.951 347 9407	9.730 411 8608	.102 770 5727	10	
.946 614 8664	10.677 026 7272	.093 659 0331	11	
.941 905 3397	11.618 932 0668	.086 066 4297	12	
.937 219 2434	12.556 151 3103	.079 642 2387	13	
.932 556 4611	13.488 707 7714	.074 136 0860	14	
.927 916 8768	14.416 624 6482	.069 364 3640	15	
.923 300 3749	15.339 925 0231	.065 189 3669	16	
.918 706 8407	16.258 631 8637	.061 505 7902	17	
.914 136 1599	17.172 768 0236	.058 231 7305	18	
.909 588 2188	18.082 356 2424	.055 302 5273	19	
.905 062 9043	18.987 419 1467	.052 666 4520	20	
.900 560 1037	19.887 979 2504	.050 281 6293	21	ANNUALLY If compounded *annually* nominal annual rate is $\frac{1}{2}\%$
.896 079 7052	20.784 058 9556	.048 113 7973	22	
.891 621 5972	21.675 680 5529	.046 134 6530	23	
.887 185 6689	22.562 866 2218	.044 320 6103	24	
.882 771 8098	23.445 638 0316	.042 651 8570	25	
.878 379 9103	24.324 017 9419	.041 111 6289	26	
.874 009 8610	25.198 027 8029	.039 685 6456	27	
.869 661 5532	26.067 689 3561	.038 361 6663	28	
.865 334 8788	26.933 024 2349	.037 129 1390	29	
.861 029 7302	27.794 053 9651	.035 978 9184	30	
.856 746 0002	28.650 799 9653	.034 903 0394	31	SEMIANNUALLY If compounded *semiannually* nominal annual rate is 1%
.852 483 5823	29.503 283 5475	.033 894 5324	32	
.848 242 3704	30.351 525 9179	.032 947 2727	33	
.844 022 2591	31.195 548 1771	.032 055 8560	34	
.839 823 1434	32.035 371 3205	.031 215 4958	35	
.835 644 9188	32.871 016 2393	.030 421 9375	36	
.831 487 4814	33.702 503 7207	.029 671 3861	37	
.827 350 7278	34.529 854 4484	.028 960 4464	38	
.823 234 5550	35.353 089 0034	.028 286 0714	39	
.819 138 8607	36.172 227 8641	.027 645 5186	40	
.815 063 5430	36.987 291 4070	.027 036 3133	41	QUARTERLY If compounded *quarterly* nominal annual rate is 2%
.811 008 5005	37.798 299 9075	.026 456 2163	42	
.806 973 6323	38.605 273 5398	.025 903 1969	43	
.802 958 8381	39.408 232 3779	.025 375 4086	44	
.798 964 0180	40.207 196 3959	.024 871 1696	45	
.794 989 0727	41.002 185 4686	.024 388 9439	46	
.791 033 9031	41.793 219 3717	.023 927 3264	47	
.787 098 4111	42.580 317 7828	.023 485 0290	48	
.783 182 4986	43.363 500 2814	.023 060 8690	49	
.779 286 0683	44.142 786 3497	.022 653 7580	50	
.775 409 0231	44.918 195 3728	.022 262 6931	51	MONTHLY If compounded *monthly* nominal annual rate is 6%
.771 551 2668	45.689 746 6396	.021 886 7486	52	
.767 712 7033	46.457 459 3429	.021 525 0686	53	
.763 893 2371	47.221 352 5800	.021 176 8606	54	
.760 092 7732	47.981 445 3532	.020 841 3897	55	
.756 311 2171	48.737 756 5704	.020 517 9735	56	
.752 548 4748	49.490 305 0452	.020 205 9777	57	
.748 804 4525	50.239 109 4977	.019 904 8114	58	$i = .005$
.745 079 0572	50.984 188 5549	.019 613 9240	59	$j_{(2)} = .01$ $j_{(4)} = .02$
.741 372 1962	51.725 560 7511	.019 332 8015	60	$j_{(12)} = .06$
$v^n = \dfrac{1}{(1+i)^n}$	$a_{\overline{n}|} = \dfrac{1-v^n}{i}$	$\dfrac{1}{a_{\overline{n}|}} = \dfrac{i}{1-v^n}$	**n**	

RATE **7/12%**	P E R I O D S	AMOUNT OF 1 *How $1 left at compound interest will grow.*	AMOUNT OF 1 PER PERIOD *How $1 deposited periodically will grow.*	SINKING FUND *Periodic deposit that will grow to $1 at future date.*
	1	1.005 833 3333	1.000 000 0000	1.000 000 0000
	2	1.011 700 6944	2.005 833 3333	.498 545 9078
.00583333	3	1.017 602 2818	3.017 534 0278	.331 396 4286
per period	4	1.023 538 2951	4.035 136 3096	.247 823 1027
	5	1.029 508 9352	5.058 674 6047	.197 680 2380
	6	1.035 514 4040	6.088 183 5399	.164 252 6040
	7	1.041 554 9047	7.123 697 9439	.140 376 5303
	8	1.047 630 6416	8.165 252 8486	.122 470 1817
	9	1.053 741 8204	9.212 883 4902	.108 543 6499
	10	1.059 888 6476	10.266 625 3106	.097 402 9898
	11	1.066 071 3314	11.326 513 9582	.088 288 4181
	12	1.072 290 0809	12.392 585 2896	.080 693 4128
	13	1.078 545 1063	13.464 875 3705	.074 267 3046
	14	1.084 836 6194	14.543 420 4768	.068 759 6155
	15	1.091 164 8331	15.628 257 0963	.063 986 6617
	16	1.097 529 9613	16.719 421 9293	.059 810 6803
	17	1.103 932 2194	17.816 951 8906	.056 126 3232
	18	1.110 371 8240	18.920 884 1100	.052 851 6529
	19	1.116 848 9929	20.031 255 9339	.049 921 9821
	20	1.123 363 9454	21.148 104 9269	.047 285 5607
ANNUALLY *If compounded annually nominal annual rate is* **7/12%**	21	1.129 916 9018	22.271 468 8723	.044 900 4960
	22	1.136 508 0837	23.401 385 7740	.042 732 5121
	23	1.143 137 7142	24.537 893 8577	.040 753 2939
	24	1.149 806 0175	25.681 031 5719	.038 939 2458
	25	1.156 513 2193	26.830 837 5894	.037 270 5472
	26	1.163 259 5464	27.987 350 8087	.035 730 4272
	27	1.170 045 2271	29.150 610 3550	.034 304 5990
	28	1.176 870 4909	30.320 655 5821	.032 980 8172
	29	1.183 735 5688	31.497 526 0730	.031 748 5252
	30	1.190 640 6929	32.681 261 6418	.030 598 5739
SEMIANNUALLY *If compounded semiannually nominal annual rate is* **1 1/6%**	31	1.197 586 0970	33.871 902 3347	.029 522 9949
	32	1.204 572 0159	35.069 488 4316	.028 514 8157
	33	1.211 598 6859	36.274 060 4475	.027 567 9091
	34	1.218 666 3449	37.485 659 1334	.026 676 8685
	35	1.225 775 2320	38.704 325 4784	.025 836 9055
	36	1.232 925 5875	39.930 100 7103	.025 043 7635
	37	1.240 117 6534	41.163 026 2978	.024 293 6463
	38	1.247 351 6730	42.403 143 9512	.023 583 1570
	39	1.254 627 8911	43.650 495 6243	.022 909 2473
	40	1.261 946 5538	44.905 123 5154	.022 269 1738
QUARTERLY *If compounded quarterly nominal annual rate is* **2 1/3%**	41	1.269 307 9087	46.167 070 0692	.021 660 4606
	42	1.276 712 2049	47.436 377 9780	.021 080 8675
	43	1.284 159 6927	48.713 090 1829	.020 528 3630
	44	1.291 650 6243	49.997 249 8756	.020 001 1001
	45	1.299 185 2529	51.288 900 4999	.019 497 3959
	46	1.306 763 8336	52.588 085 7528	.019 015 7140
	47	1.314 386 6226	53.894 849 5863	.018 554 6487
	48	1.322 053 8779	55.209 236 2089	.018 112 9113
	49	1.329 765 8588	56.531 290 0868	.017 689 3186
	50	1.337 522 8263	57.861 055 9456	.017 282 7817
MONTHLY *If compounded monthly nominal annual rate is* **7%**	51	1.345 325 0428	59.198 578 7720	.016 892 2974
	52	1.353 172 7723	60.543 903 8148	.016 516 9306
	53	1.361 066 2801	61.897 076 5871	.016 155 8519
	54	1.369 005 8334	63.258 142 8672	.015 808 2415
	55	1.376 991 7008	64.627 148 7006	.015 473 3733
	56	1.385 024 1523	66.004 140 4013	.015 150 5647
	57	1.393 103 4599	67.389 164 5537	.014 839 1808
	58	1.401 229 8967	68.782 268 0136	.014 538 6308
	59	1.409 403 7378	70.183 497 9103	.014 248 3636
	60	1.417 625 2596	71.592 901 6481	.013 967 8652
i = .00583333 $j_{(2)}$ = .01166666 $j_{(4)}$ = .02333333 $j_{(12)}$ = .07	**n**	$s=(1+i)^n$	$s_{\overline{n}|}=\dfrac{(1+i)^n-1}{i}$	$\dfrac{1}{s_{\overline{n}|}}=\dfrac{i}{(1+i)^n-1}$

PRESENT WORTH OF 1	PRESENT WORTH OF 1 PER PERIOD	PARTIAL PAYMENT	P E R I O D S	RATE
What $1 due in the future is worth today.	What $1 payable periodically is worth today.	Annuity worth $1 today. Periodic payment necessary to pay off a loan of $1.		7/12%

.994 200 4971	.994 200 4971	1.005 833 3333	1	
.988 434 6284	1.982 635 1255	.504 379 2411	2	
.982 702 1989	2.965 337 3245	.337 229 7619	3	.00583333
.977 003 0147	3.942 340 3392	.253 656 4360	4	per period
.971 336 8829	4.913 677 2220	.203 513 5714	5	
.965 703 6118	5.879 380 8338	.170 085 9373	6	
.960 103 0109	6.839 483 8447	.146 209 8636	7	
.954 534 8907	7.794 018 7355	.128 303 5150	8	
.948 999 0628	8.743 017 7983	.114 376 9832	9	
.943 495 3400	9.686 513 1383	.103 236 3231	10	
.938 023 5361	10.624 536 6744	.094 121 7514	11	
.932 583 4658	11.557 120 1402	.086 526 7461	12	
.927 174 9453	12.484 295 0856	.080 100 6379	13	
.921 797 7916	13.406 092 8771	.074 592 9488	14	
.916 451 8226	14.322 544 6997	.069 819 9950	15	
.911 136 8576	15.233 681 5573	.065 644 0136	16	
.905 852 7167	16.139 534 2740	.061 959 6565	17	
.900 599 2213	17.040 133 4953	.058 684 9863	18	
.895 376 1935	17.935 509 6888	.055 755 3154	19	
.890 183 4567	18.825 693 1454	.053 118 8941	20	
.885 020 8351	19.710 713 9805	.050 733 8294	21	ANNUALLY
.879 888 1542	20.590 602 1348	.048 565 8454	22	If compounded
.874 785 2403	21.465 387 3751	.046 586 6272	23	annually nominal annual rate is
.869 711 9208	22.335 099 2958	.044 772 5791	24	
.864 668 0240	23.199 767 3198	.043 103 8806	25	7/12%
.859 653 3793	24.059 420 6991	.041 563 7605	26	
.854 667 8170	24.914 088 5161	.040 137 9324	27	
.849 711 1685	25.763 799 6846	.038 814 1506	28	
.844 783 2661	26.608 582 9507	.037 581 8285	29	
.839 883 9431	27.448 466 8938	.036 431 9072	30	SEMIANNUALLY
.835 013 0338	28.283 479 9276	.035 356 3282	31	If compounded
.830 170 3732	29.113 650 3008	.034 348 1491	32	semiannually nominal annual rate is
.825 355 7978	29.939 006 0986	.033 401 2424	33	
.820 569 1444	30.759 575 2430	.032 510 2019	34	
.815 810 2513	31.575 385 4943	.031 670 2388	35	1 1/6 %
.811 078 9574	32.386 464 4516	.030 877 0969	36	
.806 375 1026	33.192 839 5542	.030 126 9796	37	
.801 698 5279	33.994 538 0821	.029 416 4903	38	
.797 049 0749	34.791 587 1570	.028 742 5807	39	
.792 426 5865	35.584 013 7435	.028 102 5071	40	QUARTERLY
.787 830 9062	36.371 844 6497	.027 493 7939	41	If compounded
.783 261 8786	37.155 106 5283	.026 914 2009	42	quarterly nominal annual rate is
.778 719 3490	37.933 825 8773	.026 361 6964	43	
.774 203 1639	38.708 029 0413	.025 834 4334	44	
.769 713 1704	39.477 742 2117	.025 330 7293	45	2 1/3 %
.765 249 2167	40.242 991 4284	.024 849 0474	46	
.760 811 1516	41.003 802 5800	.024 387 9820	47	
.756 398 8251	41.760 201 4051	.023 946 2447	48	
.752 012 0880	42.512 213 4931	.023 522 6519	49	
.747 650 7917	43.259 864 2848	.023 116 1151	50	MONTHLY
.743 314 7887	44.003 179 0735	.022 725 6308	51	If compounded
.739 003 9325	44.742 183 0060	.022 350 2729	52	monthly nominal annual rate is
.734 718 0770	45.476 901 0830	.021 989 1852	53	
.730 457 0774	46.207 358 1604	.021 641 5748	54	
.726 220 7895	46.933 578 9498	.021 306 7067	55	7%
.722 009 0699	47.655 588 0197	.020 983 8980	56	
.717 821 7762	48.373 409 7959	.020 672 5142	57	
.713 658 7667	49.087 068 5626	.020 371 9641	58	$i = .00583333$
.709 519 9006	49.796 588 4633	.020 081 6970	59	$j^{(2)} = .01166666$
.705 405 0379	50.501 993 5012	.019 801 1985	60	$j^{(4)} = .02333333$

$v^n = \dfrac{1}{(1+i)^n}$	$a_{\overline{n}\rceil} = \dfrac{1-v^n}{i}$	$\dfrac{1}{a_{\overline{n}\rceil}} = \dfrac{i}{1-v^n}$	n	$j^{(12)} = .07$

11

RATE 2/3%	P E R I O D S	AMOUNT OF 1 *How $1 left at compound interest will grow.*	AMOUNT OF 1 PER PERIOD *How $1 deposited periodically will grow.*	SINKING FUND *Periodic deposit that will grow to $1 at future date.*
	1	1.006 666 6667	1.000 000 0000	1.000 000 0000
	2	1.013 377 7778	2.006 666 6667	.498 338 8704
.00666666	3	1.020 133 6296	3.020 044 4444	.331 120 9548
	4	1.026 934 5205	4.040 178 0741	.247 513 8426
per period	5	1.033 780 7506	5.067 112 5946	.197 351 0518
	6	1.040 672 6223	6.100 893 3452	.163 910 4215
	7	1.047 610 4398	7.141 565 9675	.140 025 3116
	8	1.054 594 5094	8.189 176 4073	.122 112 4018
	9	1.061 625 1394	9.243 770 9167	.108 180 9587
	10	1.068 702 6404	10.305 396 0561	.097 036 5423
	11	1.075 827 3246	11.374 098 6965	.087 919 0542
	12	1.082 999 5068	12.449 926 0211	.080 321 7624
	13	1.090 219 5035	13.532 925 5279	.073 893 8523
	14	1.097 487 6335	14.623 145 0315	.068 384 7420
	15	1.104 804 2178	15.720 632 6650	.063 610 6715
	16	1.112 169 5792	16.825 436 8828	.059 433 8208
	17	1.119 584 0431	17.937 606 4620	.055 748 7980
	18	1.127 047 9367	19.057 190 5051	.052 473 6319
	19	1.134 561 5896	20.184 238 4418	.049 543 6081
	20	1.142 125 3335	21.318 800 0314	.046 906 9553
ANNUALLY *If compounded* *annually* nominal annual rate is 2/3%	21	1.149 739 5024	22.460 925 3649	.044 521 7632
	22	1.157 404 4324	23.610 664 8673	.042 953 7417
	23	1.165 120 4620	24.768 069 2998	.040 374 5640
	24	1.172 887 9317	25.933 189 7618	.038 560 6248
	25	1.180 707 1846	27.106 077 6935	.036 892 0952
	26	1.188 578 5659	28.286 784 8782	.035 352 1973
	27	1.196 502 4230	29.475 363 4440	.033 926 6385
	28	1.204 479 1058	30.671 865 8670	.032 603 1681
	29	1.212 508 9665	31.876 344 9728	.031 371 2253
	30	1.220 592 3596	33.088 853 9392	.030 221 6572
SEMIANNUALLY *If compounded* *semiannually* nominal annual rate is 1 1/3%	31	1.228 729 6420	34.309 446 2988	.029 146 4919
	32	1.236 921 1729	35.538 175 9408	.028 138 7543
	33	1.245 167 3141	36.775 097 1138	.027 192 3143
	34	1.253 468 4295	38.020 264 4279	.026 301 7634
	35	1.261 824 8857	39.273 732 8574	.025 462 3110
	36	1.270 237 0516	40.535 557 7431	.024 669 6988
	37	1.278 705 2986	41.805 794 7947	.023 920 1289
	38	1.287 230 0006	43.084 500 0934	.023 210 2032
	39	1.295 811 5340	44.371 730 0940	.022 536 8720
	40	1.304 450 2775	45.667 541 6279	.021 897 3907
QUARTERLY *If compounded* *quarterly* nominal annual rate is 2 2/3%	41	1.313 146 6127	46.971 991 9055	.021 289 2824
	42	1.321 900 9235	48.285 138 5182	.020 710 3061
	43	1.330 713 5963	49.607 039 4416	.020 158 4294
	44	1.339 585 0203	50.937 753 0379	.019 631 8043
	45	1.348 515 5871	52.277 338 0581	.019 128 7475
	46	1.357 505 6910	53.625 853 6452	.018 647 7218
	47	1.366 555 7289	54.983 359 3362	.018 187 3209
	48	1.375 666 1004	56.349 915 0651	.017 746 2557
	49	1.384 837 2078	57.725 581 1655	.017 323 3423
	50	1.394 069 4558	59.110 418 3733	.016 917 4915
MONTHLY *If compounded* *monthly* nominal annual rate is 8%	51	1.403 363 2522	60.504 487 8291	.016 527 6996
	52	1.412 719 0072	61.907 851 0813	.016 153 0401
	53	1.422 137 1339	63.320 570 0885	.015 792 6563
	54	1.431 618 0481	64.742 707 2224	.015 445 7551
	55	1.441 162 1685	66.174 325 2706	.015 111 6010
	56	1.450 769 9163	67.615 487 4390	.014 789 5111
i = .00666666 $j_{(3)}$ = .01333333 $j_{(4)}$ = .02666666 $j_{(12)}$ = .08	57	1.460 441 7157	69.066 257 3553	.014 478 8503
	58	1.470 177 9938	70.526 699 0710	.014 179 0274
	59	1.479 979 1804	71.996 877 0648	.013 889 4913
	60	1.489 845 7083	73.476 856 2452	.013 609 7276
	n	$s=(1+i)^n$	$s_{\overline{n}}=\dfrac{(1+i)^n-1}{i}$	$\dfrac{1}{s_{\overline{n}}}=\dfrac{i}{(1+i)^n-1}$

PRESENT WORTH OF 1 *What $1 due in the future is worth today.*	PRESENT WORTH OF 1 PER PERIOD *What $1 payable periodically is worth today.*	PARTIAL PAYMENT *Annuity worth $1 today.* *Periodic payment necessary to pay off a loan of $1.*	PERIODS	RATE $2/3\%$
.993 377 4834	.993 377 4834	1.006 666 6667	1	
.986 798 8246	1.980 176 3081	.505 005 5371	2	
.980 263 7331	2.960 440 0411	.337 787 6215	3	.00666666
.973 771 9203	3.934 211 9614	.254 180 5093	4	
.967 323 0996	4.901 535 0610	.204 017 7184	5	*per period*
.960 916 9864	5.862 452 0473	.170 577 0882	6	
.954 553 2977	6.817 005 3450	.146 691 9783	7	
.948 231 7527	7.765 237 0977	.128 779 0685	8	
.941 952 0722	8.707 189 1699	.114 847 6254	9	
.935 713 9790	9.642 903 1489	.103 703 2089	10	
.929 517 1977	10.572 420 3466	.094 585 7209	11	
.923 361 4547	11.495 781 8013	.086 988 4291	12	
.917 246 4781	12.413 028 2794	.080 560 5190	13	
.911 171 9981	13.324 200 2775	.075 051 4087	14	
.905 137 7465	14.229 338 0240	.070 277 3382	15	
.899 143 4568	15.128 481 4808	.066 100 4874	16	
.893 188 8644	16.021 670 3452	.062 415 4647	17	
.887 273 7063	16.908 944 0515	.059 140 2986	18	
.881 397 7215	17.790 341 7730	.056 210 2748	19	
.875 560 6505	18.665 902 4236	.053 573 6220	20	
.869 762 2356	19.535 664 6592	.051 188 4299	21	ANNUALLY
.864 002 2208	20.399 666 8800	.049 020 4083	22	If compounded
.858 280 3518	21.257 947 2317	.047 041 2307	23	*annually*
.852 596 3759	22.110 543 6077	.045 227 2915	24	nominal annual rate is
.846 950 0423	22.957 493 6500	.043 558 7619	25	$2/3\%$
.841 341 1017	23.798 834 7517	.042 018 8640	26	
.835 769 3063	24.634 604 0580	.040 593 3052	27	
.830 234 4102	25.464 838 4682	.039 269 8348	28	
.824 736 1691	26.289 574 6373	.038 037 8920	29	
.819 274 3402	27.108 848 9774	.036 888 3238	30	SEMIANNUALLY
.813 848 6823	27.922 697 6597	.035 813 1586	31	If compounded
.808 458 9559	28.731 156 6156	.034 805 4209	32	*semiannually*
.803 104 9231	29.534 261 5387	.033 858 9810	33	nominal annual rate is
.797 786 3474	30.332 047 8861	.032 968 4301	34	
.792 502 9941	31.124 550 8802	.032 128 9777	35	$1\frac{1}{3}\%$
.787 254 6299	31.911 805 5101	.031 336 3655	36	
.782 041 0231	32.693 846 5333	.030 586 7956	37	
.776 861 9435	33.470 708 4767	.029 876 8698	38	
.771 717 1624	34.242 425 6392	.029 203 5386	39	
.766 606 4527	35.009 032 0919	.028 564 0573	40	QUARTERLY
.761 529 5888	35.770 561 6807	.027 955 9491	41	If compounded
.756 486 5465	36.527 048 0272	.027 376 9728	42	*quarterly*
.751 476 5031	37.278 524 5303	.026 825 0960	43	nominal annual rate is
.746 499 8375	38.025 024 3678	.026 298 4710	44	
.741 556 1300	38.766 580 4978	.025 795 4142	45	$2\frac{2}{3}\%$
.736 645 1623	39.503 225 6601	.025 314 3885	46	
.731 766 7175	40.234 992 3776	.024 853 9876	47	
.726 920 5803	40.961 912 9579	.024 412 9223	48	
.722 106 5367	41.684 019 4946	.023 990 0089	49	
.717 324 3742	42.401 343 8688	.023 584 1582	50	MONTHLY
.712 573 8817	43.113 917 7505	.023 194 3663	51	If compounded
.707 854 8493	43.821 772 5998	.022 819 7068	52	*monthly*
.703 167 0689	44.524 939 6687	.022 459 3230	53	nominal annual rate is
.698 510 3333	45.223 450 0020	.022 112 4218	54	
.693 884 4371	45.917 334 4391	.021 778 2677	55	8%
.689 289 1759	46.606 623 6150	.021 456 1777	56	
.684 724 3469	47.291 347 9619	.021 145 5170	57	
.680 189 7486	47.971 537 7105	.020 845 6941	58	$i = .00666666$
.675 685 1807	48.647 222 8912	.020 556 1580	59	$j_{(2)} = .01333333$
.671 210 4444	49.318 433 3356	.020 276 3943	60	$j_{(4)} = .02666666$ $j_{(12)} = .08$
$v^n = \dfrac{1}{(1+i)^n}$	$a_{\overline{n}\rceil} = \dfrac{1-v^n}{i}$	$\dfrac{1}{a_{\overline{n}\rceil}} = \dfrac{i}{1-v^n}$	n	

RATE **3/4%**	P E R I O D S	AMOUNT OF 1 *How $1 left at compound interest will grow.*	AMOUNT OF 1 PER PERIOD *How $1 deposited periodically will grow.*	SINKING FUND *Periodic deposit that will grow to $1 at future date.*
	1	1.007 500 0000	1.000 000 0000	1.000 000 0000
	2	1.015 056 2500	2.007 500 0000	.498 132 0050
.0075	3	1.022 669 1719	3.022 556 2500	.330 845 7866
	4	1.030 339 1907	4.045 225 4219	.247 205 0123
per period	5	1.038 066 7346	5.075 564 6125	.197 022 4155
	6	1.045 852 2351	6.113 631 3471	.163 568 9074
	7	1.053 696 1269	7.159 483 5822	.139 674 8786
	8	1.061 598 8478	8.213 179 7091	.121 755 5241
	9	1.069 560 8392	9.274 778 5569	.107 819 2858
	10	1.077 582 5455	10.344 339 3961	.096 671 2287
	11	1.085 664 4146	11.421 921 9416	.087 550 9398
	12	1.093 806 8977	12.507 586 3561	.079 951 4768
	13	1.102 010 4494	13.601 393 2538	.073 521 8798
	14	1.110 275 5278	14.703 403 7032	.068 011 4632
	15	1.118 602 5942	15.813 679 2310	.063 236 3908
	16	1.126 992 1137	16.932 281 8252	.059 058 7855
	17	1.135 444 5545	18.059 273 9389	.055 373 2118
	18	1.143 960 3887	19.194 718 4934	.052 097 6643
	19	1.152 540 0916	20.338 678 8821	.049 167 4020
	20	1.161 184 1423	21.491 218 9738	.046 530 6319
ANNUALLY *If compounded annually nominal annual rate is* **3/4%**	21	1.169 893 0234	22.652 403 1161	.044 145 4266
	22	1.178 667 2210	23.822 296 1394	.041 977 4817
	23	1.187 507 2252	25.000 963 3605	.039 998 4587
	24	1.196 413 5294	26.188 470 5857	.038 184 7423
	25	1.205 386 6309	27.384 884 1151	.036 516 4956
	26	1.214 427 0306	28.590 270 7459	.034 976 9335
	27	1.223 535 2333	29.804 697 7765	.033 551 7578
	28	1.232 711 7476	31.028 233 0099	.032 228 7125
	29	1.241 957 0857	32.260 944 7574	.030 997 2323
	30	1.251 271 7638	33.502 901 8431	.029 848 1608
SEMIANNUALLY *If compounded semiannually nominal annual rate is* **1½%**	31	1.260 656 3021	34.754 173 6069	.028 773 5226
	32	1.270 111 2243	36.014 829 9090	.027 766 3397
	33	1.279 637 0585	37.284 941 1333	.026 820 4795
	34	1.289 234 3364	38.564 578 1918	.025 930 5313
	35	1.298 903 5940	39.853 812 5282	.025 091 7023
	36	1.308 645 3709	41.152 716 1222	.024 299 7327
	37	1.318 460 2112	42.461 361 4931	.023 550 8228
	38	1.328 348 6628	43.779 821 7043	.022 841 5732
	39	1.338 311 2778	45.108 170 3671	.022 168 9329
	40	1.348 348 6123	46.446 481 6449	.021 530 1561
QUARTERLY *If compounded quarterly nominal annual rate is* **3%**	41	1.358 461 2269	47.794 830 2572	.020 922 7650
	42	1.368 649 6861	49.153 291 4841	.020 344 5175
	43	1.378 914 5588	50.521 941 1703	.019 793 3804
	44	1.389 256 4180	51.900 855 7290	.019 267 5051
	45	1.399 675 8411	53.290 112 1470	.018 765 2073
	46	1.410 173 4099	54.689 787 9881	.018 284 9493
	47	1.420 749 7105	56.099 961 3980	.017 825 3242
	48	1.431 405 3333	57.520 711 1085	.017 385 0424
	49	1.442 140 8733	58.952 116 4418	.016 962 9194
	50	1.452 956 9299	60.394 257 3151	.016 557 8657
MONTHLY *If compounded monthly nominal annual rate is* **9%**	51	1.463 854 1068	61.847 214 2450	.016 168 8770
	52	1.474 833 0126	63.311 068 3518	.015 795 0265
	53	1.485 894 2602	64.785 901 3645	.015 435 4571
	54	1.497 038 4672	66.271 795 6247	.015 089 3754
	55	1.508 266 2557	67.768 834 0919	.014 756 0455
i = .0075 *j*(₂) = .015 *j*(₄) = .03 *j*(₁₂) = .09	56	1.519 578 2526	69.277 100 3476	.014 434 7843
	57	1.530 975 0895	70.796 678 6002	.014 124 9564
	58	1.542 457 4027	72.327 653 6897	.013 825 9704
	59	1.554 025 8332	73.870 111 0923	.013 537 2749
	60	1.565 681 0269	75.424 136 9255	.013 258 3552
	n	$s = (1+i)^n$	$s_{\overline{n}\rceil} = \dfrac{(1+i)^n - 1}{i}$	$\dfrac{1}{s_{\overline{n}\rceil}} = \dfrac{i}{(1+i)^n - 1}$

14

PRESENT WORTH OF 1 *What $1 due in the future is worth today.*	PRESENT WORTH OF 1 PER PERIOD *What $1 payable periodically is worth today.*	PARTIAL PAYMENT *Annuity worth $1 today. Periodic payment necessary to pay off a loan of $1.*	PERIODS	RATE 3/4%
.992 555 8313	.992 555 8313	1.007 500 0000	1	
.985 167 0782	1.977 722 9094	.505 632 0050	2	
.977 833 3282	2.955 556 2377	.338 345 7866	3	.0075
.970 554 1719	3.926 110 4096	.254 705 0123	4	
.963 329 2029	4.889 439 6125	.204 522 4155	5	*per period*
.956 158 0178	5.845 597 6303	.171 068 9074	6	
.949 040 2162	6.794 637 8464	.147 174 8786	7	
.941 975 4006	7.736 613 2471	.129 255 5241	8	
.934 963 1768	8.671 576 4239	.115 319 2858	9	
.928 003 1532	9.599 579 5771	.104 171 2287	10	
.921 094 9411	10.520 674 5182	.095 050 9398	11	
.914 238 1550	11.434 912 6731	.087 451 4768	12	
.907 432 4119	12.342 345 0850	.081 021 8798	13	
.900 677 3319	13.243 022 4169	.075 511 4632	14	
.893 972 5378	14.136 994 9547	.070 736 3908	15	
.887 317 6554	15.024 312 6101	.066 558 7855	16	
.880 712 3131	15.905 024 9232	.062 873 2118	17	
.874 156 1420	16.779 181 0652	.059 597 6643	18	
.867 648 7762	17.646 829 8414	.056 667 4020	19	
.861 189 8523	18.508 019 6937	.054 030 6319	20	
.854 779 0097	19.362 798 7034	.051 645 4266	21	ANNUALLY *If compounded annually nominal annual rate is*
.848 415 8905	20.211 214 5940	.049 477 4817	22	
.842 100 1395	21.053 314 7335	.047 498 4587	23	
.835 831 4040	21.889 146 1374	.045 684 7423	24	
.829 609 3340	22.718 755 4714	.044 016 4956	25	3/4%
.823 433 5821	23.542 189 0535	.042 476 9335	26	
.817 303 8036	24.359 492 8571	.041 051 7578	27	
.811 219 6562	25.170 712 5132	.039 728 7125	28	
.805 180 8001	25.975 893 3134	.038 497 2323	29	
.799 186 8984	26.775 080 2118	.037 348 1608	30	
.793 237 6163	27.568 317 8281	.036 273 5226	31	SEMIANNUALLY *If compounded semiannually nominal annual rate is*
.787 332 6216	28.355 650 4497	.035 266 3397	32	
.781 471 5847	29.137 122 0344	.034 320 4795	33	
.775 654 1784	29.912 776 2128	.033 430 5313	34	
.769 880 0778	30.682 656 2907	.032 591 7023	35	1 1/2%
.764 148 9606	31.446 805 2513	.031 799 7327	36	
.758 460 5068	32.205 265 7581	.031 050 8228	37	
.752 814 3988	32.958 080 1569	.030 341 5732	38	
.747 210 3214	33.705 290 4783	.029 668 9329	39	
.741 647 9617	34.446 938 4400	.029 030 1561	40	QUARTERLY *If compounded quarterly nominal annual rate is*
.736 127 0091	35.183 065 4492	.028 422 7650	41	
.730 647 1555	35.913 712 6046	.027 844 5175	42	
.725 208 0948	36.638 920 6994	.027 293 3804	43	
.719 809 5233	37.358 730 2227	.026 767 5051	44	
.714 451 1398	38.073 181 3625	.026 265 2073	45	3%
.709 132 6449	38.782 314 0074	.025 784 9493	46	
.703 853 7419	39.486 167 7493	.025 325 3242	47	
.698 614 1359	40.184 781 8852	.024 885 0424	48	
.693 413 5344	40.878 195 4195	.024 462 9194	49	
.688 251 6470	41.566 447 0665	.024 057 8657	50	MONTHLY *If compounded monthly nominal annual rate is*
.683 128 1856	42.249 575 2521	.023 668 8770	51	
.678 042 8641	42.927 618 1163	.023 295 0265	52	
.672 995 3986	43.600 613 5149	.022 935 4571	53	
.667 985 5073	44.268 599 0222	.022 589 3754	54	
.663 012 9105	44.931 611 9327	.022 256 0455	55	9%
.658 077 3305	45.589 689 2633	.021 934 7843	56	
.653 178 4918	46.242 867 7551	.021 624 9564	57	
.648 316 1209	46.891 183 8760	.021 325 9704	58	$i = .0075$
.643 489 9463	47.534 673 8224	.021 037 2749	59	$j_{(2)} = .015$
.638 699 6986	48.173 373 5210	.020 758 3552	60	$j_{(4)} = .03$ $j_{(12)} = .09$
$v^n = \dfrac{1}{(1+i)^n}$	$a_{\overline{n}\rceil} = \dfrac{1-v^n}{i}$	$\dfrac{1}{a_{\overline{n}\rceil}} = \dfrac{i}{1-v^n}$	n	

P E R I O D S	AMOUNT OF 1 *How $1 left at compound interest will grow.*	AMOUNT OF 1 PER PERIOD *How $1 deposited periodically will grow.*	SINKING **FUND** *Periodic deposit that will grow to $1 at future date.*
1	1.008 333 3333	1.000 000 0000	1.000 000 0000
2	1.016 736 1111	2.008 333 3333	.497 925 3112
3	1.025 208 9120	3.025 069 4444	.330 570 9235
4	1.033 752 3196	4.050 278 3565	.246 896 6110
5	1.042 366 9223	5.084 030 6761	.196 694 3285
6	1.051 053 3133	6.126 397 5984	.163 228 0609
7	1.059 812 0909	7.177 450 9117	.139 325 2301
8	1.068 643 8584	8.237 263 0027	.121 399 5474
9	1.077 549 2238	9.305 906 8610	.107 458 6298
10	1.086 528 8007	10.383 456 0849	.096 307 0477
11	1.095 583 2074	11.469 984 8856	.087 184 0730
12	1.104 713 0674	12.565 568 0930	.079 582 5539
13	1.113 919 0097	13.670 281 1604	.073 151 3850
14	1.123 201 6681	14.784 200 1701	.067 639 7768
15	1.132 561 6820	15.907 401 8382	.062 863 8171
16	1.141 999 6960	17.039 963 5201	.058 685 5716
17	1.151 516 3601	18.181 963 2161	.054 999 5613
18	1.161 112 3298	19.333 479 5763	.051 723 7467
19	1.170 788 2659	20.494 591 9061	.048 793 3600
20	1.180 544 8348	21.665 380 1720	.046 156 5868
21	1.190 382 7084	22.845 925 0067	.043 771 4822
22	1.200 302 5643	24.036 307 7151	.041 603 7277
23	1.210 305 0857	25.236 610 2794	.039 624 9730
24	1.220 390 9614	26.446 915 3651	.037 811 5930
25	1.230 560 8861	27.667 306 3264	.036 143 7427
26	1.240 815 5601	28.897 867 2125	.034 604 6299
27	1.251 155 6898	30.138 682 7726	.033 179 9504
28	1.261 581 9872	31.389 838 4624	.031 857 4433
29	1.272 095 1704	32.651 420 4496	.030 626 5389
30	1.282 695 9635	33.923 515 6200	.029 478 0768
31	1.293 385 0965	35.206 211 5835	.028 404 0786
32	1.304 163 3057	36.499 596 6800	.027 397 5630
33	1.315 031 3332	37.803 759 9857	.026 452 3952
34	1.325 989 9277	39.118 791 3189	.025 563 1620
35	1.337 039 8437	40.444 781 2465	.024 725 0688
36	1.348 181 8424	41.781 821 0903	.023 933 8539
37	1.359 416 6911	43.130 002 9327	.023 185 7160
38	1.370 745 1635	44.489 419 6238	.022 477 2543
39	1.382 168 0399	45.860 164 7873	.021 805 4166
40	1.393 686 1069	47.242 332 8272	.021 167 4560
41	1.405 300 1578	48.636 018 9341	.020 560 8934
42	1.417 010 9924	50.041 319 0919	.019 983 4860
43	1.428 819 4174	51.458 330 0843	.019 433 1996
44	1.440 726 2458	52.887 149 5017	.018 908 1849
45	1.452 732 2979	54.327 875 7475	.018 406 7569
46	1.464 838 4004	55.780 608 0454	.017 927 3772
47	1.477 045 3870	57.245 446 4458	.017 468 6383
48	1.489 354 0986	58.722 491 8329	.017 029 2501
49	1.501 765 3828	60.211 845 9315	.016 608 0276
50	1.514 280 0943	61.713 611 3142	.016 203 8808
51	1.526 899 0951	63.227 891 4085	.015 815 8050
52	1.539 623 2542	64.754 790 5036	.015 442 8729
53	1.552 453 4480	66.294 413 7578	.015 084 2272
54	1.565 390 5600	67.846 867 2058	.014 739 0741
55	1.578 435 4814	69.412 257 7658	.014 406 6773
56	1.591 589 1104	70.990 693 2472	.014 086 3535
57	1.604 852 3530	72.582 282 3576	.013 777 4670
58	1.618 226 1226	74.187 134 7106	.013 479 4261
59	1.631 711 3403	75.805 360 8332	.013 191 6792
60	1.645 308 9348	77.437 072 1734	.012 913 7114
n	$s=(1+i)^n$	$s_{\overline{n}|}=\dfrac{(1+i)^n-1}{i}$	$\dfrac{1}{s_{\overline{n}|}}=\dfrac{i}{(1+i)^n-1}$

.00833333

per period

ANNUALLY
If compounded
annually
nominal annual rate is

5/6%

SEMIANNUALLY
If compounded
semiannually
nominal annual rate is

1 2/3%

QUARTERLY
If compounded
quarterly
nominal annual rate is

3 1/3%

MONTHLY
If compounded
monthly
nominal annual rate is

10%

$i = .00833333$
$j_{(2)} = .01666666$
$j_{(4)} = .03333333$
$j_{(12)} = .1$

PRESENT WORTH OF 1 — *What $1 due in the future is worth today.*	PRESENT WORTH OF 1 PER PERIOD — *What $1 payable periodically is worth today.*	PARTIAL PAYMENT — *Annuity worth $1 today. Periodic payment necessary to pay off a loan of $1.*	PERIODS	RATE
.991 735 5372	.991 735 5372	1.008 333 3333	1	**5/6%**
.983 539 3757	1.975 274 9129	.506 258 6445	2	
.975 410 9511	2.950 685 8640	.338 904 2569	3	.00833333
.967 349 7036	3.918 035 5677	.255 229 9444	4	*per period*
.959 355 0780	4.877 390 6456	.205 027 6619	5	
.951 426 5236	5.828 817 1692	.171 561 3942	6	
.943 563 4945	6.772 380 6637	.147 658 5635	7	
.935 765 4491	7.708 146 1127	.129 732 8807	8	
.928 031 8503	8.636 177 9630	.115 791 9631	9	
.920 362 1656	9.556 540 1286	.104 640 3810	10	
.912 755 8667	10.469 295 9953	.095 517 4064	11	
.905 212 4298	11.374 508 4251	.087 915 8872	12	
.897 731 3353	12.272 239 7605	.081 484 7183	13	
.890 312 0681	13.162 551 8285	.075 973 1102	14	
.882 954 1171	14.045 505 9457	.071 197 1505	15	
.875 656 9757	14.921 162 9213	.067 018 9050	16	
.868 420 1411	15.789 583 0625	.063 332 8946	17	
.861 243 1152	16.650 826 1777	.060 057 0800	18	
.854 125 4035	17.504 951 5811	.057 126 6933	19	
.847 066 5159	18.352 018 0970	.054 489 9201	20	ANNUALLY *If compounded annually nominal annual rate is*
.840 065 9661	19.192 084 0631	.052 104 8155	21	
.833 123 2722	20.025 207 3354	.049 937 0610	22	
.826 237 9559	20.851 445 2913	.047 958 3063	23	
.819 409 5430	21.670 854 8343	.046 144 9263	24	
.812 637 5634	22.483 492 3977	.044 477 0760	25	**5/6%**
.805 921 5504	23.289 413 9481	.042 937 9632	26	
.799 261 0418	24.088 674 9898	.041 513 2837	27	
.792 655 5786	24.881 330 5684	.040 190 7767	28	
.786 104 7060	25.667 435 2745	.038 959 8723	29	
.779 607 9729	26.447 043 2474	.037 811 4102	30	
.773 164 9318	27.220 208 1793	.036 737 4119	31	SEMIANNUALLY *If compounded semiannually nominal annual rate is*
.766 775 1390	27.986 983 3183	.035 730 8963	32	
.760 438 1544	28.747 421 4727	.034 785 7286	33	
.754 153 5415	29.501 575 0142	.033 896 4953	34	
.747 920 8677	30.249 495 8819	.033 058 4022	35	**1 2/3%**
.741 739 7035	30.991 235 5853	.032 267 1872	36	
.735 609 6233	31.726 845 2086	.031 519 0494	37	
.729 530 2049	32.456 375 4135	.030 810 5877	38	
.723 501 0296	33.179 876 4431	.030 138 7500	39	
.717 521 6823	33.897 398 1254	.029 500 7893	40	
.711 591 7510	34.608 989 8764	.028 894 2267	41	QUARTERLY *If compounded quarterly nominal annual rate is*
.705 710 8275	35.314 700 7039	.028 316 8193	42	
.699 878 5066	36.014 579 2105	.027 766 5329	43	
.694 094 3867	36.708 673 5972	.027 241 5182	44	
.688 358 0694	37.397 031 6666	.026 740 0902	45	**3 1/3%**
.682 669 1598	38.079 700 8264	.026 260 7105	46	
.677 027 2659	38.756 728 0923	.025 801 9717	47	
.671 431 9992	39.428 160 0915	.025 362 5834	48	
.665 882 9745	40.094 043 0660	.024 941 3609	49	
.660 379 8094	40.754 422 8754	.024 537 2141	50	MONTHLY *If compounded monthly nominal annual rate is*
.654 922 1250	41.409 345 0003	.024 149 1383	51	
.649 509 5455	42.058 854 5458	.023 776 2062	52	
.644 141 6980	42.702 996 2438	.023 417 5605	53	
.638 818 2129	43.341 814 4566	.023 072 4074	54	
.633 538 7235	43.975 353 1801	.022 740 0107	55	**10%**
.628 302 8663	44.603 656 0464	.022 419 6868	56	
.623 110 2806	45.226 766 3270	.022 110 8003	57	
.617 960 6089	45.844 726 9359	.021 812 7594	58	i = .00833333
.612 853 4964	46.457 580 4323	.021 525 0125	59	$j_{(2)}$ = .01666666
.607 788 5915	47.065 369 0238	.021 247 0447	60	$j_{(4)}$ = .03333333
				$j_{(12)}$ = .1

| $v^n = \dfrac{1}{(1+i)^n}$ | $a_{\overline{n}|} = \dfrac{1-v^n}{i}$ | $\dfrac{1}{a_{\overline{n}|}} = \dfrac{i}{1-v^n}$ | **n** | |

P E R I O D S	AMOUNT OF 1 *How $1 left at compound interest will grow.*	AMOUNT OF 1 PER PERIOD *How $1 deposited periodically will grow.*	SINKING FUND *Periodic deposit that will grow to $1 at future date.*
1	1.010 000 0000	1.000 000 0000	1.000 000 0000
2	1.020 100 0000	2.010 000 0000	.497 512 4378
3	1.030 301 0000	3.030 100 0000	.330 022 1115
4	1.040 604 0100	4.060 401 0000	.246 281 0939
5	1.051 010 0501	5.101 005 0100	.196 039 7996
6	1.061 520 1506	6.152 015 0601	.162 548 3667
7	1.072 135 3521	7.213 535 2107	.138 628 2829
8	1.082 856 7056	8.285 670 5628	.120 690 2920
9	1.093 685 2727	9.368 527 2684	.106 740 3628
10	1.104 622 1254	10.462 212 5411	.095 582 0766
11	1.115 668 3467	11.566 834 6665	.086 454 0757
12	1.126 825 0301	12.682 503 0132	.078 848 7887
13	1.138 093 2804	13.809 328 0433	.072 414 8197
14	1.149 474 2132	14.947 421 3238	.066 901 1717
15	1.160 968 9554	16.096 895 5370	.062 123 7802
16	1.172 578 6449	17.257 864 4924	.057 944 5968
17	1.184 304 4314	18.430 443 1373	.054 258 0551
18	1.196 147 4757	19.614 747 5687	.050 982 0479
19	1.208 108 9504	20.810 895 0444	.048 051 7536
20	1.220 190 0399	22.019 003 9948	.045 415 3149
21	1.232 391 9403	23.239 194 0347	.043 030 7522
22	1.244 715 8598	24.471 585 9751	.040 863 7185
23	1.257 163 0183	25.716 301 8348	.038 885 8401
24	1.269 734 6485	26.973 464 8532	.037 073 4722
25	1.282 431 9950	28.243 199 5017	.035 406 7534
26	1.295 256 3150	29.525 631 4967	.033 868 8776
27	1.308 208 8781	30.820 887 8117	.032 445 5287
28	1.321 290 9669	32.129 096 6898	.031 124 4356
29	1.334 503 8766	33.450 387 6567	.029 895 0198
30	1.347 848 9153	34.784 891 5333	.028 748 1132
31	1.361 327 4045	36.132 740 4486	.027 675 7309
32	1.374 940 6785	37.494 067 8531	.026 670 8857
33	1.388 690 0853	38.869 008 5316	.025 727 4378
34	1.402 576 9862	40.257 698 6170	.024 839 9694
35	1.416 602 7560	41.660 275 6031	.024 003 6818
36	1.430 768 7836	43.076 878 3592	.023 214 3098
37	1.445 076 4714	44.507 647 1427	.022 468 0491
38	1.459 527 2361	45.952 723 6142	.021 761 4958
39	1.474 122 5085	47.412 250 8503	.021 091 5951
40	1.488 863 7336	48.886 373 3588	.020 455 5980
41	1.503 752 3709	50.375 237 0924	.019 851 0232
42	1.518 789 8946	51.878 989 4633	.019 275 6260
43	1.533 977 7936	53.397 779 3580	.018 727 3705
44	1.549 317 5715	54.931 757 1515	.018 204 4058
45	1.564 810 7472	56.481 074 7231	.017 705 0455
46	1.580 458 8547	58.045 885 4703	.017 227 7499
47	1.596 263 4432	59.626 344 3250	.016 771 1103
48	1.612 226 0777	61.222 607 7682	.016 333 8354
49	1.628 348 3385	62.834 833 8459	.015 914 7393
50	1.644 631 8218	64.463 182 1844	.015 512 7309
51	1.661 078 1401	66.107 814 0062	.015 126 8048
52	1.677 688 9215	67.768 892 1463	.014 756 0329
53	1.694 465 8107	69.446 581 0678	.014 399 5570
54	1.711 410 4688	71.141 046 8784	.014 056 5826
55	1.728 524 5735	72.852 457 3472	.013 726 3730
56	1.745 809 8192	74.580 981 9207	.013 408 2440
57	1.763 267 9174	76.326 791 7399	.013 101 5595
58	1.780 900 5966	78.090 059 6573	.012 805 7272
59	1.798 709 6025	79.870 960 2539	.012 520 1950
60	1.816 696 6986	81.669 669 8564	.012 244 4477
n	$s=(1+i)^n$	$s_{\overline{n}} = \dfrac{(1+i)^n - 1}{i}$	$\dfrac{1}{s_{\overline{n}}} = \dfrac{i}{(1+i)^n - 1}$

.01
per period

ANNUALLY
If compounded
annually
nominal annual rate is

1%

SEMIANNUALLY
If compounded
semiannually
nominal annual rate is

2%

QUARTERLY
If compounded
quarterly
nominal annual rate is

4%

MONTHLY
If compounded
monthly
nominal annual rate is

12%

$i = .01$
$j_{(2)} = .02$
$j_{(4)} = .04$
$j_{(12)} = .12$

PRESENT WORTH OF 1	PRESENT WORTH OF 1 PER PERIOD	PARTIAL PAYMENT	P E R I O D S	RATE
What $1 due in the future is worth today.	*What $1 payable periodically is worth today.*	*Annuity worth $1 today.* *Periodic payment necessary to pay off a loan of $1.*		**1%**
.990 099 0099	.990 099 0099	1.010 000 0000	1	
.980 296 0494	1.970 395 0593	.507 512 4378	2	
.970 590 1479	2.940 985 2072	.340 022 1115	3	.01
.960 980 3445	3.901 965 5517	.256 281 0939	4	
.951 465 6876	4.853 431 2393	.206 039 7996	5	*per period*
.942 045 2353	5.795 476 4746	.172 548 3667	6	
.932 718 0547	6.728 194 5293	.148 628 2829	7	
.923 483 2225	7.651 677 7518	.130 690 2920	8	
.914 339 8242	8.566 017 5760	.116 740 3628	9	
.905 286 9547	9.471 304 5307	.105 582 0766	10	
.896 323 7175	10.367 628 2482	.096 454 0757	11	
.887 449 2253	11.255 077 4735	.088 848 7887	12	
.878 662 5993	12.133 740 0728	.082 414 8197	13	
.869 962 9696	13.003 703 0423	.076 901 1717	14	
.861 349 4748	13.865 052 5172	.072 123 7802	15	
.852 821 2622	14.717 873 7794	.067 944 5968	16	
.844 377 4873	15.562 251 2667	.064 258 0551	17	
.836 017 3142	16.398 268 5809	.060 982 0479	18	
.827 739 9150	17.226 008 4959	.058 051 7536	19	
.819 544 4703	18.045 552 9663	.055 415 3149	20	
.811 430 1687	18.856 983 1349	.053 030 7522	21	ANNUALLY
.803 396 2066	19.660 379 3415	.050 863 7185	22	If compounded *annually*
.795 441 7887	20.455 821 1302	.048 885 8401	23	nominal annual rate is
.787 566 1274	21.243 387 2576	.047 073 4722	24	
.779 768 4430	22.023 155 7006	.045 406 7534	25	**1%**
.772 047 9634	22.795 203 6640	.043 868 8776	26	
.764 403 9241	23.559 607 5881	.042 445 5287	27	
.756 835 5684	24.316 443 1565	.041 124 4356	28	
.749 342 1470	25.065 785 3035	.039 895 0198	29	
.741 922 9178	25.807 708 2213	.038 748 1132	30	
.734 577 1463	26.542 285 3676	.037 675 7309	31	SEMIANNUALLY
.727 304 1053	27.269 589 4729	.036 670 8857	32	If compounded *semiannually*
.720 103 0745	27.989 692 5474	.035 727 4378	33	nominal annual rate is
.712 973 3411	28.702 665 8885	.034 839 9694	34	
.705 914 1991	29.408 580 0876	.034 003 6818	35	**2%**
.698 924 9496	30.107 505 0373	.033 214 3098	36	
.692 004 9006	30.799 509 9379	.032 468 0491	37	
.685 153 3670	31.484 663 3048	.031 761 4958	38	
.678 369 6702	32.163 032 9751	.031 091 5951	39	
.671 653 1389	32.834 686 1140	.030 455 5980	40	
.665 003 1078	33.499 689 2217	.029 851 0232	41	QUARTERLY
.658 418 9186	34.158 108 1403	.029 275 6260	42	If compounded *quarterly*
.651 899 9194	34.810 008 0597	.028 727 3705	43	nominal annual rate is
.645 445 4648	35.455 453 5245	.028 204 4058	44	
.639 054 9156	36.094 508 4401	.027 705 0455	45	**4%**
.632 727 6392	36.727 236 0793	.027 227 7499	46	
.626 463 0091	37.353 699 0884	.026 771 1103	47	
.620 260 4051	37.973 959 4935	.026 333 8354	48	
.614 119 2129	38.588 078 7064	.025 914 7393	49	
.608 038 8247	39.196 117 5311	.025 512 7309	50	
.602 018 6383	39.798 136 1694	.025 126 8048	51	MONTHLY
.596 058 0577	40.394 194 2271	.024 756 0329	52	If compounded *monthly*
.590 156 4928	40.984 350 7199	.024 399 5570	53	nominal annual rate is
.584 313 3592	41.568 664 0791	.024 056 5826	54	
.578 528 0784	42.147 192 1576	.023 726 3730	55	**12%**
.572 800 0776	42.719 992 2352	.023 408 2440	56	
.567 128 7898	43.287 121 0250	.023 101 5595	57	
.561 513 6532	43.848 634 6782	.022 805 7272	58	$i = .01$
.555 954 1121	44.404 588 7903	.022 520 1950	59	$j_{(2)} = .02$
.550 449 6159	44.955 038 4062	.022 244 4477	60	$j_{(4)} = .04$ $j_{(12)} = .12$
$v^n = \dfrac{1}{(1+i)^n}$	$a_{\overline{n}|} = \dfrac{1-v^n}{i}$	$\dfrac{1}{a_{\overline{n}|}} = \dfrac{i}{1-v^n}$	n	

19

P E R I O D S	AMOUNT OF 1 *How $1 left at compound interest will grow.*	AMOUNT OF 1 PER PERIOD *How $1 deposited periodically will grow.*	SINKING FUND *Periodic deposit that will grow to $1 at future date.*
1	1.012 500 0000	1.000 000 0000	1.000 000 0000
2	1.025 156 2500	2.012 500 0000	.496 894 4099
3	1.037 970 7031	3.037 656 2500	.329 201 1728
4	1.050 945 3369	4.075 626 9531	.245 361 0233
5	1.064 082 1536	5.126 572 2900	.195 062 1084
6	1.077 383 1805	6.190 654 4437	.161 533 8102
7	1.090 850 4703	7.268 037 6242	.137 588 7209
8	1.104 486 1012	8.358 888 0945	.119 633 1365
9	1.118 292 1774	9.463 374 1957	.105 670 5546
10	1.132 270 8297	10.581 666 3731	.094 503 0740
11	1.146 424 2150	11.713 937 2028	.085 368 3935
12	1.160 754 5177	12.860 361 4178	.077 758 3123
13	1.175 263 9492	14.021 115 9356	.071 320 9993
14	1.189 954 7486	15.196 379 8848	.065 805 1462
15	1.204 829 1829	16.386 334 6333	.061 026 4603
16	1.219 889 5477	17.591 163 8162	.056 846 7221
17	1.235 138 1670	18.811 053 3639	.053 160 2341
18	1.250 577 3941	20.046 191 5310	.049 884 7873
19	1.266 209 6116	21.296 768 9251	.046 955 4797
20	1.282 037 2317	22.562 978 5367	.044 320 3896
21	1.298 062 6971	23.845 015 7684	.041 937 4854
22	1.314 288 4808	25.143 078 4655	.039 772 3772
23	1.330 717 0868	26.457 366 9463	.037 796 6561
24	1.347 351 0504	27.788 084 0331	.035 986 6480
25	1.364 192 9385	29.135 435 0836	.034 322 4667
26	1.381 245 3503	30.499 628 0221	.032 787 2851
27	1.398 510 9172	31.880 873 3724	.031 366 7693
28	1.415 992 3036	33.279 384 2895	.030 048 6329
29	1.433 692 2074	34.695 376 5932	.028 822 2841
30	1.451 613 3600	36.129 068 8006	.027 678 5434
31	1.469 758 5270	37.580 682 1606	.026 609 4159
32	1.488 130 5086	39.050 440 6876	.025 607 9056
33	1.506 732 1400	40.538 571 1962	.024 667 8650
34	1.525 566 2917	42.045 303 3361	.023 783 8693
35	1.544 635 8703	43.570 869 6278	.022 951 1141
36	1.563 943 8187	45.115 505 4982	.022 165 3285
37	1.583 493 1165	46.679 449 3169	.021 422 7035
38	1.603 286 7804	48.262 942 4334	.020 719 8308
39	1.623 327 8652	49.866 229 2138	.020 053 6519
40	1.643 619 4635	51.489 557 0790	.019 421 4139
41	1.664 164 7068	53.133 176 5424	.018 820 6327
42	1.684 966 7656	54.797 341 2492	.018 249 0606
43	1.706 028 8502	56.482 308 0148	.017 704 6589
44	1.727 354 2108	58.188 336 8650	.017 185 5745
45	1.748 946 1384	59.915 691 0758	.016 690 1188
46	1.770 807 9652	61.664 637 2143	.016 216 7499
47	1.792 943 0647	63.435 445 1795	.015 764 0574
48	1.815 354 8531	65.228 388 2442	.015 330 7483
49	1.838 046 7887	67.043 743 0973	.014 915 6350
50	1.861 022 3736	68.881 789 8860	.014 517 6251
51	1.884 285 1532	70.742 812 2596	.014 135 7117
52	1.907 838 7177	72.627 097 4128	.013 768 9655
53	1.931 686 7016	74.534 936 1305	.013 416 5272
54	1.955 832 7854	76.466 622 8321	.013 077 6012
55	1.980 280 6952	78.422 455 6175	.012 751 4497
56	2.005 034 2039	80.402 736 3127	.012 437 3877
57	2.030 097 1315	82.407 770 5166	.012 134 7780
58	2.055 473 3456	84.437 867 6481	.011 843 0276
59	2.081 166 7624	86.493 340 9937	.011 561 5837
60	2.107 181 3470	88.574 507 7561	.011 289 9301
n	$s=(1+i)^n$	$s_{\overline{n}\rvert}=\dfrac{(1+i)^n-1}{i}$	$\dfrac{1}{s_{\overline{n}\rvert}}=\dfrac{i}{(1+i)^n-1}$

.0125

per period

ANNUALLY
If compounded
annually
nominal annual rate is

1¼%

SEMIANNUALLY
If compounded
semiannually
nominal annual rate is

2½%

QUARTERLY
If compounded
quarterly
nominal annual rate is

5%

MONTHLY
If compounded
monthly
nominal annual rate is

15%

$i = .0125$
$j_{(2)} = .025$
$j_{(4)} = .05$
$j_{(12)} = .15$

PRESENT WORTH OF 1	PRESENT WORTH OF 1 PER PERIOD	PARTIAL PAYMENT	P E R I O D S	RATE
What $1 due in the future is worth today.	*What $1 payable periodically is worth today.*	*Annuity worth $1 today.* *Periodic payment necessary to pay off a loan of $1.*		**1¼%**
.987 654 3210	.987 654 3210	1.012 500 0000	1	
.975 461 0578	1.963 115 3788	.509 394 4099	2	
.963 418 3287	2.926 533 7074	.341 701 1728	3	.0125
.951 524 2752	3.878 057 9826	.257 861 0233	4	*per period*
.939 777 0619	4.817 835 0446	.207 562 1084	5	
.928 174 8760	5.746 009 9206	.174 033 8102	6	
.916 715 9269	6.662 725 8475	.150 088 7209	7	
.905 398 4463	7.568 124 2938	.132 133 1365	8	
.894 220 6877	8.462 344 9815	.118 170 5546	9	
.883 180 9262	9.345 525 9077	.107 003 0740	10	
.872 277 4579	10.217 803 3656	.097 868 3935	11	
.861 508 6004	11.079 311 9660	.090 258 3123	12	
.850 872 6918	11.930 184 6578	.083 820 9993	13	
.840 368 0906	12.770 552 7485	.078 305 1462	14	
.829 993 1759	13.600 545 9244	.073 526 4603	15	
.819 746 3466	14.420 292 2710	.069 346 7221	16	
.809 626 0213	15.229 918 2924	.065 660 2341	17	
.799 630 6384	16.029 548 9307	.062 384 7873	18	
.789 758 6552	16.819 307 5859	.059 455 4797	19	
.780 008 5483	17.599 316 1342	.056 820 3896	20	
.770 378 8132	18.369 694 9474	.054 437 4854	21	**ANNUALLY** If compounded *annually* nominal annual rate is
.760 867 9636	19.130 562 9110	.052 272 3772	22	
.751 474 5320	19.882 037 4430	.050 296 6561	23	
.742 197 0686	20.624 234 5116	.048 486 6480	24	
.733 034 1418	21.357 268 6534	.046 822 4667	25	**1¼%**
.723 984 3376	22.081 252 9910	.045 287 2851	26	
.715 046 2594	22.796 299 2504	.043 866 7693	27	
.706 218 5278	23.502 517 7782	.042 548 6329	28	
.697 499 7805	24.200 017 5587	.041 322 2841	29	
.688 888 6721	24.888 906 2308	.040 178 5434	30	
.680 383 8737	25.569 290 1045	.039 109 4159	31	**SEMIANNUALLY** If compounded *semiannually* nominal annual rate is
.671 984 0728	26.241 274 1773	.038 107 9056	32	
.663 687 9731	26.904 962 1504	.037 167 8650	33	
.655 494 2944	27.560 456 4448	.036 283 8693	34	
.647 401 7723	28.207 858 2171	.035 451 1141	35	**2½%**
.639 409 1578	28.847 267 3749	.034 665 3285	36	
.631 515 2176	29.478 782 5925	.033 922 7035	37	
.623 718 7334	30.102 501 3259	.033 219 8308	38	
.616 018 5021	30.718 519 8281	.032 553 6519	39	
.608 413 3355	31.326 933 1635	.031 921 4139	40	
.600 902 0597	31.927 835 2233	.031 320 6327	41	**QUARTERLY** If compounded *quarterly* nominal annual rate is
.593 483 5158	32.521 318 7390	.030 749 0606	42	
.586 156 5588	33.107 475 2978	.030 204 6589	43	
.578 920 0581	33.686 395 3558	.029 685 5745	44	
.571 772 8968	34.258 168 2527	.029 190 1188	45	**5%**
.564 713 9722	34.822 882 2249	.028 716 7499	46	
.557 742 1948	35.380 624 4196	.028 264 0574	47	
.550 856 4886	35.931 480 9083	.027 830 7483	48	
.544 055 7913	36.475 536 6995	.027 415 6350	49	
.537 339 0531	37.012 875 7526	.027 017 6251	50	
.530 705 2376	37.543 580 9902	.026 635 7117	51	**MONTHLY** If compounded *monthly* nominal annual rate is
.524 153 3211	38.067 734 3114	.026 268 9655	52	
.517 682 2925	38.585 416 6038	.025 916 5272	53	
.511 291 1530	39.096 707 7568	.025 577 6012	54	
.504 978 9166	39.601 686 6734	.025 251 4497	55	**15%**
.498 744 6090	40.100 431 2824	.024 937 3877	56	
.492 587 2681	40.593 018 5505	.024 634 7780	57	
.486 505 9438	41.079 524 4943	.024 343 0276	58	i = .0125
.480 499 6976	41.560 024 1919	.024 061 5837	59	$j_{(2)}$ = .025
.474 567 6026	42.034 591 7945	.023 789 9301	60	$j_{(4)}$ = .05 $j_{(12)}$ = .15
$v^n = \dfrac{1}{(1+i)^n}$	$a_{\overline{n}|} = \dfrac{1-v^n}{i}$	$\dfrac{1}{a_{\overline{n}|}} = \dfrac{i}{1-v^n}$	**n**	

P E R I O D S	AMOUNT OF 1 *How $1 left at compound interest will grow.*	AMOUNT OF 1 PER PERIOD *How $1 deposited periodically will grow.*	SINKING FUND *Periodic deposit that will grow to $1 at future date.*
1	1.015 000 0000	1.000 000 0000	1.000 000 0000
2	1.030 225 0000	2.015 000 0000	.496 277 9156
3	1.045 678 3750	3.045 225 0000	.328 382 9602
4	1.061 363 5506	4.090 903 3750	.244 444 7860
5	1.077 284 0039	5.152 266 9256	.194 089 3231
6	1.093 443 2639	6.229 550 9295	.160 525 2146
7	1.109 844 9129	7.322 994 1935	.136 556 1645
8	1.126 492 5866	8.432 839 1064	.118 584 0246
9	1.143 389 9754	9.559 331 6929	.104 609 8234
10	1.160 540 8250	10.702 721 6683	.093 434 1779
11	1.177 948 9374	11.863 262 4934	.084 293 8442
12	1.195 618 1715	13.041 211 4308	.076 679 9929
13	1.213 552 4440	14.236 829 6022	.070 240 3574
14	1.231 755 7307	15.450 382 0463	.064 723 3186
15	1.250 232 0667	16.682 137 7770	.059 944 3557
16	1.268 985 5477	17.932 369 8436	.055 765 0778
17	1.288 020 3309	19.201 355 3913	.052 079 6569
18	1.307 340 6358	20.489 375 7221	.048 805 7818
19	1.326 950 7454	21.796 716 3580	.045 878 4701
20	1.346 855 0066	23.123 667 1033	.043 245 7359
21	1.367 057 8316	24.470 522 1099	.040 865 4950
22	1.387 563 6991	25.837 579 9415	.038 703 3152
23	1.408 377 1546	27.225 143 6407	.036 730 7520
24	1.429 502 8119	28.633 520 7953	.034 924 1020
25	1.450 945 3541	30.063 023 6072	.033 263 4539
26	1.472 709 5344	31.513 968 9613	.031 731 9599
27	1.494 800 1774	32.986 678 4957	.030 315 2680
28	1.517 222 1801	34.481 478 6732	.029 001 0765
29	1.539 980 5128	35.998 700 8533	.027 778 7802
30	1.563 080 2205	37.538 681 3661	.026 639 1883
31	1.586 526 4238	39.101 761 5865	.025 574 2954
32	1.610 324 3202	40.688 288 0103	.024 577 0970
33	1.634 479 1850	42.298 612 3305	.023 641 4375
34	1.658 996 3727	43.933 091 5155	.022 761 8855
35	1.683 881 3183	45.592 087 8882	.021 933 6303
36	1.709 139 5381	47.275 969 2065	.021 152 3955
37	1.734 776 6312	48.985 108 7446	.020 414 3673
38	1.760 798 2806	50.719 885 3758	.019 716 1329
39	1.787 210 2548	52.480 683 6564	.019 054 6298
40	1.814 018 4087	54.267 893 9113	.018 427 1017
41	1.841 228 6848	56.081 912 3199	.017 831 0610
42	1.868 847 1151	57.923 141 0047	.017 264 2571
43	1.896 879 8218	59.791 988 1198	.016 724 6488
44	1.925 333 0191	61.688 867 9416	.016 210 3801
45	1.954 213 0144	63.614 200 9607	.015 719 7604
46	1.983 526 2096	65.568 413 9751	.015 251 2458
47	2.013 279 1028	67.551 940 1848	.014 803 4238
48	2.043 478 2893	69.565 219 2875	.014 374 9996
49	2.074 130 4637	71.608 697 5768	.013 964 7841
50	2.105 242 4206	73.682 828 0405	.013 571 6832
51	2.136 821 0569	75.788 070 4611	.013 194 6887
52	2.168 873 3728	77.924 891 5180	.012 832 8700
53	2.201 406 4734	80.093 764 8908	.012 485 3664
54	2.234 427 5705	82.295 171 3642	.012 151 3812
55	2.267 943 9840	84.529 598 9346	.011 830 1756
56	2.301 963 1438	86.797 542 9186	.011 521 0635
57	2.336 492 5909	89.099 506 0624	.011 223 4068
58	2.371 539 9798	91.435 998 6534	.010 936 6116
59	2.407 113 0795	93.807 538 6332	.010 660 1241
60	2.443 219 7757	96.214 651 7126	.010 393 4274
n	$s=(1+i)^n$	$s_{\overline{n}|} = \dfrac{(1+i)^n-1}{i}$	$\dfrac{1}{s}$

.015
per period

ANNUALLY
If compounded *annually* nominal annual rate is
1½%

SEMIANNUALLY
If compounded *semiannually* nominal annual rate is
3%

QUARTERLY
If compounded *quarterly* nominal annual rate is
6%

MONTHLY
If compounded *monthly* nominal annual rate is
18%

$i = .015$
$j_{(2)} = .03$
$j_{(4)} = .06$
$j_{(12)} = .18$

PRESENT WORTH OF 1 *What $1 due in the future is worth today.*	PRESENT WORTH OF 1 PER PERIOD *What $1 payable periodically is worth today.*	PARTIAL PAYMENT *Annuity worth $1 today.* *Periodic payment necessary to pay off a loan of $1.*	PERIODS	RATE **1½%**
.985 221 6749	.985 221 6749	1.015 000 0000	1	
.970 661 7486	1.955 883 4235	.511 277 9156	2	
.956 316 9937	2.912 200 4173	.343 382 9602	3	.015
.942 184 2303	3.854 384 6476	.259 444 7860	4	*per period*
.928 260 3254	4.782 644 9730	.209 089 3231	5	
.914 542 1925	5.697 187 1655	.175 525 2146	6	
.901 026 7907	6.598 213 9561	.151 556 1645	7	
.887 711 1238	7.485 925 0799	.133 584 0246	8	
.874 592 2402	8.360 517 3201	.119 609 8234	9	
.861 667 2317	9.222 184 5519	.108 434 1779	10	
.848 933 2332	10.071 117 7851	.099 293 8442	11	
.836 387 4219	10.907 505 2070	.091 679 9929	12	
.824 027 0166	11.731 532 2236	.085 240 3574	13	
.811 849 2775	12.543 381 5011	.079 723 3186	14	
.799 851 5049	13.343 233 0060	.074 944 3557	15	
.788 031 0393	14.131 264 0453	.070 765 0778	16	
.776 385 2604	14.907 649 3057	.067 079 6569	17	
.764 911 5866	15.672 560 8924	.063 805 7818	18	
.753 607 4745	16.426 168 3669	.060 878 4701	19	
.742 470 4182	17.168 638 7851	.058 245 7359	20	ANNUALLY If compounded *annually* nominal annual rate is
.731 497 9490	17.900 136 7341	.055 865 4950	21	
.720 687 6345	18.620 824 3685	.053 703 3152	22	
.710 037 0783	19.330 861 4468	.051 730 7520	23	
.699 543 9195	20.030 405 3663	.049 924 1020	24	
.689 205 8320	20.719 611 1984	.048 263 4539	25	**1½%**
.679 020 5242	21.398 631 7225	.046 731 9599	26	
.668 985 7381	22.067 617 4606	.045 315 2680	27	
.659 099 2494	22.726 716 7100	.044 001 0765	28	
.649 358 8664	23.376 075 5763	.042 778 7802	29	
.639 762 4299	24.015 838 0062	.041 639 1883	30	SEMIANNUALLY If compounded *semiannually* nominal annual rate is
.630 307 8127	24.646 145 8189	.040 574 2954	31	
.620 992 9189	25.267 138 7379	.039 577 0970	32	
.611 815 6837	25.878 954 4216	.038 641 4375	33	
.602 774 0726	26.481 728 4941	.037 761 8855	34	
.593 866 0814	27.075 594 5755	.036 933 6303	35	**3%**
.585 089 7353	27.660 684 3109	.036 152 3955	36	
.576 443 0890	28.237 127 3999	.035 414 3673	37	
.567 924 2256	28.805 051 6255	.034 716 1329	38	
.559 531 2568	29.364 582 8822	.034 054 6298	39	
.551 262 3219	29.915 845 2042	.033 427 1017	40	QUARTERLY If compounded *quarterly* nominal annual rate is
.543 115 5881	30.458 960 7923	.032 831 0610	41	
.535 089 2494	30.994 050 0417	.032 264 2571	42	
.527 181 5265	31.521 231 5681	.031 724 6488	43	
.519 390 6665	32.040 622 2346	.031 210 3804	44	
.511 714 9423	32.552 337 1770	.030 719 7604	45	**6%**
.504 152 6526	33.056 489 8295	.030 251 2458	46	
.496 702 1207	33.553 191 9503	.029 803 4238	47	
.489 361 6953	34.042 553 6456	.029 374 9996	48	
.482 129 7491	34.524 683 3947	.028 964 5441	49	
.475 004 6789	34.999 688 0736	.028 571 6832	50	MONTHLY If compounded *monthly* nominal annual rate is
.467 984 9053	35.467 672 9789	.028 194 6887	51	
.461 068 8722	35.928 741 8511	.027 832 8700	52	
.454 255 0465	36.382 996 8977	.027 485 3664	53	
.447 541 9178	36.830 538 8154	.027 151 3812	54	
.440 927 9978	37.271 466 8132	.026 830 1756	55	**18%**
.434 411 8205	37.705 878 6337	.026 521 0635	56	
.427 991 9414	38.133 870 5751	.026 223 4068	57	$i = .015$
.421 666 9373	38.555 537 5124	.025 936 6116	58	$j_{(2)} = .03$
.415 435 4062	38.970 972 9186	.025 660 1241	59	$j_{(4)} = .06$
.409 295 9667	39.380 268 8853	.025 393 4274	60	$j_{(12)} = .18$
$v^n = \dfrac{1}{(1+i)^n}$	$a_{\overline{n}|} = \dfrac{1-v^n}{i}$	$\dfrac{1}{a_{\overline{n}|}} = \dfrac{i}{1-v^n}$	n	

1¾%

	P E R I O D S	AMOUNT OF 1 *How $1 left at compound interest will grow.*	AMOUNT OF 1 PER PERIOD *How $1 deposited periodically will grow.*	SINKING FUND *Periodic deposit that will grow to $1 at future date.*
	1	1.017 500 0000	1.000 000 0000	1.000 000 0000
	2	1.035 306 2500	2.017 500 0000	.495 662 9492
.0175	3	1.053 424 1094	3.052 806 2500	.327 567 4635
	4	1.071 859 0313	4.106 230 3594	.243 532 3673
per period	5	1.090 616 5643	5.178 089 3907	.193 121 4246
	6	1.109 702 3542	6.268 705 9550	.159 522 5565
	7	1.129 122 1454	7.378 408 3092	.135 530 5857
	8	1.148 881 7830	8.507 530 4546	.117 542 9233
	9	1.168 987 2142	9.656 412 2376	.103 558 1306
	10	1.189 444 4904	10.825 399 4517	.092 375 3442
	11	1.210 259 7690	12.014 843 9421	.083 230 3778
	12	1.231 439 3149	13.225 103 7111	.075 613 7738
	13	1.252 989 5030	14.456 543 0261	.069 172 8305
	14	1.274 916 8193	15.709 532 5290	.063 655 6179
	15	1.297 227 8636	16.984 449 3483	.058 877 3872
	16	1.319 929 3512	18.281 677 2119	.054 699 5764
	17	1.343 028 1149	19.601 606 5631	.051 016 2265
	18	1.366 531 1069	20.944 634 6779	.047 744 9244
	19	1.390 445 4012	22.311 165 7848	.044 820 6073
	20	1.414 778 1958	23.701 611 1860	.042 191 2246
ANNUALLY If compounded *annually* nominal annual rate is 1¾%	21	1.439 536 8142	25.116 389 3818	.039 814 6399
	22	1.464 728 7084	26.555 926 1960	.037 656 3782
	23	1.490 361 4608	28.020 654 9044	.035 687 9596
	24	1.516 442 7864	29.511 016 3642	.033 885 6510
	25	1.542 980 5352	31.027 459 1516	.032 229 5163
	26	1.569 982 6945	32.570 439 6868	.030 702 6865
	27	1.597 457 3917	34.140 422 3813	.029 290 7917
	28	1.625 412 8960	35.737 879 7730	.027 981 5145
	29	1.653 857 6217	37.363 292 6690	.026 764 2365
	30	1.682 800 1301	39.017 150 2907	.025 629 7549
SEMIANNUALLY If compounded *semiannually* nominal annual rate is 3½%	31	1.712 249 1324	40.699 950 4208	.024 570 0545
	32	1.742 213 4922	42.412 199 5532	.023 578 1216
	33	1.772 702 2283	44.154 413 0453	.022 647 7928
	34	1.803 724 5173	45.927 115 2736	.021 773 6297
	35	1.835 289 6963	47.730 839 7909	.020 950 8151
	36	1.867 407 2660	49.566 129 4873	.020 175 0673
	37	1.900 086 8932	51.433 536 7533	.019 442 5673
	38	1.933 338 4138	53.333 623 6465	.018 749 8979
	39	1.967 171 8361	55.266 962 0603	.018 093 9926
	40	2.001 597 3432	57.234 133 8963	.017 472 0911
QUARTERLY If compounded *quarterly* nominal annual rate is 7%	41	2.036 625 2967	59.235 731 2395	.016 881 7026
	42	2.072 266 2394	61.272 356 5362	.016 320 5735
	43	2.108 530 8986	63.344 622 7756	.015 786 6596
	44	2.145 430 1893	65.453 153 6742	.015 278 1026
	45	2.182 975 2176	67.598 583 8635	.014 793 2093
	46	2.221 177 2839	69.781 559 0811	.014 330 4336
	47	2.260 047 8864	72.002 736 3650	.013 888 3611
	48	2.299 598 7244	74.262 784 2514	.013 465 6950
	49	2.339 841 7021	76.562 382 9758	.013 061 2445
	50	2.380 788 9319	78.902 224 6779	.012 673 9139
MONTHLY If compounded *monthly* nominal annual rate is 21%	51	2.422 452 7382	81.283 013 6097	.012 302 6935
	52	2.464 845 6611	83.705 466 3479	.011 946 6511
	53	2.507 980 4602	86.170 312 0090	.011 604 9249
	54	2.551 870 1182	88.678 292 4691	.011 276 7169
	55	2.596 527 8453	91.230 162 5874	.010 961 2871
	56	2.641 967 0826	93.826 690 4326	.010 657 9481
	57	2.688 201 5065	96.468 657 5152	.010 366 0611
	58	2.735 245 0329	99.156 859 0217	.010 085 0310
	59	2.783 111 8210	101.892 104 0546	.009 814 3032
	60	2.831 816 2778	104.675 215 8756	.009 553 3598

$i = .0175$
$j_{(2)} = .035$
$j_{(4)} = .07$
$j_{(12)} = .21$

n	$s=(1+i)^n$	$s_{\overline{n}|}=\dfrac{(1+i)^n-1}{i}$	$\dfrac{1}{s_{\overline{n}|}}=\dfrac{i}{(1+i)^n-1}$

PRESENT WORTH OF 1 *What $1 due in the future is worth today.*	PRESENT WORTH OF 1 PER PERIOD *What $1 payable periodically is worth today.*	PARTIAL PAYMENT *Annuity worth $1 today.* *Periodic payment necessary to pay off a loan of $1.*	PERIODS	RATE
				1¾%
.982 800 9828	.982 800 9828	1.017 500 0000	1	
.965 897 7718	1.948 698 7546	.513 162 9492	2	
.949 285 2794	2.897 984 0340	.345 067 4635	3	.0175
.932 958 5056	3.830 942 5396	.261 032 3673	4	
.916 912 5362	4.747 855 0757	.210 621 4246	5	*per period*
.901 142 5417	5.648 997 6174	.177 022 5565	6	
.885 643 7756	6.534 641 3930	.153 030 5857	7	
.870 411 5731	7.405 052 9661	.135 042 9233	8	
.855 441 3495	8.260 494 3156	.121 058 1306	9	
.840 728 5990	9.101 222 9146	.109 875 3442	10	
.826 268 8934	9.927 491 8080	.100 730 3778	11	
.812 057 8805	10.739 549 6884	.095 113 7738	12	
.798 091 2830	11.537 640 9714	.086 672 8305	13	
.784 364 8973	12.322 005 8687	.081 155 6179	14	
.770 874 5919	13.092 880 4607	.076 377 3872	15	
.757 616 3066	13.850 496 7672	.072 199 5764	16	
.744 586 0507	14.595 082 8179	.068 516 2265	17	
.731 779 9024	15.326 862 7203	.065 244 9244	18	
.719 194 0073	16.046 056 7276	.062 320 6073	19	
.706 824 5772	16.752 881 3048	.059 691 2246	20	ANNUALLY <small>If compounded *annually* nominal annual rate is</small>
.694 667 8891	17.447 549 1939	.057 314 6399	21	
.682 720 2841	18.130 269 4780	.055 156 3782	22	
.670 978 1662	18.801 247 6442	.053 187 9596	23	
.659 438 0012	19.460 685 6454	.051 385 6510	24	
.648 096 3157	20.108 781 9611	.049 729 5163	25	**1¾%**
.636 949 6960	20.745 731 6571	.048 202 6865	26	
.625 994 7872	21.371 726 4443	.046 790 7917	27	
.615 228 2921	21.986 954 7364	.045 481 5145	28	
.604 646 9701	22.591 601 7066	.044 264 2365	29	
.594 247 6365	23.185 849 3431	.043 129 7549	30	SEMIANNUALLY <small>If compounded *semiannually* nominal annual rate is</small>
.584 027 1612	23.769 876 5042	.042 070 0545	31	
.573 982 4680	24.343 858 9722	.041 078 1216	32	
.564 110 5336	24.907 969 5059	.040 147 7928	33	
.554 408 3869	25.462 377 8928	.039 273 6297	34	
.544 873 1075	26.007 251 0003	.038 450 8151	35	**3½%**
.535 501 8255	26.542 752 8258	.037 675 0673	36	
.526 291 7204	27.069 044 5462	.036 942 5673	37	
.517 240 0201	27.586 284 5663	.036 249 8979	38	
.508 344 0001	28.094 628 5664	.035 593 9926	39	
.499 600 9829	28.594 229 5493	.034 972 0911	40	QUARTERLY <small>If compounded *quarterly* nominal annual rate is</small>
.491 008 3370	29.085 237 8863	.034 381 7026	41	
.482 563 4762	29.567 801 3625	.033 820 5735	42	
.474 263 8586	30.042 065 2211	.033 286 6596	43	
.466 106 9864	30.508 172 2075	.032 778 1026	44	
.458 090 4043	30.966 262 6117	.032 293 2093	45	**7%**
.450 211 6996	31.416 474 3113	.031 830 4336	46	
.442 468 5008	31.858 942 8121	.031 388 5611	47	
.434 858 4774	32.293 801 2895	.030 965 6950	48	
.427 379 3390	32.721 180 6285	.030 561 2445	49	
.420 028 8344	33.141 209 4629	.030 173 9139	50	MONTHLY <small>If compounded *monthly* nominal annual rate is</small>
.412 804 7513	33.554 014 2142	.029 802 6935	51	
.405 704 9152	33.959 719 1294	.029 446 6511	52	
.398 727 1894	34.358 446 3188	.029 104 9249	53	
.391 869 4736	34.750 315 7925	.028 776 7169	54	
.385 129 7038	35.135 445 4963	.028 461 2871	55	**21%**
.378 505 8514	35.513 951 3477	.028 157 9481	56	
.371 995 9228	35.885 947 2705	.027 866 0611	57	
.365 597 9585	36.251 545 2290	.027 585 0310	58	$i = .0175$
.359 310 0329	36.610 855 2619	.027 314 3032	59	$j_{(2)} = .035$
.353 130 2535	36.963 985 5154	.027 053 3598	60	$j_{(4)} = .07$ $j_{(12)} = .21$
$v^n = \dfrac{1}{(1+i)^n}$	$a_{\overline{n}|} = \dfrac{1-v^n}{i}$	$\dfrac{1}{a_{\overline{n}|}} = \dfrac{i}{1-v^n}$	n	

25

P E R I O D S	AMOUNT OF 1 How $1 left at compound interest will grow.	AMOUNT OF 1 PER PERIOD How $1 deposited periodically will grow.	SINKING FUND Periodic deposit that will grow to $1 at future date.
1	1.020 000 0000	1.000 000 0000	1.000 000 0000
2	1.040 400 0000	2.020 000 0000	.495 049 5050
3	1.061 208 0000	3.060 400 0000	.326 754 6726
4	1.082 432 1600	4.121 608 0000	.242 623 7527
5	1.104 080 8032	5.204 040 1600	.192 158 3941
6	1.126 162 4193	6.308 120 9632	.158 525 8123
7	1.148 685 6676	7.434 283 3825	.134 511 9561
8	1.171 659 3810	8.582 969 0501	.116 509 7991
9	1.195 092 5686	9.754 628 4311	.102 515 4374
10	1.218 994 4200	10.949 720 9997	.091 326 5279
11	1.243 374 3084	12.168 715 4197	.082 177 9428
12	1.268 241 7946	13.412 089 7281	.074 559 5966
13	1.293 606 6305	14.680 331 5227	.068 118 3527
14	1.319 478 7631	15.973 938 1531	.062 601 9702
15	1.345 868 3383	17.293 416 9162	.057 825 4723
16	1.372 785 7051	18.639 285 2545	.053 650 1259
17	1.400 241 4192	20.012 070 9596	.049 969 8408
18	1.428 246 2476	21.412 312 3788	.046 702 1022
19	1.456 811 1725	22.840 558 6264	.043 781 7663
20	1.485 947 3960	24.297 369 7989	.041 156 7181
21	1.515 666 3439	25.783 317 1949	.038 784 7689
22	1.545 979 6708	27.298 983 5388	.036 631 4005
23	1.576 899 2642	28.844 963 2096	.034 668 0976
24	1.608 437 2495	30.421 862 4738	.032 871 0973
25	1.640 605 9945	32.030 299 7232	.031 220 4384
26	1.673 418 1144	33.670 905 7177	.029 699 2308
27	1.706 886 4766	35.344 323 8321	.028 293 0862
28	1.741 024 2062	37.051 210 3087	.026 989 6716
29	1.775 844 6903	38.792 234 5149	.025 778 3552
30	1.811 361 5841	40.568 079 2052	.024 649 9223
31	1.847 588 8158	42.379 440 7893	.023 596 3472
32	1.884 540 5921	44.227 029 6051	.022 610 6073
33	1.922 231 4039	46.111 570 1972	.021 686 5311
34	1.960 676 0320	48.033 801 6011	.020 818 6728
35	1.999 889 5527	49.994 477 6331	.020 002 2092
36	2.039 887 3437	51.994 367 1858	.019 232 8526
37	2.080 685 0906	54.034 254 5295	.018 506 7789
38	2.122 298 7924	56.114 939 6201	.017 820 5663
39	2.164 744 7682	58.237 238 4125	.017 171 1439
40	2.208 039 6636	60.401 983 1807	.016 555 7478
41	2.252 200 4569	62.610 022 8444	.015 971 8836
42	2.297 244 4660	64.862 223 3012	.015 417 2945
43	2.343 189 3553	67.159 467 7673	.014 889 9334
44	2.390 053 1425	69.502 657 1226	.014 387 9391
45	2.437 854 2053	71.892 710 2651	.013 909 6161
46	2.486 611 2894	74.330 564 4704	.013 453 4159
47	2.536 343 5152	76.817 175 7598	.013 017 9220
48	2.587 070 3855	79.353 519 2750	.012 601 8355
49	2.638 811 7932	81.940 589 6605	.012 203 9639
50	2.691 588 0291	84.579 401 4537	.011 823 2097
51	2.745 419 7897	87.270 989 4828	.011 458 5615
52	2.800 328 1854	90.016 409 2724	.011 109 0856
53	2.856 334 7492	92.816 737 4579	.010 773 9189
54	2.913 461 4441	95.673 072 2070	.010 452 2618
55	2.971 730 6730	98.586 533 6512	.010 143 3732
56	3.031 165 2865	101.558 264 3242	.009 846 5645
57	3.091 788 5922	104.589 429 6107	.009 561 1957
58	3.153 624 3641	107.681 218 2029	.009 286 6706
59	3.216 696 8513	110.834 842 5669	.009 022 4335
60	3.281 030 7884	114.051 539 4183	.008 767 9658
n	$s = (1+i)^n$	$s_{\overline{n}} = \dfrac{(1+i)^n - 1}{i}$	$\dfrac{1}{s_{\overline{n}}} = \dfrac{i}{(1+i)^n - 1}$

.02
per period

ANNUALLY
If compounded
annually
nominal annual rate is
2%

SEMIANNUALLY
If compounded
semiannually
nominal annual rate is
4%

QUARTERLY
If compounded
quarterly
nominal annual rate is
8%

MONTHLY
If compounded
monthly
nominal annual rate is
24%

$i = .02$
$j_{(2)} = .04$
$j_{(4)} = .08$
$j_{(12)} = .24$

PRESENT WORTH OF 1 *What $1 due in the future is worth today.*	PRESENT WORTH OF 1 PER PERIOD *What $1 payable periodically is worth today.*	PARTIAL PAYMENT *Annuity worth $1 today.* *Periodic payment necessary to pay off a loan of $1.*	P E R I O D S	RATE **2%**
.980 392 1569	.980 392 1569	1.020 000 0000	1	
.961 168 7812	1.941 560 9381	.515 049 5050	2	
.942 322 3345	2.883 883 2726	.346 754 6726	3	.02
.923 845 4260	3.807 728 6987	.262 623 7527	4	
.905 730 8098	4.713 459 5085	.212 158 3941	5	*per period*
.887 971 3822	5.601 430 8907	.178 525 8123	6	
.870 560 1786	6.471 991 0693	.154 511 9561	7	
.853 490 3712	7.325 481 4405	.136 509 7991	8	
.836 755 2659	8.162 236 7064	.122 515 4374	9	
.820 348 2999	8.982 585 0062	.111 326 5279	10	
.804 263 0391	9.786 848 0453	.102 177 9428	11	
.788 493 1756	10.575 341 2209	.094 559 5966	12	
.773 032 5251	11.348 373 7460	.088 118 3527	13	
.757 875 0246	12.106 248 7706	.082 601 9702	14	
.743 014 7300	12.849 263 5006	.077 825 4723	15	
.728 445 8137	13.577 709 3143	.073 650 1259	16	
.714 162 5625	14.291 871 8768	.069 969 8408	17	
.700 159 3750	14.992 031 2517	.066 702 1022	18	
.686 430 7598	15.678 462 0115	.063 781 7663	19	
.672 971 3331	16.351 433 3446	.061 156 7181	20	
.659 775 8168	17.011 209 1614	.058 784 7689	21	ANNUALLY If compounded *annually* nominal annual rate is
.646 839 0361	17.658 048 1974	.056 631 4005	22	
.634 155 9177	18.292 204 1151	.054 668 0976	23	
.621 721 4879	18.913 925 6031	.052 871 0973	24	
.609 530 8705	19.523 456 4736	.051 220 4384	25	**2%**
.597 579 2848	20.121 035 7584	.049 699 2308	26	
.585 862 0440	20.706 897 8024	.048 293 0862	27	
.574 374 5529	21.281 272 3553	.046 989 6716	28	
.563 112 3068	21.844 384 6620	.045 778 3552	29	
.552 070 8890	22.396 455 5510	.044 649 9223	30	
.541 245 9696	22.937 701 5206	.043 596 3472	31	SEMIANNUALLY If compounded *semiannually* nominal annual rate is
.530 633 3035	23.468 334 8241	.042 610 6073	32	
.520 228 7289	23.988 563 5530	.041 686 5311	33	
.510 028 1656	24.498 591 7187	.040 818 6728	34	
.500 027 6134	24.998 619 3320	.040 002 2092	35	**4%**
.490 223 1504	25.488 842 4824	.039 232 8526	36	
.480 610 9317	25.969 453 4141	.038 506 7789	37	
.471 187 1880	26.440 640 6021	.037 820 5663	38	
.461 948 2235	26.902 588 8256	.037 171 1439	39	
.452 890 4152	27.355 479 2407	.036 555 7478	40	QUARTERLY If compounded *quarterly* nominal annual rate is
.444 010 2110	27.799 489 4517	.035 971 8836	41	
.435 304 1284	28.234 793 5801	.035 417 2945	42	
.426 768 7533	28.661 562 3334	.034 889 9334	43	
.418 400 7386	29.079 963 0720	.034 387 9391	44	
.410 196 8025	29.490 159 8745	.033 909 6161	45	**8%**
.402 153 7280	29.892 313 6025	.033 453 4159	46	
.394 268 3607	30.286 581 9632	.033 017 9220	47	
.386 537 6086	30.673 119 5718	.032 601 8355	48	
.378 958 4398	31.052 078 0115	.032 203 9639	49	
.371 527 6821	31.423 605 8937	.031 823 2097	50	MONTHLY If compounded *monthly* nominal annual rate is
.364 243 0217	31.787 848 9153	.031 458 5615	51	
.357 101 0017	32.144 949 9170	.031 109 0856	52	
.350 099 0212	32.495 048 9382	.030 773 9189	53	
.343 294 3345	32.838 283 2728	.030 452 2618	54	
.336 504 2496	33.174 787 5223	.030 143 3732	55	**24%**
.329 906 1270	33.504 693 6494	.029 846 5645	56	
.323 437 3794	33.828 131 0288	.029 561 1957	57	$i = .02$
.317 095 4700	34.145 226 4988	.029 286 6706	58	$j_{(2)} = .04$
.310 877 9118	34.456 104 4106	.029 022 4335	59	$j_{(4)} = .08$
.304 782 2665	34.760 886 6770	.028 767 9658	60	$j_{(12)} = .24$
$v^n = \dfrac{1}{(1+i)^n}$	$a_{\overline{n}|} = \dfrac{1-v^n}{i}$	$\dfrac{1}{a_{\overline{n}|}} = \dfrac{i}{1-v^n}$	n	

P E R I O D S	AMOUNT OF 1 *How $1 left at compound interest will grow.*	AMOUNT OF 1 PER PERIOD *How $1 deposited periodically will grow.*	SINKING FUND *Periodic deposit that will grow to $1 at future date.*
1	1.022 500 0000	1.000 000 0000	1.000 000 0000
2	1.045 506 2500	2.022 500 0000	.494 437 5773
3	1.069 030 1406	3.068 006 2500	.325 944 5772
4	1.093 083 3188	4.137 036 3906	.241 718 9277
5	1.117 677 6935	5.230 119 7094	.191 200 2125
6	1.142 825 4416	6.347 797 4029	.157 534 9584
7	1.168 539 0140	7.490 622 8444	.133 500 2470
8	1.194 831 1418	8.659 161 8584	.115 484 6181
9	1.221 714 8425	9.853 993 0003	.101 481 7039
10	1.249 203 4265	11.075 707 8428	.090 287 6831
11	1.277 310 5036	12.324 911 2692	.081 136 4868
12	1.306 049 9899	13.602 221 7728	.073 517 4015
13	1.335 436 1147	14.908 271 7627	.067 076 8561
14	1.365 483 4272	16.243 707 8773	.061 562 2989
15	1.396 206 8044	17.609 191 3046	.056 788 5250
16	1.427 621 4575	19.005 398 1089	.052 616 6300
17	1.459 742 9402	20.433 019 5664	.048 940 3926
18	1.492 587 1564	21.892 762 5066	.045 677 1958
19	1.526 170 3674	23.385 349 6630	.042 761 8152
20	1.560 509 2007	24.911 520 0304	.040 142 0708
21	1.595 620 6577	26.472 029 2311	.037 775 7214
22	1.631 522 1225	28.067 649 8888	.035 628 2056
23	1.668 231 3703	29.699 172 0113	.033 670 9724
24	1.705 766 5761	31.367 403 3816	.031 880 2289
25	1.744 146 3240	33.073 169 9577	.030 235 9889
26	1.783 389 6163	34.817 316 2817	.028 721 3406
27	1.823 515 8827	36.600 705 8980	.027 321 8774
28	1.864 544 9901	38.424 221 7807	.026 025 2506
29	1.906 497 2523	40.288 766 7708	.024 820 8143
30	1.949 393 4405	42.195 264 0232	.023 699 3422
31	1.993 254 7929	44.144 657 4637	.022 652 7978
32	2.038 103 0258	46.137 912 2566	.021 674 1493
33	2.083 960 3439	48.176 015 2824	.020 757 2169
34	2.130 849 4516	50.259 975 6262	.019 896 5477
35	2.178 793 5643	52.390 825 0778	.019 087 3115
36	2.227 816 4194	54.569 618 6421	.018 325 2151
37	2.277 942 2889	56.797 435 0615	.017 606 4289
38	2.329 195 9904	59.075 377 3504	.016 927 5262
39	2.381 602 9002	61.404 573 3408	.016 285 4319
40	2.435 188 9654	63.786 176 2410	.015 677 3781
41	2.489 980 7171	66.221 365 2064	.015 100 8666
42	2.546 005 2833	68.711 345 9235	.014 553 6372
43	2.603 290 4022	71.257 351 2068	.014 033 6398
44	2.661 864 4362	73.860 641 6090	.013 539 0105
45	2.721 756 3860	76.522 506 0452	.013 068 0508
46	2.782 995 9047	79.244 262 4312	.012 619 2101
47	2.845 613 3126	82.027 258 3359	.012 191 0694
48	2.909 639 6121	84.872 871 6484	.011 782 3279
49	2.975 106 5034	87.782 511 2605	.011 391 7908
50	3.042 046 3997	90.757 617 7639	.011 018 3588
51	3.110 492 4437	93.799 664 1636	.010 661 0190
52	3.180 478 5237	96.910 156 6073	.010 318 8359
53	3.252 039 2904	100.090 635 1309	.009 990 9447
54	3.325 210 1745	103.342 674 4214	.009 676 5446
55	3.400 027 4034	106.667 884 5958	.009 374 8930
56	3.476 528 0200	110.067 911 9993	.009 085 3000
57	3.554 749 9004	113.544 440 0192	.008 807 1243
58	3.634 731 7732	117.099 189 9197	.008 539 7687
59	3.716 513 2381	120.733 921 6929	.008 282 6764
60	3.800 134 7859	124.450 434 9310	.008 035 3275
n	$s=(1+i)^n$	$s_{\overline{n}|}=\dfrac{(1+i)^n-1}{i}$	$\dfrac{1}{s_{\overline{n}|}}=\dfrac{i}{(1+i)^n-1}$

.0225

per period

ANNUALLY
If compounded *annually* nominal annual rate is

2¼%

SEMIANNUALLY
If compounded *semiannually* nominal annual rate is

4½%

QUARTERLY
If compounded *quarterly* nominal annual rate is

9%

MONTHLY
If compounded *monthly* nominal annual rate is

27%

$i = .0225$
$j_{(2)} = .045$
$j_{(4)} = .09$
$j_{(12)} = .27$

PRESENT WORTH OF 1	PRESENT WORTH OF 1 PER PERIOD	PARTIAL PAYMENT	P E R I O D S	RATE
What $1 due in the future is worth today.	*What $1 payable periodically is worth today.*	*Annuity worth $1 today.* *Periodic payment necessary to pay off a loan of $1.*		$2\frac{1}{4}\%$
.977 995 1100	.977 995 1100	1.022 500 0000	1	
.956 474 4352	1.934 469 5453	.516 937 5773	2	
.935 427 3205	2.869 896 8658	.348 444 5772	3	.0225
.914 843 3453	3.784 740 2110	.264 218 9277	4	*per period*
.894 712 3181	4.679 452 5291	.213 700 2125	5	
.875 024 2720	5.554 476 8011	.180 034 9584	6	
.855 769 4591	6.410 246 2602	.156 000 2470	7	
.836 938 3464	7.247 184 6066	.137 984 6181	8	
.818 521 6101	8.065 706 2167	.123 981 7039	9	
.800 510 1322	8.866 216 3489	.112 787 6831	10	
.782 894 9948	9.649 111 3436	.103 636 4868	11	
.765 667 4765	10.414 778 8202	.096 017 4015	12	
.748 819 0480	11.163 597 8681	.089 576 8561	13	
.732 341 3672	11.895 939 2354	.084 062 2989	14	
.716 226 2760	12.612 165 5113	.079 288 5250	15	
.700 465 7956	13.312 631 3069	.075 116 6300	16	
.685 052 1228	13.997 683 4298	.071 440 3926	17	
.669 977 6262	14.667 661 0560	.068 177 1958	18	
.655 234 8423	15.322 895 8983	.065 261 8152	19	
.640 816 4717	15.963 712 3700	.062 642 0708	20	ANNUALLY
.626 715 3757	16.590 427 7457	.060 275 7214	21	If compounded *annually* nominal annual rate is
.612 924 5728	17.203 352 3185	.058 128 2056	22	
.599 437 2350	17.802 789 5536	.056 170 9724	23	
.586 246 6846	18.389 036 2382	.054 380 2289	24	
.573 346 3908	18.962 382 6291	.052 735 9889	25	$2\frac{1}{4}\%$
.560 729 9666	19.523 112 5957	.051 221 3406	26	
.548 391 1654	20.071 503 7610	.049 821 8774	27	
.536 323 8781	20.607 827 6392	.048 525 2506	28	
.524 522 1302	21.192 349 7693	.047 320 8143	29	
.512 980 0784	21.645 329 8478	.046 199 3422	30	SEMIANNUALLY
.501 692 0082	22.147 021 8560	.045 152 7978	31	If compounded *semiannually* nominal annual rate is
.490 652 3308	22.637 674 1868	.044 174 1493	32	
.479 855 5802	23.117 529 7670	.043 257 2169	33	
.469 296 4110	23.586 826 1780	.042 396 5477	34	
.458 969 5951	24.045 795 7731	.041 587 3115	35	$4\frac{1}{2}\%$
.448 870 0197	24.494 665 7928	.040 825 2151	36	
.438 992 6843	24.933 658 4771	.040 106 4289	37	
.429 332 6985	25.362 991 1756	.039 427 5262	38	
.419 885 2798	25.782 876 4554	.038 785 4319	39	
.410 645 7504	26.193 522 2057	.038 177 3781	40	QUARTERLY
.401 609 5358	26.595 131 7416	.037 600 8666	41	If compounded *quarterly* nominal annual rate is
.392 772 1622	26.987 903 9037	.037 053 6372	42	
.384 129 2540	27.372 033 1577	.036 533 6398	43	
.375 676 5320	27.747 709 6897	.036 039 0105	44	
.367 409 8112	28.115 119 5009	.035 568 0508	45	9%
.359 324 9988	28.474 444 4997	.035 119 2101	46	
.351 418 0917	28.825 862 5913	.034 691 0694	47	
.343 685 1753	29.169 547 7666	.034 282 3279	48	
.336 122 4208	29.505 670 1874	.033 891 7908	49	
.328 726 0839	29.834 396 2713	.033 518 3588	50	MONTHLY
.321 492 5026	30.155 888 7739	.033 161 0190	51	If compounded *monthly* nominal annual rate is
.314 418 0954	30.470 306 8693	.032 818 8359	52	
.307 499 3598	30.777 806 2291	.032 490 9447	53	
.300 732 8703	31.078 539 0994	.032 176 5446	54	
.294 115 2765	31.372 654 3760	.031 874 8930	55	27%
.287 643 3022	31.660 297 6782	.031 585 3000	56	
.281 313 7430	31.941 611 4212	.031 307 1243	57	
.275 123 4651	32.216 734 8863	.031 039 7687	58	$i = .0225$
.269 069 4035	32.485 804 2898	.030 782 6764	59	$j_{(2)} = .045$
.263 148 5609	32.748 952 8506	.030 535 3275	60	$j_{(4)} = .09$
$v^n = \dfrac{1}{(1+i)^n}$	$a_{\overline{n}\rceil} = \dfrac{1-v^n}{i}$	$\dfrac{1}{a_{\overline{n}\rceil}} = \dfrac{i}{1-v^n}$	n	$j_{(12)} = .27$

P E R I O D S	AMOUNT OF 1 *How $1 left at compound interest will grow.*	AMOUNT OF 1 PER PERIOD *How $1 deposited periodically will grow.*	SINKING FUND *Periodic deposit that will grow to $1 at future date.*
1	1.025 000 0000	1.000 000 0000	1.000 000 0000
2	1.050 625 0000	2.025 000 0000	.493 827 1605
3	1.076 890 6250	3.075 625 0000	.325 137 1672
4	1.103 812 8906	4.152 515 6250	.240 817 8777
5	1.131 408 2129	5.256 328 5156	.190 246 8609
6	1.159 693 4182	6.387 736 7285	.156 549 9711
7	1.188 685 7537	7.547 430 1467	.132 495 4296
8	1.218 402 8975	8.736 115 9004	.114 467 3458
9	1.248 862 9699	9.954 518 7979	.100 456 8900
10	1.280 084 5442	11.203 381 7679	.089 258 7632
11	1.312 086 6578	12.483 466 3121	.080 105 9558
12	1.344 888 8242	13.795 552 9699	.072 487 1270
13	1.378 511 0449	15.140 441 7941	.066 048 2708
14	1.412 973 8210	16.518 952 8390	.060 536 5249
15	1.448 298 1665	17.931 926 6599	.055 766 4561
16	1.484 505 6207	19.380 224 8264	.051 598 9886
17	1.521 618 2612	20.864 730 4471	.047 927 7699
18	1.559 658 7177	22.386 348 7083	.044 670 0805
19	1.598 650 1856	23.946 007 4260	.041 760 6151
20	1.638 616 4403	25.544 657 6116	.039 147 1287
21	1.679 581 8513	27.183 274 0519	.036 787 3273
22	1.721 571 3976	28.862 855 9032	.034 646 6061
23	1.764 610 6825	30.584 427 3008	.032 696 3781
24	1.808 725 9496	32.349 037 9833	.030 912 8204
25	1.853 944 0983	34.157 763 9329	.029 275 9210
26	1.900 292 7008	36.011 708 0312	.027 768 7467
27	1.947 800 0183	37.912 000 7320	.026 376 8722
28	1.996 495 0188	39.859 800 7503	.025 087 9327
29	2.046 407 3942	41.856 295 7690	.023 891 2685
30	2.097 567 5791	43.902 703 1633	.022 777 6407
31	2.150 006 7686	46.000 270 7424	.021 739 0025
32	2.203 756 9378	48.150 277 5109	.020 768 3123
33	2.258 850 8612	50.354 034 4487	.019 859 3819
34	2.315 322 1327	52.612 885 3099	.019 006 7508
35	2.373 205 1861	54.928 207 4426	.018 205 5823
36	2.432 535 3157	57.301 412 6287	.017 451 5767
37	2.493 348 6986	59.733 947 9444	.016 740 8992
38	2.555 682 4161	62.227 296 6430	.016 070 1180
39	2.619 574 4765	64.782 979 0591	.015 436 1534
40	2.685 063 8384	67.402 553 5356	.014 836 2332
41	2.752 190 4343	70.087 617 3740	.014 267 8555
42	2.820 995 1952	72.839 807 8083	.013 728 7567
43	2.891 520 0751	75.660 803 0035	.013 216 8833
44	2.963 808 0770	78.552 323 0786	.012 730 3683
45	3.037 903 2789	81.516 131 1556	.012 267 5106
46	3.113 850 8609	84.554 034 4345	.011 826 7568
47	3.191 697 1324	87.667 885 2954	.011 406 6855
48	3.271 489 5607	90.859 582 4277	.011 005 9938
49	3.353 276 7997	94.131 071 9884	.010 623 4847
50	3.437 108 7197	97.484 348 7881	.010 258 0569
51	3.523 036 4377	100.921 457 5078	.009 908 6956
52	3.611 112 3486	104.444 493 9455	.009 574 4635
53	3.701 390 1574	108.055 606 2942	.009 254 4944
54	3.793 924 9113	111.756 996 4515	.008 947 9856
55	3.888 773 0341	115.550 921 3628	.008 654 1932
56	3.985 992 3599	119.439 694 3969	.008 372 4260
57	4.085 642 1689	123.425 686 7568	.008 102 0412
58	4.187 783 2231	127.511 328 9257	.007 842 4404
59	4.292 477 8037	131.699 112 1489	.007 593 0656
60	4.399 789 7488	135.991 589 9526	.007 353 3959
n	$s=(1+i)^n$	$s_{\overline{n}|}=\dfrac{(1+i)^n-1}{i}$	$\dfrac{1}{s_{\overline{n}|}}=\dfrac{i}{(1+i)^n-1}$

.025
per period

ANNUALLY
If compounded
annually
nominal annual rate is

2½%

SEMIANNUALLY
If compounded
semiannually
nominal annual rate is

5%

QUARTERLY
If compounded
quarterly
nominal annual rate is

10%

MONTHLY
If compounded
monthly
nominal annual rate is

30%

$i = .025$
$j_{(2)} = .05$
$j_{(4)} = .1$
$j_{(12)} = .3$

PRESENT WORTH OF 1	PRESENT WORTH OF 1 PER PERIOD	PARTIAL PAYMENT	P E R I O D S	RATE
What $1 due in the future is worth today.	What $1 payable periodically is worth today.	Annuity worth $1 today. Periodic payment necessary to pay off a loan of $1.		$2\frac{1}{2}\%$

PRESENT WORTH OF 1	PRESENT WORTH OF 1 PER PERIOD	PARTIAL PAYMENT	n	
.975 609 7561	.975 609 7561	1.025 000 0000	1	
.951 814 3962	1.927 424 1523	.518 827 1605	2	
.928 599 4109	2.856 023 5632	.350 137 1672	3	.025
.905 950 6448	3.761 974 2080	.265 817 8777	4	per period
.883 854 2876	4.645 828 4956	.215 246 8609	5	
.862 296 8660	5.508 125 3616	.181 549 9711	6	
.841 265 2351	6.349 390 5967	.157 495 4296	7	
.820 746 5708	7.170 137 1675	.139 467 3458	8	
.800 728 3618	7.970 865 5292	.125 456 8900	9	
.781 198 4017	8.752 063 9310	.114 258 7632	10	
.762 144 7822	9.514 208 7131	.105 105 9558	11	
.743 555 8850	10.257 764 5982	.097 487 1270	12	
.725 420 3757	10.983 184 9738	.091 048 2708	13	
.707 727 1958	11.690 912 1696	.085 536 5249	14	
.690 465 5568	12.381 377 7264	.080 766 4561	15	
.673 624 9335	13.055 002 6599	.076 598 9886	16	
.657 195 0571	13.712 197 7170	.072 927 7699	17	
.641 165 9093	14.353 363 6264	.069 670 0805	18	
.625 527 7164	14.978 891 3428	.066 760 6151	19	
.610 270 9429	15.589 162 2856	.064 147 1287	20	
.595 386 2857	16.184 548 5714	.061 787 3273	21	ANNUALLY
.580 864 6690	16.765 413 2404	.059 646 6061	22	If compounded annually
.566 697 2380	17.332 110 4784	.057 696 3781	23	nominal annual rate is
.552 875 3542	17.884 985 8326	.055 912 8204	24	
.539 390 5894	18.424 376 4220	.054 275 9210	25	$2\frac{1}{2}\%$
.526 234 7214	18.950 611 1434	.052 768 7467	26	
.513 399 7282	19.464 010 8717	.051 376 8722	27	
.500 877 7836	19.964 888 6553	.050 087 9327	28	
.488 661 2523	20.453 549 9076	.048 891 2685	29	
.476 742 6852	20.930 292 5928	.047 777 6407	30	
.465 114 8148	21.395 407 4076	.046 739 0025	31	SEMIANNUALLY
.453 770 5510	21.849 177 9586	.045 768 3123	32	If compounded semiannually
.442 702 9766	22.291 880 9352	.044 859 3819	33	nominal annual rate is
.431 905 3430	22.723 786 2783	.044 006 7508	34	
.421 371 0664	23.145 157 3447	.043 205 5823	35	5%
.411 093 7233	23.556 251 0680	.042 451 5767	36	
.401 067 0471	23.957 318 1151	.041 740 8992	37	
.391 284 9240	24.348 603 0391	.041 070 1180	38	
.381 741 3893	24.730 344 4284	.040 436 1534	39	
.372 430 6237	25.102 775 0521	.039 836 2332	40	
.363 346 9499	25.466 122 0020	.039 267 8555	41	QUARTERLY
.354 484 8292	25.820 606 8313	.038 728 7567	42	If compounded quarterly
.345 838 8578	26.166 445 6890	.038 216 8833	43	nominal annual rate is
.337 403 7637	26.503 849 4527	.037 730 3683	44	
.329 174 4036	26.833 023 8563	.037 267 5106	45	10%
.321 145 7596	27.154 169 6159	.036 826 7568	46	
.313 312 9362	27.467 482 5521	.036 406 6855	47	
.305 671 1573	27.773 153 7094	.036 005 9938	48	
.298 215 7632	28.071 369 4726	.035 623 4847	49	
.290 942 2080	28.362 311 6805	.035 258 0569	50	MONTHLY
.283 846 0566	28.646 157 7371	.034 908 6956	51	If compounded monthly
.276 922 9820	28.923 080 7191	.034 574 4635	52	nominal annual rate is
.270 168 7629	29.193 249 4821	.034 254 4944	53	
.263 579 2809	29.456 828 7630	.033 947 9856	54	
.257 150 5180	29.713 979 2810	.033 654 1932	55	30%
.250 878 5541	29.964 857 8351	.033 372 4260	56	
.244 759 5650	30.209 617 4001	.033 102 0412	57	$i = .025$
.238 789 8195	30.448 407 2196	.032 842 4404	58	$j_{(2)} = .05$
.232 965 6776	30.681 372 8972	.032 593 0656	59	$j_{(4)} = .1$
.227 283 5879	30.908 656 4851	.032 353 3959	60	$j_{(12)} = .3$
$v^n = \dfrac{1}{(1+i)^n}$	$a_{\overline{n}|} = \dfrac{1-v^n}{i}$	$\dfrac{1}{a_{\overline{n}|}} = \dfrac{i}{1-v^n}$	n	

P E R I O D S	AMOUNT OF 1 *How $1 left at compound interest will grow.*	AMOUNT OF 1 PER PERIOD *How $1 deposited periodically will grow.*	SINKING FUND *Periodic deposit that will grow to $1 at future date.*
1	1.030 000 0000	1.000 000 0000	1.000 000 0000
2	1.060 900 0000	2.030 000 0000	.492 610 8374
3	1.092 727 0000	3.090 900 0000	.323 530 3633
4	1.125 508 8100	4.183 627 0000	.239 027 0452
5	1.159 274 0743	5.309 135 8100	.188 354 5714
6	1.194 052 2965	6.468 409 8843	.154 597 5005
7	1.229 873 8654	7.662 462 1808	.130 506 3538
8	1.266 770 0814	8.892 336 0463	.112 456 3888
9	1.304 773 1838	10.159 106 1276	.098 433 8570
10	1.343 916 3793	11.463 879 3115	.087 230 5066
11	1.384 233 8707	12.807 795 6908	.078 077 4478
12	1.425 760 8868	14.192 029 5615	.070 462 0855
13	1.468 533 7135	15.617 790 4484	.064 029 5440
14	1.512 589 7249	17.086 324 1618	.058 526 3390
15	1.557 967 4166	18.598 913 8867	.053 766 5805
16	1.604 706 4391	20.156 881 3033	.049 610 8493
17	1.652 847 6323	21.761 587 7424	.045 952 5294
18	1.702 433 0612	23.414 435 3747	.042 708 6959
19	1.753 506 0531	25.116 868 4359	.039 813 8806
20	1.806 111 2347	26.870 374 4890	.037 215 7076
21	1.860 294 5717	28.676 485 7236	.034 871 7765
22	1.916 103 4089	30.536 780 2954	.032 747 3948
23	1.973 586 5111	32.452 883 7042	.030 813 9027
24	2.032 794 1065	34.426 470 2153	.029 047 4159
25	2.093 777 9297	36.459 264 3218	.027 427 8710
26	2.156 591 2675	38.553 042 2515	.025 938 2903
27	2.221 289 0056	40.709 633 5190	.024 564 2103
28	2.287 927 6757	42.930 922 5246	.023 293 2334
29	2.356 565 5060	45.218 850 2003	.022 114 6711
30	2.427 262 4712	47.575 415 7063	.021 019 2593
31	2.500 080 3453	50.002 678 1775	.019 998 9288
32	2.575 082 7557	52.502 758 5228	.019 046 6183
33	2.652 335 2384	55.077 841 2785	.018 156 1219
34	2.731 905 2955	57.730 176 5169	.017 321 9633
35	2.813 862 4544	60.462 081 8124	.016 539 2916
36	2.898 278 3280	63.275 944 2668	.015 803 7942
37	2.985 226 6778	66.174 222 5948	.015 111 6244
38	3.074 783 4782	69.159 449 2726	.014 459 3401
39	3.167 026 9825	72.234 232 7508	.013 843 8516
40	3.262 037 7920	75.401 259 7333	.013 262 3779
41	3.359 898 9258	78.663 297 5253	.012 712 4089
42	3.460 695 8935	82.023 196 4511	.012 191 6731
43	3.564 516 7703	85.483 892 3446	.011 698 1103
44	3.671 452 2734	89.048 409 1149	.011 229 8469
45	3.781 595 8417	92.719 861 3884	.010 785 1757
46	3.895 043 7169	96.501 457 2300	.010 362 5378
47	4.011 895 0284	100.396 500 9469	.009 960 5065
48	4.132 251 8793	104.408 395 9753	.009 577 7738
49	4.256 219 4356	108.540 647 8546	.009 213 1383
50	4.383 906 0187	112.796 867 2902	.008 865 4944
51	4.515 423 1993	117.180 773 3089	.008 533 8232
52	4.650 885 8952	121.696 196 5082	.008 217 1837
53	4.790 412 4721	126.347 082 4035	.007 914 7059
54	4.934 124 8463	131.137 494 8756	.007 625 5841
55	5.082 148 5917	136.071 619 7218	.007 349 0710
56	5.234 613 0494	141.153 768 3135	.007 084 4726
57	5.391 651 4409	146.388 381 3629	.006 831 1432
58	5.553 400 9841	151.780 032 8038	.006 588 4819
59	5.720 003 0136	157.333 433 7879	.006 355 9281
60	5.891 603 1040	163.053 436 8015	.006 132 9587
n	$s=(1+i)^n$	$s_{\overline{n}|}=\dfrac{(1+i)^n-1}{i}$	$\dfrac{1}{s_{\overline{n}|}}=\dfrac{i}{(1+i)^n-1}$

.03

per period

ANNUALLY
If compounded
annually
nominal annual rate is

3%

SEMIANNUALLY
If compounded
semiannually
nominal annual rate is

6%

QUARTERLY
If compounded
quarterly
nominal annual rate is

12%

MONTHLY
If compounded
monthly
nominal annual rate is

36%

$i = .03$
$j_{(2)} = .06$
$j_{(4)} = .12$
$j_{(12)} = .36$

PRESENT WORTH OF 1 *What $1 due in the future is worth today.*	PRESENT WORTH OF 1 PER PERIOD *What $1 payable periodically is worth today.*	PARTIAL PAYMENT *Annuity worth $1 today. Periodic payment necessary to pay off a loan of $1.*	P E R I O D S	RATE **3%**
.970 873 7864	.970 873 7864	1.030 000 0000	1	
.942 595 9091	1.913 469 6955	.522 610 8374	2	
.915 141 6594	2.828 611 3549	.353 530 3633	3	.03
.888 487 0479	3.717 098 4028	.269 027 0452	4	
.862 608 7844	4.579 707 1872	.218 354 5714	5	*per period*
.837 484 2567	5.417 191 4439	.184 597 5005	6	
.813 091 5113	6.230 282 9552	.160 506 3538	7	
.789 409 2343	7.019 692 1895	.142 456 3888	8	
.766 416 7323	7.786 108 9219	.128 433 8570	9	
.744 093 9149	8.530 202 8368	.117 230 5066	10	
.722 421 2766	9.252 624 1134	.108 077 4478	11	
.701 379 8802	9.954 003 9936	.100 462 0855	12	
.680 951 3400	10.634 955 3336	.094 029 5440	13	
.661 117 8058	11.296 073 1394	.088 526 3390	14	
.641 861 9474	11.937 935 0868	.083 766 5805	15	
.623 166 9392	12.561 102 0260	.079 610 8493	16	
.605 016 4458	13.166 118 4718	.075 952 5294	17	
.587 394 6076	13.753 513 0795	.072 708 6959	18	
.570 286 0268	14.323 799 1063	.069 813 8806	19	
.553 675 7542	14.877 474 8605	.067 215 7076	20	ANNUALLY *If compounded annually nominal annual rate is*
.537 549 2759	15.415 024 1364	.064 871 7765	21	
.521 892 5009	15.936 916 6372	.062 747 3948	22	
.506 691 7484	16.443 608 3857	.060 813 9027	23	
.491 933 7363	16.935 542 1220	.059 047 4159	24	
.477 605 5693	17.413 147 6913	.057 427 8710	25	**3%**
.463 694 7274	17.876 842 4187	.055 938 2903	26	
.450 189 0558	18.327 031 4745	.054 564 2103	27	
.437 076 7532	18.764 108 2277	.053 293 2334	28	
.424 346 3623	19.188 454 5900	.052 114 6711	29	
.411 986 7595	19.600 441 3495	.051 019 2593	30	SEMIANNUALLY *If compounded semiannually nominal annual rate is.*
.399 987 1452	20.000 428 4946	.049 998 9288	31	
.388 337 0341	20.388 765 5288	.049 046 6183	32	
.377 026 2467	20.765 791 7755	.048 156 1219	33	
.366 044 8997	21.131 836 6752	.047 321 9633	34	
.355 383 3978	21.487 220 0731	.046 539 2916	35	**6%**
.345 032 4251	21.832 252 4981	.045 803 7942	36	
.334 982 9369	22.167 235 4351	.045 111 6244	37	
.325 226 1524	22.492 461 5874	.044 459 3401	38	
.315 753 5460	22.808 215 1334	.043 843 8516	39	
.306 556 8408	23.114 771 9742	.043 262 3779	40	QUARTERLY *If compounded quarterly nominal annual rate is*
.297 628 0008	23.412 399 9750	.042 712 4089	41	
.288 959 2240	23.701 359 1990	.042 191 6731	42	
.280 542 9360	23.981 902 1349	.041 698 1103	43	
.272 371 7825	24.254 273 9174	.041 229 8469	44	
.264 438 6238	24.518 712 5412	.040 785 1757	45	**12%**
.256 736 5279	24.775 449 0691	.040 362 5378	46	
.249 258 7650	25.024 707 8341	.039 960 5065	47	
.241 998 8009	25.266 706 6350	.039 577 7738	48	
.234 950 2922	25.501 656 9272	.039 213 1383	49	
.228 107 0798	25.729 764 0070	.038 865 4944	50	MONTHLY *If compounded monthly nominal annual rate is*
.221 463 1843	25.951 227 1913	.038 533 8232	51	
.215 012 8003	26.166 239 9915	.038 217 1837	52	
.208 750 2915	26.374 990 2830	.037 914 7059	53	
.202 670 1859	26.577 660 4690	.037 625 5841	54	
.196 767 1708	26.774 427 6398	.037 349 0710	55	**36%**
.191 036 0882	26.965 463 7279	.037 084 4726	56	
.185 471 9303	27.150 935 6582	.036 831 1432	57	
.180 069 8352	27.331 005 4934	.036 588 4819	58	$i = .03$
.174 825 0827	27.505 830 5761	.036 355 9281	59	$j_{(2)} = .06$
.169 733 0900	27.675 563 6661	.036 132 9587	60	$j_{(4)} = .12$ $j_{(12)} = .36$
$v^n = \dfrac{1}{(1+i)^n}$	$a_{\overline{n}\|} = \dfrac{1-v^n}{i}$	$\dfrac{1}{a_{\overline{n}\|}} = \dfrac{i}{1-v^n}$	n	

3½%

	P E R I O D S	AMOUNT OF 1 *How $1 left at compound interest will grow.*	AMOUNT OF 1 PER PERIOD *How $1 deposited periodically will grow.*	SINKING FUND *Periodic deposit that will grow to $1 at future date.*
.035 *per period*	1	1.035 000 0000	1.000 000 0000	1.000 000 0000
	2	1.071 225 0000	2.035 000 0000	.491 400 4914
	•3	1.108 717 8750	3.106 225 0000	.321 934 1806
	4	1.147 523 0006	4.214 942 8750	.237 251 1395
	5	1.187 686 3056	5.362 465 8756	.186 481 3732
	6	1.229 255 3263	6.550 152 1813	.152 668 2087
	7	1.272 279 2628	7.779 407 5076	.128 544 4938
	8	1.316 809 0370	9.051 686 7704	.110 476 6465
	9	1.362 897 3533	10.368 495 8073	.096 446 0051
	10	1.410 598 7606	11.731 393 1606	.085 241 3679
	11	1.459 969 7172	13.141 991 9212	.076 091 9658
	12	1.511 068 6573	14.601 961 6385	.068 483 9493
	13	1.563 956 0604	16.113 030 2958	.062 061 5726
	14	1.618 694 5225	17.676 986 3562	.056 570 7287
	15	1.675 348 8308	19.295 680 8786	.051 825 0694
	16	1.733 986 0398	20.971 029 7094	.047 684 8306
	17	1.794 675 5512	22.705 015 7492	.044 043 1317
	18	1.857 489 1955	24.499 691 3004	.040 816 8408
	19	1.922 501 3174	26.357 180 4960	.037 940 3252
	20	1.989 788 8635	28.279 681 8133	.035 361 0768
ANNUALLY *If compounded annually nominal annual rate is* **3½%**	21	2.059 431 4737	30.269 470 6768	.033 036 5870
	22	2.131 511 5753	32.328 902 1505	.030 932 0742
	23	2.206 114 4804	34.460 413 7257	.029 018 8042
	24	2.283 328 4872	36.666 528 2061	.027 272 8303
	25	2.363 244 9843	38.949 856 6933	.025 674 0354
	26	2.445 958 5587	41.313 101 6776	.024 205 3963
	27	2.531 567 1083	43.759 060 2363	.022 852 4103
	28	2.620 171 9571	46.290 627 3446	.021 602 6452
	29	2.711 877 9756	48.910 799 3017	.020 445 3825
	30	2.806 793 7047	51.622 677 2772	.019 371 3316
SEMIANNUALLY *If compounded semiannually nominal annual rate is* **7%**	31	2.905 031 4844	54.429 470 9819	.018 372 3998
	32	3.006 707 5863	57.334 502 4663	.017 441 5048
	33	3.111 942 3518	60.341 210 0526	.016 572 4221
	34	3.220 860 3342	63.453 152 4044	.015 759 6583
	35	3.333 590 4459	66.674 012 7386	.014 998 3473
	36	3.450 266 1115	70.007 603 1845	.014 284 1628
	37	3.571 025 4254	73.457 869 2959	.013 613 2454
	38	3.696 011 3152	77.028 894 7213	.012 982 1414
	39	3.825 371 7113	80.724 906 0365	.012 387 7506
	40	3.959 259 7212	84.550 277 7478	.011 827 2823
QUARTERLY *If compounded quarterly nominal annual rate is* **14%**	41	4.097 833 8114	88.509 537 4690	.011 298 2174
	42	4.241 257 9948	92.607 371 2804	.010 798 2765
	43	4.389 702 0246	96.848 629 2752	.010 325 3914
	44	4.543 341 5955	101.238 331 2998	.009 877 6816
	45	4.702 358 5513	105.781 672 8953	.009 453 4334
	46	4.866 941 1006	110.484 031 4467	.009 051 0817
	47	5.037 284 0392	115.350 972 5473	.008 669 1944
	48	5.213 588 9805	120.388 256 5864	.008 306 4580
	49	5.396 064 5948	125.601 845 5670	.007 961 6665
	50	5.584 926 8557	130.997 910 1618	.007 633 7096
MONTHLY *If compounded monthly nominal annual rate is* **42%**	51	5.780 399 2956	136.582 837 0175	.007 321 5641
	52	5.982 713 2710	142.363 236 3131	.007 024 2854
	53	6.192 108 2354	148.345 949 5840	.006 740 9997
	54	6.408 832 0237	154.538 057 8195	.006 470 8979
	55	6.633 141 1445	160.946 889 8432	.006 213 2297
$i = .035$ $j_{(2)} = .07$ $j_{(4)} = .14$ $j_{(12)} = .42$	56	6.865 301 0846	167.580 030 9877	.005 967 2981
	57	7.105 586 6225	174.445 332 0722	.005 732 4549
	58	7.354 282 1543	181.550 918 6948	.005 508 0966
	59	7.611 682 0297	188.905 200 8491	.005 293 6605
	60	7.878 090 9008	196.516 882 8788	.005 088 6213
	n	$s=(1+i)^n$	$s_{\overline{n}}=\dfrac{(1+i)^n-1}{i}$	$\dfrac{1}{s_{\overline{n}}}=\dfrac{i}{(1+i)^n-1}$

PRESENT WORTH OF 1 — What $1 due in the future is worth today.	PRESENT WORTH OF 1 PER PERIOD — What $1 payable periodically is worth today.	PARTIAL PAYMENT — Annuity worth $1 today. Periodic payment necessary to pay off a loan of $1.	PERIODS
.966 183 5749	.966 183 5749	1.035 000 0000	1
.933 510 7004	1.899 694 2752	.526 400 4914	2
.901 942 7057	2.801 636 9809	.356 934 1806	3
.871 442 2277	3.673 079 2086	.272 251 1395	4
.841 973 1669	4.515 052 3755	.221 481 3732	5
.813 500 6443	5.328 553 0198	.187 668 2087	6
.785 990 9607	6.114 543 9805	.163 544 4938	7
.759 411 5562	6.873 955 5367	.145 476 6465	8
.733 730 9722	7.607 686 5089	.131 446 0051	9
.708 918 8137	8.316 605 3226	.120 241 3679	10
.684 945 7137	9.001 551 0363	.111 091 9658	11
.661 783 2983	9.663 334 3346	.103 483 9493	12
.639 404 1529	10.302 738 4875	.097 061 5726	13
.617 781 7903	10.920 520 2778	.091 570 7287	14
.596 890 6186	11.517 410 8964	.086 825 0694	15
.576 705 9117	12.094 116 8081	.082 684 8306	16
.557 203 7794	12.651 320 5876	.079 043 1317	17
.538 361 1396	13.189 681 7271	.075 816 8408	18
.520 155 6904	13.709 837 4175	.072 940 3252	19
.502 565 8844	14.212 403 3020	.070 361 0768	20
.485 570 9028	14.697 974 2048	.068 036 5870	21
.469 150 6308	15.167 124 8355	.065 932 0742	22
.453 285 6336	15.620 410 4691	.064 018 8042	23
.437 957 1339	16.058 367 6030	.062 272 8303	24
.423 146 9893	16.481 514 5923	.060 674 0354	25
.408 837 6708	16.890 352 2631	.059 205 3963	26
.395 012 2423	17.285 364 5054	.057 852 4103	27
.381 654 3404	17.667 018 8458	.056 602 6452	28
.368 748 1550	18.035 767 0008	.055 445 3825	29
.356 278 4106	18.392 045 4114	.054 371 3316	30
.344 230 3484	18.736 275 7598	.053 372 3998	31
.332 589 7086	19.068 865 4684	.052 441 5048	32
.321 342 7136	19.390 208 1820	.051 572 4221	33
.310 476 0518	19.700 684 2338	.050 759 6583	34
.299 976 8617	20.000 661 0955	.049 998 3473	35
.289 832 7166	20.290 493 8121	.049 284 1628	36
.280 031 6102	20.570 525 4223	.048 613 2454	37
.270 561 9422	20.841 087 3645	.047 982 1414	38
.261 412 5046	21.102 499 8691	.047 387 7506	39
.252 572 4682	21.355 072 3373	.046 827 2823	40
.244 031 3702	21.599 103 7075	.046 298 2174	41
.235 779 1017	21.834 882 8092	.045 798 2765	42
.227 805 8953	22.062 688 7046	.045 325 3914	43
.220 102 3143	22.282 791 0189	.044 877 6816	44
.212 659 2409	22.495 450 2598	.044 453 4334	45
.205 467 8656	22.700 918 1254	.044 051 0817	46
.198 519 6769	22.899 437 8023	.043 669 1944	47
.191 806 4511	23.091 244 2535	.043 306 4580	48
.185 320 2426	23.276 564 4961	.042 961 6665	49
.179 053 3745	23.455 617 8706	.042 633 7096	50
.172 998 4295	23.628 616 3001	.042 321 5641	51
.167 148 2411	23.795 764 5412	.042 024 2854	52
.161 495 8851	23.957 260 4263	.041 740 9997	53
.156 034 6716	24.113 295 0978	.041 470 8979	54
.150 758 1368	24.264 053 2346	.041 213 2297	55
.145 660 0355	24.409 713 2702	.040 967 2981	56
.140 734 3339	24.550 447 6040	.040 732 4549	57
.135 975 2018	24.686 422 8058	.040 508 0966	58
.131 377 0066	24.817 799 8124	.040 293 6605	59
.126 934 3059	24.944 734 1182	.040 088 6213	60
$v^n=\dfrac{1}{(1+i)^n}$	$a_{\overline{n}\rceil}=\dfrac{1-v^n}{i}$	$\dfrac{1}{a_{\overline{n}\rceil}}=\dfrac{i}{1-v^n}$	n

RATE

3½%

.035

per period

ANNUALLY
If compounded
annually
nominal annual rate is

3½%

SEMIANNUALLY
If compounded
semiannually
nominal annual rate is

7%

QUARTERLY
If compounded
quarterly
nominal annual rate is

14%

MONTHLY
If compounded
monthly
nominal annual rate is

42%

$i = .035$
$j_{(2)} = .07$
$j_{(4)} = .14$
$j_{(12)} = .42$

P E R I O D S	AMOUNT OF 1 *How $1 left at compound interest will grow.*	AMOUNT OF 1 PER PERIOD *How $1 deposited periodically will grow.*	SINKING FUND *Periodic deposit that will grow to $1 at future date.*
1	1.040 000 0000	1.000 000 0000	1.000 000 0000
2	1.081 600 0000	2.040 000 0000	.490 196 0784
3	1.124 864 0000	3.121 600 0000	.320 348 5392
4	1.169 858 5600	4.246 464 0000	.235 490 0454
5	1.216 652 9024	5.416 322 5600	.184 627 1135
6	1.265 319 0185	6.632 975 4624	.150 761 9025
7	1.315 931 7792	7.898 294 4809	.126 609 6120
8	1.368 569 0504	9.214 226 2601	.108 527 8320
9	1.423 311 8124	10.582 795 3105	.094 492 9927
10	1.480 244 2849	12.006 107 1230	.083 290 9443
11	1.539 454 0563	13.486 351 4079	.074 149 0393
12	1.601 032 2186	15.025 805 4642	.066 552 1727
13	1.665 073 5073	16.626 837 6828	.060 143 7278
14	1.731 676 4476	18.291 911 1901	.054 668 9731
15	1.800 943 5055	20.023 587 6377	.049 941 1004
16	1.872 981 2457	21.824 531 1432	.045 819 9992
17	1.947 900 4956	23.697 512 3889	.042 198 5221
18	2.025 816 5154	25.645 412 8845	.038 993 3281
19	2.106 849 1760	27.671 229 3998	.036 138 6184
20	2.191 123 1430	29.778 078 5758	.033 581 7503
21	2.278 768 0688	31.969 201 7189	.031 280 1054
22	2.369 918 7915	34.247 969 7876	.029 198 8111
23	2.464 715 5432	36.617 888 5791	.027 309 0568
24	2.563 304 1649	39.082 604 1223	.025 586 8313
25	2.665 836 3315	41.645 908 2872	.024 011 9628
26	2.772 469 7847	44.311 744 6187	.022 567 3805
27	2.883 368 5761	47.084 214 4034	.021 238 5406
28	2.998 703 3192	49.967 582 9796	.020 012 9752
29	3.118 651 4519	52.966 286 2987	.018 879 9342
30	3.243 397 5100	56.084 937 7507	.017 830 0991
31	3.373 133 4104	59.328 335 2607	.016 855 3524
32	3.508 058 7468	62.701 468 6711	.015 948 5897
33	3.648 381 0967	66.209 527 4180	.015 103 5665
34	3.794 316 3406	69.857 908 5147	.014 314 7715
35	3.946 088 9942	73.652 224 8553	.013 577 3224
36	4.103 932 5540	77.598 313 8495	.012 886 8780
37	4.268 089 8561	81.702 246 4035	.012 239 5655
38	4.438 813 4504	85.970 336 2596	.011 631 9191
39	4.616 365 9884	90.409 149 7100	.011 060 8274
40	4.801 020 6279	95.025 515 6984	.010 523 4893
41	4.993 061 4531	99.826 536 3264	.010 017 3765
42	5.192 783 9112	104.819 597 7794	.009 540 2007
43	5.400 495 2676	110.012 381 6906	.009 089 8859
44	5.616 515 0783	115.412 876 9582	.008 664 5444
45	5.841 175 6815	121.029 392 0365	.008 262 4558
46	6.074 822 7087	126.870 567 7180	.007 882 0488
47	6.317 815 6171	132.945 390 4267	.007 521 8855
48	6.570 528 2418	139.263 206 0438	.007 180 6476
49	6.833 349 3714	145.833 734 2855	.006 857 1240
50	7.106 683 3463	152.667 083 6570	.006 550 2004
51	7.390 950 6801	159.773 767 0032	.006 258 8497
52	7.686 588 7073	167.164 717 6834	.005 982 1236
53	7.994 052 2556	174.851 306 3907	.005 719 1451
54	8.313 814 3459	182.845 358 6463	.005 469 1025
55	8.646 366 9197	191.159 172 9922	.005 231 2426
56	8.992 221 5965	199.805 539 9119	.005 004 8662
57	9.351 910 4603	208.797 761 5083	.004 789 3234
58	9.725 986 8787	218.149 671 9687	.004 584 0087
59	10.115 026 3539	227.875 658 8474	.004 388 3581
60	10.519 627 4081	237.990 685 2013	.004 201 8451
n	$s=(1+i)^n$	$s_{\overline{n}\|}=\dfrac{(1+i)^n-1}{i}$	$\dfrac{1}{s_{\overline{n}\|}}=\dfrac{i}{(1+i)^n-1}$

.04

per period

ANNUALLY
If compounded
annually
nominal annual rate is

4%

SEMIANNUALLY
If compounded
semiannually
nominal annual rate is

8%

QUARTERLY
If compounded
quarterly
nominal annual rate is

16%

MONTHLY
If compounded
monthly
nominal annual rate is

48%

$i = .04$
$j_{(2)} = .08$
$j_{(4)} = .16$
$j_{(12)} = .48$

36

PRESENT WORTH OF 1 *What $1 due in the future is worth today.*	PRESENT WORTH OF 1 PER PERIOD *What $1 payable periodically is worth today.*	PARTIAL PAYMENT *Annuity worth $1 today.* *Periodic payment necessary to pay off a loan of $1.*	PERIODS	RATE **4%**
.961 538 4615	.961 538 4615	1.040 000 0000	1	
.924 556 2130	1.886 094 6746	.530 196 0784	2	
.888 996 3587	2.775 091 0332	.360 348 5392	3	.04
.854 804 1910	3.629 895 2243	.275 490 0454	4	
.821 927 1068	4.451 822 3310	.224 627 1135	5	*per period*
.790 314 5257	5.242 136 8567	.190 761 9025	6	
.759 917 8132	6.002 054 6699	.166 609 6120	7	
.730 690 2050	6.732 744 8750	.148 527 8320	8	
.702 586 7356	7.435 331 6105	.134 492 9927	9	
.675 564 1688	8.110 895 7794	.123 290 9443	10	
.649 580 9316	8.760 476 7109	.114 149 0393	11	
.624 597 0496	9.385 073 7605	.106 552 1727	12	
.600 574 0861	9.985 647 8466	.100 143 7278	13	
.577 475 0828	10.563 122 9295	.094 668 9731	14	
.555 264 5027	11.118 387 4322	.089 941 1004	15	
.533 908 1757	11.652 295 6079	.085 819 9992	16	
.513 373 2459	12.165 668 8537	.082 198 5221	17	
.493 628 1210	12.659 296 9747	.078 993 3281	18	
.474 642 4240	13.133 939 3988	.076 138 6184	19	
.456 386 9462	13.590 326 3450	.073 581 7503	20	
.438 833 6021	14.029 159 9471	.071 280 1054	21	ANNUALLY If compounded *annually* nominal annual rate is
.421 955 3867	14.451 115 3337	.069 198 8111	22	
.405 726 3333	14.856 841 6671	.067 309 0568	23	
.390 121 4743	15.246 963 1414	.065 586 8313	24	
.375 116 8023	15.622 079 9437	.064 011 9628	25	**4%**
.360 689 2329	15.982 769 1766	.062 567 3805	26	
.346 816 5701	16.329 585 7467	.061 238 5406	27	
.333 477 4713	16.663 063 2180	.060 012 9752	28	
.320 651 4147	16.983 714 6327	.058 879 9342	29	
.308 318 6680	17.292 033 3007	.057 830 0991	30	SEMIANNUALLY If compounded *semiannually* nominal annual rate is
.296 460 2577	17.588 493 5583	.056 855 3524	31	
.285 057 9401	17.873 551 4984	.055 948 5897	32	
.274 094 1731	18.147 645 6715	.055 103 5665	33	
.263 552 0896	18.411 197 7611	.054 314 7715	34	
.253 415 4707	18.664 613 2318	.053 577 3224	35	**8%**
.243 668 7219	18.908 281 9537	.052 886 8780	36	
.234 296 8479	19.142 578 8016	.052 239 5655	37	
.225 285 4307	19.367 864 2323	.051 631 9191	38	
.216 620 6064	19.584 484 8388	.051 060 8274	39	
.208 289 0447	19.792 773 8834	.050 523 4893	40	QUARTERLY If compounded *quarterly* nominal annual rate is
.200 277 9276	19.993 051 8110	.050 017 3765	41	
.192 574 9303	20.185 626 7413	.049 540 2007	42	
.185 168 2023	20.370 794 9436	.049 089 8859	43	
.178 046 3483	20.548 841 2919	.048 664 5444	44	
.171 198 4118	20.720 039 7038	.048 262 4558	45	**16%**
.164 613 8575	20.884 653 5613	.047 882 0488	46	
.158 282 5553	21.042 936 1166	.047 521 8855	47	
.152 194 7647	21.195 130 8814	.047 180 6476	48	
.146 341 1199	21.341 472 0013	.046 857 1240	49	
.140 712 6153	21.482 184 6167	.046 550 2004	50	MONTHLY If compounded *monthly* nominal annual rate is
.135 300 5917	21.617 485 2083	.046 258 8497	51	
.130 096 7228	21.747 581 9311	.045 982 1236	52	
.125 093 0027	21.872 674 9337	.045 719 1451	53	
.120 281 7333	21.992 956 6671	.045 469 1025	54	
.115 655 5128	22.108 612 1799	.045 231 2426	55	**48%**
.111 207 2239	22.219 819 4037	.045 004 8662	56	
.106 930 0229	22.326 749 4267	.044 789 3234	57	$i = .04$
.102 817 3297	22.429 566 7564	.044 584 0087	58	$j_{(2)} = .08$
.098 862 8171	22.528 429 5735	.044 388 3581	59	$j_{(4)} = .16$
.095 060 4010	22.623 489 9745	.044 201 8451	60	$j_{(12)} = .48$
$v^n = \dfrac{1}{(1+i)^n}$	$a_{\overline{n}\rceil} = \dfrac{1-v^n}{i}$	$\dfrac{1}{a_{\overline{n}\rceil}} = \dfrac{i}{1-v^n}$	n	

P E R I O D S	AMOUNT OF 1 *How $1 left at compound interest will grow.*	AMOUNT OF 1 PER PERIOD *How $1 deposited periodically will grow.*	SINKING FUND *Periodic deposit that will grow to $1 at future date.*
1	1.045 000 0000	1.000 000 0000	1.000 000 0000
2	1.092 025 0000	2.045 000 0000	.488 997 5550
3	1.141 166 1250	3.137 025 0000	.318 773 3601
4	1.192 518 6006	4.278 191 1250	.233 743 6479
5	1.246 181 9377	5.470 709 7256	.182 791 6395
6	1.302 260 1248	6.716 891 6633	.148 878 3875
7	1.360 861 8305	8.019 151 7881	.124 701 4680
8	1.422 100 6128	9.380 013 6186	.106 609 6533
9	1.486 095 1404	10.802 114 2314	.092 574 4700
10	1.552 969 4217	12.288 209 3718	.081 378 8217
11	1.622 853 0457	13.841 178 7936	.072 248 1817
12	1.695 881 4328	15.464 031 8393	.064 666 1886
13	1.772 196 0972	17.159 913 2721	.058 275 3528
14	1.851 944 9216	18.932 109 3693	.052 820 3160
15	1.935 282 4431	20.784 054 2909	.048 113 8081
16	2.022 370 1530	22.719 336 7340	.044 015 3694
17	2.113 376 8099	24.741 706 8870	.040 417 5833
18	2.208 478 7664	26.855 083 6970	.037 236 8975
19	2.307 860 3108	29.063 562·4633	.034 407 3443
20	2.411 714 0248	31.371 422 7742	.031 876 1443
21	2.520 241 1560	33.783 136 7990	.0?9 600 5669
22	2.633 652 0080	36.303 377 9550	.027 545 6461
23	2.752 166 3483	38.937 029 9629	.025 682 4930
24	2.876 013 8340	41.689 196 3113	.023 987 0299
25	3.005 434 4565	44.565 210 1453	.022 439 0280
26	3.140 679 0071	47.570 644 6018	.021 021 3674
27	3.282 009 5624	50.711 323 6089	.019 719 4616
28	3.429 699 9927	53.993 333 1713	.018 520 8051
29	3.584 036 4924	57.423 033 1640	.017 414 6147
30	3.745 318 1345	61.007 069 6564	.016 391 5429
31	3.913 857 4506	64.752 387 7909	.015 443 4459
32	4.089 981 0359	68.666 245 2415	.014 563 1962
33	4.274 030 1825	72.756 226 2774	.013 744 5281
34	4.466 361 5407	77.030 256 4599	.012 981 9119
35	4.667 347 8100	81.496 618 0005	.012 270 4478
36	4.877 378 4615	86.163 965 8106	.011 605 7796
37	5.096 860 4922	91.041 344 2720	.010 984 0206
38	5.326 219 2144	96.138 204 7643	.010 401 6920
39	5.565 899 0790	101.464 423 9787	.009 855 6712
40	5.816 364 5376	107.030 323 0577	.009 343 1466
41	6.078 100 9418	112.846 687 5953	.008 861 5804
42	6.351 615 4842	118.924 788 5371	.008 408 6759
43	6.637 438 1810	125.276 404 0213	.007 982 3492
44	6.936 122 8991	131.913 842 2022	.007 580 7056
45	7.248 248 4296	138.849 965 1013	.007 202 0184
46	7.574 419 6089	146.098 213 5309	.006 844 7107
47	7.915 268 4913	153.672 633 1398	.006 507 3395
48	8.271 455 5734	161.587 901 6311	.006 188 5821
49	8.643 671 0742	169.859 357 2045	.005 887 2235
50	9.032 636 2725	178.503 028 2787	.005 602 1459
51	9.439 104 9048	187.535 664 5512	.005 332 3191
52	9.863 864 6255	196.974 769 4560	.005 076 7923
53	10.307 738 5337	206.838 634 0815	.004 834 6867
54	10.771 586 7677	217.146 372 6152	.004 605 1886
55	11.256 308 1722	227.917 959 3829	.004 387 5437
56	11.762 842 0400	239.174 267 5551	.004 181 0518
57	12.292 169 9318	250.937 109 5951	.003 985 0622
58	12.845 317 5787	263.229 279 5269	.003 798 9695
59	13.423 356 8698	276.074 597 1056	.003 622 2094
60	14.027 407 9289	289.497 953 9753	.003 454 2558
n	$s=(1+i)^n$	$s_{\overline{n}\mid}=\dfrac{(1+i)^n-1}{i}$	$\dfrac{1}{s_{\overline{n}\mid}}=\dfrac{i}{(1+i)^n-1}$

.045

per period

ANNUALLY
If compounded
annually
nominal annual rate is

$4\frac{1}{2}\%$

SEMIANNUALLY
If compounded
semiannually
nominal annual rate is

9%

QUARTERLY
If compounded
quarterly
nominal annual rate is

18%

MONTHLY
If compounded
monthly
nominal annual rate is

54%

$i\ =.045$
$j_{(2)} =.09$
$j_{(4)} =.18$
$j_{(12)} =.54$

PRESENT WORTH OF 1 *What $1 due in the future is worth today.*	PRESENT WORTH OF 1 PER PERIOD *What $1 payable periodically is worth today.*	PARTIAL PAYMENT *Annuity worth $1 today.* *Periodic payment necessary to pay off a loan of $1.*	PERIODS	RATE 4½%
.956 937 7990	.956 937 7990	1.045 000 0000	1	
.915 729 9512	1.872 667 7503	.533 997 5550	2	
.876 296 6041	2.748 964 3543	.363 773 3601	3	.045
.838 561 3436	3.587 525 6979	.278 743 6479	4	*per period*
.802 451 0465	4.389 976 7444	.227 791 6395	5	
.767 895 7383	5.157 872 4827	.193 878 3875	6	
.734 828 4577	5.892 700 9404	.169 701 4680	7	
.703 185 1270	6.595 886 0674	.151 609 6533	8	
.672 904 4277	7.268 790 4951	.137 574 4700	9	
.643 927 6820	7.912 718 1771	.126 378 8217	10	
.616 198 7388	8.528 916 9159	.117 248 1817	11	
.589 663 8649	9.118 580 7808	.109 666 1886	12	
.564 271 6410	9.682 852 4218	.103 275 3528	13	
.539 972 8622	10.222 825 2840	.097 820 3160	14	
.516 720 4423	10.739 545 7263	.093 113 8081	15	
.494 469 3228	11.234 015 0491	.089 015 3694	16	
.473 176 3854	11.707 191 4346	.085 417 5833	17	
.452 800 3688	12.159 991 8034	.082 236 8975	18	
.433 301 7884	12.593 293 5918	.079 407 3443	19	
.414 642 8597	13.007 936 4515	.076 876 1443	20	
.396 787 4255	13.404 723 8770	.074 600 5669	21	ANNUALLY If compounded *annually* nominal annual rate is 4½%
.379 700 8857	13.784 424 7627	.072 545 6461	22	
.363 350 1298	14.147 774 8925	.070 682 4930	23	
.347 703 4735	14.495 478 3660	.068 987 0299	24	
.332 730 5967	14.828 208 9627	.067 439 0280	25	
.318 402 4849	15.146 611 4476	.066 021 3674	26	
.304 691 3731	15.451 302 8206	.064 719 4616	27	
.291 570 6919	15.742 873 5126	.063 520 8051	28	
.279 015 0162	16.021 888 5288	.062 414 6147	29	
.267 000 0155	16.288 888 5443	.061 391 5429	30	
.255 502 4072	16.544 390 9515	.060 443 4459	31	SEMIANNUALLY If compounded *semiannually* nominal annual rate is 9%
.244 499 9112	16.788 890 8627	.059 563 1962	32	
.233 971 2069	17.022 862 0695	.058 744 5281	33	
.223 895 8917	17.246 757 9613	.057 981 9119	34	
.214 254 4419	17.461 012 4031	.057 270 4478	35	
.205 028 1740	17.666 040 5772	.056 605 7796	36	
.196 199 2096	17.862 239 7868	.055 984 0206	37	
.187 750 4398	18.049 990 2266	.055 401 6920	38	
.179 665 4926	18.229 655 7192	.054 855 6712	39	
.171 928 7011	18.401 584 4203	.054 343 1466	40	QUARTERLY If compounded *quarterly* nominal annual rate is 18%
.164 525 0728	18.566 109 4931	.053 861 5804	41	
.157 440 2611	18.723 549 7542	.053 408 6759	42	
.150 660 5369	18.874 210 2911	.052 982 3492	43	
.144 172 7626	19.018 383 0536	.052 580 7056	44	
.137 964 3661	19.156 347 4198	.052 202 0184	45	
.132 023 3169	19.288 370 7366	.051 844 7107	46	
.126 338 1023	19.414 708 8389	.051 507 3395	47	
.120 897 7055	19.535 606 5444	.051 188 5821	48	
.115 691 5842	19.651 298 1286	.050 887 2235	49	
.110 709 6500	19.762 007 7785	.050 602 1459	50	MONTHLY If compounded *monthly* nominal annual rate is 54%
.105 942 2488	19.867 950 0273	.050 332 3191	51	
.101 380 1424	19.969 330 1697	.050 076 7923	52	
.097 014 4903	20.066 344 6600	.049 834 6867	53	
.092 836 8328	20.159 181 4928	.049 605 1886	54	
.088 839 0745	20.248 020 5673	.049 387 5437	55	
.085 013 4684	20.333 034 0357	.049 181 0518	56	$i = .045$
.081 352 6013	20.414 386 6370	.048 985 0622	57	$j_{(2)} = .09$
.077 849 3793	20.492 236 0163	.048 798 9695	58	$j_{(4)} = .18$
.074 497 0137	20.566 733 0299	.048 622 2094	59	$j_{(12)} = .54$
.071 289 0083	20.638 022 0382	.048 454 2558	60	
$v^n = \dfrac{1}{(1+i)^n}$	$a_{\overline{n}|} = \dfrac{1-v^n}{i}$	$\dfrac{1}{a_{\overline{n}|}} = \dfrac{i}{1-v^n}$	n	

P E R I O D S	AMOUNT OF 1 *How $1 left at compound interest will grow.*	AMOUNT OF 1 PER PERIOD *How $1 deposited periodically will grow.*	SINKING FUND *Periodic deposit that will grow to $1 at future date.*
1	1.050 000 0000	1.000 000 0000	1.000 000 0000
2	1.102 500 0000	2.050 000 0000	.487 804 8780
3	1.157 625 0000	3.152 500 0000	.317 208 5646
4	1.215 506 2500	4.310 125 0000	.232 011 8326
5	1.276 281 5625	5.525 631 2500	.180 974 7981
6	1.340 095 6406	6.801 912 8125	.147 017 4681
7	1.407 100 4227	8.142 008 4531	.122 819 8184
8	1.477 455 4438	9.549 108 8758	.104 721 8136
9	1.551 328 2160	11.026 564 3196	.090 690 0800
10	1.628 894 6268	12.577 892 5355	.079 504 5750
11	1.710 339 3581	14.206 787 1623	.070 388 8915
12	1.795 856 3260	15.917 126 5204	.062 825 4100
13	1.885 649 1423	17.712 982 8465	.056 455 7652
14	1.979 931 5994	19.598 631 9888	.051 023 9695
15	2.078 928 1794	21.578 563 5882	.046 342 2876
16	2.182 874 5884	23.657 491 7676	.042 269 9080
17	2.292 018 3178	25.840 366 3560	.038 699 1417
18	2.406 619 2337	28.132 384 6738	.035 546 2223
19	2.526 950 1954	30.539 003 9075	.032 745 0104
20	2.653 297 7051	33.065 954 1029	.030 242 5872
21	2.785 962 5904	35.719 251 8080	.027 996 1071
22	2.925 260 7199	38.505 214 3984	.025 970 5086
23	3.071 523 7559	41.430 475 1184	.024 136 8219
24	3.225 099 9437	44.501 998 8743	.022 470 9008
25	3.386 354 9409	47.727 098 8180	.020 952 4573
26	3.555 672 6879	51.113 453 7589	.019 564 3207
27	3.733 456 3223	54.669 126 4468	.018 291 8599
28	3.920 129 1385	58.402 582 7692	.017 122 5304
29	4.116 135 5954	62.322 711 9076	.016 045 5149
30	4.321 942 3752	66.438 847 5030	.015 051 4351
31	4.538 039 4939	70.760 789 8782	.014 132 1204
32	4.764 941 4686	75.298 829 3721	.013 280 4189
33	5.003 188 5420	80.063 770 8407	.012 490 0437
34	5.253 347 9691	85.066 959 3827	.011 755 4454
35	5.516 015 3676	90.320 307 3518	.011 071 7072
36	5.791 816 1360	95.836 322 7194	.010 434 4571
37	6.081 406 9428	101.628 138 8554	.009 839 7945
38	6.385 477 2899	107.709 545 7982	.009 284 2282
39	6.704 751 1544	114.095 023 0881	.008 764 6242
40	7.039 988 7121	120.799 774 2425	.008 278 1612
41	7.391 988 1477	127.839 762 9546	.007 822 2924
42	7.761 587 5551	135.231 751 1023	.007 394 7131
43	8.149 666 9329	142.993 338 6575	.006 993 3328
44	8.557 150 2795	151.143 005 5903	.006 616 2506
45	8.985 007 7935	159.700 155 8699	.006 261 7347
46	9.434 258 1832	168.685 163 6633	.005 928 2036
47	9.905 971 0923	178.119 421 8465	.005 614 2109
48	10.401 269 6469	188.025 392 9388	.005 318 4306
49	10.921 333 1293	198.426 662 5858	.005 039 6453
50	11.467 399 7858	209.347 995 7151	.004 776 7355
51	12.040 769 7750	220.815 395 5008	.004 528 6697
52	12.642 808 2638	232.856 165 2759	.004 294 4966
53	13.274 948 6770	245.498 973 5397	.004 073 3368
54	13.938 696 1108	258.773 922 2166	.003 864 3770
55	14.635 630 9164	272.712 618 3275	.003 666 8637
56	15.367 412 4622	287.348 249 2439	.003 480 0978
57	16.135 783 0853	302.715 661 7060	.003 303 4300
58	16.942 572 2396	318.851 444 7913	.003 136 2568
59	17.789 700 8515	335.794 017 0309	.002 978 0161
60	18.679 185 8941	353.583 717 8825	.002 828 1845
n	$s=(1+i)^n$	$s_{\overline{n}} = \dfrac{(1+i)^n - 1}{i}$	$\dfrac{1}{s_{\overline{n}}} = \dfrac{i}{(1+i)^n - 1}$

.05

per period

ANNUALLY
If compounded *annually* nominal annual rate is

5%

SEMIANNUALLY
If compounded *semiannually* nominal annual rate is

10%

QUARTERLY
If compounded *quarterly* nominal annual rate is

20%

MONTHLY
If compounded *monthly* nominal annual rate is

60%

$i = .05$
$j_{(2)} = .1$
$j_{(4)} = .2$
$j_{(12)} = .6$

PRESENT WORTH OF 1 *What $1 due in the future is worth today.*	PRESENT WORTH OF 1 PER PERIOD *What $1 payable periodically is worth today.*	PARTIAL PAYMENT *Annuity worth $1 today.* *Periodic payment necessary to pay off a loan of $1.*	P E R I O D S	RATE
				5%
.952 380 9524	.952 380 9524	1.050 000 0000	1	
.907 029 4785	1.859 410 4308	.537 804 8780	2	.05
.863 837 5985	2.723 248 0294	.367 208 5646	3	*per period*
.822 702 4748	3.545 950 5042	.282 011 8326	4	
.783 526 1665	4.329 476 6706	.230 974 7981	5	
.746 215 3966	5.075 692 0673	.197 017 4681	6	
.710 681 3301	5.786 373 3974	.172 819 8184	7	
.676 839 3620	6.463 212 7594	.154 721 8136	8	
.644 608 9162	7.107 821 6756	.140 690 0800	9	
.613 913 2535	7.721 734 9292	.129 504 5750	10	
.584 679 2891	8.306 414 2183	.120 388 8915	11	
.556 837 4182	8.863 251 6364	.112 825 4100	12	
.530 321 3506	9.393 572 9871	.106 455 7652	13	
.505 067 9530	9.898 640 9401	.101 023 9695	14	
.481 017 0981	10.379 658 0382	.096 342 2876	15	
.458 111 5220	10.837 769 5602	.092 269 9080	16	
.436 296 6876	11.274 066 2478	.088 699 1417	17	
.415 520 6549	11.689 586 9027	.085 546 2223	18	
.395 733 9570	12.085 320 8597	.082 745 0104	19	
.376 889 4829	12.462 210 3425	.080 242 5872	20	ANNUALLY
.358 942 3646	12.821 152 7072	.077 996 1071	21	If compounded *annually* nominal annual rate is
.341 849 8711	13.163 002 5783	.075 970 5086	22	
.325 571 3058	13.488 573 8841	.074 136 8219	23	
.310 067 9103	13.798 641 7943	.072 470 9008	24	
.295 302 7717	14.093 944 5660	.070 952 4573	25	**5%**
.281 240 7350	14.375 185 3010	.069 564 3207	26	
.267 848 3190	14.643 033 6200	.068 291 8599	27	
.255 093 6371	14.898 127 2571	.067 122 5304	28	
.242 946 3211	15.141 073 5782	.066 045 5149	29	
.231 377 4487	15.372 451 0269	.065 051 4351	30	SEMIANNUALLY
.220 359 4749	15.592 810 5018	.064 132 1204	31	If compounded *semiannually* nominal annual rate is
.209 866 1666	15.802 676 6684	.063 280 4189	32	
.199 872 5396	16.002 549 2080	.062 490 0437	33	
.190 354 7996	16.192 904 0076	.061 755 4454	34	
.181 290 2854	16.374 194 2929	.061 071 7072	35	**10%**
.172 657 4146	16.546 851 7076	.060 434 4571	36	
.164 435 6330	16.711 287 3405	.059 839 7945	37	
.156 605 3647	16.867 892 7053	.059 284 2282	38	
.149 147 9664	17.017 040 6717	.058 764 6242	39	
.142 045 6823	17.159 086 3540	.058 278 1612	40	QUARTERLY
.135 281 6022	17.294 367 9562	.057 822 2924	41	If compounded *quarterly* nominal annual rate is
.128 839 6211	17.423 207 5773	.057 394 7131	42	
.122 704 4011	17.545 911 9784	.056 993 3328	43	
.116 861 3344	17.662 773 3128	.056 616 2506	44	
.111 296 5089	17.774 069 8217	.056 261 7347	45	**20%**
.105 996 6752	17.880 066 4968	.055 928 2036	46	
.100 949 2144	17.981 015 7113	.055 614 2109	47	
.096 142 1090	18.077 157 8203	.055 318 4306	48	
.091 563 9133	18.168 721 7336	.055 039 6453	49	
.087 203 7270	18.255 925 4606	.054 776 7355	50	MONTHLY
.083 051 1685	18.338 976 6291	.054 528 6697	51	If compounded *monthly* nominal annual rate is
.079 096 3510	18.418 072 9801	.054 294 4966	52	
.075 329 8581	18.493 402 8382	.054 073 3368	53	
.071 742 7220	18.565 145 5602	.053 864 3770	54	
.068 326 4019	18.633 471 9621	.053 666 8637	55	**60%**
.065 072 7637	18.698 544 7258	.053 480 0978	56	
.061 974 0607	18.760 518 7865	.053 303 4300	57	
.059 022 9149	18.819 541 7014	.053 136 2568	58	$i = .05$
.056 212 2999	18.875 754 0013	.052 978 0161	59	$j^{(2)} = .1$ $j^{(4)} = .2$
.053 535 5237	18.929 289 5251	.052 828 1845	60	$j^{(12)} = .6$
$v^n = \dfrac{1}{(1+i)^n}$	$a_{\overline{n}|} = \dfrac{1-v^n}{i}$	$\dfrac{1}{a_{\overline{n}|}} = \dfrac{i}{1-v^n}$	**n**	

RATE **6%**	P E R I O D S	AMOUNT OF 1 *How $1 left at compound interest will grow.*	AMOUNT OF 1 PER PERIOD *How $1 deposited periodically will grow.*	SINKING FUND *Periodic deposit that will grow to $1 at future date.*
.06 *per period*	1	1.060 000 0000	1.000 000 0000	1.000 000 0000
	2	1.123 600 0000	2.060 000 0000	.485 436 8932
	3	1.191 016 0000	3.183 600 0000	.314 109 8128
	4	1.262 476 9600	4.374 616 0000	.228 591 4924
	5	1.338 225 5776	5.637 092 9600	.177 396 4004
	6	1.418 519 1123	6.975 318 5376	.143 362 6285
	7	1.503 630 2590	8.393 837 6499	.119 135 0181
	8	1.593 848 0745	9.897 467 9088	.101 035 9426
	9	1.689 478 9590	11.491 315 9834	.087 022 2350
	10	1.790 847 6965	13.180 794 9424	.075 867 9582
	11	1.898 298 5583	14.971 642 6389	.066 792 9381
	12	2.012 196 4718	16.869 941 1973	.059 277 0294
	13	2.132 928 2601	18.882 137 6691	.052 960 1053
	14	2.260 903 9558	21.015 065 9292	.047 584 9090
	15	2.396 558 1931	23.275 969 8850	.042 962 7640
	16	2.540 351 6847	25.672 528 0731	.038 952 1436
	17	2.692 772 7858	28.212 879 7628	.035 444 8042
	18	2.854 339 1529	30.905 652 5485	.032 356 5406
	19	3.025 599 5021	33.759 991 7015	.029 620 8604
	20	3.207 135 4722	36.785 591 2035	.027 184 5570
ANNUALLY *If compounded annually nominal annual rate is* **6%**	21	3.399 563 6005	39.992 726 6758	.025 004 5467
	22	3.603 537 4166	43.392 290 2763	.023 045 5685
	23	3.819 749 6616	46.995 827 6929	.021 278 4847
	24	4.048 934 6413	50.815 577 3545	.019 679 0050
	25	4.291 870 7197	54.864 511 9957	.018 226 7182
	26	4.549 382 9629	59.156 382 7155	.016 904 3467
	27	4.822 345 9407	63.705 765 6784	.015 697 1663
	28	5.111 686 6971	68.528 111 6191	.014 592 5515
	29	5.418 387 8990	73.639 798 3162	.013 579 6135
	30	5.743 491 1729	79.058 186 2152	.012 648 9115
SEMIANNUALLY *If compounded semiannually nominal annual rate is* **12%**	31	6.088 100 6433	84.801 677 3881	.011 792 2196
	32	6.453 386 6819	90.889 778 0314	.011 002 3374
	33	6.840 589 8828	97.343 164 7133	.010 272 9950
	34	7.251 025 2758	104.183 754 5961	.009 598 4254
	35	7.686 086 7923	111.434 779 8719	.008 973 8590
	36	8.147 251 9999	119.120 866 6642	.008 394 8348
	37	8.636 087 1198	127.268 118 6640	.007 857 4274
	38	9.154 252 3470	135.904 205 7839	.007 358 1240
	39	9.703 507 4879	145.058 458 1309	.006 893 7724
	40	10.285 717 9371	154.761 965 6188	.006 461 5359
QUARTERLY *If compounded quarterly nominal annual rate is* **24%**	41	10.902 861 0134	165.047 683 5559	.006 058 8551
	42	11.557 032 6742	175.950 544 5692	.005 683 4152
	43	12.250 454 6346	187.507 577 2434	.005 333 1178
	44	12.985 481 9127	199.758 031 8780	.005 006 0565
	45	13.764 610 8274	212.743 513 7907	.004 700 4958
	46	14.590 487 4771	226.508 124 6181	.004 414 8527
	47	15.465 916 7257	241.098 612 0952	.004 147 6805
	48	16.393 871 7293	256.564 528 8209	.003 897 6549
	49	17.377 504 0330	272.958 400 5502	.003 663 5619
	50	18.420 154 2750	290.335 904 5832	.003 444 2864
MONTHLY *If compounded monthly nominal annual rate is* **72%**	51	19.525 363 5315	308.756 058 8582	.003 238 8028
	52	20.696 885 3434	328.281 422 3897	.003 046 1669
	53	21.938 698 4640	348.978 307 7331	.002 865 5076
	54	23.255 020 3718	370.917 006 1970	.002 696 0209
	55	24.650 321 5941	394.172 026 5689	.002 536 9634
i = .06 $j_{(2)}$ = .12 $j_{(4)}$ = .24 $j_{(12)}$ = .72	56	26.129 340 8898	418.822 348 1630	.002 387 6472
	57	27.697 101 3432	444.951 689 0528	.002 247 4350
	58	29.358 927 4238	472.648 790 3959	.002 115 7359
	59	31.120 463 0692	502.007 717 8197	.001 992 0012
	60	32.987 690 8533	533.128 180 8889	.001 875 7215
	n	$s=(1+i)^n$	$s_{\overline{n}\|} = \dfrac{(1+i)^n-1}{i}$	$\dfrac{1}{s_{\overline{n}\|}} = \dfrac{i}{(1+i)^n-1}$

PRESENT WORTH OF 1	PRESENT WORTH OF 1 PER PERIOD	PARTIAL PAYMENT	P E R I O D S	RATE
What $1 due in the future is worth today.	*What $1 payable periodically is worth today.*	*Annuity worth $1 today.* *Periodic payment necessary to pay off a loan of $1.*		**6%**
.943 396 2264	.943 396 2264	1.060 000 0000	1	
.889 996 4400	1.833 392 6664	.545 436 8932	2	
.839 619 2830	2.673 011 9495	.374 109 8128	3	.06
.792 093 6632	3.465 105 6127	.288 591 4924	4	
.747 258 1729	4.212 363 7856	.237 396 4004	5	*per period*
.704 960 5404	4.917 324 3260	.203 362 6285	6	
.665 057 1136	5.582 381 4396	.179 135 0181	7	
.627 412 3713	6.209 793 8110	.161 035 9426	8	
.591 898 4635	6.801 692 2745	.147 022 2350	9	
.558 394 7769	7.360 087 0514	.135 867 9582	10	
.526 787 5254	7.886 874 5768	.126 792 9381	11	
.496 969 3636	8.383 843 9404	.119 277 0294	12	
.468 839 0222	8.852 682 9626	.112 960 1053	13	
.442 300 9644	9.294 983 9270	.107 584 9090	14	
.417 265 0607	9.712 248 9877	.102 962 7640	15	
.393 646 2837	10.105 895 2715	.098 952 1436	16	
.371 364 4186	10.477 259 6901	.095 444 8042	17	
.350 343 7911	10.827 603 4812	.092 356 5406	18	
.330 513 0105	11.158 116 4917	.089 620 8604	19	
.311 804 7269	11.469 921 2186	.087 184 5570	20	
.294 155 4027	11.764 076 6213	.085 004 5467	21	ANNUALLY
.277 505 0969	12.041 581 7182	.083 045 5685	22	If compounded *annually*
.261 797 2612	12.303 378 9794	.081 278 4847	23	nominal annual rate is
.246 978 5483	12.550 357 5278	.079 679 0050	24	
.232 998 6305	12.783 356 1583	.078 226 7182	25	**6%**
.219 810 0288	13.003 166 1870	.076 904 3467	26	
.207 367 9517	13.210 534 1387	.075 697 1663	27	
.195 630 1431	13.406 164 2818	.074 592 5515	28	
.184 556 7388	13.590 721 0206	.073 579 6135	29	
.174 110 1309	13.764 831 1515	.072 648 9115	30	SEMIANNUALLY
.164 254 8405	13.929 085 9920	.071 792 2196	31	If compounded *semiannually*
.154 957 3967	14.084 043 3887	.071 002 3374	32	nominal annual rate is
.146 186 2233	14.230 229 6119	.070 272 9350	33	
.137 911 5314	14.368 141 1433	.069 598 4254	34	
.130 105 2183	14.498 246 3616	.068 973 8590	35	**12%**
.122 740 7720	14.620 987 1336	.068 394 8348	36	
.115 793 1811	14.736 780 3147	.067 857 4274	37	
.109 238 8501	14.846 019 1648	.067 358 1240	38	
.103 055 5190	14.949 074 6838	.066 893 7724	39	
.097 222 1877	15.046 296 8715	.066 461 5359	40	QUARTERLY
.091 719 0450	15.138 015 9165	.066 058 8551	41	If compounded *quarterly*
.086 527 4010	15.224 543 3175	.065 683 4152	42	nominal annual rate is
.081 629 6235	15.306 172 9410	.065 333 1178	43	
.077 009 0788	15.383 182 0198	.065 006 0565	44	
.072 650 0743	15.455 832 0942	.064 700 4958	45	**24%**
.068 537 8060	15.524 369 9002	.064 414 8527	46	
.064 658 3075	15.589 028 2077	.064 147 6805	47	
.060 998 4033	15.650 026 6110	.063 897 6549	48	
.057 545 6635	15.707 572 2746	.063 663 5619	49	
.054 288 3618	15.761 860 6364	.063 444 2864	50	MONTHLY
.051 215 4357	15.813 076 0721	.063 238 8028	51	If compounded *monthly*
.048 316 4488	15.861 392 5208	.063 046 1669	52	nominal annual rate is
.045 581 5554	15.906 974 0762	.062 865 5076	53	
.043 001 4674	15.949 975 5436	.062 696 0209	54	
.040 567 4221	15.990 542 9657	.062 536 9634	55	**72%**
.038 271 1529	16.028 814 1186	.062 387 6472	56	
.036 104 8612	16.064 918 9798	.062 247 4350	57	
.034 061 1898	16.098 980 1696	.062 115 7359	58	i = .06
.032 133 1979	16.131 113 3676	.061 992 0012	59	$j_{(2)}$ = .12
.030 314 3377	16.161 427 7052	.061 875 7215	60	$j_{(4)}$ = .24 $j_{(12)}$ = .72
$v^n = \dfrac{1}{(1+i)^n}$	$a_{\overline{n}|} = \dfrac{1-v^n}{i}$	$\dfrac{1}{a_{\overline{n}|}} = \dfrac{i}{1-v^n}$	**n**	

P E R I O D S	AMOUNT OF 1 *How $1 left at compound interest will grow.*	AMOUNT OF 1 PER PERIOD *How $1 deposited periodically will grow.*	SINKING FUND *Periodic deposit that will grow to $1 at future date.*
1	1.070 000 0000	1.000 000 0000	1.000 000 0000
2	1.144 900 0000	2.070 000 0000	.483 091 7874
3	1.225 043 0000	3.214 900 0000	.311 051 6657
4	1.310 796 0100	4.439 943 0000	.225 228 1167
5	1.402 551 7307	5.750 739 0100	.173 890 6944
6	1.500 730 3518	7.153 290 7407	.139 795 7998
7	1.605 781 4765	8.654 021 0925	.115 553 2196
8	1.718 186 1798	10.259 802 5690	.097 467 7625
9	1.838 459 2124	11.977 988 7489	.083 486 4701
10	1.967 151 3573	13.816 447 9613	.072 377 5027
11	2.104 851 9523	15.783 599 3186	.063 356 9048
12	2.252 191 5890	17.888 451 2709	.055 901 9887
13	2.409 845 0002	20.140 642 8598	.049 650 8481
14	2.578 534 1502	22.550 487 8600	.044 344 9386
15	2.759 031 5407	25.129 022 0102	.039 794 6247
16	2.952 163 7486	27.888 053 5509	.035 857 6477
17	3.158 815 2110	30.840 217 2995	.032 425 1931
18	3.379 932 2757	33.999 032 5105	.029 412 6017
19	3.616 527 5350	37.378 964 7862	.026 753 0148
20	3.869 684 4625	40.995 492 3212	.024 392 9257
21	4.140 562 3749	44.865 176 7837	.022 289 0017
22	4.430 401 7411	49.005 739 1586	.020 405 7732
23	4.740 529 8630	53.436 140 8997	.018 713 9263
24	5.072 366 9534	58.176 670 7627	.017 189 0207
25	5.427 432 6401	63.249 037 7160	.015 810 5172
26	5.807 352 9249	68.676 470 3562	.014 561 0279
27	6.213 867 6297	74.483 823 2811	.013 425 7340
28	6.648 838 3638	80.697 690 9108	.012 391 9283
29	7.114 257 0492	87.346 529 2745	.011 448 6518
30	7.612 255 0427	94.460 786 3237	.010 586 4035
31	8.145 112 8956	102.073 041 3664	.009 796 9061
32	8.715 270 7983	110.218 154 2621	.009 072 9155
33	9.325 339 7542	118.933 425 0604	.008 408 0653
34	9.978 113 5370	128.258 764 8146	.007 796 7381
35	10.676 581 4846	138.236 878 3516	.007 233 9596
36	11.423 942 1885	148.913 459 8363	.006 715 3097
37	12.223 618 1417	160.337 402 0248	.006 236 8480
38	13.079 271 4117	172.561 020 1665	.005 795 0515
39	13.994 820 4105	185.640 291 5782	.005 386 7616
40	14.974 457 8392	199.635 111 9887	.005 009 1389
41	16.022 669 8880	214.609 569 8279	.004 659 6245
42	17.144 256 7801	230.632 239 7158	.004 335 9072
43	18.344 354 7547	247.776 496 4959	.004 035 8953
44	19.628 459 5875	266.120 851 2507	.003 757 6913
45	21.002 451 7587	285.749 310 8382	.003 499 5710
46	22.472 623 3818	306.751 762 5969	.003 259 9650
47	24.045 707 0185	329.224 385 9787	.003 037 4421
48	25.728 906 5098	353.270 092 9972	.002 830 6953
49	27.529 929 9655	378.998 999 5070	.002 638 5294
50	29.457 025 0631	406.528 929 4724	.002 459 8495
51	31.519 016 8175	435.985 954 5355	.002 293 6519
52	33.725 347 9947	467.504 971 3530	.002 139 0147
53	36.086 122 3543	501.230 319 3477	.001 995 0908
54	38.612 150 9191	537.316 441 7021	.001 861 1007
55	41.315 001 4835	575.928 592 6212	.001 736 3264
56	44.207 051 5873	617.243 594 1047	.001 620 1059
57	47.301 545 1984	661.450 645 6920	.001 511 8286
58	50.612 653 3623	708.752 190 8905	.001 410 9304
59	54.155 539 0977	759.364 844 2528	.001 316 8900
60	57.946 426 8345	813.520 383 3505	.001 229 2255
n	$s=(1+i)^n$	$s_{\overline{n}} = \dfrac{(1+i)^n - 1}{i}$	$\dfrac{1}{s_{\overline{n}}} = \dfrac{i}{(1+i)^n - 1}$

ANNUALLY
If compounded annually nominal annual rate is

7%

SEMIANNUALLY
If compounded semiannually nominal annual rate is

14%

QUARTERLY
If compounded quarterly nominal annual rate is

28%

MONTHLY
If compounded monthly nominal annual rate is

84%

$i = .07$
$j_{(2)} = .14$
$j_{(4)} = .28$
$j_{(12)} = .84$

PRESENT WORTH OF 1	PRESENT WORTH OF 1 PER PERIOD	PARTIAL PAYMENT	P E R I O D S	RATE 7%
What $1 due in the future is worth today.	*What $1 payable periodically is worth today.*	*Annuity worth $1 today.* *Periodic payment necessary to pay off a loan of $1.*		
.934 579 4393	.934 579 4393	1.070 000 0000	1	
.873 438 7283	1.808 018 1675	.553 091 7874	2	
.816 297 8769	2.624 316 0444	.381 051 6657	3	.07
.762 895 2120	3.387 211 2565	.295 228 1167	4	
.712 986 1795	4.100 197 4359	.243 890 6944	5	*per period*
.666 342 2238	4.766 539 6598	.209 795 7998	6	
.622 749 7419	5.389 289 4016	.185 553 2196	7	
.582 009 1046	5.971 298 5062	.167 467 7625	8	
.543 933 7426	6.515 232 2488	.153 486 4701	9	
.508 349 2921	7.023 581 5409	.142 377 5027	10	
.475 092 7964	7.498 674 3373	.133 356 9048	11	
.444 011 9592	7.942 686 2966	.125 901 9887	12	
.414 964 4479	8.357 650 7444	.119 650 8481	13	
.387 817 2410	8.745 467 9855	.114 344 9386	14	
.362 446 0196	9.107 914 0051	.109 794 6247	15	
.338 734 5978	9.446 648 6029	.105 857 6477	16	
.316 574 3905	9.763 222 9934	.102 425 1931	17	
.295 863 9163	10.059 086 9097	.099 412 6017	18	
.276 508 3330	10.335 595 2427	.096 753 0148	19	
.258 419 0028	10.594 014 2455	.094 392 9257	20	ANNUALLY *If compounded annually nominal annual rate is*
.241 513 0867	10.835 527 3323	.092 289 0017	21	
.225 713 1652	11.061 240 4974	.090 405 7732	22	
.210 946 8833	11.272 187 3808	.088 713 9263	23	
.197 146 6199	11.469 334 0007	.087 189 0207	24	
.184 249 1775	11.653 583 1783	.085 810 5172	25	7%
.172 195 4930	11.825 778 6713	.084 561 0279	26	
.160 930 3673	11.986 709 0386	.083 425 7340	27	
.150 402 2124	12.137 111 2510	.082 391 9283	28	
.140 562 8154	12.277 674 0664	.081 448 6518	29	
.131 367 1172	12.409 041 1835	.080 586 4035	30	SEMIANNUALLY *If compounded semiannually nominal annual rate is*
.122 773 0067	12.531 814 1902	.079 796 9061	31	
.114 741 1277	12.646 555 3179	.079 072 9155	32	
.107 234 6988	12.753 790 0168	.078 408 0653	33	
.100 219 3447	12.854 009 3615	.077 796 7381	34	
.093 662 9390	12.947 672 3004	.077 233 9596	35	14%
.087 535 4570	13.035 207 7574	.076 715 3097	36	
.081 808 8383	13.117 016 5957	.076 236 8480	37	
.076 456 8582	13.193 473 4539	.075 795 0515	38	
.071 455 0077	13.264 928 4616	.075 386 7616	39	
.066 780 3810	13.331 708 8426	.075 009 1389	40	QUARTERLY *If compounded quarterly nominal annual rate is*
.062 411 5710	13.394 120 4137	.074 659 6245	41	
.058 328 5711	13.452 448 9847	.074 335 9072	42	
.054 512 6832	13.506 961 6680	.074 035 8953	43	
.050 946 4329	13.557 908 1009	.073 757 6913	44	
.047 613 4887	13.605 521 5896	.073 499 5710	45	28%
.044 498 5876	13.650 020 1772	.073 259 9650	46	
.041 587 4650	13.691 607 6423	.073 037 4421	47	
.038 866 7898	13.730 474 4320	.072 830 6953	48	
.036 324 1026	13.766 798 5346	.072 638 5294	49	
.033 947 7594	13.800 746 2940	.072 459 8495	50	MONTHLY *If compounded monthly nominal annual rate is*
.031 726 8780	13.832 473 1720	.072 293 6519	51	
.029 651 2878	13.862 124 4598	.072 139 0147	52	
.027 711 4839	13.889 835 9437	.071 995 0908	53	
.025 898 5831	13.915 734 5269	.071 861 1007	54	
.024 204 2833	13.939 938 8102	.071 736 3264	55	84%
.022 620 8255	13.962 559 6357	.071 620 1059	56	
.021 140 9584	13.983 700 5941	.071 511 8286	57	
.019 757 9051	14.003 458 4991	.071 410 9304	58	$i\ = .07$
.018 465 3318	14.021 923 8310	.071 316 8900	59	$j_{(2)} = .14$
.017 257 3195	14.039 181 1504	.071 229 2255	60	$j_{(4)} = .28$ $j_{(12)} = .84$
$v^n = \dfrac{1}{(1+i)^n}$	$a_{\overline{n}|} = \dfrac{1-v^n}{i}$	$\dfrac{1}{a_{\overline{n}|}} = \dfrac{i}{1-v^n}$	n	

P E R I O D S	AMOUNT OF 1 *How $1 left at compound interest will grow.*	AMOUNT OF 1 PER PERIOD *How $1 deposited periodically will grow.*	SINKING FUND *Periodic deposit that will grow to $1 at future date.*
1	1.080 000 0000	1.000 000 0000	1.000 000 0000
2	1.166 400 0000	2.080 000 0000	.480 769 2308
3	1.259 712 0000	3.246 400 0000	.308 033 5140
4	1.360 488 9600	4.506 112 0000	.221 920 8045
5	1.469 328 0768	5.866 600 9600	.170 456 4546
6	1.586 874 3229	7.335 929 0368	.136 315 3862
7	1.713 824 2688	8.922 803 3597	.112 072 4014
8	1.850 930 2103	10.636 627 6285	.094 014 7606
9	1.999 004 6271	12.487 557 8388	.080 079 7092
10	2.158 924 9973	14.486 562 4659	.069 029 4887
11	2.331 638 9971	16.645 487 4632	.060 076 3421
12	2.518 170 1168	18.977 126 4602	.052 695 0169
13	2.719 623 7262	21.495 296 5771	.046 521 8052
14	2.937 193 6243	24.214 920 3032	.041 296 8528
15	3.172 169 1142	27.152 113 9275	.036 829 5449
16	3.425 942 6433	30.324 283 0417	.032 976 8720
17	3.700 018 0548	33.750 225 6850	.029 629 4315
18	3.996 019 4992	37.450 243 7398	.026 702 0959
19	4.315 701 0591	41.446 263 2390	.024 127 6275
20	4.660 957 1438	45.761 964 2981	.021 852 2088
21	5.033 833 7154	50.422 921 4420	.019 832 2503
22	5.436 540 4126	55.456 755 1573	.018 032 0684
23	5.871 463 6456	60.893 295 5699	.016 422 1692
24	6.341 180 7372	66.764 759 2155	.014 977 9616
25	6.848 475 1962	73.105 939 9527	.013 678 7791
26	7.396 353 2119	79.954 415 1490	.012 507 1267
27	7.988 061 4689	87.350 768 3609	.011 448 0962
28	8.627 106 3864	95.338 829 8297	.010 488 9057
29	9.317 274 8973	103.965 936 2161	.009 618 5350
30	10.062 656 8891	113.283 211 1134	.008 827 4334
31	10.867 669 4402	123.345 868 0025	.008 107 2841
32	11.737 082 9954	134.213 537 4427	.007 450 8132
33	12.676 049 6350	145.950 620 4381	.006 851 6324
34	13.690 133 6059	158.626 670 0732	.006 304 1101
35	14.785 344 2943	172.316 803 6790	.005 803 2646
36	15.968 171 8379	187.102 147 9733	.005 344 6741
37	17.245 625 5849	203.070 319 8112	.004 924 4025
38	18.625 275 6317	220.315 945 3961	.004 538 9361
39	20.115 297 6822	238.941 221 0278	.004 185 1297
40	21.724 521 4968	259.056 518 7100	.003 860 1615
41	23.462 483 2165	280.781 040 2068	.003 561 4940
42	25.339 481 8739	304.243 523 4233	.003 286 8407
43	27.366 640 4238	329.583 005 2972	.003 034 1370
44	29.555 971 6577	356.949 645 7210	.002 801 5156
45	31.920 449 3903	386.505 617 3787	.002 587 2845
46	34.474 085 3415	418.426 066 7690	.002 389 9085
47	37.232 012 1688	452.900 152 1105	.002 207 9922
48	40.210 573 1423	490.132 164 2793	.002 040 2660
49	43.427 418 9937	530.342 737 4217	.001 885 5731
50	46.901 612 5132	573.770 156 4154	.001 742 8582
51	50.653 741 5143	620.671 768 9286	.001 611 1575
52	54.706 040 8354	671.325 510 4429	.001 489 5903
53	59.082 524 1023	726.031 551 2783	.001 377 3506
54	63.809 126 0304	785.114 075 3806	.001 273 7003
55	68.913 856 1129	848.923 201 4111	.001 177 9629
56	74.426 964 6019	917.837 057 5239	.001 089 5180
57	80.381 121 7701	992.264 022 1259	.001 007 7963
58	86.811 611 5117	1072.645 143 8959	.000 932 2748
59	93.756 540 4326	1159.456 755 4076	.000 862 4729
60	101.257 063 6672	1253.213 295 8402	.000 797 9488
n	$s=(1+i)^n$	$s_{\overline{n}\rceil}=\dfrac{(1+i)^n-1}{i}$	$\dfrac{1}{s_{\overline{n}\rceil}}=\dfrac{i}{(1+i)^n-1}$

.08

per period

ANNUALLY
If compounded *annually* nominal annual rate is

8%

SEMIANNUALLY
If compounded *semiannually* nominal annual rate is

16%

QUARTERLY
If compounded *quarterly* nominal annual rate is

32%

MONTHLY
If compounded *monthly* nominal annual rate is

96%

$i = .08$
$j_{(2)} = .16$
$j_{(4)} = .32$
$j_{(12)} = .96$

PRESENT WORTH OF 1 *What $1 due in the future is worth today.*	PRESENT WORTH OF 1 PER PERIOD *What $1 payable periodically is worth today.*	PARTIAL PAYMENT *Annuity worth $1 today.* *Periodic payment necessary to pay off a loan of $1.*	PERIODS	RATE **8%**
.925 925 9259	.925 925 9259	1.080 000 0000	1	
.857 338 8203	1.783 264 7462	.560 769 2308	2	
.793 832 2410	2.577 096 9872	.388 033 5140	3	.08
.735 029 8528	3.312 126 8400	.301 920 8045	4	*per period*
.680 583 1970	3.992 710 0371	.250 456 4546	5	
.630 169 6269	4.622 879 6640	.216 315 3862	6	
.583 490 3953	5.206 370 0592	.192 072 4014	7	
.540 268 8845	5.746 638 9437	.174 014 7606	8	
.500 248 9671	6.246 887 9109	.160 079 7092	9	
.463 193 4881	6.710 081 3989	.149 029 4887	10	
.428 882 8593	7.138 964 2583	.140 076 3421	11	
.397 113 7586	7.536 078 0169	.132 695 0169	12	
.367 697 9247	7.903 775 9416	.126 521 8052	13	
.340 461 0414	8.244 236 9830	.121 296 8528	14	
.315 241 7050	8.559 478 6879	.116 829 5449	15	
.291 890 4676	8.851 369 1555	.112 976 8720	16	
.270 268 9514	9.121 638 1069	.109 629 4315	17	
.250 249 0291	9.371 887 1360	.106 702 0959	18	
.231 712 0640	9.603 599 2000	.104 127 6275	19	
.214 548 2074	9.818 147 4074	.101 852 2088	20	
.198 655 7476	10.016 803 1550	.099 832 2503	21	ANNUALLY
.183 940 5070	10.200 743 6621	.098 032 0684	22	If compounded *annually*
.170 315 2843	10.371 058 9464	.096 422 1692	23	nominal annual rate is
.157 699 3373	10.528 758 2837	.094 977 9616	24	
.146 017 9049	10.674 776 1886	.093 678 7791	25	**8%**
.135 201 7638	10.809 977 9524	.092 507 1267	26	
.125 186 8183	10.935 164 7707	.091 448 0962	27	
.115 913 7207	11.051 078 4914	.090 488 9057	28	
.107 327 5192	11.158 406 0106	.089 618 5350	29	
.099 377 3325	11.257 783 3431	.088 827 4334	30	
.092 016 0487	11.349 799 3918	.088 107 2841	31	SEMIANNUALLY
.085 200 0451	11.434 999 4368	.087 450 8132	32	If compounded *semiannually*
.078 888 9306	11.513 888 3674	.086 851 6324	33	nominal annual rate is
.073 045 3061	11.586 933 6736	.086 304 1101	34	
.067 634 5427	11.654 568 2163	.085 803 2646	35	**16%**
.062 624 5766	11.717 192 7928	.085 344 6741	36	
.057 985 7190	11.775 178 5119	.084 924 4025	37	
.053 690 4806	11.828 868 9925	.084 538 9361	38	
.049 713 4080	11.878 582 4004	.084 185 1297	39	
.046 030 9333	11.924 613 3337	.083 860 1615	40	
.042 621 2345	11.967 234 5683	.083 561 4940	41	QUARTERLY
.039 464 1061	12.006 698 6743	.083 286 8407	42	If compounded *quarterly*
.036 540 8389	12.043 239 5133	.083 034 1370	43	nominal annual rate is
.033 834 1101	12.077 073 6234	.082 801 5156	44	
.031 327 8797	12.108 401 5032	.082 587 2845	45	**32%**
.029 007 2961	12.137 408 7992	.082 389 9085	46	
.026 858 6075	12.164 267 4067	.082 207 9922	47	
.024 869 0810	12.189 136 4877	.082 040 2660	48	
.023 026 9268	12.212 163 4145	.081 885 5731	49	
.021 321 2286	12.233 484 6431	.081 742 8582	50	MONTHLY
.019 741 8783	12.253 226 5214	.081 611 1575	51	If compounded *monthly*
.018 279 5169	12.271 506 0383	.081 489 5903	52	nominal annual rate is
.016 925 4786	12.288 431 5169	.081 377 3506	53	
.015 671 7395	12.304 103 2564	.081 273 7003	54	**96%**
.014 510 8699	12.318 614 1263	.081 177 9629	55	
.013 435 9906	12.332 050 1170	.081 089 5180	56	
.012 440 7321	12.344 490 8490	.081 007 7963	57	$i = .08$
.011 519 1964	12.356 010 0454	.080 932 2748	58	$j_{(2)} = .16$
.010 665 9226	12.366 675 9680	.080 862 4729	59	$j_{(4)} = .32$
.009 875 8542	12.376 551 8222	.080 797 9488	60	$j_{(12)} = .96$
$v^n = \dfrac{1}{(1+i)^n}$	$a_{\overline{n}|} = \dfrac{1-v^n}{i}$	$\dfrac{1}{a_{\overline{n}|}} = \dfrac{i}{1-v^n}$	n	

	P E R I O D S	AMOUNT OF 1 *How $1 left at compound interest will grow.*	AMOUNT OF 1 PER PERIOD *How $1 deposited periodically will grow.*	SINKING FUND *Periodic deposit that will grow to $1 at future date.*
	1	1.090 000 0000	1.000 000 0000	1.000 000 0000
.09	2	1.188 100 0000	2.090 000 0000	.478 468 8995
	3	1.295 029 0000	3.278 100 0000	.305 054 7573
per period	4	1.411 581 6100	4.573 129 0000	.218 668 6621
	5	1.538 623 9549	5.984 710 6100	.167 092 4570
	6	1.677 100 1108	7.523 334 5649	.132 919 7833
	7	1.828 039 1208	9.200 434 6757	.108 690 5168
	8	1.992 562 6417	11.028 473 7966	.090 674 3778
	9	2.171 893 2794	13.021 036 4382	.076 798 8021
	10	2.367 363 6746	15.192 929 7177	.065 820 0899
	11	2.580 426 4053	17.560 293 3923	.056 946 6567
	12	2.812 664 7818	20.140 719 7976	.049 650 6585
	13	3.065 804 6121	22.953 384 5794	.043 566 5597
	14	3.341 727 0272	26.019 189 1915	.038 433 1730
	15	3.642 482 4597	29.360 916 2188	.034 058 8827
	16	3.970 305 8811	33.003 398 6784	.030 299 9097
	17	4.327 633 4104	36.973 704 5595	.027 046 2485
	18	4.717 120 4173	41.301 337 9699	.024 212 2907
	19	5.141 661 2548	46.018 458 3871	.021 730 4107
	20	5.604 410 7678	51.160 119 6420	.019 546 4750
ANNUALLY If compounded *annually* nominal annual rate is **9%**	21	6.108 807 7369	56.764 530 4098	.017 616 6348
	22	6.658 600 4332	62.873 338 1466	.015 904 9930
	23	7.257 874 4722	69.531 938 5798	.014 381 8800
	24	7.911 083 1747	76.789 813 0520	.013 022 5607
	25	8.623 080 6604	84.700 896 2267	.011 806 2505
	26	9.399 157 9198	93.323 976 8871	.010 715 3599
	27	10.245 082 1326	102.723 134 8069	.009 734 9054
	28	11.167 139 5246	112.968 216 9396	.008 852 0473
	29	12.172 182 0818	124.135 356 4641	.008 055 7226
	30	13.267 678 4691	136.307 538 5459	.007 336 3514
SEMIANNUALLY If compounded *semiannually* nominal annual rate is **18%**	31	14.461 769 5314	149.575 217 0150	.006 685 5995
	32	15.763 328 7892	164.036 986 5464	.006 096 1861
	33	17.182 028 3802	179.800 315 3356	.005 561 7255
	34	18.728 410 9344	196.982 343 7158	.005 076 5971
	35	20.413 967 9185	215.710 754 6502	.004 635 8375
	36	22.251 225 0312	236.124 722 5687	.004 235 0500
	37	24.253 835 2840	258.375 947 5999	.003 870 3293
	38	26.436 680 4595	282.629 782 8839	.003 538 1975
	39	28.815 981 7009	309.066 463 3434	.003 235 5500
	40	31.409 420 0540	337.882 445 0443	.002 959 6092
QUARTERLY If compounded *quarterly* nominal annual rate is **36%**	41	34.236 267 8588	369.291 865 0983	.002 707 8853
	42	37.317 531 9661	403.528 132 9572	.002 478 1420
	43	40.676 109 8431	440.845 664 9233	.002 268 3675
	44	44.336 959 7290	481.521 774 7664	.002 076 7493
	45	48.327 286 1046	525.858 734 4954	.001 901 6514
	46	52.676 741 8540	574.186 020 6000	.001 741 5959
	47	57.417 648 6209	626.862 762 4540	.001 595 2455
	48	62.585 236 9967	684.280 411 0748	.001 461 3892
	49	68.217 908 3264	746.865 648 0716	.001 338 9289
	50	74.357 520 0758	815.083 556 3980	.001 226 8681
MONTHLY If compounded *monthly* nominal annual rate is **108%**	51	81.049 696 8826	889.441 076 4738	.001 124 3016
	52	88.344 169 6021	970.490 773 3565	.001 030 4065
	53	96.295 144 8663	1058.834 942 9585	.000 944 4343
	54	104.961 707 9042	1155.130 087 8248	.000 865 7034
	55	114.408 261 6156	1260.091 795 7290	.000 793 5930
$i = .09$ $j_{(2)} = .18$ $j_{(4)} = .36$ $j_{(12)} = 1.08$	56	124.705 005 1610	1374.500 057 3447	.000 727 5373
	57	135.928 455 6255	1499.205 062 5057	.000 667 0202
	58	148.162 016 6318	1635.133 518 1312	.000 611 5709
	59	161.496 598 1287	1783.295 534 7630	.000 560 7595
	60	176.031 291 9602	1944.792 132 8917	.000 514 1938
	n	$s=(1+i)^n$	$s_{\overline{n}|}=\dfrac{(1+i)^n-1}{i}$	$\dfrac{1}{s_{\overline{n}|}}=\dfrac{i}{(1+i)^n-1}$

PRESENT WORTH OF 1 _What $1 due in the future is worth today._	PRESENT WORTH OF 1 PER PERIOD _What $1 payable periodically is worth today._	PARTIAL PAYMENT _Annuity worth $1 today._ _Periodic payment necessary to pay off a loan of $1._	PERIODS	RATE 9%
.917 431 1927	.917 431 1927	1.090 000 0000	1	
.841 679 9933	1.759 111 1859	.568 468 8995	2	
.772 183 4801	2.531 294 6660	.395 054 7573	3	.09
.708 425 2111	3.239 719 8771	.308 668 6621	4	_per period_
.649 931 3863	3.889 651 2634	.257 092 4570	5	
.596 267 3269	4.485 918 5902	.222 919 7833	6	
.547 034 2448	5.032 952 8351	.198 690 5168	7	
.501 866 2797	5.534 819 1147	.180 674 3778	8	
.460 427 7795	5.995 246 8943	.166 798 8021	9	
.422 410 8069	6.417 657 7012	.155 820 0899	10	
.387 532 8504	6.805 190 5515	.146 946 6567	11	
.355 534 7251	7.160 725 2766	.139 650 6585	12	
.326 178 6469	7.486 903 9235	.133 566 5597	13	
.299 246 4650	7.786 150 3885	.128 433 1730	14	
.274 538 0413	8.060 688 4299	.124 058 8827	15	
.251 869 7627	8.312 558 1925	.120 299 9097	16	
.231 073 1768	8.543 631 3693	.117 046 2485	17	
.211 993 7402	8.755 625 1094	.114 212 2907	18	
.194 489 6699	8.950 114 7793	.111 730 4107	19	
.178 430 8898	9.128 545 6691	.109 546 4750	20	
.163 698 0640	9.292 243 7331	.107 616 6348	21	ANNUALLY If compounded _annually_ nominal annual rate is 9%
.150 181 7101	9.442 425 4432	.105 904 9930	22	
.137 781 3854	9.580 206 8286	.104 381 8800	23	
.126 404 9408	9.706 611 7694	.103 022 5607	24	
.115 967 8356	9.822 579 6049	.101 806 2505	25	
.106 392 5097	9.928 972 1146	.100 715 3599	26	
.097 607 8070	10.026 579 9217	.099 734 9054	27	
.089 548 4468	10.116 128 3685	.098 852 0473	28	
.082 154 5384	10.198 282 9069	.098 055 7226	29	
.075 371 1361	10.273 654 0430	.097 336 3514	30	SEMIANNUALLY If compounded _semiannually_ nominal annual rate is 18%
.069 147 8313	10.342 801 8743	.096 685 5995	31	
.063 438 3773	10.406 240 2517	.096 096 1861	32	
.058 200 3462	10.464 440 5979	.095 561 7255	33	
.053 394 8130	10.517 835 4109	.095 076 5971	34	
.048 986 0670	10.566 821 4779	.094 635 8375	35	
.044 941 3459	10.611 762 8237	.094 235 0500	36	
.041 230 5925	10.652 993 4163	.093 870 3293	37	
.037 826 2317	10.690 819 6480	.093 538 1975	38	
.034 702 9648	10.725 522 6128	.093 235 5500	39	
.031 837 5824	10.757 360 1952	.092 959 6092	40	QUARTERLY If compounded _quarterly_ nominal annual rate is 36%
.029 208 7912	10.786 568 9865	.092 707 8853	41	
.026 797 0562	10.813 366 0426	.092 478 1420	42	
.024 584 4552	10.837 950 4978	.092 268 3675	43	
.022 554 5461	10.860 505 0439	.092 076 7493	44	
.020 692 2441	10.881 197 2880	.091 901 6514	45	
.018 983 7102	10.900 180 9981	.091 741 5959	46	
.017 416 2479	10.917 597 2460	.091 595 2455	47	
.015 978 2090	10.933 575 4550	.091 461 3892	48	
.014 658 9074	10.948 234 3624	.091 338 9289	49	
.013 448 5389	10.961 682 9013	.091 226 8681	50	MONTHLY If compounded _monthly_ nominal annual rate is 108%
.012 338 1091	10.974 021 0104	.091 124 3016	51	
.011 319 3661	10.985 340 3765	.091 030 4065	52	
.010 384 7396	10.995 725 1160	.090 944 4343	53	
.009 527 2840	11.005 252 4000	.090 865 7034	54	
.008 740 6275	11.013 993 0276	.090 793 5930	55	
.008 018 9243	11.022 011 9519	.090 727 5373	56	
.007 356 8113	11.029 368 7632	.090 667 0202	57	
.006 749 3682	11.036 118 1314	.090 611 5709	58	$i = .09$
.006 192 0809	11.042 310 2123	.090 560 7595	59	$j_{(2)} = .18$
.005 680 8082	11.047 991 0204	.090 514 1938	60	$j_{(4)} = .36$ $j_{(12)} = 1.08$
$v^n = \dfrac{1}{(1+i)^n}$	$a_{\overline{n}} = \dfrac{1-v^n}{i}$	$\dfrac{1}{a_{\overline{n}}} = \dfrac{i}{1-v^n}$	n	

49

TABLE 3 ADDITIONAL COMPOUND INTEREST AND ANNUITY TABLES

N	AMOUNT OF 1	AMOUNT OF 1 PER PERIOD	PRESENT WORTH OF 1 PER PERIOD
1	1.0050000000	1.0000000	0.9950249
2	1.0100250000	2.0050000	1.9850994
3	1.0150751250	3.0150250	2.9702481
4	1.0201505006	4.0301001	3.9504957
5	1.0252512531	5.0502506	4.9258663
6	1.0303775094	6.0755019	5.8963844
7	1.0355293969	7.1058794	6.8620740
8	1.0407070439	8.1414088	7.8229592
9	1.0459105791	9.1821158	8.7790639
10	1.0511401320	10.2280264	9.7304119
11	1.0563958327	11.2791665	10.6770267
12	1.0616778119	12.3355624	11.6189321
18	1.0939289396	18.7857879	17.1727680
24	1.1271597762	25.4319552	22.5628662
30	1.1614000829	32.2800166	27.7940540
36	1.1966805248	39.3361050	32.8710162
42	1.2330326987	46.6065397	37.7982999
48	1.2704891611	54.0978322	42.5803178
54	1.3090834575	61.8166915	47.2213526
60	1.3488501525	69.7700305	51.7255608
66	1.3898248607	77.9649721	56.0969762
72	1.4320442785	86.4088557	60.3395139
78	1.4755462170	95.1092434	64.4569735
84	1.5203696361	104.0739272	68.4530424
90	1.5665546790	113.3109358	72.3312996
96	1.6141427085	122.8285417	76.0952183
102	1.6631763438	132.6352688	79.7481694
108	1.7136994988	142.7398993	83.2934245
114	1.7657574214	153.1514843	86.7341586
120	1.8193967340	163.8793468	90.0734533
132	1.9316131435	186.3226287	96.4595987
144	2.0507508156	210.1501631	102.4747432
156	2.1772366385	235.4473277	108.1404398
168	2.3115238303	262.3047661	113.4769898
180	2.4540935622	290.8187124	118.5035147
192	2.6054566833	321.0913367	123.2380253
204	2.7661555504	353.2311101	127.6974861
216	2.9367659720	387.3531944	131.8978761
228	3.1178992711	423.5798542	135.8542459
240	3.3102044758	462.0408952	139.5807717
252	3.5143706447	502.8741289	143.0908062
264	3.7311293361	546.2258672	146.3969265
276	3.9612572294	592.2514459	149.5109789
288	4.2055789075	641.1157815	152.4441214
300	4.4649698122	692.9939624	155.2068640
360	6.0225752123	1004.5150425	166.7916144
420	8.1235514938	1424.7102988	175.3802262
480	10.9574536717	1991.4907343	181.7475842

N	AMOUNT OF 1	AMOUNT OF 1 PER PERIOD	PRESENT WORTH OF 1 PER PERIOD	RATE 13/24%
1	1.0054166667	1.0000000	0.9946125	
2	1.0108626736	2.0054167	1.9838666	
3	1.0163381798	3.0162793	2.9677910	
4	1.0218433449	4.0326175	3.9464146	
5	1.0273783297	5.0544609	4.9197659	
6	1.0329432956	6.0818392	5.8878732	
7	1.0385384052	7.1147825	6.8507649	
8	1.0441638215	8.1533209	7.8084691	
9	1.0498197089	9.1974847	8.7610136	
10	1.0555062323	10.2473044	9.7084263	
11	1.0612235577	11.3028107	10.6507348	
12	1.0669718520	12.3640342	11.5879666	
18	1.1021214212	18.8531854	17.1062689	
24	1.1384289330	25.5561107	22.4485780	
30	1.1759325339	32.4798524	27.6205067	
36	1.2146716270	39.6316850	32.6274889	
42	1.2546869135	47.0191225	37.4747851	
48	1.2960204354	54.6499265	42.1674883	
54	1.3387156198	62.5321144	46.7105287	
60	1.3828173242	70.6739675	51.1086796	
66	1.4283718841	79.0840401	55.3665618	
72	1.4754271614	87.7711683	59.4886488	
78	1.5240325946	96.7444790	63.4792716	
84	1.5742392509	106.0134002	67.3426229	
90	1.6260998799	115.5876701	71.0827616	
96	1.6796689690	125.4773481	74.7036175	
102	1.7350028004	135.6928247	78.2089946	
108	1.7921595106	146.2448327	81.6025760	
114	1.8511991512	157.1444587	84.8879271	
120	1.9121837521	168.4031542	88.0684997	
132	2.0402462394	192.0454596	94.1285693	
144	2.1768853086	217.2711339	99.8082596	
156	2.3226753493	244.1862183	105.1314461	
168	2.4782292190	272.9038558	110.1205061	
180	2.6442008195	303.5447667	114.7964120	
192	2.8212878455	336.2377561	119.1788199	
204	3.0102347175	371.1202555	123.2861522	
216	3.2118357115	408.3389006	127.1356748	
228	3.4269382974	448.0501472	130.7435700	
240	3.6564467019	490.4209296	134.1250043	
252	3.9013257093	535.6293617	137.2941922	
264	4.1626047173	583.8654863	140.2644560	
276	4.4413820644	635.3320734	143.0482819	
288	4.7388296467	690.2454732	145.6573721	
300	5.0561978444	748.8365251	148.1026946	
360	6.9917979739	1106.1780875	158.2108195	
420	9.6683793656	1600.3161906	165.5206245	
480	13.3696024838	2283.6189201	170.8067927	

N	AMOUNT OF 1	AMOUNT OF 1 PER PERIOD	PRESENT WORTH OF 1 PER PERIOD
1	1.0058333333	1.0000000	0.9942005
2	1.0117006944	2.0058333	1.9826351
3	1.0176022818	3.0175340	2.9653373
4	1.0235382951	4.0351363	3.9423403
5	1.0295089352	5.0586746	4.9136772
6	1.0355144040	6.0881835	5.8793808
7	1.0415549047	7.1236979	6.8394838
8	1.0476306416	8.1652528	7.7940187
9	1.0537418204	9.2128835	8.7430178
10	1.0598886476	10.2666253	9.6865131
11	1.0660713314	11.3265140	10.6245367
12	1.0722900809	12.3925853	11.5571201
18	1.1103718240	18.9208841	17.0401335
24	1.1498060175	25.6810316	22.3350993
30	1.1906406929	32.6812616	27.4484669
36	1.2329255875	39.9301007	32.3864645
42	1.2767122049	47.4363780	37.1551065
48	1.3220538779	55.2092362	41.7602014
54	1.3690058334	63.2581429	46.2073582
60	1.4176252596	71.5929016	50.5019935
66	1.4679713758	80.2236644	54.6493384
72	1.5201055043	89.1609436	58.6544443
78	1.5740911452	98.4156249	62.5221895
84	1.6299940541	107.9989807	66.2572851
90	1.6878823214	117.9226837	69.8642803
96	1.7478264560	128.1988210	73.3475687
102	1.8098994709	138.8399093	76.7113928
108	1.8741769719	149.8589095	79.9598500
114	1.9407372500	161.2692429	83.0968967
120	2.0096613767	173.0848074	86.1263541
132	2.1549399601	197.9897074	91.8771340
144	2.3107207441	224.6949847	97.2402162
156	2.4777629335	253.3307886	102.2417380
168	2.6568806163	284.0366771	106.9060745
180	2.8489467309	316.9622967	111.2559576
192	3.0548973204	352.2681121	115.3125867
204	3.2757360947	390.1261877	119.0957319
216	3.5125393219	430.7210266	122.6238306
228	3.7664610734	474.2504697	125.9140770
240	4.0387388490	520.9266598	128.9825065
252	4.3306996069	570.9770755	131.8440731
264	4.6437662317	624.6456397	134.5127228
276	4.9794644680	682.1939088	137.0014613
288	5.3394303571	743.9023469	139.3224178
300	5.7254182093	810.0716930	141.4869034
360	8.1164974754	1219.9709958	150.3075679
420	11.5061518407	1801.0546013	156.5297092
480	16.3114114903	2624.8133983	160.9188389

N	AMOUNT OF 1	AMOUNT OF 1 PER PERIOD	PRESENT WORTH OF 1 PER PERIOD	RATE 5/8%
1	1.0062500000	1.0000000	0.9937888	
2	1.0125390625	2.0062500	1.9814050	
3	1.0188674316	3.0187891	2.9628870	
4	1.0252353531	4.0376565	3.9382728	
5	1.0316430740	5.0628918	4.9076003	
6	1.0380908433	6.0945349	5.8709071	
7	1.0445789110	7.1326258	6.8282307	
8	1.0511075292	8.1772047	7.7796081	
9	1.0576769513	9.2283122	8.7250764	
10	1.0642874322	10.2859892	9.6646722	
11	1.0709392287	11.3502766	10.5984320	
12	1.0776325989	12.4212158	11.5263920	
18	1.1186805333	18.9888853	16.9743593	
24	1.1612920181	25.8067229	22.2224234	
30	1.2055266104	32.8842577	27.2779194	
36	1.2514461355	40.2313817	32.1479132	
42	1.2991147741	47.8583639	36.8392114	
48	1.3485991513	55.7758642	41.3583711	
54	1.3999684302	63.9949488	45.7117085	
60	1.4532944083	72.5271053	49.9053082	
66	1.5086516178	81.3842588	53.9450314	
72	1.5661174301	90.5787888	57.8365243	
78	1.6257721636	100.1235462	61.5852260	
84	1.6876991963	110.0318714	65.1963760	
90	1.7519850819	120.3176131	68.6750215	
96	1.8187196710	130.9951474	72.0260244	
102	1.8879962369	142.0793979	75.2540684	
108	1.9599116057	153.5858569	78.3636652	
114	2.0345662914	165.5306066	81.3591611	
120	2.1120646371	177.9303419	84.2447427	
132	2.2760297039	204.1647526	89.7021477	
144	2.4527238048	232.4358088	94.7664015	
156	2.6431351281	262.9016205	99.4658267	
168	2.8483285772	295.7325724	103.8267055	
180	3.0694517271	331.1122763	107.8734268	
192	3.3077412417	369.2385987	111.6286226	
204	3.5645297906	410.3247665	115.1132942	
216	3.8412535020	454.6005603	118.3469303	
228	4.1394599942	502.3135991	121.3476153	
240	4.4608170314	553.7307250	124.1321312	
252	4.8071218506	609.1394961	126.7160507	
264	5.1803112129	668.8497941	129.1138247	
276	5.5824722352	733.1955576	131.3388633	
288	6.0158540628	802.5366501	133.4036101	
300	6.4828804481	877.2608717	135.3196127	
360	9.4215339047	1347.4454248	143.0176273	
420	13.6922625411	2030.7620066	148.3145682	
480	19.8988885877	3023.8221740	151.9593499	

N	AMOUNT OF 1	AMOUNT OF 1 PER PERIOD	PRESENT WORTH OF 1 PER PERIOD
1	1.0066666667	1.0000000	0.9933775
2	1.0133777778	2.0066667	1.9801763
3	1.0201336296	3.0200444	2.9604400
4	1.0269345205	4.0401781	3.9342120
5	1.0337807506	5.0671126	4.9015351
6	1.0406726223	6.1008933	5.8624520
7	1.0476104398	7.1415660	6.8170053
8	1.0545945094	8.1891764	7.7652371
9	1.0616251394	9.2437709	8.7071892
10	1.0687026404	10.3053961	9.6429031
11	1.0758273246	11.3740987	10.5724203
12	1.0829995068	12.4499260	11.4957818
18	1.1270479367	19.0571905	16.9089441
24	1.1728879317	25.9331898	22.1105436
30	1.2205923596	33.0888539	27.1088490
36	1.2702370516	40.5355577	31.9118055
42	1.3219009235	48.2851385	36.5270480
48	1.3756661004	56.3499151	40.9619130
54	1.4316180481	64.7427072	45.2234500
60	1.4898457083	73.4768562	49.3184333
66	1.5504416401	82.5662460	53.2533724
72	1.6135021673	92.0253251	57.0345221
78	1.6791275315	101.8691297	60.6678932
84	1.7474220514	112.1133077	64.1592611
90	1.8184942885	122.7741433	67.5141759
96	1.8924572199	133.8685830	70.7379705
102	1.9694284176	145.4142626	73.8357695
108	2.0495302358	157.4295354	76.8124971
114	2.1328900050	169.9335007	79.6728853
120	2.2196402345	182.9460352	82.4214809
132	2.4038692793	210.5803919	87.6006003
144	2.6033892439	240.5083866	92.3827995
156	2.8194692672	272.9203901	96.7984979
168	3.0534838258	308.0225739	100.8757837
180	3.3069214774	346.0382216	104.6405922
192	3.5813943291	387.2091494	108.1168712
204	3.8786482921	431.7972438	111.3267333
216	4.2005741874	480.0861281	114.2905962
228	4.5492197733	532.3829660	117.0273129
240	4.9268027708	589.0204156	119.5542917
252	5.3357249709	650.3587456	121.8876065
264	5.7785875120	716.7881268	124.0420994
276	6.2582074255	788.7311138	126.0314752
288	6.7776355553	866.6453333	127.8683881
300	7.3401759637	951.0263946	129.5645226
360	10.9357296578	1490.3594487	136.2834941
420	16.2925498978	2293.8824847	140.7933380
480	24.2733855425	3491.0078314	143.8203923

	AMOUNT	AMOUNT	PRESENT WORTH	RATE
N	OF 1	OF 1 PER PERIOD	OF 1 PER PERIOD	17/24%
1	1.0070833333	1.0000000	0.9929665	
2	1.0142168403	2.0070833	1.9789489	
3	1.0214008762	3.0213002	2.9579965	
4	1.0286357991	4.0427010	3.9301578	
5	1.0359219693	5.0713368	4.8954815	
6	1.0432597500	6.1072588	5.8540156	
7	1.0506495065	7.1505186	6.8058078	
8	1.0580916072	8.2011681	7.7509055	
9	1.0655864227	9.2592597	8.6893559	
10	1.0731343266	10.3248461	9.6212057	
11	1.0807356947	11.3979804	10.5465013	
12	1.0883909059	12.4787161	11.4652889	
18	1.1354744243	19.1258011	16.8438854	
24	1.1845947640	26.0604373	21.9994534	
30	1.2358400373	33.2950641	26.9412408	
36	1.2893021683	40.8426591	31.6781124	
42	1.3450770578	48.7167611	36.2185652	
48	1.4032647550	56.9314948	40.5707438	
54	1.4639696374	65.5015959	44.7424552	
60	1.5273005979	74.4424373	48.7411826	
66	1.5933712398	83.7700574	52.5740991	
72	1.6623000813	93.5011879	56.2480800	
78	1.7342107672	103.6532848	59.7697158	
84	1.8092322913	114.2445588	63.1453238	
90	1.8874992279	125.2940086	66.3809589	
96	1.9691519725	136.8214549	69.4824254	
102	2.0543369945	148.8475757	72.4552866	
108	2.1432070992	161.3939434	75.3048753	
114	2.2359217025	174.4830639	78.0363032	
120	2.3326471162	188.1384164	80.6544698	
132	2.5388319080	217.2468576	85.5696105	
144	2.7632415602	248.9282203	90.0855806	
156	3.0074869849	283.4099273	94.2347976	
168	3.2733214840	320.9395036	98.0470465	
180	3.5626533352	361.7863532	101.5496932	
192	3.8775594909	406.2436928	104.7678814	
204	4.2203004870	454.6306570	107.7247126	
216	4.5933366702	507.2945887	110.4414122	
228	4.9993458595	564.6135331	112.9374820	
240	5.4412425689	626.9989509	115.2308398	
252	5.9221989288	694.8986723	117.3379484	
264	6.4456674569	768.8001116	119.2739335	
276	7.0154058425	849.2337660	121.0526925	
288	7.6355039202	936.7770240	122.6869941	
300	8.3104130286	1032.0583099	124.1885700	
360	12.6924987871	1650.7057111	130.0536434	
420	19.3852609860	2595.5662568	133.8938000	
480	29.6071206937	4038.6523332	136.4081423	

N	AMOUNT OF 1	AMOUNT OF 1 PER PERIOD	PRESENT WORTH OF 1 PER PERIOD
1	1.0075000000	1.0000000	0.9925558
2	1.0150562500	2.0075000	1.9777229
3	1.0226691719	3.0225563	2.9555562
4	1.0303391907	4.0452254	3.9261104
5	1.0380667346	5.0755646	4.8894396
6	1.0458522351	6.1136313	5.8455976
7	1.0536961269	7.1594836	6.7946378
8	1.0615988478	8.2131797	7.7366132
9	1.0695608392	9.2747786	8.6715764
10	1.0775825455	10.3443394	9.5995796
11	1.0856644146	11.4219219	10.5206745
12	1.0938068977	12.5075864	11.4349127
18	1.1439603887	19.1947185	16.7791811
24	1.1964135294	26.1884706	21.8891461
30	1.2512717638	33.5029018	26.7750802
36	1.3086453709	41.1527161	31.4468053
42	1.3686496861	49.1532915	35.9137126
48	1.4314053333	57.5207111	40.1847819
54	1.4970384672	66.2717956	44.2685990
60	1.5656810269	75.4241369	48.1733735
66	1.6374710015	84.9961335	51.9069550
72	1.7125527068	95.0070276	55.4768488
78	1.7910770762	105.4769435	58.8902314
84	1.8732019633	116.4269284	62.1539646
90	1.9590924602	127.8789947	65.2746092
96	2.0489212282	139.8561638	68.2584386
102	2.1428688461	152.3825128	71.1114509
108	2.2411241722	165.4832230	73.8393816
114	2.3438847247	179.1846300	76.4477144
120	2.4513570781	193.5142771	78.9416927
132	2.6813112807	224.1748374	83.6064201
144	2.9328367736	257.7115698	87.8710920
156	3.2079570928	294.3942790	91.7700177
168	3.5088855955	334.5180794	95.3345643
180	3.8380432675	378.4057690	98.5934088
192	4.1980781995	426.4104266	101.5727689
204	4.5918868916	478.9182522	104.2966135
216	5.0226375554	536.3516740	106.7868561
228	5.4937956026	599.1727470	109.0635310
240	6.0091515245	667.8868699	111.1449540
252	6.5728513866	743.0468515	113.0478704
264	7.1894301840	825.2573579	114.7875891
276	7.8638483256	915.1797768	116.3781063
288	8.6015315408	1013.5375388	117.8322179
300	9.4084145299	1121.1219373	119.1616222
360	14.7305761230	1830.7434831	124.2818657
420	23.0633835518	2941.7844736	127.5521637
480	36.1099020441	4681.3202725	129.6409020

N	AMOUNT OF 1	AMOUNT OF 1 PER PERIOD	PRESENT WORTH OF 1 PER PERIOD	RATE 19/24%
1	1.0079166667	1.0000000	0.9921455	
2	1.0158960069	2.0079167	1.9764982	
3	1.0239385170	3.0238127	2.9531194	
4	1.0320446969	4.0477512	3.9220697	
5	1.0402150508	5.0797959	4.8834093	
6	1.0484500866	6.1200109	5.8371982	
7	1.0567503164	7.1684610	6.7834955	
8	1.0651162565	8.2252113	7.7223602	
9	1.0735484268	9.2903276	8.6538505	
10	1.0820473519	10.3638760	9.5780245	
11	1.0906135601	11.4459234	10.4949395	
12	1.0992475841	12.5365369	11.4046527	
18	1.1525062247	19.2639442	16.7148287	
24	1.2083452511	26.3172949	21.7796154	
30	1.2668896832	33.7123810	26.6103525	
36	1.3282705980	41.4657597	31.2178556	
42	1.3926254235	49.5947903	35.6124407	
48	1.4600982459	58.1176732	39.8039470	
54	1.5308401323	67.0534904	43.8017589	
60	1.6050094693	76.4222488	47.6148273	
66	1.6827723171	86.2449243	51.2516895	
72	1.7643027816	96.5435092	54.7204880	
78	1.8497834041	107.3410616	58.0289894	
84	1.9394055702	118.6617562	61.1846011	
90	2.0333699380	130.5309395	64.1943884	
96	2.1318868876	142.9751858	67.0650899	
102	2.2351769919	156.0223569	69.8031330	
108	2.3434715107	169.7016645	72.4146480	
114	2.4570129084	184.0437358	74.9054818	
120	2.5760553965	199.0806817	77.2812114	
132	2.8317226711	231.3754953	81.7083882	
144	3.1127643050	266.8754912	85.7358492	
156	3.4216986421	305.8987758	89.3996836	
168	3.7612939658	348.7950273	92.7327219	
180	4.1345933049	395.9486280	95.7648307	
192	4.5449417016	447.7821097	98.5231801	
204	4.9960161852	504.7599392	101.0324868	
216	5.4918587216	567.3926806	103.3152361	
228	6.0369124319	636.2415703	105.3918833	
240	6.6360614060	711.9235460	107.2810365	
252	7.2946744684	795.1167750	108.9996241	
264	8.0186532861	886.5667309	110.5630458	
276	8.8144852523	987.0928740	111.9853112	
288	9.6893016185	1097.5959939	113.2791647	
300	10.6509413955	1219.0662815	114.4562003	
360	17.0948617968	2033.0351743	118.9266809	
420	27.4374150602	3339.4629550	121.7120107	
480	44.0373109848	5436.2919139	123.4474084	

N	AMOUNT OF 1	AMOUNT OF 1 PER PERIOD	PRESENT WORTH OF 1 PER PERIOD
1	1.0083333333	1.0000000	0.9917355
2	1.0167361111	2.0083333	1.9752749
3	1.0252089120	3.0250694	2.9506859
4	1.0337523196	4.0502784	3.9180356
5	1.0423669223	5.0840307	4.8773906
6	1.0510533133	6.1263976	5.8288172
7	1.0598120909	7.1774509	6.7723807
8	1.0686438584	8.2372630	7.7081461
9	1.0775492238	9.3059069	8.6361780
10	1.0865288007	10.3834561	9.5565401
11	1.0955832074	11.4699849	10.4692960
12	1.1047130674	12.5655681	11.3745084
18	1.1611123298	19.3334796	16.6508262
24	1.2203909614	26.4469154	21.6708548
30	1.2826959635	33.9235156	26.4470432
36	1.3481818424	41.7818211	30.9912356
42	1.4170109924	50.0413191	35.3147007
48	1.4893540986	58.7224918	39.4281601
54	1.5653905600	67.8468672	43.3418145
60	1.6453089348	77.4370722	47.0653690
66	1.7293074073	87.5168889	50.6080576
72	1.8175942802	98.1113136	53.9786655
78	1.9103884905	109.2466189	57.1855512
84	2.0079201527	120.9504183	60.2366674
90	2.1104311294	133.2517355	63.1395802
96	2.2181756310	146.1810757	65.9014884
102	2.3314208465	159.7705016	68.5292412
108	2.4504476055	174.0537127	71.0293549
114	2.5755510749	189.0661290	73.4080294
120	2.7070414909	204.8449789	75.6711634
132	2.9905041091	238.8604931	79.8729861
144	3.3036489675	276.4378761	83.6765282
156	3.6495841847	317.9501022	87.1195419
168	4.0317433395	363.8092007	90.2362006
180	4.4539195517	414.4703462	93.0574388
192	4.9203031301	470.4363756	95.6112587
204	5.4355231636	532.2627796	97.9230083
216	6.0046934672	600.5632161	100.0156327
228	6.6334633392	676.0156007	101.9099023
240	7.3280736332	759.3688360	103.6246187
252	8.0954187018	851.4502442	105.1768013
264	8.9431148263	953.1737792	106.5818563
276	9.8795758123	1065.5490975	107.8537295
288	10.9140965006	1189.6915801	109.0050450
300	12.0569450235	1326.8334028	110.0472301
360	19.8373993733	2260.4879248	113.9508200
420	32.6386504317	3796.6380518	116.3233774
480	53.7006631743	6324.0795809	117.7653907

N	AMOUNT OF 1	AMOUNT OF 1 PER PERIOD	PRESENT WORTH OF 1 PER PERIOD	RATE 7/8%
1	1.0087500000	1.0000000	0.9913259	
2	1.0175765625	2.0087500	1.9740529	
3	1.0264803574	3.0263266	2.9482557	
4	1.0354620605	4.0528069	3.9140081	
5	1.0445223536	5.0882690	4.8713835	
6	1.0536619242	6.1327913	5.8204545	
7	1.0628814660	7.1864533	6.7612932	
8	1.0721816788	8.2493347	7.6939710	
9	1.0815632685	9.3215164	8.6185586	
10	1.0910269471	10.4030797	9.5351262	
11	1.1005734329	11.4941066	10.4437435	
12	1.1102034505	12.5946801	11.3444793	
18	1.1697791038	19.4033262	16.5871711	
24	1.2325517014	26.5773373	21.5628580	
30	1.2986927973	34.1363197	26.2851382	
36	1.3683831517	42.1009316	30.7669176	
42	1.4418132247	50.4929400	35.0204445	
48	1.5191836966	59.3352796	39.0573436	
54	1.6007060169	68.6521162	42.8886476	
60	1.6866029818	78.4689122	46.5248272	
66	1.7771093432	88.8124964	49.9758198	
72	1.8724724500	99.7111371	53.2510570	
78	1.9729529246	111.1946200	56.3594897	
84	2.0788253749	123.2943286	59.3096130	
90	2.1903791445	136.0433308	62.1094896	
96	2.3079191041	149.4764690	64.7667714	
102	2.4317664840	163.6304553	67.2887205	
108	2.5622597527	178.5439717	69.6822293	
114	2.6997555412	194.2577761	71.9538392	
120	2.8446296184	210.8148135	74.1097583	
132	3.1581176176	246.6420134	78.0977922	
144	3.5061530760	286.4174944	81.6899571	
156	3.8925432428	330.5763706	84.9255487	
168	4.3215149391	379.6017073	87.8399618	
180	4.7977607966	434.0298053	90.4650781	
192	5.3264905908	494.4560675	92.8296144	
204	5.9134882328	561.5415123	94.9594368	
216	6.5651750402	636.0200046	96.8778442	
228	7.2886799825	718.7062837	98.6058224	
240	8.0919176658	810.5048761	100.1622742	
252	8.9836749133	912.4199901	101.5642261	
264	9.9737068865	1025.5665013	102.8270144	
276	11.0728437992	1151.1821485	103.9644530	
288	12.2931093922	1290.6410734	104.9889847	
300	13.6478524640	1445.4688530	105.9118170	
360	23.0185086616	2516.4009899	109.3207656	
420	38.8230853463	4322.6383253	111.3419577	
480	65.4791315096	7369.0436011	112.5403381	

N	AMOUNT OF 1	AMOUNT OF 1 PER PERIOD	PRESENT WORTH OF 1 PER PERIOD
1	1.0091666667	1.0000000	0.9909166
2	1.0184173611	2.0091667	1.9728323
3	1.0277528536	3.0275840	2.9458289
4	1.0371739214	4.0553369	3.9099873
5	1.0466813490	5.0925108	4.8653879
6	1.0562759281	6.1391922	5.8121103
7	1.0659584574	7.1954681	6.7502331
8	1.0757297433	8.2614265	7.6798346
9	1.0855905992	9.3371563	8.6009922
10	1.0955418464	10.4227469	9.5137825
11	1.1055843133	11.5182887	10.4182816
12	1.1157188362	12.6238730	11.3145648
18	1.1785069492	19.4734854	16.5238613
24	1.2448285214	26.7085660	21.4556186
30	1.3148824018	34.3508075	26.1246233
36	1.3888786292	42.4231232	30.5448743
42	1.4670390630	50.9497160	34.7296246
48	1.5495980478	59.9561507	38.6914211
54	1.6368031160	69.4694308	42.4421423
60	1.7289157305	79.5180797	45.9930338
66	1.8262120677	90.1322256	49.3547421
72	1.9289838467	101.3436924	52.5373463
78	2.0375392028	113.1860949	55.5503888
84	2.1522036124	125.6949395	58.4029033
90	2.2733208681	138.9077311	61.1034426
96	2.4012541097	152.8640847	63.6601033
102	2.5363869133	167.6058451	66.0805511
108	2.6791244407	183.1772117	68.3720431
114	2.8298946550	199.6248715	70.5414497
120	2.9891496030	216.9981385	72.5952754
132	3.3350505163	254.7327836	76.3804873
144	3.7209786807	296.8340379	79.7731090
156	4.1515660031	343.8072003	82.8138587
168	4.6319803894	396.2160425	85.5392314
180	5.1679877693	454.6895748	87.9819371
192	5.7660212995	519.9295963	90.1712930
204	6.4332585737	592.7191171	92.1335759
216	7.1777077688	673.9317566	93.8923370
228	8.0083037584	764.5422282	95.4686849
240	8.9350153492	865.6380381	96.8815390
252	9.9689649268	978.4325375	98.1478563
264	11.1225619462	1104.2794850	99.2828352
276	12.4096518701	1244.6892949	100.3000977
288	13.8456823421	1401.3471646	101.2118529
300	15.4478885890	1576.1333006	102.0290437
360	26.7080975839	2804.5197364	105.0063460
420	46.1760500432	4928.2963684	106.7284093
480	79.8344992899	8600.1271953	107.7244458

N	AMOUNT OF 1	AMOUNT OF 1 PER PERIOD	PRESENT WORTH OF 1 PER PERIOD	RATE 23/24%
1	1.0095833333	1.0000000	0.9905076	
2	1.0192585069	2.0095833	1.9716130	
3	1.0290264010	3.0288418	2.9434054	
4	1.0388879040	4.0578682	3.9059731	
5	1.0488439131	5.0967561	4.8594038	
6	1.0588953339	6.1456001	5.8037842	
7	1.0690430808	7.2044954	6.7392002	
8	1.0792880770	8.2735385	7.6657369	
9	1.0896312544	9.3528266	8.5834786	
10	1.1000735540	10.4424578	9.4925087	
11	1.1106159255	11.5425314	10.3929100	
12	1.1212593281	12.6531473	11.2847643	
18	1.1872962706	19.5439587	16.4608945	
24	1.2572224809	26.8406067	21.3491304	
30	1.3312670187	34.5669933	25.9654846	
36	1.4096724343	42.7484279	30.3250790	
42	1.4926955630	51.4117109	34.4421945	
48	1.5806083666	60.5852209	38.3303177	
54	1.6736988241	70.2990077	42.0021851	
60	1.7722718752	80.5848913	45.4698246	
66	1.8766504190	91.4765655	48.7445954	
72	1.9871763720	103.0097084	51.8372248	
78	2.1042117879	115.2220996	54.7578434	
84	2.2281400438	128.1537437	57.5160184	
90	2.3593670956	141.8470013	60.1207847	
96	2.4983228085	156.3467278	62.5806750	
102	2.6454623645	171.7004206	64.9037472	
108	2.8012677537	187.9583743	67.0976111	
114	2.9662493534	205.1738456	69.1694531	
120	3.1409475995	223.4032278	71.1260601	
132	3.5218167951	263.1461004	74.7188499	
144	3.9488699335	307.7081670	77.9230950	
156	4.4277072485	357.6737998	80.7808149	
168	4.9646080547	413.6982318	83.3294849	
180	5.5666130918	476.5161487	85.6025272	
192	6.2416168554	546.9513240	87.6297499	
204	6.9984711217	625.9274214	89.4377373	
216	7.8471010280	714.4801073	91.0501986	
228	8.7986352264	813.7706323	92.4882793	
240	9.8655518225	925.1010597	93.7708378	
252	11.0618420082	1049.9313400	94.9146932	
264	12.4031935381	1189.8984562	95.9348455	
276	13.9071964533	1346.8378908	96.8446728	
288	15.5935737515	1522.8076958	97.6561063	
300	17.4844400279	1720.1154812	98.3797867	
360	30.9871813142	3129.0971806	100.9803747	
420	54.9177099335	5626.1958191	102.4477500	
480	97.3291127629	10051.7335057	103.2757129	

N	AMOUNT OF 1	AMOUNT OF 1 PER PERIOD	PRESENT WORTH OF 1 PER PERIOD
1	1.0100000000	1.0000000	0.9900990
2	1.0201000000	2.0100000	1.9703951
3	1.0303010000	3.0301000	2.9409852
4	1.0406040100	4.0604010	3.9019656
5	1.0510100501	5.1010050	4.8534312
6	1.0615201506	6.1520151	5.7954765
7	1.0721353521	7.2135352	6.7281945
8	1.0828567056	8.2856706	7.6516778
9	1.0936852727	9.3685273	8.5660176
10	1.1046221254	10.4622125	9.4713045
11	1.1156683467	11.5668347	10.3676282
12	1.1268250301	12.6825030	11.2550775
18	1.1961474757	19.6147476	16.3982686
24	1.2697346485	26.9734649	21.2433873
30	1.3478489153	34.7848915	25.8077082
36	1.4307687836	43.0768784	30.1075050
42	1.5187898946	51.8789895	34.1581081
48	1.6122260777	61.2226078	37.9739595
54	1.7114104688	71.1410469	41.5686641
60	1.8166966986	81.6696699	44.9550384
66	1.9284601531	92.8460153	48.1451562
72	2.0470993121	104.7099312	51.1503915
78	2.1730371701	117.3037170	53.9814590
84	2.3067227440	130.6722744	56.6484528
90	2.4486326746	144.8632675	59.1608815
96	2.5992729256	159.9272926	61.5277030
102	2.7591805874	175.9180587	63.7573559
108	2.9289257927	192.8925793	65.8577898
114	3.1091137485	210.9113749	67.8364936
120	3.3003868946	230.0386895	69.7005220
132	3.7189585619	271.8958562	73.1107518
144	4.1906155936	319.0615594	76.1371575
156	4.7220905425	372.2090543	78.8229389
168	5.3209698179	432.0969818	81.2064335
180	5.9958019754	499.5801975	83.3216640
192	6.7562197415	575.6219742	85.1988236
204	7.6130775138	661.3077514	86.8647075
216	8.5786062989	757.8606299	88.3430948
228	9.6665883013	866.6588301	89.6550886
240	10.8925536539	989.2553654	90.8194163
252	12.2740020992	1127.4002099	91.8526982
264	13.8306527853	1283.0652785	92.7696833
276	15.5847257416	1458.4725742	93.5834610
288	17.5612590533	1656.1259053	94.3056475
300	19.7884662619	1878.8466262	94.9465513
360	35.9496413277	3494.9641328	97.2183311
420	65.3095947146	6430.9594715	98.4688314
480	118.6477251025	11764.7725103	99.1571688

N	AMOUNT OF 1	AMOUNT OF 1 PER PERIOD	PRESENT WORTH OF 1 PER PERIOD	RATE 1¹/₂₄%
1	1.0104166667	1.0000000	0.9896907	
2	1.0209418403	2.0104167	1.9691784	
3	1.0315766511	3.0313585	2.9385684	
4	1.0423222412	4.0629352	3.8979646	
5	1.0531797646	5.1052574	4.8474701	
6	1.0641503871	6.1584372	5.7871869	
7	1.0752352870	7.2225876	6.7172159	
8	1.0864356546	8.2978228	7.6376570	
9	1.0977526926	9.3842585	8.5486089	
10	1.1091876165	10.4820112	9.4501697	
11	1.1207416542	11.5911988	10.3424360	
12	1.1324160464	12.7119405	11.2255036	
18	1.2050609742	19.6858535	16.3359813	
24	1.2823661022	27.1071458	21.1383830	
30	1.3646303841	35.0045169	25.6512806	
36	1.4521719515	43.4085073	29.8921263	
42	1.5453293443	52.3516171	33.8773202	
48	1.6444628200	61.8684307	37.6222740	
54	1.7499557465	71.9957517	41.1414699	
60	1.8622160851	82.7727442	44.4485175	
66	1.9816779679	94.2410849	47.5562056	
72	2.1088033767	106.4451242	50.4765524	
78	2.2440839297	119.4320572	53.2208514	
84	2.3880427825	133.2521071	55.7997152	
90	2.5412366515	147.9587185	58.2231169	
96	2.7042579664	163.6087648	60.5004281	
102	2.8777371618	180.2627675	62.6404558	
108	3.0623451148	197.9851310	64.6514758	
114	3.2587957394	216.8443910	66.5412650	
120	3.4678487477	236.9134798	68.3171317	
132	3.9270475684	280.9965666	71.5541540	
144	4.4470516815	330.9169614	74.4126637	
156	5.0359126834	387.4476176	76.9369213	
168	5.7027483310	451.4638398	79.1660115	
180	6.4578837187	523.9568370	81.1344490	
192	7.3130111489	606.0490703	82.8727125	
204	8.2813711727	699.0116326	84.4077168	
216	9.3779576023	804.2839298	85.7632295	
228	10.6197496714	923.4959685	86.9602389	
240	12.0259749368	1058.4935939	88.0172792	
252	13.6184069922	1211.3670713	88.9507174	
264	15.4217026046	1384.4834500	89.7750064	
276	17.4637834925	1580.5232153	90.5029094	
288	19.7762686580	1802.5217912	91.1456970	
300	22.3949639666	2053.9165408	91.7133220	
360	41.7042621243	3907.6091639	93.6980770	
420	77.6623477459	7359.5853836	94.7638798	
480	144.6240731807	13787.9110253	95.3362101	

N	AMOUNT OF 1	AMOUNT OF 1 PER PERIOD	PRESENT WORTH OF 1 PER PERIOD
1	1.0108333333	1.0000000	0.9892828
2	1.0217840278	2.0108333	1.9679632
3	1.0328533547	3.0326174	2.9361548
4	1.0440425994	4.0654707	3.8939701
5	1.0553530609	5.1095133	4.8415203
6	1.0667860524	6.1648664	5.7789154
7	1.0783429013	7.2316524	6.7062642
8	1.0900249494	8.3099953	7.6236744
9	1.1018335530	9.4000203	8.5312525
10	1.1137700832	10.5018538	9.4291039
11	1.1258359258	11.6156239	10.3173328
12	1.1380324816	12.7414598	11.1960423
18	1.2140371786	19.7572780	16.2740305
24	1.2951179292	27.2416550	21.0341116
30	1.3816137431	35.2258840	25.4961882
36	1.4738862710	43.7433481	29.6789169
42	1.5723213167	52.8296600	33.5997862
48	1.6773304506	62.5228108	37.2751898
54	1.7893527299	72.8633289	40.7204950
60	1.9088565351	83.8944494	43.9501072
66	2.0363415277	95.6622949	46.9775298
72	2.1723407397	108.2160683	49.8154209
78	2.3174228022	121.6082587	52.4756460
84	2.4721943229	135.8948606	54.9693280
90	2.6373024226	151.1356082	57.3068932
96	2.8134374404	167.3942253	59.4981153
102	3.0013358207	184.7386911	61.5521562
108	3.2017831921	203.2415254	63.4776040
114	3.4156176522	222.9800910	65.2825092
120	3.6437332717	244.0369174	66.9744186
132	4.1466868176	290.4633985	70.0471030
144	4.7190642895	343.2982421	72.7471001
156	5.3704484442	403.4260102	75.1196133
168	6.1117447704	471.8533634	77.2043633
180	6.9553640680	549.7259140	79.0362530
192	7.9154302308	638.3474059	80.6459519
204	9.0080167087	739.2015423	82.0604098
216	10.2514156094	853.9768255	83.3033074
228	11.6664439460	984.5948258	84.3954533
240	13.2767921555	1133.2423528	85.3551324
252	15.1094207245	1302.4080669	86.1984116
264	17.1950115629	1494.9241443	86.9394091
276	19.5684816803	1714.0136936	87.5905306
288	22.2695677681	1963.3447171	88.1626773
300	25.3434914715	2247.0915205	88.6654281
360	48.3770893186	4373.2697833	90.3996054
420	92.3449230965	8431.8390551	91.3080955
480	176.2732099391	16179.0655328	91.7840297

N	AMOUNT OF 1	AMOUNT OF 1 PER PERIOD	PRESENT WORTH OF 1 PER PERIOD	RATE 1 1/8 %
1	1.0112500000	1.0000000	0.9888752	
2	1.0226265625	2.0112500	1.9667492	
3	1.0341311113	3.0338766	2.9337446	
4	1.0457650863	4.0680077	3.8899823	
5	1.0575299436	5.1137728	4.8355820	
6	1.0694271554	6.1713027	5.7706621	
7	1.0814582109	7.2407299	6.6953395	
8	1.0936246158	8.3221881	7.6097300	
9	1.1059278927	9.4158127	8.5139481	
10	1.1183695815	10.5217406	9.4081069	
11	1.1309512393	11.6401102	10.2923183	
12	1.1436744407	12.7710614	11.1666930	
18	1.2230765039	19.8290226	16.2124139	
24	1.3079912264	27.3769979	20.9305669	
30	1.3988013366	35.4490077	25.3424177	
36	1.4959161344	44.0814342	29.4678513	
42	1.5997733363	53.3131854	33.3254620	
48	1.7108410484	63.1858710	36.9326367	
54	1.8296198757	73.7439890	40.3056339	
60	1.9566451792	85.0351270	43.4596563	
66	2.0924894881	97.1101767	46.4089197	
72	2.2377650810	110.0235628	49.1667171	
78	2.3931267451	123.8334885	51.7454785	
84	2.5592747276	138.6021980	54.1568267	
90	2.7369578918	154.3962571	56.4116304	
96	2.9269770928	171.2868527	58.5200523	
102	3.1301887863	189.3501143	60.4915956	
108	3.3475088896	208.6674569	62.3351464	
114	3.5799169096	229.3259475	64.0590140	
120	3.8284603572	251.4186984	65.6709682	
132	4.3785122580	300.3122007	68.5877264	
144	5.0075925579	356.2304496	71.1380659	
156	5.7270556181	420.1827216	73.3680183	
168	6.5498871312	493.3233005	75.3178323	
180	7.4909385017	576.9723113	77.0227003	
192	8.5671949015	672.6395468	78.5133938	
204	9.7980818377	782.0517189	79.8168184	
216	11.2058157661	907.1836237	80.9565000	
228	12.8158050794	1050.2937848	81.9530087	
240	14.6571087068	1213.9652184	82.8243307	
252	16.7629606032	1401.1520536	83.5861926	
264	19.1713695930	1615.2328527	84.2523454	
276	21.9258053976	1860.0715909	84.8348125	
288	25.0759832259	2140.0873979	85.3441071	
300	28.6787610920	2460.3343193	85.7894214	
360	56.1141596356	4899.0364121	87.3048165	
420	109.7954999350	9670.7111053	88.0793030	
480	214.8308356439	19007.1853906	88.4751266	

N	AMOUNT OF 1	AMOUNT OF 1 PER PERIOD	PRESENT WORTH OF 1 PER PERIOD
1	1.0116666667	1.0000000	0.9884679
2	1.0234694444	2.0116667	1.9655366
3	1.0354099213	3.0351361	2.9313377
4	1.0474897037	4.0705460	3.8860010
5	1.0597104169	5.1180357	4.8296550
6	1.0720737051	6.1777462	5.7624267
7	1.0845812317	7.2498199	6.6844416
8	1.0972346794	8.3344011	7.5958236
9	1.1100357506	9.4316358	8.4966955
10	1.1229861677	10.5416715	9.3871784
11	1.1360876730	11.6646577	10.2673922
12	1.1493420292	12.8007454	11.1374552
18	1.2321793677	19.9010887	16.1511296
24	1.3209871001	27.5131800	20.8277431
30	1.4161955348	35.6739030	25.1899558
36	1.5182659942	44.4227995	29.2589044
42	1.6276930497	53.8022614	33.0543043
48	1.7450069186	63.8577359	36.5945460
54	1.8707760327	74.6379457	39.8967831
60	2.0056097928	86.1951251	42.9770165
66	2.1501615216	98.5852733	45.8501709
72	2.3051316291	111.8684254	48.5301681
78	2.4712710064	126.1089434	51.0299935
84	2.6493846642	141.3758284	53.3617599
90	2.8403356332	157.7430543	55.5367656
96	3.0450491461	175.2899268	57.5655493
102	3.2645171203	194.1014675	59.4579413
108	3.4998029646	214.2688255	61.2231110
114	3.7520467314	235.8897198	62.8696114
120	4.0224706412	259.0689121	64.4054203
132	4.6231945691	310.5595345	67.1742298
144	5.3136318275	369.7398709	69.5832686
156	6.1071803871	437.7583189	71.6792842
168	7.0192390988	515.9347799	73.5029499
180	8.0675065093	605.7862722	75.0896540
192	9.2723243021	709.0563688	76.4701865
204	10.6570720288	827.7490310	77.6713368
216	12.2486207910	964.1674964	78.7164133
228	14.0778546749	1120.9589721	79.6256957
240	16.1802700590	1301.1660051	80.4168287
252	18.5966644227	1508.2855219	81.1051642
264	21.3739280241	1746.3366878	81.7040595
276	24.5659538073	2019.9388978	82.2251362
288	28.2346831983	2334.4014170	82.6785057
300	32.4513080812	2695.8264070	83.0729658
360	65.0846612783	5492.9709667	84.3973197
420	130.5344340237	11102.9514877	85.0576445
480	261.8011391815	22354.3833584	85.3868835

N	AMOUNT OF 1	AMOUNT OF 1 PER PERIOD	PRESENT WORTH OF 1 PER PERIOD

N	AMOUNT OF 1	AMOUNT OF 1 PER PERIOD	PRESENT WORTH OF 1 PER PERIOD
1	1.0120833333	1.0000000	0.9880609
2	1.0243126736	2.0120833	1.9643253
3	1.0366897851	3.0363960	2.9289340
4	1.0492164533	4.0730858	3.8820262
5	1.0618944855	5.1223022	4.8237394
6	1.0747257105	6.1841967	5.7542093
7	1.0877119795	7.2589224	6.6735704
8	1.1008551659	8.3466344	7.5819551
9	1.1141571658	9.4474896	8.4794945
10	1.1276198983	10.5616468	9.3663182
11	1.1412453054	11.6892667	10.2425540
12	1.1550353528	12.8305120	11.1083284
18	1.2413461902	19.9734778	16.0901753
24	1.3341066662	27.6502069	20.7256343
30	1.4337987347	35.9005849	25.0387897
36	1.5409403639	44.7674784	29.0520512
42	1.6560882274	54.2969568	32.7862706
48	1.7798405969	64.5385322	36.2608496
54	1.9128404500	75.5454166	39.4938410
60	2.0557788117	87.3747982	42.5020424
66	2.2093983441	100.0881388	45.3010835
72	2.3744972051	113.7514928	47.9055071
78	2.5519331958	128.4358507	50.3288452
84	2.7426282170	144.2175076	52.5836884
90	2.9475730592	161.1784601	54.6817524
96	3.1678325503	179.4068317	56.6339378
102	3.4045510883	198.9973314	58.4503878
108	3.6589585873	220.0517452	60.1405400
114	3.9323768674	242.6794649	61.7131758
120	4.2262265228	266.9980571	63.1764662
132	4.8814410428	321.2227070	65.8048933
144	5.6382369771	383.8540947	68.0805181
156	6.5123630360	456.1955616	70.0506957
168	7.5220095369	539.7525134	71.7564250
180	8.6881869392	636.2637467	73.2332017
192	10.0351630666	747.7376331	74.5117571
204	11.5909681130	876.4939128	75.6186976
216	13.3879779438	1025.2119678	76.5770583
228	15.4635878276	1196.9865788	77.4067824
240	17.8609906221	1395.3923273	78.1251363
252	20.6300756046	1624.5579811	78.7470687
264	23.8284666543	1889.2524128	79.2855218
276	27.5227213889	2194.9838391	79.7517007
288	31.7897162095	2548.1144449	80.1553065
300	36.7182460776	2955.9927788	80.5047380
360	75.4845922907	6164.2421206	81.6622563
420	155.1796254442	12759.6931402	82.2253121
480	319.0149860023	26318.4816002	82.4992015

N	AMOUNT OF 1	AMOUNT OF 1 PER PERIOD	PRESENT WORTH OF 1 PER PERIOD
1	1.0125000000	1.0000000	0.9876543
2	1.0251562500	2.0125000	1.9631154
3	1.0379707031	3.0376563	2.9265337
4	1.0509453369	4.0756270	3.8780580
5	1.0640821536	5.1265723	4.8178350
6	1.0773831805	6.1906544	5.7460099
7	1.0908504703	7.2680376	6.6627258
8	1.1044861012	8.3588881	7.5681243
9	1.1182921774	9.4633742	8.4623450
10	1.1322708297	10.5816664	9.3455259
11	1.1464242150	11.7139372	10.2178034
12	1.1607545177	12.8603614	11.0793120
18	1.2505773941	20.0461915	16.0295489
24	1.3473510504	27.7880840	20.6242345
30	1.4516133600	36.1290688	24.8889062
36	1.5639438187	45.1155055	28.8472674
42	1.6849667656	54.7973412	32.5213187
48	1.8153548531	65.2283882	35.9314809
54	1.9558327854	76.4666228	39.0967078
60	2.1071813470	88.5745078	42.0345918
66	2.2702417416	101.6193393	44.7614619
72	2.4459202681	115.6736215	47.2924743
78	2.6351933578	130.8154686	49.6416964
84	2.8391130012	147.1290401	51.8221853
90	3.0588125952	164.7050076	53.8460604
96	3.2955132425	183.6410594	55.7245703
102	3.5505305387	204.0424431	57.4681561
108	3.8252818844	226.0225508	59.0865085
114	4.1212943632	249.7035491	60.5886227
120	4.4402132289	275.2170583	61.9828472
132	5.1539975651	332.3198052	64.4780679
144	5.9825259581	398.6020766	66.6277220
156	6.9442440332	475.5395227	68.4796675
168	8.0605626337	564.8450107	70.0751345
180	9.3563344925	668.5067594	71.4496430
192	10.8604075315	788.8326025	72.6337939
204	12.6062671065	928.5013685	73.6539501
216	14.6327814955	1090.6225196	74.5328234
228	16.9850672278	1278.8053782	75.2899804
240	19.7154935184	1497.2394815	75.9422776
252	22.8848481707	1750.7878537	76.5042372
264	26.5636909015	2045.0952721	76.9883703
276	30.8339242213	2386.7139377	77.4054551
288	35.7906168390	2783.2493471	77.7647773
300	41.5441201880	3243.5296150	78.0743364
360	87.5409951357	6923.2796109	79.0861424
420	184.4647520434	14677.1801635	79.5663128
480	388.7006846759	31016.0547741	79.7941861

N	AMOUNT OF 1	AMOUNT OF 1 PER PERIOD	PRESENT WORTH OF 1 PER PERIOD	RATE 1 7/24%
1	1.0129166667	1.0000000	0.9872480	
2	1.0260001736	2.0129167	1.9619068	
3	1.0392526759	3.0389168	2.9241367	
4	1.0526763563	4.0781695	3.8740962	
5	1.0662734259	5.1308459	4.8119420	
6	1.0800461243	6.1971193	5.7378284	
7	1.0939967200	7.2771654	6.6519079	
8	1.1081275110	8.3711621	7.5543311	
9	1.1224408247	9.4792897	8.4452467	
10	1.1369390187	10.6017305	9.3248013	
11	1.1516244810	11.7386695	10.1931399	
12	1.1664996305	12.8902940	11.0504055	
18	1.2598734049	20.1192313	15.9692484	
24	1.3607213881	27.9268171	20.5235380	
30	1.4696418614	36.3593699	24.7402928	
36	1.5872809965	45.4669159	28.6445286	
42	1.7143366884	55.3034855	32.2594073	
48	1.8515626959	65.9274345	35.6063744	
54	1.9997731136	77.4017894	38.7052856	
60	2.1598472008	89.7946220	41.5745253	
66	2.3327345982	103.1794528	44.2311152	
72	2.5194609617	117.6356874	46.6908157	
78	2.7211340470	133.2490875	48.9682188	
84	2.9389502810	150.1122798	51.0768354	
90	3.1742018605	168.3253053	53.0291748	
96	3.4282844170	187.9962129	54.8368193	
102	3.7027052975	209.2417005	56.5104926	
108	3.9990925059	232.1878069	58.0601240	
114	4.3192043616	256.9706603	59.4949066	
120	4.6649399306	283.7372850	60.8233523	
132	5.4416507056	343.8697320	63.1921729	
144	6.3476835377	414.0142094	65.2228812	
156	7.4045705015	495.8377162	66.9637376	
168	8.6374287544	591.2848068	68.4561139	
180	10.0755574509	702.6238026	69.7354768	
192	11.7531340440	832.5007002	70.8322305	
204	13.7100265201	984.0020532	71.7724398	
216	15.9927408706	1160.7283255	72.5784489	
228	18.6555263170	1366.8794568	73.2694127	
240	21.7616645564	1607.3546753	73.8617522	
252	25.3849736652	1887.8689289	74.3695445	
264	29.6115624019	2215.0887021	74.8048574	
276	34.5418766018	2596.7904466	75.1780361	
288	40.2930862944	3042.0453905	75.4979494	
300	47.0018702761	3561.4351181	75.7722001	
360	101.5168579462	7781.9502926	76.6567292	
420	219.2609014652	16897.6181780	77.0662625	
480	473.5700442658	36586.0679432	77.2558746	

N	AMOUNT OF 1	AMOUNT OF 1 PER PERIOD	PRESENT WORTH OF 1 PER PERIOD
1	1.0133333333	1.0000000	0.9868421
2	1.0268444444	2.0133333	1.9606994
3	1.0405357037	3.0401778	2.9217429
4	1.0544095131	4.0807135	3.8701410
5	1.0684683066	5.1351230	4.8060602
6	1.0827145507	6.2035913	5.7296647
7	1.0971507447	7.2863059	6.6411164
8	1.1117794213	8.3834566	7.5405754
9	1.1266031469	9.4952360	8.4281994
10	1.1416245222	10.6218392	9.3041442
11	1.1568461825	11.7634637	10.1685633
12	1.1722707983	12.9203099	11.0216086
18	1.2692346506	20.1925988	15.9092716
24	1.3742188245	28.0664118	20.4235391
30	1.4878867171	36.5915038	24.5929367
36	1.6109565983	45.8217449	28.4438109
42	1.7442061495	55.8154612	32.0004956
48	1.8884773775	66.6358033	35.2854655
54	2.0446819352	78.3511451	38.3194783
60	2.2138068828	91.0355162	41.1217062
66	2.3969209244	104.7690693	43.7098564
72	2.5951811617	119.6385871	46.1002834
78	2.8098404054	135.7380304	48.3080926
84	3.0422550920	153.1691319	50.3472350
90	3.2938938550	172.0420391	52.2305960
96	3.5663468052	192.4760104	53.9700766
102	3.8613355788	214.6001684	55.5766688
108	4.1807242162	238.5543162	57.0605244
114	4.5265309413	264.4898206	58.4310201
120	4.9009409143	292.5705686	59.6968161
132	5.7452299178	355.8922438	61.9456922
144	6.7349652619	430.1223946	63.8640851
156	7.8952031038	517.1402328	65.5005610
168	9.2553160449	619.1487034	66.8965490
180	10.8497367281	738.7302546	68.0873899
192	12.7188295352	878.9122151	69.1032310
204	14.9099124521	1043.2434339	69.9697894
216	17.4784549722	1235.8841229	70.7090029
228	20.4894823626	1461.7111772	71.3395854
240	24.0192218451	1726.4416384	71.8775008
252	28.1570323660	2036.7774274	72.3363670
264	33.0076668083	2400.5750106	72.7278006
276	38.6939239180	2827.0442938	73.0617112
288	45.3597570791	3326.9817809	73.3465520
300	53.1739186399	3913.0438980	73.5895341
360	117.7167870698	8753.7590302	74.3628776
420	260.6022334344	19470.1675076	74.7122051
480	576.9230180464	43194.2263535	74.8700000

N	AMOUNT OF 1	AMOUNT OF 1 PER PERIOD	PRESENT WORTH OF 1 PER PERIOD

RATE 1 3/8%

N	AMOUNT OF 1	AMOUNT OF 1 PER PERIOD	PRESENT WORTH OF 1 PER PERIOD
1	1.0137500000	1.0000000	0.9864365
2	1.0276890625	2.0137500	1.9594935
3	1.0418197871	3.0414391	2.9193524
4	1.0561448092	4.0832588	3.8661922
5	1.0706668003	5.1394037	4.8001896
6	1.0853884688	6.2100705	5.7215187
7	1.1003125603	7.2954589	6.6303514
8	1.1154418580	8.3957715	7.5268571
9	1.1307791835	9.5112133	8.4112031
10	1.1463273973	10.6419925	9.2835542
11	1.1620893990	11.7883199	10.1440732
12	1.1780681282	12.9504093	10.9929205
18	1.2786615619	20.2662954	15.8496165
24	1.3878445148	28.2068738	20.3242319
30	1.5063504328	36.8254860	24.4468254
36	1.6349753898	46.1800283	28.2450908
42	1.7745834349	56.3333407	31.7445433
48	1.9261123971	67.3536289	34.9686908
54	2.0905801855	79.3149226	37.9391918
60	2.2690916265	92.2975728	40.6760008
66	2.4628458860	106.3887917	43.1975027
72	2.6731445252	121.6832382	45.5206357
78	2.9014002431	138.2836540	47.6610059
84	3.1491463673	156.3015540	49.6329912
90	3.4180471536	175.8579748	51.4498387
96	3.7099089664	197.0842885	53.1237532
102	4.0266924125	220.1230845	54.6659794
108	4.3705255120	245.1291281	56.0868773
114	4.7437179933	272.2703995	57.3959919
120	5.1487768093	301.7292225	58.6021173
132	6.0656098584	368.4079897	60.7371721
144	7.1457016524	446.9601202	62.5495077
156	8.4181233706	539.4998815	64.0879039
168	9.9171228424	648.5180249	65.3937674
180	11.6830463444	776.9488250	66.5022463
192	13.7634245389	928.2490574	67.4431756
204	16.2142517846	1106.4910389	68.2418809
216	19.1014932506	1316.4722364	68.9198598
228	22.5028604002	1563.8443927	69.4953604
240	26.5099026315	1855.2656459	69.9838725
252	31.2304713727	2198.5797362	70.3985447
264	36.7916229538	2603.0271239	70.7505382
276	43.3430383878	3079.4937009	71.0493268
288	51.0610521053	3640.8037895	71.3029528
300	60.1533980793	4302.0653149	71.5182426
360	136.4935718845	9854.0779552	72.1944471
420	309.7164210281	22452.1033475	72.4924538
480	702.7749375307	51038.1772750	72.6237869

N	AMOUNT OF 1	AMOUNT OF 1 PER PERIOD	PRESENT WORTH OF 1 PER PERIOD
1	1.0141666667	1.0000000	0.9860312
2	1.0285340278	2.0141667	1.9582888
3	1.0431049265	3.0427007	2.9169651
4	1.0578822463	4.0858056	3.8622499
5	1.0728689115	5.1436879	4.7943302
6	1.0880678877	6.2165568	5.7133905
7	1.1034821828	7.3046247	6.6196127
8	1.1191148470	8.4081068	7.5131760
9	1.1349689740	9.5272217	8.3942574
10	1.1510477012	10.6621907	9.2630311
11	1.1673542103	11.8132384	10.1196691
12	1.1838917282	12.9805926	10.9643410
18	1.2881545720	20.3403227	15.7902811
24	1.4015996242	28.3482088	20.2256110
30	1.5250355425	37.0613324	24.3019467
36	1.6593422014	46.5418025	28.0483449
42	1.8054769640	56.8571975	31.4915109
48	1.9644815065	68.0810475	34.6559880
54	2.1374892432	80.2933583	37.5643333
60	2.3257334059	93.5811816	40.2372780
66	2.5305558343	108.0392354	42.6938754
72	2.7534165413	123.7705794	44.9516365
78	2.9959041201	140.8873497	47.0266551
84	3.2597470677	159.5115577	48.9337223
90	3.5468261063	179.7759604	50.6864321
96	3.8591875896	201.8250063	52.2972780
102	4.1990580888	225.8158651	53.7777426
108	4.5688602650	251.9195481	55.1383788
114	4.9712301377	280.3221274	56.3888856
120	5.4090358752	311.2260618	57.5381767
132	6.4037128304	381.4385527	59.5652183
144	7.5813026500	464.5625400	61.2774033
156	8.9754414966	562.9723409	62.7236377
168	10.6259509451	679.4788902	63.9452312
180	12.5799754286	817.4100303	64.9770769
192	14.8933288514	980.7055660	65.8486478
204	17.6320888331	1174.0298000	66.5848392
216	20.8744841211	1402.9047615	67.2066794
228	24.7131290823	1673.8679352	67.7319302
240	29.2576690994	1994.6589953	68.1755949
252	34.6379124344	2374.4408777	68.5503459
264	41.0075380146	2824.0615069	68.8668875
276	48.5484850509	3356.3636507	69.1342613
288	57.4761498704	3986.5517556	69.3601044
300	68.0455384026	4732.6262402	69.5508677
360	158.2557817840	11100.4081259	70.1421964
420	368.0607583685	25910.1711790	70.3964511
480	856.0112011306	60353.7318445	70.5057735

N	AMOUNT OF 1	AMOUNT OF 1 PER PERIOD	PRESENT WORTH OF 1 PER PERIOD
1	1.0145833333	1.0000000	0.9856263
2	1.0293793403	2.0145833	1.9570855
3	1.0443911223	3.0439627	2.9145811
4	1.0596218262	4.0883538	3.8583141
5	1.0750746445	5.1479756	4.7884820
6	1.0907528164	6.2230503	5.7052800
7	1.1066596283	7.3138031	6.6089002
8	1.1227984145	8.4204627	7.4995321
9	1.1391725581	9.5432611	8.3773622
10	1.1557854912	10.6824337	9.2425747
11	1.1726406963	11.8382192	10.0953508
12	1.1897417065	13.0108599	10.9358694
18	1.2977141171	20.4146823	15.7312632
24	1.4154853281	28.4904225	20.1276707
30	1.5439446082	37.2990588	24.1582882
36	1.6840619297	46.9071038	27.8535503
42	1.8368952928	57.3871058	31.2413593
48	2.0035987140	68.8181975	34.3472957
54	2.1854309402	81.2866930	37.1948120
60	2.3837649531	94.8867396	39.8054093
66	2.6000983362	109.7210288	42.1987997
72	2.8360645831	125.9015714	44.3930551
78	3.0934454315	143.5505439	46.4047442
84	3.3741843167	162.8012103	48.2490567
90	3.6804010465	183.7989289	49.9399187
96	4.0144078069	206.7022496	51.4900976
102	4.3787266215	231.6841112	52.9112985
108	4.7761083946	258.9331471	54.2142526
114	5.2095536827	288.6551097	55.4087984
120	5.6823353516	321.0744241	56.5039555
132	6.7605113578	395.0064931	58.4284934
144	8.0432623194	482.9665590	60.0461032
156	9.5694046374	587.6163180	61.4057342
168	11.3851198031	712.1225008	62.5485294
180	13.5453518628	860.2526992	63.5090700
192	16.1154700398	1036.4893742	64.3164221
204	19.1732468255	1246.1654966	64.9950166
216	22.8112113966	1495.6259243	65.5653879
228	27.1394495733	1792.4193993	66.0447956
240	32.2889350477	2145.5269747	66.4477466
252	38.4154926834	2565.6337840	66.7864345
264	45.7045138196	3065.4523762	67.0711079
276	54.3765662646	3660.1074010	67.3103812
288	64.6940687390	4367.5932850	67.5114948
300	76.9692317393	5209.3187478	67.6805345
360	183.4765570863	12512.6782002	68.1976946
420	437.3649864956	29922.1705026	68.4146455
480	1042.5753265160	71422.3081040	68.5056574

RATE 1¹¹/₂₄%

N	AMOUNT OF 1	AMOUNT OF 1 PER PERIOD	PRESENT WORTH OF 1 PER PERIOD
1	1.0150000000	1.0000000	0.9852217
2	1.0302250000	2.0150000	1.9558834
3	1.0456783750	3.0452250	2.9122004
4	1.0613635506	4.0909034	3.8543846
5	1.0772840039	5.1522669	4.7826450
6	1.0934432639	6.2295509	5.6971872
7	1.1098449129	7.3229942	6.5982140
8	1.1264925866	8.4328391	7.4859251
9	1.1433899754	9.5593317	8.3605173
10	1.1605408250	10.7027217	9.2221846
11	1.1779489374	11.8632625	10.0711178
12	1.1956181715	13.0412114	10.9075052
18	1.3073406358	20.4893757	15.6725609
24	1.4295028119	28.6335208	20.0304054
30	1.5630802205	37.5386814	24.0158380
36	1.7091395381	47.2759692	27.6606843
42	1.8688471151	57.9231410	30.9940500
48	2.0434782893	69.5652193	34.0425536
54	2.2344275705	82.2951714	36.8305388
60	2.4432197757	96.2146517	39.3802689
66	2.6715222061	111.4348137	41.7121046
72	2.9211579607	128.0771974	43.8446668
78	3.1941204950	146.2746997	45.7949848
84	3.4925895395	166.1726360	47.5786330
90	3.8189485057	187.9299004	49.2098545
96	4.1758035189	211.7202346	50.7016754
102	4.5660042293	237.7336153	52.0660086
108	4.9926665676	266.1777712	53.3137488
114	5.4591976275	297.2798418	54.4548599
120	5.9693228723	331.2881915	55.4984541
132	7.1370308975	409.1353932	57.3257142
144	8.5331638313	502.2109221	58.8540115
156	10.2024057368	613.4937158	60.1322601
168	12.1981816915	746.5454461	61.2013712
180	14.5843676891	905.6245126	62.0955623
192	17.4373350284	1095.8223352	62.8434525
204	20.8483946218	1323.2263081	63.4689784
216	24.9267194557	1595.1146304	63.9921604
228	29.8028387361	1920.1892491	64.4297433
240	35.6328155540	2308.8543703	64.7957321
252	42.6032417767	2773.5494518	65.1018405
264	50.9372100314	3329.1473354	65.3578658
276	60.9014539171	3993.4302611	65.5720021
288	72.8148849717	4787.6589981	65.7511030
300	87.0587996251	5737.2533083	65.9009007
360	212.7037808918	14113.5853928	66.3532417
420	519.6820833389	34578.8055893	66.5383831
480	1269.6975443068	84579.8362871	66.6141607

N	AMOUNT OF 1	AMOUNT OF 1 PER PERIOD	PRESENT WORTH OF 1 PER PERIOD

N	AMOUNT OF 1	AMOUNT OF 1 PER PERIOD	PRESENT WORTH OF 1 PER PERIOD
1	1.0154166667	1.0000000	0.9848174
2	1.0310710069	2.0154167	1.9546827
3	1.0469666850	3.0464877	2.9098229
4	1.0631074214	4.0934544	3.8504617
5	1.0794969941	5.1565618	4.7768190
6	1.0961392394	6.2360588	5.6891119
7	1.1130380527	7.3321980	6.5875538
8	1.1301973894	8.4452361	7.4723550
9	1.1476212658	9.5754335	8.3437226
10	1.1653137603	10.7230547	9.2018606
11	1.1832790141	11.8883685	10.0469698
12	1.2015212322	13.0716475	10.8792480
18	1.3170345697	20.5644045	15.6141722
24	1.4436532715	28.7775095	19.9338096
30	1.5824449990	37.7802162	23.8745841
36	1.7345800577	47.6484362	27.4697244
42	1.9013412651	58.4653794	30.7495453
48	2.0841347683	70.3222552	33.7417025
54	2.2845018998	83.3190421	36.4714261
60	2.5041321749	97.5653303	38.9617334
66	2.7448775376	113.1812457	41.2336230
72	3.0087679764	130.2984633	43.3062517
78	3.2980286413	149.0613173	45.1970960
84	3.6150986065	169.6280177	46.9220998
90	3.9626514371	192.1719851	48.4958085
96	4.3436177323	216.8833124	49.9314916
102	4.7612098375	243.9703678	51.2412551
108	5.2189489301	273.6615522	52.4361430
114	5.7206947109	306.2072245	53.5262306
120	6.2706779494	341.8818129	54.5207098
132	7.5343526966	423.8499046	56.2556495
144	9.0526847361	522.3363072	57.6996021
156	10.8769929191	640.6698110	58.9013724
168	13.0689379350	782.8500282	59.9015798
180	15.7026064116	953.6825780	60.7340306
192	18.8670150048	1158.9415138	61.4268613
204	22.6691191169	1405.5644833	62.0034892
216	27.2374279348	1701.8872174	62.4834041
228	32.7263479749	2057.9252740	62.8828269
240	39.3214019451	2485.7125586	63.2152577
252	47.2454993178	2999.7080639	63.4919327
264	56.7664705575	3617.2845767	63.7222033
276	68.2061196533	4359.3158694	63.9138525
288	81.9511009311	5250.8822226	64.0733579
300	98.4659877730	6322.1181258	64.2061108
360	246.5718481162	15928.9847427	64.6017981
420	617.4484982938	39985.8485380	64.7598118
480	1546.1726509246	100227.4151951	64.8229130

N	AMOUNT OF 1	AMOUNT OF 1 PER PERIOD	PRESENT WORTH OF 1 PER PERIOD
1	1.0158333333	1.0000000	0.9844135
2	1.0319173611	2.0158333	1.9534833
3	1.0482560527	3.0477507	2.9074487
4	1.0648534402	4.0960067	3.8465451
5	1.0817136196	5.1608602	4.7710042
6	1.0988407519	6.2425738	5.6810541
7	1.1162390638	7.3414146	6.5769196
8	1.1339128490	8.4576536	7.4588216
9	1.1518664691	9.5915665	8.3269778
10	1.1701043549	10.7434329	9.1816024
11	1.1886310072	11.9135373	10.0229064
12	1.2074509981	13.1021683	10.8510973
18	1.3267963627	20.6397703	15.5560950
24	1.4579379129	28.9223945	19.8378780
30	1.6020415925	38.0236795	23.7345146
36	1.7603885881	48.0245424	27.2806486
42	1.9343867199	59.0138981	30.5078077
48	2.1255829578	71.0894500	33.4446838
54	2.3356771757	84.3585585	36.1173879
60	2.5665372640	98.9391956	38.5496821
66	2.8202157371	114.9609939	40.7631914
72	3.0989679812	132.5663988	42.7775955
78	3.4052723067	151.9119352	44.6108039
84	3.7418519821	173.1695989	46.2791152
90	4.1116994456	196.5283860	47.7973618
96	4.5181029106	222.1959733	49.1790421
102	4.9646755996	250.4005642	50.4364402
108	5.4553878691	281.3929180	51.5807354
114	5.9946025082	315.4485795	52.6221011
120	6.5871135277	352.8703281	53.5697960
132	7.9536168038	439.1757981	55.2171181
144	9.6036025485	543.3854241	56.5814153
156	11.5958794828	669.2134410	57.7113139
168	14.0014562557	821.1446056	58.6470857
180	16.9060723312	1004.5940420	59.4220835
192	20.4132539108	1226.1002470	60.0639297
204	24.6480038097	1493.5581353	60.5955008
216	29.7612568019	1816.5004296	61.0357433
228	35.9352592310	2206.4374251	61.4003481
240	43.3900646265	2677.2672396	61.7023105
252	52.3913768422	3245.7711690	61.9523930
264	63.2600202615	3932.2118060	62.1595091
276	76.3833746065	4761.0552383	62.3310408
288	92.2291819092	5761.8430679	62.4731018
300	111.3622177529	6970.2453318	62.5907554
360	285.8152816684	17988.3335791	62.9369202
420	733.5555710326	46266.6676442	63.0717964
480	1882.6977082955	118844.0657871	63.1243482

N	AMOUNT OF 1	AMOUNT OF 1 PER PERIOD	PRESENT WORTH OF 1 PER PERIOD	RATE $1^{5}/_{8}\%$
1	1.0162500000	1.0000000	0.9840098	
2	1.0327640625	2.0162500	1.9522852	
3	1.0495464785	3.0490141	2.9050777	
4	1.0666016088	4.0985605	3.8426349	
5	1.0839338849	5.1651621	4.7652004	
6	1.1015478106	6.2490960	5.6730139	
7	1.1194479625	7.3506438	6.5663113	
8	1.1376389919	8.4700918	7.4453248	
9	1.1561256255	9.6077308	8.3102827	
10	1.1749126669	10.7638564	9.1614098	
11	1.1940049977	11.9387691	9.9989272	
12	1.2134075790	13.1327741	10.8230526	
18	1.3366264619	20.7154746	15.4983274	
24	1.4723579527	29.0681817	19.7426052	
30	1.6218726791	38.2690879	23.5956179	
36	1.7865702987	48.4043261	27.0934349	
42	1.9679926010	59.5687754	30.2688005	
48	2.1678379408	71.8669502	33.1514404	
54	2.3879771374	85.4139777	35.7683398	
60	2.6304709873	100.3366761	38.1439965	
66	2.8975895569	116.7747420	40.3006498	
72	3.1918334323	134.8820574	42.2584888	
78	3.5159571290	154.8281310	44.0358415	
84	3.8729948775	176.7996848	45.6493464	
90	4.2662890276	201.0024017	47.1141079	
96	4.6995213376	227.6628515	48.4438383	
102	5.1767474402	257.0306117	49.6509854	
108	5.7024348085	289.3806036	50.7468500	
114	6.2815045782	325.0156664	51.7416906	
120	6.9193776152	364.2693917	52.6448204	
132	8.3960252400	455.1400148	54.2089860	
144	10.1878006593	565.4031175	55.4980546	
156	12.3619545330	699.1972020	56.5604088	
168	15.0000893210	861.5439582	57.4359219	
180	18.2012220672	1058.5367426	58.1574544	
192	22.0855008027	1297.5692802	58.7520877	
204	26.7987140591	1587.6131729	59.2421401	
216	32.5177627457	1939.5546305	59.6460047	
228	39.4572997664	2366.6030625	59.9788398	
240	47.8777865819	2884.7868666	60.2531377	
252	58.0952691022	3513.5550217	60.4791935	
264	70.4932398303	4276.5070665	60.6654919	
276	85.5370314755	5202.2788600	60.8190251	
288	103.7912822741	6325.6173707	60.9455557	
300	125.9411285414	7688.6848333	61.0498327	
360	331.2844847402	20325.1990609	61.3527044	
420	871.4342256632	53565.1831177	61.4678441	
480	2292.2824479773	141001.9967986	61.5116156	

N	AMOUNT OF 1	AMOUNT OF 1 PER PERIOD	PRESENT WORTH OF 1 PER PERIOD
1	1.0166666667	1.0000000	0.9836066
2	1.0336111111	2.0166667	1.9510884
3	1.0508379630	3.0502778	2.9027099
4	1.0683519290	4.1011157	3.8387311
5	1.0861577945	5.1694677	4.7594076
6	1.1042604244	6.2556255	5.6649911
7	1.1226647648	7.3598859	6.5557289
8	1.1413758442	8.4825507	7.4318645
9	1.1603987750	9.6239265	8.2936372
10	1.1797387545	10.7843253	9.1412825
11	1.1994010671	11.9640640	9.9750320
12	1.2193910849	13.1634651	10.7951134
18	1.3465253169	20.7915190	15.4408675
24	1.4869146179	29.2148771	19.6479857
30	1.6419409671	38.5164580	23.4578823
36	1.8131304291	48.7878257	26.9080619
42	2.0021681772	60.1300906	30.0324874
48	2.2109150811	72.6549049	32.8619156
54	2.4414260257	86.4855615	35.4241991
60	2.6959701393	101.7582084	37.7445606
66	2.9770531302	118.6231878	39.8458417
72	3.2874419531	137.2465172	41.7487272
78	3.6301920463	157.8115228	43.4719488
84	4.0086774097	180.5206446	45.0324698
90	4.4266238178	205.5974291	46.4456519
96	4.8881454957	233.2887297	47.7254063
102	5.3977856196	263.8671372	48.8843307
108	5.9605610391	297.6336623	49.9338335
114	6.5820116628	334.9206998	50.8842459
120	7.2682549922	376.0952995	51.7449236
132	8.8628453403	471.7707204	53.2301651
144	10.8072745948	588.4364757	54.4481840
156	13.1782942930	730.6976576	55.4470587
168	16.0694945752	904.1696745	56.2662174
180	19.5949984239	1115.6999054	56.9379941
192	23.8939663868	1373.6379832	57.4889058
204	29.1360895951	1688.1653757	57.9406983
216	35.5282879013	2071.6972741	58.3112049
228	43.3228775288	2539.3726517	58.6150504
240	52.8275306311	3109.6518379	58.8642286
252	64.4174198891	3805.0451933	59.0685749
264	78.5500275253	4653.0016515	59.2361556
276	95.7832032835	5686.9921970	59.3735854
288	116.7971841675	6947.8310501	59.4862890
300	142.4214451159	8485.2867070	59.5787151
360	383.9639632327	22977.8377940	59.8437353
420	1035.1553794543	62049.3227673	59.9420377
480	2790.7479925758	167384.8795545	59.9785004

TABLE 4 AUXILIARY TABLES

Time Interval	Amount of 1	Payment Equivalent to 1 per Period	Equivalent per Period to a Payment of 1
Fractional Parts of a Unit Period.	*How 1 left at compound interest will grow for a time interval which is a fractional part of a unit period.*	*Payment at the end of each time interval equivalent to 1 at the end of each period.*	*Payment at the end of each period equivalent to 1 at the end of each time interval.*

$\frac{1}{2}\%$ per Period $i = .005$

1-12	1.000 415 7148	.083 142 9689	12.027 475 2355
1-6	1.000 831 6025	.166 320 5017	6.012 487 8775
1-4	1.001 247 6631	.249 532 6125	4.007 492 2070
1-3	1.001 663 8966	.332 779 3159	3.004 994 4583
1-2	1.002 496 8828	.499 376 5576	2.002 496 8828

$\frac{7}{12}\%$ per Period $i = .00583333$

1-12	1.000 484 8163	.083 111 3592	12.032 049 6401
1-6	1.000 969 8676	.166 263 0122	6.014 566 8401
1-4	1.001 455 1540	.249 454 9785	4.008 739 3972
1-3	1.001 940 6758	.332 687 2775	3.005 825 7936
1-2	1.002 912 4256	.499 272 9523	2.002 912 4256

$\frac{2}{3}\%$ per Period $i = .00666666$

1-12	1.000 553 8652	.083 079 7830	12.036 622 6774
1-6	1.001 108 0372	.166 205 5810	6.016 645 1334
1-4	1.001 662 5161	.249 377 4195	4.009 986 1572
1-3	1.002 217 3022	.332 595 3239	3.006 656 8229
1-2	1.003 327 7962	.499 169 4329	2.003 327 7962

$\frac{3}{4}\%$ per Period $i = .0075$

1-12	1.000 622 8618	.083 048 2402	12.041 194 3491
1-6	1.001 246 1116	.166 148 2079	6.018 722 7583
1-4	1.001 869 7495	.249 299 9354	4.011 232 4875
1-3	1.002 493 7759	.332 503 4550	3.007 487 5467
1-2	1.003 742 9950	.499 065 9992	2.003 742 9950

$\frac{5}{6}\%$ per Period $i = .00833333$

1-12	1.000 691 8061	.083 016 7306	12.045 764 6570
1-6	1.001 384 0908	.166 090 8928	6.020 799 7155
1-4	1.002 076 8544	.249 222 5261	4.012 478 3886
1-3	1.002 770 0973	.332 411 6704	3.008 317 9652
1-2	1.004 158 0221	.498 962 6511	2.004 158 0221

1% per Period $i = .01$

1-12	1.000 829 5381	.082 953 8114	12.054 901 1879
1-6	1.001 659 7644	.165 976 4362	6.024 951 6304
1-4	1.002 490 6793	.249 067 9314	4.014 968 9053
1-3	1.003 322 2835	.332 228 3542	3.009 977 8882
1-2	1.004 987 5621	.498 756 2112	2.004 987 5621

TABLE 4 AUXILIARY TABLES *(cont.)*

Time Interval	Amount of 1	Payment Equivalent to 1 per Period	Equivalent per Period to a Payment of 1
Fractional Parts of a Unit Period.	*How 1 left at compound interest will grow for a time interval which is a fractional part of a unit period.*	*Payment at the end of each time interval equivalent to 1 at the end of each period.*	*Payment at the end of each period equivalent to 1 at the end of each time interval.*

1¼% per Period   *i* = .0125

1-12	1.001 035 7460	.082 859 6812	12.068 595 7972
1-6	1.002 072 5648	.165 805 1839	6.031 174 5161
1-4	1.003 110 4575	.248 836 5972	4.018 701 4747
1-3	1.004 149 4251	.331 954 0099	3.012 465 4931
1-2	1.006 230 5899	.498 447 1900	2.006 230 5899

1½% per Period   *i* = .015

1-12	1.001 241 4877	.082 765 8478	12.082 278 2225
1-6	1.002 484 5167	.165 634 4483	6.037 391 4376
1-4	1.003 729 0889	.248 605 9292	4.022 430 2099
1-3	1.004 975 2063	.331 680 4182	3.014 950 3715
1-2	1.007 472 0840	.498 138 9320	2.007 472 0840

1¾% per Period   *i* = .0175

1-12	1.001 446 7654	.082 672 3096	12.095 948 5087
1-6	1.002 895 6240	.165 464 2266	6.043 602 4169
1-4	1.004 346 5787	.248 375 9242	4.026 155 1251
1-3	1.005 799 6326	.331 407 5755	3.017 432 5334
1-2	1.008 712 0501	.497 831 4338	2.008 712 0501

2% per Period   *i* = .02

1-12	1.001 651 5813	.082 579 0651	12.109 606 7004
1-6	1.003 305 8903	.165 294 5162	6.049 807 4758
1-4	1.004 962 9316	.248 146 5787	4.029 876 2344
1-3	1.006 622 7096	.331 135 4780	3.019 911 9890
1-2	1.009 950 4938	.497 524 6918	2.009 950 4938

2¼% per Period   *i* = .0225

1-12	1.001 855 9375	.082 486 1127	12.123 252 8421
1-6	1.003 715 3196	.165 125 3144	6.056 006 6360
1-4	1.005 578 1525	.247 917 8894	4.033 593 5518
1-3	1.007 444 4427	.330 864 1222	3.022 388 7480
1-2	1.011 187 4208	.497 218 7026	2.011 187 4208

2½% per Period   *i* = .025

1-12	1.002 059 8363	.082 393 4508	12.136 886 9779
1-6	1.004 123 9155	.164 956 6186	6.062 199 9193
1-4	1.006 192 2463	.247 689 8530	4.037 307 0910
1-3	1.008 264 8376	.330 593 5044	3.024 862 8204
1-2	1.012 422 8366	.496 913 4626	2.012 422 8366

3% per Period   *i* = .03

1-12	1.002 466 2698	.082 208 9924	12.164 119 4069
1-6	1.004 938 6220	.164 620 7344	6.074 568 9406
1-4	1.007 417 0718	.247 235 7259	4.044 722 8905
1-3	1.009 901 6340	.330 054 4683	3.029 802 9445
1-2	1.014 889 1565	.496 305 2170	2.014 889 1565

TABLE 4 AUXILIARY TABLES *(cont.)*

Time Interval	Amount of 1	Payment Equivalent to 1 per Period	Equivalent per Period to a Payment of 1
Fractional Parts of a Unit Period.	*How 1 left at compound interest will grow for a time interval which is a fractional part of a unit period.*	*Payment at the end of each time interval equivalent to 1 at the end of each period.*	*Payment at the end of each period equivalent to 1 at the end of each time interval.*

$3\frac{1}{2}\%$ per Period $\qquad i = .035$

1-12	1.002 870 8987	.082 025 6777	12.191 304 3353
1-6	1.005 750 0395	.164 286 8428	6.086 914 7098
1-4	1.008 637 4460	.246 784 1714	4.052 123 7423
1-3	1.011 533 1419	.329 518 3414	3.034 732 4392
1-2	1.017 349 4975	.495 699 9277	2.017 349 4975

4% per Period $\qquad i = .04$

1-12	1.003 273 7398	.081 843 4946	12.218 442 1063
1-6	1.006 558 1969	.163 954 9234	6.099 237 3951
1-4	1.009 853 4065	.246 335 1637	4.059 509 7544
1-3	1.013 159 4038	.328 985 0955	3.039 651 3814
1-2	1.019 803 9027	.495 097 5680	2.019 803 9027

$4\frac{1}{2}\%$ per Period $\qquad i = .045$

1-12	1.003 674 8094	.081 662 4311	12.245 533 0594
1-6	1.007 363 1230	.163 624 9561	6.111 537 1626
1-4	1.011 064 9905	.245 888 6778	4.066 881 0338
1-3	1.014 780 4616	.328 454 7029	3.044 559 8469
1-2	1.022 252 4150	.494 498 1114	2.022 252 4150

5% per Period $\qquad i = .05$

1-12	1.004 074 1238	.081 482 4757	12.272 577 5296
1-6	1.008 164 8461	.163 296 9210	6.123 814 1763
1-4	1.012 272 2344	.245 444 6886	4.074 237 6858
1-3	1.016 396 3568	.327 927 1363	3.049 457 9110
1-2	1.024 695 0766	.493 901 5319	2.024 695 0766

6% per Period $\qquad i = .06$

1-12	1.004 867 5506	.081 125 8428	12.326 528 3420
1-6	1.009 758 7942	.162 646 5697	6.148 300 5890
1-4	1.014 673 8462	.244 564 1028	4.088 907 5237
1-3	1.019 612 8224	.326 880 3737	3.059 223 1301
1-2	1.029 563 0141	.492 716 9016	2.029 563 0141

7% per Period $\qquad i = .07$

1-12	1.005 654 1454	.080 773 5055	12.380 297 1455
1-6	1.011 340 2601	.162 003 7162	6.172 697 9071
1-4	1.017 058 5250	.243 693 2143	4.103 520 0870
1-3	1.022 809 1218	.325 844 5967	3.068 947 6213
1-2	1.034 408 0433	.491 543 4754	2.034 408 0433

8% per Period $\qquad i = .08$

1-12	1.006 434 0301	.080 425 3764	12.433 886 4805
1-6	1.012 909 4570	.161 368 2120	6.197 007 3742
1-4	1.019 426 5469	.242 831 8364	4.118 076 1757
1-3	1.025 985 5680	.324 819 6001	3.078 631 9538
1-2	1.039 230 4845	.490 381 0568	2.039 230 4845

9% per Period $\qquad i = .09$

1-12	1.007 207 3233	.080 081 3702	12.487 298 8282
1-6	1.014 466 5921	.160 739 9127	6.221 230 2053
1-4	1.021 778 1809	.241 979 7874	4.132 576 5710
1-3	1.029 142 4666	.323 805 1841	3.088 276 6831
1-2	1.044 030 6509	.489 229 4544	2.044 030 6509

TABLE 5   PRESENT WORTH OF 1

n	4%	6%	8%	10%	12%	14%	16%	18%	20%	22%	24%
1	.962	.943	.926	.909	.893	.877	.862	.847	.833	.820	.806
2	.925	.890	.857	.826	.797	.769	.743	.718	.694	.672	.650
3	.889	.840	.794	.751	.712	.675	.641	.609	.579	.551	.524
4	.855	.792	.735	.683	.636	.592	.552	.516	.482	.451	.423
5	.822	.747	.681	.621	.567	.519	.476	.437	.402	.370	.341
6	.790	.705	.630	.564	.507	.456	.410	.370	.335	.303	.275
7	.760	.665	.583	.513	.452	.400	.354	.314	.279	.249	.222
8	.731	.627	.540	.467	.404	.351	.305	.266	.233	.204	.179
9	.703	.592	.500	.424	.361	.308	.263	.225	.194	.167	.144
10	.676	.558	.463	.386	.322	.270	.227	.191	.162	.137	.116
11	.650	.527	.429	.350	.287	.237	.195	.162	.135	.112	.094
12	.625	.497	.397	.319	.257	.208	.168	.137	.112	.092	.076
13	.601	.469	.368	.290	.229	.182	.145	.116	.093	.075	.061
14	.577	.442	.340	.263	.205	.160	.125	.099	.078	.062	.049
15	.555	.417	.315	.239	.183	.140	.108	.084	.065	.051	.040
16	.534	.394	.292	.218	.163	.123	.093	.071	.054	.042	.032
17	.513	.371	.270	.198	.146	.108	.080	.060	.045	.034	.026
18	.494	.350	.250	.180	.130	.095	.069	.051	.038	.028	.021
19	.475	.331	.232	.164	.116	.083	.060	.043	.031	.023	.017
20	.456	.312	.215	.149	.104	.073	.051	.037	.026	.019	.014
21	.439	.294	.199	.135	.093	.064	.044	.031	.022	.015	.011
22	.422	.278	.184	.123	.083	.056	.038	.026	.018	.013	.009
23	.406	.262	.170	.112	.074	.049	.033	.022	.015	.010	.007
24	.390	.247	.158	.102	.066	.043	.028	.019	.013	.008	.006
25	.375	.233	.146	.092	.059	.038	.024	.016	.010	.007	.005
26	.361	.220	.135	.084	.053	.033	.021	.014	.009	.006	.004
27	.347	.207	.125	.076	.047	.029	.018	.011	.007	.005	.003
28	.333	.196	.116	.069	.042	.026	.016	.010	.006	.004	.002
29	.321	.185	.107	.063	.037	.022	.014	.008	.005	.003	.002
30	.308	.174	.099	.057	.033	.020	.012	.007	.004	.003	.002
31	.296	.164	.092	.052	.030	.017	.010	.006	.004	.002	.001
32	.285	.155	.085	.047	.027	.015	.009	.005	.003	.002	.001
33	.274	.146	.079	.043	.024	.013	.007	.004	.002	.001	.001
34	.264	.138	.073	.039	.021	.012	.006	.004	.002	.001	.001
35	.253	.130	.068	.036	.019	.010	.006	.003	.002	.001	.001
36	.244	.123	.063	.032	.017	.009	.005	.003	.001	.001	—
37	.234	.116	.058	.029	.015	.008	.004	.002	.001	.001	—
38	.225	.109	.054	.027	.013	.007	.004	.002	.001	.001	—
39	.217	.103	.050	.024	.012	.006	.003	.002	.001	—	—
40	.208	.097	.046	.022	.011	.005	.003	.001	.001	—	—
41	.200	.092	.043	.020	.010	.005	.002	.001	.001	—	—
42	.193	.087	.039	.018	.009	.004	.002	.001	—	—	—
43	.185	.082	.037	.017	.008	.004	.002	.001	—	—	—
44	.178	.077	.034	.015	.007	.003	.001	.001	—	—	—
45	.171	.073	.031	.014	.006	.003	.001	.001	—	—	—
46	.165	.069	.029	.012	.005	.002	.001	—	—	—	—
47	.158	.065	.027	.011	.005	.002	.001	—	—	—	—
48	.152	.061	.025	.010	.004	.002	.001	—	—	—	—
49	.146	.058	.023	.009	.004	.002	.001	—	—	—	—
50	.141	.054	.021	.009	.003	.001	.001	—	—	—	—

n	25%	30%	35%	40%	45%	50%	60%	70%	80%	90%	100%
1	.800	.769	.741	.714	.690	.667	.625	.588	.556	.526	.500
2	.640	.592	.549	.510	.476	.444	.391	.346	.309	.277	.250
3	.512	.455	.406	.364	.328	.296	.244	.204	.171	.146	.125
4	.410	.350	.301	.260	.226	.198	.153	.120	.095	.077	.063
5	.328	.269	.223	.186	.156	.132	.095	.070	.053	.040	.031
6	.262	.207	.165	.133	.108	.088	.060	.041	.029	.021	.016
7	.210	.159	.122	.095	.074	.059	.037	.024	.016	.011	.008
8	.168	.123	.091	.068	.051	.039	.023	.014	.009	.006	.004
9	.134	.094	.067	.048	.035	.026	.015	.008	.005	.003	.002
10	.107	.073	.050	.035	.024	.017	.009	.005	.003	.002	.001
11	.086	.056	.037	.025	.017	.012	.006	.003	.002	.001	—
12	.069	.043	.027	.018	.012	.008	.004	.002	.001	—	—
13	.055	.033	.020	.013	.008	.005	.002	.001	—	—	—
14	.044	.025	.015	.009	.006	.003	.001	.001	—	—	—
15	.035	.020	.011	.006	.004	.002	.001	—	—	—	—
16	.028	.015	.008	.005	.003	.002	.001	—	—	—	—
17	.023	.012	.006	.003	.002	.001	—	—	—	—	—
18	.018	.009	.005	.002	.001	.001	—	—	—	—	—
19	.014	.007	.003	.002	.001	—	—	—	—	—	—
20	.012	.005	.002	.001	.001	—	—	—	—	—	—

TABLE 5 PRESENT WORTH OF
1 PER PERIOD *(cont.)*

n	4%	6%	8%	10%	12%	14%	16%	18%	20%	22%	24%
1	.962	.943	.926	.909	.893	.877	.862	.847	.833	.820	.806
2	1.886	1.833	1.783	1.736	1.690	1.647	1.605	1.566	1.528	1.492	1.457
3	2.775	2.673	2.577	2.487	2.402	2.322	2.246	2.174	2.106	2.042	1.981
4	3.630	3.465	3.312	3.170	3.037	2.914	2.798	2.690	2.589	2.494	2.404
5	4.452	4.212	3.993	3.791	3.605	3.433	3.274	3.127	2.991	2.864	2.745
6	5.242	4.917	4.623	4.355	4.111	3.889	3.685	3.498	3.326	3.167	3.020
7	6.002	5.582	5.206	4.868	4.564	4.288	4.039	3.812	3.605	3.416	3.242
8	6.733	6.210	5.747	5.335	4.968	4.639	4.344	4.078	3.837	3.619	3.421
9	7.435	6.802	6.247	5.759	5.328	4.946	4.607	4.303	4.031	3.786	3.566
10	8.111	7.360	6.710	6.145	5.650	5.216	4.833	4.494	4.192	3.923	3.682
11	8.760	7.887	7.139	6.495	5.938	5.453	5.029	4.656	4.327	4.035	3.776
12	9.385	8.384	7.536	6.814	6.194	5.660	5.197	4.793	4.439	4.127	3.851
13	9.986	8.853	7.904	7.103	6.424	5.842	5.342	4.910	4.533	4.203	3.912
14	10.563	9.295	8.244	7.367	6.628	6.002	5.468	5.008	4.611	4.265	3.962
15	11.118	9.712	8.559	7.606	6.811	6.142	5.575	5.092	4.675	4.315	4.001
16	11.652	10.106	8.851	7.824	6.974	6.265	5.668	5.162	4.730	4.357	4.033
17	12.166	10.477	9.122	8.022	7.120	6.373	5.749	5.222	4.775	4.391	4.059
18	12.659	10.828	9.372	8.201	7.250	6.467	5.818	5.273	4.812	4.419	4.080
19	13.134	11.158	9.604	8.365	7.366	6.550	5.877	5.316	4.843	4.442	4.097
20	13.590	11.470	9.818	8.514	7.469	6.623	5.929	5.353	4.870	4.460	4.110
21	14.029	11.764	10.017	8.649	7.562	6.687	5.973	5.384	4.891	4.476	4.121
22	14.451	12.042	10.201	8.772	7.645	6.743	6.011	5.410	4.909	4.488	4.130
23	14.857	12.303	10.371	8.883	7.718	6.792	6.044	5.432	4.925	4.499	4.137
24	15.247	12.550	10.529	8.985	7.784	6.835	6.073	5.451	4.937	4.507	4.143
25	15.622	12.783	10.675	9.077	7.843	6.873	6.097	5.467	4.948	4.514	4.147
26	15.983	13.003	10.810	9.161	7.896	6.906	6.118	5.480	4.956	4.520	4.151
27	16.330	13.211	10.935	9.237	7.943	6.935	6.136	5.492	4.964	4.524	4.154
28	16.663	13.406	11.051	9.307	7.984	6.961	6.152	5.502	4.970	4.528	4.157
29	16.984	13.591	11.158	9.370	8.022	6.983	6.166	5.510	4.975	4.531	4.159
30	17.292	13.765	11.258	9.427	8.055	7.003	6.177	5.517	4.979	4.534	4.160
31	17.588	13.929	11.350	9.479	8.085	7.020	6.187	5.523	4.982	4.536	4.161
32	17.874	14.084	11.435	9.526	8.112	7.035	6.196	5.528	4.985	4.538	4.162
33	18.148	14.230	11.514	9.569	8.135	7.048	6.203	5.532	4.988	4.539	4.163
34	18.411	14.368	11.587	9.609	8.157	7.060	6.210	5.536	4.990	4.540	4.164
35	18.665	14.498	11.655	9.644	8.176	7.070	6.215	5.539	4.992	4.541	4.164
36	18.908	14.621	11.717	9.677	8.192	7.079	6.220	5.541	4.993	4.542	4.165
37	19.143	14.737	11.775	9.706	8.208	7.087	6.224	5.543	4.994	4.543	4.165
38	19.368	14.846	11.829	9.733	8.221	7.094	6.228	5.545	4.995	4.543	4.165
39	19.584	14.949	11.879	9.757	8.233	7.100	6.231	5.547	4.996	4.544	4.166
40	19.793	15.046	11.925	9.779	8.244	7.105	6.233	5.548	4.997	4.544	4.166
41	19.993	15.138	11.967	9.799	8.253	7.110	6.236	5.549	4.997	4.544	4.166
42	20.186	15.225	12.007	9.817	8.262	7.114	6.238	5.550	4.998	4.544	4.166
43	20.371	15.306	12.043	9.834	8.270	7.117	6.239	5.551	4.998	4.545	4.166
44	20.549	15.383	12.077	9.849	8.276	7.120	6.241	5.552	4.998	4.545	4.166
45	20.720	15.456	12.108	9.863	8.283	7.123	6.242	5.552	4.999	4.545	4.166
46	20.885	15.524	12.137	9.875	8.288	7.126	6.243	5.553	4.999	4.545	4.166
47	21.043	15.589	12.164	9.887	8.293	7.128	6.244	5.553	4.999	4.545	4.166
48	21.195	15.650	12.189	9.897	8.297	7.130	6.245	5.554	4.999	4.545	4.167
49	21.341	15.708	12.212	9.906	8.301	7.131	6.246	5.554	4.999	4.545	4.167
50	21.482	15.762	12.233	9.915	8.304	7.133	6.246	5.554	4.999	4.545	4.167

n	25%	30%	35%	40%	45%	50%	60%	70%	80%	90%	100%
1	.800	.769	.741	.714	.690	.667	.625	.588	.556	.526	.500
2	1.440	1.361	1.289	1.224	1.165	1.111	1.016	.934	.864	.803	.750
3	1.952	1.816	1.696	1.589	1.493	1.407	1.260	1.138	1.036	.949	.875
4	2.362	2.166	1.997	1.849	1.720	1.605	1.412	1.258	1.131	1.026	.938
5	2.689	2.436	2.220	2.035	1.876	1.737	1.508	1.328	1.184	1.066	.969
6	2.951	2.643	2.385	2.168	1.983	1.824	1.567	1.369	1.213	1.087	.984
7	3.161	2.802	2.508	2.263	2.057	1.883	1.605	1.394	1.230	1.099	.992
8	3.329	2.925	2.598	2.331	2.109	1.922	1.628	1.408	1.239	1.105	.996
9	3.463	3.019	2.665	2.379	2.144	1.948	1.642	1.417	1.244	1.108	.998
10	3.571	3.092	2.715	2.414	2.168	1.965	1.652	1.421	1.246	1.109	.999
11	3.656	3.147	2.752	2.438	2.185	1.977	1.657	1.424	1.248	1.110	1.000
12	3.725	3.190	2.779	2.456	2.196	1.985	1.661	1.426	1.249	1.111	1.000
13	3.780	3.223	2.799	2.469	2.204	1.990	1.663	1.427	1.249	1.111	1.000
14	3.824	3.249	2.814	2.478	2.210	1.993	1.664	1.428	1.250	1.111	1.000
15	3.859	3.268	2.825	2.484	2.214	1.995	1.665	1.428	1.250	1.111	1.000
16	3.887	3.283	2.834	2.489	2.216	1.997	1.666	1.428	1.250	1.111	1.000
17	3.910	3.295	2.840	2.492	2.218	1.998	1.666	1.428	1.250	1.111	1.000
18	3.928	3.304	2.844	2.494	2.219	1.999	1.666	1.428	1.250	1.111	1.000
19	3.942	3.311	2.848	2.496	2.220	1.999	1.666	1.429	1.250	1.111	1.000
20	3.954	3.316	2.850	2.497	2.221	1.999	1.667	1.429	1.250	1.111	1.000

TABLE 6 EXPONENTIAL FUNCTION

x	e^x	e^{-x}	x	e^x	e^{-x}
.000	1.0000000000	1.0000000000	.16	1.1735108710	.8521437890
.001	1.0010005002	.9990004998	.17	1.1853048513	.8436648166
.002	1.0020020013	.9980019987	.18	1.1972173631	.8352702114
.003	1.0030045045	.9970044955	.19	1.2092495977	.8269591339
.004	1.0040080107	.9960079893	.20	1.2214027582	.8187307531
.005	1.0050125209	.9950124792	.21	1.2336780600	.8105842460
.006	1.0060180361	.9940179641	.22	1.2460767306	.8025187980
.007	1.0070245573	.9930244429	.23	1.2586000099	.7945336025
.008	1.0080320855	.9920319148	.24	1.2712491503	.7866278611
.009	1.0090406218	.9910403788	.25	1.2840254167	.7788007831
.01	1.0100501671	.9900498337	.26	1.2969300867	.7710515858
.02	1.0202013400	.9801986733	.27	1.3099644507	.7633794943
.03	1.0304545340	.9704455335	.28	1.3231298123	.7557837415
.04	1.0408107742	.9607894392	.29	1.3364274880	.7482635676
.05	1.0512710964	.9512294245	.30	1.3498588076	.7408182207
.06	1.0618365465	.9417645336	.31	1.3634251141	.7334469562
.07	1.0725081813	.9323938199	.32	1.3771277643	.7261490371
.08	1.0832870677	.9231163464	.33	1.3909681285	.7189237334
.09	1.0941742837	.9139311853	.34	1.4049475906	.7117703228
.10	1.1051709181	.9048374180	.35	1.4190675486	.7046880897
.11	1.1162780705	.8958341353	.36	1.4333294146	.6976763261
.12	1.1274968516	.8869204367	.37	1.4477346147	.6907343306
.13	1.1388283833	.8780954309	.38	1.4622845894	.6838614092
.14	1.1502737989	.8693582354	.39	1.4769807939	.6770568745
.15	1.1618342427	.8607079764	.40	1.4918246976	.6703200460

TABLE 6   EXPONENTIAL FUNCTION *(cont.)*

x	e^x	e^{-x}	x	e^x	e^{-x}
.41	1.5068177851	.6636502501	.71	2.0339912586	.4916441975
.42	1.5219615556	.6570468198	.72	2.0544332106	.4867522560
.43	1.5372575235	.6505090947	.73	2.0750806077	.4819089901
.44	1.5527072185	.6440364211	.74	2.0959355145	.4774139155
.45	1.5683121855	.6376281516	.75	2.1170000166	.4723665527
.46	1.5840739850	.6312836455	.76	2.1382762205	.4676664270
.47	1.5999941932	.6250022683	.77	2.1597662538	.4630130683
.48	1.6160744022	.6187833918	.78	2.1814722655	.4584060113
.49	1.6323162200	.6126263942	.79	2.2033964263	.4538447953
.50	1.6487212707	.6065306597	.80	2.2255409285	.4493289641
.51	1.6652911949	.6004955788	.81	2.2479079867	.4448580662
.52	1.6820276497	.5945205480	.82	2.2704998375	.4404316545
.53	1.6989323086	.5886049697	.83	2.2933187403	.4360492863
.54	1.7160068622	.5827482524	.84	2.3163669768	.4317105234
.55	1.7332530179	.5769498104	.85	2.3396468519	.4274149319
.56	1.7506725003	.5712090638	.86	2.3631606937	.4231620823
.57	1.7682670514	.5655254387	.87	2.3869108535	.4189515492
.58	1.7860384308	.5598983666	.88	2.4108897064	.4147829117
.59	1.8039884154	.5543272847	.89	2.4351296513	.4106557528
.60	1.8221188004	.5488116361	.90	2.4596031112	.4065696597
.61	1.8404313988	.5433508691	.91	2.4843225334	.4025242240
.62	1.8589280418	.5379444376	.92	2.5092903899	.3985190411
.63	1.8776105793	.5325918010	.93	2.5345091776	.3945537104
.64	1.8964808793	.5272924240	.94	2.5599814183	.3906278354
.65	1.9155408290	.5220457768	.95	2.5857096593	.3867410235
.66	1.9347923344	.5168513345	.96	2.6116964734	.3828928860
.67	1.9542373206	.5117085778	.97	2.6379444594	.3790830381
.68	1.9738777322	.5066169924	.98	2.6644562419	.3753110989
.69	1.9937155332	.5015760691	.99	2.6912344723	.3715766910
.70	2.0137527075	.4965853038	1.00	2.7182818285	.3678794412

TABLE 7 1958 COMMISSIONERS STANDARD ORDINARY (CSO) MORTALITY TABLE

Values for females age 0 to 14 are in the complete tables of the Society of Actuaries from which these data are reproduced with permission of the Society.

Age x M	F	Number Living l_x	Number Dying d_x	Deaths per 1000 $1000q_x$	Age x M	F	Number Living l_x	Number Dying d_x	Deaths per 1000 $1000q_x$
0		10 000 000	70 800	7.08	50	53	8 762 306	72 902	8.32
1		9 929 200	17 475	1.76	51	54	8 689 404	79 160	9.11
2		9 911 725	15 066	1.52	52	55	8 610 244	85 758	9.96
3		9 896 659	14 449	1.46	53	56	8 524 486	92 832	10.89
4		9 882 210	13 835	1.40	54	57	8 431 654	100 337	11.90
5		9 868 375	13 322	1.35	55	58	8 331 317	108 307	13.00
6		9 855 053	12 812	1.30	56	59	8 223 010	116 849	14.21
7		9 842 241	12 401	1.26	57	60	8 106 161	125 970	15.54
8		9 829 840	12 091	1.23	58	61	7 980 191	135 663	17.00
9		9 817 749	11 879	1.21	59	62	7 844 528	145 830	18.59
10		9 805 870	11 865	1.21	60	63	7 698 698	156 592	20.34
11		9 794 005	12 047	1.23	61	64	7 542 106	167 736	22.24
12	15	9 781 958	12 325	1.26	62	65	7 374 370	179 271	24.31
13	16	9 769 633	12 896	1.32	63	66	7 195 099	191 174	26.57
14	17	9 756 737	13 562	1.39	64	67	7 003 925	203 394	29.04
15	18	9 743 175	14 225	1.46	65	68	6 800 531	215 917	31.75
16	19	9 728 950	14 983	1.54	66	69	6 584 614	228 749	34.74
17	20	9 713 967	15 737	1.62	67	70	6 355 865	241 777	38.04
18	21	9 698 230	16 390	1.69	68	71	6 114 088	254 835	41.68
19	22	9 681 840	16 846	1.74	69	72	5 859 253	267 241	45.61
20	23	9 664 994	17 300	1.79	70	73	5 592 012	278 426	49.79
21	24	9 647 694	17 655	1.83	71	74	5 313 586	287 731	54.15
22	25	9 630 039	17 912	1.86	72	75	5 025 855	294 766	58.65
23	26	9 612 127	18 167	1.89	73	76	4 731 089	299 289	63.26
24	27	9 593 960	18 324	1.91	74	77	4 431 800	301 894	68.12
25	28	9 575 636	18 481	1.93	75	78	4 129 906	303 011	73.37
26	29	9 557 155	18 732	1.96	76	79	3 826 895	303 014	79.18
27	30	9 538 423	18 981	1.99	77	80	3 523 881	301 997	85.70
28	31	9 519 442	19 324	2.03	78	81	3 221 884	299 829	93.06
29	32	9 500 118	19 760	2.08	79	82	2 922 055	295 683	101.19
30	33	9 480 358	20 193	2.13	80	83	2 626 372	288 848	109.98
31	34	9 460 165	20 718	2.19	81	84	2 337 524	278 983	119.35
32	35	9 439 447	21 239	2.25	82	85	2 058 541	265 902	129.17
33	36	9 418 208	21 850	2.32	83	86	1 792 639	249 858	139.38
34	37	9 396 358	22 551	2.40	84	87	1 542 781	231 433	150.01
35	38	9 373 807	23 528	2.51	85	88	1 311 348	211 311	161.14
36	39	9 350 279	24 685	2.64	86	89	1 100 037	190 108	172.82
37	40	9 325 594	26 112	2.80	87	90	909 929	168 455	185.13
38	41	9 299 482	27 991	3.01	88	91	741 474	146 997	198.25
39	42	9 271 491	30 132	3.25	89	92	594 477	126 303	212.46
40	43	9 241 359	32 622	3.53	90	93	468 174	106 809	228.14
41	44	9 208 737	35 362	3.84	91	94	361 365	88 813	245.77
42	45	9 173 375	38 253	4.17	92	95	272 552	72 480	265.93
43	46	9 135 122	41 382	4.53	93	96	200 072	57 881	289.30
44	47	9 093 740	44 741	4.92	94	97	142 191	45 026	316.66
45	48	9 048 999	48 412	5.35	95	98	97 165	34 128	351.24
46	49	9 000 587	52 473	5.83	96	99	63 037	25 250	400.56
47	50	8 948 114	56 910	6.36	97	100	37 787	18 456	488.42
48	51	8 891 204	61 794	6.95	98	101	19 331	12 916	668.15
49	52	8 829 410	67 104	7.60	99	102	6 415	6 415	1000.00

TABLE 8 COMMUTATION COLUMNS, INTEREST AT $2\frac{1}{2}\%$

Values for females age 0 to 14 are in the complete tables of the Society of Actuaries from which these data are reproduced with permission of the Society.

Age M	x F	D_x	N_x	C_x	M_x	Annuity Due $\ddot{a}_x$	Life Insurance $1000A_x$
0		10 000 000.0	324 850 105.9	69 073.171	2 076 826.724	32.48 5011	207.68 267
1		9 687 024.4	314 850 105.9	16 632.957	2 007 753.553	32.50 2252	207.26 216
2		9 434 122.6	305 163 081.5	13 990.279	1 991 120.596	32.34 6737	211.05 520
3		9 190 031.7	295 728 958.9	13 090.081	1 977 130.317	32.17 9319	215.13 857
4		8 952 794.5	286 538 927.2	12 228.124	1 964 040.236	32.00 5529	219.37 734
5		8 722 205.6	277 586 132.7	11 487.519	1 951 812.112	31.82 5222	223.77 506
6		8 497 981.4	268 863 927.1	10 778.290	1 940 324.593	31.63 8564	228.32 771
7		8 279 935.2	260 365 945.7	10 178.078	1 929 546.303	31.44 5409	233.03 882
8		8 067 807.5	252 086 010.5	9 681.607	1 919 368.225	31.24 5913	237.90 456
9		7 861 350.1	244 018 203.0	9 279.856	1 909 686.618	31.04 0241	242.92 095
10		7 660 330.0	236 156 852.9	9 042.848	1 900 406.762	30.82 8548	248.08 419
11		7 464 449.8	228 496 522.9	8 957.618	1 891 363.914	30.61 1301	253.38 290
12	15	7 273 432.5	221 032 073.1	8 940.806	1 882 406.296	30.38 8963	258.80 577
13	16	7 087 090.9	213 758 640.6	9 126.850	1 873 465.490	30.16 1690	264.34 901
14	17	6 905 108.2	206 671 549.7	9 364.094	1 864 338.640	29.93 0241	269.99 412
15	18	6 727 326.8	199 766 441.5	9 582.315	1 854 974.546	29.69 4773	275.73 724
16	19	6 553 663.3	193 039 114.7	9 846.754	1 845 392.231	29.45 5147	281.58 179
17	20	6 383 971.1	186 485 451.4	10 090.028	1 835 545.477	29.21 1512	287.52 409
18	21	6 218 174.5	180 101 480.3	10 252.399	1 825 455.449	28.96 3722	293.56 774
19	22	6 056 259.3	173 883 305.8	10 280.624	1 815 203.050	28.71 1338	299.72 347
20	23	5 898 265.0	167 827 046.5	10 300.183	1 804 922.426	28.45 3629	306.00 904
21	24	5 744 104.7	161 928 781.5	10 255.166	1 794 622.243	28.19 0430	312.42 854
22	25	5 593 749.4	156 184 676.8	10 150.681	1 784 367.077	27.92 1286	318.99 303
23	26	5 447 165.8	150 590 927.4	10 044.086	1 774 216.396	27.64 5740	325.71 368
24	27	5 304 264.0	145 143 761.6	9 883.793	1 764 172.310	27.36 3601	332.59 512
25	28	5 165 008.0	139 839 497.6	9 725.344	1 754 288.517	27.07 4401	339.64 875
26	29	5 029 306.8	134 674 489.6	9 617.004	1 744 563.173	26.77 7943	346.87 945
27	30	4 897 023.8	129 645 182.8	9 507.161	1 734 946.169	26.47 4281	354.28 584
28	31	4 768 077.0	124 748 159.0	9 442.890	1 725 439.008	26.16 3201	361.87 314
29	32	4 642 339.5	119 980 082.0	9 420.436	1 715 996.118	25.84 4745	369.64 038
30	33	4 519 691.4	115 337 742.5	9 392.064	1 706 575.682	25.51 8942	377.58 677
31	34	4 400 062.9	110 818 051.1	9 401.218	1 697 183.618	25.18 5561	385.71 804
32	35	4 283 343.1	106 417 988.2	9 402.569	1 687 782.400	24.84 4610	394.03 390
33	36	4 169 468.7	102 134 645.1	9 437.132	1 678 379.831	24.49 5842	402.54 046
34	37	4 058 337.2	97 965 176.4	9 502.339	1 668 942.699	24.13 9240	411.23 806
35	38	3 949 851.1	93 906 839.2	9 672.213	1 659 440.360	23.77 4780	420.12 732
36	39	3 843 841.0	89 956 988.1	9 900.340	1 649 768.147	23.40 2890	429.19 781
37	40	3 740 188.5	86 113 147.1	10 217.232	1 639 867.807	23.02 3745	438.44 523
38	41	3 638 747.1	82 372 958.6	10 685.323	1 629 650.575	22.63 7726	447.86 036
39	42	3 539 311.9	78 734 211.5	11 222.079	1 618 965.252	22.24 5627	457.42 373
40	43	3 441 765.1	75 194 899.6	11 853.104	1 607 743.173	21.84 7772	467.12 751
41	44	3 345 966.5	71 753 134.5	12 535.293	1 595 890.069	21.44 4666	476.95 937
42	45	3 251 822.3	68 407 168.0	13 229.374	1 583 354.776	21.03 6564	486.91 307
43	46	3 159 280.2	65 155 345.7	13 962.442	1 570 125.402	20.62 3478	496.98 833
44	47	3 068 262.1	61 996 065.5	14 727.592	1 556 162.960	20.20 5596	507.18 058
45	48	2 978 698.8	58 927 803.4	15 547.309	1 541 435.368	19.78 3069	517.48 615
46	49	2 890 500.4	55 949 104.6	16 440.470	1 525 888.059	19.35 6200	527.89 754
47	50	2 803 559.9	53 058 604.2	17 395.746	1 509 447.589	18.92 5440	538.40 390
48	51	2 717 784.6	50 255 044.3	18 427.945	1 492 051.843	18.49 1180	548.99 562
49	52	2 633 069.2	47 537 259.7	19 523.386	1 473 623.898	18.05 3935	559.66 015

TABLE 8 COMMUTATION COLUMNS *(cont.)*

Age x						Annuity Due	Life Insurance
M	F	D_x	N_x	C_x	M_x	$\ddot{a}_x$	$1000A_x$
50	53	2 549 324.7	44 904 190.5	20 692.945	1 454 100.512	17.61 4151	570.38 655
51	54	2 466 453.1	42 354 865.8	21 921.223	1 433 407.567	17.17 2378	581.16 149
52	55	2 384 374.4	39 888 412.7	23 169.133	1 411 486.344	16.72 9089	591.97 345
53	56	2 303 049.8	37 504 038.3	24 468.592	1 388 317.211	16.28 4510	602.81 684
54	57	2 222 409.3	35 200 988.5	25 801.712	1 363 848.619	15.83 9111	613.68 022
55	58	2 142 402.5	32 978 579.2	27 171.903	1 338 046.907	15.39 3270	624.55 440
56	59	2 062 976.8	30 836 176.7	28 599.910	1 310 875.004	14.94 7418	635.42 886
57	60	1 984 060.4	28 773 199.9	30 080.354	1 282 275.094	14.50 2179	646.28 834
58	61	1 905 588.4	26 789 139.5	31 604.823	1 252 194.740	14.05 8198	657.11 711
59	62	1 827 505.8	24 883 551.1	33 144.766	1 220 589.917	13.61 6127	667.89 934
60	63	1 749 787.7	23 056 045.3	34 722.724	1 187 445.151	13.17 6482	678.62 241
61	64	1 672 387.3	21 306 257.6	36 286.629	1 152 722.427	12.74 0026	689.26 763
62	65	1 595 310.7	19 633 870.3	37 836.114	1 116 435.798	12.30 7239	699.82 342
63	66	1 518 564.6	18 038 559.6	39 364.201	1 078 599.684	11.87 8691	710.27 580
64	67	1 442 162.2	16 519 995.0	40 858.920	1 039 235.483	11.45 5019	720.60 929
65	68	1 366 128.5	15 077 832.8	42 316.694	998 376.563	11.03 6907	730.80 721
66	69	1 290 491.7	13 711 704.3	43 738.131	956 059.869	10.62 5178	740.84 930
67	70	1 215 278.1	12 421 212.6	45 101.621	912 321.738	10.22 0881	750.71 026
68	71	1 140 535.6	11 205 934.5	46 378.038	867 220.117	9.82 5151	760.36 216
69	72	1 066 339.6	10 065 398.9	47 449.596	820 842.079	9.43 9206	769.77 548
70	73	992 881.8	8 999 059.3	48 229.787	773 392.483	9.06 3576	778.93 711
71	74	920 435.3	8 006 177.5	48 625.978	725 162.696	8.69 8251	787.84 755
72	75	849 359.7	7 085 742.2	48 599.883	676 536.718	8.34 2452	796.52 557
73	76	780 043.7	6 236 382.5	48 142.066	627 936.835	7.99 4914	805.00 212
74	77	712 876.2	5 456 338.8	47 376.675	579 794.769	7.65 3978	813.31 761
75	78	648 112.3	4 743 462.6	46 392.163	532 418.094	7.31 8890	821.49 049
76	79	585 912.5	4 095 350.3	45 261.095	486 025.931	6.98 9696	829.51 965
77	80	526 360.9	3 509 437.8	44 008.963	440 764.836	6.66 7360	837.38 142
78	81	469 513.8	2 983 076.9	42 627.343	396 755.873	6.35 3545	845.03 559
79	82	415 434.9	2 513 563.1	41 012.583	354 128.530	6.05 0438	852.42 846
80	83	364 289.8	2 098 128.2	39 087.353	313 115.947	5.75 9503	859.52 433
81	84	316 317.3	1 733 838.4	36 831.617	274 028.594	5.48 1327	866.30 922
82	85	271 770.7	1 417 521.1	34 248.438	237 196.977	5.21 5872	872.78 348
83	86	230 893.7	1 145 750.4	31 397.029	202 948.539	4.96 2242	878.96 958
84	87	193 865.1	914 856.7	28 372.443	171 551.510	4.71 9038	884.90 146
85	88	160 764.2	720 991.6	25 273.751	143 179.067	4.48 4777	890.61 537
86	89	131 569.4	560 227.4	22 183.195	117 905.316	4.25 8037	896.14 543
87	90	106 177.2	428 658.0	19 177.136	95 722.121	4.03 7194	901.53 179
88	91	84 410.4	322 480.8	16 326.175	76 544.985	3.82 0392	906.81 936
89	92	66 025.4	238 070.4	13 685.661	60 218.810	3.60 5740	912.05 521
90	93	50 729.4	172 045.0	11 291.096	46 533.149	3.39 1426	917.28 167
91	94	38 201.0	121 315.6	9 159.693	35 242.053	3.17 5718	922.54 268
92	95	28 109.5	83 114.6	7 292.874	26 082.360	2.95 6815	927.88 417
93	96	20 131.1	55 005.1	5 681.888	18 789.486	2.73 2344	933.35 615
94	97	13 958.2	34 874.0	4 312.173	13 107.598	2.49 8460	939.06 077
95	98	9 305.6	20 915.8	3 188.745	8 795.425	2.24 7657	945.17 549
96	99	5 889.9	11 610.2	2 301.688	5 606.680	1.97 1205	951.91 429
97	100	3 444.5	5 720.3	1 641.341	3 304.992	1.66 0705	959.49 833
98	101	1 719.2	2 275.8	1 120.638	1 663.651	1.32 3755	967.68 904
99	102	556.6	556.6	543.013	543.013	1.00 0000	975.58 929

TABLE 9 SIX-PLACE LOGARITHMS OF NUMBERS 100–1000

N	0	1	2	3	4	5	6	7	8	9	D
100	00 0000	00 0434	00 0868	00 1301	00 1734	00 2166	00 2598	00 3029	00 3461	00 3891	432
101	4321	4751	5181	5609	6038	6466	6894	7321	7748	8174	428
102	8600	9026	9451	9876	01 0300	01 0724	01 1147	01 1570	01 1993	01 2415	424
103	01 2837	01 3259	01 3680	01 4100	4521	4940	5360	5779	6197	6616	420
104	7033	7451	7868	8284	8700	9116	9532	9947	02 0361	02 0775	416
105	02 1189	02 1603	02 2016	02 2428	02 2841	02 3252	02 3664	02 4075	4486	4896	412
106	5306	5715	6125	6533	6942	7350	7757	8164	8571	8978	408
107	9384	9789	03 0195	03 0600	03 1004	03 1408	03 1812	03 2216	03 2619	03 3021	404
108	03 3424	03 3826	4227	4628	5029	5430	5830	6230	6629	7028	400
109	7426	7825	8223	8620	9017	9414	9811	04 0207	04 0602	04 0998	397
110	04 1393	04 1787	04 2182	04 2576	04 2969	04 3362	04 3755	4148	4540	4932	393
111	5323	5714	6105	6495	6885	7275	7664	8053	8442	8830	390
112	9218	9606	9993	05 0380	05 0766	05 1153	05 1538	05 1924	05 2309	05 2694	386
113	05 3078	05 3463	05 3846	4230	4613	4996	5378	5760	6142	6524	383
114	6905	7286	7666	8046	8426	8805	9185	9563	9942	06 0320	379
115	06 0698	06 1075	06 1452	06 1829	06 2206	06 2582	06 2958	06 3333	06 3709	4083	376
116	4458	4832	5206	5580	5953	6326	6699	7071	7443	7815	373
117	8186	8557	8928	9298	9668	07 0038	07 0407	07 0776	07 1145	07 1514	370
118	07 1882	07 2250	07 2617	07 2985	07 3352	3718	4085	4451	4816	5182	366
119	5547	5912	6276	6640	7004	7368	7731	8094	8457	8819	363
120	9182	9543	9904	08 0266	08 0626	08 0987	08 1347	08 1707	08 2067	08 2426	360
121	08 2785	08 3144	08 3503	3861	4219	4576	4934	5291	5647	6004	357
122	6360	6716	7071	7426	7781	8136	8490	8845	9198	9552	355
123	9905	09 0258	09 0611	09 0963	09 1315	09 1667	09 2018	09 2370	09 2721	09 3071	352
124	09 3422	3772	4122	4471	4820	5169	5518	5866	6215	6562	349
125	6910	7257	7604	7951	8298	8644	8990	9335	9681	10 0026	346
126	10 0371	10 0715	10 1059	10 1403	10 1747	10 2091	10 2434	10 2777	10 3119	3462	343
127	3804	4146	4487	4828	5169	5510	5851	6191	6531	6871	341
128	7210	7549	7888	8227	8565	8903	9241	9579	9916	11 0253	338
129	11 0590	11 0926	11 1263	11 1599	11 1934	11 2270	11 2605	11 2940	11 3275	3609	335
130	3943	4277	4611	4944	5278	5611	5943	6276	6608	6940	333
131	7271	7603	7934	8265	8595	8926	9256	9586	9915	12 0245	330
132	12 0574	12 0903	12 1231	12 1560	12 1888	12 2216	12 2544	12 2871	12 3198	3525	328
133	3852	4178	4504	4830	5156	5481	5806	6131	6456	6781	325
134	7105	7429	7753	8076	8399	8722	9045	9368	9690	13 0012	323
135	13 0334	13 0655	13 0977	13 1298	13 1619	13 1939	13 2260	13 2580	13 2900	3219	321
136	3539	3858	4177	4496	4814	5133	5451	5769	6086	6403	318
137	6721	7037	7354	7671	7987	8303	8618	8934	9249	9564	316
138	9879	14 0194	14 0508	14 0822	14 1136	14 1450	14 1763	14 2076	14 2389	14 2702	314
139	14 3015	3327	3639	3951	4263	4574	4885	5196	5507	5818	311
140	6128	6438	6748	7058	7367	7676	7985	8294	8603	8911	309
141	9219	9527	9835	15 0142	15 0449	15 0756	15 1063	15 1370	15 1676	15 1982	307
142	15 2288	15 2594	15 2900	3205	3510	3815	4120	4424	4728	5032	305
143	5336	5640	5943	6246	6549	6852	7154	7457	7759	8061	303
144	8362	8664	8965	9266	9567	9868	16 0168	16 0469	16 0769	16 1068	301
145	16 1368	16 1667	16 1967	16 2266	16 2564	16 2863	3161	3460	3758	4055	299
146	4353	4650	4947	5244	5541	5838	6134	6430	6726	7022	297
147	7317	7613	7908	8203	8497	8792	9086	9380	9674	9968	295
148	17 0262	17 0555	17 0848	17 1141	17 1434	17 1726	17 2019	17 2311	17 2603	17 2895	293
149	3186	3478	3769	4060	4351	4641	4932	5222	5512	5802	291
150	6091	6381	6670	6959	7248	7536	7825	8113	8401	8689	289

Proportional Parts

n\d	435	430	425	420
1	44	43	43	42
2	87	86	85	84
3	131	129	128	126
4	174	172	170	168
5	218	215	213	210
6	261	258	255	252
7	305	301	298	294
8	348	344	340	336
9	392	387	383	378

n\d	415	410	405	400
1	42	41	41	40
2	83	82	81	80
3	125	123	122	120
4	166	164	162	160
5	208	205	203	200
6	249	246	243	240
7	291	287	284	280
8	332	328	324	320
9	374	369	365	360

n\d	395	390	385	380
1	40	39	39	38
2	79	78	77	76
3	119	117	116	114
4	158	156	154	152
5	198	195	193	190
6	237	234	231	228
7	277	273	270	266
8	316	312	308	304
9	356	351	347	342

n\d	375	370	365	360
1	38	37	37	36
2	75	74	73	72
3	113	111	110	108
4	150	148	146	144
5	188	185	183	180
6	225	222	219	216
7	263	259	256	252
8	300	296	292	288
9	338	333	329	324

n\d	355	350	345	340
1	36	35	35	34
2	71	70	69	68
3	107	105	104	102
4	142	140	138	136
5	178	175	173	170
6	213	210	207	204
7	249	245	242	238
8	284	280	276	272
9	320	315	311	306

n\d	335	330	325	320
1	34	33	33	32
2	67	66	65	64
3	101	99	98	96
4	134	132	130	128
5	168	165	163	160
6	201	198	195	192
7	235	231	228	224
8	268	264	260	256
9	302	297	293	288

n\d	315	310	305	300
1	32	31	31	30
2	63	62	61	60
3	95	93	92	90
4	126	124	122	120
5	158	155	153	150
6	189	186	183	180
7	221	217	214	210
8	252	248	244	240
9	284	279	275	270

Six-Place Logarithms of Numbers 150-200   Proportional Parts

N	0	1	2	3	4	5	6	7	8	9	D
150	17 6091	17 6381	17 6670	17 6959	17 7248	17 7536	17 7825	17 8113	17 8401	17 8689	289
151	8977	9264	9552	9839	18 0126	18 0413	18 0699	18 0986	18 1272	18 1558	287
152	18 1844	18 2129	18 2415	18 2700	2985	3270	3555	3839	4123	4407	285
153	4691	4975	5259	5542	5825	6108	6391	6674	6956	7239	283
154	7521	7803	8084	8366	8647	8928	9209	9490	9771	19 0051	281
155	19 0332	19 0612	19 0892	19 1171	19 1451	19 1730	19 2010	19 2289	19 2567	2846	279
156	3125	3403	3681	3959	4237	4514	4792	5069	5346	5623	278
157	5900	6176	6453	6729	7005	7281	7556	7832	8107	8382	276
158	8657	8932	9206	9481	9755	20 0029	20 0303	20 0577	20 0850	20 1124	274
159	20 1397	20 1670	20 1943	20 2216	20 2488	2761	3033	3305	3577	3848	272
160	4120	4391	4663	4934	5204	5475	5746	6016	6286	6556	271
161	6826	7096	7365	7634	7904	8173	8441	8710	8979	9247	269
162	9515	9783	21 0051	21 0319	21 0586	21 0853	21 1121	21 1388	21 1654	21 1921	267
163	21 2188	21 2454	2720	2986	3252	3518	3783	4049	4314	4579	266
164	4844	5109	5373	5638	5902	6166	6430	6694	6957	7221	264
165	7484	7747	8010	8273	8536	8798	9060	9323	9585	9846	262
166	22 0108	22 0370	22 0631	22 0892	22 1153	22 1414	22 1675	22 1936	22 2196	22 2456	261
167	2716	2976	3236	3496	3755	4015	4274	4533	4792	5051	259
168	5309	5568	5826	6084	6342	6600	6858	7115	7372	7630	258
169	7887	8144	8400	8657	8913	9170	9426	9682	9938	23 0193	256
170	23 0449	23 0704	23 0960	23 1215	23 1470	23 1724	23 1979	23 2234	23 2488	2742	255
171	2996	3250	3504	3757	4011	4264	4517	4770	5023	5276	253
172	5528	5781	6033	6285	6537	6789	7041	7292	7544	7795	252
173	8046	8297	8548	8799	9049	9299	9550	9800	24 0050	24 0300	250
174	24 0549	24 0799	24 1048	24 1297	24 1546	24 1795	24 2044	24 2293	2541	2790	249
175	3038	3286	3534	3782	4030	4277	4525	4772	5019	5266	248
176	5513	5759	6006	6252	6499	6745	6991	7237	7482	7728	246
177	7973	8219	8464	8709	8954	9198	9443	9687	9932	25 0176	245
178	25 0420	25 0664	25 0908	25 1151	25 1395	25 1638	25 1881	25 2125	25 2368	2610	243
179	2853	3096	3338	3580	3822	4064	4306	4548	4790	5031	242
180	5273	5514	5755	5996	6237	6477	6718	6958	7198	7439	241
181	7679	7918	8158	8398	8637	8877	9116	9355	9594	9833	239
182	26 0071	26 0310	26 0548	26 0787	26 1025	26 1263	26 1501	26 1739	26 1976	26 2214	238
183	2451	2688	2925	3162	3399	3636	3873	4109	4346	4582	237
184	4818	5054	5290	5525	5761	5996	6232	6467	6702	6937	235
185	7172	7406	7641	7875	8110	8344	8578	8812	9046	9279	234
186	9513	9746	9980	27 0213	27 0446	27 0679	27 0912	27 1144	27 1377	27 1609	233
187	27 1842	27 2074	27 2306	2538	2770	3001	3233	3464	3696	3927	232
188	4158	4389	4620	4850	5081	5311	5542	5772	6002	6232	230
189	6462	6692	6921	7151	7380	7609	7838	8067	8296	8525	229
190	8754	8982	9211	9439	9667	9895	28 0123	28 0351	28 0578	28 0806	228
191	28 1033	28 1261	28 1488	28 1715	28 1942	28 2169	2396	2622	2849	3075	227
192	3301	3527	3753	3979	4205	4431	4656	4882	5107	5332	226
193	5557	5782	6007	6232	6456	6681	6905	7130	7354	7578	225
194	7802	8026	8249	8473	8696	8920	9143	9366	9589	9812	223
195	29 0035	29 0257	29 0480	29 0702	29 0925	29 1147	29 1369	29 1591	29 1813	29 2034	222
196	2256	2478	2699	2920	3141	3363	3584	3804	4025	4246	221
197	4466	4687	4907	5127	5347	5567	5787	6007	6226	6446	220
198	6665	6884	7104	7323	7542	7761	7979	8198	8416	8635	219
199	8853	9071	9289	9507	9725	9943	30 0161	30 0378	30 0595	30 0813	218
200	30 1030	30 1247	30 1464	30 1681	30 1898	30 2114	2331	2547	2764	2980	217

Proportional Parts

n\d	295	290	285	280
1	30	29	29	28
2	59	58	57	56
3	89	87	86	84
4	118	116	114	112
5	148	145	143	140
6	177	174	171	168
7	207	203	200	196
8	236	232	228	224
9	266	261	257	252

n\d	275	270	265	260
1	28	27	27	26
2	55	54	53	52
3	83	81	80	78
4	110	108	106	104
5	138	135	133	130
6	165	162	159	156
7	193	189	186	182
8	220	216	212	208
9	248	243	239	234

n\d	255	250	248	246
1	26	25	25	25
2	51	50	50	49
3	77	75	74	74
4	102	100	99	98
5	128	125	124	123
6	153	150	149	148
7	179	175	174	172
8	204	200	198	197
9	230	225	223	221

n\d	244	242	240	238
1	24	24	24	24
2	49	48	48	48
3	73	73	72	71
4	98	97	96	95
5	122	121	120	119
6	146	145	144	143
7	171	169	168	167
8	195	194	192	190
9	220	218	216	214

n\d	236	234	232	230
1	24	23	23	23
2	47	47	46	46
3	71	70	70	69
4	94	94	93	92
5	118	117	116	115
6	142	140	139	138
7	165	164	162	161
8	189	187	186	184
9	212	211	209	207

n\d	228	226	224	222
1	23	23	22	22
2	46	45	45	44
3	68	68	67	67
4	91	90	90	89
5	114	113	112	111
6	137	136	134	133
7	160	158	157	155
8	182	181	179	178
9	205	203	202	200

n\d	220	218	216	214
1	22	22	22	21
2	44	44	43	43
3	66	65	65	64
4	88	87	86	86
5	110	109	108	107
6	132	131	130	128
7	154	153	151	150
8	176	174	173	171
9	198	196	194	193

Six-Place Logarithms of Numbers 200-250

N	0	1	2	3	4	5	6	7	8	9	D
200	30 1030	30 1247	30 1464	30 1681	30 1898	30 2114	30 2331	30 2547	30 2764	30 2980	217
201	3196	3412	3628	3844	4059	4275	4491	4706	4921	5136	216
202	5351	5566	5781	5996	6211	6425	6639	6854	7068	7282	215
203	7496	7710	7924	8137	8351	8564	8778	8991	9204	9417	213
204	9630	9843	31 0056	31 0268	31 0481	31 0693	31 0906	31 1118	31 1330	31 1542	212
205	3i 1754	31 1966	2177	2389	2600	2812	3023	3234	3445	3656	211
206	3867	4078	4289	4499	4710	4920	5130	5340	5551	5760	210
207	5970	6180	6390	6599	6809	7018	7227	7436	7646	7854	209
208	8063	8272	8481	8689	8898	9106	9314	9522	9730	9938	208
209	32 0146	32 0354	32 0562	32 0769	32 0977	32 1184	32 1391	32 1598	32 1805	32 2012	207
210	2219	2426	2633	2839	3046	3252	3458	3665	3871	4077	206
211	4282	4488	4694	4899	5105	5310	5516	5721	5926	6131	205
212	6336	6541	6745	6950	7155	7359	7563	7767	7972	8176	204
213	8380	8583	8787	8991	9194	9398	9601	9805	33 0008	33 0211	203
214	33 0414	33 0617	33 0819	33 1022	33 1225	33 1427	33 1630	33 1832	2034	2236	202
215	2438	2640	2842	3044	3246	3447	3649	3850	4051	4253	202
216	4454	4655	4856	5057	5257	5458	5658	5859	6059	6260	201
217	6460	6660	6860	7060	7260	7459	7659	7858	8058	8257	200
218	8456	8656	8855	9054	9253	9451	9650	9849	34 0047	34 0246	199
219	34 0444	34 0642	34 0841	34 1039	34 1237	34 1435	34 1632	34 1830	2028	2225	198
220	2423	2620	2817	3014	3212	3409	3606	3802	3999	4196	197
221	4392	4589	4785	4981	5178	5374	5570	5766	5962	6157	196
222	6353	6549	6744	6939	7135	7330	7525	7720	7915	8110	195
223	8305	8500	8694	8889	9083	9278	9472	9666	9860	35 0054	194
224	35 0248	35 0442	35 0636	35 0829	35 1023	35 1216	35 1410	35 1603	35 1796	1989	193
225	2183	2375	2568	2761	2954	3147	3339	3532	3724	3916	193
226	4108	4301	4493	4685	4876	5068	5260	5452	5643	5834	192
227	6026	6217	6408	6599	6790	6981	7172	7363	7554	7744	191
228	7935	8125	8316	8506	8696	8886	9076	9266	9456	9646	190
229	9835	36 0025	36 0215	36 0404	36 0593	36 0783	36 0972	36 1161	36 1350	36 1539	189
230	36 1728	1917	2105	2294	2482	2671	2859	3048	3236	3424	188
231	3612	3800	3988	4176	4363	4551	4739	4926	5113	5301	188
232	5488	5675	5862	6049	6236	6423	6610	6796	6983	7169	187
233	7356	7542	7729	7915	8101	8287	8473	8659	8845	9030	186
234	9216	9401	9587	9772	9958	37 0143	37 0328	37 0513	37 0698	37 0883	185
235	37 1068	37 1253	37 1437	37 1622	37 1806	1991	2175	2360	2544	2728	184
236	2912	3096	3280	3464	3647	3831	4015	4198	4382	4565	184
237	4748	4932	5115	5298	5481	5664	5846	6029	6212	6394	183
238	6577	6759	6942	7124	7306	7488	7670	7852	8034	8216	182
239	8398	8580	8761	8943	9124	9306	9487	9668	9849	38 0030	181
240	38 0211	38 0392	38 0573	38 0754	38 0934	38 1115	38 1296	38 1476	38 1656	1837	181
241	2017	2197	2377	2557	2737	2917	3097	3277	3456	3636	180
242	3815	3995	4174	4353	4533	4712	4891	5070	5249	5428	179
243	5606	5785	5964	6142	6321	6499	6677	6856	7034	7212	178
244	7390	7568	7746	7923	8101	8279	8456	8634	8811	8989	178
245	9166	9343	9520	9698	9875	39 0051	39 0228	39 0405	39 0582	39 0759	177
246	39 0935	39 1112	39 1288	39 1464	39 1641	1817	1993	2169	2345	2521	176
247	2697	2873	3048	3224	3400	3575	3751	3926	4101	4277	176
248	4452	4627	4802	4977	5152	5326	5501	5676	5850	6025	175
249	6199	6374	6548	6722	6896	7071	7245	7419	7592	7766	174
250	7940	8114	8287	8461	8634	8808	8981	9154	9328	9501	173

Proportional Parts

n\d	220	218	216	214
1	22	22	22	21
2	44	44	43	43
3	66	65	65	64
4	88	87	86	86
5	110	109	108	107
6	132	131	130	128
7	154	153	151	150
8	176	174	173	171
9	198	196	194	193

n\d	212	210	208	206
1	21	21	21	21
2	42	42	42	41
3	64	63	62	62
4	85	84	83	82
5	106	105	104	103
6	127	126	125	124
7	148	147	146	144
8	170	168	166	165
9	191	189	187	185

n\d	204	202	200	198
1	20	20	20	20
2	41	40	40	40
3	61	61	60	59
4	82	81	80	79
5	102	101	100	99
6	122	121	120	119
7	143	141	140	139
8	163	162	160	158
9	184	182	180	178

n\d	196	194	192	190
1	20	19	19	19
2	39	39	38	38
3	59	58	58	57
4	78	78	77	76
5	98	97	96	95
6	118	116	115	114
7	137	136	134	133
8	157	155	154	152
9	176	175	173	171

n\d	188	186	184	182
1	19	19	18	18
2	38	37	37	36
3	56	56	55	55
4	75	74	74	73
5	94	93	92	91
6	113	112	110	109
7	132	130	129	127
8	150	149	147	146
9	169	167	166	164

n\d	180	178	176	175
1	18	18	18	18
2	36	36	35	35
3	54	53	53	53
4	72	71	70	70
5	90	89	88	88
6	108	107	106	105
7	126	125	123	123
8	144	142	141	140
9	162	160	158	158

n\d	174	173	172	171
1	17	17	17	17
2	35	35	34	34
3	52	52	52	51
4	70	69	69	68
5	87	87	86	86
6	104	104	103	103
7	122	121	120	120
8	139	138	138	137
9	157	156	155	154

Six-Place Logarithms of Numbers 250-300

Six-Place Logarithms of Numbers 250-300

Proportional Parts

N	0	1	2	3	4	5	6	7	8	9	D
250	39 7940	39 8114	39 8287	39 8461	39 8634	39 8808	39 8981	39 9154	39 9328	39 9501	173
251	9674	9847	40 0020	40 0192	40 0365	40 0538	40 0711	40 0883	40 1056	40 1228	173
252	40 1401	40 1573	1745	1917	2089	2261	2433	2605	2777	2949	172
253	3121	3292	3464	3635	3807	3978	4149	4320	4492	4663	171
254	4834	5005	5176	5346	5517	5688	5858	6029	6199	6370	171
255	6540	6710	6881	7051	7221	7391	7561	7731	7901	8070	170
256	8240	8410	8579	8749	8918	9087	9257	9426	9595	9764	169
257	9933	41 0102	41 0271	41 0440	41 0609	41 0777	41 0946	41 1114	41 1283	41 1451	169
258	41 1620	1788	1956	2124	2293	2461	2629	2796	2964	3132	168
259	3300	3467	3635	3803	3970	4137	4305	4472	4639	4806	167
260	4973	5140	5307	5474	5641	5808	5974	6141	6308	6474	167
261	6641	6807	6973	7139	7306	7472	7638	7804	7970	8135	166
262	8301	8467	8633	8798	8964	9129	9295	9460	9625	9791	165
263	9956	42 0121	42 0286	42 0451	42 0616	42 0781	42 0945	42 1110	42 1275	42 1439	165
264	42 1604	1768	1933	2097	2261	2426	2590	2754	2918	3082	164
265	3246	3410	3574	3737	3901	4065	4228	4392	4555	4718	164
266	4882	5045	5208	5371	5534	5697	5860	6023	6186	6349	163
267	6511	6674	6836	6999	7161	7324	7486	7648	7811	7973	162
268	8135	8297	8459	8621	8783	8944	9106	9268	9429	9591	162
269	9752	9914	43 0075	43 0236	43 0398	43 0559	43 0720	43 0881	43 1042	43 1203	161
270	43 1364	43 1525	1685	1846	2007	2167	2328	2488	2649	2809	161
271	2969	3130	3290	3450	3610	3770	3930	4090	4249	4409	160
272	4569	4729	4888	5048	5207	5367	5526	5685	5844	6004	159
273	6163	6322	6481	6640	6799	6957	7116	7275	7433	7592	159
274	7751	7909	8067	8226	8384	8542	8701	8859	9017	9175	158
275	9333	9491	9648	9806	9964	44 0122	44 0279	44 0437	44 0594	44 0752	158
276	44 0909	44 1066	44 1224	44 1381	44 1538	1695	1852	2009	2166	2323	157
277	2480	2637	2793	2950	3106	3263	3419	3576	3732	3889	157
278	4045	4201	4357	4513	4669	4825	4981	5137	5293	5449	156
279	5604	5760	5915	6071	6226	6382	6537	6692	6848	7003	155
280	7158	7313	7468	7623	7778	7933	8088	8242	8397	8552	155
281	8706	8861	9015	9170	9324	9478	9633	9787	9941	45 0095	154
282	45 0249	45 0403	45 0557	45 0711	45 0865	45 1018	45 1172	45 1326	45 1479	1633	154
283	1786	1940	2093	2247	2400	2553	2706	2859	3012	3165	153
284	3318	3471	3624	3777	3930	4082	4235	4387	4540	4692	153
285	4845	4997	5150	5302	5454	5606	5758	5910	6062	6214	152
286	6366	6518	6670	6821	6973	7125	7276	7428	7579	7731	152
287	7882	8033	8184	8336	8487	8638	8789	8940	9091	9242	151
288	9392	9543	9694	9845	9995	46 0146	46 0296	46 0447	46 0597	46 0748	151
289	46 0898	46 1048	46 1198	46 1348	46 1499	1649	1799	1948	2098	2248	150
290	2398	2548	2697	2847	2997	3146	3296	3445	3594	3744	150
291	3893	4042	4191	4340	4490	4639	4788	4936	5085	5234	149
292	5383	5532	5680	5829	5977	6126	6274	6423	6571	6719	149
293	6868	7016	7164	7312	7460	7608	7756	7904	8052	8200	148
294	8347	8495	8643	8790	8938	9085	9233	9380	9527	9675	148
295	9822	9969	47 0116	47 0263	47 0410	47 0557	47 0704	47 0851	47 0998	47 1145	147
296	47 1292	47 1438	1585	1732	1878	2025	2171	2318	2464	2610	146
297	2756	2903	3049	3195	3341	3487	3633	3779	3925	4071	146
298	4216	4362	4508	4653	4799	4944	5090	5235	5381	5526	146
299	5671	5816	5962	6107	6252	6397	6542	6687	6832	6976	145
300	7121	7266	7411	7555	7700	7844	7989	8133	8278	8422	145

Proportional Parts

n\d	170	169	168	167
1	17	17	17	17
2	34	34	34	33
3	51	51	50	50
4	68	68	67	67
5	85	85	84	84
6	102	101	101	100
7	119	118	118	117
8	136	135	134	134
9	153	152	151	150

n\d	166	165	164	163
1	17	17	16	16
2	33	33	33	33
3	50	50	49	49
4	66	66	66	65
5	83	83	82	82
6	100	99	98	98
7	116	116	115	114
8	133	132	131	130
9	149	149	148	147

n\d	162	161	160	159
1	16	16	16	16
2	32	32	32	32
3	49	48	48	48
4	65	64	64	64
5	81	81	80	80
6	97	97	96	95
7	113	113	112	111
8	130	129	128	127
9	146	145	144	143

n\d	158	157	156	155
1	16	16	16	16
2	32	31	31	31
3	47	47	47	47
4	63	63	62	62
5	79	79	78	78
6	95	94	94	93
7	111	110	109	109
8	126	126	125	124
9	142	141	140	140

n\d	154	153	152	151
1	15	15	15	15
2	31	31	30	30
3	46	46	46	45
4	62	61	61	60
5	77	77	76	76
6	92	92	91	91
7	108	107	106	106
8	123	122	122	121
9	139	138	137	136

n\d	150	149	148	147
1	15	15	15	15
2	30	30	30	29
3	45	45	44	44
4	60	60	59	59
5	75	75	74	74
6	90	89	89	88
7	105	104	104	103
8	120	119	118	118
9	135	134	133	132

n\d	146	145	144
1	15	15	14
2	29	29	29
3	44	44	43
4	58	58	58
5	73	73	72
6	88	87	86
7	102	102	101
8	117	116	115
9	131	131	130

Six-Place Logarithms of Numbers 300–350

Proportional Parts

N	0	1	2	3	4	5	6	7	8	9	D
300	47 7121	47 7266	47 7411	47 7555	47 7700	47 7844	47 7989	47 8133	47 8278	47 8422	145
301	8566	8711	8855	8999	9143	9287	9431	9575	9719	9863	144
302	48 0007	48 0151	48 0294	48 0438	48 0582	48 0725	48 0869	48 1012	48 1156	48 1299	144
303	1443	1586	1729	1872	2016	2159	2302	2445	2588	2731	143
304	2874	3016	3159	3302	3445	3587	3730	3872	4015	4157	143
305	4300	4442	4585	4727	4869	5011	5153	5295	5437	5579	142
306	5721	5863	6005	6147	6289	6430	6572	6714	6855	6997	142
307	7138	7280	7421	7563	7704	7845	7986	8127	8269	8410	141
308	8551	8692	8833	8974	9114	9255	9396	9537	9677	9818	141
309	9958	49 0099	49 0239	49 0380	49 0520	49 0661	49 0801	49 0941	49 1081	49 1222	140
310	49 1362	1502	1642	1782	1922	2062	2201	2341	2481	2621	140
311	2760	2900	3040	3179	3319	3458	3597	3737	3876	4015	139
312	4155	4294	4433	4572	4711	4850	4989	5128	5267	5406	139
313	5544	5683	5822	5960	6099	6238	6376	6515	6653	6791	139
314	6930	7068	7206	7344	7483	7621	7759	7897	8035	8173	138
315	8311	8448	8586	8724	8862	8999	9137	9275	9412	9550	138
316	9687	9824	9962	50 0099	50 0236	50 0374	50 0511	50 0648	50 0785	50 0922	137
317	50 1059	50 1196	50 1333	1470	1607	1744	1880	2017	2154	2291	137
318	2427	2564	2700	2837	2973	3109	3246	3382	3518	3655	136
319	3791	3927	4063	4199	4335	4471	4607	4743	4878	5014	136
320	5150	5286	5421	5557	5693	5828	5964	6099	6234	6370	136
321	6505	6640	6776	6911	7046	7181	7316	7451	7586	7721	135
322	7856	7991	8126	8260	8395	8530	8664	8799	8934	9068	135
323	9203	9337	9471	9606	9740	9874	51 0009	51 0143	51 0277	51 0411	134
324	51 0545	51 0679	51 0813	51 0947	51 1081	51 1215	1349	1482	1616	1750	134
325	1883	2017	2151	2284	2418	2551	2684	2818	2951	3084	133
326	3218	3351	3484	3617	3750	3883	4016	4149	4282	4415	133
327	4548	4681	4813	4946	5079	5211	5344	5476	5609	5741	133
328	5874	6006	6139	6271	6403	6535	6668	6800	6932	7064	132
329	7196	7328	7460	7592	7724	7855	7987	8119	8251	8382	132
330	8514	8646	8777	8909	9040	9171	9303	9434	9566	9697	131
331	9828	9959	52 0090	52 0221	52 0353	52 0484	52 0615	52 0745	52 0876	52 1007	131
332	52 1138	52 1269	1400	1530	1661	1792	1922	2053	2183	2314	131
333	2444	2575	2705	2835	2966	3096	3226	3356	3486	3616	130
334	3746	3876	4006	4136	4266	4396	4526	4656	4785	4915	130
335	5045	5174	5304	5434	5563	5693	5822	5951	6081	6210	129
336	6339	6469	6598	6727	6856	6985	7114	7243	7372	7501	129
337	7630	7759	7888	8016	8145	8274	8402	8531	8660	8788	129
338	8917	9045	9174	9302	9430	9559	9687	9815	9943	53 0072	128
339	53 0200	53 0328	53 0456	53 0584	53 0712	53 0840	53 0968	53 1096	53 1223	1351	128
340	1479	1607	1734	1862	1990	2117	2245	2372	2500	2627	128
341	2754	2882	3009	3136	3264	3391	3518	3645	3772	3899	127
342	4026	4153	4280	4407	4534	4661	4787	4914	5041	5167	127
343	5294	5421	5547	5674	5800	5927	6053	6180	6306	6432	126
344	6558	6685	6811	6937	7063	7189	7315	7441	7567	7693	126
345	7819	7945	8071	8197	8322	8448	8574	8699	8825	8951	126
346	9076	9202	9327	9452	9578	9703	9829	9954	54 0079	54 0204	125
347	54 0329	54 0455	54 0580	54 0705	54 0830	54 0955	54 1080	54 1205	1330	1454	125
348	1579	1704	1829	1953	2078	2203	2327	2452	2576	2701	125
349	2825	2950	3074	3199	3323	3447	3571	3696	3820	3944	124
350	4068	4192	4316	4440	4564	4688	4812	4936	5060	5183	124

Proportional Parts

n\d	145	144	143	142
1	15	14	14	14
2	29	29	29	28
3	44	43	43	43
4	58	58	57	57
5	73	72	72	71
6	87	86	86	85
7	102	101	100	99
8	116	115	114	114
9	131	130	129	128

n\d	141	140	139	138
1	14	14	14	14
2	28	28	28	28
3	42	42	42	41
4	56	56	56	55
5	71	70	70	69
6	85	84	83	83
7	99	98	97	97
8	113	112	111	110
9	127	126	125	124

n\d	137	136	135	134
1	14	14	14	13
2	27	27	27	27
3	41	41	41	40
4	55	54	54	54
5	69	68	68	67
6	82	82	81	80
7	96	95	95	94
8	110	109	108	107
9	123	122	122	121

n\d	133	132	131	130
1	13	13	13	13
2	27	26	26	26
3	40	40	39	39
4	53	53	52	52
5	67	66	66	65
6	80	79	79	78
7	93	92	92	91
8	106	106	105	104
9	120	119	118	117

n\d	129	128	127
1	13	13	13
2	26	26	25
3	39	38	38
4	52	51	51
5	65	64	64
6	77	77	76
7	90	90	89
8	103	102	102
9	116	115	114

n\d	126	125	124
1	13	13	12
2	25	25	25
3	38	38	37
4	50	50	50
5	63	63	62
6	76	75	74
7	88	88	87
8	101	100	99
9	113	113	112

Proportional Parts

N	0	1	2	3	4	5	6	7	8	9	D
350	54 4068	54 4192	54 4316	54 4440	54 4564	54 4688	54 4812	54 4936	54 5060	54 5183	124
351	5307	5431	5555	5678	5802	5925	6049	6172	6296	6419	124
352	6543	6666	6789	6913	7036	7159	7282	7405	7529	7652	123
353	7775	7898	8021	8144	8267	8389	8512	8635	8758	8881	123
354	9003	9126	9249	9371	9494	9616	9739	9861	9984	55 0106	123
355	55 0228	55 0351	55 0473	55 0595	55 0717	55 0840	55 0962	55 1084	55 1206	1328	122
356	1450	1572	1694	1816	1938	2060	2181	2303	2425	2547	122
357	2668	2790	2911	3033	3155	3276	3398	3519	3640	3762	121
358	3883	4004	4126	4247	4368	4489	4610	4731	4852	4973	121
359	5094	5215	5336	5457	5578	5699	5820	5940	6061	6182	121
360	6303	6423	6544	6664	6785	6905	7026	7146	7267	7387	120
361	7507	7627	7748	7868	7988	8108	8228	8349	8469	8589	120
362	8709	8829	8948	9068	9188	9308	9428	9548	9667	9787	120
363	9907	56 0026	56 0146	56 0265	56 0385	56 0504	56 0624	56 0743	56 0863	56 0982	119
364	56 1101	1221	1340	1459	1578	1698	1817	1936	2055	2174	119
365	2293	2412	2531	2650	2769	2887	3006	3125	3244	3362	119
366	3481	3600	3718	3837	3955	4074	4192	4311	4429	4548	119
367	4666	4784	4903	5021	5139	5257	5376	5494	5612	5730	118
368	5848	5966	6084	6202	6320	6437	6555	6673	6791	6909	118
369	7026	7144	7262	7379	7497	7614	7732	7849	7967	8084	118
370	8202	8319	8436	8554	8671	8788	8905	9023	9140	9257	117
371	9374	9491	9608	9725	9842	9959	57 0076	57 0193	57 0309	57 0426	117
372	57 0543	57 0660	57 0776	57 0893	57 1010	57 1126	1243	1359	1476	1592	117
373	1709	1825	1942	2058	2174	2291	2407	2523	2639	2755	116
374	2872	2988	3104	3220	3336	3452	3568	3684	3800	3915	116
375	4031	4147	4263	4379	4494	4610	4726	4841	4957	5072	116
376	5188	5303	5419	5534	5650	5765	5880	5996	6111	6226	115
377	6341	6457	6572	6687	6802	6917	7032	7147	7262	7377	115
378	7492	7607	7722	7836	7951	8066	8181	8295	8410	8525	115
379	8639	8754	8868	8983	9097	9212	9326	9441	9555	9669	114
380	9784	9898	58 0012	58 0126	58 0241	58 0355	58 0469	58 0583	58 0697	58 0811	114
381	58 0925	58 1039	1153	1267	1381	1495	1608	1722	1836	1950	114
382	2063	2177	2291	2404	2518	2631	2745	2858	2972	3085	114
383	3199	3312	3426	3539	3652	3765	3879	3992	4105	4218	113
384	4331	4444	4557	4670	4783	4896	5009	5122	5235	5348	113
385	5461	5574	5686	5799	5912	6024	6137	6250	6362	6475	113
386	6587	6700	6812	6925	7037	7149	7262	7374	7486	7599	112
387	7711	7823	7935	8047	8160	8272	8384	8496	8608	8720	112
388	8832	8944	9056	9167	9279	9391	9503	9615	9726	9838	112
389	9950	59 0061	59 0173	59 0284	59 0396	59 0507	59 0619	59 0730	59 0842	59 0953	112
390	59 1065	1176	1287	1399	1510	1621	1732	1843	1955	2066	111
391	2177	2288	2399	2510	2621	2732	2843	2954	3064	3175	111
392	3286	3397	3508	3618	3729	3840	3950	4061	4171	4282	111
393	4393	4503	4614	4724	4834	4945	5055	5165	5276	5386	110
394	5496	5606	5717	5827	5937	6047	6157	6267	6377	6487	110
395	6597	6707	6817	6927	7037	7146	7256	7366	7476	7586	110
396	7695	7805	7914	8024	8134	8243	8353	8462	8572	8681	110
397	8791	8900	9009	9119	9228	9337	9446	9556	9665	9774	109
398	9883	9992	60 0101	60 0210	60 0319	60 0428	60 0537	60 0646	60 0755	60 0864	109
399	60 0973	60 1082	1191	1299	1408	1517	1625	1734	1843	1951	109
400	2060	2169	2277	2386	2494	2603	2711	2819	2928	3036	108

n\d	124	123	122
1	12	12	12
2	25	25	24
3	37	37	37
4	50	49	49
5	62	62	61
6	74	74	73
7	87	86	85
8	99	98	98
9	112	111	110

n\d	121	120	119
1	12	12	12
2	24	24	24
3	36	36	36
4	48	48	48
5	61	60	60
6	73	72	71
7	85	84	83
8	97	96	95
9	109	108	107

n\d	118	117	116
1	12	12	12
2	24	23	23
3	35	35	35
4	47	47	46
5	59	59	58
6	71	70	70
7	83	82	81
8	94	94	93
9	106	105	104

n\d	115	114	113
1	12	11	11
2	23	23	23
3	35	34	34
4	46	46	45
5	58	57	57
6	69	68	68
7	81	80	79
8	92	91	90
9	104	103	102

n\d	112	111	110
1	11	11	11
2	22	22	22
3	34	33	33
4	45	44	44
5	56	56	55
6	67	67	66
7	78	78	77
8	90	89	88
9	101	100	99

n\d	109	108
1	11	11
2	22	22
3	33	32
4	44	43
5	55	54
6	65	65
7	76	76
8	87	86
9	98	97

Six-Place Logarithms of Numbers 400-450 — Proportional Parts

N	0	1	2	3	4	5	6	7	8	9	D
400	60 2060	60 2169	60 2277	60 2386	60 2494	60 2603	60 2711	60 2819	60 2928	60 3036	108
401	3144	3253	3361	3469	3577	3686	3794	3902	4010	4118	108
402	4226	4334	4442	4550	4658	4766	4874	4982	5089	5197	108
403	5305	5413	5521	5628	5736	5844	5951	6059	6166	6274	108
404	6381	6489	6596	6704	6811	6919	7026	7133	7241	7348	107
405	7455	7562	7669	7777	7884	7991	8098	8205	8312	8419	107
406	8526	8633	8740	8847	8954	9061	9167	9274	9381	9488	107
407	9594	9701	9808	9914	61 0021	61 0128	61 0234	61 0341	61 0447	61 0554	107
408	61 0660	61 0767	61 0873	61 0979	1086	1192	1298	1405	1511	1617	106
409	1723	1829	1936	2042	2148	2254	2360	2466	2572	2678	106
410	2784	2890	2996	3102	3207	3313	3419	3525	3630	3736	106
411	3842	3947	4053	4159	4264	4370	4475	4581	4686	4792	106
412	4897	5003	5108	5213	5319	5424	5529	5634	5740	5845	105
413	5950	6055	6160	6265	6370	6476	6581	6686	6790	6895	105
414	7000	7105	7210	7315	7420	7525	7629	7734	7839	7943	105
415	8048	8153	8257	8362	8466	8571	8676	8780	8884	8989	105
416	9093	9198	9302	9406	9511	9615	9719	9824	9928	62 0032	104
417	62 0136	62 0240	62 0344	62 0448	62 0552	62 0656	62 0760	62 0864	62 0968	1072	104
418	1176	1280	1384	1488	1592	1695	1799	1903	2007	2110	104
419	2214	2318	2421	2525	2628	2732	2835	2939	3042	3146	104
420	3249	3353	3456	3559	3663	3766	3869	3973	4076	4179	103
421	4282	4385	4488	4591	4695	4798	4901	5004	5107	5210	103
422	5312	5415	5518	5621	5724	5827	5929	6032	6135	6238	103
423	6340	6443	6546	6648	6751	6853	6956	7058	7161	7263	103
424	7366	7468	7571	7673	7775	7878	7980	8082	8185	8287	102
425	8389	8491	8593	8695	8797	8900	9002	9104	9206	9308	102
426	9410	9512	9613	9715	9817	9919	63 0021	63 0123	63 0224	63 0326	102
427	63 0428	63 0530	63 0631	63 0733	63 0835	63 0936	1038	1139	1241	1342	102
428	1444	1545	1647	1748	1849	1951	2052	2153	2255	2356	101
429	2457	2559	2660	2761	2862	2963	3064	3165	3266	3367	101
430	3468	3569	3670	3771	3872	3973	4074	4175	4276	4376	101
431	4477	4578	4679	4779	4880	4981	5081	5182	5283	5383	101
432	5484	5584	5685	5785	5886	5986	6087	6187	6287	6388	100
433	6488	6588	6688	6789	6889	6989	7089	7189	7290	7390	100
434	7490	7590	7690	7790	7890	7990	8090	8190	8290	8389	100
435	8489	8589	8689	8789	8888	8988	9088	9188	9287	9387	100
436	9486	9586	9686	9785	9885	9984	64 0084	64 0183	64 0283	64 0382	99
437	64 0481	64 0581	64 0680	64 0779	64 0879	64 0978	1077	1177	1276	1375	99
438	1474	1573	1672	1771	1871	1970	2069	2168	2267	2366	99
439	2465	2563	2662	2761	2860	2959	3058	3156	3255	3354	99
440	3453	3551	3650	3749	3847	3946	4044	4143	4242	4340	98
441	4439	4537	4636	4734	4832	4931	5029	5127	5226	5324	98
442	5422	5521	5619	5717	5815	5913	6011	6110	6208	6306	98
443	6404	6502	6600	6698	6796	6894	6992	7089	7187	7285	98
444	7383	7481	7579	7676	7774	7872	7969	8067	8165	8262	98
445	8360	8458	8555	8653	8750	8848	8945	9043	9140	9237	97
446	9335	9432	9530	9627	9724	9821	9919	65 0016	65 0113	65 0210	97
447	65 0308	65 0405	65 0502	65 0599	65 0696	65 0793	65 0890	0987	1084	1181	97
448	1278	1375	1472	1569	1666	1762	1859	1956	2053	2150	97
449	2246	2343	2440	2536	2633	2730	2826	2923	3019	3116	97
450	3213	3309	3405	3502	3598	3695	3791	3888	3984	4080	96

Proportional Parts

n\d	109	108	107
1	11	11	11
2	22	22	21
3	33	32	32
4	44	43	43
5	55	54	54
6	65	65	64
7	76	76	75
8	87	86	86
9	98	97	96

n\d	106	105	104
1	11	11	10
2	21	21	21
3	32	32	31
4	42	42	42
5	53	53	52
6	64	63	62
7	74	74	73
8	85	84	83
9	95	95	94

n\d	103	102
1	10	10
2	21	20
3	31	31
4	41	41
5	52	51
6	62	61
7	72	71
8	82	82
9	93	92

n\d	101	100
1	10	10
2	20	20
3	30	30
4	40	40
5	51	50
6	61	60
7	71	70
8	81	80
9	91	90

n\d	99	98
1	9.9	9.8
2	19.8	19.6
3	29.7	29.4
4	39.6	39.2
5	43.5	49.0
6	59.4	58.8
7	69.3	68.6
8	79.2	78.4
9	89.1	88.2

n\d	97	96
1	9.7	9.6
2	19.4	19.2
3	29.1	28.8
4	38.8	38.4
5	48.5	48.0
6	58.2	57.6
7	67.9	67.2
8	77.6	76.8
9	87.3	86.4

N	0	1	2	3	4	5	6	7	8	9	D
450	65 3213	65 3309	65 3405	65 3502	65 3598	65 3695	65 3791	65 3888	65 3984	65 4080	96
451	4177	4273	4369	4465	4562	4658	4754	4850	4946	5042	96
452	5138	5235	5331	5427	5523	5619	5715	5810	5906	6002	96
453	6098	6194	6290	6386	6482	6577	6673	6769	6864	6960	96
454	7056	7152	7247	7343	7438	7534	7629	7725	7820	7916	96
455	8011	8107	8202	8298	8393	8488	8584	8679	8774	8870	95
456	8965	9060	9155	9250	9346	9441	9536	9631	9726	9821	95
457	9916	66 0011	66 0106	66 0201	66 0296	66 0391	66 0486	66 0581	66 0676	66 0771	95
458	66 0865	0960	1055	1150	1245	1339	1434	1529	1623	1718	95
459	1813	1907	2002	2096	2191	2286	2380	2475	2569	2663	95
460	2758	2852	2947	3041	3135	3230	3324	3418	3512	3607	94
461	3701	3795	3889	3983	4078	4172	4266	4360	4454	4548	94
462	4642	4736	4830	4924	5018	5112	5206	5299	5393	5487	94
463	5581	5675	5769	5862	5956	6050	6143	6237	6331	6424	94
464	6518	6612	6705	6799	6892	6986	7079	7173	7266	7360	94
465	7453	7546	7640	7733	7826	7920	8013	8106	8199	8293	93
466	8386	8479	8572	8665	8759	8852	8945	9038	9131	9224	93
467	9317	9410	9503	9596	9689	9782	9875	9967	67 0060	67 0153	93
468	67 0246	67 0339	67 0431	67 0524	67 0617	67 0710	67 0802	67 0895	0988	1080	93
469	1173	1265	1358	1451	1543	1636	1728	1821	1913	2005	93
470	2098	2190	2283	2375	2467	2560	2652	2744	2836	2929	92
471	3021	3113	3205	3297	3390	3482	3574	3666	3758	3850	92
472	3942	4034	4126	4218	4310	4402	4494	4586	4677	4769	92
473	4861	4953	5045	5137	5228	5320	5412	5503	5595	5687	92
474	5778	5870	5962	6053	6145	6236	6328	6419	6511	6602	92
475	6694	6785	6876	6968	7059	7151	7242	7333	7424	7516	91
476	7607	7698	7789	7881	7972	8063	8154	8245	8336	8427	91
477	8518	8609	8700	8791	8882	8973	9064	9155	9246	9337	91
478	9428	9519	9610	9700	9791	9882	9973	68 0063	68 0154	68 0245	91
479	68 0336	68 0426	68 0517	68 0607	68 0698	68 0789	68 0879	0970	1060	1151	91
480	1241	1332	1422	1513	1603	1693	1784	1874	1964	2055	90
481	2145	2235	2326	2416	2506	2596	2686	2777	2867	2957	90
482	3047	3137	3227	3317	3407	3497	3587	3677	3767	3857	90
483	3947	4037	4127	4217	4307	4396	4486	4576	4666	4756	90
484	4845	4935	5025	5114	5204	5294	5383	5473	5563	5652	90
485	5742	5831	5921	6010	6100	6189	6279	6368	6458	6547	89
486	6636	6726	6815	6904	6994	7083	7172	7261	7351	7440	89
487	7529	7618	7707	7796	7886	7975	8064	8153	8242	8331	89
488	8420	8509	8598	8687	8776	8865	8953	9042	9131	9220	89
489	9309	9398	9486	9575	9664	9753	9841	9930	69 0019	69 0107	89
490	69 0196	69 0285	69 0373	69 0462	69 0550	69 0639	69 0728	69 0816	0905	0993	89
491	1081	1170	1258	1347	1435	1524	1612	1700	1789	1877	88
492	1965	2053	2142	2230	2318	2406	2494	2583	2671	2759	88
493	2847	2935	3023	3111	3199	3287	3375	3463	3551	3639	88
494	3727	3815	3903	3991	4078	4166	4254	4342	4430	4517	88
495	4605	4693	4781	4868	4956	5044	5131	5219	5307	5394	88
496	5482	5569	5657	5744	5832	5919	6007	6094	6182	6269	87
497	6356	6444	6531	6618	6706	6793	6880	6968	7055	7142	87
498	7229	7317	7404	7491	7578	7665	7752	7839	7926	8014	87
499	8101	8188	8275	8362	8449	8535	8622	8709	8796	8883	87
500	8970	9057	9144	9231	9317	9404	9491	9578	9664	9751	87

Proportional Parts

n\d	97	96
1	9.7	9.6
2	19.4	19.2
3	29.1	28.8
4	38.8	38.4
5	48.5	48.0
6	58.2	57.6
7	67.9	67.2
8	77.6	76.8
9	87.3	86.4

n\d	95	94
1	9.5	9.4
2	19.0	18.8
3	28.5	28.2
4	38.0	37.6
5	47.5	47.0
6	57.0	56.4
7	66.5	65.8
8	76.0	75.2
9	85.5	84.6

n\d	93	92
1	9.3	9.2
2	18.6	18.4
3	27.9	27.6
4	37.2	36.8
5	46.5	46.0
6	55.8	55.2
7	65.1	64.4
8	74.4	73.6
9	83.7	82.8

n\d	91	90
1	9.1	9.0
2	18.2	18.0
3	27.3	27.0
4	36.4	36.0
5	45.5	45.0
6	54.6	54.0
7	63.7	63.0
8	72.8	72.0
9	81.9	81.0

n\d	89	88
1	8.9	8.8
2	17.8	17.6
3	26.7	26.4
4	35.6	35.2
5	44.5	44.0
6	53.4	52.8
7	62.3	61.6
8	71.2	70.4
9	80.1	79.2

n\d	87	86
1	8.7	8.6
2	17.4	17.2
3	26.1	25.8
4	34.8	34.4
5	43.5	43.0
6	52.2	51.6
7	60.9	60.2
8	69.6	68.8
9	78.3	77.4

Six-Place Logarithms of Numbers 500–550

N	0	1	2	3	4	5	6	7	8	9	D
500	69 8970	69 9057	69 9144	69 9231	69 9317	69 9404	69 9491	69 9578	69 9664	69 9751	87
501	9838	9924	70 0011	70 0098	70 0184	70 0271	70 0358	70 0444	70 0531	70 0617	87
502	70 0704	70 0790	0877	0963	1050	1136	1222	1309	1395	1482	86
503	1568	1654	1741	1827	1913	1999	2086	2172	2258	2344	86
504	2431	2517	2603	2689	2775	2861	2947	3033	3119	3205	86
505	3291	3377	3463	3549	3635	3721	3807	3893	3979	4065	86
506	4151	4236	4322	4408	4494	4579	4665	4751	4837	4922	86
507	5008	5094	5179	5265	5350	5436	5522	5607	5693	5778	86
508	5864	5949	6035	6120	6206	6291	6376	6462	6547	6632	85
509	6718	6803	6888	6974	7059	7144	7229	7315	7400	7485	85
510	7570	7655	7740	7826	7911	7996	8081	8166	8251	8336	85
511	8421	8506	8591	8676	8761	8846	8931	9015	9100	9185	85
512	9270	9355	9440	9524	9609	9694	9779	9863	9948	71 0033	85
513	71 0117	71 0202	71 0287	71 0371	71 0456	71 0540	71 0625	71 0710	71 0794	0879	85
514	0963	1048	1132	1217	1301	1385	1470	1554	1639	1723	84
515	1807	1892	1976	2060	2144	2229	2313	2397	2481	2566	84
516	2650	2734	2818	2902	2986	3070	3154	3238	3323	3407	84
517	3491	3575	3659	3742	3826	3910	3994	4078	4162	4246	84
518	4330	4414	4497	4581	4665	4749	4833	4916	5000	5084	84
519	5167	5251	5335	5418	5502	5586	5669	5753	5836	5920	84
520	6003	6087	6170	6254	6337	6421	6504	6588	6671	6754	83
521	6838	6921	7004	7088	7171	7254	7338	7421	7504	7587	83
522	7671	7754	7837	7920	8003	8086	8169	8253	8336	8419	83
523	8502	8585	8668	8751	8834	8917	9000	9083	9165	9248	83
524	9331	9414	9497	9580	9663	9745	9828	9911	9994	72 0077	83
525	72 0159	72 0242	72 0325	72 0407	72 0490	72 0573	72 0655	72 0738	72 0821	0903	83
526	0986	1068	1151	1233	1316	1398	1481	1563	1646	1728	82
527	1811	1893	1975	2058	2140	2222	2305	2387	2469	2552	82
528	2634	2716	2798	2881	2963	3045	3127	3209	3291	3374	82
529	3456	3538	3620	3702	3784	3866	3948	4030	4112	4194	82
530	4276	4358	4440	4522	4604	4685	4767	4849	4931	5013	82
531	5095	5176	5258	5340	5422	5503	5585	5667	5748	5830	82
532	5912	5993	6075	6156	6238	6320	6401	6483	6564	6646	82
533	6727	6809	6890	6972	7053	7134	7216	7297	7379	7460	81
534	7541	7623	7704	7785	7866	7948	8029	8110	8191	8273	81
535	8354	8435	8516	8597	8678	8759	8841	8922	9003	9084	81
536	9165	9246	9327	9408	9489	9570	9651	9732	9813	9893	81
537	9974	73 0055	73 0136	73 0217	73 0298	73 0378	73 0459	73 0540	73 0621	73 0702	81
538	73 0782	0863	0944	1024	1105	1186	1266	1347	1428	1508	81
539	1589	1669	1750	1830	1911	1991	2072	2152	2233	2313	81
540	2394	2474	2555	2635	2715	2796	2876	2956	3037	3117	80
541	3197	3278	3358	3438	3518	3598	3679	3759	3839	3919	80
542	3999	4079	4160	4240	4320	4400	4480	4560	4640	4720	80
543	4800	4880	4960	5040	5120	5200	5279	5359	5439	5519	80
544	5599	5679	5759	5838	5918	5998	6078	6157	6237	6317	80
545	6397	6476	6556	6635	6715	6795	6874	6954	7034	7113	80
546	7193	7272	7352	7431	7511	7590	7670	7749	7829	7908	79
547	7987	8067	8146	8225	8305	8384	8463	8543	8622	8701	79
548	8781	8860	8939	9018	9097	9177	9256	9335	9414	9493	79
549	9572	9651	9731	9810	9889	9968	74 0047	74 0126	74 0205	74 0284	79
550	74 0363	74 0442	74 0521	74 0600	74 0678	74 0757	0836	0915	0994	1073	79

Proportional Parts

n\d	87	86
1	8.7	8.6
2	17.4	17.2
3	26.1	25.8
4	34.8	34.4
5	43.5	43.0
6	52.2	51.6
7	60.9	60.2
8	69.6	68.8
9	78.3	77.4

n\d	85	84
1	8.5	8.4
2	17.0	16.8
3	25.5	25.2
4	34.0	33.6
5	42.5	42.0
6	51.0	50.4
7	59.5	58.8
8	68.0	67.2
9	76.5	75.6

n\d	83	82
1	8.3	8.2
2	16.6	16.4
3	24.9	24.6
4	33.2	32.8
5	41.5	41.0
6	49.8	49.2
7	58.1	57.4
8	66.4	65.6
9	74.7	73.8

n\d	81	80
1	8.1	8.0
2	16.2	16.0
3	24.3	24.0
4	32.4	32.0
5	40.5	40.0
6	48.6	48.0
7	56.7	56.0
8	64.8	64.0
9	72.9	72.0

n\d	79
1	7.9
2	15.8
3	23.7
4	31.6
5	39.5
6	47.4
7	55.3
8	63.2
9	71.1

Six-Place Logarithms of Numbers 550-600

N	0	1	2	3	4	5	6	7	8	9	D
550	74 0363	74 0442	74 0521	74 0600	74 0678	74 0757	74 0836	74 0915	74 0994	74 1073	79
551	1152	1230	1309	1388	1467	1546	1624	1703	1782	1860	79
552	1939	2018	2096	2175	2254	2332	2411	2489	2568	2647	79
553	2725	2804	2882	2961	3039	3118	3196	3275	3353	3431	79
554	3510	3588	3667	3745	3823	3902	3980	4058	4136	4215	78
555	4293	4371	4449	4528	4606	4684	4762	4840	4919	4997	78
556	5075	5153	5231	5309	5387	5465	5543	5621	5699	5777	78
557	5855	5933	6011	6089	6167	6245	6323	6401	6479	6556	78
558	6634	6712	6790	6868	6945	7023	7101	7179	7256	7334	78
559	7412	7489	7567	7645	7722	7800	7878	7955	8033	8110	78
560	8188	8266	8343	8421	8498	8576	8653	8731	8808	8885	77
561	8963	9040	9118	9195	9272	9350	9427	9504	9582	9659	77
562	9736	9814	9891	9968	75 0045	75 0123	75 0200	75 0277	75 0354	75 0431	77
563	75 0508	75 0586	75 0663	75 0740	0817	0894	0971	1048	1125	1202	77
564	1279	1356	1433	1510	1587	1664	1741	1818	1895	1972	77
565	2048	2125	2202	2279	2356	2433	2509	2586	2663	2740	77
566	2816	2893	2970	3047	3123	3200	3277	3353	3430	3506	77
567	3583	3660	3736	3813	3889	3966	4042	4119	4195	4272	77
568	4348	4425	4501	4578	4654	4730	4807	4883	4960	5036	76
569	5112	5189	5265	5341	5417	5494	5570	5646	5722	5799	76
570	5875	5951	6027	6103	6180	6256	6332	6408	6484	6560	76
571	6636	6712	6788	6864	6940	7016	7092	7168	7244	7320	76
572	7396	7472	7548	7624	7700	7775	7851	7927	8003	8079	76
573	8155	8230	8306	8382	8458	8533	8609	8685	8761	8836	76
574	8912	8988	9063	9139	9214	9290	9366	9441	9517	9592	76
575	9668	9743	9819	9894	9970	76 0045	76 0121	76 0196	76 0272	76 0347	75
576	76 0422	76 0498	76 0573	76 0649	76 0724	0799	0875	0950	1025	1101	75
577	1176	1251	1326	1402	1477	1552	1627	1702	1778	1853	75
578	1928	2003	2078	2153	2228	2303	2378	2453	2529	2604	75
579	2679	2754	2829	2904	2978	3053	3128	3203	3278	3353	75
580	3428	3503	3578	3653	3727	3802	3877	3952	4027	4101	75
581	4176	4251	4326	4400	4475	4550	4624	4699	4774	4848	75
582	4923	4998	5072	5147	5221	5296	5370	5445	5520	5594	75
583	5669	5743	5818	5892	5966	6041	6115	6190	6264	6338	74
584	6413	6487	6562	6636	6710	6785	6859	6933	7007	7082	74
585	7156	7230	7304	7379	7453	7527	7601	7675	7749	7823	74
586	7898	7972	8046	8120	8194	8268	8342	8416	8490	8564	74
587	8638	8712	8786	8860	8934	9008	9082	9156	9230	9303	74
588	9377	9451	9525	9599	9673	9746	9820	9894	9968	77 0042	74
589	77 0115	77 0189	77 0263	77 0336	77 0410	77 0484	77 0557	77 0631	77 0705	0778	74
590	0852	0926	0999	1073	1146	1220	1293	1367	1440	1514	74
591	1587	1661	1734	1808	1881	1955	2028	2102	2175	2248	73
592	2322	2395	2468	2542	2615	2688	2762	2835	2908	2981	73
593	3055	3128	3201	3274	3348	3421	3494	3567	3640	3713	73
594	3786	3860	3933	4006	4079	4152	4225	4298	4371	4444	73
595	4517	4590	4663	4736	4809	4882	4955	5028	5100	5173	73
596	5246	5319	5392	5465	5538	5610	5683	5756	5829	5902	73
597	5974	6047	6120	6193	6265	6338	6411	6483	6556	6629	73
598	6701	6774	6846	6919	6992	7064	7137	7209	7282	7354	73
599	7427	7499	7572	7644	7717	7789	7862	7934	8006	8079	72
600	8151	8224	8296	8368	8441	8513	8585	8658	8730	8802	72

Proportional Parts

n\d	79	78
1	7.9	7.8
2	15.8	15.6
3	23.7	23.4
4	31.6	31.2
5	39.5	39.0
6	47.4	46.8
7	55.3	54.6
8	63.2	62.4
9	71.1	70.2

n\d	77	76
1	7.7	7.6
2	15.4	15.2
3	23.1	22.8
4	30.8	30.4
5	38.5	38.0
6	46.2	45.6
7	53.9	53.2
8	61.6	60.8
9	69.3	68.4

n\d	75	74
1	7.5	7.4
2	15.0	14.8
3	22.5	22.2
4	30.0	29.6
5	37.5	37.0
6	45.0	44.4
7	52.5	51.8
8	60.0	59.2
9	67.5	66.6

n\d	73
1	7.3
2	14.6
3	21.9
4	29.2
5	36.5
6	43.8
7	51.1
8	58.4
9	65.7

n\d	72
1	7.2
2	14.4
3	21.6
4	28.8
5	36.0
6	43.2
7	50.4
8	57.6
9	64.8

Six-Place Logarithms of Numbers 600-650

N	0	1	2	3	4	5	6	7	8	9	D
600	77 8151	77 8224	77 8296	77 8368	77 8441	77 8513	77 8585	77 8658	77 8730	77 8802	72
601	8874	8947	9019	9091	9163	9236	9308	9380	9452	9524	72
602	9596	9669	9741	9813	9885	9957	78 0029	78 0101	78 0173	78 0245	72
603	78 0317	78 0389	78 0461	78 0533	78 0605	78 0677	0749	0821	0893	0965	72
604	1037	1109	1181	1253	1324	1396	1468	1540	1612	1684	72
605	1755	1827	1899	1971	2042	2114	2186	2258	2329	2401	72
606	2473	2544	2616	2688	2759	2831	2902	2974	3046	3117	72
607	3189	3260	3332	3403	3475	3546	3618	3689	3761	3832	71
608	3904	3975	4046	4118	4189	4261	4332	4403	4475	4546	71
609	4617	4689	4760	4831	4902	4974	5045	5116	5187	5259	71
610	5330	5401	5472	5543	5615	5686	5757	5828	5899	5970	71
611	6041	6112	6183	6254	6325	6396	6467	6538	6609	6680	71
612	6751	6822	6893	6964	7035	7106	7177	7248	7319	7390	71
613	7460	7531	7602	7673	7744	7815	7885	7956	8027	8098	71
614	8168	8239	8310	8381	8451	8522	8593	8663	8734	8804	71
615	8875	8946	9016	9087	9157	9228	9299	9369	9440	9510	71
616	9581	9651	9722	9792	9863	9933	79 0004	79 0074	79 0144	79 0215	70
617	79 0285	79 0356	79 0426	79 0496	79 0567	79 0637	0707	0778	0848	0918	70
618	0988	1059	1129	1199	1269	1340	1410	1480	1550	1620	70
619	1691	1761	1831	1901	1971	2041	2111	2181	2252	2322	70
620	2392	2462	2532	2602	2672	2742	2812	2882	2952	3022	70
621	3092	3162	3231	3301	3371	3441	3511	3581	3651	3721	70
622	3790	3860	3930	4000	4070	4139	4209	4279	4349	4418	70
623	4488	4558	4627	4697	4767	4836	4906	4976	5045	5115	70
624	5185	5254	5324	5393	5463	5532	5602	5672	5741	5811	70
625	5880	5949	6019	6088	6158	6227	6297	6366	6436	6505	69
626	6574	6644	6713	6782	6852	6921	6990	7060	7129	7198	69
627	7268	7337	7406	7475	7545	7614	7683	7752	7821	7890	69
628	7960	8029	8098	8167	8236	8305	8374	8443	8513	8582	69
629	8651	8720	8789	8858	8927	8996	9065	9134	9203	9272	69
630	9341	9409	9478	9547	9616	9685	9754	9823	9892	9961	69
631	80 0029	80 0098	80 0167	80 0236	80 0305	80 0373	80 0442	80 0511	80 0580	80 0648	69
632	0717	0786	0854	0923	0992	1061	1129	1198	1266	1335	69
633	1404	1472	1541	1609	1678	1747	1815	1884	1952	2021	69
634	2089	2158	2226	2295	2363	2432	2500	2568	2637	2705	68
635	2774	2842	2910	2979	3047	3116	3184	3252	3321	3389	68
636	3457	3525	3594	3662	3730	3798	3867	3935	4003	4071	68
637	4139	4208	4276	4344	4412	4480	4548	4616	4685	4753	68
638	4821	4889	4957	5025	5093	5161	5229	5297	5365	5433	68
639	5501	5569	5637	5705	5773	5841	5908	5976	6044	6112	68
640	6180	6248	6316	6384	6451	6519	6587	6655	6723	6790	68
641	6858	6926	6994	7061	7129	7197	7264	7332	7400	7467	68
642	7535	7603	7670	7738	7806	7873	7941	8008	8076	8143	68
643	8211	8279	8346	8414	8481	8549	8616	8684	8751	8818	67
644	8886	8953	9021	9088	9156	9223	9290	9358	9425	9492	67
645	9560	9627	9694	9762	9829	9896	9964	81 0031	81 0098	81 0165	67
646	81 0233	81 0300	81 0367	81 0434	81 0501	81 0569	81 0636	0703	0770	0837	67
647	0904	0971	1039	1106	1173	1240	1307	1374	1441	1508	67
648	1575	1642	1709	1776	1843	1910	1977	2044	2111	2178	67
649	2245	2312	2379	2445	2512	2579	2646	2713	2780	2847	67
650	2913	2980	3047	3114	3181	3247	3314	3381	3448	3514	67

n\d	73	72
1	7.3	7.2
2	14.6	14.4
3	21.9	21.6
4	29.2	28.8
5	36.5	36.0
6	43.8	43.2
7	51.1	50.4
8	58.4	57.6
9	65.7	64.8

n\d	71	70
1	7.1	7.0
2	14.2	14.0
3	21.3	21.0
4	28.4	28.0
5	35.5	35.0
6	42.6	42.0
7	49.7	49.0
8	56.8	56.0
9	63.9	63.0

n\d	69	68
1	6.9	6.8
2	13.8	13.6
3	20.7	20.4
4	27.6	27.2
5	34.5	34.0
6	41.4	40.8
7	48.3	47.6
8	55.2	54.4
9	62.1	61.2

n\d	67
1	6.7
2	13.4
3	20.1
4	26.8
5	33.5
6	40.2
7	46.9
8	53.6
9	60.3

n\d	66
1	6.6
2	13.2
3	19.8
4	26.4
5	33.0
6	39.6
7	46.2
8	52.8
9	59.4

Six-Place Logarithms of Numbers 650-700 — Proportional Parts

N	0	1	2	3	4	5	6	7	8	9	D
650	81 2913	81 2980	81 3047	81 3114	81 3181	81 3247	81 3314	81 3381	81 3448	81 3514	67
651	3581	3648	3714	3781	3848	3914	3981	4048	4114	4181	67
652	4248	4314	4381	4447	4514	4581	4647	4714	4780	4847	67
653	4913	4980	5046	5113	5179	5246	5312	5378	5445	5511	66
654	5578	5644	5711	5777	5843	5910	5976	6042	6109	6175	66
655	6241	6308	6374	6440	6506	6573	6639	6705	6771	6838	66
656	6904	6970	7036	7102	7169	7235	7301	7367	7433	7499	66
657	7565	7631	7698	7764	7830	7896	7962	8028	8094	8160	66
658	8226	8292	8358	8424	8490	8556	8622	8688	8754	8820	66
659	8885	8951	9017	9083	9149	9215	9281	9346	9412	9478	66
660	9544	9610	9676	9741	9807	9873	9939	82 0004	82 0070	82 0136	66
661	82 0201	82 0267	82 0333	82 0399	82 0464	82 0530	82 0595	0661	0727	0792	66
662	0858	0924	0989	1055	1120	1186	1251	1317	1382	1448	66
663	1514	1579	1645	1710	1775	1841	1906	1972	2037	2103	65
664	2168	2233	2299	2364	2430	2495	2560	2626	2691	2756	65
665	2822	2887	2952	3018	3083	3148	3213	3279	3344	3409	65
666	3474	3539	3605	3670	3735	3800	3865	3930	3996	4061	65
667	4126	4191	4256	4321	4386	4451	4516	4581	4646	4711	65
668	4776	4841	4906	4971	5036	5101	5166	5231	5296	5361	65
669	5426	5491	5556	5621	5686	5751	5815	5880	5945	6010	65
670	6075	6140	6204	6269	6334	6399	6464	6528	6593	6658	65
671	6723	6787	6852	6917	6981	7046	7111	7175	7240	7305	65
672	7369	7434	7499	7563	7628	7692	7757	7821	7886	7951	65
673	8015	8080	8144	8209	8273	8338	8402	8467	8531	8595	64
674	8660	8724	8789	8853	8918	8982	9046	9111	9175	9239	64
675	9304	9368	9432	9497	9561	9625	9690	9754	9818	9882	64
676	9947	83 0011	83 0075	83 0139	83 0204	83 0268	83 0332	83 0396	83 0460	83 0525	64
677	83 0589	0653	0717	0781	0845	0909	0973	1037	1102	1166	64
678	1230	1294	1358	1422	1486	1550	1614	1678	1742	1806	64
679	1870	1934	1998	2062	2126	2189	2253	2317	2381	2445	64
680	2509	2573	2637	2700	2764	2828	2892	2956	3020	3083	64
681	3147	3211	3275	3338	3402	3466	3530	3593	3657	3721	64
682	3784	3848	3912	3975	4039	4103	4166	4230	4294	4357	64
683	4421	4484	4548	4611	4675	4739	4802	4866	4929	4993	64
684	5056	5120	5183	5247	5310	5373	5437	5500	5564	5627	63
685	5691	5754	5817	5881	5944	6007	6071	6134	6197	6261	63
686	6324	6387	6451	6514	6577	6641	6704	6767	6830	6894	63
687	6957	7020	7083	7146	7210	7273	7336	7399	7462	7525	63
688	7588	7652	7715	7778	7841	7904	7967	8030	8093	8156	63
689	8219	8282	8345	8408	8471	8534	8597	8660	8723	8786	63
690	8849	8912	8975	9038	9101	9164	9227	9289	9352	9415	63
691	9478	9541	9604	9667	9729	9792	9855	9918	9981	84 0043	63
692	84 0106	84 0169	84 0232	84 0294	84 0357	84 0420	84 0482	84 0545	84 0608	0671	63
693	0733	0796	0859	0921	0984	1046	1109	1172	1234	1297	63
694	1359	1422	1485	1547	1610	1672	1735	1797	1860	1922	63
695	1985	2047	2110	2172	2235	2297	2360	2422	2484	2547	62
696	2609	2672	2734	2796	2859	2921	2983	3046	3108	3170	62
697	3233	3295	3357	3420	3482	3544	3606	3669	3731	3793	62
698	3855	3918	3980	4042	4104	4166	4229	4291	4353	4415	62
699	4477	4539	4601	4664	4726	4788	4850	4912	4974	5036	62
700	5098	5160	5222	5284	5346	5408	5470	5532	5594	5656	62

Proportional Parts

n\d	67
1	6.7
2	13.4
3	20.1
4	26.8
5	33.5
6	40.2
7	46.9
8	53.6
9	60.3

n\d	66
1	6.6
2	13.2
3	19.8
4	26.4
5	33.0
6	39.6
7	46.2
8	52.8
9	59.4

n\d	65
1	6.5
2	13.0
3	19.5
4	26.0
5	32.5
6	39.0
7	45.5
8	52.0
9	58.5

n\d	64
1	6.4
2	12.8
3	19.2
4	25.6
5	32.0
6	38.4
7	44.8
8	51.2
9	57.6

n\d	63
1	6.3
2	12.6
3	18.9
4	25.2
5	31.5
6	37.8
7	44.1
8	50.4
9	56.7

n\d	62
1	6.2
2	12.4
3	18.6
4	24.8
5	31.0
6	37.2
7	43.4
8	49.6
9	55.8

Six-Place Logarithms of Numbers 700-750

N	0	1	2	3	4	5	6	7	8	9	D
700	84 5098	84 5160	84 5222	84 5284	84 5346	84 5408	84 5470	84 5532	84 5594	84 5656	62
701	5718	5780	5842	5904	5966	6028	6090	6151	6213	6275	62
702	6337	6399	6461	6523	5685	6646	6708	6770	6832	6894	62
703	6955	7017	7079	7141	7202	7264	7326	7388	7449	7511	62
704	7573	7634	7696	7758	7819	7881	7943	8004	8066	8128	62
705	8189	8251	8312	8374	8435	8497	8559	8620	8682	8743	62
706	8805	8866	8928	8989	9051	9112	9174	9235	9297	9358	61
707	9419	9481	9542	9604	9665	9726	9788	9849	9911	9972	61
708	85 0033	85 0095	85 0156	85 0217	85 0279	85 0340	85 0401	85 0462	85 0524	85 0585	61
709	0646	0707	0769	0830	0891	0952	1014	1075	1136	1197	61
710	1258	1320	1381	1442	1503	1564	1625	1686	1747	1809	61
711	1870	1931	1992	2053	2114	2175	2236	2297	2358	2419	61
712	2480	2541	2602	2663	2724	2785	2846	2907	2968	3029	61
713	3090	3150	3211	3272	3333	3394	3455	3516	3577	3637	61
714	3698	3759	3820	3881	3941	4002	4063	4124	4185	4245	61
715	4306	4367	4428	4488	4549	4610	4670	4731	4792	4852	61
716	4913	4974	5034	5095	5156	5216	5277	5337	5398	5459	61
717	5519	5580	5640	5701	5761	5822	5882	5943	6003	6064	61
718	6124	6185	6245	6306	6366	6427	6487	6548	6608	6668	60
719	6729	6789	6850	6910	6970	7031	7091	7152	7212	7272	60
720	7332	7393	7453	7513	7574	7634	7694	7755	7815	7875	60
721	7935	7995	8056	8116	8176	8236	8297	8357	8417	8477	60
722	8537	8597	8657	8718	8778	8838	8898	8958	9018	9078	60
723	9138	9198	9258	9318	9379	9439	9499	9559	9619	9679	60
724	9739	9799	9859	9918	9978	86 0038	86 0098	86 0158	86 0218	86 0278	60
725	86 0338	86 0398	86 0458	86 0518	86 0578	0637	0697	0757	0817	0877	60
726	0937	0996	1056	1116	1176	1236	1295	1355	1415	1475	60
727	1534	1594	1654	1714	1773	1833	1893	1952	2012	2072	60
728	2131	2191	2251	2310	2370	2430	2489	2549	2608	2668	60
729	2728	2787	2847	2906	2966	3025	3085	3144	3204	3263	60
730	3323	3382	3442	3501	3561	3620	3680	3739	3799	3858	59
731	3917	3977	4036	4096	4155	4214	4274	4333	4392	4452	59
732	4511	4570	4630	4689	4748	4808	4867	4926	4985	5045	59
733	5104	5163	5222	5282	5341	5400	5459	5519	5578	5637	59
734	5696	5755	5814	5874	5933	5992	6051	6110	6169	6228	59
735	6287	6346	6405	6465	6524	6583	6642	6701	6760	6819	59
736	6878	6937	6996	7055	7114	7173	7232	7291	7350	7409	59
737	7467	7526	7585	7644	7703	7762	7821	7880	7939	7998	59
738	8056	8115	8174	8233	8292	8350	8409	8468	8527	8586	59
739	8644	8703	8762	8821	8879	8938	8997	9056	9114	9173	59
740	9232	9290	9349	9408	9466	9525	9584	9642	9701	9760	59
741	9818	9877	9935	9994	87 0053	87 0111	87 0170	87 0228	87 0287	87 0345	59
742	87 0404	87 0462	87 0521	87 0579	0638	0696	0755	0813	0872	0930	58
743	0989	1047	1106	1164	1223	1281	1339	1398	1456	1515	58
744	1573	1631	1690	1748	1806	1865	1923	1981	2040	2098	58
745	2156	2215	2273	2331	2389	2448	2506	2564	2622	2681	58
746	2739	2797	2855	2913	2972	3030	3088	3146	3204	3262	58
747	3321	3379	3437	3495	3553	3611	3669	3727	3785	3844	58
748	3902	3960	4018	4076	4134	4192	4250	4308	4366	4424	58
749	4482	4540	4598	4656	4714	4772	4830	4888	4945	5003	58
750	5061	5119	5177	5235	5293	5351	5409	5466	5524	5582	58

n\d	62	61
1	6.2	6.1
2	12.4	12.2
3	18.6	18.3
4	24.8	24.4
5	31.0	30.5
6	37.2	36.6
7	43.4	42.7
8	49.6	48.8
9	55.8	54.9

n\d	60
1	6.0
2	12.0
3	18.0
4	24.0
5	30.0
6	36.0
7	42.0
8	48.0
9	54.0

n\d	59
1	5.9
2	11.8
3	17.7
4	23.6
5	29.5
6	35.4
7	41.3
8	47.2
9	53.1

n\d	58
1	5.8
2	11.6
3	17.4
4	23.2
5	29.0
6	34.8
7	40.6
8	46.4
9	52.2

n\d	57
1	5.7
2	11.4
3	17.1
4	22.8
5	28.5
6	34.2
7	39.9
8	45.6
9	51.3

Six-Place Logarithms of Numbers 750-800 — Proportional Parts

N	0	1	2	3	4	5	6	7	8	9	D
750	87 5061	87 5119	87 5177	87 5235	87 5293	87 5351	87 5409	87 5466	87 5524	87 5582	58
751	5640	5698	5756	5813	5871	5929	5987	6045	6102	6160	58
752	6218	6276	6333	6391	6449	6507	6564	6622	6680	6737	58
753	6795	6853	6910	6968	7026	7083	7141	7199	7256	7314	58
754	7371	7429	7487	7544	7602	7659	7717	7774	7832	7889	58
755	7947	8004	8062	8119	8177	8234	8292	8349	8407	8464	57
756	8522	8579	8637	8694	8752	8809	8866	8924	8981	9039	57
757	9096	9153	9211	9268	9325	9383	9440	9497	9555	9612	57
758	9669	9726	9784	9841	9898	9956	88 0013	88 0070	88 0127	88 0185	57
759	88 0242	88 0299	88 0356	88 0413	88 0471	88 0528	0585	0642	0699	0756	57
760	0814	0871	0928	0985	1042	1099	1156	1213	1271	1328	57
761	1385	1442	1499	1556	1613	1670	1727	1784	1841	1898	57
762	1955	2012	2069	2126	2183	2240	2297	2354	2411	2468	57
763	2525	2581	2638	2695	2752	2809	2866	2923	2980	3037	57
764	3093	3150	3207	3264	3321	3377	3434	3491	3548	3605	57
765	3661	3718	3775	3832	3888	3945	4002	4059	4115	4172	57
766	4229	4285	4342	4399	4455	4512	4569	4625	4682	4739	57
767	4795	4852	4909	4965	5022	5078	5135	5192	5248	5305	57
768	5361	5418	5474	5531	5587	5644	5700	5757	5813	5870	57
769	5926	5983	6039	6096	6152	6209	6265	6321	6378	6434	56
770	6491	6547	6604	6660	6716	6773	6829	6885	6942	6998	56
771	7054	7111	7167	7223	7280	7336	7392	7449	7505	7561	56
772	7617	7674	7730	7786	7842	7898	7955	8011	8067	8123	56
773	8179	8236	8292	8348	8404	8460	8516	8573	8629	8685	56
774	8741	8797	8853	8909	8965	9021	9077	9134	9190	9246	56
775	9302	9358	9414	9470	9526	9582	9638	9694	9750	9806	56
776	9862	9918	9974	89 0030	89 0086	89 0141	89 0197	89 0253	89 0309	89 0365	56
777	89 0421	89 0477	89 0533	0589	0645	0700	0756	0812	0868	0924	56
778	0980	1035	1091	1147	1203	1259	1314	1370	1426	1482	56
779	1537	1593	1649	1705	1760	1816	1872	1928	1983	2039	56
780	2095	2150	2206	2262	2317	2373	2429	2484	2540	2595	56
781	2651	2707	2762	2818	2873	2929	2985	3040	3096	3151	56
782	3207	3262	3318	3373	3429	3484	3540	3595	3651	3706	56
783	3762	3817	3873	3928	3984	4039	4094	4150	4205	4261	55
784	4316	4371	4427	4482	4538	4593	4648	4704	4759	4814	55
785	4870	4925	4980	5036	5091	5146	5201	5257	5312	5367	55
786	5423	5478	5533	5588	5644	5699	5754	5809	5864	5920	55
787	5975	6030	6085	6140	6195	6251	6306	6361	6416	6471	55
788	6526	6581	6636	6692	6747	6802	6857	6912	6967	7022	55
789	7077	7132	7187	7242	7297	7352	7407	7462	7517	7572	55
790	7627	7682	7737	7792	7847	7902	7957	8012	8067	8122	55
791	8176	8231	8286	8341	8396	8451	8506	8561	8615	8670	55
792	8725	8780	8835	8890	8944	8999	9054	9109	9164	9218	55
793	9273	9328	9383	9437	9492	9547	9602	9656	9711	9766	55
794	9821	9875	9930	9985	90 0039	90 0094	90 0149	90 0203	90 0258	90 0312	55
795	90 0367	90 0422	90 0476	90 0531	0586	0640	0695	0749	0804	0859	55
796	0913	0968	1022	1077	1131	1186	1240	1295	1349	1404	55
797	1458	1513	1567	1622	1676	1731	1785	1840	1894	1948	54
798	2003	2057	2112	2166	2221	2275	2329	2384	2438	2492	54
799	2547	2601	2655	2710	2764	2818	2873	2927	2981	3036	54
800	3090	3144	3199	3253	3307	3361	3416	3470	3524	3578	54

Proportional Parts

n\d	58	57	56	55	54
1	5.8	5.7	5.6	5.5	5.4
2	11.6	11.4	11.2	11.0	10.8
3	17.4	17.1	16.8	16.5	16.2
4	23.2	22.8	22.4	22.0	21.6
5	29.0	28.5	28.0	27.5	27.0
6	34.8	34.2	33.6	33.0	32.4
7	40.6	39.9	39.2	38.5	37.8
8	46.4	45.6	44.8	44.0	43.2
9	52.2	51.3	50.4	49.5	48.6

Proportional Parts

N	0	1	2	3	4	5	6	7	8	9	D
800	90 3090	90 3144	90 3199	90 3253	90 3307	90 3361	90 3416	90 3470	90 3524	90 3578	54
801	3633	3687	3741	3795	3849	3904	3958	4012	4066	4120	54
802	4174	4229	4283	4337	4391	4445	4499	4553	4607	4661	54
803	4716	4770	4824	4878	4932	4986	5040	5094	5148	5202	54
804	5256	5310	5364	5418	5472	5526	5580	5634	5688	5742	54
805	5796	5850	5904	5958	6012	6066	6119	6173	6227	6281	54
806	6335	6389	6443	6497	6551	6604	6658	6712	6766	6820	54
807	6874	6927	6981	7035	7089	7143	7196	7250	7304	7358	54
808	7411	7465	7519	7573	7626	7680	7734	7787	7841	7895	54
809	7949	8002	8056	8110	8163	8217	8270	8324	8378	8431	54
810	8485	8539	8592	8646	8699	8753	8807	8860	8914	8967	54
811	9021	9074	9128	9181	9235	9289	9342	9396	9449	9503	54
812	9556	9610	9663	9716	9770	9823	9877	9930	9984	91 0037	53
813	91 0091	91 0144	91 0197	91 0251	91 0304	91 0358	91 0411	91 0464	91 0518	0571	53
814	0624	0678	0731	0784	0838	0891	0944	0998	1051	1104	53
815	1158	1211	1264	1317	1371	1424	1477	1530	1584	1637	53
816	1690	1743	1797	1850	1903	1956	2009	2063	2116	2169	53
817	2222	2275	2328	2381	2435	2488	2541	2594	2647	2700	53
818	2753	2806	2859	2913	2966	3019	3072	3125	3178	3231	53
819	3284	3337	3390	3443	3496	3549	3602	3655	3708	3761	53
820	3814	3867	3920	3973	4026	4079	4132	4184	4237	4290	53
821	4343	4396	4449	4502	4555	4608	4660	4713	4766	4819	53
822	4872	4925	4977	5030	5083	5136	5189	5241	5294	5347	53
823	5400	5453	5505	5558	5611	5664	5716	5769	5822	5875	53
824	5927	5980	6033	6085	6138	6191	6243	6296	6349	6401	53
825	6454	6507	6559	6612	6664	6717	6770	6822	6875	6927	53
826	6980	7033	7085	7138	7190	7243	7295	7348	7400	7453	53
827	7506	7558	7611	7663	7716	7768	7820	7873	7925	7978	52
828	8030	8083	8135	8188	8240	8293	8345	8397	8450	8502	52
829	8555	8607	8659	8712	8764	8816	8869	8921	8973	9026	52
830	9078	9130	9183	9235	9287	9340	9392	9444	9496	9549	52
831	9601	9653	9706	9758	9810	9862	9914	9967	92 0019	92 0071	52
832	92 0123	92 0176	92 0228	92 0280	92 0332	92 0384	92 0436	92 0489	0541	0593	52
833	0645	0697	0749	0801	0853	0906	0958	1010	1062	1114	52
834	1166	1218	1270	1322	1374	1426	1478	1530	1582	1634	52
835	1686	1738	1790	1842	1894	1946	1998	2050	2102	2154	52
836	2206	2258	2310	2362	2414	2466	2518	2570	2622	2674	52
837	2725	2777	2829	2881	2933	2985	3037	3089	3140	3192	52
838	3244	3296	3348	3399	3451	3503	3555	3607	3658	3710	52
839	3762	3814	3865	3917	3969	4021	4072	4124	4176	4228	52
840	4279	4331	4383	4434	4486	4538	4589	4641	4693	4744	52
841	4796	4848	4899	4951	5003	5054	5106	5157	5209	5261	52
842	5312	5364	5415	5467	5518	5570	5621	5673	5725	5776	52
843	5828	5879	5931	5982	6034	6085	6137	6188	6240	6291	51
844	6342	6394	6445	6497	6548	6600	6651	6702	6754	6805	51
845	6857	6908	6959	7011	7062	7114	7165	7216	7268	7319	51
846	7370	7422	7473	7524	7576	7627	7678	7730	7781	7832	51
847	7883	7935	7986	8037	8088	8140	8191	8242	8293	8345	51
848	8396	8447	8498	8549	8601	8652	8703	8754	8805	8857	51
849	8908	8959	9010	9061	9112	9163	9215	9266	9317	9368	51
850	9419	9470	9521	9572	9623	9674	9725	9776	9827	9879	51

n\d	55
1	5.5
2	11.0
3	16.5
4	22.0
5	27.5
6	33.0
7	38.5
8	44.0
9	49.5

n\d	54
1	5.4
2	10.8
3	16.2
4	21.6
5	27.0
6	32.4
7	37.8
8	43.2
9	48.6

n\d	53
1	5.3
2	10.6
3	15.9
4	21.2
5	26.5
6	31.8
7	37.1
8	42.4
9	47.7

n\d	52
1	5.2
2	10.4
3	15.6
4	20.8
5	26.0
6	31.2
7	36.4
8	41.6
9	46.8

n\d	51
1	5.1
2	10.2
3	15.3
4	20.4
5	25.5
6	30.6
7	35.7
8	40.8
9	45.9

Six-Place Logarithms of Numbers 850-900   Proportional Parts

N	0	1	2	3	4	5	6	7	8	9	D
850	92 9419	92 9470	92 9521	92 9572	92 9623	92 9674	92 9725	92 9776	92 9827	92 9879	51
851	9930	9981	93 0032	93 0083	93 0134	93 0185	93 0236	93 0287	93 0338	93 0389	51
852	93 0440	93 0491	0542	0592	0643	0694	0745	0796	0847	0898	51
853	0949	1000	1051	1102	1153	1204	1254	1305	1356	1407	51
854	1458	1509	1560	1610	1661	1712	1763	1814	1865	1915	51
855	1966	2017	2068	2118	2169	2220	2271	2322	2372	2423	51
856	2474	2524	2575	2626	2677	2727	2778	2829	2879	2930	51
857	2981	3031	3082	3133	3183	3234	3285	3335	3386	3437	51
858	3487	3538	3589	3639	3690	3740	3791	3841	3892	3943	51
859	3993	4044	4094	4145	4195	4246	4296	4347	4397	4448	51
860	4498	4549	4599	4650	4700	4751	4801	4852	4902	4953	50
861	5003	5054	5104	5154	5205	5255	5306	5356	5406	5457	50
862	5507	5558	5608	5658	5709	5759	5809	5860	5910	5960	50
863	6011	6061	6111	6162	6212	6262	6313	6363	6413	6463	50
864	6514	6564	6614	6665	6715	6765	.6815	6865	6916	6966	50
865	7016	7066	7117	7167	7217	7267	7317	7367	7418	7468	50
866	7518	7568	7618	7668	7718	7769	7819	7869	7919	7969	50
867	8019	8069	8119	8169	8219	8269	8320	8370	8420	8470	50
868	8520	8570	8620	8670	8720	8770	8820	8870	8920	8970	50
869	9020	9070	9120	9170	9220	9270	9320	9369	9419	9469	50
870	9519	9569	9619	9669	9719	9769	9819	9869	9918	9968	50
871	94 0018	94 0068	94 0118	94 0168	94 0218	94 0267	94 0317	94 0367	94 0417	94 0467	50
872	0516	0566	0616	0666	0716	0765	0815	0865	0915	0964	50
873	1014	1064	1114	1163	1213	1263	1313	1362	1412	1462	50
874	1511	1561	1611	1660	1710	1760	1809	1859	1909	1958	50
875	2008	2058	2107	2157	2207	2256	2306	2355	2405	2455	50
876	2504	2554	2603	2653	2702	2752	2801	2851	2901	2950	50
877	3000	3049	3099	3148	3198	3247	3297	3346	3396	3445	49
878	3495	3544	3593	3643	3692	3742	3791	3841	3890	3939	49
879	3989	4038	4088	4137	4186	4236	4285	4335	4384	4433	49
880	4483	4532	4581	4631	4680	4729	4779	4828	4877	4927	49
881	4976	5025	5074	5124	5173	5222	5272	5321	5370	5419	49
882	5469	5518	5567	5616	5665	5715	5764	5813	5862	5912	49
883	5961	6010	6059	6108	6157	6207	6256	6305	6354	6403	49
884	6452	6501	6551	6600	6649	6698	6747	6796	6845	6894	49
885	6943	6992	7041	7090	7140	7189	7238	7287	7336	7385	49
886	7434	7483	7532	7581	7630	7679	7728	7777	7826	7875	49
887	7924	7973	8022	8070	8119	8168	8217	8266	8315	8364	49
888	8413	8462	8511	8560	8609	8657	8706	8755	8804	8853	49
889	8902	8951	8999	9048	9097	9146	9195	9244	9292	9341	49
890	9390	9439	9488	9536	9585	9634	9683	9731	9780	9829	49
891	9878	9926	9975	95 0024	95 0073	95 0121	95 0170	95 0219	95 0267	95 0316	49
892	95 0365	95 0414	95 0462	0511	0560	0608	0657	0706	0754	0803	49
893	0851	0900	0949	0997	1046	1095	1143	1192	1240	1289	49
894	1338	1386	1435	1483	1532	1580	1629	1677	1726	1775	49
895	1823	1872	1920	1969	2017	2066	2114	2163	2211	2260	48
896	2308	2356	2405	2453	2502	2550	2599	2647	2696	2744	48
897	2792	2841	2889	2938	2986	3034	3083	3131	3180	3228	48
898	3276	3325	3373	3421	3470	3518	3566	3615	3663	3711	48
899	3760	3808	3856	3905	3953	4001	4049	4098	4146	4194	48
900	4243	4291	4339	4387	4435	4484	4532	4580	4628	4677	48

Proportional Parts

n\d 52	
1	5.2
2	10.4
3	15.6
4	20.8
5	26.0
6	31.2
7	36.4
8	41.6
9	46.8

n\d 51	
1	5.1
2	10.2
3	15.3
4	20.4
5	25.5
6	30.6
7	35.7
8	40.8
9	45.9

n\d 50	
1	5.C
2	10.0
3	15.0
4	20.0
5	25.0
6	30.0
7	35.0
8	40.0
9	45.0

n\d 49	
1	4.9
2	9.8
3	14.7
4	19.6
5	24.5
6	29.4
7	34.3
8	39.2
9	44.1

n\d 48	
1	4.8
2	9.6
3	14.4
4	19.2
5	24.0
6	28.8
7	33.6
8	38.4
9	43.2

Proportional Parts

N	0	1	2	3	4	5	6	7	8	9	D
900	95 4243	95 4291	95 4339	95 4387	95 4435	95 4484	95 4532	95 4580	95 4628	95 4677	48
901	4725	4773	4821	4869	4918	4966	5014	5062	5110	5158	48
902	5207	5255	5303	5351	5399	5447	5495	5543	5592	5640	48
903	5688	5736	5784	5832	5880	5928	5976	6024	6072	6120	48
904	6168	6216	6265	6313	6361	6409	6457	6505	6553	6601	48
905	6649	6697	6745	6793	6840	6888	6936	6984	7032	7080	48
906	7128	7176	7224	7272	7320	7368	7416	7464	7512	7559	48
907	7607	7655	7703	7751	7799	7847	7894	7942	7990	8038	48
908	8086	8134	8181	8229	8277	8325	8373	8421	8468	8516	48
909	8564	8612	8659	8707	8755	8803	8850	8898	8946	8994	48
910	9041	9089	9137	9185	9232	9280	9328	9375	9423	9471	48
911	9518	9566	9614	9661	9709	9757	9804	9852	9900	9947	48
912	9995	96 0042	96 0090	96 0138	96 0185	96 0233	96 0280	96 0328	96 0376	96 0423	48
913	96 0471	0518	0566	0613	0661	0709	0756	0804	0851	0899	48
914	0946	0994	1041	1089	1136	1184	1231	1279	1326	1374	48
915	1421	1469	1516	1563	1611	1658	1706	1753	1801	1848	47
916	1895	1943	1990	2038	2085	2132	2180	2227	2275	2322	47
917	2369	2417	2464	2511	2559	2606	2653	2701	2748	2795	47
918	2843	2890	2937	2985	3032	3079	3126	3174	3221	3268	47
919	3316	3363	3410	3457	3504	3552	3599	3646	3693	3741	47
920	3788	3835	3882	3929	3977	4024	4071	4118	4165	4212	47
921	4260	4307	4354	4401	4448	4495	4542	4590	4637	4684	47
922	4731	4778	4825	4872	4919	4966	5013	5061	5108	5155	47
923	5202	5249	5296	5343	5390	5437	5484	5531	5578	5625	47
924	5672	5719	5766	5813	5860	5907	5954	6001	6048	6095	47
925	6142	6189	6236	6283	6329	6376	6423	6470	6517	6564	47
926	6611	6658	6705	6752	6799	6845	6892	6939	6986	7033	47
927	7080	7127	7173	7220	7267	7314	7361	7408	7454	7501	47
928	7548	7595	7642	7688	7735	7782	7829	7875	7922	7969	47
929	8016	8062	8109	8156	8203	8249	8296	8343	8390	8436	47
930	8483	8530	8576	8623	8670	8716	8763	8810	8856	8903	47
931	8950	8996	9043	9090	9136	9183	9229	9276	9323	9369	47
932	9416	9463	9509	9556	9602	9649	9695	9742	9789	9835	47
933	9882	9928	9975	97 0021	97 0068	97 0114	97 0161	97 0207	97 0254	97 0300	47
934	97 0347	97 0393	97 0440	0486	0533	0579	0626	0672	0719	0765	46
935	0812	0858	0904	0951	0997	1044	1090	1137	1183	1229	46
936	1276	1322	1369	1415	1461	1508	1554	1601	1647	1693	46
937	1740	1786	1832	1879	1925	1971	2018	2064	2110	2157	46
938	2203	2249	2295	2342	2388	2434	2481	2527	2573	2619	46
939	2666	2712	2758	2804	2851	2897	2943	2989	3035	3082	46
940	3128	3174	3220	3266	3313	3359	3405	3451	3497	3543	46
941	3590	3636	3682	3728	3774	3820	3866	3913	3959	4005	46
942	4051	4097	4143	4189	4235	4281	4327	4374	4420	4466	46
943	4512	4558	4604	4650	4696	4742	4788	4834	4880	4926	46
944	4972	5018	5064	5110	5156	5202	5248	5294	5340	5386	46
945	5432	5478	5524	5570	5616	5662	5707	5753	5799	5845	46
946	5891	5937	5983	6029	6075	6121	6167	6212	6258	6304	46
947	6350	6396	6442	6488	6533	6579	6625	6671	6717	6763	46
948	6808	6854	6900	6946	6992	7037	7083	7129	7175	7220	46
949	7266	7312	7358	7403	7449	7495	7541	7586	7632	7678	46
950	7724	7769	7815	7861	7906	7952	7998	8043	8089	8135	46

n\d	49
1	4.9
2	9.8
3	14.7
4	19.6
5	24.5
6	29.4
7	34.3
8	39.2
9	44.1

n\d	48
1	4.8
2	9.6
3	14.4
4	19.2
5	24.0
6	28.8
7	33.6
8	38.4
9	43.2

n\d	47
1	4.7
2	9.4
3	14.1
4	18.8
5	23.5
6	28.2
7	32.9
8	37.6
9	42.3

n\d	46
1	4.6
2	9.2
3	13.8
4	18.4
5	23.0
6	27.6
7	32.2
8	36.8
9	41.4

n\d	45
1	4.5
2	9.0
3	13.5
4	18.0
5	22.5
6	27.0
7	31.5
8	36.0
9	40.5

Six-Place Logarithms of Numbers 950-1000

N	0	1	2	3	4	5	6	7	8	9	D
950	97 7724	97 7769	97 7815	97 7861	97 7906	97 7952	97 7998	97 8043	97 8089	97 8135	46
951	8181	8226	8272	8317	8363	8409	8454	8500	8546	8591	46
952	8637	8683	8728	8774	8819	8865	8911	8956	9002	9047	46
953	9093	9138	9184	9230	9275	9321	9366	9412	9457	9503	46
954	9548	9594	9639	9685	9730	9776	9821	9867	9912	9958	46
955	98 0003	98 0049	98 0094	98 0140	98 0185	98 0231	98 0276	98 0322	98 0367	98 0412	45
956	0458	0503	0549	0594	0640	0685	0730	0776	0821	0867	45
957	0912	0957	1003	1048	1093	1139	1184	1229	1275	1320	45
958	1366	1411	1456	1501	1547	1592	1637	1683	1728	1773	45
959	1819	1864	1909	1954	2000	2045	2090	2135	2181	2226	45
960	2271	2316	2362	2407	2452	2497	2543	2588	2633	2678	45
961	2723	2769	2814	2859	2904	2949	2994	3040	3085	3130	45
962	3175	3220	3265	3310	3356	3401	3446	3491	3536	3581	45
963	3626	3671	3716	3762	3807	3852	3897	3942	3987	4032	45
964	4077	4122	4167	4212	4257	4302	4347	4392	4437	4482	45
965	4527	4572	4617	4662	4707	4752	4797	4842	4887	4932	45
966	4977	5022	5067	5112	5157	5202	5247	5292	5337	5382	45
967	5426	5471	5516	5561	5606	5651	5696	5741	5786	5830	45
968	5875	5920	5965	6010	6055	6100	6144	6189	6234	6279	45
969	6324	6369	6413	6458	6503	6548	6593	6637	6682	6727	45
970	6772	6817	6d61	6906	6951	6996	7040	7085	7130	7175	45
971	7219	7264	7309	7353	7398	7443	7488	7532	7577	7622	45
972	7666	7711	7756	7800	7845	7890	7934	7979	8024	8068	45
973	8113	8157	8202	8247	8291	8336	8381	8425	8470	8514	45
974	8559	8604	8648	8693	8737	8782	8826	8871	8916	8960	45
975	9005	9049	9094	9138	9183	9227	9272	9316	9361	9405	45
976	9450	9494	9539	9583	9628	9672	9717	9761	9806	9850	44
977	9895	9939	9983	99 0028	99 0072	99 0117	99 0161	99 0206	99 0250	99 0294	44
978	99 0339	99 0383	99 0428	0472	0516	0561	0605	0650	0694	0738	44
979	0783	0827	0871	0916	0960	1004	1049	1093	1137	1182	44
980	1226	1270	1315	1359	1403	1448	1492	1536	1580	1625	44
981	1669	1713	1758	1802	1846	1890	1935	1979	2023	2067	44
982	2111	2156	2200	2244	2288	2333	2377	2421	2465	2509	44
983	2554	2598	2642	2686	2730	2774	2819	2863	2907	2951	44
984	2995	3039	3083	3127	3172	3216	3260	3304	3348	3392	44
985	3436	3480	3524	3568	3613	3657	3701	3745	3789	3833	44
986	3877	3921	3965	4009	4053	4097	4141	4185	4229	4273	44
987	4317	4361	4405	4449	4493	4537	4581	4625	4669	4713	44
988	4757	4801	4845	4889	4933	4977	5021	5065	5108	5152	44
989	5196	5240	5284	5328	5372	5416	5460	5504	5547	5591	44
990	5635	5679	5723	5767	5811	5854	5898	5942	5986	6030	44
991	6074	6117	6161	6205	6249	6293	6337	6380	6424	6468	44
992	6512	6555	6599	6643	6687	6731	6774	6818	6862	6906	44
993	6949	6993	7037	7080	7124	7168	7212	7255	7299	7343	44
994	7386	7430	7474	7517	7561	7605	7648	7692	7736	7779	44
995	7823	7867	7910	7954	7998	8041	8085	8129	8172	8216	44
996	8259	8303	8347	8390	8434	8477	8521	8564	8608	8652	44
997	8695	8739	8782	8826	8869	8913	8956	9000	9043	9087	44
998	9131	9174	9218	9261	9305	9348	9392	9435	9479	9522	44
999	9565	9609	9652	9696	9739	9783	9826	9870	9913	9957	43
1000	00 0000	00 0043	00 0087	00 0130	00 0174	00 0217	00 0260	00 0304	00 0347	00 0391	43

Proportional Parts

n\d	46
1	4.6
2	9.2
3	13.8
4	18.4
5	23.0
6	27.6
7	32.2
8	36.8
9	41.4

n\d	45
1	4.5
2	9.0
3	13.5
4	18.0
5	22.5
6	27.0
7	31.5
8	36.0
9	40.5

n\d	44
1	4.4
2	8.8
3	13.2
4	17.6
5	22.0
6	26.4
7	30.8
8	35.2
9	39.6

n\d	43
1	4.3
2	8.6
3	12.9
4	17.2
5	21.5
6	25.8
7	30.1
8	34.4
9	38.7